MEMORANDUM
ON THE
PROGRESS OF THE MADRAS PRESIDENCY

DURING THE LAST FORTY YEARS OF BRITISH ADMINISTRATION

MEMORANDUM
ON THE
PROGRESS OF THE MADRAS PRESIDENCY

DURING THE LAST FORTY YEARS OF BRITISH ADMINISTRATION

S. SRINIVASA RAGHAVAIYANGAR

GYAN

Published by

GYAN

Gyan Publishing House
5, Ansari Road
Daryaganj, New Delhi-110002
Phone: 011-47034999, 9811692060
E-mail: books@gyanbooks.com

Distribution Network
gyanbooks.com
India, USA, Canada, UK, Australia, France

ISBN : 978-81-212-4536-4 (HB)
First Published, London, 1893

2nd Impression 2020

Printed at: Gyan Press, Delhi.

Memorandum on the Progress of the Madras President
Author: S. Srinivasa Raghavaiyangar

MEMORANDUM
ON THE
PROGRESS OF THE MADRAS PRESIDENCY
DURING THE LAST FORTY YEARS
OF BRITISH ADMINISTRATION

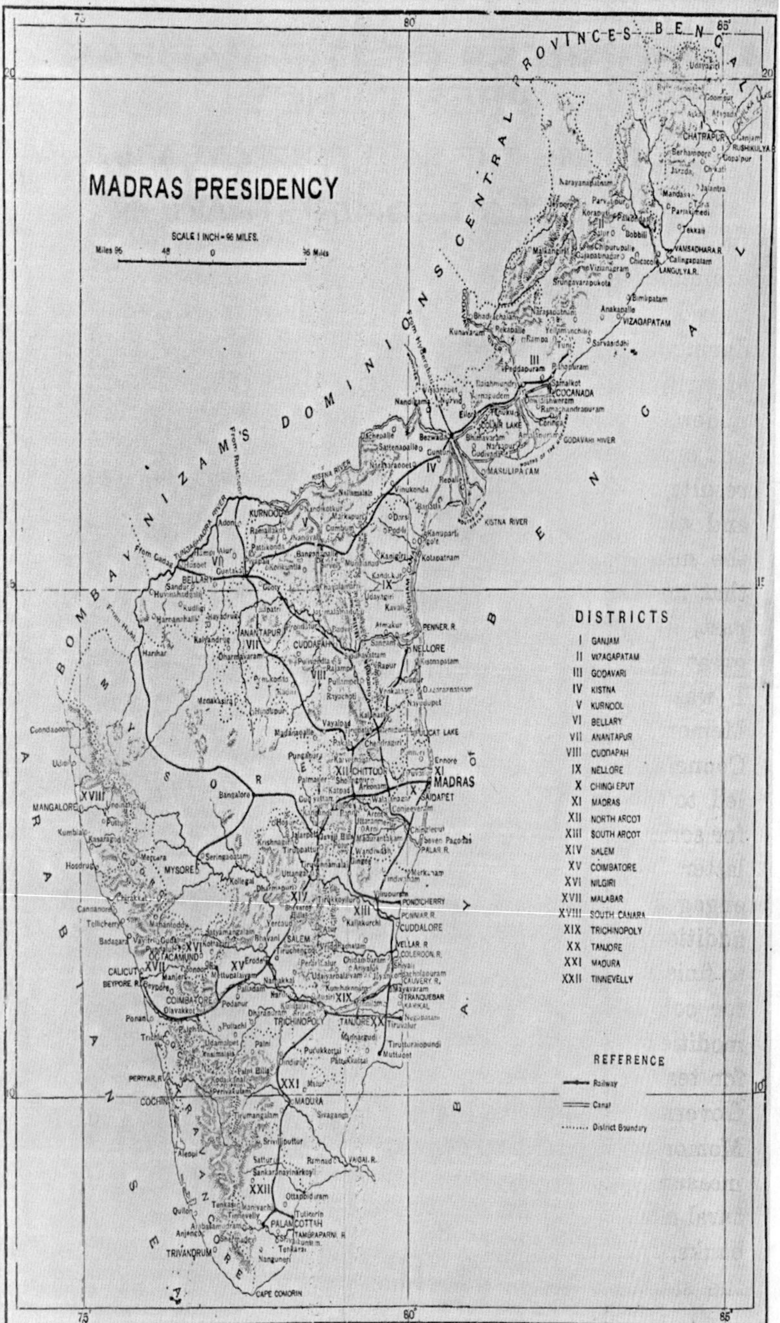

Reg. No. 878 _ Copies 1,500

Survey Office Madras
1893

PREFACE TO THE FIRST EDITION.

In July 1890, Lord Connemara entrusted to me the task of examining whether the economic condition of the Madras Presidency has, on the whole, improved or deteriorated during the last 40 or 50 years of British administration and of writing a Memorandum on the subject. I was given to understand that the conclusions arrived at should be based not only on information officially on record but also on the results of independent inquiries. To ascertain whether any and what improvement has taken place in the condition of the masses of the population, it was, of course, necessary that an idea should be formed as to their condition in the past, and, for this purpose, I had to collect and read up a great mass of old reports. This took up a deal of time, and I was able to write only the preliminary portion of this Memorandum before the end of 1890. The departure of Lord Connemara to England and pressure of other official work led to the preparation of this Memorandum being laid aside for some time, and I was able to resume the work only in the latter half of 1891. Since then I have been more or less engaged on it, but as the work has had to be carried on in addition to my other official duties, it has not been possible to finish it earlier. The interval, however, has been utilized for collecting information on such matters as prices of commodities, wages of labour, &c., in order that it might be used for testing information obtained from official sources. The Government has permitted me to add another section to this Memorandum containing suggestions as to certain special measures to be adopted for the amelioration of the agricultural classes in connection with land settlements, agricultural banks, agricultural and industrial education, &c., and to revise the statistics given in the appendices to the Memorandum with reference to the results of the last census. This will be done as soon as the results of the census become available, which will be very shortly, and the Memorandum will then be issued in a complete form.

2. I have endeavoured to make the statistics given in the memorandum as accurate as possible, but I can scarcely hope that I have fully succeeded. The information given as regards the state of things in former centuries, though derived from sources which are the best available, is admittedly imperfect, but this does not invalidate in any way the general conclusions arrived at.

3. The subject being many-sided, it is, of course, not possible in a first attempt to do more than break ground as regards the various questions dealt with. I have, therefore, printed as appendices to the Memorandum such official and other papers as throw light on the questions discussed, for purposes of easy reference in subsequent inquiries. This accounts also for the large quantity of statistical information and the large number of quotations given in the earlier portions of my Memorandum. Much of this information is new to the generation that is growing up, though not new to the generation that is passing away.

4. In conclusion, I wish to point out that the subject dealt with is the improvement in the *material* condition of the Presidency, and though there are other points of view from which the question of national well-being has to be considered, improvement in the *material* condition is the foundation on which improvement in other respects should be built up. I venture to think that if the question be impartially considered, there can be no two opinions as to the very great advance made by the country during the last 40 years.

MADRAS,
11*th April* 1892.

S. S.

PREFACE TO THE SECOND EDITION.

The additional section containing suggestions as to measures to be adopted for the amelioration of the condition of the agricultural classes has now been completed, and the Memorandum is accordingly issued in a complete form.

I have made a few verbal changes in portions of the Memorandum already issued and added foot-notes in three or four places to make my meaning clearer on some points to prevent misapprehension. I have also given in the appendix extracts from a reply published by me in the *Madras Mail* to some criticisms which appeared in the *Calcutta Review* on the question of pressure of population and one or two important matters bearing on the condition of the agricultural population.

The statistics given in the appendices have been revised, as far as possible, with reference to the results of the last census. The Board of Revenue having furnished revised figures as regards the acreage of holdings for some of the earlier years, these have been adopted in the statement of acreage of holdings printed in the appendix. I have retained the life-table for the population of the Presidency taken from the census report of 1881, as the table prepared in connection with the census of 1891 relates to the population of the Madras city alone. The comparative table of persons classified under various occupations in 1871 and 1881 has also been retained unaltered, as owing to a radical change of classification adopted for the census of 1891, a comparison between the results of this census and those of the earlier censuses has not been found possible.

No pains have been spared to render the statistics as accurate as possible, but considering the great mass of figures dealt with, it is not possible to say that all chances of error have been excluded. If any errors are brought to notice, I shall thankfully correct them and issue an erratum.

Though the work has outgrown the limits of a Memorandum, the original form has been retained, the object throughout being not so much to furnish cut and dry conclusions as to indicate the methods of investigation to be pursued and furnish materials as far as possible for forming a judgment as to the improvement which has taken place in the condition of the agricultural classes, and as to the further measures to be taken for their amelioration. On some of the subjects dealt with under the latter head, such as agricultural and technical education and widening the scope of local administration, my remarks are necessarily general, as my intention is to point out the necessity for increased attention in certain directions, and not to lay down the precise measures to be adopted, the determination of which must, of course, be based on a thorough investigation of the conditions of the localities to which they are to be applied. It is hardly necessary to add that the views I have expressed on these and other matters are my individual opinions submitted for the consideration of Government, and are not to be understood as reflecting the opinions of the Government itself.

I must in conclusion express my grateful acknowledgments to several gentlemen who have favoured me with the results of their observation and experience in connection with the inquiry forming the subject-matter of the Memorandum, and to Mr. Hill, the Superintendent of the Government Press, for the ready and willing assistance afforded by him in passing this work through the press. My thanks are also due to Mr. Cardozo, by whose kindness I have been enabled to prefix a map of the Presidency to the Memorandum.

PALMANÉR, S. S.
21st May 1893.

CONTENTS.

APPENDICES.

MEMORANDUM.

In this memorandum I propose to examine whether the economic condition of the Madras Presidency, and especially of the agricultural classes, has improved or deteriorated during the last 40 years of British administration, and whether, if there has been improvement, it is proceeding on right lines.

Section I.—*The state of the country and the condition of the people in former centuries.*

Scantiness of information as to the condition of the people in former centuries.

2. It is generally admitted that the last century, which immediately preceded the establishment of British power in Southern India, was a period of anarchy and of suffering to the masses of the population; but it would be interesting to learn what was the condition of the people in the preceding centuries under native rulers. Information on the subject is, however, exceedingly scanty, the very names of some of the dynasties which bore sway in Southern India having been forgotten[1]; and it is only recently by a laborious study of ancient inscriptions, Indian archæologists have been endeavouring to construct a South Indian history. The results of their researches, so far as they have gone, have been summarized by Mr. R. Sewell, M.C.S., in his *Lists of Antiquities of the Madras Presidency*, and I have ventured to extract Mr. Sewell's remarks in an appendix[2] to this memorandum. It will be seen from Mr. Sewell's account, that from the earliest historical times Southern India was divided into a number of small kingdoms, which, like the kingdoms of the Heptarchy, were continually at war with one another; that each dynasty aspired for universal dominion and asserted it as opportunities offered; that the pressure of immigration of tribes from Northern India added to the distracted state of the country caused by internecine wars; and that from the 14th century, when the Muhammadans pushed their arms to Southern India and founded Muhammadan kingdoms in the Northern Deccan, to the beginning of the 19th century, the country seldom enjoyed peace.

[1] The Pallava dynasty appears to have been a powerful one and ruled over all the East Coast districts from the Kistna to the Coleroon and to have had its capital at Conjeeveram. Even the name of the dynasty has gone completely out of the memory of the people of the country over whom it ruled.

[2] *Vide* appendix A, section I.

3. Among the various dynasties which have successively ruled in Southern India, the times of the Pandiyans in the Madura and Tinnevelly districts, of the Cholas in the Tanjore district and of the Vijianagar kings in the Southern Deccan, live in tradition as a sort of "golden age." That the Pandiyans were a powerful dynasty, and that their country under Budhist at first, and subsequently under Brahminic, influences, attained to a very considerable degree of civilization, and kept up commercial intercourse with the Greeks and Romans, seem certain. They were also great patrons of the Tamil literature, and it was during their time that the famous "Sangham" or College of Poets was established, and the greatest Tamil poems were composed. The Cholas, who rose to great power in the 11th, 12th and 13th centuries and held sway over nearly the whole of Southern India, were the builders of most of the great temples that exist in such numbers in the Tanjore district, and of the anicut across the Cauvery. They excavated several channels for irrigation, which are known by their names—Virasholanar, Vikramanar, Kirtimanar, Mudikondanar—and established agricultural colonies and Brahmin agraharams for the spread of Aryan civilization. The powerful Vijianagar dynasty stemmed the tide of Muhammadan conquest for two centuries, *i.e.*, 15th and 16th, until it was overwhelmed by a confederation of the Muhammadan sovereigns of the Deccan, and its magnificent capital was sacked and utterly destroyed. All these dynasties rendered important services to South Indian civilization, and, as during their times some of the greatest religious teachers and scholars and dialecticians—Sankaracharya, Ramanujacharya and Vidiaranya—lived and flourished, it is no wonder that the people of Southern India recall the memory of those times with pleasure and pride.

Pandya, Chola and Vijianagar dynasties.

4. Every dynasty, however, when it attained to supreme power, drew to itself all the wealth of the surrounding provinces and adorned its capital with magnificent buildings, but the conquered provinces were generally oppressed. One of the Pandiyan kings in an inscription boasts, among his other exploits, of having set Tanjore and Uraiyur (the Chola capitals) on fire; demolished the houses, high walls, storied houses and palaces; made the tears of the wives of refractory kings flow like a river; caused the sites of the buildings to be ploughed with asses and sown with cowries; driven the Chola from his dominions into a barren place and taken away his crown of gold and given it to a poet, who sang in praise of him, &c. One of the Chola kings in the same manner, in his turn,

Frequency of wars and backward state of the country.

humbled the Pandiyans and assumed the title of Madurantaka (death of the Madura city). Allowing for great exaggeration, the language of the inscriptions shows that even the best days of the ancient dynasties were those of wars and violence, that the ambition of every king was to humble the pride of his neighbours and to spoil their territories, and that these exhausting wars must have entailed on the people an immense amount of misery, which, of course, was borne with patience and resignation, as they had had no experience of a happier condition. Large portions of the country were also covered with jungle or inhabited by tribes hardly reclaimed from savagery. From a letter of a Jesuit missionary, written in the beginning of the 18th century, it appears that on the Tinnevelly coast, which is now a fully cultivated and densely populated tract, "a large jungle had for some time past been infested by tigers to such a degree that after sunset no inhabitant of any village situated in its neighbourhood dared to move outside his door. Watch was kept in every village at night and large fires were lighted for the purpose of scaring the monsters away. Even in the daytime travelling was not quite safe, and numbers of people had disappeared who had, without doubt, been seized and devoured in lonely places." The country lying on the outskirts of Trichinopoly town appears to have been covered with jungle and infested by robbers in the middle of the 16th century. The same was the case in the Coimbatore district also. Marauders were so numerous that a traveller by night was almost certain to fall into their hands. Wild beasts were so common that one missionary lost thirty of his acquaintances by their ravages within six months. Both in the Pandiya and Chola countries large tracts were, and still are, inhabited by Kallers, whom Father Martin, who lived in the 18th century in the vicinity of Kaller country, described as more barbarous than any savages in any part of the globe. His assertion is corroborated by Ward and Connor's survey account, which states that "a horrible custom exists among the females of the Colleries. When a quarrel or dissension arises between them, the insulted woman brings her child to the house of the aggressor and kills it at her door to avenge herself, although her vengeance is attended with the most cruél barbarity. She immediately thereafter proceeds to a neighbouring village with all her goods, &c. In this attempt she is opposed by her neighbours, which gives rise to clamour and outrage. The complaint is then carried to the head Ombalakar, who lays it before the elders of the village and solicits their interference to terminate the quarrel. In the course of this investigation, if the husband finds that sufficient evidence has been brought against his wife and that she had given cause for provocation and aggression, then he proceeds unobserved by the assembly to his house and brings one of his children, and in the presence of the witnesses, kills his child at the door of the woman who had first killed her child at his; by this mode of procedure he considers that he has saved himself much trouble and expense, which would otherwise have devolved on him. The circumstance is soon brought to the notice of the tribunal, which proclaims that the offence committed is sufficiently avenged. But should this voluntary retribution of revenge not be executed by the convicted person, the tribunal is prorogued to a limited time—fifteen days generally. Before the expiration of that period one of the children of the convicted person must be killed; at the same time he is to bear all expenses for providing food, &c., for the assembly during three days. Such is their inhuman barbarity in avenging outrage, which proves the innate cruelty and the unrestrained barbarity of their manners and morals."

Famines and epidemics very destructive in former times.

5. There cannot be the slightest doubt that famines and epidemics were far more frequent and destructive in former centuries than at present. Allusions to terrible famines occur in ancient Hindu writings. The Ramayana mentions a severe and prolonged drought which occurred in Northern India. According to the Orissa legends severe famines occurred between the years 1107 and 1143 A.D. The memory of a terrible 12 years' famine [3] "Dvadasavarsha Panjam" lives in tradition in Southern India. Duff in his history of the Mahrattas states that "in 1396 the dreadful famine distinguished from all others by the name Durga Devee commenced in Maharashtra. It lasted, according to Hindu legends, for 12 years. At the end of that time the periodical rains returned; but whole districts were entirely depopulated and a very scanty revenue was obtained from the territory between the Godávari and the Kistna for upwards of 30 years afterwards. The hill forts and

[3] The story is as follows: There was a terrible 12 years' famine in the land, the "nine" planets who rule the destinies of men having decreed that the human race should be destroyed. At the close of the 12th year, the "planets" went on a tour of inspection to see if the work of destruction was complete. All was desolation, but there was one green spot at a distance. They repaired to the place to see what it was. There, a ryot, who was a great astrologer, had, by his art, foreseen that a great famine was coming and had taken precautions against it. In years of abundance he saved the grain (ragi) and built up the walls of his house with this grain mixed with mud and planted prickly-pear round his gardens and fields. When the drought came the man fed his goats with prickly-pear, which flourishes even during times of drought, and boiled the grain scraped from the walls of his house with the milk yielded by the goats and ate the boiled ragi and thus lived; for there was not a drop of water to be had anywhere. When the man saw the "planets," he knew who they were and offered to feed them too. They accepted his hospitality and after a full meal lay down to sleep in crooked and inauspicious positions. When they were fast asleep the ryot put them all in auspicious positions and thus the famine came to an end and the world began once more to prosper.

strong places previously conquered by the Muhammadans had fallen into the hands of Poligars and robbers, and the returning cultivators were driven from their villages." In the works of the Hindu astronomer Varaha Mihira, there are passages tending to show that the theory of the connection between sun spots and droughts was known at the time, and this knowledge must have been the result of observations made during long periods of time. The Muhammadan historian Ferishta records two famines as having occurred in the 15th century. He states that, in 1423 A.D., no rain falling, a grievous famine was experienced throughout the Deccan, and multitudes of cattle died on the parched plains for want of water. The king (Ahmed I of the Bahmini dynasty), in consequence, increased the pay of his troops and opened public stores of grain for the use of the poor. The next year also, there being no rain, the people became seditious, complaining that the present reign was unlucky and the conduct of the prince displeasing to God. The king felt this bitterly, repaired to the mosque and prayed to God for rain. Rain came and the people were satisfied and the king was thenceforward surnamed the "saint." In 1474 A.D., there occurred a famine still more terrible. The following account is given of it by Ferishta: "When the royal standard reached the city of Bijapore, Mahomed Shah (Bahmini dynasty), at the request of Khajwa Mahomed Khan, halted to repose his fatigues, and the minister endeavoured to soothe his grief for the death of his mother. Admiring the situation of Bijapore, the king would willingly have remained there during the rainy season, but so severe a drought prevailed throughout the Deccan that the wells dried up, and the king, contrary to his inclination, moved with his army to Ahmedabad Beder. No rain fell during the next year either, and the towns in consequence became almost depopulated. Many of the inhabitants died of famine and numbers emigrated for food to Malwa, Jajnagger and Guzerat. In Telingana, Maharashtra and throughout the Bahmini, no grain was sown for two years; and, in the third, when the Almighty showered his mercy on the earth, scarcely any farmers remained in the country to cultivate the lands."

In 1570 a great famine appears (from the records of the Portuguese Mission) to have raged on the Tinnevelly coast. Father Henriques, a Portuguese missionary, established famine relief houses, in some of which 50 persons were daily fed. The records of the Madura Jesuit Mission contain accounts of some famines which occurred in the 17th and 18th centuries. In 1648 there was a famine in the Coimbatore district when a great part of the population died or deserted the country. In

1659 the Muhammadans of Golconda invaded the southern countries. "The cruel devastation of the country round Trichinopoly and in the direction of Vallam led to a local famine, which within a short time compelled the population to emigrate in a body, some to the Marava country and some to the Madura country, and some to Satyamangalam; and then the Muhammadans themselves were reduced to great extremities. Their horses died from want of forage, their camp-followers ran away and thousands of them died of actual starvation. So numerous were their deaths that it was impossible to bury their corpses, which were accordingly left in great heaps in the open fields. The effluvium arising from their decomposition, combined with the ill-health resulting from want of proper food, rapidly engendered a pestilence, which carried off large numbers." The sufferings of the people during the years 1659 to 1662 appear to have been terrible. The privations undergone by the Christians are described by the Jesuit missionaries as heart-rending; upwards of 10,000 of them died of want and starvation. Tanjore appears to have suffered even more than Madura, and almost the entire Christian population of that kingdom was driven out of it either by the fear of Muhammadans or by the pangs of hunger. The Hindus also persecuted the Christians for having offended the local deities and brought drought and famine on the land by their impiety, in the same manner as Christians in European countries appear to have persecuted the Jews in the middle ages, whenever famines and plagues occurred.

In 1677 the Madura country was invaded by the Mysoreans. An extraordinary fall of rain on the Western Ghauts inundated the country and swept away the low-lying villages with their entire population. This was followed by famine and pestilence, and it is stated that many of the half-starved wretches, who survived these calamities, took to brigandage and overran the kingdom unchecked. From 1709, for nearly 12 years, the Marava country, Ramnad and Sivaganga, suffered from terrible droughts alternating with floods, and large numbers of the inhabitants emigrated to Tanjore and Madura. The droughts appear to have been entirely due to the capriciousness of the seasons, as irrigation works in the Marava country were in those days in an excellent condition. Father Martin wrote in 1713:[4] "Nowhere have more precautions been taken than in Marava not to let a drop of water escape and to collect all the

---

[1] These and other quotations from the records of the Madura Jesuit Mission are translations of extracts in French given in Mr. Nelson's *Madura Manual*. They contain the most authentic information as to the condition of the Madura district in the 17th century and I have therefore given them at length in this memorandum.

water formed by the rains in brooks and torrents. Here there is to be seen a pretty large river called Vaigaiyaru. After crossing a part of Madura, it enters Marava, and when its bed is full, which ordinarily happens a whole month every year, it is as large as the Seine. Yet, by means of canals dug by our Indians far away from their tanks, this river is so drained on all sides that it loses itself entirely and does not reach its mouth till it has spent several weeks in filling the reservoirs towards which it is diverted. The most common tanks have banks half a league long; there are others which are a league and more in length. I have seen three, more than three leagues in length. One of these tanks furnishes enough water to irrigate the fields of more than 60 plantations. As rice (paddy) must have its stem in water until it has acquired perfect maturity, after the first reaping, when there is still water in the tanks, they manure the lands and commence sowing again, for all times of the year are adapted to the growing of paddy, provided there is no deficiency of water." That prices of agricultural produce were subject to the most violent fluctuations on account of want of outlet for produce in years of abundance is evident from the following extract from the Jesuit missionary's letter:—"It is owing to the abundance of water, which the ryots caused to flow from their tanks into the fields, that they are able to grow a prodigious quantity of rice. When the rain is abundant, the price of rice and other provisions is low. They get eight merkals [5] or large measures of unhusked rice for one fanam, which suffice to nourish a man for more than 15 days. But as soon as the rain fails, the dearness is so great that I have seen the price of one of these measures of rice rise to 8 fanams (eighteen sous)." This shows that in years of scarcity the price rose to 64 times of what it was in ordinary times! In 1733, there was a scarcity in the Chingleput district, which is stated to have been caused more by the neglect of irrigation works under the rule of the Nabobs of Arcot than by the failure of the seasons. The price of paddy rose to 40 pagodas per garce, while the ordinary price was 25 pagodas per garce. Twenty years before 1733, it is stated that 25 pagodas per garce would have been reckoned as famine price. In 1780 occurred Hyder's desolating invasion of the Carnatic followed by the grievous famine, the horrors

---

[5] Mr. Nelson takes the price quoted as equivalent to 96 lb. for $2\frac{1}{4}d$. Father Martin says that 8 merkals will suffice to nourish a man for more than 15 days. If we take the quantity of rice required by a person at 3 lb. per diem, the quantity required for 15 days would be 45 lb. Even if this reduced quantity were worth $2\frac{1}{4}d.$, the price would have been 480 lb. per rupee or $\frac{1}{12}$th of the price at the present time; in other words the purchasing value of the rupee would have been in the beginning of the 18th century 12 times what it is now.

of which were described by Burke in one of his well known orations. From 1789 to 1792, a terrible famine raged in the Northern Circars. The famine does not appear to have extended to the north of Ganjam, and at Puri the people lived in the midst of plenty. In the Ichápur and Chicacole countries, however, the people died in thousands. The country was plunged in a state of misery and desolation truly deplorable. Whole tracts were depopulated, and when the famine came to an end, people were not forthcoming to cultivate the lands. The reports of the Collector of Rajahmundry in the beginning of the century show that many villages in the fertile delta of the Godávari had become depopulated and great difficulty was felt in arranging for the cultivation of lands.

Epidemics also were very frequent and destructive. Small-pox was very virulent, so much so that, on the Western Coast, till within recent times, on the first appearance of the epidemic in villages, the villagers used to desert them, leaving the sufferers to shift for themselves as best they could or die. So recently as the beginning of this century a fever of a very malignant type decimated the populations of Madura, Tinnevelly and Coimbatore districts. A committee was appointed by Government to inquire into the causes of the epidemic, and it reported that the primary cause was the highly insalubrious condition of the atmosphere resulting from the continued and extraordinary deviations from the regular course of the seasons and the miasmata arising from the marshy grounds, the thick jungles on the hill sides and from the salt marshes on the sea coast. The committee added that there were not wanting also predisposing causes in the debilitated condition of the population owing to insufficient diet, exposure to cold and damp, and fear and anxiety. The wretched ryots were only too well prepared to imbibe the poison by their poor condition and careless habits of life, and this was conclusively shown by the fact that, on one occasion, while the ryots were dying by thousands, soldiers, convicts and others scarcely suffered at all.

The land tax collected by Native sovereigns heavy and oppressive.

6. There is also ample evidence to show that the land tax taken, not only by the Muhammadan but also by the Hindu sovereigns, was fully one-half the gross produce. Menu's proportion of one-sixth (which in the case of unirrigated lands must have operated as a heavy tax on industry and not on rent, for rent, owing to the abundance of cultivable lands and the sparseness of population, could not have come into existence) must, if it ever was observed in practice, have for several centuries been exceeded, and half the gross produce come to

be recognized as the legal rate. Dr. Burnell, in his *South Indian Palæography*, has stated "that the land tax (for such it originally was in South India, not *rent*) should amount to half the produce, has long been quoted as an instance of rapacity of Muhammadan and English Governments, from the illustrious B. Neiburh's early letters down to modern public discussions, by people ignorant of Indian history. But it has nothing to do with either. The inscriptions at Tanjore show that the indigenous Chola kings of the 11th century took about half the produce, and F. W. Ellis long ago asserted, on other grounds, that the tax was always more than the sixth or fourth permitted by the Sanskrit lawyers. A consideration of royal grants would also conclusively show (as Sanskrit lawyers asserted) that the Government never had any right to the land." In the Northern Circars also the native dynasties, long before the Muhammadan conquest, appear to have taken half the gross produce as the land tax, and this rule was in force in several zemindaries and principalities which had never, or only for a short time, been under Muhammadan domination—the Ramnad zemindari for instance. The only instance in which the rule laid down by the Shastras was adopted in rating lands for the revenue was in South Canara, and in this case, the Shastraic rule was resorted to with a view to enhance the land tax which had till then been levied. In South Canara, cultivation has to be carried on under more difficult conditions than elsewhere. The country is extremely rocky and uneven, and, owing to excessive rainfall, cattle are scarce and cannot be employed at all seasons of the year. The ground has to be levelled at great expense to make it fit for cultivation, and this operation has to be continually repeated, as, owing to heavy rainfall and mountain torrents, the land is constantly cut up into deep gullies. Reclamation of land could, under these circumstances, have been possible only if the land tax had been extremely moderate, and accordingly the original land tax appears to have been fixed at $\frac{1}{6}$th of the gross produce till about A.D. 1252, when the country was conquered by a Pandiyan prince. He ruled that the $\frac{1}{6}$th share should be delivered in rice and not in unhusked paddy, and thus increased the tax by about 10 per cent. When the country became a dependency of Vijianagar, the king Hari Har Roy fixed the land-tax at $\frac{1}{4}$th of gross produce, *i.e.*, $\frac{1}{6}$th the king's share proper, and $\frac{1}{12}$th the share allotted by the Shastras for the support of temples and Brahmins, thus enhancing the tax by 50 per cent. From information extracted by Dr. Buchanan from certain old accounts in the possession of a shanbogue at Gokurna and given in his "Journey through Mysore, Malabar and Canara in 1800," it appears, however, that in certain parts of North Canara, according to a valuation of Krishna Raya, the king of Vijianagar, while the tax on rice lands was $\frac{1}{4}$th of the gross produce, that on cocoanut plantations was quite half the gross produce.

The character of the revenue administration under the Vijianagar sovereigns.

7. The following extracts from the records of the Madura Jesuit Mission give the particulars connected with the land revenue administration of the Madura country under the rule of the viceroys of the Vijianagar kings in the 17th century: "The King or Grand Nayakar of Madura has but a few domains which depend immediately on him, that is to say, which form his property (for, in this country, the great are sole proprietors, and the people are only tenants or farmers); all the other lands are the domains of a multitude of petty princes, or tributary lords; these latter have each in his own domains the full administration of the police and of justice, if justice there is at all; they levy contributions which comprise at least the half of the produce of the lands; of this they make three parts, the first of which is reserved as tribute to the Grand Nayakar; the second is employed in supporting troops, which the lord is bound to furnish him with in case of war; the third belongs to the lord. The Grand Nayakars of Madura, like those of Tanjore and Gingee, are themselves tributaries of Vijianagar, to whom they pay, or ought to pay, each one an annual tribute of from 6 to 10 millions of francs. But they are not punctual in this payment; often they delay, and even sometimes refuse insolently; then Vijianagar arrives or sends one of his generals at the head of a hundred thousand men to enforce payment of all arrears, with interest, and in such cases, which are frequent, it is the poor people who are to expiate the fault of their princes; the whole country is devastated and the population is either pillaged or massacred." The revenue administration of the Mahratta chief, Ekoji, a half-brother of Sivaji, in Tanjore, appears from a letter of a Jesuit missionary in 1683 to have been, if possible, even more oppressive. The missionary states: "Tanjore is in the possession of Ekoji with the exception of a few provinces which have been seized by the Marava. Here is a short sketch of the administration of this country. Ekoji appropriates four-fifths of the produce. This is not all. Instead of accepting these four-fifths in kind, he insists that they should be paid in money; and as he takes care to fix the price himself much beyond that which the proprietor can realize, the result is that the sale of the entire produce does not suffice to pay the entire contri-

bution. The cultivators then remain under the weight of a heavy debt; and often they are obliged to prove their inability to pay by submitting to the most barbarous tortures. It would be difficult for you to conceive such an oppression, and yet I must add that this tyranny is more frightful and revolting in the kingdom of Gingee. For the rest this is all I can say, for I cannot find words to express all that is horrible in it."

Even the rule of Tirumal Nayak, who may be fitly called the "magnificent," was oppressive. Tirumal Nayak was partial to Christianity and treated the Jesuit missionaries with marked kindness; and he was even suspected of having embraced Christianity secretly. And yet this is the account given by Father Proenza in a letter, dated Trichinopoly, 1659: "Tirumal Nayakar was not spared to enjoy the victory; he was called upon to render an account to God of the evils which his treacherous policy had drawn on his people and on the neighbouring kingdoms. He died at the age of 75 years after a reign of 30 years. We cannot but acknowledge that he possessed great qualities; but he tarnished their glory towards the end of his life by vices and follies which nothing could justify. His reign was illustrious by works of truly royal magnificence, among them being the pagoda of Madura, and, above all, the royal palace, whose colossal proportions and gigantic strength recall to memory the ancient monuments of Thebes. He loved and protected the Christian religion, the excellence of which he recognized, but never had the courage to accept the consequence of this conviction. The greatest obstacle to his conversion arose from his two hundred wives, the most distinguished of whom were burnt over his funeral pile according to the barbarous custom of these nations." The Government of Coimbatore under the Naiks[6] of Satyamangalam appears to have been no better.

---

[6] *Vide Coimbatore District Manual*, pp. 89 and 90. There were, of course, also some kings and queens whose names are revered to this day. The wisdom of Kistna Deva Raya in council and his prowess in war form the theme of many a legend in the Telugu country. Of Queen Rudramma, of the Warangal dynasty, who governed the kingdom as regent during the minority of her grandson (A.D. 1257-1295), Marco Polo writes as follows: "This kingdom was under the rule of a king, and since his death forty years ago, it has been under his queen, a lady of much distinction, who for the great love she bore him never would marry another husband, and I can assure you that during all that space of 40 years she had administered her realm as well as her husband did, or better, and as she was a lover of justice, of equity and of peace, she was more beloved by those of her kingdom than ever was lady or lord of theirs before." Of Queen Regent Mangammal (A.D. 1689-1704) Bishop Caldwell in his *History of Tinnevelly* states: "She eschewed wars and cultivated the arts of peace, and all through Tinnevelly, as well as in Madura and the adjacent districts, she achieved a reputation which survives to the present day as the greatest maker of roads, planter of avenues, digger of wells and builder of choultries the royal houses of Madura ever produced. It has become customary to attribute to her every avenue found anywhere in the country. I have found, for instance, that all the avenues in the neighbourhood of Courtallum are attributed to Mangammal. Having done so much, she is supposed to have done all."

The enormous revenue of former rulers.

8. The above long extracts show not only what the real character of the administration of the Nayak dynasty, who adorned their capitals with such magnificent buildings, was, but also the enormous revenue which former Hindu rulers derived from land. According to the statements contained in the letters of the Jesuit missionaries, the three viceroyalties of Madura, Tanjore and Gingee were each bound to pay a tribute, varying between 6 and 10 millions of francs or between £240,000 and £400,000 to the Vijianagar sovereign, and if the Madura province, which was the most extensive of the three, paid the higher sum, it is clear that the revenue taken from the ryots of that province must have been at least three times that sum or £1,200,000. In fact, most of the lands comprised within the Madura province were in the hands of Poligars, who, it is stated, paid to the local viceroys only one-third of the revenue of their polliems, and out of this one-third, the viceroys had to pay the tribute after defraying their own expenses. The Madura province comprised the present districts, Madura, Tinnevelly, Trichinopoly and a portion of the Salem district. The land revenue of these districts aggregates now 87½ lakhs of rupees only, and when it is remembered that in the 16th and 17th centuries much of the country now under cultivation was covered with jungle and that the purchasing power of the precious metals was several times higher than it is at present, an idea may be formed of the large share of the gross produce which the Government of those days appropriated as revenue. It seems probable, as, indeed, the records of the Jesuit Mission state, that the tribute was seldom regularly paid, but was exacted by the Vijianagar king by force of arms whenever he was able to do so; but the large amount of tribute fixed shows that practically the only limit to the exactions which could be made from the ryots was their ability to pay. The amount of revenue taken by the sovereigns of the Madura and Tanjore countries would be hardly credible, were it not for the fact that there is ample evidence to show that in other parts of the peninsula the revenue taken by other sovereigns was equally great, if not greater. In Orissa, it appears that in the 12th century the Gangetic dynasty had a land revenue of about £450,000, or a little less than three times the revenue derived by the British Government from the same province, while the purchasing power of the rupee was then 8 times of what it is now.[7] The land revenue of the whole of British India is 23 millions of

[7] *Vide* extracts (appendix B, section I) from Hunter's *Orissa* as regards the revenue derived by the Gangetic kings in the 12th century and the purchasing power of silver in those days.

tens of rupees. In the time of the Emperor Akbar, the land revenue of the territories subject to his rule, which did not extend south of the Vindhya mountains, was $16\frac{1}{2}$ millions Rx. in 1594 and $17\frac{1}{2}$ millions in 1605. In Jehangir's time the land tax continued at $17\frac{1}{2}$ millions. In the earlier years of Aurangzebe's reign (1655) the land revenue was 24 millions. It rose to $34\frac{1}{2}$ millions in 1670 and to $38\frac{3}{4}$ millions in 1697. In the last year of Aurangzebe's reign (1707) the revenue fell to 30 millions. It is stated that in the official statement of the revenues of the empire presented to the Afghan invader, Ahmed Shah Abdali,[8] when he entered Delhi in 1761, the land revenue of the empire was entered as $34\frac{1}{2}$ millions. The significance of the above figures will be rightly estimated when it is remembered that between the years 1593 and 1605 the price of wheat averaged between 186 to 224 lb. per rupee and barley $275\frac{1}{2}$ lb. per rupee, *i.e.*, the price of wheat and barley in the end of the 16th century was between one-sixth and one-seventh of what it is at present.

The devices resorted to with a view to increase revenue.

9. The Hindu Shastras consigned the king, who exacted more than one-sixth or one-fourth of the produce, to infamy in this world and the torments of hell in the next, but the Muhammadan law had no such scruples. The Hedaia states: "*The learned in the law* allege that the utmost extent of tributo is one-half of the actual product, nor is it allowable to exact more; but the taking of a half is no more than strict justice and is not tyrannical, because, as it is lawful to take the whole of the person and property of infidels and distribute them

---

[8] The revenues of the Moghul emperors appear to have been carefully investigated by Mr. Edward Thomas in his book, entitled *The Revenue Resources of the Moghul Empire.* The particulars available as regards the revenue of the several provinces during the time of the Moghuls have been extracted from the article on "India" in Hunter's *Gazetteer* and printed in the appendix C, section I. The figures quoted appear indeed fabulous. Take, for instance, the land revenue of Orissa—£450,000—which, allowing for the depreciation in the value of the precious metals, would at the present day be equivalent to £3,600,000. The present area of cultivation in Orissa is $2\frac{1}{2}$ millions of acres. If the whole area had been under cultivation in the 12th century, the land tax per acre would be £ 1-9-0; if only half, which is more likely, it would be £2-18-0. The tax would represent a much larger proportion of the gross produce than one-half. This seems likely; in the beginning of the present century the tax represented nearly $\frac{5}{8}$ths of the gross produce, and the cultivators were left only the barest means of subsistence and often not even that, a portion of the so-called land tax being met out of the earnings from dairy produce and domestic industries, such as weaving. Much of the revenue consisted of payments in kind, and the Government sold the grain at monopoly rates. The revenue shown in the accounts also were, to a great extent, nominal and much of it probably remained unrealized, because it was impossible to realize it. The fact, however, of the demand being fixed so high as to absorb nearly the whole of the gross produce shows that the Government took all that it could. Even the principle laid down by the Emperor Akbar, who was immeasurably in advance of his time, for regulating land assessment will not, according to modern standards, be accepted as liberal. He said: "There shall be left for every man who cultivates his lands as much as he requires for his own support till the next crop be reaped, and that of his family and for seed. This much shall be left to him; what remains is the land tax and shall go to the public treasury."

among the Mussalmans, it follows that taking half their incomes is lawful *a fortiori*." The hint given as to the lawfulness of taking the whole of the property of the infidels was of course not likely to be lost on the ever necessitous Muhammadan sovereigns. Emperor Akbar abolished many vexatious taxes and fixed the land tax at about one-third of the gross produce, but his successors re-imposed all the abolished taxes. The devices resorted to for enhancing taxation were innumerable. In the provinces of Agra and Delhi the money assessment had been fixed by Todar Mull at so much per beigah of 3,600 square ells (each ell between 38½ to 41 inches) or nearly an acre; the tax was enhanced by the simple expedient[9] of reducing the *beigah* to one-third of its original dimensions.

Temples, palaces, &c., erected by means of forced labour.

10. It is the enormous revenue which former rulers derived from land, coupled with unlimited command of forced labour, that enabled them to execute the stupendous works, whether palaces, temples, anicuts or tanks, which strike us with astonishment. The celebrated temple at Tanjore built by the Cholas in the 11th century is stated to have taken 12 years to complete. The architect, who designed the building and supervised its execution, was one Soma Varman of Conjeeveram. A village, called Sárapallam (literally the hollow at the base of the scaf-

---

[9] *Vide* Grant's *Political Survey of the Northern Circars*. Appendix to the "Fifth Report" of the Parliamentary Committee on Indian affairs published by Messrs. Higginbotham & Co., page 233. Colonel Wilks in his *History of Mysore* mentions 20 additional taxes imposed by Chick Deo Raj, the able ruler of Mysore in 1672-1704. Four of the taxes may be mentioned here as the reasons given in justification of them are very characteristic:—

(1) *Hul Hanna*, a tax upon straw produced on land which had already paid kandaya or the regular land tax, on the pretence that a share of the straw as well as of the grain belonged to Government.

(2) *Deo Rai Wutta* is literally loss or difference of exchange on defective coins. Deo Raj exacted this tax as a reimbursement. This was soon after permanently added to the ryot's payments. It averaged 2 per cent. of the regular assessment.

(3) *Beargee*.—A potail, for example, farmed his village or engaged for the payment of a fixed sum to Government. When his actual receipts fell short of the amount, he compelled or induced the ryots to make good the loss by a proportional contribution. This contribution was called Beargee, and the largest amount that was ever contributed was collected under that name in addition to the kandaya of each ryot.

(4) *Yeare Sunca*.—Sunca is properly a duty on transit of goods or grain. *Yeare* is a plough. The ryot instead of carrying grain to where a transit duty is payable often sold it or consumed it in his own village. A tax of one to two gold fanams on each plough was imposed as an equivalent for the transit duty that would have been payable on the produce if it had been carried outside the village. This was called *Yeare Sunca*.

There is of course something to be said for these artifices resorted to with a view to enhance taxation. Where law is professedly based on customary usages and there is no direct legislation, if the revenue levied at customary rates becomes, owing to the fall in the value of the precious metals or otherwise, inadequate, the only way in which custom could be circumvented and a re-adjustment of taxation brought about would be the adoption of legal fictions of some sort or other.

For a list (a long one) of taxes levied by Native sovereigns in former centuries see appendices D and E, section I, to this memorandum. A grant in the reign of Rajarajadeva Chola, A.D. 1373, mentions revenue in paddy, tolls, small tax for the village police, including three handfuls of paddy, the money from water and land, the tax on looms, the tax on shops, the tax on goldsmiths, the tax on Ajivakas (Jains), the tax on oilmills, the money from the sale of fish in tanks, the money from documents, &c.

folding), 4 miles from Tanjore, is believed to be the place where the scaffolding, over which the block of granite, estimated to weigh 80 tons, was carried to the top of the tower, 200 feet high, rested. After visiting the Sun temple at Kunarak in Orissa, Abul Fazl, the famous minister of Akbar, is stated to have written as follows: "Near to Jagganath is the temple of the Sun, in the erection of which was expended the whole revenue of Orissa for 12 years. No one can behold this immense building without being struck with amazement." Dr. Hunter, in his "Orissa," mentions that the eastern entrance of the temple was till lately surmounted by a chlorite slab elaborately carved, and that its beauty tempted some English antiquarians to attempt to remove it to the Museum at Calcutta. A grant of public money was obtained for the purpose, but it sufficed only to drag the massive block a couple of 100 yards, where it now lies quite apart from the temple and as far as ever from the shore. Dr. Hunter states that the builders of the 12th century had excavated it in the quarries of the Hill States and carried it by a land journey across swamps and over unbridged rivers for a distance of 80 miles. It is evident that, to make this possible, human life and labour must have been quite as cheap in the 12th century as in the time of the Pharaohs when the Great Pyramid [10] was built. Impressment of labour for public works was till recently resorted to even under British rule, and there cannot be the slightest doubt that in previous centuries all public works were carried out by this means. Hyder, when he invaded the Carnatic, seized many artisans and carried them away to his own territories to work there. Colonel Wilks, in his history of Mysore, gives an account of the frightful oppressions caused by the impressment of labour by Tippu for carrying out the fortifications of Seringapatam, where 20,000 labourers were kept employed for years.

Tavernier's account of the state of the country and the condition of the people.

11. In Tavernier's account of his travels we have a bird's eye view of the state of India during the reigns of Shah Jehan and Aurangzebe, when the Moghul empire was at the height of its power and glory. Tavernier was a French goldsmith, who for purposes of trade made five voyages between 1631—1668 to India, and resided several months and

---

[10] "Senefru reigned 19 years, and his successor Khufu was the Cheops of the Greek lists, the builder of the Great Pyramid at Gizeh. How he lived we know but dimly, and the traditions preserved are not favorable, but he resolved to be buried grandly. Human labour was abundant and cheap, for it was supplied by slaves and captives and by the wretched peasantry, whose condition was little better. The huge masses of stone required for the building of the pyramidal tomb were dragged from the quarries by thousands of men harnessed by ropes to the rudely constructed cars and goaded by the whips of the task-masters. If they fainted and fell, they were left to die by the wayside and other conscripts took their places."—*Henry N. Inman.*

even years there on each occasion. He visited almost all parts of India. Masulipatam was in his time a great port and had the best anchorage on the Bay of Bengal. It was the only place from which vessels sailed for Pegu, Siam, Arrakan, Bengal, Cochin China, Mecca, Hormuz, Madagascar, Sumatra and the Manillas. Wheeled carriages could not travel between Golgonda and Masulipatam. It was with great difficulty that Tavernier was able to take a small cart to Golgonda, and he was obliged to take it to pieces in several places and carry them. There were no wagons in the country between Golgonda and Cape Comorin. Either oxen or pack horses were used for the conveyance of merchandize. But in default of chariots, says Tavernier, "you have the convenience of much larger palanquins than in the rest of India; for one is carried much more easily, more quickly and at less cost." Palanquin bearers were paid Rs. 5 each per mensem, and if the journey was long and likely to occupy more than 60 days, they were paid at the rate of Rs. 6. The most powerful of the sovereigns south of the Ganges was the Rajah of Vellore (Vijianagar dynasty), whose authority extended to Cape Comorin, but in his country there was no trade. Shah Jehan reigned for 40 years, less as a king over his subjects than as a father over his children. His dominions were well cultivated, but there were no roads or bridges. The journey from Surat to Agra occupied from thirty-five to forty days, and one had to pay between 40 and 45 rupees for carriage for the whole journey. Burhanpore was a much ruined town, where, however, an enormous quantity of very transparent muslins was made and exported to Persia, Turkey, Muskovie, Poland, Arabia, Grand Cairo and other places. There was abundance of cotton in the neighbourhood of Burhanpore. In Sironj there were a great many merchants and artisans, and that was the reason why it contained some houses of stone and brick. There was a large trade in colored calicoes called *chites* which were sent to Persia and Turkey. There was also made in this place a description of muslin "so fine that when it is on the person you see the skin as though it were uncovered." The merchants, however, were not allowed to export it, and the Governor sent it all for the use of the Great Moghul's seraglio and of the principal courtiers. Ahmedabad was a large town with considerable trade in silken stuffs, gold and silver tapestries, saltpetre, sugar, indigo, &c. In Benares, cottons, silken stuffs, and other merchandize were sold. The manufacturers, before exposing anything for sale, had to go to the person who had the Government contract to get the king's stamp impressed on the pieces of calico or silk manufactured, in default of which they were fined and flogged. Patna was one of the largest towns in India. The houses, however, were not better than in the majority of other towns and were nearly all roofed with thatch or bamboo. In Dacca the houses were miserable huts made of bamboo and mud. Sales were conditional on payments being made in coins coined during the current year. Foreign coins brought into the country had to be taken to the king's mint and there recoined, the expenses and seigniorage both in Persia and India amounting to ten per cent. These regulations were, however, generally evaded. In places where there were no money-changers, people would not take silver coins without putting them in the fire to test whether the silver was good. Bitter almonds and cowries were used as small change. Almonds were brought from Persia, and these were so bitter that there was no danger of children eating them. Thirty-five or forty almonds went to the *paisa* which was $\frac{1}{48}$ of a rupee. Of cowries, from 50 to 80 were exchangeable for a *paisa*, according to the distance of the place from the coast. "In India," says Tavernier, "a village must be very small if it has not a money-changer, whom they call *shroff*, who acts as broker to make remittances of money and issue letters of exchange. As in general these changers have an understanding with the Governors of provinces, they enhance at their will the rate of exchange of the rupee for the paisa and of the paisa for these shells. All the Jews who occupy themselves with money in the empire of the Grand Seignior pass for being very sharp, but in India they would be scarcely apprentices to these money-changers." Merchants were frequently plundered by the rajahs of the territories through which they had to pass. The Rajah of Kalabagh was oppressive to merchants, but since Aurangzebe came to the throne, says Tavernier, "he cut off his head and those of a large number of his subjects. They have set up towers near the town, on the high road, and these towers are pierced all round by several windows where they have placed in each the head of a man at every two feet. On my last journey in 1665, it was not long since the execution had taken place when I passed by Kalabagh, for all the heads were still entire and gave out an unpleasant odour." The dispensation of justice was very summary and unencumbered with forms. There were no jails, for the custom of the country was not to keep men in prison. Immediately the accused was taken he was examined and sentence pronounced on him and executed without delay. Tavernier went to see Meer Jumla, Nabob of Gundikot, a place in the Cuddapah district, who was a General under the King of Golgonda at first and subsequently under Emperor Aurangzebe, and to whom he had shown some diamonds for sale and of whose abilities he speaks highly. While he was with the Nabob, it was announced that 4 prisoners had arrived. "The Nabob remained silent for half an hour without replying, writing continually and making his secretaries write, but at length he suddenly ordered the criminals to be brought in, and after having questioned them and made them confess with their mouths the crimes of which they were accused, he remained nearly an hour without saying anything and continuing to write and making his secretaries write." Among these 4 prisoners was one who had entered a house and slain a mother and her three infants. He was condemned forthwith to have his hands and feet cut off and to be thrown into a field near the high road to end his days. Another had stolen on the high road, and the Nabob ordered him to have his stomach slit open and flung in a drain. Tavernier says that he could not ascertain what the others had done, but the heads of both of them were cut off. The men who worked at the diamond mines at Golgonda earned only 2*s*. 3*d*. per mensem, though, says Tavernier, they were men who thoroughly understood their work. The wages being so small the men did not manifest any scruple about concealing a stone found when they could, which they did by putting it in their mouths, as they had little or no clothing on their bodies. Tavernier gives the following account of the peasantry and of the common soldiers: "One hundred of our European soldiers would scarcely have any difficulty in vanquishing 1,000 of these Indian soldiers; but it is true, on the other hand, that they would have much difficulty in accustoming themselves to so abstemious a life as theirs. For the horseman, as well as the infantry, supports himself with a little flour kneaded with a little water and black sugar, of which he makes balls, and in the evening they make *kichri*, which consists of rice cooked with dholl in water with a little salt. When eating it, they dip their fingers in melted butter. Such is the ordinary food of both soldiers and the poor people. To which it should be added that the heat would kill our soldiers, who would be unable to remain in the heat of the sun as these Indians do. I should say, *en passant*, that the peasants have for their sole garment a scrap of cloth tied round their loins, and that they are reduced to great poverty because, if the Governors become aware that they possess any property, they seize it straightway by right or by force. You may see in India whole provinces like deserts, from whence the peasants have fled on account of the oppressions of the Governors. Under cover of the fact that they are themselves Muhammadans, they persecute the poor idolators to the utmost, and if any of the latter become Muhammadans, it is in order not to work any more; they become soldiers or fakirs, who are people who make profession of having renounced the world and live upon alms, but in reality they are great rascals. It is estimated that there are 800,000 Muhammadan fakirs and 1,200,000 among the idolators." Tavernier was a devout French Protestant Christian, and he adds: "Although these idolators are in the depths of blindness to a knowledge of the true God, that does not prevent them from living morally well; when married, they are rarely unfaithful to their wives, and adultery is very rare among them."

SECTION II.—*The condition of the Presidency at the end of the 18th century when most of the provinces of Southern India were acquired by the British.*

12. In the appendix A, section II, will be found extracts from official reports describing in some detail the state of the country at the commencement of the present century when most of the provinces of Southern India came under British occupation. In the earlier centuries, although the country had suffered from frequent wars, it had, with some intervals of anarchy, the advantage of a more or less settled government. In the 18th century, however, the completest anarchy prevailed and the condition of the people was miserable in the extreme. In the beginning of the century, the Moghul General Zulfikar Khan, who had command of the Payen Ghât or the country between the Kistna and the Coleroon rivers, was engaged in incessant and destructive wars for 19 years till the death of the Emperor Aurangzebe. "The express statement," says Colonel Wilks, "of 19 actions fought and three thousand coss (6,000 miles) marched by this officer in the course of six months only may afford some faint idea of the wretchedness in which the unfortunate inhabitants were involved during that period, and these miseries of war, in the ordinary course of human calamity, were necessarily followed by a long and destructive famine and pestilence. Within this period Zulfikar Khan appears to have made three different expeditions to the south of the Cauvery, levying heavy contributions on Tanjore and Trichinopoly." Soon after the Moghul conquest the Moghul power rapidly declined under the assaults made on it by the Mahrattas. When the emperor appointed a jaghirdar over a tract of country, the Mahrattas appointed another, and both of them fleeced the cultivators who often had no alternative left but to leave off cultivating and become plunderers in their turn. Shortly after followed the wars consequent on disputed succession to the soubah of the Deccan and the nabobship of the Carnatic and the struggle for

supremacy between the English and the French. In the language of the "Fifth Report," when the Northern Circars were handed over by the Nizam to the English in 1766, "the whole system of internal management had become disorganized. Not only the forms but even the remembrance of civil authority seemed to be wholly lost." The Chingleput district had almost entirely been depopulated by the wars with Hyder, so much so that "hardly any other signs were left in many parts of the country of its having been inhabited by human beings than the bones of the bodies that had been massacred or the naked walls of the houses, choultries and temples which had been burnt."[11] The terrible memories of "Hyder kalábam," or the ravages of Hyder's cavalry, still live in stories current among the common people at the present day. Tanjore, which was in the possession of the Nabob of Arcot in the years 1774 and 1775, was almost ruined by "his inhuman exactions;" and, according to Rev. Schwartz, the famous Luthern missionary and an eyewitness, the people would have preferred Hyder's invasion to the Nabob's occupation. In the second year, the Nabob extorted from the landholders no less than 81 lakhs of rupees which is nearly double the present land revenue of the district. It will have been seen from the extracts from the letters of the Jesuit missionaries already given, that Ekoji took 80 per cent. of the gross produce as revenue, leaving only 20 per cent. to the mirasidars. On the accession of Pratap Singh to the musnud the mirasidars' varam appears to have been 30 per cent. of the pisanam and 45 per cent. of the kar crop, and the rate for the pisanam crop was raised by him and his successors till it amounted to 40 per cent. in the time of Amir Singh. How little the rights of the mirasidars were, owing to misgovernment, understood at the time will be seen from the fact that the English commissioners, who reported on the resources of the country on the deposition of Amir Singh and the installation of Surfoji under British auspices. characterized the settlement made by Amir Singh fixing the Government share of the produce at 60 per cent. and the mirasidars' varam at 40 per cent., as a "profligate remission." In the zemindar and poligar countries the only limit to the exactions to which the ryots were subjected was their ability to pay; the customary share of the produce belonging to Government was nominally half, but additional taxes were levied on various pretexts, reducing

---

[11] Even in the Tanjore delta a large part of the population must have died of famine. In 1781, the year before Hyder's invasions the outturn of crop in the Tanjore delta was 11,909,085 kalams of paddy. In 1781-82 the outturn was 1,808,808 kalams, and in 1782-83 only 1,563,122 kalams. The outturn gradually rose again till it reached 10,416,746 kalams in 1796-97.—*Vide Tanjore District Manual*, page 813.

the share enjoyed by the ryots to $\frac{1}{5}$ or $\frac{1}{6}$. Where there were no zemindars, renters were employed, especially by Muhammadan Governments, to collect the revenue and these renters mercilessly fleeced the people. Mr. Wallace, the Collector of Trichinopoly, writing in 1802, has given an account of the revenue administration of the district under the Nabob. The Government tax on wet lands was received in grain, and the whole of the grain produced was a strict Government monopoly, so strict, indeed, that if one ryot lent to another a small quantity of grain for consumption, he was severely fined. The ryots were compelled to pay in grain even the taxes on swarnadayam (literally money-rented) or garden lands which were ordinarily payable in money. The grain was taken from the mirasidars at a valuation of 7 or 8 fanams per kalam and sold back from the Government granaries at 9 or 10 fanams per kalam. When Mr. Wallace settled the Government revenue he had to base his settlement on the prices of grain in the adjoining district of Tanjore, as the natural prices of grain in the Trichinopoly district itself could not be ascertained in consequence of the Government monopoly of grain which had long been subsisting there. Of all the portions of the Presidency the most prosperous were perhaps Malabar and South Canara, which, owing to their isolated position, had not suffered from frequent and destructive wars like other provinces. Both these districts were, however, ruined by the exactions of Hyder and Tippoo, and, more especially, by the attempt of the latter to convert all the inhabitants to Islamism. Most of the landholders in Malabar fled to Travancore and Tippoo carried away nearly 60,000 Christians of South Canara into captivity to Mysore. Colonel, afterwards Sir Thomas, Munro, who was Collector of Canara, wrote: "Canara has completely fallen from its state of prosperity. The evils which have been continually accumulating upon it, since it became a province of Mysore, have destroyed a great part of its former population and rendered its remaining inhabitants as poor as those of neighbouring countries. Its lands, which are now saleable, are reduced to a very small portion and lie chiefly between the Kundapur and Chandragiri rivers and within 5 or 6 miles of the sea. It is not to be supposed, however, that the whole of this tract can be sold, but only that saleable lands are scattered throughout every part of it, thinner in some places and thicker in others, particularly in the Mangalore district. There is scarcely any saleable land, even on the sea coast, any where to the northward of Kundapur, or any where inland from one end of Canara to the other, excepting on the banks of the Mangalore and some other great rivers. It is reckoned that the population of the country has been diminished one-third within the last 40 years and there can be little doubt that its property has suffered much greater reduction. Garisappa, Ankola and Kundapur, formerly flourishing places, contain now only a few beggarly inhabitants. Honawar, once the second town in trade after Mangalore, has not a single house; and Mangalore itself is greatly decayed."

13. Dr. Buchanan, who travelled from the East to the West Coast in 1800, mentions that the country was infested by gangs of marauders to such an extent that "the smallest village of 5 or 6 houses is fortified. The defence of such a village consists of a round stone wall, perhaps 40 feet in diameter and 6 feet high. On the top of this is a parapet of mud with a door-way in it, to which the only access is by a ladder. In case of a plundering party coming near the village, the people ascend this tower with their families and most valuable effects and having drawn up the ladder defend themselves with stones, which even the women throw with great force and dexterity. Larger villages have square forts, with round towers at the angles. In those still larger or in towns, the defences are more numerous and the fort serves as a citadel; while the village or pettah is surrounded by a weaker defence of mud. The inhabitants consider fortifications as necessary to their existence and are at the expense of building and the risk of defending them. The country indeed, for a long series of years, has been in a constant state of warfare and the poor inhabitants have suffered too much from all parties to trust in any." The internal trade was greatly restricted by the number of choukies or custom-houses existing in the country and the absence of a recognized currency. Every petty poligar levied customs duty on goods passing through his estate. In the Salem district there were no less than 25 choukies on 206 miles of road or one for every 8 miles. Colonel Reade, Collector of Salem, in 1797, calculates that the customs duties alone levied on goods sent from Salem to the coast, a distance of 150 miles, added 40 per cent. to the cost price of articles exclusive of the cost of carriage, and the result was that it did not pay to send most of the articles in demand to the coast. In Salem and the Ceded districts no less than 40 different descriptions of coins were current, and, as most of them did not bear to one another the relation of multiples or sub-multiples, the shroffs were enabled to cheat poor people right and left. Tippoo Sultan used to change the value of the coins in a very arbitrary manner. When he was about to pay his troops the nominal value of every coin was raised very high and kept at that level for a few days, and during

this period, the soldiery were allowed to pay off their debts at the high valuation. Under the designation *moturpha*, taxes[12] were levied on all artisans and laborers, and these bore hardest on the poorest classes.

There were no courts of justice, the settlement of disputes being left entirely to the villagers themselves and the heads of castes and clans. Even in the province of Tanjore, where, owing to its comparative prosperity, it might be supposed that the necessity for regular courts of justice would have been felt, a court was established by the Rajah of Tanjore only about the close of the last century at the suggestion of Rev. Schwartz. Colonel Reade states: "When the district (Salem) was ceded to the Company the Chetties of certain castes, exercising judicial authority over their clients, were in the practice of levying taxes on the pullers, a caste of husbandmen, on the five castes of artisans, viz., goldsmiths, blacksmiths, carpenters, braziers, and stone-cutters, and on washermen, barbers, pariahs, chucklers and others. The Chetties likewise exacted fines for murder, theft, adultery, breach of marriage contract, also for killing brahmani kites, monkeys, snakes, &c. The Government, in consideration of these privileges, had imposed a tax on the Chetties; but, conceiving that I and my assistants might administer justice with greater impartiality than the Chetties, their judicial powers were annulled and with them the tax on castes."

14. The early reports teem with evidence of the extreme poverty of the vast majority of the agricultural classes. Dr. Buchanan states that "the peasantry here as in almost every part of India are miserably poor. One great cause indeed of the poverty of the farmers and the consequent poverty of crops in many parts of India is the custom of forcing land on people who have no means of cultivating it." Grant, in his Survey of the Northern Circars, writes in 1784 that the peasantry, "in order to carry on the common practices of husbandry

---

[12] No less than thirty-five taxes of Coimbatore district were abolished by Major McLeod. These were—(1) tax on potters, (2) Nama and Vibhuti khancha or taxes on those wearing the Namam and sacred ash marks, (3) fees at weekly markets, (4) tax on dye stuffs, (5) on ghee, (6) on tobacco, (7) on heaps of grain, (8) on chunam, (9) on taliaries, (10) on nirgantis, (11) on pack-bullock keepers, (12) on dancing girls, (13) on labour maistries, (14) on women committing adultery, (15) rents of lotus leaves, (16) on gardens in backyards and plantations in river banks, (17) on cattle grazing in paddy fields, (18) on young palmyra nuts, (19) on tamarinds, (20) on balapam (pot stone or soap stone), (21) on betel nuts, (22) tax on the measurement of grain on the sharing system, (23) on offerings at Mahadeveswaramalai, (24) levies for charity, (25) taxes on mamoties (hoes), (26) on village fees to village artisans, (27) on the sale of cattle, (28) on cattle stalls, (29) on water lifts, (30) on fishing, (31) on looms, (32) contributions levied by amuldars from ryots whenever there was any deficiency in the amount agreed to be paid by the latter to Government, (33) contributions levied for the expenses of the Tahsildar, (34) payment of one fanam by each ryot with his first instalment of assessment and (35) plough tax (*vide Coimbatore District Manual*). See also appendix B, section II, for a list of the taxes levied and the rates at which they were assessed.

in places where the culture is simple and the meanest as in the Circars, find it expedient, at the different seasons, to borrow money at high interest in proportion to the risk incurred by the lender, and never under two per cent." Sir Thomas Munro, writing in 1797, says "many of the ryots are so poor that it is always doubtful whether next year they will be in the rank of cultivators or laborers, and few of them so rich as not to be liable to be forced by one or two bad seasons to throw up a considerable part of their farms. Many of the middling class of ryots often fail from the most trifling accidents. The loss of a bullock, or of a member of the family who worked in the fields, or confinement to bed by a fit of sickness, frequently disable them from paying their usual rent during the ensuing year." The realization of Government revenue by means of torture was one of the recognized institutions of the country and the practice indeed continued, though in a mitigated form, down to 1855. Mr. Forbes, the Collector of Tanjore, writing in that year, states that "the ryot will often appear in the cutcherry with his full liabilities in his possession, tied up in small sums about his person, to be doled out rupee by rupee according to the *urgency* of the demand, and will sometimes return to his village, having left a balance undischarged, not because he could not pay it, but because he was not forced to do so." The above quotation will serve to show how abject and demoralized was the condition of the agricultural classes in those days.

SECTION III.—*The Condition of the Agricultural Classes under British Administration during the first half of the present century.*

Early land settlements and the condition of the country during the first 30 years of the century.

15. The bulk of the territories under the Government of Madras, with the exception of the Northern Circars, the Chingleput jaghir, and a few trading settlements, were acquired by the English between the years 1792 and 1803. At the conclusion of the first war with Tippoo in 1792, the districts of Salem, Dindigul and Malabar were acquired. The second Mysore war in 1799 added Canara and Coimbatore. In 1800 the whole territory south of the Kistna and Tungabhadra rivers, comprising the districts of Cuddapah, Bellary and Anantapur and portions of Kurnool, were ceded by the Nizam. In 1799 the Rajah of Tanjore resigned his sovereign rights over that province to the English, and in 1801 the Nabob of the Carnatic made over to them the districts of Nellore, North Arcot, South Arcot, Trichinopoly, Madura and Tinnevelly. The British power may thus be said to have been

fully established in this Presidency in the beginning of the century, the only territorial changes that have since occurred being the annexation of Kurnool Proper in 1838, the transfer of North Canara to the Bombay Presidency in 1862, and the addition of Bhadráchalam and Rékapalle taluks transferred from the Central Provinces to the Godávari district in 1874. Previous to the reforms in the Civil Service introduced by Lord Cornwallis, there was little to choose between English administration and that of the Native Princes so far as the agricultural classes were concerned. English writers and factors, who were paid £10 and £20 per annum and were allowed liberty to carry on private trade, found themselves suddenly transformed into governors of provinces and were not slow to make the most of their opportunities. Within a short time, however, after Lord Cornwallis' reforms, the administration had wonderfully improved and a succession of great administrators, among whom may be mentioned Reade, Munro, Graham, Hurdis, Wallace, Hodgson, Thackeray, came to the front. Their first measures were directed towards the pacification of the country and the suppression of the power of the poligars, who, with large bands of armed followers, plundered the country, committing the greatest excesses; there were in the Ceded districts alone 80 poligars, who had under their command 30,000 armed peons. The poligars in the Madura and Tinnevelly districts especially, fought desperately for their independence, but were finally reduced to submission. Next followed settlements of land revenue, in the introduction of which many grievous mistakes were committed. The resources of the country had been brought to the last stage of exhaustion by the previous mis-government wars and famines, and, before there was time to ascertain the true revenue capabilities of the several districts, orders were received from Bengal for the immediate carrying out of the permanent settlement of the revenue with zemindars if such were in existence and for creating zemindars where they did not exist. The Governor-General declared that he was determined to dismiss every officer who neglected or delayed to carry out these orders. The districts of Chingleput, Salem and Dindigul were divided into a number of mittahs and sold to the highest bidders. Most of the purchasers, after pillaging the ryots, failed in the course of a year or two and the whole settlement collapsed. The system of village leases was next tried, but with the same result. In the Ceded districts especially, where, in supersession of the ryotwar system introduced by Colonel, afterwards Sir Thomas, Munro, village leases were introduced, the results were disastrous. It was expected that the villagers as a body would agree to the leases, but, as the assessment was high, the leases were taken up by mere speculators, the renters were ruined, the ryots impoverished, and the villages returned to Government. In the Ráyadrug taluk alone Sir Thomas Munro states "nearly half the ryots had emigrated, most of the headmen were reduced to poverty, and many of them had been sent to jail. The substantial ryots, whose stock supported the agriculture of the villages, were gone." The fact was that the old assessments, which were continued in their entirety or with only slight reductions in the first years of British administration, were excessive. Under the loose systems of revenue administration which had prevailed under Native Governments, although the full demand was occasionally realized, the ryot had a great many opportunities of cheating the Government of its dues with the connivance of the revenue agents. Under the more regular system introduced by the British, however, opportunities for evasion and peculation were less frequent. Sir Thomas Munro calculated that out of Rs. 100, the value of the gross produce, the Government assessment was represented by Rs. 45–12–0 and the expenses of cultivation by Rs. 40, leaving a profit to the ryot of only Rs. 14–4–0.[13] The profit was liable to be turned into loss not only in bad seasons, which were by no means infrequent, but also in good seasons when the prices of produce fell. He was of opinion that to encourage cultivation of land and give it saleable value, the Government demand should be limited to one-third of the gross produce, and strongly urged on Government, in 1807, the desirability of reducing the assessment on wet and dry lands by 25 and on garden lands by $33\frac{1}{3}$ per cent. The Government, while acquiescing in the justice of the recommendation, was unable to sanction it in consequence

[13] Mr. G. E. Russel, the Collector of Masulipatam, writing in 1819, estimates the average profit of cultivation made by the ryots in the zemindari villages in the Kistna delta at even less. His calculations are as follows for wet lands :—

	RS.	A.	P.	RS.	A.	P.
Value of gross produce				160	0	0
Government assessment	80	0	0			
Durbar charges and other taxes..	27	3	0			
				107	3	0
Expenses of cultivation				42	8	0
Ryot's profit ..				10	5	0

A ryot's family, consisting of five persons, will cost for grain alone Rs. 33. Mr. Russel adds: "The plough itself affords little towards his support, and were it not that it gives him a valuable right of pasture for his cattle and ground for his pumpkins, he could not subsist. A single she-buffalo will yield him Rs. 8 per annum in ghee alone, and the profit he derives from this source added to the labour of his women enable him to procure the necessaries of life, but even these aids will not always afford him the means of subsistence, and for 2 or 3 months in the year the fruit from his pumpkin garden, mixed up with his buttermilk or a very small proportion of meat, is the daily diet of his family."

Dr. Macleane in his *Manual of Administration* states of the ryots of Nellore: "Historically it is said that the farmers devoted themselves to cattle breeding in despair of obtaining remunerative prices from agriculture."

of orders received from England for the remittance of an additional sum of a million sterling annually, accompanied by a threat from the Court of Directors, that unless this were done they would take the question of reducing the establishments in their own hands. When Sir Thomas Munro became Governor of Madras in 1822, he sanctioned the proposals made by himself for the reduction of assessment in the Ceded districts and granted alleviations in other districts also. These measures, though they averted the further decline of the country, had, owing to adverse circumstances, little effect in improving the condition of the ryots. Within 24 years there were no less than four famines, viz., those of 1799, of 1804–7, of 1811–12 and of 1824. Nine years later in 1833–34 occurred the famine known as the Guntúr famine, which, though confined to a small area, was more destructive in its effects than that of 1876–78. The mortality and suffering [14] caused by it were terrible. In the Guntúr portion of the Kistna district from one-third to half of the whole population perished.

Agricultural depression between 1834 to 1854 and its causes.

16. From 1834 down to 1854 there was no famine of a severe type, though the country suffered from a series of unfavorable seasons. There was a severe agricultural depression on account of the low prices which then ruled of agricultural produce. This was due to causes which were in operation throughout India and were not merely confined to this Presidency. Owing to the slow development of export trade and the remittance of considerable amount of specie to England, the currency of the country had become quite insufficient for its requirements, under the altered conditions brought about by English rule, viz., the development of internal traffic consequent on a quarter of a century of peace and the substitution of cash payments for payments in kind both in the receipt of taxes and the disbursements of Government. On this subject Mr. Pedder writes: "India does not produce the precious metals and can obtain her currency only in exchange for exports. Before the introduction of British rule there was comparatively little trade; much of what trade there was was carried on by barter, and a considerable portion of the receipts and disbursements of Government was in kind, not in

---

[14] Captain (afterwards Colonel) Walter Campbell, who was an eye-witness, describes the horrors of the famine at Masulipatam in the centre of the Kistna delta. He states: "The description in 'the siege of Corinth' of dogs gnawing human skulls is mild as compared with the scenes of horror we are daily forced to witness in our morning and evening rides. . . . It is dreadful to see what revolting food human beings may be driven to partake of. Dead dogs and horses are greedily devoured by these starving wretches; and the other day an unfortunate donkey having strayed from the fort, they fell upon him like a pack of wolves, tore him limb from limb and devoured him on the spot."

cash. Hence, if the circulating medium was limited in quantity, its 'duty,' that is, the number and amount of the transactions in which it had to be exchanged for goods or labour, was still more limited and prices were high. After the general introduction of British rule, a heavier 'duty' was thrown upon the circulating medium by the extension of trade, by the greater demands of the revenue for cash (especially of the land revenue, assessments in kind being converted into assessments in coin), by the system of the British Government of paying its army and its officers in money. The circulating medium could not expand to the extent demanded by this altered state of things; importation of bullion was not sufficient to make up the amount annually withdrawn from circulation by waste, by being hoarded or by being converted into ornaments; or at any rate was not sufficient to increase the currency in proportion to the greater 'duty' thrown on it, while at the same time, with peace and a settled government there was a great extension of cultivation and consequent increase of production. Hence prices steadily fell."[15] This period was one of acute suffering to the agricultural classes and the revenues declined greatly in several districts.

17. In the reports of the Collectors on the state of the several districts during this period, and those of the Commissioners appointed to enquire into the causes of the decline of the revenues in the several parts of the Presidency, we have full information regarding the condition of the ryots in those days. I shall here mention the principal facts gathered from these reports as regards typical districts. Notwithstanding the large remissions sanctioned by Sir Thomas Munro in the assessment of the Ceded districts, we find the Collector of Cuddapah, Mr. Dalzell, writing to the Board in 1828 as follows: "The present system of revenue management is clearly favorable to the more substantial class of ryots in a degree beyond that of our predecessors (Hyder and Tippoo), but it is to be feared that the case is different with the poorer cultivators. . . . Our system, it is true, admits of the entire remission of rent when cultivation is prevented or crops are actually destroyed by want of water, but it does not allow much for deficient crops. . . . The ryots are more in the hands of merchants than perhaps you are prepared to hear. . . . The peasantry are too poor to more than keep up their cultivation with Takavi when they have met with no extraordinary losses.

---

[15] *Vide Statement of Moral and Material Progress of India* for 1882-83, vol. I, page 201. For a more detailed explanation of the causes of the fall of prices between 1830 and 1850, see also the Article from the *Bombay Quarterly Journal*, 1857, printed in the appendix A, section III.

When they have met with such losses from the death of cattle or other cause, it is impossible to repair them without assistance from Takavi." By 1854, however, the condition of the ryots in this district had considerably improved. The orders of the Court of Directors allowing to the ryots the full benefits of the improvements to land carried out by them at their own expense had led to the construction of substantial wells and the increase of the produce of lands irrigated by them. The cultivation of indigo had increased and the poorer ryots had been assisted by advances by European firms and thus freed from the clutches of usurious money-lenders. Sir Thomas Munro estimated the value of indigo exported in 1805 from the Ceded districts at Rs. 4,37,500. The exports in 1851 from the Cuddapah district alone were valued at Rs. 13,75,182, notwithstanding the fact that the price of indigo had decreased considerably since 1805. The cultivation of sugarcane had also considerably increased, the exports of jaggery in 1851 amounting to 11 lakhs of maunds. The trade of the district was, however, much hampered by want of roads. The Collector writes in 1852: "At present the journey to Madras is dreaded by the ryots, and they object to allow their cattle to be employed in conveying indigo and other produce to the Presidency where it is required for shipment to Europe. The small number of carts and the heavy rate for carriage together with the small quantity that can be placed on the loaded cart on account of the badness of the road act as a prohibition to the export of the various kinds of oil-seeds, &c., which would find a ready market in the ports of the sea coast. In the neighbourhood of the Presidency I am informed that 50 or 55 maunds (of 25 lb.) is the usual cart-load, whilst here, with good bullocks, under 40 can only be placed in a cart. The hire per gow of 10 miles in the south is 8 annas, whilst here not less than 10 annas is accepted and they demand often 1 rupee. The hire from Cuddapah to Madras has of late been as high as 20 and 24 rupees which raises the hire of cart per gow to the exorbitant sum of about Rs. 1–8–0, nearly tripling the current rate in the south." In the Bellary district, on the other hand, the ryots had made no progress. The incidence of the land revenue assessments, notwithstanding Sir Thomas Munro's reductions, continued, owing to the heavy fall in the prices of produce, oppressive, while this district enjoyed no special advantages like Cuddapah in regard to good subsoil water-supply, and extension of indigo cultivation. Mr. Mellor, the Collector, reported in 1845: "The universal complaint and request of the ryots is to be allowed to reduce their farms, a convincing proof that cultivation is not profitable.

Land has never been saleable. Ryots, formerly substantial and capable of laying out their capital on the lands and liquidating their Sircar demand, reserving their produce until they could get a favorable price, are now sunk in debt bearing heavy interest, entirely subject to their creditors; and were it not for the aid of the Collector through his revenue subordinates, one-half, or at least one-third of the highly assessed lands would ere this have been thrown up. Husbandry is not carried on efficiently, and consequently the land seldom returns what it ought and is capable of. The number of puttah holders has increased, but they are a poor class who seek a maintenance only in husbandry with less spirit, and by no means to be compared with the substantial farmers who have fallen into difficulties and disappeared from the rent roll of the district. With regard to food and raiment the majority of them are poorly clad and ill-fed, and it is impossible to arrive at any other conclusion than that poverty is the cause. It is no new doctrine; Sir Thomas Munro declared that the ryots of the Ceded districts were the poorest of the Company's subjects." Writing in 1851, or six years later, Mr. Pelly gives the following account of the Bellary ryots: "I find that out of the whole body of farmers only 17 per cent. are in what may be termed to be good circumstances, substantial ryots who have capital enabling them to discharge their kists without recourse to the money-lender. About 49 per cent. are obliged to borrow money by mortgaging their crops and stock and 34 per cent. are obliged to sell their crops as soon as reaped and even their stock to pay their kists." Rajahmundry, *i.e.*, the present Godávari district, which may now be said to be the garden of the Madras Presidency, appears, from the report of Sir Henry Montgomery in 1844, to have been on the verge of ruin. Of the ten years between 1831–1840, 1831 and 1832 were famine years, in 1835, 1836 and 1837 the season is described as "unfavorable," and in 1838, 1839 and 1840 as "calamitous." The population which in 1830 had been 695,016 had decreased in 1840 to 533,836. The closing of the Government weaving factories in consequence of the abrogation of the Company's trading privileges in 1833 had thrown large numbers of weavers out of employment, and money to the extent of 7 lakhs of rupees on an average per annum, which was in circulation in connection with the maintenance of the factories, was withdrawn. The value of exports of piece-goods had decreased from Rs. 9,74,075 to Rs. 1,59,312. Notwithstanding a series of bad harvests, prices of grain continuously declined owing to the competition of cheap rice from Arrakan. Of the condition of the ryots under the zemindars Sir Henry Montgomery writes:

"The system of management was formed on the sole principle of extracting from the ryots the utmost possible amount of present revenue. In adverse seasons all that could be taken of the ryots was claimed on the part of the zemindar whose demand purposely exceeded the means of the ryots in ordinary seasons. In years of abundant produce, the deficiency of bad seasons was made good, so that in either case the ryot was left but the barest means of subsistence. . . . The Visabadi kist, which remained the standard beriz, was itself immoderately heavy, exceeding the possible amount of ordinary collections and not likely to be equalled in extraordinarily favorable times, by the over-rated value of the gross produce which itself was also over-estimated. It served, however, for a never-failing pretext for the demand of balances against those who, by industry or any fortuitous circumstances, procured the means of answering it in part, and was with this view continued." He, however, adds: "Though a grievous and oppressive dependence of the ryot characterized the management of zemindars and proprietors, yet the pressing wants of the ryot were in some degree seasonably supplied. Cultivation was compulsory and maintained by seasonable advances, and though the ryot was left little more than what was absolutely necessary for his maintenance, some care was taken against the discouragement of agriculture by his distress." Sir Henry Montgomery recommended the construction of the Godávari anicut, and from 1844 the condition of the district rapidly improved; from that year the seasons began to improve; French ships flocked to Cocanada for cargoes of grain, and the large expenditure on public works afforded work to thousands of the labouring classes. Sir Walter Elliot's report on Guntúr shows that the terrible famine of 1833 had utterly prostrated the district, and the epidemic which broke out in the following year and prevailed to such an extent that "a man in perfect health was hardly to be seen anywhere," rendered the recovery of the country impossible for a long series of years even under the most favorable circumstances. In Nellore, the ryots had become impoverished by the low prices of grain which ruled. Indigo cultivation was tolerably remunerative, but sugarcane cultivation had entirely ceased, owing to its inability to compete with jaggery imported from the Ceded districts. The total cropped area of the district had, however, risen from 244,319 acres in 1801 to 389,802 acres in 1850. Garden lands had entirely ceased to be cultivated owing to the increased pressure of the assessment consequent on the fall in the prices of grain. As regards North Arcot, the Collector, Mr. Bourdillon, reported: "The ryots are in worse condition than they were at the beginning of the century. However this may be, their present condition is indubitably bad and must be improved. The great body of them are certainly poor; their food is deficient in quantity as well as coarse; their clothing is scanty and poor, and their dwellings extremely mean; all this combined with gross ignorance." The unequal pressure of the assessment had the effect of throwing out of cultivation lands of the better qualities. The Collector of South Arcot, however, writing in 1840, gave a somewhat more favorable account of the ryots in his district. The population in 20 years had increased from 455,020 to 591,667, and cultivating ryots from 60,000 to 90,000. The price of labour had increased by 25 per cent. In the use of spring carriages, fine cloths, the style of houses, furniture and ornaments, there were indications of improvement. Agriculture was, however, in a backward condition owing to heavy and unequal assessment and two thirds of the cultivable lands were waste. Tanjore did not suffer to the same extent as other districts from agricultural depression owing to the improvements to irrigation works carried out by Government and increased production, and to the extension of communications and the growth of an export trade in grain with Madras and Ceylon. As regards the Coimbatore district, the Collector writing in 1840 remarks that of the previous ten seasons nine had been bad ones, and that the land revenue had fallen in consequence. There was not much variation in the value of the trade in piece-goods. The trade in coarse piece-goods exported to Bombay had improved, but that in fine goods had been annihilated by English manufactures. Prices of agricultural produce had risen owing to a succession of bad seasons. The wages of labour had also risen. "In India" the Collector remarks "greater income does not lead to improvement in the style of living, but increase of expenditure on marriages and religious ceremonies and in feeding poor relations." Bandies were coming into use; 30 years before they were not used by merchants. Money was said to be more easily procurable than before; the rate of interest on loans was from 12 to 18 per cent., while formerly the rates were from 24 to 30 per cent. on the security of jewels or landed property. In Malabar the population had increased from 465,594 in 1802 to 1,165,489 in 1837. The value of exports of cotton goods, which were manufactured in Coimbatore, Salem, Madura and Tinnevelly districts increased from Rs. 4,363 in 1804 to Rs. 22,81,000 in 1837. The price of labour had not increased with the increase of cultivation. This result was due to the increase of population and cheapness of grain. The improved state of communications—roads and navigation—and the introduction, though on a small scale, of pack bullocks and carts reduced the cost of carriage of goods to 50 per cent. of what it was 20 or 30 years before. The Collector remarks that cheap prices increased the consumption of luxuries and ameliorated the condition of the lower orders. Taking the Presidency as a whole, however, there can be no doubt that between 1830 and 1850, and more especially between 1835 and 1845, the condition of the agricultural classes was wretched. For detailed particulars regarding the income and the style of living of the different classes of ryots, reference may be made to the account of Mr. Bourdillon printed as appendix B, section III, to this memorandum.

The measures taken to ameliorate the condition of ryots and the state of communications.

18. The principal measures adopted by Government during this period for the development of the country and the amelioration of the condition of the agricultural classes were (1) the abolition of the sayer duties and of the duties on interportal trade; (2) the abolition of the tobacco monopoly in South Canara and Malabar and of a large number of petty and vexatious imposts; (3) the relinquishment of the right claimed by former Governments to tax improvements to lands carried out solely at the expense of the landholders; and (4) the construction of the Cauvery, Godávari and Kistna anicuts. Sir Charles Trevelyan's famous report on the sayer or inland transit duties in 1834 contains a graphic account of the frightful oppressions suffered by the people and the demoralization caused by the levy of these duties. "If we were to encourage swamps," says Sir Charles Trevelyan, "or accumulate mountains between the different districts of the country, we could not paralyse their industry so effectually as by this scheme of finance." These duties were abolished in the Madras Presidency in 1844 or ten years after the issue of Sir Charles Trevelyan's report. In the report of the Public Works Commission in 1852, we have an account of the state of communications and of the measures taken to improve them. At the time when most of the districts were acquired by the British, says this report, "there was not one complete road throughout the whole Presidency on which it would have been possible to employ wheeled carriages; their use was therefore very limited, and the distant traffic of the country had nowhere the advantage of them. Trucks were used by those who collected stone for the dams and the tank embankments, and in some localities the harvest was brought in by carts upon wheels either formed of solid pieces of timber or cut from a single block of stone. These carts were drawn by several pairs of bullocks and carried nearly a ton, but they were never used for distant journeys. Even the main streets of the largest towns

were not practicable for wheels, and when the most wealthy used light carriages, they rarely left the precincts of their villages. The only 'made roads,' if they deserved the name, were the mountain passes which in the later wars were opened for the passage of artillery, but they had generally been destroyed by the monsoon rains before the country came into the possession of the Company. The only proof of attention to the great roads was to be seen in the fine avenues of trees, which in some districts measured several hundred miles in length; but as the roadways beneath them had never been properly formed or drained, and bridges had not been built, nor care taken to keep the pathway practicable, they were roads no longer; but in most cases from being worn down by former traffic and washed by the rains of the monsoon, they had become the drain of the country that they passed and were so much more rugged than the land on either side that their only use was as a guide to travellers who took a course as nearly parallel as the ground permitted." Prior to 1823, the English Government too had paid little or no attention to the improvement of communications, and its efforts in that direction up to the date of the report of the Public Works Commission had been feeble and intermittent. The Commissioners state that "in 1846 there were 3,110 miles of road called made road, but a large part of even this small extent was totally unbridged and totally unmade, consisting of tracks over a firm soil not considered to need making for the light traffic then using them;" that, with the exception of the districts of Salem, Madura, Tanjore and South Canara, the roads in the several districts were practically impassable during the rainy season; and that in most parts "the tracks by which the carts travel had never been made or improved, but are such as the carts are able to strike out for themselves, winding their way as best they can through the natural obstacles of the country, which are in some parts greater, in others less; in some parts rocks and hills, in others swamps and muddy streams, in others rice flats and irrigation channels." "Through, or round, or over these various difficulties" add the Commissioners "the carts find their way as best they can, changing their line from time to time at particular points, as the old tracks there become impracticable, and gradually deviating more and more from a straight line. On such roads the carts can only carry one-third of the load that they could on a good road and travel one-half the distance in a day, and there are many days in a year in which they cannot travel at all, and all perishable goods, sugar, cotton and even grain are much exposed to damage." In illustration of their remarks, the Commissioners give the following particulars extracted from the accounts of a Madras merchant regarding the great saving effected in the cost of carriage of goods from Madras to Wallajahnugger—a great centre of trade in those days—by the gradual improvement of the road between the two towns :—

In 1823 the hire of a cart from Wallajahnugger to Madras—a distance of 70 miles—carrying 37½ maunds or 900 lb. was Rs. 7-0-0 or Rs. 17-6-9 per ton.

In 1835 the hire of a cart from Wallajahnugger to Madras—a distance of 70 miles—carrying 37½ maunds or 900 lb. was Rs. 6-10-0 or Rs. 16-7-9 per ton.

In 1837 the hire of a cart from Wallajahnugger to Madras—a distance of 70 miles—carrying 37½ maunds or 900 lb. was Rs. 5-0-0 or Rs. 12-7-1 per ton.

In 1844 the hire of a cart from Wallajahnugger to Madras—a distance of 70 miles—carrying 1,000 lb. was Rs. 4-8-0 or Rs. 10-1-3 per ton.

In 1847 the hire of a cart from Wallajahnugger to Madras—a distance of 70 miles—carrying 1,000 lb. was Rs. 4-0-0 or Rs. 8-15-4 per ton.

In 1851 the hire of a cart from Wallajahnugger to Madras—a distance of 70 miles—carrying 1,600 lb. was Rs. 3-10-0 or Rs. 5-1-2 per ton.

The Commissioners, among whom were Mr. Bourdillon and Sir Arthur Cotton, earnestly drew the attention of Government to the extent to which the trade of the country was being hampered by the want of communications, and urged that much greater and more strenuous efforts should be made for their improvement than had been done in the past. Another important question to which the Commissioners drew attention was the system of *corvée* or impressment of labour for public works. Their inquiries showed that there was no district in which labour was not obtained more or less by compulsion. "Little coercion is actually used," say the Commissioners, "but it is known that it will be used if required, and indeed the workpeople themselves from long custom consider themselves under a sort of obligation to work for Government on the established terms, but where the remuneration is inadequate, they work unwillingly and slowly." The Commissioners then recount the various ways in which the labourers were cheated of the wages due to them; 1st, the rate allowed was too low, as in Madura where it was fixed at one-third of the rate paid by private persons; 2ndly, the device of short measurement was adopted and the work done was undervalued; 3rdly, artificers, bricklayers in particular, were often required to leave their towns, where they could get constant work, to go to a distant part of the taluk, to be separated from their friends and to submit to privations; 4thly, there was great delay in payment; and 5thly, much of the wages entered in the accounts as having been paid was never really received by the labourers, who submitted to various deductions, which had become customary, in favour of officers employed on or about the work and in the disbursement of the money.

SECTION IV.—*Narrative of the principal facts bearing on the condition of the Agricultural classes from the middle of the present century to the present time.*

The cessation of the period of agricultural depression and the commencement of a period of prosperity and internal reforms.

19. There was a famine in 1854, but it was restricted in its effects to the district of Bellary and was not of long duration; the chief losses were in cattle, four-fifths of which are stated to have died. The agricultural depression from which the country was suffering came to an end about this time, and a period of great prosperity for the agricultural classes commenced. For this there were several causes. The discovery of gold mines in Australia and California had increased the demand for Indian commodities in European countries whose stocks of gold had been enlarged, and this movement was accelerated by the Crimean war which stimulated exports of jute and oil-seeds, and by the cotton famine in England caused by the American war, which increased the demand for Indian cotton enormously. The merchandise exported from India, which amounted to only $13\frac{1}{2}$ millions sterling in 1840–41, rose to 68 millions in 1864–65. The result was a great influx of silver into India which she was able to obtain on advantageous terms in exchange for her commodities, as the cheap new gold had, to a considerable extent, taken the place of silver in European countries and made the latter metal available for export to this country. Further, about this time loans on a large scale were raised in England for the construction of public works. For railways alone, 90 millions were raised, and it is calculated that more than half this sum was remitted to India for payment of wages to men employed on the works. The influx of all this money enabled India to replenish her insufficient currency and the prices of Indian produce rose to nearly three times of what they were in the years immediately preceding 1850. This period was also remarkable for the great reforms carried out in the internal administration of the country, which gave a great impetus to the extension of cultivation and trade. The land assessments were reduced wherever they were found to be heavy, notably in the Bellary, North Arcot, South Arcot, Trichinopoly and Kurnool Districts. The effects of these reductions under the stimulus of

high prices were almost immediately felt on the acreage under cultivation and the amount of revenue. In South Arcot seven lakhs of rupees, amounting to nearly one-third of the revenue on cultivated lands, and 8¼ lakhs on waste lands were remitted in 1854. The area under cultivation the very next year rose from 632,180 to 810,707 acres. The Collector reported in 1857 that "the demand for fresh land since the reduction of assessment, and especially where the reduction was most liberal, had been very great; that the relief had given a decided impetus to industry; that the condition of the people had been indisputably improved, as was evident from the substantial houses they were building in every direction and by the independent manner in which they deported themselves; and that labour was in great demand and emigration to Bourbon had ceased." The Collector of Kurnool in the same year stated that since the reduction of assessment, cultivable lands had become every year more difficult to obtain, that the revenue came in readily, and that wells, topes of trees and indigo vats were increasing in number. Similar reports in regard to the favorable turn in the circumstances of the ryots were received from other Collectors also. The Collector of Godávari reported in 1859, "it is very gratifying to me to be able to bear testimony to the rapid increase of prosperity among the people of this district. This has been perhaps more especially apparent during the last two years and is accounted for in various ways —by the great demand for labour, by the great increase in the rate of wages and in the prices of all commodities and in the general appearance of the people. The high prices of all kinds of agricultural produce during the last few years may have aided in obtaining this result; but that the main cause is the work at Dowlaishweram no one can, I think, for a moment doubt." In the Coimbatore district the relinquishment by Government of the right to tax improvements to land effected by the ryots had led to a great extension of cultivation. Mr. E. B. Thomas, who perhaps had done more to develop the resources of this district than any other Collector, wrote in 1856, "a great many new wells continue to be dug in punjah fields, and some of the old deserted and exhausted wells are being opened, and fences restored; and garden crops are again appearing on fields long waste, some 30 or 40 years. A great proof of the practical value and policy of the garden remissions is exhibited in lands (fit for new wells or with old wells in them) becoming more saleable, and in discussions now arising on old dormant claims to lands long since waste." Again in 1857 he said, "the district only wants *rain*. With a moderate assessment and most of the oppressive taxes relieved, the moturpha alone remaining, improvements and investment of capital now encouraged, the district holds up, though this is the *fourth* successive bad year of short rain. During the last 4 years, 18 inches of rain in the 12 months have been the maximum; this year there were only 16 inches and the land is parched, the crops scanty, wells nearly dry and cattle dying for want of grass and water in large numbers; but with good prices, great industry and much energy among the cultivating classes, the rental, notwithstanding all difficulties, keeps up and is collected without oppression or any balances to speak of." The testimony afforded by the reports of the Collectors in other districts in regard to the improvement in the condition of the agricultural classes which had set in about this time is equally emphatic. The ryots were granted complete freedom in the matter of taking up lands or relinquishing them. Numerous petty and vexatious imposts, grouped under the general head of moturpha, were abolished. The titles to inams or favorably assessed lands were placed on a secure basis. The Settlement Department was organized with the professed object of alleviating the heavy burdens on land and of removing inequalities in the assessments. The revenue remitted between the years 1844 to 1860 in consequence of the above measures amounted to 68 lakhs[16] of rupees. As a consequence of the recommendations of the Public Works Commission already referred to, greater attention was paid to the maintenance of irrigation works and the construction of roads, railways and canals. The system of impressment of labour for Government works and the payment of discretionary wages was abolished. A new Police force was organized, which, whatever its shortcomings may be when judged by a high standard of efficiency, is incomparably superior to the unspeakably corrupt Police which it superseded; and the magistracy were relieved of police duties. In consequence of the revelations of the Torture Commissioners, who submitted their report in 1855, the employment of illegal pressure and coercion,[17] whether in the collection of Government revenue or detection of crime, was prohibited under stringent penalties. The revenue and magisterial establishments were revised, the taluk and village accounts were simplified, and a scheme of examinations for qualifying for public service was brought into force in view to securing the services of a more honest and capable class of officers than were available under the old *régime*. All these reforms, it will be seen, were in the direction of freeing the ryots from official dependence and

---

[16] A detailed statement showing the revenue remitted is printed in the appendix A, section IV.

[17] See extracts from the report given in the appendix D, section IV.

trammels, while at the same time affording them every facility by the improvement of communications to take the produce to the best markets. Owing to the operation of the economic causes and the administrative improvements above referred to, both cultivation and trade increased enormously and the agricultural and trading classes enjoyed great prosperity. The ryots in the single district of Bellary made 1½ million sterling by the sale of cotton in the 3 years of the American war. There was a considerable improvement in the condition of non-agricultural labourers also, as, owing to the construction of several railways and other public works, the demand for labour was great and continuous, and the rise in wages kept pace with the rise in the price of food-grains, the old system of impressment of labour at discretionary wages having, as already stated, been swept away. The Board of Revenue, Madras, instituted careful inquiries in 1863 regarding the rates of wages prevailing in the several districts in their relation to the prices of food-grains. The results were as follows. Agricultural labourers continued to be paid generally in kind and, therefore, the increase in the price of food did not materially affect their condition. Payment in *money* was very rare, and, where it obtained, the rates of hire had more than doubled. Grain wages also had in some instances risen, though not in the same ratio as the payment in money. In consequence of the greater demand for labour, the condition of the agricultural labourers had not deteriorated, but on the contrary had generally improved; and this was no less the case with other classes of labourers, whose wages had fully kept pace with the enhanced price of food, being in some cases doubled and trebled. A carpenter who would have received 4 annas before the rise of prices would not take less than 6 or 8 annas, while the hire of the common cooly had risen from 2 or 3 annas to 4 annas a day. The Board considered that this state of things was a satisfactory indication of the generally improved circumstances of the people. The only class which suffered by the high prices was the lower Government officials who, notwithstanding the recent enhancement of their salaries, were in no case in a better, generally in a considerably worse, position than before. Mr. Dalyell, writing in 1866, estimated that the ryot was in twice as good a position as he was in 1854. His remarks on the condition of the general mass of the population have been extracted in the appendix E, section IV.

The reaction.

20. There was a drought again in 1865 and 1866 all along the East Coast of the Presidency to the north of Madras and extending as far inland as the Mysore plateau, the area affected being about 43,000

square miles and the population 6 millions. The effects of the famine were most severely felt in the Ganjam district on account of its comparatively isolated position; in the Ceded districts, however, in which the ryots had made large gains owing to the high price of cotton which ruled during the years of the American war, the famine was comparatively mild. The period of high prices continued till about 1870 when there was a sudden reaction. The loans for public works, which had caused the influx of silver into India, ceased; and remittances of large sums to England for the payment of Home charges and the interest on loans already contracted became necessary; and on account of these and other causes prices fell heavily. There was considerable uneasiness caused also by the continual increase of taxation, which, though lighter than it was before 1850, was still severely felt, as the increase synchronized with a period of falling prices. The fact was that the inflated prices of the years of the cotton famine had led to extravagance and when the reaction came, the ryots were unable to adapt themselves to the altered conditions. In the Bombay Presidency especially, the agricultural classes, finding that their lands had acquired value, borrowed largely on them from Marwadi soukars, and the repeal of the usury laws and the enforcement by the Civil Courts of extortionate contracts without considering whether the terms agreed to were equitable, had led to distress and riots. In the Madras Presidency, however, the agricultural classes who were not in the hands of soukars to the same extent did not suffer similarly. But that they felt considerably upset even in the comparatively prosperous district of Tanjore will be evident from the following remarks of the Collector of that district extracted from a report written by him in 1871. "So long as prices ruled at between double and treble the commutation rate, and *pro tanto* reduced the Government demand to between one-third and one-half of what it used to be, the Tanjore mirasidar could well afford to pay his kists in advance and at the same time indulge in the luxuries of litigation as well as in a high style of living. A deficiency in the outturn of his harvest was then a matter of comparative indifference to him. Now, however, a marked decline in prices has considerably altered this state of things. Not even the wealthier landed proprietors escaped the process of distraint under Act II of 1864 this year, and it is a fact that in April and May, the months of heavy kists, jewels of no small value came into the money market for loans which were obtained on 12 and, in several instances, as much as 24 per cent. interest. I, of course, do not mean to say that the Government demand does not, on the whole, now leave a liberal margin of profit to the mirasidars; for, as market prices still average 70 per cent. over the settlement commutation rate, they must be able to gain so much more beyond their mirasi-waram share as originally fixed; but this estimate of their profits holds good only as regards the well irrigated delta taluks. There are parts of the district, especially those situated at the remote ends of irrigation channels, where irrigation is from its nature precarious, and the present system of conservancy under the direction of a highly centralized, but in point of numerical strength utterly inadequate, professional agency is necessarily inefficient. In such parts there can be no question that the recent high prices of agricultural produce have alone enabled the landholders to punctually discharge the Government dues." The decline in prices, however, benefited the landless classes whose wages had risen during the years of high prices, but did not decline when the prices fell. Inquiries[18] were instituted at this time by the Government of India regarding the pressure of taxation. The Board of Revenue reported "there can be no doubt that there is a feeling of uneasiness and perplexity abroad among the tax-payers which is strong enough to warrant grave anxiety. This feeling is the result not so much of the nature or weight of the taxes as of the rapid changes in the law which have been taking place of late years. When a tax is new it is bitterly felt, but as the people get more and more used to it, their dissatisfaction wears away. The great bulk of the population being engaged in agriculture, the cultivation statistics, which are recorded with great minuteness, would show if the burden of taxation were too great; but there is no evidence that this is the case. On the other hand, any considerable fall in the prices of produce would make the burden unbearable, and it may safely be said that the load cannot be increased or even shifted without danger." The Madras Government expressed a similar opinion. It remarked "with the exception of the income-tax, in condemning which there is a very general consensus of opinion, comparatively little soreness seems to be felt in the country at any existing Imperial taxation. The stamp duties perplex the people and probably would produce more with less annoyance, were the schedules framed on some more easily intelligible principle. The system irritates, but the tax cannot be called burdensome on the masses. The rise in prices of late years has indirectly tended to alleviate the burdens on the land, whether for local or Imperial purposes, while the concurrent improvement in wages has prevented the increase in prices from telling hard on the lower classes.

[18] An abstract of the reports of Collectors and other officers in regard to the condition of agricultural classes in 1872 is given in the appendix F, section IV.

The salt-tax has probably in this Presidency been raised to the highest point at which it will not injuriously affect consumption. The greater facilities for carriage afforded by the extension of railways have, doubtless, tended and must continue to reduce the tax to the inland consumer, but consumption is nevertheless not increasing proportionately with the increase of wealth and population. The tax, however, being an indirect one, is not likely to be the subject of complaint unless enhanced to a prohibitive rate, but it is deserving of serious consideration whether it is not now so high as to be a financial mistake in this Presidency. The other Imperial taxes, except the income-tax, do not seem to call for remark ; but as regards this latter tax, the opinions collected are almost universally condemnatory of it, not so much as being in its present form felt as a heavy burden, but as being unequal in incidence and incapable of fair adjustment, as calculated to demoralize those who assess and those who pay, as aggravating the burden of municipal taxation, as maintaining a feeling of distrust as to the financial policy of Government. . . . . The experiment of local taxation is of much more recent introduction and the time has not yet arrived for forming a just judgment as to its merits. It cannot be doubted that the pressure of this taxation is more severely felt, and it must be confessed that the house-tax, as a method of providing funds for elementary education beyond the limits of municipalities, is at present regarded with strong dislike by the great majority of rate-payers. The application of the tax up to the present time has been comparatively limited and its extension will be gradual and cautious."

Famine of 1876-78.

21. Before the country had time to recover from the shock caused by the sudden fall in prices below the inflated level they had attained in the sixties, by the new and unfamiliar forms of taxation and by the succession of laws issuing out of the legislature, it was visited with the famine of 1876–78, the most terrible in point of magnitude, intensity and duration, that was known for upwards of a century. This calamity was the result of a drought extending over three successive years and affecting a tract of country 200,000 square miles in extent with a population of 36 millions ; and no country which is purely agricultural can, of course, expect to make head against a disaster on such a scale. The area which suffered in the Madras Presidency alone was 74,000 square miles containing a population of 16 millions. Notwithstanding the gigantic efforts made by the Government, three-quarter million of persons on an average having been relieved daily for a period of 22 months, and the cost of the famine including revenue remitted amounting to

8 millions sterling, the loss of the population was nearly 4 millions. The progress of the agricultural classes in the affected districts and of the landless classes in other parts of the Presidency received a severe check, from the effects of which, however, they have since recovered with astonishing rapidity, as is evident from the increase in population, acreage of cultivation and land revenue, and from the self-reliant manner in which the Presidency has, during the last two years, borne itself against the partial drought which has prevailed in several districts.

SECTION V.—*Statistics showing the improvement in the condition of the people since* 1850.

22. In the previous pages I have endeavoured to show in a general manner, by the evidence of official reports and other publications, what was the condition of the agricultural classes both before and after the establishment of British power in this Presidency. I will now more particularly examine what progress has been made during the last 40 years under the following heads, viz., (*a*) population, (*b*) acreage of cultivation, (*c*) prices of produce, (*d*) improvement in the processes of production and in communications, (*e*) foreign and domestic trade, (*f*) taxation, and (*g*) the standard of living of the different classes of the population. I shall first mention what strike me as note-worthy facts in connection with the heads above enumerated, and then point out their bearing on the economic condition of the people. Detailed statistics bearing on these matters are given in appendix V.

Increase of population.

23. A fairly correct census was taken in 1871 and the population of the Presidency was found to be 31¼ millions. Owing to the famine of 1876–78 the population decreased in 1881 to 30¾ millions. The loss of population was specially heavy in the districts of Kurnool, Bellary and Anantapur, Salem and Cuddapah, the percentage of loss ranging between 17 and 26. The census taken in 1891 shows that during the last decade the population has increased by no less than 4¾ millions or 15·6 per cent. The rates of increase in the districts which had suffered severely from the last famine are specially remarkable. These high rates are no doubt mainly due to the fact that the famine killed off disproportionately large numbers of the juvenile and aged population, leaving among the survivors a larger proportion than usual of adults of the productive ages. The rapid recovery of the population of a country after great calamities seems to be a well attested fact and has often been noticed.

Mr. Thorold Rogers, in his *Six Centuries of Work and Wages*, observes : "We learn from contemporary accounts that rapid growth of population followed on the destruction of the Black Death (in England in the 13th century). It is said that after this event double and triple births were frequent, that marriages were singularly fertile, and that in a short time the void made by the pestilence was no longer visible. The repressive check of a high standard of living was removed by the ease with which the survivors could obtain that standard and accumulate from a considerable margin beyond it. . . . I make no doubt that the population speedily righted itself, as it has done on many other occasions, when a sudden or abnormal destruction of human life has occurred in a people and the people has a recuperative power." For a consideration of the question as to what conclusions bearing on the economic condition of the people, the increase in the population during the last decade leads to, we must await the publication of the detailed results of the census. It seems, however, to be pretty clear that the normal rate of increase, viz., ·8 per cent. per annum, given in the census report of this Presidency for 1881, is much below the mark. Mr. Hardy, in the chapter on the rate of increase of population contributed by him to the report on the census of British India taken in 1881, has calculated the rate of increase for the whole of the Madras Presidency to be ·6 per cent. and for the tracts not afflicted with famine, ·8 per cent. Between 1856 and 1871, the population had increased at the rate of 1·2 per cent. That this rate must have been higher than the rate which had obtained previously when the country suffered from severe agricultural depression is evident from the fact that the proportion of the population under 20 years of age, that is, born subsequent to 1851, to the total population censused in 1871, was found to be as high as 52½ per cent., while, according to the life table, the proportion should have been something like 45 per cent. The increase of population during the last decade has been at the rate of 1·44 per cent. and, during the last 35 years, of ·84 per cent. not merely in the non-famine tracts but throughout the whole Presidency. So severe a famine as that of 1876-78 is not likely to occur except once in a century and it would probably be nearer the mark to assume the normal increase of population under present conditions to be not much less than 1 per cent., even making allowance for mortality from droughts and scarcities, such as those that usually occur. At this rate the population will double itself in 70 years. This high rate of increase, while showing that the means of subsistence at the present day are more plentiful than in times past, shows at the same time that the pressure of population is likely to become more severe in the future than in the past, especially when it is considered how universal is the custom of early marriages and how difficult it is to introduce salutary changes in this custom. Dr. Farr has pointed out that undue increase or decrease of population in England is capable of being remedied by regulating the number of marriages. He says: "at present (in England) one-fifth of the women who attain the age of 24·3 years never marry; if one-half of the women who attained that age never married, and if illegitimate births did not increase, the births would ultimately not exceed the deaths, and the population would remain stationary. But the same end would be almost as effectually, and less harshly, attained though four-fifths of the women who arrived at the mean age continued to marry, if instead of beginning to marry at 18, none married under 23, and the mean age of marriage were raised to 30 years; for the interval from generation to generation would be thus extended, the children to a marriage diminished and the number of women at 30 would be reduced by the loss of the younger lives" (see Farr's *Vital Statistics*). He adds that under the pressure of circumstances, the population in England, to a considerable extent, regulates itself in the manner above pointed out to prevent any impairment of the standard of living and frequently with a view to bring about a rise in that standard. Such a process of adjustment is of course much more difficult of application in India, where the marriage customs are less flexible. In England the average age of marriage for women is about 25 years, and only 18 per cent. of women of ages between 15 and 25 are married and ·2 per cent. are widowed. Further, of the women who reach 25 years of age, 20 per cent. never marry. In this Presidency nearly 80 per cent. of women between the ages of 15 and 25 are married and 5 per cent. are widowed, and a considerable proportion of the widows are debarred by the customs of the country from re-marrying. I have been informed that 50 or even 40 years ago men married much later (generally [19] after 30 years) than

[19] The Hindu Sastras recommend marriages between men of 32 years of age and girls of 10 years, or men of 24 years and girls of 8. There is an inscription at Virinjipuram, North Arcot district, dated during the reign of Veerapratapa Devaraja Maharajah of Vijianagar, A.D. 1419. which shows that the practice of paying money to parents of girls to induce them to give them in marriage was widely prevalent in former times. The inscription states "in the reign of the illustrious Veerapratapa Devaraja Maharajah, the great men of all branches of sacred studies of the Kingdom drew up in the presence of Gopinatha of Arkapushkarani, a document containing an agreement regarding the sacred law. According to this, if the Brahmins of this kingdom of Padaividu, viz., Kannadigas, Tamiras, Telungas, Ilalas, &c., of all Gotras, Sutras and Sakhas, conclude a marriage, they shall from this day forward do it by Kanyadanam (gift of girls). Those who do not adopt Kanyadanam, *i.e.*, both those who give away a girl after having received gold, and those who conclude a marriage after having given gold, shall be liable to punishment by the King and shall be excluded from the community of the Brahmins." The inscription is interesting as showing in what manner legislation on social matters was effected in the old days.

they do now, while women were married as early as at present, even among the higher classes; the reason being poverty and the difficulty of procuring sufficient money to pay to the parents of girls for purchasing their consent to the marriage. This, combined with the system of enforced widowhood, had the effect of putting a check on the inordinate increase of population by abridging the duration of married life. The great disparity in the ages of the married couple which is said to influence the sex of the offspring, possibly accounts also for the scarcity of girls which, if current belief is to be credited, existed in former times.[20] During later years, however, it became quite the fashion among the well-to-do to marry their sons while still very young, though in view of the prejudicial effect which very early marriages have on the education of boys, a slight change for the better has recently become perceptible.[21] In India as in England, increase in the means of subsistence leads to increase in the number of marriages among the lower classes. In England, this tendency is, to some extent, counteracted by the example of the middle classes who postpone

[20] Sir Thomas Munro notices this fact. He says with reference to the census of the Ceded districts taken when he was Collector of these districts : "It is a general opinion among the inhabitants that the number of males is actually one-tenth greater than that of females. I was at first inclined to believe that the difference might have arisen from the seclusion of females, but it is not particularly great among those castes who follow this practice, but extends to every caste and every district. I examined the details of several villages in different parts of the country, and though in one village the females were more numerous than the males, and in a few others equal in number to them, yet the average result was the same as in whole districts. The coincidence of so many unconnected accounts is certainly a strong argument in favor of the popular notion, of the males being one-tenth more numerous than females."

[21] In England the number of persons under 21 years of age who contract marriages appears to have increased as shown below :—

	Persons under 21 years who marry per 1,000.	
	Men.	Women.
1850-52	7·6	24·3
1860-62	9·5	29·6
1870-72	11·8	34·1

The increase of early marriages is stated to be entirely due to the prosperous condition of the lower classes, the middle classes, unlike those in India, preferring to postpone marriage on account of the continual increase in the standard of living. Professor Marshall remarks : "In the middle classes a man's income seldom reaches its maximum till he is 40 or 50 years old ; and the expense of bringing up his children is heavy and lasts for many years. The artisan earns nearly as much at 21 as he ever does, unless he rises to a responsible post, but he does not earn much before he is 21 ; his children are likely to be a considerable expense to him till about the age of 15 ; unless they are sent to a factory where they may pay their way at a very early age ; and lastly the labourer earns nearly full wages at 18, while his children begin to pay their expenses very early. In consequence, the average age of marriage is highest among the middle classes, it is low among the artisans and still lower among the unskilled labourers." It will have been inferred from my remarks that, looking at the question purely from the point of view of preventing undue increase of population, the evils of compulsory early marriages of Hindu women are mitigated by the system of enforced widowhood, and a relaxation of the restrictions on widow marriage necessitates relaxation of the system of early marriages by postponing marriages of girls for some years after the period at which by present opinion they are recognized as marriageable. This, of course, is no objection to widow re-marriage reform but only shows why the progress of the reform is so slow. There are various adjustments in other directions necessary before the reform is likely to be generally accepted

marriages in order that the standard of living may not deteriorate. In India, on the contrary, with the classes corresponding to middle-classes in England, early marriage of girls is a religious obligation, and their example in this respect is the reverse of beneficial. These considerations will bring home to our minds the futility of the expectation that great changes can be produced in the condition of the masses, within the periods of time which are insufficient for effecting a transformation in deep-rooted national habits, and will enable us to estimate rightly the value of the advance made under such difficulties.

Increase in the acreage of cultivation.

24. We have next to consider whether the increase in agricultural production has kept pace with the increase of population. According to the calculations already referred to, the population in 1856 must have amounted to 26½ millions, and as there was a famine in 1854, the population in 1852 may be taken at about this figure. Between 1852 and 1891 the population has increased from 26½ to 35½ millions or by 30 per cent. Statistics of acreage of cultivation are not available for zemindaris and inam villages, and therefore it is not possible to calculate the increase in production with any very great accuracy. Nevertheless an analysis of the statistics of acreage available in regard to ryotwar lands serves to show roughly that the increase in the cultivated area, making allowance for the increased productiveness of irrigated as compared with unirrigated lands, is quite on a par with it if it does not exceed the increase in population. Excluding South Canara and Malabar, for which districts, owing to the absence of a survey, statistics of acreage are not available, the ryotwar cultivation was in 1852, 12·2 million acres, of which 9·5 million acres were unirrigated, 2·3 million acres were irrigated from Government sources of irrigation and ·4 million of acres irrigated by private sources, but were taxed at specially high rates on account of the valuable crops grown. These areas require a double correction to be applied to them, first, because they include portions of fields left waste which were charged for, though not cultivated, and which are excluded from cultivation statistics for later years, and secondly, because the areas given in the old surveys have been found, by the recent surveys, to be somewhat below the truth. On this account, on a rough calculation, it is found that ¾ million of acres has to be added to the acreage of 1852, to admit of its being compared with the acreage of more recent years in districts which have been surveyed. In 1890 the area of cultivated lands classed as dry, *i.e.*, not irrigated by Government sources of irrigation, was 13·64

millions of acres, of which 12·64 millions were unirrigated and 1 million was irrigated by wells constructed by the ryots at their own expense and 3·44 millions of acres of lands irrigated by Government sources. The increase in the area of cultivation is thus—(1) 25 per cent. in unirrigated lands, (2) 41 per cent. in lands irrigated by Government sources of irrigation, and (3) 138 per cent. in lands irrigated by private wells. Nearly the whole of the increase under the second head amounting to upwards of a million of acres is due to the extension of cultivation in tracts commanded by the great anicut systems—Godávari, Kistna, Cauvery, Pennér, Pálár and Támbraparni—which secure an almost unfailing supply of water, and every acre of irrigated lands in these tracts produces, on an average, not less than four times as much as they would do if they were unirrigated. Moreover the increase of production due to the great irrigation systems cannot be measured merely by the increase in the acreage of cultivation, as the increase of produce, consequent on an assured supply to lands which before the anicuts were constructed were dependent on a precarious supply of water, and on additional supply of water for a second crop to lands cultivated formerly with a single crop, amounting in all to about 1½ millions of acres, must be taken into account. Similarly, the million acres irrigated by private wells produce as much at least as 4 millions of acres of unirrigated lands. Making allowance for these considerations and taking into account the increase in the cultivated area under such articles as cotton, indigo, ground-nut, coffee, sugarcane, tea and cinchona, it seems to me that the percentage of increase in production cannot be less than 3 or 4 times the increase in population. There are no means of making an exact calculation; all that can be stated is that the increased production is very considerable. The area under cotton, which in 1852 was a little less than a million of acres, has increased to more than 1¾ millions of acres. The area under indigo has increased from about 200,000 acres to more than 500,000 acres or by 150 per cent.; ground-nut which in former years was cultivated to a small extent to meet local demands has now become a very remunerative commercial crop. It is chiefly cultivated in the South Arcot district where the acreage under it has risen from about 6,700 acres in 1852 to 190,000 acres in 1889–90. The area under sugarcane has risen from 38,400 to 70,000 acres. Though the acreage under this crop may appear small, the crop itself is very valuable, the value of the outturn per acre being more than 20 times the outturn on dry lands. The area under coffee and tea is 55,000 and 5,000 acres respectively. These crops are of course extremely valuable.

25. In this connection there are two prevalent notions which deserve some notice. These are (1) that the rainfall has sensibly diminished of late years, and (2) that the fertility of the soil, under the improvident and non-restorative systems of native cultivation, has deteriorated.[22] Both these notions have been shown, by scientific men who have given close attention to the subject, to be unfounded to a great extent. The prevalence of these impressions is sufficiently accounted for by the habit of old people in all countries of asserting that "in the days of their youth the fields were greener and the sun warmer" (or as we should say in India "less intense"). We have statistics of the rainfall for some stations for the last 80 years, and they do not show that there has been any appreciable diminution in the quantity of annual rainfall during this period. The complaint of deficient rainfall is also, it must be remembered, not a new one. The following passages extracted from Buchanan's "Journey" in 1800 show that people complained in much the same way then, that they do now. "*Tarkeri* (Coimbatore district). The people say that since the death of Hyder (*i.e.*, since 1782 or for 18 years) they have had one year with a proper fall of rain. This year there has been abundance, but it came too late by two months." "*Dharapuram.* Owing to the want of rain and of stock the farmers are not able to cultivate all that they rent, &c." "*Pryapattana*, *Grishmaritu* (summer season) contains the two months including the summer solstice. It is said that formerly during this period the weather used to be constantly clouded, with a regular unremitting drizzling rain; but for the last half a century such seasons have occurred only once in 4 or 5 years; and in the intervening ones, although the cloudy weather continues, the constant rain has ceased, and in its place heavy showers have come at intervals of 3 or 4 days, and these are succeeded by some thunder. *Varsharitu* (rainy season). Formerly the rains used to be incessant and heavy; of late years they have not been so copious oftener than once in 4 or 5 years; still they are almost always sufficient to produce a good crop of grass and dry grains, and one crop

Alleged decrease of rainfall.

---

[22] A third impression which is prevalent, though not confined to this country, is that men in past times were giants in stature, had more robust health and lived longer than their degenerate descendants do now. In England it was currently believed that the knights of the middle ages were men of great stature, until it was shown that the armour worn by them was too small to fit the present race of men in the upper classes of society. In European countries, the average duration of life has increased owing to diminution in infant mortality. It may be that the diminution of risks to life has had the effect of prolonging to adult age frail lives which under the old conditions would have had no chance of surviving to that age, but as the conditions favorable to the life of frail infants are also conditions which diminish the risks to which fairly healthy persons are subject, their general effect on the whole population cannot be other than beneficial. These remarks, in so far as the present conditions differ from the past, are equally applicable to this country.

of rice. Pryapattana has therefore been termed the chosen city of the natives of Karnata who suffer from scarcity of rain." . . . "*Haltoray. Change of climate.* The natives say that formerly the rains were so copious that by means of small tanks a great part of the country could be cultivated with rice. These tanks were only sufficient to contain 8 or 10 days water, and to supply the fields when such short intervals of fair weather occurred. For 40 years past, however, a change having taken place in the climate, no rice has been cultivated except by means of large reservoirs." Buchanan adds "the truth of this allegation is confirmed by the number of small tanks, the ruins of which are now visible; and by the plots of ground levelled for rice which are near these tanks and which are now quite waste." Possibly this was the result of the clearance of forests which are stated to have some effect in regulating and conserving local falls of rain but no influence in modifying the general features of climate. Dr. Brandis, who might be expected to claim for forests all the merit they could justly lay claim to, states: "There is no proof that forests modify the climate to any great extent. The great features of climate depend on cosmic causes, which are independent of local circumstances. Large extent of forests or large areas of irrigated lands may, however, have some effect in increasing the rainfall at certain seasons, and there is no doubt that in the vicinity of dense forests and on irrigated lands, the air near the ground is generally moister during the dry season and the dew heavier." In the Godávari district, where forests had been extensively cleared in recent times, Mr. Henry Forbes, the Sub-Collector, reported in 1848 that the forest had receded, but that he thought it open to question whether the diminution in the streams which came from the hills was not in the time which the stream took to exhaust itself, instead of in the body of water passing down to its bed; whether the rain was not said to be less in quantity only because, falling on the hills and no longer restrained by the trunks and roots of trees and allowed no time to percolate through the soil and fissures of rocks and to supply the reservoirs of springs, it poured down in torrents and left the water-courses dry as soon as the rains had ceased to fall. Moreover, the want of communications during the rainy season, and the difficulty in crossing unbridged rivers, and the liability of the country to inundations in past times were all calculated to produce an exaggerated impression regarding the quantity of rainfall. The accounts of famines in past centuries given in the previous portion of this memorandum will show that large portions of Southern India were liable to severe and prolonged droughts quite as much in past times as at present.

Mr. Graham writing in 1797, *i.e.*, nearly a century ago, says of Salem: "A person who had not experienced the contrary would be led to suppose that the Baramahal possessed peculiar advantages of situation, and that, lying between Mysore and the Carnatic, the soil would experience the best effects from a participation of both monsoons. We know, however, that the rains are extremely precarious, and that when they do fall, they are either partial and scanty, or if plentiful, that the season has passed; and the only purpose they serve, as at present, is from their violence to destroy half the tanks in the country. How often has the farmer, deceived by a passing shower, imprudently committed his seed to the ground, and how often have his hopes of a return been blasted by a succeeding drought, equally fatal to his crop as to his cattle! How frequently have we observed whole fields of grain apparently vigorous, and rapidly advancing to perfection, destroyed in one night by devouring insects, and the seemingly full-eared cumbu, which one would pronounce in a few days fit for reaping, exhibiting when rubbed between the hands nothing but a useless powder, the consequence of its premature formation!" I have examined the accounts given in the old reports[23] regarding the character of the agricultural season each year from the beginning of the century, and I find that there is no reason to believe either that the rainfall has diminished or that unfavorable seasons are more frequent now than in the past. There were then as prolonged and frequent droughts as now. If the drought was of short duration and affected small portions of country, the people managed to get on; if, however, by a combination of circumstances the drought continued over two or three years and affected simultaneously large portions of the country, the result was famine. The destruction of forests appears, however, to have affected the supply of subsoil water in the vicinity of hills and led to the drying up of streams fed by springs. Dr. Brandis remarks that "in the Coimbatore district the Noyel river, the main channel of which rises in the Bolampatti valley, probably has less water now in the dry season than it had 30 years ago. In the Palladam taluk the old anicuts now remaining unused attest this." The importance of forests in subserving the needs of agriculture cannot of course be over-estimated, but there is, on the whole, no

---

[23] Surgeon-General Edward Balfour, after instituting careful enquiries in 1849, came to the conclusion that "it may be confidently stated that in India within the present century, the rainfall has not diminished, nor has the quantity annually falling now become more uncertain, but that man, partly ignorant and wholly reckless, has denuded the soil of its trees and shrubs and bared the surface to the sun's rays, thus depriving the country of its conservative agents and making the extremes of floods and droughts of more frequent occurrence and more severe."

reason to suppose that their clearance has diminished the rainfall [24] to such an extent as materially to affect the yield of lands. The disappearance of forests has undoubtedly improved the public health, for many tracts of country, in the Madura district for instance, now perfectly healthy were, 60 or 70 years ago, notoriously feverish.

Alleged deterioration of the soil by over-cropping.

26. If then, there is no sufficient evidence in regard to any diminution in the annual rainfall, there is still less evidence to show that there has been any sensible deterioration in the productive capacity of lands. The arguments based on a comparison of the rates of average outturn per acre for the several grains given in the Ayeen Akbari with the outturns assumed at the present day, will not bear examination. According to the Ayeen Akbari tables, the average outturn per acre in the middle of the 16th century was for rice (apparently unhusked) 1,338 lb., for wheat 1,155 lb., for cotton unpicked 670 lb. The averages in these tables have been arrived at with reference to the rates for good, bad and middling lands, but without any attempt being made to find out under which of these classes the area predominated. Moreover, with the immense increase in the acreage of cultivation especially of inferior soils, the average outturn must necessarily decrease, while to establish a deterioration it must be shown that lands under cultivation in former times yield less now than they did before. In the case of wheat, especially, irrigation makes a great difference, the yield of irrigated wheat being from 50 to 300 per cent. in excess of the outturn of unirrigated wheat. The dominions of the Emperor Akbar did not extend to the south of the Vyndhia Mountains, and the Ayeen Akbari rates cannot therefore be applied to South India. If the rate for rice, 1,338 lb., given in these tables refer to unhusked rice, the Madras settlement average (1,621 lb.) is considerably higher. Cotton is frequently sown as a mixed crop, and it is difficult to calculate its average outturn. There is nothing, however, to show that its outturn has diminished. In a recent report [25] on the cultivation of

---

[24] Mr. Mackenzie in the *Kistna District Manual* remarks: "It would no doubt be interesting to find any indication of change of climate, for it is supposed that in former centuries, before the forests were cleared, there was a much heavier rainfall. Hiouen Tsang's description of Dhanakacheka with trees and gushing fountains supports this idea, but we have seen that even in the 13th century there were quarrels about pasture land, bitter enough to cause war, and we shall see in the following chapter that the Muhammadan historians described the famines in A.D. 1423 and 1474 in language that might have applied to the Guntúr famine of 1832. We cannot say therefore that there is historical evidence that the climate has become worse."

[25] In a note to the report of the Agricultural Inspector it is stated that the year to which the report related was a good year and that therefore the estimate of average yield of cotton should be accepted with some caution.

cotton in the Tinnevelly district submitted to the Madras Agricultural Department by an Agricultural Inspector, it is stated, "cotton soils of the best quality sell for Rs. 1,000 a sanghili (3·64 acres); ordinary soils for Rs. 500, while inferior soils sell below Rs. 200. In fertile soils and under good treatment 1,000 lb. seed cotton per acre is no unusual outturn; an ordinary good yield of cotton may be taken to vary from 750 lb. to 900 lb. of seed cotton, while 500 lb. may be taken as a fair average of yield taking all soils into consideration. These figures have been arrived at from the statements of different classes of ryots and include the first and second courses of pickings. It is assumed by dealers that 6 podis (of about 328 lb. each) of seed cotton are required to produce 500 lb. of lint, and therefore the average outturn of an acre is 125 lb. of lint. In the United States, the average outturn of cotton is about 567 lb. seed cotton or 189 lb. lint per acre." In [26] 1862 the average outturn of Tinnevelly cotton was reported to be 300 lb. of seed cotton or 75 lb. of lint. The Agricultural Inspector adds "that the outturn in Tinnevelly is somewhat greater than formerly is admitted by the ryots, and unless this were a well known fact they would make no such admission. The explanation may be found in the fact that the system of adding all kinds of earthy matter to the manure heaps, by which the quantity is not only largely increased but is also better decomposed, is only a recent practice. Moreover all soils are now kept much cleaner than before owing to closer and better tillage." The allegation regarding the diminished outturn of lands is based to a great extent upon the *a priori* reasoning that when the ingredients forming plant food abstracted from the soil by continuous cropping are not restored to it by artificial manuring, it must necessarily deteriorate. Recent enquiries made into agricultural practices in this country by scientific agricultural experts have, however, resulted in showing that the injurious effects attributed to native methods of agriculture are grossly exaggerated. Professor Wallace in his *India in 1887* emphatically denies that the fertility of the

---

[26] Mr. Nicholson in his valuable "Preliminary Note" printed in the *Report of the Madras Agricultural Committee* remarks: "Forty years ago the yield of cotton in Bellary, Cuddapah, Coimbatore and Tinnevelly was 90, 50, 50 and 80 lb. per acre respectively (Collector's reports in Wheeler's Hand-book) while the present average even on good black cotton soil in those districts is not above 62½ lb. per acre." The statement appended to Wheeler's Hand-book, however, shows that the outturn of clean cotton per acre was estimated at only 46, 50, 27 and 75 lb. respectively. The average outturn is not less now. Sir Thomas Munro in 1806 estimated the average outturn in the Ceded districts at less than 20 lb. per acre. Mr. Rundall, Commercial Resident in the Ceded districts, writing in 1819, states that the native produce of cotton is not more than 30 lb. (clean cotton) per acre.

soil is being exhausted by native practices. He quotes from the report of Mr. Chisholm, the Settlement officer of Bilsapur, the following remarks as to how the outturn is affected by the continuous cropping of irrigated lands. "When fresh soil is broken up for rice cultivation, the ground can never be got into proper order during the first year, and the yield is less than in the old fields. In the second year the outturn rises about one-eighth above that of the old fields and increases gradually year by year until the fifth, when it reaches 50 per cent. above the old fields. It then commences to decline, and in about another five years has subsided to the level of the old fields, and at that level it remains unchanged for ever. Many fields for instance are believed to have been continuously cultivated for 150 years[27] and more, and yet they are in no way inferior to land reclaimed from the jungle but 15 years ago." Professor Wallace[28] goes on to remark that 5 lb. of nitrogen is required for an acre, combined by electric action. Thunderstorms being common during the south-west monsoon months, India has a natural advantage over the British and American wheat growers, whose supply of nitrogen is, in a great measure, drawn from vegetable accumulations in a virgin soil, which is, in consequence of a system of close cropping, becoming exhausted. More recently, Dr. Voelcker has expressed an opinion to a similar effect. He states: "the possibility of soil exhaustion going on (in India) can only be determined by a careful study of what is removed from the land, and how far this is replaced by the forces of nature and by the artificial nourishment of manuring. I have mentioned the deficiency of nitrogen which I observed in the case of several Indian soils, but it is worthy of note too, how very large a proportion of the crops annually grown, also of the trees and shrubs and even of the weeds, are leguminous in character, and

---

[27] In an inscription (*vide* appendix I.–D.) recording a grant to a Jain temple at Negapatam by Kulottungachola (A.D. 1084) the produce of certain villages which can now be identified is given. Comparing the present outturn with the rates given in the inscription, it is found that on the whole the produce has increased and not diminished. There is a popular impression in the Godávari district that the construction of anicuts and locks has diminished the quantity of silt deposited on lands under irrigation. I have also heard a story—apocryphal, no doubt, but still significant. It appears that an astute Tanjore Mirassidar paid a handsome bribe to the subordinate officers of the Public Works Department, to be allowed to breach the bank of a river when in full flood and that, though he got no produce from his lands the first year, he made a great profit in subsequent years. This, of course, is a very dangerous way of manuring lands. The inundations of the Nile fertilize the lands subject to them, but they often do as much harm as good.

[28] The question is entirely a scientific one and is at present in an experimental stage. Recent investigations, it is stated, with certain kinds of leguminous plants, have shown that they derive their nitrogen from the atmosphere and enrich the soil in which they are grown—*Vide Journal of the Royal Agricultural Society* for December 1891.

may thus, if recent investigations be correct, possibly derive their nitrogen from the atmosphere." Dr. Voelcker has given high praise to the native methods of cultivation which he considers are excellent, the problem of improving native agriculture being a more difficult one than the problem of improving English agriculture. The "garden" cultivation, *i.e.*, cultivation with the aid of wells, presents, in his opinion, "some of the most splendid features of careful and high class cultivation that one can possibly see in any part of the world." "Garden" cultivation has, as already remarked, greatly increased in this Presidency. To take one district, Coimbatore. The number of irrigation wells in good order, which were 22,000 in number in 1801, increased to 28,719 in 1821, to 31,507 in 1852, to 58,385 in 1882, and to 60,283 in 1888–89.[29] This means on about 15 per cent. of the area under cultivation, the outturn was quadrupled or even quintupled. It was owing to the existence of these wells that Coimbatore, though one of the driest districts in the Presidency, suffered so little from the famine of 1876–78; since the famine, cultivation by means of wells has been extending in other districts also. Dr. Brandis, who travelled through the several districts of the Presidency in 1880, writes in his report on Forest management, "I was much gratified to see in Bellary, Salem and other districts the large number of new wells made since the famine, and old wells deepened; and it seemed to me that the people fully recognize the value of wells for irrigation. Many of the wells in the dry inland districts are large and beautifully built, 30 feet square and 25 feet deep or more, and such wells cost from Rs. 500 to Rs. 1,000." The Board's report [30] on the Revenue Settlement of the Presidency for the year ending 30th June 1890 shows that 3,176 wells were excavated in that year by Government ryots at a cost of Rs. 2,63,677; and of this number, three-fourths were in Salem, Coimbatore and Chingleput. The same report shows that in seven districts, from which alone returns had been received, the number of wells in use for supplementing irrigation from Government works was no less than 48,220, showing beyond doubt that the policy recently adopted by Government of doing away with the last remnant of restrictive regulations calculated to impede the extension of well irrigation used for the purpose of supple-

---

[29] I examined the accounts of 10 villages in the Coimbatore taluk and found that the number of wells had increased from 208 in 1860 to 315 in 1890.

[30] Recent official reports show that about 20,000 wells were excavated during the last two years of drought by means of advances, amounting to upwards of 30 lakhs of rupees granted by Government, and it was found on inspection by the Commissioner of Revenue Settlement and Agriculture that the wells were in proper order. The 900 wells constructed in the Ponneri taluk have since been found to be mud wells estimated to last for from 10 to 15 years, but excavated on hard soil.

menting the deficiency of irrigation from Government works and saving the Government as well as the ryots from loss, was an eminently wise one. I am informed that large numbers of wells have been excavated in the Chingleput, North Arcot, Coimbatore, Madura and Tinnevelly districts during the last two years with the aid of loans obtained under the very favorable rules which have been framed for the purpose. In the single taluk of Ponnéri, which is liable more or less to drought, it appears that no less than 900 wells have been excavated during the last six months. This is a great boon to that taluk which will henceforth, to a great extent, be protected from the effects of partial droughts. The increase of produce under the great irrigation systems has already been noticed. Of late years considerable attention has been paid to the repair of minor irrigation works also, and when the project for the restoration of tanks throughout the Presidency at a cost of 26 lakhs of rupees, which is now under execution, is completed, there is no doubt that the efficiency of the tanks and the produce of the lands under them will be greatly increased. As regards dry or unirrigated lands, it is true that there is now less fallowing than formerly, though the practice of leaving lands fallow prevails even now to a much greater extent than is generally supposed. Thus out of 17 millions of unirrigated lands held by Government ryots no less than 3 millions were left fallow in 1890. In the Godávari district one-half, and in the Tinnevelly district one-third of the ryots' holdings is left fallow annually.[31] There is, besides, a large area of lands on the margin of cultivation which are taken up for cultivation or relinquished by the ryots as it suits them. Cultivation under a system of fallows is of course poor and slovenly cultivation, and with the increase of population and the decrease in the area of waste, must necessarily be displaced by cultivation under improved methods. My enquiries tend to show that, under the stress of necessity and the additional incentives to individual exertion promoted by the breakup of the joint family system, greater care is now bestowed on cultivation of lands in the Tanjore district than in times past; and this is to some extent the case in other districts also. If any marked results have not been obtained in this direction, it is not because the ryots are so very unintelligent that they could not be induced to adopt improved methods of cultivation, but

[31] The Madras Board of Revenue have since the above was written instituted enquiries as to the reason for such a large proportion of dry land being left fallow in the Godávari and Tinnevelly districts. The results of the enquiries are not yet known. In Tinnevelly, however, it is stated that land planted with palmyrah trees, though included in ryots' holdings, is treated in the revenue accounts as 'waste,' that is, fallow. This will however, account for the area of land left fallow only in a portion of the district.

because the pressure of population has not enhanced the prices of agricultural produce to such an extent as to make *intensive* cultivation[32] necessary or profitable.

Prices.

27. *Prices* of commodities appear to have varied enormously in different parts of the country in previous centuries owing to the difficulty of communication and general insecurity; they were comparatively high in such districts as Malabar and South Canara which exported spices much in demand in Europe, receiving in return gold and silver. In the districts in the interior, prices were exceedingly low. We find, for instance, that the commutation rate adopted by Hari Har Roy, the Vijianagar Sovereign, for the settlement of land revenue in Canara in the middle of the 14th century was 3 kattis for 1 ghetti pagoda, or 30 seers of 80 tolas of rice per rupee, while the present price is 15 seers per rupee. Buchanan states that in the 15th century the price adopted for fixing the tax on cocoanut plantations was 6 pagodas or 24 rupees per 1,000 cocoanuts. The price is not much higher at present. In the Ramnad country on the other hand, it will be seen from the letter of the Jesuit Missionary already quoted that in 1713, 8 markals of excellent husked rice could be purchased for 1 fanam, and Mr. Nelson, the compiler of the *Madura District Manual*, says that the rate is equivalent to 96 lb. for $2\frac{1}{4}d.$, or 512 seers of 80 tolas for 1 rupee, which is nearly one-twenty-third of the present price. In the Chingleput district, it appears that in 1733 paddy was sold at 25 pagodas per garce, which is about one-half of the present price. Twenty years previously, however, it would seem that this would have been reckoned a famine price. The price of paddy in the last quarter of the last century in the Ganjam district appears to have averaged 8*d*. per cwt., or 168 seers of 80 tolas per rupee or about one-sixth of the present

---

[32] The English example is very instructive. The average price of wheat in the beginning of the 15th century was only 6*s*. a quarter and in particular years it went down as low as 1*s*. 2*d*. Between 1459 and 1560, the average price rose to 9*s*. 2*d*. in consequence mainly of the debasement of the currency. From 1561 to 1601 the average price was 47*s*. 6*d*. In the 17th and 18th centuries prices were at the same level. In the first half of the present century the average price was 60*s*. The greatest improvements in agriculture were effected in the 17th and 18th centuries and the first half of the 19th century. The price, however, has since under the stress of foreign competition gone down as low as 30*s*. a quarter. The consequence is that high cultivation does not pay in England. "The soil is weakly farmed, undermanned, and understocked, partly because capital has dwindled, partly because farmers are compelled to realize something, even if the sales are premature. Land is going back: it is falling out of condition, if not out of cultivation, and farmers are too poor, too weak and dispirited to restore or maintain it. Its produce per acre is diminishing and the number of sheep has decreased by more than two millions since 1875. High farming at present prices appears waste of money; agriculture cannot hold its own by *intension* against *extension*. The progress of centuries seems thrown away; the instrument becomes useless just when it is perfected and able to double the existing produce."—Prothero's *Pioneers and Progress of English Farming.*

price. Comparatively high prices appear to have ruled at this time in the Southern districts owing to the devastating wars and famines from which they suffered. Since the beginning of the century we have continuous records of the prices of food-grains. The old prices are, strictly speaking, not comparable with recent prices on account of the variety of the measures in terms of which the prices were quoted in the old days, and the uncertainty as to their contents, but they nevertheless give a fairly correct general idea of the changes that have occurred. In the appendix V (C) I have given tables showing the average prices of the four principal food-grains for quinquennial periods, leaving out of account famine years. From these tables it will be seen that prices were at their lowest level for some years before 1850, in consequence of the insufficiency of the currency to meet the requirements of the country. Representing the average prices of the food-grains in the five years ending 1853 by 100, the average prices at the quinquennial periods referred to will be indicated by the numbers shown in the subjoined table :—

Grains.	Average for five years ending						
	1813.	1823.	1832.	1853.	1865.	1874.	1888.
Paddy	128	134	117	100	264	216	234
Cholum	135	141	118	100	227	182	189
Ragi	133	141	114	100	233	180	192
Cumbu	123	137	110	100	227	185	200
All four grains ..	129	138	115	100	238	191	204

The above table clearly brings out the following conclusions. *First*, from about 1828 to 1853, or for a period of nearly 25 years, the prices rapidly declined till they reached a level which was one-fourth[33] less than the prices in the early years of the century on which the land settlements were based. The result was the acute agricultural depression already described and the collapse of the settlements; *secondly*, prices rose rapidly after 1853 till they reached their culmination in the five years ending 1865, when they were two-and-a-half times what they were prior to 1853 and twice as high as in the early years of

[33] As the figures given in the table represent averages of prices differing widely and relating to large tracts of country, they must be taken as indicating the direction of the movement of prices and not as a strict measure of their rise or fall. I have endeavoured to obtain information regarding the course of prices from the accounts kept by land-holders and merchants. The results which are given in the appendix V.-C. (e) to (k) are confirmatory of the inferences derivable from the table given here.

the century. The causes of this sudden rise have already been mentioned; they may be briefly recapitulated as follows. The gold discoveries of America and Australia in 1848 led to a large influx of gold into Europe, raising prices and creating a demand for Indian productions. The substitution of gold for silver in the currencies of the principal European countries cheapened the latter metal and made it available for export to India. The Crimean War at the same time led to the development of the trade of India in jute and oil-seeds. The Indian Mutiny necessitated large remittances in silver for expenditure in India, and the construction of public works, especially railways, had the same effect. The American War and the consequent Cotton famine in England developed an enormous trade in the somewhat hitherto despised Indian cotton. The net imports into India of gold and silver which in the decade ending 1849 was 21 millions sterling rose successively to 70 millions in the decade ending 1859, and to 159 millions in the decade ending 1869. *Thirdly*, after 1870, prices fell by about 20 per cent. from the level they had attained in 1865, but were nevertheless nearly twice as high as in 1853, and 50 per cent. higher than in the earlier years of the century. The re-action was brought about of course by the cessation of the causes which had led to the influx into India of the precious metals in the previous decade. The cotton famine in England ended with the American war and the United States resumed their position as the chief suppliers of cotton to England, and the loans for the construction of public works in India ceased. India, instead of receiving large sums of money, had to remit large sums in payment of interest on the obligations already contracted and to meet the increased charges incurred in England as a consequence of the amalgamation of the Indian Army with that in England. The net imports of gold and silver amounted in the five years ending 1874 only to 15 and 18 millions against 29 and 50 millions respectively in the previous five years. *Fourthly*, leaving out of account the last two years of drought, the average prices of the previous five years show a slight increase as compared with those in the five years ending 1874, *i.e.*, the years immediately preceding the great famine of 1876–78.

Effect of the improvement of communications on prices.

28. The great benefits conferred on the country by the improvement of communications are too obvious to need detailed consideration. Nevertheless a few facts gleaned from the old reports will here be given to enable us to realize what immense advance there has been in this direction. Owing to

the absence of roads, pack bullocks and coolies were the only means of conveyance 60 or 70 years ago, and the cost of transport of bulky articles for long distances was consequently prohibitive. Buchanan, writing in 1800, states that the wage of a cooly in the Coimbatore district for carrying a man's load 10 miles was 2 gopali fanams or 5 annas 4 pies. The pacification of the country led to a revival of trade and the increase in the means of conveyance, and we accordingly find that the rate was reduced to 2 annas 6 pies in 1804 and to 2 annas in 1839. The hire of a bullock carrying, say, 200 lb. 10 miles was 5 annas in 1809 and 4 annas in 1839. The Collector of Coimbatore writing in the latter year gives the following as the cost of carriage for 100 miles of 1 ton of goods by men, pack bullocks and carts—by coolies Rs. 21–14–0; by pack bullocks Rs. 10–15–0; by bandies Rs. 8–12–0. The figures show, as might be expected, that carriage by coolies even in those days was the most expensive of all modes of conveyance. In Nellore the cost of carrying 1 putti of grain (742 Madras measures) was 1 star pagoda and 5 fanams or Rs. 4 for every 8 miles in 1805. Carts were not used in the district then or for a long time afterwards. The Collector writing in 1847 mentions as a novelty that he had for the first time used carts during his tours. The cost of carriage of grain by means of pack bullocks for a distance of 8 miles amounted to one-third of the value of the grain which could not therefore be profitably transported to places distant even 24 miles, unless the price at the place of import was more than double that at the place of production. Piece-goods manufactured at Nellore were carried all the way to Madras—a distance of 110 miles—on the heads of coolies. Wálajáh was a great emporium of trade and consequently the cost of carriage to that station was lower than to other places. Buchanan mentions that in 1800 the hire of a bullockload of 8 maunds or 200 lb. from Bangalore to Wálajáh—a distance of 145 miles—was Rs. 1–4–0 or Rs. 1–8–0 according to the nature of the goods carried, and these rates, allowing for the fall in the purchasing power of the rupee, would be equivalent to Rs. 2 or Rs. 2–8–0 at the present day. In the case of grain the cost of carriage often exceeded the value of the grain. The result was violent fluctuations in one direction or the other in prices according as the harvests were good or bad, and it often happened that, while in one tract of country people were in the midst of plenty, in an adjoining tract not far distant the inhabitants were suffering the direst distress. When the terrible famine of 1833 was raging in Guntúr, there was plenty of grain in Malabar and South Canara where it was being sold at ordinary prices. The report of the Cotton Committee of 1848 mentions that when grain was selling at from 6*s.* to 8*s.* a quarter at Kandeish, the price at Poona was from 64*s.* to 70*s.* a quarter. Mr. Nicholson in his *Manual of the Coimbatore District* has so well described the revolution in trade effected by the improvement of communications in that district that his remarks may be usefully quoted here. He states: "From various reports it is known that in 1800 there were practically no roads, but merely tracks; there was not a cart in the district, and what traffic existed was carried on by pack bullocks, and by ponies and by basket boats on the Cauvery. The result was not only that all imported commodities were dear, but export trade was insignificant, and only in valuable articles such as gheе, spices and so forth. Grain could not be moved, so that prices depended on local scarcity or abundance, with the result that substantial ryots were no worse off in bad years than in good, for storage was a necessity, so that deficient crops were supplemented from the surplus of good years, which then fetched very high prices; while in good years, especially if consecutive, the markets were glutted, prices fell heavily, and the ryots who were compelled to sell in order to meet the Government and other demands were ruined by their own superabundance. This reproach remained for many years, so that average prices between 1849–53 were lower than at any previous time, while in times of famine, as in 1824 and 1837, the difference in prices between famine and non-famine districts was very serious. There are now (1887) in the district above 1,500 miles of metalled or gravelled roads in good order, besides numerous cross roads and village lanes and 147 miles of railway—Madras and South Indian. The result of this improvement is an immense internal traffic between the various trade centres, such as weekly markets and towns, and a considerable import and export trade in which thousands of carts take part with railways. Every village has several and every town hundreds of carts which are extensively built in many places. The value of the rail-borne traffic has not been ascertained, but one or two facts may be noted—(1) that in the late famine grain was poured by thousands of tons, while the price of rice at the height of famine differed from that at Tanjore, whence it was supplied by only about 3 lb. per rupee; (2) that private trade has been so stimulated by the railway that at the least hint of scarcity in any other district or province grain is at once moved, *e.g.*, in the early months of 1884, scarcity seemed imminent in Northern India, and the Coimbatore Railway Stations were crammed with grain *en route* northwards; (3) that trades such as the considerable tanning industry, coffee growing, &c., have been begotten by the railway, which carries the produce cheaply to the coast; (4) that upon the making of the railway, prices, to the great advantage of the ryot, speedily doubled owing to export facilities; with this great rise in grain prices, land prices also rose, so that land, especially near the railways, is now worth from 6 to 10 times its value when the Madras Railway was made; (5) that the production of valuable crops has been greatly stimulated, tobacco, which has long been grown largely owing to the West Coast demand, being excepted. It is to be noted that railways cannot yet compete with carts for local traffic of say 30 miles' run, owing to the necessary delay in getting trains and the low rates at which ryots can afford to hire out their carts during the non-cultivation season." Mr. Nicholson's observations which have reference to the Coimbatore district are equally applicable to the other parts of the Presidency. We have already seen that in the beginning of the century roads were practically non-existent, and that in 1852 there were only 3,000 miles of roads hardly deserving the name. There are now 25,000 miles of road in the Presidency maintained by the Local Fund Boards in fair order, 2,000 miles of railway, and 1,500 miles of canals. As pointed out by Mr. Nicholson, the number of carts has enormously increased coincidentally with increase in the mileage of railways. In the Presidency as a whole there were only 90,000 carts in 1850; in 1877–78 there were 284,000 and there are now 436,000 or nearly 5 times as many as in 1850. There was not a single cart in South Canara in 1838; there are now 3,000 carts. In Salem a tax on carts at the rate of 1 rupee was levied in 1836 and the number of carts in the district was ascertained to be 1,189. The number had increased to 3,296 in 1847 and the number in use at present is 12,400.[34] The hire of a cart which was As. 14 per diem in 1838 was reduced to As. 8 in 1847, while the load of a cart which was no more than 300 lb. at the former had increased to 1,000 lb. at the latter date. The rate in force in 1838 was thus 6 times the rate in 1847. In the latter year the purchasing power of money was 2½ times at least as high as it is now, and consequently As. 8 then would be equivalent to Rs. 1–4–0 now. The ordinary rate of hire for a cart is 1 rupee per diem at present, and as a cart-load is about 1,000 lb. and the distance hauled every day 15 miles on an

---

[34] The argument which is sometimes put forward that railways by superseding carts have rendered the breeding of cattle for draught unnecessary and prejudicially affected agriculture is, it will be seen from the above remarks, to a great extent unfounded.

average, this rate is equivalent to about As. 2–5 per ton per mile, while the cost of carriage by railway is about 8 pies per ton per mile or a little more than one-fourth of the cost of carriage by carts. The cost of carriage in boats on the canals is about half of that on railways. Confining our attention to the main railways and canals in this Presidency, the quantity of goods and the number of passengers carried in 1888–89 were for the Madras Railway—passengers 8,003,205 over an average distance of 39·1 miles and goods 1,088,774 tons over an average distance of 105 miles; for the South Indian Railway—passengers 7,212,299 over an average distance of 35·12 miles and goods 1,349,433 tons over an average distance of 46·9 miles. In the Godávari, Kistna and Buckingham canals, the number of passengers carried was 480,000 and the ton-mileage of goods 36 millions. Leaving out of consideration the passenger traffic, the saving in the cost of carriage of goods alone caused by the substitution of carriage by railways and canals for conveyance by carts may roughly be estimated at 27 millions of rupees every year; that is more than one-half the entire land revenue of the Presidency. If the saving in time, and the diminished risk of loss[35] by robbery and of damage by exposure to the weather be taken into account, the real saving in cost will be found to be very much greater. Of course, under the old conditions it would have been impossible to carry anything like the quantity of goods now sent from place to place, or in other words, the immense trade that now exists would not have been possible but for the extension of communications. It is a well known fact that silver has fallen considerably in value since 1873, and, under ordinary circumstances, we should have expected that the prices of the principal commodities in India would have risen in the same proportion. The cheapening of the cost of carriage has, however, been so great as to neutralize almost wholly the rise in prices, and the consequence is that the prices of food grains during recent years are slightly, if at all, in excess of the prices in 1873.

---

[35] Even as regards passengers, the risks in travelling by railways are incomparably smaller than the risks of travelling by other conveyances, notwithstanding the terrible railway accidents that occasionally occur. The number of passengers carried by the Madras and South Indian Railways in 1889–90 was upwards of 16½ millions, while the number of persons killed was 32. In England the number of persons killed by railway accidents during the years 1882 to 1885 was 1 in 60 millions of passengers. Mr. Henry Ward in his article on "Locomotion and Transport," in the jubilee volume entitled *The Reign of Queen Victoria*, says: "From a comparison between the number of accidents and the average train mileage, it may be deduced that a man in order to secure his death must begin to travel as soon as he is born and move day and night at the rate of 20 miles an hour for 466 years. Even to make the risks from railway travelling equal to those from general causes, he must pursue the practice for 9 years. Very few have time even to get injured by the railway."

Trade. Its dimensions.

29. The statistics available as regards the sea-borne trade of the several provinces included in this Presidency for the last century are, as might be expected, fragmentary and imperfect. In the *Political Survey of the Northern Circars* written by Mr. Grant and printed as appendix to the "Fifth Report," and in Buchanan's *Journey* in 1800, we have scattered accounts of both sea-borne and inland trade which was carried on [36] on a very small scale. According to Grant the value of the sea-borne and inland trade of the Northern Circars amounted only to 75 lakhs of rupees made up as follows: Exports by Europeans of fine cloth manufactures 30 lakhs; coasting trade to Madras chiefly in grain valued at 25 lakhs; exports of coarser cloths for the Eastern markets 10 lakhs; and inland trade in salt and piece-goods 10 lakhs. In 1889–90, in the single port of Cocanada, the value of the sea-borne trade amounted to 200 lakhs. Fairly reliable statistics are available in regard to sea-borne trade since the beginning of the century, and the rapid

---

[36] We must be on our guard against accepting too literally the exaggerated accounts given of the trade of India by ancient writers. The want of communications, as we have already seen, made it impossible for any extensive trade being carried on in bulky articles in general demand among the people. The chief articles of export were cotton muslins of the finest texture and printed cloths, silk and spices, and latterly coarse cloths and indigo. India received the value of the exports in gold and silver, as all necessaries of life were produced in the country, the imports being small quantities of tin, lead, glass, amber, steel for arms and frankincense from Arabia. In these circumstances, the trade of India, in former times, though large perhaps as compared with the trade of other countries, must have been of small proportions when judged by modern standards, and was carried on intermittently; for, other countries could not afford to be sending precious metals continually to India, as the rise of prices in India under such circumstances must have extinguished the trade, unless there was a large demand for the productions of Europe in India. The articles in demand in Europe were such as only the richest classes forming an insignificant portion of the population could purchase. For instance, spices were much esteemed in Europe, the Indian trade being there known as the *spice trade*. The price of such articles as pepper, cardamoms, &c., was as high as 11*s*. a lb. in the 14th century, that is more than ten times the price in India, taking the nominal values, while the purchasing power of money was between 8 and 12 times of what it is at present. The difference between the prices of articles in India and in Europe was reduced after the discovery of the Cape of Good Hope, but still it was very considerable. For instance, the price of pepper which was 8*s*. a lb. was reduced to 1*s*. 8*d*. a lb. In 1621 Mr. Munn, one of the Directors of the East India Company, estimated the quantity of Indian articles imported and their prices at the places of export and import as follows:—

	Price in India per lb.	Price in England per lb.
250,000 lb. of pepper	2½*d*.	1*s*. 3*d*.
150,000 ,, of cloves	9*d*.	6*s*. 0*d*.
150,000 ,, of nutmegs	4*d*.	2*s*. 6*d*.
50,000 ,, of mace	8*d*.	6*s*. 0*d*.
200,000 ,, of indigo	1*s*. 2*d*.	5*s*. 0*d*.
107,140 ,, of China raw silk ..	7*s*. 0*d*.	20*s*. 0*d*.

Ordinary coarse cloths called "calicoes" which cost 7*s*. in India were sold in England at 21*s*. a piece. In the first quarter of the century the value of articles exported from India to Europe was estimated at about half a million sterling. The value of bullion and merchandize imported by the East India Company into Madras from 1708 to 1811, a period of 104 years, was 20 millions sterling—bullion 12 millions and merchandize 8 millions.

progress made in this direction will be seen from the figures given in the subjoined table :

Average of 10 years		Foreign trade— millions, Rx.	Coasting trade— millions, Rx.	Total millions, Rx.
Ending 31st March ..	1810 ..	1·72	2·41	4·13
	1820 ..	1·64	1·26	2·90
	1830 ..	1·98	1·52	3·50
	1840 ..	1·80	1·89	3·69
	1850 ..	2·42	2·24	4·66
	1860 ..	4·12	3·07	7·19
	1870 ..	9·17	5·39	14·56
	1880 ..	10·79	11·07	21·86
	1890 ..	14·54	10·41	24·95
For the year 1889–1890	..	18·23	11·37	29·60

Note.—The figures shown above under "coasting trade" represent the value of imports from and exports to ports within the Presidency as well as ports in other parts of India. As, however, in the former case the imports of one port are the exports of another, the value of interportal trade within the Presidency is reckoned twice over. For instance, in the 11·37 millions, Rx. shown as the value of the coasting trade, 4·6 million, Rx. represents the aggregate value of import and export trade as between ports within the Presidency and half of it should be deducted from the total trade.

The table above given shows that, during the first half of the century, there was not only no improvement in sea-borne trade, but that it showed a tendency to decline. The East India Company was deprived of its commercial privileges except as regards the China trade in 1813, and the monopoly of the China trade also was abolished in 1833. The internal trade of the country, owing to the want of communications and the levy of the oppressive transit duties, was very restricted, and the Presidency itself was suffering from agricultural depression. Since 1850, however, in consequence of the development of communications, the abolition of transit duties and customs duties on interportal trade and other causes which have been already more than once referred to, the trade has advanced by "leaps and bounds." This will be still more manifest if we take one port, Tuticorin for instance, and examine how its trade has progressed. In the early years of the century the trade of the whole district of Tinnevelly, both by sea and land, was very small. There were only 16 ships (native craft) engaged in sea traffic, and the trade was chiefly in jaggery with Madras and in cloth with Colombo. The total exports by sea and land amounted only to 14 lakhs of rupees, of which about 4 lakhs represented the Company's investments. The trade by land consisted of raw cotton valued at Rs. 80,000 and tobacco valued at Rs. 75,000. The imports were insignificant, consisting of small quantities of pepper and occasionally rice. The progress of sea-borne trade since 1830 has been as follows :—1830—Exports 21 lakhs of rupees, imports 2 lakhs, total 23 lakhs; 1850–51—Exports 15 lakhs, imports 2 lakhs, total 17 lakhs; 1875–76—Exports 75 lakhs, imports 51 lakhs, total 126 lakhs; 1889–90—Exports 200 lakhs and imports 32 lakhs, total 232 lakhs. In 1830 the chief articles of exports were jaggery 1·16 lakhs; cotton 8·48 lakhs; cotton goods 10·18 lakhs and miscellaneous articles 1·38 lakhs. In 1889–90[37] the exports were jaggery 17 lakhs; cotton 146 lakhs; cotton goods 7·46 lakhs and other articles 29·54 lakhs. The trade of the other ports of the Presidency, with the exception of Masulipatam, has likewise increased very considerably.

As regards inland trade, the distant traffic carried on by means of railways between groups of districts into which the Presidency is divided for purposes of registration of this traffic amounted in 1889–90 to 31·85 millions of Indian maunds as shown below:

	Million maunds.
External trade—	
Imports into Madras Presidency, excluding the chief sea-port towns	2·60
Imports into Madras chief sea-port towns	1·18
	3·78
Exports from Madras excluding the chief sea-port towns	3·07
Exports from Madras sea-port towns	1·24
	4·31
Internal trade—	
Of Madras Presidency, excluding chief sea-port towns ...	10·86
Of Madras chief sea-port towns	12·90
	23·76

The traffic borne on the Godávari, Kistna and Buckingham canals in 1889–90 was 21·44 millions of maunds valued at 6·41 crores of rupees and the ton mileage 36·03 millions. The carriage alone of this merchandize at 4 pies per ton per mile must have cost not less than 75 lakhs of rupees. The trade with the French Settlements was valued at 2·15 crores of rupees.

Besides the above, there is an immense traffic carried on by roads which is not registered. In 1888–89 an attempt was made to register the traffic on some of the more important roads in the Ganjam, South Canara, Cuddapah, North Arcot and Madura districts. The registration was necessarily imperfect, but the quantity of the registered traffic was found to be above 4 million maunds. The traffic registered represents of course only a very small portion of the total road traffic of the

[37] It must be noted that the season of 1889-90 in the Tinnevelly district was a good one, and the exports of cotton and jaggery were somewhat larger than usual.

country. Moreover, there is a large amount of petty local traffic for distribution of merchandize in retail by means of weekly fairs held in several places in the Presidency. We have no means of estimating the value of traffic which is not carried on the main lines of communication, but there can be no doubt that its aggregate amount is very large.

The advantages of trade.

30. Now, of the abovementioned sea-borne and inland traffic, it will be quite within the mark to state that nine-tenths has sprung up since 1850; and this statement is applicable in a greater degree to inland than to sea-borne traffic, as land carriage in former years owing to want of communication was more expensive than sea carriage, and the land traffic was in consequence restricted to articles of small bulk and high value. It seems almost an act of supererogation to attempt to *prove* that all this development of traffic has been of benefit to the country, but as the increase of traffic, and especially foreign traffic, is sometimes spoken of as if it were an evil and not a benefit by persons who ought to know better, it may not be considered altogether unnecessary to examine in what the advantages of trade consist, and whether these advantages are outweighed by any counterbalancing evils. The following remarks of Professor Thorold Rogers explain succinctly what are the advantages of trade in general and of foreign trade in particular. He says: "The economical benefits of trade and of that understanding between nations, which leads to the exchange of products, which protects merchants and merchandize and gives temporarily to the foreigner, under more or less easy conditions, opportunities of commerce, are obvious and trite. The distribution of products to the greatest possible reciprocal advantage is the first and most enduring stimulant to trade. In all acts of exchange, the buyer has the strongest inducement to get what he most needs, and in commerce, both parties buy and both parties sell. Trade is again the most efficient instructor as to the natural benefits of soil, climate and material, and it teaches this with the greatest rapidity and accuracy. The greatest service which unimpeded trade does to a community which has accepted it, is that it informs the people who desire to exchange their products, what are the best kinds of material on which to exercise their industry and develop that utility which is the sole end of economical labour. Hence it supplies the answer to the important problem—Has the industry in which a country is engaged been determined on in the most productive direction, does it produce the greatest possible results with the least possible expenditure of force? Hence it acts as a stimulant for the discovery of labour—saving instru-

ments and of cost-saving processes, for any waste is labour needlessly and unprofitably expended. It leads to the discovery of natural resources, as in this country (England) coal, salt and iron, the last two of which, before certain discoveries were made, were imported into this country." Bearing these remarks in mind, I will endeavour to show by an analysis of the statistics of trade in the principal articles of export and import to what extent the country has benefited by the increase of trade.

The progress of trade in the principal articles of export.

31. *Cotton.*—Among the articles of export, *cotton* is the most important. In 1855–56 the exports of cotton were only 21 million lb. valued at 25 lakhs of rupees, whereas now the exports are 98 million lb. valued at $2\frac{1}{2}$ crores of rupees; and of this increased value a larger share reaches the cultivator now than it did in former years. For instance, in 1848, Dr. Forbes Watson, Reporter of the Economic Products of India, stated that the cost of raising cotton in the Bombay Presidency was $1\frac{1}{4}d.$ per lb.; the cost of carriage to Bombay was $1\frac{1}{2}d.$ or 120 per cent. of the cost of the article at the place of production; and freight to England and connected charges were 1*d.* a lb.; so that Indian cotton could not be sold in England at less than 4*d.* a lb. The producer thus obtained for his article only about 31 per cent. of the price at which it was sold in England, the remainder being absorbed in the cost of carriage and the profits of middlemen. Now owing to the great cheapening of the cost of carriage by land by the introduction of railways, and of sea freight by improvements in the construction of steamers, the producer in India secures something like 66 per cent.[38] of the price realized in the English market. The development of the export trade in cotton has also led to the establishment of 41 cotton presses in which the quantity of cotton pressed amounts to $95\frac{3}{4}$ million lb.

---

[38] I append below the calculations given by an agricultural inspector in his report on cotton cultivation in the Tinnevelly district:

	RS.	A.	P.
Value of 1 candy (500 lb.) of lint at $5\frac{1}{4}d.$ per lb. in the English market, the exchange being at 1*s.* 6*d.* per rupee	146	0	0
Deduct charges—			
Pressing charge	2	0	0
Railway transit	1	2	0
Freight, commission, &c.	13	14	0
Firm's profit	4	0	0
Principal dealer's profit	1	0	0
Other charges borne by the sub-dealer	2	0	0
Cleaning charges	10	0	0
Sub-dealer's profit	3	0	0
Bagging and cartage	1	0	0
	38	0	0
Balance, being the value to the ryot of 1 candy of clean cotton	**108**	**0**	**0**

Coffee.—The cultivation and trade in coffee, as is well known, have been entirely created and developed within the last 40 years. The value of the coffee exported in 1889–90 amounted to 1½ crores of rupees. It is estimated that the amount expended on the maintenance of coffee plantations on the Nílgiris alone is 20 lakhs of rupees, of which about one-third is paid as wages to coolies and goes to support 14,000 labouring families from the plains. 23 large works for curing coffee have been established, the outturn being estimated at 18½ million lb. valued at nearly one crore of rupees. These works afford employment to 7,500 hands.

Indigo is another article of export which has rapidly progressed within the last 40 years. In 1855–56 the exports were 2·9 million lb. valued at 43 lakhs of rupees. In 1889–90 the quantity exported was 6·1 million lb. and the value 1·19 crores. The Collector of Cuddapah, in which district indigo is extensively manufactured, writing in 1853, states that at the commencement of the century "the manufacture of indigo was in its rudest state, and the plant from which it is extracted grown to a limited extent; the cultivation of this plant was formerly confined to the south-eastern portion of the district, but now is gradually extending to the north and west. The indigo itself was manufactured in earthen pots with great labour and considerable expense, and was of inferior quality, but in later years a more improved and better system of manufacture has been introduced and the culture of the plant greatly increased. The produce of this plant from its quality is well known in the European markets, and its culture has proved of the greatest benefit to the cultivators both rich and poor, as a ready market is found for any quantity which may be grown; the poorer ryots receive advances without interest from the wealthy firms who have established indigo manufactories, and who, should their crop be insufficient to repay the advances received, are seldom pressed for payment, unless it is ascertained that they are endeavouring to defraud those from whom they have received liberal advances, by disposing of their crop to another party. This system to a considerable extent relieves the poorer ryots from the exorbitant interest demanded by village bakalls and shroffs, and thus, instead of being ruined by usurious interest, they with a little care and management may repay all their advances from their crops during the following year, and obtain sufficient profit to satisfy the Sircar demand and to maintain themselves and families." The manufacture of indigo has, however, since passed entirely into the hands of natives, while the area under indigo and the production of the dye have increased. The reason why European agencies cannot cope with natives is explained by an agent of an European firm to be that "the latter can do things cheaper. They manufacture the produce of their own lands, work their own factories and are assisted by relatives and friends who are paid little or nothing, though, of course, they expect assistance in return. At an European agency the weed is purchased, and the cost of supervision and labour is very great. The weed, as is often the case, during some seasons, yields little or no dye. European agencies suffer heavy losses, while natives do not feel the loss so heavily." There are now six [39] indigo factories and 6,393 indigo vats at work in the Presidency, the quantity of indigo manufactured being estimated at 3·8 million lb. valued at 51 lakhs of rupees. Besides the persons employed in the cultivation of the plant, the manufacture of the dye gives employment to 90,000 persons during the working season. Cultivation being perfectly voluntary, no difficulties or disturbances similar to those frequently experienced in Bengal, where indigo planters who had secured leases of land on zemindari tenure endeavoured to force the cultivation of indigo on ryots against their will, have ever been experienced in this Presidency. The indigo manufactured in Madras is supplanting the indigo of Bengal, and it would, doubtless, soon take possession of the market were it not for the fact that Madras indigo is extensively adulterated by dealers. Indigo cultivation is very profitable to the ryot not only on account of the dye, but also because it enriches the soil and increases the yield of cereals, especially rice, grown in rotation.

Seeds to the quantity of 613,000 cwts. valued at 16¾ lakhs of rupees were exported in 1855–56. The exports in 1889–90 had increased to a little less than 2 million cwts. valued at 1·19 crores of rupees. The trade, in earth-nuts especially, has developed within the last few years and assumed large dimensions. Forty years ago, earth-nuts were unknown to European commerce. The cultivation of this crop has extended rapidly in the South Arcot district where the acreage under this crop has increased from about 6,700 acres to 190,000 acres. As ground-nuts do not require irrigation or much care in cultivation, and as they grow on dry, sandy soil, the trade in this article has increased the profits and the value of inferior lands. Besides the exports of earth-nuts from British ports, large quantities, the produce chiefly of the South Arcot district, are shipped from Pondicherry. In 1889 and 1890 the exports were valued at 14 and 9½ million francs, the diminished exports in the latter year being due to diminished production owing to

[39] There is reason to believe that the number of indigo factories is much in excess of the number officially returned.

adverse agricultural season. The value of exports of vegetable oils which was 6¼ lakhs of rupees in 1855–56 increased in 1889–90 to 51½ lakhs of rupees, which is less than half the value of exports of seeds. There are 16 lamp-oil manufactories in the Godávari district turning out about 10 lakhs' worth of oil, and there are a few mills in other districts doing a small business. The large export of seeds, however, shows that there is much scope for the establishment of additional oil-mills at convenient centres, for, the substitution of exports of oils for exports of seeds will cause a saving in the cost of carriage, while providing employment to a large number of labourers in this country and enabling the ryots to utilize the refuse of the oil-mills as manure or as food for cattle.

Sugar is both an article of export and import in this Presidency. In 1855–56 about 500,000 cwts. were exported, the value being nearly 32 lakhs of rupees. In 1889–90 the exports were nearly three times as much,—1,350,000 cwts.. valued at 86 lakhs of rupees. The imports by sea in 1889–90 were valued at 5¼ lakhs of rupees. About 155,000 maunds or 110,000 cwts. were also received by land from Mysore where sugar, both refined and unrefined, is extensively manufactured. There are 6 large sugar factories for the manufacture of refined sugar, and these give employment to about 2,000 persons. Tho art of manufacturing crystallized and refined sugar was in the beginning of the century a mystery known to very few. Buchanan states that sugar-candy made at Chickabalapura in Mysore "is equal to the Chinese and the clayed sugar is very white and fine. The art of making it is kept a secret. The price at which they sell it precludes an extensive sale. Chinese sugar-candy is sold at Seringapatam cheaper than the local produce is sold here." The Chinese sugar-candy was sold at Bangalore at £5–1–1, or say Rs. 50 per cwt., while the present price is not more than Rs. 20 per cwt., *i.e.*, the present price of the article, allowing for the fall in the purchasing power of money in India, is a little more than one-fourth of what it was in the beginning of the century. The production of unrefined sugar has greatly increased, especially in the Godávari district. The rail-borne inland traffic in this article in this Presidency amounted to 1½ million maunds. Iron mills are rapidly superseding the old inefficient wooden mills in extracting the juice of canes. There is great scope for the cultivation of cane and manufacture of sugar in this Presidency in the lands commanded by the great irrigation systems. Two years ago Messrs. Travers and Sons of London pointed out that under proper arrangements India ought to be able to produce all the refined sugar it wants, instead of exporting both crude sugar and labour to Mauritius, and receiving back refined sugar. The explanation for this is to be found in the fact that the price of refined sugar has enormously fallen, owing to the competition of bounty-fed beet sugar in France and Germany and the difficulty of getting cane grown near factories on a sufficiently large scale to make the manufacture of sugar by improved processes profitable. The latter difficulty is not, however, very formidable, and if a satisfactory solution of the sugar bounty question in Europe is arrived at, a considerable extension of the sugar industry in this Presidency might be hoped for.[40]

Spices.—The trade in spices is an ancient one in this Presidency. The exports were in 1855–56 of the value of 24 lakhs of rupees and in 1889–90, 71 lakhs.

Food-grains.—The net exports of food-grains have not increased, but on the contrary show a slight decline, owing to competition of cheap rice from Burma and Bengal.

Piece-goods.—The exports of cotton piece-goods were in 1855–56, 1,894,504 pieces and 223,140 yards valued at 21½ lakhs of rupees. In 1889–90, 1,100,165 pieces and 13,638,070 yards valued at 45 lakhs of rupees were exported. The cloths were partly the products of hand looms and cotton mills established in the country and partly foreign manufactures dyed in the country and re-exported. There were at the end of 1889-90 8 cotton mills worked by steam. The number of persons employed was 6,000, and the quantity of cotton worked up

---

[40] A recent enquiry instituted by the Government of India showed that the difficulties in the way of the introduction of improved methods of manufacture of sugar on an extensive scale were the following :

"(*a*) The cultivation of sugar-cane is limited by the supply not only of water for irrigation, but also of manure. (*b*) As cultivation in India is confined to small farms or holdings, each cultivator who is able to grow the crop at all can only find manure enough for a small area, generally less than half an acre, of sugar-cane. The plots of sugar-cane are, therefore, greatly scattered even in a canal irrigated tract. (*c*) A central factory has accordingly to bring in its supplies of cane in small quantities over varying distances, in many cases the distances being great. (*d*) The carriage of canes over a long distance, even in a climate like that of the Mauritius, is detrimental to the juice for purposes of sugar-making. It is much more so in India, where the canes ripen at the season when the atmosphere is driest and suffer, therefore, the maximum of injury. (*e*) The Mauritius system of growing large canes at intervals is not adapted to the greater part of India, where in order to prevent the ingress of dry air into the fields, small canes have to be grown in close contact. (*f*) The amount of cane which can be grown, limited as it is by the supply of water and manure, barely suffices for the wants of the Indian population. It seems to be at present as profitable to produce coarse sugar for their use as highly refined sugar for export. There is, therefore, no sufficient inducement to capital to embark on the more difficult and expensive system."

Mr. Tucker in his report on the inland trade of India, for 1888-89, adds—"a further obstacle to sugar refining in India exists in the high differential rate, which the conditions of the Indian excise system require to be placed on spirits made on the European method as compared with that levied on spirits manufactured by the indigenous process. The sugar refiner in India is thus placed at a disadvantage in respect to the utilization of his molasses in the form of spirits." In this Presidency, however, the so-called country liquor is mostly made from molasses according to European methods of distillation, and the other difficulties in regard to the cultivation of sugar-cane will not be difficult to overcome if the bounty system in European countries be abolished.

amounted to $20\frac{1}{4}$ million lb. Additional mills have since been established.

Of less important articles of export, the value of *tobacco* has risen from a little over 2 lakhs in 1855–56 to 17 lakhs in 1889–90, and *tea* from $\frac{1}{2}$ a lakh to 5 lakhs. *Cinchona* is a plant very recently introduced, and the exports of this drug from this Presidency amounted to 12 lakhs of rupees. In connection with the manufacture of tobacco, there are 32 factories in which cigars to the value of upwards of 7 lakhs of rupees are manufactured.

The progress of trade in imported articles and the low cost at which they are now obtained.

32. The value of the sea-borne imports of the Presidency amounted in 1889–90 to $9\frac{1}{2}$ crores of rupees, of which 4·15 crores or nearly one-half consisted of cotton manufactures. Cotton piece-goods have increased from about 28 lakhs in 1855–56 to 2·68 crores in 1889–90; cotton twist from 23 lakhs to 1·47 crores; metals from 11 to 58 lakhs; liquors from 13 to 21 lakhs. The other articles imported in 1889–90 were railway materials 40 lakhs; timber and wood 21 lakhs; hardware and cutlery 20 lakhs; coal, machinery and mill work 34 lakhs; salt 28 lakhs; apparel 28 lakhs; kerosine and other oils 20 lakhs; spices and areca-nuts 19 lakhs; gunny bags 17 lakhs; stationery 14 lakhs; provisions 14 lakhs; drugs and medicines 9 lakhs; woollen goods 8 lakhs; sugar 5 lakhs; raw silk 12 lakhs; books 3 lakhs; other minor commodities 9 lakhs. Some of the articles, such as machinery and mill-work, could not of course have been procured except by means of foreign trade. In the case of other articles, the cost, that is, not merely nominal prices but real values, allowing for change in the purchasing power of money, has been enormously reduced. For instance, the money price of cotton goods, it will be seen from the statement given in the appendix, V.–D. (e), is now about two-thirds of the price in 1850, and as the purchasing power of money estimated in terms of food-grains is now only two-fifth of what it was in 1850, it is clear that a ryot on the coast has now to give in exchange for cloth a little more than one-fourth of the quantity of grain he gave in 1850 and a ryot in the interior even less. The same proportion holds good as regards the exchangeable value of metals and other imported goods more or less. The fall in the value of imported goods has been specially great since 1873, owing to economies effected (1) in the cost of production in European countries by the adoption of labour-saving processes in the manufacture of commodities, and (2) in the cost of carriage by the opening of the Suez Canal and improvements in the construction of steamers. There are, says Sir Lyon Playfair in his book entitled *Subject of*

Social Welfare, in explanation of the causes which have brought about a temporary depression of particular trades in England, two immediate causes of depression in all machine-using countries. The first is the changes produced by science in the economy of distribution. By the opening of the Suez Canal, the old route round the Cape of Good Hope has been superseded by the shorter and more economical route through the Suez Canal. The time occupied during the voyage—from six to eight months for sailing vessels—has been shortened to thirty days. By the substitution of iron steamers carrying the commerce of the Western Hemisphere through the Suez Canal, a tonnage estimated at two millions was practically destroyed, and vast arrangements in commercial industry were displaced. In the old system of long voyages, large storehouses of goods had to be provided for the shipping interest, not only in foreign ports, but also in England, which became the centre of banking, ware-housing and exchange. All this was altered by electricity. The discoveries and appliances in the science of electricity—the telegraph, telephone and electric lighting—have created new labour, but have at the same time displaced a great amount of other labour. In the United Kingdom upwards of 42,000 persons are employed on work depending on electricity, while probably throughout the world more than 300,000 persons win their subsistence by the recent applications of this science. The amount of labour which it has displaced cannot be calculated. The whole method of effecting exchanges has been altered, because communication with other countries is now immediate; the consumer and the producer in opposite parts of the globe making their bargains in a single hour without the intervention of mercantile agencies or the large ware-house system, which former methods of commerce required. The Suez Canal and improved telegraphy made great demands for quick and economical distribution of material. Numerous steamers were built between 1870—73 for this purpose, but so rapid were the improvements that they were all displaced two years afterwards (1875–76) and sold at half their cost. Iron has been largely substituted by steel, both on land and at sea, Bessemer's invention having destroyed wealth; but like the phœnix new wealth has arisen from its ashes. A ship which in 1883 cost £24,000 can now be built for £14,000. The economy of fuel has been very great. Shortly before the opening of the Suez Canal, the best steamers crossing the Atlantic expended 200 tons of coal to carry an amount of cargo which can now be driven across for 35 tons. The application of compound engines to steamers has also produced an enormous economy of fuel. In 1850, the fine steamer the *Persia* carried over cargo at an expenditure of 14,500 lb. of coal to a ton; a modern steamer does the same work for 300 or 400 lb. The effect of this economy on haulage by land and transit by sea is immense. In an experiment lately made on the London and North-Western Railway, a compound locomotive dragged a ton of goods for 1 mile by the combustion of 2 ounces of coal. In ocean navigation there is a much larger economy. A cube of coal which passes through a ring of the size of a shilling will drive a ton of cargo two miles in our most improved steamers. The cost of transit of a ton of wheat from Calcutta to England was 71*s.* 3*d.* in 1881 and 27*s.* in 1885. The haulage of a thousand miles from Chicago to New York brings a whole year's supply of food for one man at a cost of a single day's wage. A ton is hauled for less than a farthing per mile. The fall in the prices of ocean transit from New York to Liverpool has been as follows:

	1880.	1886.
Grain per bushel	$9\frac{1}{4}$*d.*	1*d.*
Flour per ton	25*s.*	7*s.* 6*d.*
Cheese	50*s.*	15*s.*
Cotton per lb.	$\frac{3}{8}$*d.*	$\frac{7}{64}$*d.*
Bacon and lard per ton ...	45*s.*	7*s.* 6*d.*

India, it is needless to say, has immensely benefited by these improvements. In 1850, freight from Calcutta to England was sometimes as high as £5 a ton for wheat. In 1879 it had fallen to 22*s.* 6*d.* for transport *viâ* the Cape and to £1–10–0 *viâ* the Suez Canal. In 1849 Colonel Sykes calculated that a ton of wheat costing 61*s.* in India could not be landed in England at a less cost than 161*s.* or in other words, freight was 164 per cent. of the first cost of wheat at the Indian port. Mr. T. Comber, one of the witnesses examined by the English Royal Commission on the value of the precious metals, put in a statement which showed that the cost of carriage of wheat from Jubbulpore to Bombay was reduced from 9*s.* 8*d.* per quarter in 1873 to 4*s.* 11*d.* in 1887 by the development of railways in India, and the sea freight from Bombay to the United Kingdom was reduced from 13*s.* to 4*s.* 6*d.*, the total saving in the cost of carriage from India to England being 13*s.* 3*d.* From the evidence of Mr. Waterfield, the Financial Secretary of the India Office, it appears that the saving in the cost of carriage of wheat exported from Calcutta to England was about the same. He stated that in June 1881 and June 1886 the prices of Cawnpore wheat at Calcutta were at the same level, viz., 2·9 rupees per maund of 80 lb. The cost of Indian wheat in London in 1881 was 42*s.* a quarter and 31*s.* 6*d.* in 1886, showing a difference of 10*s.* 6*d.* or 25 per cent.

In 1881 the rate of freight from India to London was 60*s.* per ton, and 30*s.* in 1886, a difference of 30*s.* per ton or 6*s.* 6*d.* per quarter. Between 1879 and 1886 the charge for the transport of grain by railway from Cawnpore to Calcutta was reduced to the extent of about 2*s.* a quarter which was equivalent to a saving to the producer in the cost of production of the same amount. There was a further reduction of about 6*d.* a quarter in the price of gunny bags, the total saving to the producer being thus 9*s.* The freights for rice exported from Rangoon to England have been reduced from 72*s.* 6*d.* per ton in 1873 to 32*s.* 6*d.* per ton in 1891; and coal freights from England to Bombay from 22*s.* 6*d.* to 12*s.* 6*d.* per ton in the case of steamers and from 24*s.* to 16*s.* in the case of sailing vessels. The Indian producer has thus doubly benefited; *first* by the higher value realised by him for his productions; and secondly, by the lower value paid by him for the imported commodities which he obtains at far less cost measured not merely by money values [41] but by actual sacrifice of time and labour than would have been incurred if he had produced them himself.

How far the rapid expansion of foreign trade is "enforced."

33. It has, however, been represented by a certain class of persons, both in India and England, that the rapid expansion of foreign trade in India, which the last 40 years have witnessed, far from being a blessing is a matter for the gravest anxiety; that much of it, instead of being brought about by the development of the resources of the country in directions which will conduce to its prosperity, is really "enforced" or in other words is the outcome of the necessity which its political relation with England imposes on it for finding the wherewithal to meet the remittances to be made to England, in payment of services of a non-commercial character rendered

[41] It is hardly necessary to say that in comparing prices at different periods, the purchasing power of money at those periods should be taken into account. For all rough calculations, the purchasing power of money in this Presidency may, I think, be measured by the average prices of food grains given in paragraph 27 of this memorandum, as the bulk of the income of the country is expended on food, the secondary wants of the population being very few. As already stated, these prices can be relied on only as showing the general direction of the movement as regards purchasing power and not as accurately defining its amount. An increase in prices, when caused by the increased production of the precious metals throughout the world, would not mean an increase of wealth or of exchange value, nor would decrease of prices due to diminution in the cost of production owing to the adoption of labour-saving processes in the manufacture of commodities mean diminution of wealth. On the contrary, in the latter case the decrease of prices would really mean increased power of production. The demonetization of certain kinds of precious metals, *e.g.*, silver, in favour of other metals, *e.g.*, gold, would, by decreasing the demand for the former and increasing the demand for the latter, depreciate the first and give increased value to the second. The demand for precious metals again for currency purposes is affected by the extension of the use of instruments of credit. It would be impossible to assign correct values to all these factors, and their relative values can be inferred only from general considerations. This accounts for the divergence of views among the members of the Royal Commission on the value of the precious metals.

by Englishmen temporarily resident here; that the trade is to a great extent monopolized by foreigners, who have ousted the natives of the soil from their legitimate fields of enterprise; that the destruction of indigenous manufactures has had the effect of impoverishing the artisan classes and driving them to crowd on agriculture, which, owing to the capriciousness of the seasons, is a precarious industry; and that the result is that the population as a whole is growing poorer and pocrer every day, and losing in stamina. It is, therefore, necessary to examine whether there is any truth in these serious statements; to what extent the evils complained of are real, and how far they are temporary and incidental to a period of transition from a lower to a higher stage of industrial development, and whether they are not outweighed by unquestionable benefits enjoyed by the general population. In considering the above questions, the trade of India must be dealt with as a whole.

Balance of trade.

34. The question of the international indebtedness of India is one of great complexity, and a full consideration of it in its various phases will require more space than can be afforded in this memorandum. I will therefore content myself with mentioning its most salient features without entering into the minutiæ of the subject. It is a well known fact that the value of the exports of India habitually exceeds the value of the imports, the excess being due mainly to remittances which India has to make to England, not with a view to redress balances accruing in the ordinary operations of commerce, but on account of (1) payment of interest due on loans contracted by the Government of India for the ordinary purposes of Government and for the construction of productive works, and (2) payment for services of a political and non-commercial character rendered by England to India. The payments made under these heads amount to 14½ millions sterling, equivalent at the rate of exchange prevailing during the last few years to about 21 crores of rupees. Besides these, there are the remittances on account of private capital invested in commercial and industrial undertakings by Europeans temporarily resident in India, as also of savings out of income made by them in India in the various professions. The amount of these latter remittances is not ascertainable, there being no data for making even a rough estimate. All these payments are made in commodities and not in money, according to a well known law applicable to international trade, the operation of which may be briefly explained as follows. The passage of money from one country to another lessens the stock of money material in the remitting and increases the

stock in the receiving country, the result being that prices are depressed in the former, and elevated in the latter country owing to the diminution and augmentation, respectively, of the volume of the currency. By this double effect, a great divergence of prices of commodities and of labour in the two countries is established, and it becomes profitable for the receiving country to receive the value of the remittances in goods instead of in money. The disadvantage of this state of things to the remitting country consists in its having to exchange its productions on less advantageous terms than it would have done, if it had no payments of a non-commercial character to make. The exact measure of this disadvantage may be seen from the following hypothetical case. Suppose a country has a currency of 200 millions sterling and that the amount is just sufficient for its requirements. If this country has to make an annual payment of a non-commercial character to another country to the extent of 20 millions sterling, the abstraction of so much money-material depresses prices and the country has to give in exchange for the commodities of other countries a larger quantity of its products than it would otherwise have to do. If the currency be replenished with a view to establish the old scale of prices, the sum of 20 millions would have to be procured by giving in exchange for it commodities at the lowered prices, or in other words by giving a larger quantity of goods than would have had to be given at the old scale of prices. Thus, for instance, if prices were depressed one-tenth, one-ninth more of commodities would have to be given in return. In determining, therefore, whether the payments in question amount to a "drain of the resources of the remitting country" or whether they are really a "necessary outlay" incurred for securing a large net profit, the amount of such payments together with the increased cost at which the quantity of money to be replaced has to be procured—the two together constituting the maximum sacrifice incurred—will have to be taken into account. Having regard to these considerations, the following analysis will show the effect of the several items of remittances to England grouped under the general designation of "Home charges."

(*a*) The expenditure of 21 millions Rx. under this head comprises, (1) 11½ millions on account of interest on the debt owed by the Government of India and payments made to railway companies to make good the guaranteed interest; (2) 5½ millions on account of charges incurred in England for the army; (3) 2½ millions on account of furlough and superannuation allowances of Indian officers; (4) ¾ million on account of general administration; and (5) $\frac{3}{4}$ million on account of miscellaneous charges including cost of stationery and stores purchased in England for the Government of India.

(*b*) The total debt of India amounted at the end of 1889–90 to 201 millions, of which 98 millions were in sterling and 103 millions Rx. in rupees. The whole of the sterling debt and about 75 per cent. of the rupee debt are held by Europeans. Of the total sum of 201 millions, 122 millions have been incurred for the construction of productive works—95 millions for railways and 27 millions for irrigation works—the remaining 79 millions being incurred for the purposes of general administration, principally wars and military defence works. The Government of India has further guaranteed an interest of 5 per cent. on capital amounting to 71 millions invested by certain railway companies in railways in India.

(*c*) The total outlay on railways in India, whether classed as productive or not, was up to the end of 1890, 213 millions Rx. The mileage open was 16,277, and 2,272 miles were under construction. The net receipts from railways amounted to about $10\frac{1}{2}$ millions Rx. which is 4·8 per cent. on the capital cost. The loss to Government on this account is about 1·8 millions Rx., and this is chiefly due to fall in the rate of exchange. During the last 10 years there has been rapid progress in railway construction, the mileage open having increased from 9,000 to 16,500 or by 83 per cent. Railways cannot be expected to commence [42] to pay until some time after they have been completed, and, as already stated, there is a mileage of nearly 2,500 yet to be completed. Moreover, many of the lines have been undertaken not as paying concerns, but for purposes of military defence and famine protection of backward and inaccessible tracts which trade cannot reach when the bullock power of the country for draught becomes paralyzed during times of severe drought. Notwithstanding these drawbacks, the railways as a whole mostly pay their way, and they would fully meet their charges and leave a surplus profit to Government but for the loss by exchange. If the traffic improves within the next 5 or 10 years by 25 per cent., which is not an improbable result, the resulting gain will be such as will repay the entire cost of construction in the course of 50 years and leave to the country a large revenue unencumbered with any charges on account of interest.

---

[42] In 1881, the Government of India laid down that productive public works to be undertaken by Government should, if railways, pay their expenses including interest on capital cost within five years. For irrigation works the period fixed was ten years.

(*d*) The amount of remittances to England on account of railways is $5\frac{1}{2}$ million sterling, equivalent to 8 millions Rx. at the average rate of exchange. Now, there cannot be the slightest doubt that the gain to the country caused by the immense development of traffic greatly outweighs the interest payable on the railway capital, as well as the disadvantage arising from the slightly enhanced cost at which, on account of remittances to England, the productions of other countries have to be obtained by India. During the last ten years the number of passengers carried by railways in India has increased from 43 to 104 millions; the number of live stock has increased from three-quarters of a million to nearly a million; and the quantity of goods carried from $8\frac{3}{4}$ to $22\frac{1}{2}$ million tons. The cost of carriage of this quantity of goods alone is 13 millions Rx., and as the cost of transport of goods by railway is about one-fourth of the cost of transport by ordinary carts, the saving under this head may be calculated at nearly 40 millions Rx., supposing it to be at all possible that there could have been so much merchandize to carry with the old means of conveyance. This great reduction in the cost of transport is an immense gain to the country and benefits all parties, the producers by securing to them a higher value for their commodities and the importers by enabling them to obtain the imported articles on easier terms. In the internal trade, the gain is enjoyed wholly by this country; and in foreign trade it is shared between this country and the country with which the trade is carried on. Thus, if the exchange value of Indian goods be lowered 2 per cent. on account of remittances to England of interest on railway capital, and the saving in cost of carriage and consequent increase of exchange value of the labour of the Indian producer be enhanced 10 per cent., there is on the whole a net gain of 8 per cent. to the country owing to the investment of foreign capital in railways. The figures taken are purely hypothetical and have been used merely for purposes of illustration, but such as they are, they probably understate and not overstate the gain.

(*e*) Similar considerations apply also to remittances to England necessitated by the outlay on productive irrigation works. The capital laid out on the works amounted at the end of 1889–90 to $32\frac{1}{2}$ millions Rx., and the net revenue from the works was 4 per cent. on the outlay. The irrigation works in the Cauvery, Kistna and Godávari deltas and in Sindh yield returns of more than 10 per cent.; and the great canals in Upper India, where they have been completed, yield a return of $4\frac{1}{2}$ per cent. There would be no loss whatever on this account, but on the contrary a large gain, were it not for the capital outlay amounting to nine millions on the Orissa, Kurnool and Sone canals which have proved disastrous[43] failures. The benefit to the country by the construction of irrigation works cannot, however, be measured simply by the revenue realized by Government, inasmuch as the Government does not take the whole of the net profit due to the provision of irrigation, but only a share of it which is nominally half but really much less. For instance, the capital outlay on the Godávari and Kistna works up to the end of 1889–90 was $2\frac{1}{4}$ millions Rx and the irrigation revenue derived from the works 35 lakhs of rupees. During 1876–77, when the Presidency was suffering from a severe famine, the production of rice in the Kistna and Godávari deltas was valued at upwards of five millions Rx. Since 1876 the area under irrigation in the Godávari and Kistna deltas has increased by upwards of 50 per cent., the increase in the past ten years amounting to 250,000 acres or upwards of 29 per cent. Allowing for the decrease in the prices of food-grains now as compared with the prices in 1876, the value of the produce in these deltas due to irrigation

---

[43] That much money was wasted in useless and unprofitable undertakings, and more would have been but for the late Mr. Fawcett's persistent efforts amidst much discouragement to enforce economy in Indian administration, there can be no doubt. The view which he endeavoured to force on the attention of the British public was that India was one of the poorest countries in the world, and administered as it was by perhaps the richest nation, the utmost vigilance was necessary to keep down expenditure by dispensing with costly luxuries which a rich country might, but a poor country could not, afford. The following facts taken from Leslie Stephen's *Life of Fawcett* show what great necessity there was for discouraging undertakings of a speculative character which were likely in the long run to prove disastrous to the finances of India. The Secretary of State had given a guarantee for the Mutlah Railway which was to connect Calcutta with Port Canning. It never paid its working expenses, and the Government was at last forced by the terms of the contract to buy it for £500,000 or £600,000. The port was finally abandoned. The Carnatic Railway Company had received a guarantee, in regard to which the Indian Government was not consulted, and the result had been that Government had paid £43,500 to the proprietors, whilst the aggregate net profit from the working of the railway was only £2,600. Some three-quarters of a million had been spent on the Godávari navigation works from which there was no return, whilst the anticipated result of opening up a new line of traffic had not been attained. It was thought better to abandon the three-quarters of a million than to spend another quarter in the faint hope of obtaining some better result from a completion of the works. Government had guaranteed interest on £1,000,000 to the Madras Irrigation Company. It had been forced to lend the Company £600,000 to save it from collapse. Though part of it had been repaid, the final result was that £1,372,000 was swallowed up without return. The irrigation canal has since been purchased by Government, &c. Mr. Leslie Stephen remarks that the evidence of official witnesses before the Finance Committee of 1872, and especially the testimony of General Strachey, indisputably showed that "the accounts hitherto given (of the irrigation and other works) were unsatisfactory and would not show whether a fair profit had been obtained; that disastrous bargains had been forced upon the Government by the pressure of interested persons; that the worst extravagance had occurred when the opinions of Indian officials had been overridden by the Home Government." All this is, however, ancient history, the Parlimentary Committees of 1872 and 1884 on Indian public works having strictly defined the conditions under which public works, whether irrigation works or railways, should be undertaken. It must be remembered also that if the history of Public Works Administration of any country for a period of half a century be examined, it would be easy to point out failures even more disastrous than those of the Indian Government.

works may still be estimated at five millions Rx. Even if only half of this sum be taken as the net gain to the ryots, it will be seen that the share of the profit derived by Government is only one-seventh of the total profit. In the Punjab during the four years ending 1885–86, the area under irrigation increased from $1\frac{3}{4}$ million to $2\frac{3}{4}$ million acres or by 57 per cent. It is hardly necessary to point out the value of irrigation works as a means of protection against famine.

(*f*) The remittances, necessitated by the payment of interest on the capital borrowed for productive works, are therefore, on the whole, in no way injurious to the country. On the contrary, these works bid fair in the course of a few years to prove highly remunerative.

(*g*) The ordinary debt has not increased during the last 30 years. Before the mutiny, the registered debt amounted to $51\frac{1}{2}$ millions sterling. The mutiny added $38\frac{1}{2}$ millions to the account, and accordingly the total debt stood at 90 millions sterling in 1860. The debt excluding sums borrowed for productive public works or transferred to that head now stands at only 75 millions. The purposes for which the debts were incurred were mainly wars and the strengthening of the defences of the Empire owing to the advance of Russia towards the Indian frontier. The ordinary debt is less than two years' net revenue of India, and no country in the world has a lighter burden of debt. The interest on debt amounts to about $4\frac{1}{2}$ millions Rx or 10 per cent. of the net revenue of India. If the interest on capital borrowed for productive works be taken into account, the ratio is 25 per cent.[44] The fact that much of the debt of India is held in England doubtless makes a difference; but, in the circumstances of India, this may be really an advantage. The dearth of capital in this country makes it undesirable that any portion of it, that is or is likely to be employed in industrial undertakings, should be invested in Government securities. In so far as the capital that is hoarded is attracted by Government loans and invested in Government securities (as in the

---

[44] The percentage of interest on debt to annual revenue of some of the European countries in 1881–82 was as follows:

	Per cent.
United Kingdom	35
Italy	43
Egypt	41
France	40
Japan	39
Spain	37
Portugal	36

case of the Gwalior loan), the result would no doubt be beneficial, but even in that case it is better that such capital should seek investment in industrial undertakings. If loans have to be contracted in foreign markets, it is desirable that Government with its superior credit should contract the loans rather than private individuals who cannot command equally favorable terms.

(*h*) There is one further consideration to be borne in mind in connection with remittances for interest on debt, viz., that the influx of money into the country when loans are contracted and consequent rise in prices is a set-off against the depression due to remittances on account of interest in subsequent years.

(*i*) As regards remittances made to England to meet the charges in connection with the army, superannuation and furlough allowances of European officers employed by the Government of India, and the establishments of the Secretary of State for India and his Council, amounting in all to nine millions Rx, it is not necessary to say much, as they are all charges necessary to secure that peace and that good government which have rendered the increased production and the increased trade, which have taken place within the last forty years, possible. That the gain to the country from the increased production and increased trade is far in excess of the charges referred to, there cannot be the slightest doubt. The additional production from the extension of canal irrigation alone amounts to twenty millions Rx. I do not, of course, mean to say that the charges are not capable of being reduced, and that, in so far as they are unnecessary or unduly high, persistent efforts should not be made to enforce economy. Considering the question merely from the point of view of the benefits conferred by foreign trade, apart from the desirability of keeping all governmental expenditure at the lowest point consistent with the efficient discharge of the duties which the circumstances of this country require to be undertaken by Government, and apart also from the higher considerations which render it necessary that the natives of the country should be entrusted with positions of high trust and responsibility in the Civil and Military services, in a liberal and not grudging spirit, both as a matter of justice and as a means of accelerating the advance of the nation in moral and material well-being, I have no hesitation in stating that the sacrifices involved in the payment of the Home charges are repaid manifoldly by the benefits secured to the country, and that

if a saving of even a couple of millions, which is, perhaps, the utmost that could be expected, be effected in these charges, its effect on the foreign trade would hardly be appreciable.[45]

---

[45] The question of military defence is one of paramount importance, and no one that is not fully acquainted with the necessities of the case can venture to pronounce an opinion on the charges incurred in connection with it. The unequal, and not quite equitable, distribution of charges incurred in England, has, however, formed the subject of complaint by successive Finance Ministers and by the Military authorities in India. The opinions of many high authorities might be referred to in support of this statement, but it will suffice here to quote those of Sir John Strachey and of the Indian Army Commission of 1879, presided over by Sir Ashley Eden, and having among its members such eminent military men as Sir Frederick Roberts and Sir Peter Lumsden. Sir John Strachey, in his *Finance and Public Works of India*, says, "I know how the powers of obstruction and *laissez faire*, both in India and in England, are apt to stop attempts at army reform, and to frustrate efforts to diminish the immense military charges now imposed on the country. I am not sanguine that we shall soon see them very largely decrease, but that they ought to be decreased, there can be no doubt whatever. It is not only in India that attention to the subject of military expenditure is required. The Government of India has never concealed its opinion that in apportioning the charges which have to be shared between the two countries, and when the interests of Indian and English rate-payers have been at stake, India has sometimes received a scant measure of justice. That feeling has been increased by the knowledge learned by the experience of the past that in this matter India is helpless. It is a fact, the gravity of which can hardly be exaggerated, that the Indian revenues are liable to have great charges thrown upon them, without the Government of India having any power of effectual remonstrance. The extension to India of the numerous measures taken in England to improve the position of officers and soldiers of the army was, no doubt, right and unavoidable, but the fact that heavy additional expenditure has thus been incurred by India gives her a claim to expect that no efforts shall be spared to diminish the charges which are unnecessary, or of which she bears too large a share." On some of the measures above referred to, the Army Commission remarks as follows: "The short-service system has increased the cost, and has materially reduced the efficiency of the British troops in India. We cannot resist the feeling that, in the introduction of this system, the interests of the Indian tax-payers were entirely left out of consideration. . . . . We believe that the whole system of staff corps is radically unsound. . . . . There can be no doubt that it has been the cause of serious financial embarassments. . . . . Its practical working has a discouraging effect on the army and is ruinous to the State. . . . . It involves a considerable expenditure for which there is little or no return. . . . . We cannot fail to see that the substitution of local (European) troops for twenty or thirty thousands of Her Majesty's British subjects would cause a saving of from £160,000 to £240,000, but we feel that any such change would seriously disturb the military system of the parent country and would deprive a great part of the British Army of the valuable training which Indian service now furnishes. We think that the portion of the British Army employed in this country should be organized and administered with due regard to the interests of the people of India, and not for the purpose of supplying defects in the system of Home defence, and, above all, that it should not be made the means of obtaining, at the cost of India, advantages for the Army at Home, which do not directly affect the interests of this country." The advance of Russia towards the Indian frontier renders an augmentation of the means of defence unavoidable; but this makes it all the more necessary that the army should be organised on the most economical basis, consistent with efficiency. Sir Charles Dilke, who has written (in his *Problems of Greater Britain*,) apparently with a full knowledge of the difficulties of Indian problems, says, "when we contemplate the increase of the Indian Army in the event of Russia being allowed to settle herself in Herat, we cannot do so without taking into view the desirability of the creation of a separate army which is indeed forced upon us by financial considerations. The present system is too ruinous to India to allow of a sufficient force being kept on foot, and we shall court disaster unless we speedily change it, though already, perhaps, too late to do so with safety. India, with an increased British force, will be drained dry by the money asked of her for a system which is not suited to her needs. When I say a separate army, of course, I do not advocate a return to the old Company's system. But the Home short service army and the army in India would be under the same supreme authority of the throne. They would be alike in drill, exercise and discipline, but separate in the existence of the two systems of recruiting, one for not more than three years for Home service, and one for long service in India and the Colonies."

35. The private remittances to England comprise the savings of Europeans resident in India in the service of Government and in other capacities, the dividends on Indian investments due to residents in England, and remittances by banks and merchants made in the course of commercial dealings. As already stated, it is not possible to make even a rough estimate of these remittances. Calculations, based on the recorded values of exports and imports, have been found to yield results which are obviously unreliable, these values not being sufficiently accurate for purposes of calculations of this kind. The total value of imports and exports of India is 185 millions Rx, and it is obvious that even so small an error in the values declared by merchants as $2\frac{1}{2}$ per cent., may vitiate the result to the extent of 5 millions. Theoretically, the relation that should subsist between exports and imports may be stated as follows:—The value of exports, including bullion of a country, on an average of years sufficiently large to eliminate the temporary fluctuations of trade in one direction or the other, should exactly balance the average value of imports of merchandise and treasure, provided, *first*, the country has no share in the carrying trade; *secondly*, that it does not levy any duty on exports of merchandise; and *thirdly* that it has not lent or borrowed from other countries, and has no money to remit or receive on account of loans or for other purposes. If the country has a share in the carrying trade, the imports will be in excess by the amount of freight earned. The same consideration applies also to export duties which will increase the imports by an equivalent amount, for, as the export duty is not included in the customs[46] house valuation of the exported merchandise, and, as it must be eventually recovered from the foreign countries in which the exported commodities are consumed, it must, *pro tanto*, increase the imports. The levy of import duties does not affect the balance of trade, as they are paid or recovered from the people of the country which imports the merchandise. The exports of a borrowing country will fall short of or exceed the imports, according as the money received, by way of loan, during the period for which the

Effect of private remittances to England.

---

[46] The valuation is made under section 30 of the Customs Act VIII of 1878, which is noted below for convenience of reference.

"For the purposes of the Customs Act, the real value shall be deemed to be—

(*a*) the wholesale cash price less trade discount, for which goods of the like kind and quality are sold, or are capable of being sold, at the time and place of importation, or exportation, as the case may be, without any abatement or deduction whatever except (in the case of goods imported) of the amount of duties payable on the importation thereof; or

(*b*) where such price is not ascertainable, the cost at which goods of the like kind and quality could be delivered at such place, without any abatement or deduction except as aforesaid."

account is taken, exceeds or falls short of the remittances on account of interest due for previous borrowings or for other purposes. India has practically little or no share in the carrying trade, the tonnage of British Indian shipping bearing only the proportion of 3·8 per cent. to the total tonnage of the foreign trade, amounting to $7\frac{1}{2}$ million tons. As regards the duty on exports, the only article that pays duty is rice, the revenue derived from this source being about $\frac{3}{4}$ million Rx. The duty on opium is an excise duty, and it is included in the values shown in the customs house returns. India has, of course, borrowed, and is borrowing largely, from England for the construction of productive works. In the statement of the trade of British India for 5 years ending 1888–89, presented to Parliament, the following account of the balance of trade, based on the statistics of 12 years ending 1888–89, is given :—

	Rx millions.
Exports of merchandise excluding Government transactions.	965
Do. of treasure	21
Indian securities enfaced for payment in England	45
Total ...	1,031
Imports of merchandise excluding Government transactions.	638
Do. of treasure	151
India Council bills	218
Government securities retransferred to India	32
Bills for interest on enfaced paper	10
Total ...	1,049
Balance of Imports ...	18

In the above account, the values of Government exports and imports have been excluded from the values of exports and imports of merchandise shown, as the *net* value of Government imports has been included in the amount of the bills drawn on India by the Secretary of State. Similarly, the loans raised in England on account of India have been excluded, as the amount of the Secretary of State's bills represents the difference between the amount of remittances to be made to England and the proceeds of the loans. The bills drawn by the Bank of England for the payment in England of interest on Indian securities enfaced for that purpose will increase exports from India by a corresponding amount, while the securities themselves will increase the imports or exports according as they are transferred to England or retransferred to India *for value*. If, however, such securities are taken over to England by persons holding them, there will be no effect produced on the balance of trade beyond increasing the exports to the amount of the interest due on the securities which will have to be remitted by Government. Out of the sum of 18 millions, which the above account shows as the excess of *imports* above *exports*, about 12 millions will have to be deducted on account of the export duty on rice and the freight earned by the Indian shipping, leaving about 6 millions for 12 years, or half a million per annum, without taking account of remittances on account of private savings and profits of trade of Europeans in India. This shows either that the private capital brought into the country exceeded the amount of the savings and profits above referred to during the 12 years for which the account is made up, or that the declared values of imported and exported merchandise are, as already observed, incorrect. Sir Richard Temple estimated the private remittances from India above referred to at 1½ millions in 1870. The salaries of Europeans employed in Government service in India aggregated 5½ millions in 1886, and if one-fifth of these salaries is remitted to England, the remittances under this head will amount to one million. These remittances, of course, stand on the same footing as furlough and superannuation charges, included in the Secretary of State's drawings already referred to. As regards interest or profits on foreign capital invested in industrial undertakings in India, it may be stated that it is almost impossible that the remittances on their account can have any prejudicial effect on India. For, if the undertakings are successful, the increased continuous [47] employment provided for labour in the country must exceed greatly in value the remittances on account of interest and profits, while the influx of the capital itself will alter the balance of trade for the time in favour of India. If, on the other hand, the undertakings are unsuccessful, there will be no remittances to make, while the capital brought into the country, in so far as it has been employed in the payment of labour, will have been [48] a gain.

---

[47] The accumulation of capital in England is so great that interest is continually falling, and by competition the profits on investments are reduced. This means that the profits must be very much less than the annual expenditure in industrial undertakings carried on with foreign capital in India.

[48] Mr. Dadhaboy Nowrojee, of Bombay, who was examined before the Royal Commission on the Value of the Precious Metals, presented an account of the balance of trade in which he claimed credit, on behalf of India, for 10 per cent. on the value of exported merchandise, for freight, commission and insurance charges, and for another 10 per cent. for the profits of trade. His contention was, "From the very commencement of ploughing—for ploughing, seed, reaping, cart or railway carriage,—to the port of shipment, carriage across the seas, all charges on both sides, commission, insurance and profits, *i.e.*, for all labour and materials for all these purposes payment has to be made from the exported produce itself. Every one of these items takes its share out of that produce. Putting it another way, every item is paid out of the value or proceeds of the produce. If the produce does not realize sufficient proceeds to pay for all the above items, the exporter has to pay the deficit from his own pocket besides getting no profit." When it was pointed out to Mr. Nowrojee that India could not fairly claim credit for freight,

36. One further effect of the drawings of the Secretary of State requires to be noticed, viz., its influence on the rate of exchange as between gold and silver. So long as the Latin Union kept up the legal relation between the value of gold and silver, the oscillations in the rate of exchange, caused by the international trade balances, were confined within the limits of the cost of transport of silver to France for the purpose of being coined; but when the Latin Convention was broken up, and silver was demonetized in Europe, the limits referred to were done away with. The India Council bills compete with silver as a mode of remittance, and in so far as they displace silver they lower its value, and there is no longer any means of preventing the rate of exchange falling below a fixed level as was the case when the Latin Union was in force. There is no means of estimating to what extent the increase in the Secretary of State's drawings in recent years has contributed to the fall in the rate of exchange, but that it does exercise considerable influence there seems to be little reason to doubt. But, at the same time, it must be remembered that the portion of the Home charges and private remittances which represents investments of capital may, and in fact does, increase the exports of merchandise, so as, *pro tanto*, to create a balance of trade in favour of India. Sir David Barbour, in his minute, appended to the Report of the Commissioners on the Value of the Precious Metals, puts this matter in a clear light. He says:—

The effect of remittances to England on the rates of exchange.

---

insurance, &c., not *earned* by her, in respect of goods purchased by English merchants at the Indian ports and carried to England by them at their own expense and risk, and sold by them to English consumers at prices sufficient to cover these additional charges, he was willing to give up the claim as regards freight and insurance, but not as regards the profits of trade. If his contention were correct, it would follow that India would be entitled to the profits of retail trade in England and also to the profits of English cotton manufactures, because Indian cotton is turned into cloth. There is no doubt that Mr. Nowrojee did good service in 1872, in calling the attention of the Parliamentary Committee on Indian Finance pointedly to the disadvantage resulting to India from the constant increase in Home remittances, at a time when there was considerable risk of Government wasting borrowed money on so-called productive works; and the position he took up was unassailable and reaffirmed by the Parliamentary Committees on Public Works in 1879 and 1884. Mr. Nowrojee, however, has since made very exaggerated statements regarding the evil effects of these remittances. Mr. M. G. Ranade pointed this out very clearly and his remarks are worth-quoting. He said: "There are people who think that so long as we have a heavy tribute to pay to England, which takes away nearly 20 crores of our surplus exports, we are doomed and can do nothing to help ourselves. This is, however, hardly a fair or a manly position to take up. A portion of the burden represents interest on moneys advanced to, or invested in, our country, and so far from complaining, we have reason to be thankful that we have a creditor who supplies our needs at such a low rate of interest. Another portion represents the value of stores supplied to us, the like of which we cannot produce here. The remainder is alleged to be more or less necessary for the purposes of defence and payment of pensions and though there is good cause for complaint that it is not all necessary, we should not forget the fact that we are enabled by reason of this British connection to levy an equivalent tribute from China by our opium monopoly."

"A considerable amount of imports (such as railway plant and machinery) really represents the investment of English capital in India, is not paid for at the time, and, consequently, has no effect on the exchange of the year. Of course, all investments of foreign capital affect the exchange in subsequent years, when profits or interest come to be remitted from India; but such investments are generally made in industries connected with the international trade, and, so far as they increase Indian exports, they counteract the tendency to a fall in the exchange owing to the remittance of profits. It is quite possible, and even probable, that an investment of foreign capital in India might so increase the exports as to favorably influence the exchange. For example, if one million sterling is invested in jute mills, and such investment increases the exports of India by £200,000 yearly, while only necessitating a remittance of £50,000 yearly on account of profits, the international account has been altered in India's favour to the extent of £150,000, and the tendency is to raise and not to lower exchange. The investment of foreign capital in tea gardens in India is a case in point. The whole of the exports of tea from India are due to this cause and the value of these exports is much more than sufficient to cover the remittance of profits and pay for such articles of import as are required in the manufacture of tea. The international equation has, therefore, been altered to the advantage of India and not to her disadvantage by these investments."

As regards the general effect of the remittances to England on the trade of India, Sir David Barbour observes: "It is commonly said that if one country has a payment to make to another, the country which has the payment to make trades at a disadvantage. The theory, as a theory, is unassailable. But in practice there are many more important factors which influence international trade, and, if the payment is made on account of foreign capital judiciously *invested*, the net effect of the whole transaction may be to improve the relative position of the country which has the payment to make.

"Payments, for which no direct commercial equivalent is received, are made in an increasing amount to England every year by foreign countries, and consequently the relative position of England in the international trade must be improving, and England should be receiving an increasing quantity of foreign produce in exchange for her exports. Yet, the facts since 1873 do not bear out this contention. If we take the price of a certain quantity of English exports in 1873 at £100, and the price of a certain quantity of English imports at the same figure, the prices of the same quantities in 1886 will be £62 and £69, respectively, according to Mr. Giffen's figures.

We thus see that if a certain quantity of English exports exchanged for a certain quantity of imports in 1873, the same quantity of exports would in 1886 have failed to exchange for the same quantity of imports in the proportion of 62 to 69. In other words, goods for goods, England was making a worse bargain internationally in 1886 than in 1873 by 11 per cent.

"It is true, that, in 1873 England was exchanging her exports for foreign products on specially favorable terms, but the figures just given show that the question of the relative indebtedness of different nations is a comparatively minor factor in determining the conditions of international trade.

"There are no figures of equal authority which can be used in determining on what terms India is now trading with other countries as compared with former times, but all the enquiries I have[49] made point in the same direction, viz., that a certain quantity of Indian produce laid down at Calcutta or Bombay will, at the present time, exchange for a larger quantity of imported goods than it would have done in 1870 or 1873. The theory that India is hampered in her foreign trade by the drawings of the India Council appears, therefore, to be without foundation. *That India would be wealthier if these drawings ceased, while India retained the advantages arising from the causes which have brought about the drawings, may certainly be admitted. That India would now be importing more goods of all kinds, including silver, if the causes which have led to the drawings of the India Council had never come into operation, is not merely unproved, but is absolutely opposed to the facts so far as they can be ascertained.*" I have ventured to italicize the last portion of the quotation as it contains the gist of the argument.

---

[49] I have assumed in other portions of this memorandum that the prices of food-grains are now 2½ times what they were in 1850, or in other words, the purchasing power of silver, as measured by the quantity of food-grains silver would purchase, has fallen 60 per cent. The fall would have been greater but for the cheapening of the cost of transport and consequent lowering of prices of commodities at the principal markets. If the reduction in prices, due to saving in the cost of transport, be taken at 25 per cent., the fall in the purchasing power of silver in India would be really 70 per cent. In England, prices of commodities measured in gold rose during 1850 to 1873, when they were 20 per cent. higher than they were before the Australian and Californian gold discoveries. Since then they have fallen to about the level of 1850. One sovereign, however, was equivalent in 1850 to Rs. 10; now 1 sovereign is equivalent to Rs. 15. Since 1850, the purchasing power of silver in England has therefore fallen by one-third or 33⅓ per cent. Taking account of the saving in the cost of production and transport which may be assumed to be 30 per cent., silver has really fallen in value in England 53⅓ per cent. as against 70 per cent. in India, that is, silver has fallen in value in India in a higher ratio than in England, or in other words, the advantage derived by England in the trade of India by abundance of money and consequent higher scale of prices, is diminishing notwithstanding the so-called "*tribute*," as foreign trade has enabled India to replenish her insufficient currency. Thus taking the higher efficiency of production in England as compared with India since 1850 into account, the silver value of a unit of productive power in India as compared with silver value of a unit of power in England has risen in the ratio of 30 to 46⅔ or as 9 to 14. These calculations are very rough and some of the figures taken are hypothetical. They merely serve to illustrate the principle.

37. Another proof of the fact that India has not been impoverished but enriched by foreign trade is found in the large imports of gold and silver since 1850. The value of gold imported into India from Europe and not re-exported from 1565 to 1835, a period of 270 years, has been estimated at 112 millions sterling. Mr. Claremont Daniell in his *Industrial Competition of Asia* conjectures that of this amount about 50 millions were probably taken over to China and other places. Including the gold obtained from China, Burma and other Asiatic sources, the total gold in India in 1835 is estimated at 140 millions. Since 1835 and up to the end of 1890-91, the net imports of gold have amounted to upwards of 140 millions, and nearly the whole of this amount has been imported since 1850. As gold is not used for purposes of currency in India, the imports have been made for the purpose of manufacture into ornaments or hoarding. The total annual production of gold at present is estimated at 20 millions sterling, of which one-fourth is sent to India. The total net imports of silver into India since 1850 amount to 302 millions Rx. The value of silver coined in British India has been estimated at 317 millions Rx or Rs. 15 per head of the population. If India had chosen to take the imports in commodities instead of in gold and silver, it would not show that she was deriving no advantage; on the contrary, it would doubtless be a great boon to the country if the value that is locked up in ornaments and coinage were turned into capital useful for industrial undertakings; but the large quantity of imports of gold and silver, amounting to a considerable proportion of the total production of the precious metals, unquestionably shows that India is not losing but gaining by international trade.

Imports of gold and silver into India.

38. The complaint that European exploitation has had the effect of driving out natives from their legitimate fields of industrial enterprise is not true of the Madras Presidency, nor is it true of other parts of India to any great extent. The chief undertakings in which Europeans are engaged are the cultivation of coffee, tea and cinchona, and gold-mining, and these are all fields which were previously unoccupied, and which would not be occupied if it were not for the importation of European capital and enterprise. We have already seen that indigo manufacture in this Presidency in which Europeans once took part has now, to a great extent, passed into the hands of the natives of the country. Coffee cultivation has not been remunerative of late years, and it has also, to a considerable extent, passed into native hands. The

European exploitation.

natives who can work the estates cheaply have a great advantage over Europeans, and with daily increasing knowledge and experience they will doubtless take an increasing share in enterprises of this kind. The natives are also beginning to take a larger share in mercantile transactions connected with articles of export and import trade, the opening of the Suez Canal and the increase in the direct trade of India with the principal countries of Continental Europe having taken away from what of the character of monopoly which long established European houses of agency may have once possessed. Mr. Slagg in his article on Cotton Industry contributed to the jubilee volume, entitled *The Reign of Queen Victoria*, gives the following account of the changes that have taken place in this respect as regards the cotton trade. He states: "In many cases the cotton spinner and manufacturer of India deals directly with the cotton producer on the one hand, and the merchant shipper on the other, and in nearly all cases the old charges for brokerage and agency have experienced a considerable reduction. Fifty years ago the commission charged for selling goods in India, including guarantee of sales and discount on remittances, amounted to from 8½ to 5 per cent., to which was added about 2½ per cent. for sundry charges, landing, storing and godown rent. These are now reduced to a total of about 4 per cent., though the downward tendency of the latter charges was checked by the Indian mutiny. The charges for packing and shipment have also been diminished by 1½ or 2 per cent., while the opening of the Suez Canal and the consequent development and competition in steam transit have produced a marvellous economy of cost and time on the old system of shipment. Mr. Goschen has observed that the carriage of a ton of goods from Manchester to Bombay, including the railway to Liverpool, the Suez Canal dues and the freight, is now little more than the price of a second class ticket from London to Manchester. The shortening of the voyage by the substitution of steamers for sailing vessels and the adoption of the Suez Canal route instead of the old route round the Cape of Good Hope has reduced the time taken in the delivery of goods, which is equivalent to a diminution of about 2½ per cent., if the additional rent and insurance under the old system, added to the loss of interest, be taken into consideration. The increase of telegraphic communication, and to some extent the use of the telephone, have tended to destroy the old custom of keeping large stocks of goods stored in the warehouses of Manchester or in the 'godowns' in India, and sales are often made in Calcutta or Bombay of goods which have yet to be manufactured or even bleached or dyed in Lancashire.

The 'Banias' or native dealers now send to England a considerable number of direct orders, and several of the principal 'Banias' have their own agents or representatives in Manchester who ship direct to their orders." In the Madras town, I am informed that with the aid of the facilities afforded by the Bank of Madras and other banks for obtaining loans, native merchants with small means are in increasing numbers carrying on a trade in articles of foreign merchandise. In Cocanada, which is daily rising in importance as a commercial centre, the competition of native merchants has led to the closing of some European firms. The direct trade of India with the countries of Continental Europe has made it more difficult for English merchants to combine to keep natives out of mercantile pursuits in which the latter may not hitherto have had a share. For instance until April 1885, with a view to keep Indian cotton manufactures out of the China market, the freight to China was kept by a combination of English steamer companies at the prohibitive rate of Rs. 15 a ton, and repeated efforts on the part of the Bombay mill owners failed to effect a reduction lower than Rs. 12. The Italian line of steamers then stepped in and accepted freight at Rs. 8 and the consequence has been that the English companies themselves have since reduced the rate to Rs. 5.

Decadence of old indigenous industries.

39. There is, however, very considerable truth in the complaint that foreign trade has affected prejudicially the old manufacturing industries of the country and impoverished the classes engaged in them. The spinning and weaving trades, especially, have suffered severely from foreign competition, and the former as a separate profession is rapidly disappearing, what remains of it being confined to the spinning of fine thread for cloths of superior texture and extreme tenuity such as could not be produced by machinery, and of coarse thread for the coarse thick cloths woven for the use of the lower classes of the agricultural population. The demand for very costly cloths of superior texture worn by men of the higher classes has considerably fallen, not so much owing to Manchester competition as to the change of fashion, English broad cloth having, to a considerable extent, superseded them as articles of dress. On the other hand, there has been considerable extension of demand for female colored cloths made with imported fine yarn, Kornadu cloths for instance; and in particular centres of industry such as Kornadu, Kuttalam and other places, the position of the weavers has really improved. Large sections of the agricultural population still use coarse cloths made of country yarn which, if

somewhat dearer than machine-made cloths, are preferred to the latter as being more durable and warmer. The coarse thread is spun by the agriculturists themselves and given to weavers who weave them into cloth on being paid about one rupee or its equivalent in grain for each cloth. These cloths are extensively in use in the Ceded districts, Kurnool, Coimbatore and Salem, where the cold in the winter months is severer than in other parts of the Presidency. The amount of weaving done in the country has not probably diminished sensibly of late years, but the profits of the weavers, both on account of the Manchester competition and the additional pressure on the weaving industry due to the collapse of the spinning industry, have undoubtedly been much reduced.[50] The Madras Board of Revenue, who instituted enquiries into the condition of the weaving industry in 1871 and again in 1890, have reported to the same effect. In 1871, the number of looms at work was nearly 280,000 or nearly 42 per cent. higher than the number at work between 1856-57 and 1860-61, as ascertained for the purpose of assessing the old moturpha tax. The returns for the earlier years, however, were imperfect and not fully to be relied on, and the Board estimated the real increase at between 20 and 25 per cent. and attributed the advance to the abolition of the vexatious and inquisitorial moturpha tax. The total quantity of twist worked up into cloth was estimated at 31½ million lb., of which 11½ millions were imported and 20 millions spun in the country. In 1889 the number of looms at work was ascertained to be 300,000 exhibiting an increase since 1871 of 7 per cent., while the increase in the population is 14 per cent. The quantity of twist worked up into cloth was estimated at 34½ millions—an increase of a little less than 10 per cent.—of which 19 millions were imported, 1 million was manufactured in the Indian mills and 14½ millions were hand-made. Since 1871, the outturn of hand-made yarn has, therefore, diminished by 22½ per cent. For the whole of India the total production of cotton was estimated in 1869 at 7·1 million cwt., of which 5 millions were exported and 2·1 million cwt. consumed in India—¼ million by the Indian mills and 1·8 million by the hand-looms. In 1888-89, the total production was estimated at 9½ million cwts., of which 5½ millions were exported to foreign countries, 3 millions were consumed by the Indian mills and 1 million by the hand-looms in India. This shows that hand-spun yarn is being rapidly superseded by yarn made in the Indian mills, and that what the hereditary spinning classes have to fear now is not the

---

[50] See appendix V.-F. (17) for a note on the condition of weavers in the Madura town.

competition of Manchester, but that of the Indian mills. The extension of the cotton mill industry in India during the last 15 years has been truly remarkable. In 1870 the number of cotton mills in Bombay was only 12 with 319,394 spindles and 4,199 looms. The number of persons employed was 8,199 and the quantity of cotton worked up 220,000 cwts. The industry then was by no means in a thriving condition, and of the paid up capital, $1\frac{1}{3}$ million Rx, the then value at the market quotations of the shares was only $\frac{3}{4}$ million Rx, showing a loss of more than half a million. The return for capital invested was 4 per cent., while the Government stock at 4 per cent. was selling at 8 discount. In the other Provinces there were a few mills which, however, did not do any real business. Now there are 124 mills in the whole of India with 3,274,196 spindles and 23,142 looms. The number of persons employed is 112,000, and the quantity of cotton worked up $3\frac{1}{2}$ million cwts. The capital invested in these mills is estimated at about 12 millions Rx, a very considerable portion of which is native capital. The exports of cotton goods from India chiefly to China, Japan, and the East Coast of Africa, which amounted to 1·3 million Rx in 1870, have increased to 8·5 million Rx. The requirements of India as regards cotton cloth have been estimated at 3,200 million yards, of which about 2,000 millions are imported and the remainder made in the country. About 600 million yards were in 1890–91 exported from India to foreign countries. There is every prospect of the products of Indian mills not only taking entire possession, at no distant date, of the markets in China, Japan and East Africa, but also of driving out the Manchester cloths of all but the finest kinds from India. A majority of the Committee appointed by the Manchester Chamber of Commerce to enquire into the causes of the rapid development of the mill industry in India, has recently reported after full investigation that the main cause, which has favored the increase of mills and enabled them to a great extent to supply China and Japan with yarns formerly shipped from Lancashire, is their geographical position which places them in close proximity to the cotton fields on the one hand and the consuming countries on the other. The net advantage to the Indian spinner from these circumstances over his competitor in England, after allowing for the extra outlay on machinery, and consequent enhanced interest and depreciation, as well as greater expenditure on such items as imported coal, stores, &c., was estimated by the committee as equal to at least $\frac{3}{4}d.$ per lb. on the portion that is shipped to China and Japan, and $\frac{13}{16}d.$ to $\frac{7}{8}d.$ per lb. on what is consumed in India itself.[51] The import trade in English piece goods has for the last 5 or 6 years shown no progress. In the review of the Indian trade for 1890-91 Mr. O'Conor remarks: "It may be said that, if it had not been for the competition of the Indian mills, the trade in piece goods in 1890-91 should have been at least 10 per cent. larger than it was, and that to this extent at any rate the cloth woven in the Indian mills, or from yarn spun there, has within 5 years taken the place of imported cloths in our markets. The extent of the diversion, is, however, probably greater. In other kinds of cotton goods, there has been a moderate increase, these being mainly of descriptions which are not woven in India either from locally spun or imported yarns, but these kinds are relatively of trifling dimensions. It would seem in fact that the time is not very far distant when the imports of the coarser and medium cottons which form the bulk of the trade will gradually disappear, and that the trade will be limited to the finer qualities and therefore of

---

[51] See Well's *Recent Economic Changes*. Mr. Wells remarks: "Other circumstances, such as cheaper labour and longer factory hours, may have also favored the Indian manufactures; but these differences as respects the conditions of labour in England and India have existed from time immemorial; and the real novelty of the present situation is, that India, with rail-roads and factories, and the advantage of cheap ocean freights, is now emancipating herself from chronic sluggishness and beginning to participate in the world's progress; and under English auspices, and largely with English capital, is, for the first time, extensively utilizing her geographical position and her cheap and abundant labour in connection with labour-saving machinery." Mr. T. Comber who was examined by the Royal Commission on the value of the Precious metals presented the following statement showing the comparative cost of manufacturing 1 lb. of 20's yarn in Bombay and England, and of its transport to China, the rate of exchange being taken at 1*s*. 5*d*. per rupee :—

	English spinner.	Indian spinner.
	d.	*d.*
Cotton $1\frac{1}{4}$ lb.	5·69	5·00
Depreciation and interest on mill and machinery ..	·42	·64
Coals	·05	·16
Wages	1·11	·99
Stores	·28	·46
Sundries	·40	·25
	7·95	7·50
Packing and carriage to Bombay	·50	..
Delivered at Bombay	8·45	7·50
Packing and carriage to China .. .. (·70—·50) ..	·20	·26
Delivered in China	8·65	7·76
Advantage in favour of the Indian produce		·89

The English spinner has an advantage in interest and depreciation and coals, but the Indian spinner has a still greater advantage in wages and cost of transport both of the raw material and the manufactured product. The factory hands in India are not individually as efficient as the English operatives, but as the rate of wages is much lower, the net advantage to the Indian spinner is 10 per cent. Moreover, it is stated, that, by longer training, the Indian hand has become more effective than formerly, and recent improvements in machinery have rendered it so automatic that much which formerly had to be done by hand, is now done by machine and this greatly diminishes the superior skill of the Lancashire hand.

small dimensions." This condition of things has, as might be naturally expected, excited the greatest alarm among the Manchester manufacturers, and in proof of it Mr. O'Conor quotes the following passages from a letter of the Commercial correspondent in London of the *Times of India:* "Several specimens of dhooties manufactured in India were laid on the table for inspection at the meeting of the Blackburn Chamber of Commerce on Wednesday. Mr. Alexander Harrison, who presided, said that during the last ten years it has been the general opinion in Lancashire that it is impossible for mill-owners in India to make dhooties from 40's or the 50's yarns, but here before their eyes were remarkably good specimens of dhooties made from 40's twist and 50's Egyptian weft. Mr. Harrison added that in his mind there never had been any insuperable difficulty that would prevent Indian manufacturers from producing fine counts, and he owned the opinion that in India in time they will grow their own cotton and weave these fine counts. The manufacturers of Lancashire should carefully watch the doings of the Indian manufacturers, or they will find not only that the coarse yarn trade has gone, but that the medium trade will go also. And he urged that it is time for Lancashire manufacturers to consider their situation and to take means to fortify themselves against encroachments on their interest." What the means referred to are intended to be, whether they are the pressure brought to bear on the Indian Government to enact stringent factory [52] laws not suited to the conditions of labour in this country, or less illegitimate methods, has not been stated; but whatever they may be, it is devoutly to be hoped that no artificial obstacles will be placed in the way of the development of the nascent factory industries in India, which may enable Indian manufacturers to regain much of the ground they have lost under the stress of Manchester competition.

The decay of hand-loom weavers, a necessary stage in industrial development.

40. It is clear, however, that the hereditary spinning and weaving castes have nothing to hope for in the future, even if India should manufacture all the clothing required for the use of her own population as well as to meet the demands of foreign markets. The deterioration of these classes has now been going on for over a hundred years. Mr. White (one of the members of Council of the Governor of

[52] In this connection the following passage from a speech of the President of the Blackburn Chamber of Commerce will be read with some amusement. He said: "They (the Lancashire manufacturers) felt not one jot of opposition as being hostile to Indian industry; but they did protest against any industry being fostered upon the lives of little children and women, upon the blood and sinews of the men who had to work in the mill stoves and dust-holes of the cotton jenny workshops of India."

Madras), writing in 1793, states that the mortality occasioned by the famine that had occurred just then fell heaviest on the weaving and spinning classes. They were in the best of times a poverty-stricken class. The fluctuations in the weaving trade of India are very instructive. Cotton manufactures before the seventeenth century were practically unknown in England, and woollen manufacture was the great national industry, so much so, that cotton cloths were designated "linens" and raw cotton was believed to be a kind of "wool." In 1621, Mr. Munn, one of the Directors of the East India Company, estimated the annual importation at 50,000 pieces of cotton cloth, the average cost of each piece on board in India being 7*s.* and the selling price in England 20*s.* The importation in 1674-75 had increased to the value of £160,000. The silk and wool weavers became alarmed for their trade and serious riots took place in various parts of England, and in consequence the further introduction of Indian goods into England was interdicted in 1700. In 1721, another statute was enacted, enforcing the prohibition by a penalty of £5 for each offence on the part of the wearer of Indian goods and a penalty of £20 on the seller of such goods. The exports of cotton goods to England were thus much restricted. In 1767 and 1769 Hargreaves' and Arkwright's inventions—spinning jenny and spinning frame—came into use, and England began to manufacture cotton cloth on an extensive scale. India's export trade was then confined to supplying some of the Asiatic countries, and soon after, England took possession of these markets. This dealt the first blow to the weaving classes in India and the effect of it was enhanced by the breaking up of the trading establishments of the East India Company when its trading privileges were abolished in 1813 and 1833. The rapid development of machinery and manufactures and the cheapness with which cotton cloths were produced in England led to India being flooded with Manchester goods to the further injury of the weaving classes here. Now the tide has turned, and the development of factories in India bids fair to enable her to manufacture the goods required for her own population, even more cheaply than England, and to compete with England in foreign markets. This means that India, by means of the advantages conferred by foreign trade, has been enabled to organize her productive powers on the most economical basis; but as every factory hand will displace 30 or more weavers and spinners, it is clear that the deterioration of these classes will be even more rapid than in the past. Spinning as a bye industry may be carried on by agriculturists to provide themselves with the coarse but durable cloths which mills do not turn out, and the weaving of superior cloths for women will doubtless still exist; but on the whole the trade of the hand-loom weavers will have shrunk to small dimensions. The sufferings of the weavers are great and such as to excite commiseration, but these sufferings are no more than have always been caused to protected classes whenever labour-saving machinery has been brought into use. In England, for instance, the sufferings of weavers were even more intense than those of the corresponding classes in India, owing to the simultaneous introduction of machinery both in manufactures and agriculture and the consequent economising of labour in both directions.[53] A writer describing the condition of the weavers in the early years of the present century states: "The most miserable class of artizans were the hand-loom weavers, who long continued to carry on their trade at home. The use of power looms was slowly adopted; and even after they were generally introduced, the hand-loom weaver could not change his mode of life, but continued to practise his craft at home. He could only earn miserable wages. He lived an isolated, degraded life, and it was the hand-loom weavers who were the foremost in the destruction of machinery and the burning of mills. The Luddites, authors of the most destructive riots which began at Nottingham, were, for the most part, hand-loom weavers. As prices rose and distress became more general, these men more and more looked upon the machinery as the cause of all their woes, and joined eagerly in their destruction." In India the abundance of waste lands and the possibility of a portion of the weaving population finding work in the cultivation of lands is some mitigation, however inadequate, of their unfortunate position.

41. Another industry which has suffered from foreign-competition is the manufacture of iron. India contains an abundant supply of iron ore and native works for iron smelting were not very long ago scattered all over the Peninsula, and Indian steel was famous. Dr. Buchanan has described minutely the processes employed by native manufacturers in 1800 for smelting iron in the districts of Salem, Coimbatore, Malabar and South Canara. The charcoal used was very great in comparison with the results obtained. In Salem, it is stated that iron ore containing 72 per cent. of metal, yields only 15 per cent. of bar iron. The clearance of forests and the consequent rise in the price of charcoal have nearly extinguished this industry; and iron smelters in many regions are the hardest

The decline in the manufacture of iron.

---

[53] See Mrs. Creighton's *Social History of England*.

worked, but the poorest among the population. The iron (which is of very good quality and superior to the imported article) is sold at a high price; nevertheless the amount of iron produced bears but a miserable proportion to the labour, time and material expended. The class that has suffered is, however, numerically a small one, while the benefit to the general population by the fall in the price of imported iron and by the prevention of the indiscriminate felling of forests for charcoal burning has been very great. The extent of the benefit may be estimated from the following figures: During the past 18 years, the imports of iron into India have been doubled both in quantity and value, while those of steel have increased more than 15 times in quantity, but less than 4 times in value, thus showing that the value of imported steel is only about one-fourth of what it was before. The imports of hardware and cutlery have increased more than two-fold, while those of railway and rolling stock have increased more than 5 times. The imports of machinery have increased from about 5 lakhs in 1850–51, to nearly 2½ crores in 1888–89, thus showing an immense advance in the steam-power of the country. There are also indications that this country will ere long be able to manufacture iron on a larger scale than hitherto by the adoption of improved processes. The discovery of coal in various parts of the country and the methods invented for its economical use afford promise of a great future for the iron industry. Fifty years ago the Madras Government spent considerable sums of money in subsidizing the Porto Novo Company in the hope of creating and developing an iron manufacturing industry according to European processes. The scheme failed owing to the difficulty of obtaining charcoal. Recently, however, it appears that near Pondicherry, not far from Porto Novo, extensive beds of coal, 10,000 acres in extent, capable of producing 250 million tons have been discovered; whether this will lead to an iron manufacturing industry being re-established in those parts it is difficult to say, but considering the startling rapidity with which methods for developing and utilizing natural resources are being discovered by science at the present day, it is not too much to hope that the rich iron ores of Southern India will not long remain unutilized.

The shipping industry.

42. The shipping trade of India has suffered also. Mr. O'Conor in the Trade Report of India for 1890–91 writes: "The native craft employed in the foreign trade do not increase. They represent less than 2¼ per cent. of the total tonnage. Except for intercourse with the Straits and the Malayan Archipelago,

Ceylon, the Maldives and the Coast from Karachi to Muscat, these craft will eventually disappear from the foreign carrying trade." This is not a result to be much regretted, as the employment of these small craft of burden averaging 50 tons each is not compatible with the enormous growth of the foreign trade of India, and as further it is the use of steam vessels for carriage that has developed the trade with China in Indian cotton manufactures. The small craft, however, will continue to be used in the carriage of the cheapest and bulkiest articles between the smaller ports which steamers do not enter.

The development of factory industries.

43. Against the disadvantage to the indigenous industries above referred to, have to be set off the new industries which foreign trade has created. The new industries which have sprung up in the Madras Presidency have already been noticed. Taking India as a whole, three important new industries may be mentioned, viz., jute, tea and coal. The export of jute in 1828 was 364 cwts. valued at 62 Rx. In 1850–51 the value of the exports of raw jute amounted to 197,071 Rx and of manufactured jute to 215,978 Rx. In 1890–91 the values were 7·6 millions Rx and 2·5 millions Rx, respectively. Jute cultivation is entirely carried on by the natives of the country, without any extraneous help. Baboo Hem Chunder Kerr in his report on the jute cultivation in Bengal writes: "It is usual with some to descant on the apathy, ignorance and want of enterprise of the people of this country, and of the ryots in particular, but the figures here given prove beyond the shadow of a cavil, that they are, notwithstanding their alleged or real defects, sufficiently long-headed thoroughly to understand their interest and capable of creating and extending in five and forty years a trade to the value of nearly $4\frac{1}{4}$ million sterling (now 10 million Rx) without any aid from without. That they are capable, likewise, of sustaining this trade and extending it if required and made worth their while, no one will, I feel certain, venture to question. As long as the trade is profitable, they will do all that is needed, but strong common sense and long-headedness will not accept theories for facts, nor adopt new methods or systems, because they are new, or because they are told to adopt them. The new methods and systems must be proved to be real improvements calculated for certain, to add to their profits, or they will have none of them." Tea on the other hand, is an industry created entirely by English enterprise and capital. The value of the exports amounts now to $5\frac{1}{4}$ million Rx. Indian and Ceylon teas have been rapidly driving the China tea out of the English market as will be seen from the following figures. In 1864 the imports

into England were: China 85·80 and Indian 2·80; total 88·60 million lb. The imports in 1890 were: China 73·74, Indian 101·77, and Ceylon 42·49; total 218 million lb. It is stated that the tea from India produces a stronger liquid than that of China, that is, a small quantity of the former is equal for purposes of consumption to a larger quntity of the latter; and as a high import duty, amounting to nearly 25 per cent. of the value is levied in England on all teas irrespective of their quality, the Indian tea is benefited. The duty which was 6*d.* per lb. has also been reduced to 4*d.* The establishment of collieries in India has been effected in recent years, the output of coal in 1889 amounting to 2 million tons and the value ·69 million Rx. The average value per ton of Indian coal is 3·4 rupees while that of imported coal is 22·4 rupees, while in point of heating power the latter has an advantage of not more than one-half. As railway communications further develop, India might be expected to use her own coal for manufacturing purposes. In India there were at the end of 1889–90, 114 cotton-mills and 27 jute mills worked by steam, 315 cotton and jute presses, 51 rice mills, 60 saw mills, 21 breweries, 2 woollen mills, 6 silk mills, 3 soap factories, 6 large tanneries, 48 iron and brass foundries, 14 large sugar factories, 23 coffee works, 66 cutch and lac factories, 61 oil mills, 41 flour mills, 24 ice factories, 23 pottery and tile factories, 15 bone-crushing factories and 34 tobacco and cigar factories, besides a large number of indigo and tea factories worked on indigo and tea plantations. The establishment of these factories affords cogent proof of the fact that India is emancipating herself, as Mr. Wells put it, from her chronic sluggishness and entering on a new era of industrial improvement.

44. *Taxation.*—The growth of taxation in this Presidency has next to be considered. The principal sources of revenue are (1) the land tax and provincial rates; (2) the income-tax; (3) the salt duties; (4) the excise on spirits and drugs; (5) the customs duties; (6) the stamp duties; and (7) fees for the registration of documents. It will be convenient to take each of these sources of revenue and examine to what extent they affect the economic condition of the several classes of the population.

Land revenue. Tax or rent?

45. Among these sources of revenue, the land revenue is, of course, by far the most important. There has been much discussion as to whether the ryot has a right in the soil and whether the payments made by him fall under the category of *tax* or of *rent*. In the opinion of the Famine Commissioners, 1880, the land revenue is a source of income

which in India must be distinguished from taxation properly so called, as by immemorial and unquestioned prescription, the Government is entitled to receive from the occupier of the land whatever it requires of the surplus profit left after defraying the expenses of cultivation; and consequently land revenue may with more propriety be regarded as a *rent* paid by a tenant, often a highly favored tenant, to the paramount owner, than as a *tax* paid by the owner to the State. This extreme view of the rights of the State, which was dissented from by the Madras member of the Famine Commission, is in consonance neither with the conclusions of the best authorities, nor with the practice of the English administrators in this Presidency; and indeed as regards the latter, Madras has been more fortunate than many other parts of India. Sir Thomas Munro, who is generally believed to have denied that the ryot had any right in the soil he cultivated, says: "The ryot of India unites in his own person the characters of laborer, farmer, and landlord; he receives the wages of the laborer, the profit of the farmer on his stock, and a small surplus from 1 to 20 per cent. on the gross produce as rent, but on an average not more than 5 or 6 per cent." Again in another place, he remarks: "The Collector looks upon the ryot as a mere tenant, and hence he infers that the occupation of land in India may be regulated as in England. But the station of the ryot is not so low as is made by his plan. The ryot is certainly not like the landlord in England, but neither is he like the English tenant. If the name of landlord belongs to any person in India, it is to the ryot. He divides with Government all the rights of the land. Whatever is not reserved by Government belongs to him. He is not a tenant at will, or for a term of years. He is not removable because another offers more." The fact is, that the relationship between the ryot and Government, or between the ryot and the Zemindar who is the assignee of the rights of Government, is not that of landlord and tenant, but that of partnership.[54] Professor Marshall puts this matter in a

---

[54] James Mill in writing to a son who was reading in the East India Company's College at Haileybury explained this very clearly: He said, "Do not allow yourself to be taken in, as many people are, by an ambiguity in the word '*property*.' Englishmen in general incline to think that where *property* is not entire, especially in the land, there is no *property*. But *property* may be as perfectly *property*, when it includes only a part, as when it includes the whole. There is no doubt that the ryot has a *property* in the soil, though it is a limited *property*. There is no doubt that the Government has a *property* in the soil—that also limited—the one limited by the other. It is therefore a case of *joint property*. Hence the controversies." As regards the proprietary rights of the ryots in the soil they cultivate, the following authorities may be referred to: Bhaskarappa *v.* The Collector of North Canara, XII Bombay High Court Reports appendix; the judgment of the Madras High Court in the Attapadi valley case; the judgment of the Madras High Court in A.S. No. 82 of 1883; Sir Charles Turner's

clear light. He says: "In early times, and in backward countries, even in our own age, all rights to property depend on general understandings rather than on precise laws and documents. In so far as these understandings can be reduced to definite terms and expressed in the language of modern business, they are generally to the following effect: The ownership of land is vested, not in an individual, but in a firm of which one member or group of members is the sleeping partner, while another member or group of members (it may be a whole family) is the working partner. The sleeping partner is sometimes the ruler of the State, sometimes he is an individual who inherits what was once the duty of collecting payments due to this ruler from the cultivators of a certain part of the soil, but what, in the course of silent time, has become a right of ownership, more or less definite, more or less absolute. If, as is generally the case, he retains the duty of making certain payments to the ruler of the State, the partnership may be regarded as containing three members, of whom two are sleeping partners. The sleeping partner, or one of them, is generally called the proprietor, or landholder or landlord, or even landowner. But this is an incorrect way of speaking, if he is restrained by law, or by custom which has the force of law, from turning the cultivator out of his holding, either by an arbitrary enhancement of the payments exacted from him or by any other means. In that case, the property in the land vests, not in him alone, but in the whole of the firm, of which he is only a sleeping partner; the payment made by the working partner is not rent at all, but is that fixed sum, or that part of the gross proceeds, as the case may be, which the constitution of the firm binds him to pay; and in so far as custom or law, which regulates these payments, is fixed and unalterable, the theory

---

minute on the Bill relating to Malabar Land tenures; and G.O., dated 21st September 1882, No. 1008, Revenue. The last paper is most important as containing the declarations of Government on the subject of ryot's rights after full inquiry. The conclusions stated by Government are—(1) that the State cannot, without violating the rule and practice dating from time immemorial, assert in this Presidency an exclusive right to minerals in unoccupied lands, but that it is fully entitled to a share in such products as in any other produce of the land; (2) that subject to the payment of a stated proportion of the produce to meet the necessities of the administration, the proprietary right of the ryot in the soil of his holding is absolute and complete; (3) that he is able to mortgage, sell, devise or otherwise alienate the land; (4) that, on these principles, property has been changing hands from time immemorial, and for the Government to put forward a claim now, which has never been asserted and which does not rest in law, practice or precedent, would undoubtedly raise a feeling of distrust and discontent which would take long to allay; (5) that it would be straining the State's privileges to attach the condition of recognition of any exclusive right to minerals on the terms on which lands may be newly occupied, although in the interests of the general public, it may in particular instances be justifiable to do so, in view to the development of ascertained mineral resources; and (6) that as regards the vast bulk of the land occupied or likely to be occupied for cultivation, such reservation would be absolutely objectless and would only have the effect of creating widespread distrust in the minds of the people.

of rent has but little direct application." It is the fashion to say that it matters little by what name the payment made by the ryot to Government is called, *i.e.*, whether it is designated *revenue* or *rent*; but, in practice, the point of view from which the question is regarded involves most important consequences. "To the modern statesman," says Lord Salisbury in reference to this question, "the refined distinctions of the economical school are a solid living reality, from which he can as little separate his thoughts as from his mother tongue. To us it may seem indifferent whether we call a payment *revenue* or *rent*, so we get the money; but it is not indifferent by what name we call it within *his* hearing. If we say that it is *rent*, he will hold the Government in strictness entitled to all that remains after wages and profits have been paid, and he will do what he can to hasten the advent of the day when the State shall no longer be kept by any weak compromises from the enjoyment of its undoubted rights. If we persuade him that it is *revenue*, he will note the vast disproportion of its incidence as compared to that of other taxes, and his efforts will tend to remedy the inequality and to lay upon other classes and interests a more equitable share of the public burden. I prefer the latter tendency to the former. So far as it is possible to change the Indian fiscal system, it is desirable that the cultivator should pay a smaller proportion of the whole national charge. It is not in itself a thrifty policy to draw the mass of revenue from the rural districts where capital is scarce, sparing the towns where it is often redundant and runs to waste in luxury. The injury is exaggerated in the case of India, where so much of the revenue is exported without a direct equivalent." The above views of Lord Salisbury, which seem to me to be perfectly sound, I shall have occasion to refer to again when I have to consider the effect of land settlements. When the relation between the ryot and the Government is regarded as one of *partnership*, it results that the payment made by the former to the latter is neither *rent* nor *tax* but a share of the profits. As the Government, which is the "*sleeping partner*" according to Professor Marshall's phraseology, has, however, power to assess the profits and determine the portion to be paid to it as its share, the public interests require that the assessment should be made with as much scrupulosity as in the case of a tax to prevent the share of the profits of the "*working partner*" or the private owner, being unduly abridged and the incentives to increased production being weakened; and this object is best attained by regarding the

14

Government assessment of land as being more in the nature of a *tax* than a *rent*.

Growth of land revenue.

46. The subjoined statement shows the average land revenue for decennial periods since the beginning of the century:

				Millions Rx.
Average of 10 years ending		1809-10	...	3·74
Do.	do.	1819-20	...	3·74
Do.	do.	1829-30	...	3·68
Do.	do.	1839-40	...	3·16
Do.	do.	1849-50	...	3·43
Do.	do.	1859-60	...	3·66
Do.	do.	1869-70	...	4·16
Do.	do.	1879-80	...	4·39
Do.	do.	1889-90	...	4·81
1889-90	...	... ...	...	5·03

The figures for the first three decades include the proceeds of the moturpha taxes and of the revenue from the tobacco monopoly. Kurnool having been annexed to British territory in 1838, the revenue of that district is not included in the figures of the years previous to 1838. North Canara, on the other hand, was transferred to Bombay in 1862, and the revenue of this district is included in the figures given for the previous years. Making allowances for these circumstances, it will be seen that during the first 20 years of the century the revenue was nearly 3¾ millions Rx, when lands were rack-rented, that it then began to decline and fell to 3·16 millions in the decade ending 1839-40 owing to the severe agricultural depression which then prevailed, that it took another 20 years to rise to the level at which it was at the beginning of the century, and that since 1859-60 it has been rapidly rising, the increase amounting to 1·15 million Rx or 31·5 per cent. The rise in the revenue may be due to (1) the extension of the area under cultivation, (2) the extension of the area under irrigation, and (3) the increase in the rates of assessment imposed by the settlement department with reference to the increase in the prices of agricultural produce. The following remarks will show to what extent the increase is due to each of the above causes.

The land revenue consists of two portions, one practically permanent and not liable to enhancement, and the other fluctuating. The first head comprises the peshcush on permanently-settled estates, and the quit-rents on inam villages and on inam lands found interspersed with ryotwar lands in ryotwar villages. The permanently-settled estates or zemindaris cover an area of 43,000 square miles or nearly one-third of the whole area of the Presidency. The area under cultivation in the zemindaris was estimated in 1880 at about $5\frac{1}{2}$ millions of acres, or a little more than one-fourth of ryotwar holdings, and the acreage at present is probably somewhat more. The inam areas aggregate nearly 8 million acres, of which the portion actually cultivated may be taken at 5 millions. The land revenue derived from permanently-settled estates is about $50\frac{1}{2}$ lakhs of rupees, from inam villages $6\frac{1}{2}$ lakhs, and from minor inams $21\frac{1}{2}$ lakhs, making a total of $78\frac{1}{2}$ lakhs. The revenue payable to Government on these lands is fixed, except that where unirrigated lands are irrigated by water derived from Government works newly constructed, a water-rate is levied. The water-rate thus levied fluctuates from year to year and may ordinarily be taken at $7\frac{1}{2}$ lakhs of rupees. For the purposes of the assessment of the Local Fund land cess, the rental of zemindari estates has been ascertained to be 161 lakhs of rupees; of inam villages to be $41\frac{1}{2}$ lakhs of rupees; and of minor inams to be 96 lakhs of rupees. The land revenue therefore bears the proportion of one-third, one-sixth and one-fifth, respectively, to the rental of zemindaris, inam villages and minor inams. As regards the inam lands which were held on uncertain tenure, by far the greatest portion of them has been confirmed to the holders in perpetuity with full right of alienation on condition of their paying a light quit-rent. Inam lands held on condition of rendering service to the State have also, in most districts, been enfranchised, that is to say, freed from the condition of service and rendered heritable and transferable property on payment of a quit-rent amounting to five-eighths of the regulated assessment. The only additional tax laid on both zemindari and inam lands is the local land cess at $6\frac{1}{4}$ per cent. of the assessment for local improvements, which they in common with ryotwar lands are liable to pay. The zemindars are charged with only a portion of the cess at the rate of $3\frac{1}{8}$ per cent. on the difference between the assessment paid to them by the ryots and the peshcush paid by the former to Government, while the ryots pay at the rate of $3\frac{1}{8}$ per cent. on the assessment paid to the zemindars. The zemindari ryots thus pay the cess at only half the rates at which the Government ryots are assessed in consideration of the fact of the land assessment levied by zemindars being much heavier than those of ryotwar lands. The amount of the cess is $12\frac{1}{2}$ lakhs of rupees, while the prices of produce, and, as a consequence, the annual money value of the lands have risen by 150 per cent. since 1850.

The ryotwar land revenue, which was 3 crores of rupees in 1852-53, increased to 3·76 crores in 1872-73 and to 4 crores in 1889-90. As already observed, prior to 1850, the land revenue, owing to the agricultural depression and the low prices of the food-grains, pressed with extreme severity on the agricultural classes; and under the liberal policy which was inaugurated about that time, extensive reductions were made in the land assessments, the remissions granted between 1850 and 1858 amounting to 28 lakhs of rupees. Between 1858 and 1872-73 further remissions of taxation were made to the extent of 24½ lakhs in districts not brought under the new settlement as shown below; the abolition of the olungu system in Tanjore and Tinnevelly districts, 7 lakhs; the reduction of assessment on unirrigated lands in South Arcot and Guntúr, Rs. 95,000; the reduction of assessment of garden lands, 7½ lakhs; the abolition of the pullary tax in Nellore, Rs. 97,000; the reduction of assessment of manavari lands in Chingleput, Rs. 15,000; and the abolition of the tobacco monopoly, 8 lakhs of rupees. On the other hand, the increase of assessment due to the new settlement, not taking into account the local cesses, was, up to 1872-73, 5½ lakhs, and from that year up to the end of 1889-90, 7 lakhs, making a total of 12½ lakhs. On the whole, therefore, the net amount of land taxation remitted since 1850 is 40 lakhs. This shows that the increase in the ryotwar land revenue is entirely due to the extension of irrigation and extension of cultivation and not in any degree to the increase of taxation. Out of 1 crore of rupees, by which the ryotwar revenue demand in 1889-90 exceeds the demand in 1852-53, more than 40 lakhs are due to irrigation provided by irrigation works constructed by Government and classed as productive; irrigation works constructed since 1850, but not classed as productive, have also brought in a considerable revenue, the amount of which is not ascertainable; and there is the revenue due to the increase in the acreage of holdings, which has risen from less than 13 to 21 millions of acres, or by about 60 per cent. As compared with 1852-53, the rate per acre of unirrigated land has fallen from [55] 2*s.* 6*d.* to 2*s.* 0¾*d.* and of irrigated land from 12*s.* 5*d.* to 10*s.* and of land of both descriptions from 4*s.* 9*d.* to 3*s.* 9⅕*d.*

The provincial rates, which affect ryotwar lands in rural tracts, are (1) the local fund land cess, (2) the village service cess, and (3) the irrigation cess. The last is a voluntary cess of trifling amount paid in a few places to keep up an

[55] £1 is taken as equivalent to Rs. 10.

establishment for the conservancy of, and distribution of water in, irrigation channels and may be left out of the calculation. Land cess is levied for the maintenance of roads, bridges, hospitals and other services administered by the Local Fund Boards. The village service cess is utilised for the maintenance of the village establishments and supersedes in part at least the merahs and grain fees, which, according to the custom of the country, the ryots were bound to pay for the maintenance of village servants. The two cesses on ryotwar lands amount to 52½ lakhs of rupees. The whole amount is not a new charge, as the value of the old merahs customarily paid before the village-cess was introduced and which are now no longer paid must be deducted. The increase of taxation on ryotwar land, taking both land revenue proper and provincial rates together, cannot be more than 10 lakhs of rupees, if even so much. Practically, therefore, the incidence of the land taxes remains the same now as it was in 1850 in nominal money value, while owing to the fall in the purchasing power of money, 2½ rupees now being equivalent to 1 rupee before, a ryot has to sell only two-fifths of the crop he would have had to sell formerly to discharge the Government dues.

Pressure of the land tax and selling prices of land.

47. The considerations referred to above clearly show that the pressure of the land tax is very much less at present than it was in the year 1850, even after making allowance for the fact that the area of land actually cultivated was in excess of the recorded area in former years. That the tax is in itself moderate is shown by the high prices obtained for much of the land under cultivation. I have collected and given in the appendix V.–E. (d) such statistics as could be obtained as regards the value of lands in a few districts from the records of the Registration department. In 1830, land had little or no value throughout the greater portion of the Presidency with the exception of the districts of Tanjore, Malabar, South Canara and the river-irrigated portions of Madura and Tinnevelly. In the rich deltas of the Kistna and the Godávari, transfers of land by sale appear to have been almost unknown till about 1850. In 1853 Sir Walter Elliott, the Commissioner of the Northern Circars, reported that in the Kistna district land was generally unsaleable, and that, in the only instances which had come to his notice, the area sold was 15 acres of dry and 56½ acres of wet land, the price obtained being Rs. 203. Again the same officer reported in 1854 that the only case of sale of assessed lands

occurred in Guntúr, where 10 acres of dry and 2 acres of wet land yielding a gross outturn of Rs. 55, and bearing an assessment of Rs. 34 fetched a price of Rs. 78. In the dry districts, such as the Ceded Districts, &c., the only lands that had any saleable value were inam lands, and lands irrigated by private wells or on which cocoanut and areca plantations had been formed, almost the entire value in these cases being due to the capital and labour laid out by the ryots in improving the lands. In the Tanjore district the statistics given in the appendix V.–E. (d 1 and 2) show that the value of lands in most places has risen to not less than ten times what it was in the early years of the century. In the deltas of the Kistna and the Godávari, lands which were unsaleable have, during the last 30 years, acquired a high value, though in the former district there are still large tracts where, owing to the sparseness of the population, the value has not risen to anything like the height it has attained in Tanjore. As regards the rise in the value of lands in the Coimbatore district, Mr. Nicholson remarks "(1) that whereas up to 1850, or at least in 1839, only about one-eighth of the dry land, three-fourths of the gardens, and one-fourth of the wet land was saleable, in 1884 the bulk of the dry land has a price ranging from As. 4 to Rs. 50 per acre; all gardens are saleable, and are worth from Rs. 50 to 100 per acre, inclusive of the well, while the wet land is wholly saleable at an average of from Rs. 250 to Rs. 300; (2) that a very large proportion of the lands bears a rental of one-half of the gross produce, whereas in 1839 a smaller proportion bore a rental of one-half the net produce, *i.e.*, after deducting cultivation expenses; (3) that interest has decreased, mortgages on landed property being now freely accepted at 9 per cent., whereas in 1839 interest on such transactions was from 12 to 18 per cent. and higher; (4) that trading capital now turns to land as an investment, and is willing to accept from it a return of 6 per cent., whereas in 1839 it was declared that trading capital did not invest in land; (5) that wells have increased from about 22,000 to about 55,000 in actual use, representing capital permanently sunk since 1800 of at least 100 lakhs, besides that sunk in wells not now in use; (6) that thousands of acres have been turned from dry into wet; (7) that the cultivation of very valuable products, such as sugar-cane, turmeric, cocoanuts, plantains, &c., has largely increased; and (8) that in the recent unprecedented famine (1877-78), it was not the ryot class who suffered severely, save only those who depended solely on dry land." All these beneficial results have been produced by the removal of the special tax on garden cultivation in a district which is known to be one of the driest in the Presidency, and in which out of 62 years beginning with 1803 and ending with 1865 the season in 9 had been described as bad, in 40 as unfavourable, and only in 11 as favourable and in 2 as "bumper." Mr. Nicholson estimates the average value of wet land at Rs. 255 per acre, of dry land at Rs. 19 per acre, and of garden land at Rs. 46 per acre. The poorest lands on the margin of cultivation have of course little or no value, and, allowing for this, he puts the average value of dry land at Rs. 12 per acre. The total capitalized value of the lands under occupation he estimates at 6·3 crores of rupees. In the densely populated districts, such as Tanjore, lands rapidly rose in value when the prices of food grains ruled high between 1860 and 1870; since then the rise in value has not been quite so great. In other districts, however, which have been opened up by extension of communications, the rise in land values during recent years has been very great. The increase in the value of land of course is to some extent due to the fact of its being a "safe" investment. In the Tanjore district, for instance, persons investing money in land do not expect to get a greater return than 4 or 5 per cent.; and in South Canara the return is stated to be as low as $3\frac{1}{8}$ per cent. Nevertheless the rise in the price of land is a sure indication of the abundance of circulating capital and of the moderation of the land tax.

Relation between Government assessment and rental.

48. The proportion which the land assessment bears to the rent value of the lands is even a better gauge of the pressure of the land tax than land prices. Statistics showing this proportion for all the districts of the Presidency are not easily procurable. I have, however, obtained the required particulars for one district, viz., Coimbatore, from leases registered in 1889, and the results are given in the appendix V.–E. (e 4). The number of leases examined was 700, of which 270 related to dry lands, 3,084 acres in extent, 301 to garden lands of 3,675 acres, and 129 to wet lands of 375 acres. In the case of dry lands, the rent was 3·4 times the Government assessment, for garden it was 5·1 times and for wet lands 5 times. Of the extent of land leased out, only in a small proportion of cases are written engagements exchanged, and of such written engagements only a small proportion is registered. Moreover it is only the better classes of lands that are leased out. Nevertheless, the figures above given show that the lands have not been over-assessed. In the case of dry lands leased

out, the average assessment comes to about 1 rupee, while the average dry assessment of the district is 14 annas 10 pies. The wet lands leased out do not seem to be of exceptionally good quality, for while their average assessment comes to Rs. 6-3-2, the average wet rate for the district is Rs. 7-7-0. The following statement shows that in a considerable number of cases the rental exceeds even ten times the assessment:

—	Description of lands.		
	Dry.	Garden.	Wet.
Number of cases in which the rent stipulated to be paid is less than twice the Government assessment ...	70	19	4
Do. do. do. between 3 and 2 ...	68	45	9
Do. do. do. do. 4 and 3 ...	45	29	26
Do. do. do. do. 5 and 4 ...	29	41	20
Do. do. do. do. 6 and 5 ...	20	25	25
Do. do. do. do. 7 and 6 ...	16	33	17
Do. do. do. do. 8 and 7 ...	5	19	12
Do. do. do. do. 9 and 8 ...	3	18	9
Do. do. do. do. 10 and 9 ...	5	11	...
Do. do. do. do. 15 and 10 ...	9	43	6
Do. do. do. over 15 ...	...	18	1
Total ...	270	301	129

NOTE.—In all these cases the lessor pays the Government assessment out of the rent stipulated.

49. The proportion of Government assessment to the gross produce was estimated by the Famine Commission at 6·3 per cent., taking the value of the gross outturn at 50 crores of rupees, and the land revenue at 3·16 crores. They have excluded from land revenue 1·37 crores as being water charge and not forming part of land tax proper. Including this amount, the proportion is 9·2 per cent. In these calculations, however, the outturn of favourably assessed inam lands and of zemindari lands, which now pay to Government a smaller revenue than ryotwar lands, has been included. Taking the ryotwar lands alone, the average rate of assessment for wet lands is Rs. 5 per acre and for dry lands 1 rupee per acre, and these rates are between one-fourth and one-fifth and one-fourth and one-sixth, respectively, of the gross outturn according to settlement calculations after deducting from the average outturn 16⅔ per cent. in the case of wet and 25 per cent. in the case of dry lands as allowance for vicissitudes of season. The average outturn of lands is, however, extremely difficult to calculate on account of the wide variety of soils and of seasons, the produce even in a small cycle of

Ratio of Government assessment to gross produce.

years varying from almost nothing to a bumper crop; but though, as I shall have hereafter occasion to show, I do not believe that the values assigned by the settlement department to the various factors which enter into the calculations from which the Government assessment is deduced are even approximately correct, there is no reason to suppose that the proportion of the assessment of ryotwar lands to the gross produce is higher than those above given. In the [56] case of lands in the poorer dry districts it is very much less.

50. *The Income-tax.*—The revenue derived from this source amounts to 18½ lakhs of rupees. The portion of the tax relating to trades is not a new one, but is the representative of the old moturpha, some account of which has already been given. Unpopular as the income-tax is, it is nothing so unbearable as the old all-embracing moturpha, which, in an ably drawn up petition, presented by the Madras Native Association to the Committee of the House of Commons, appointed to enquire into Indian affairs in 1853, is described as "a tax on trades and occupations; embracing weavers, carpenters, all workers in metals, all salesmen, whether possessing shops, which are also taxed separately, or vending by the roadside, &c., &c., some paying impost on their tools, others for permission to sell, extending to the most trifling articles of trade, and the cheapest tools the mechanic can employ; the cost of which is frequently exceeded six times over by the moturpha, under which the use of them is permitted." The tax, according to Mr. Dykes, the Collector of

	LAKHS.
Tax on salaries and pensions ...	6¼
Tax on Companies	½
Tax on interest on Government securities.	½
Tax on profits of trades, &c. ...	11¼
Total ...	18½

[56] Of course the small proportion of the assessment to the gross produce does not necessarily show that the assessment is light as there is a vast extent of poor lands in arid tracts, which are on the margin of cultivation. The only use of these calculations is to show that the land revenue now taken by the British Government does not exceed much, if at all, the one-sixth share prescribed by Menu, the Hindu lawgiver, and which I suppose must have had reference to unirrigated lands and not to lands for which irrigation is provided by expensive irrigation-works constructed and maintained by Government. The statements of Sir Thomas Munro and Mr. Russell referred to in a previous part of this memorandum show that the ryots in former days paid between 45 and 60 per cent. of the crop to Government, and that the Government share was further enhanced by the unduly high money valuation put on the crop. The ryots, on the other hand, cheated the Government by holding more lands than they paid for, and further the large area of inam lands enabled the better classes of ryots to exist. It was a case of perpetual struggle between the Government officers and the ryots, the former by means of forced cultivation and torture trying to extort the revenue which was impossible of realization except occasionally and in a spasmodic way, and the latter by practising all manner of deception and by concealment of property trying to evade payment of Government dues. Even Sir Thomas Munro, whose one object was to give saleable value to lands, and encourage enterprise in the ryots, found it necessary to prohibit the cultivation of inam lands to the neglect of lands which paid the full assessment.

Salem, who was examined by the Select Committee, varied in each district and in every village, and its assessment was, in the highest degree, arbitrary. The mode of assessment was often as follows: A man's father had paid the tax and the son was generally assessed at the same amount. If the latter was considered to be an energetic man and was believed to drive a better trade, the matter was reported to the Collector the next time he visited that part of the district. If the trader was a man of any sense, I use Mr. Dykes' words, he bought off the village authorities and did not get his assessment raised, the extent of his dealings not being reported. Sir Thomas Munro mentions that in the Bellary district, the tax amounted to between 15 and 20 per cent. of the income in some taluks and little or nothing in others, the reason for indulgent treatment in the latter cases being that the merchants were obliged to furnish at a low rate whatever articles were required for the public service, to take the Sirkar share of the crops, damaged stores, &c., at 10 per cent. above the market rate, and to pay "occasional" contributions. Sir Thomas Munro proposed to impose a uniform tax of 15 per cent. throughout the district. In one village in the Coimbatore district barbers, carpenters and blacksmiths paid Rs. 2-5-8 each; pariah labourers paid As. 14-2 and chucklers paid each Rs. 2-5-8. The Public Works Commissioners of 1852 give some interesting statistics regarding the oppressive character of this tax. They state, "In connection with the important object of increasing the class of consumers not directly concerned with the growth of food, we cannot but observe that the moturpha or tax on tradesmen and artizans appears singularly objectionable. In a country where the classes engaged in trade, manufactures and the useful arts are extremely few in number compared with those occupied in agriculture, the disfavour of the former branches of industry is increased by a special impost levied on those employed in them. It amounts in all to £116,000 and this trifling sum is collected from no fewer than 994,224 individuals being only 1⅛ R. or 2*s.* 4*d.* from each contributor." The Commissioners go on to remark "a large part of the moturpha is paid by the weavers and forms an addition to the difficulties with which they have to contend in competing with the English manufacturer. In this case too, the tax is more than usually inquisitorial, as the amount varies with the number of looms employed by each payer; houses are frequently entered in order to discover concealed looms, as the Indian loom is easily dismantled and put away." The grossly unequal incidence of the tax in the several districts will be seen from the subjoined table. The number of payees of income tax in the districts referred to and the incidence per head are added for purposes of comparison:

Names of districts.	Number of payees of moturpha tax.	Amount paid.	Rate per head of payee.	Number of payees of income tax, Part IV.	Amount paid.	Rate per head of payee.
		RS.	RS. A. P.		RS.	RS. A. P.
Tanjore	232,321	43,313	0 2 11¾	2,819	71,746	25 7 3
Bellary	145,300	2,72,576	1 14 0	2,889	60,446	20 14 9
Trichinopoly ...	5,834	6,525	1 1 10¾	973	18,742	19 4 2
Kurnool ..	12,104	55,992	4 10 0	1,620	28,338	17 7 11
Canara	28,301	16,567	0 9 4½	1,077	24,033	22 5 0
Malabar ...	211,152	1,15,742	0 8 9¼	2,015	48,078	23 13 9

The number of payees of the income-tax throughout the Presidency in 1890-91 was 56,809 and the average assessment, Rs. 28-10-6 per head. Besides the income-tax, a tax on arts, trades and professions is levied in Municipal towns; the amount collected in 1889-90 was Rs. 1,80,557, and the number of payees 43,932, and the average payment Rs. 4-1-9 per head. The exemption of incomes below Rs. 500 from assessment has minimized much of the inquisition and oppression incidental to the levy of a tax of this kind, and if the state of the finances permit, the limit of exemption may be extended to Rs. 1,000. If this were done, the revenue from this tax would be reduced by a fourth. This is the only direct tax paid by the official, professional and the trading classes who are bound to contribute their fair share to the public burdens, and it is therefore quite sound in principle. There is no difficulty in assessing official salaries and professional incomes; and as regards trade profits, the exemption of incomes below Rs. 500 secures to a great extent from oppression the classes least able to protect themselves. The people are becoming accustomed to the tax, and, though the revenue derived is small, it is collected without much additional cost, and if, as I believe it will, the country makes a rapid advance in industrial development, this source of revenue might in course of time, be expected to become important. It must, therefore, be once for allrecognized as permanently incorporated into the system of taxation of the Empire and not be periodically threatened with extinction.

Salt Revenue.

51. The Government salt monopoly in this Presidency was created in 1805. Previously under native Governments the manufacture of salt was farmed out in some places, but on no defined system, and in other places various persons had been allowed the

privilege of manufacture without any payment. In the Northern Circars it was the policy of the Muhammadan Government to limit the manufacture of salt to its own havelly or home farm lands, and to prohibit the making of salt in Zemindaris. At Nowpada in 1787 the price of salt was Rs. 40 per garce of 120 maunds (1 maund=82$\frac{2}{7}$lb.). The price of salt inland was four and often eight times the price on the coast varying according to the distance from the coast. Before the Government monopoly came into force, the price of salt at Calicut in 1800 was, according to Buchanan, 4 annas a maund. In Mangalore, Bombay salt was sold for less than 4 annas and Goa salt less than 3 annas a maund. At Taikulam (near Bangalore) the price of earth salt was 10 annas 8 pies per maund, and of Madras sea salt 2 rupees or three times as much. After the creation of the Government monopoly the price at the Government factories was fixed * at 9$\frac{1}{3}$ annas at first, and it has been continually enhanced till it amounts now to 2 rupees 11 annas. Till 1882, the manufacture of salt except on Government account was prohibited. Between 1882 and 1886, the system of manufacture and sale of salt by private individuals on payment of an excise duty was substituted for the Government monopoly system throughout the Presidency, with the exception of half a dozen places where the old system is still maintained. The growth of the salt revenue since the beginning of the century will be seen from the figures given below :

—	Millions Rx.	Quantity exported and sold Millions lb.
Average of ten years ending 1809-10	·13	360
Do. do. 1819-20	·33	322
Do. do. 1829-30	·36	442
Do. do. 1839-40	·38	401
Do. do. 1849-50	·44	408
Do. do. 1859-60	·53	476
Do. do. 1869-70	·99	565
Do. do. 1879-80	1·33	526
Do. do. 1889-90	1·50	537
For the year 1889-90	1·76	579

* The Government monopoly price of salt fixed from time to time has been as follows :

	Per maund. RS.	A.	P.
From 1805 to Nov. 1809 ...	0	9	4
Do. Nov. 1809 to 1820 ...	0	14	0
Do. 1820 to June 1828	0	9	4
Do. June 1828 to 31st March 1844 ...	0	14	0
Do. April 1844 to July 1859	1	0	0
Do. August 1859 to April 1861	1	2	0
Do. April 1861 to June 1861	1	6	0
Do. June 1861 to 1865-66.	1	8	0
Do. 1865-66 to Oct. 1869.	1	11	0
Do. Oct. 1869 to Dec. 1877	2	0	0
Do. Dec. 1877 to March 1882	2	11	0
Do. March 1882 to January 1888	2	3	0
Do. January 1888 to date.	2	11	0

Since 1820, the consumption of salt cannot be said to have increased as much as might be expected from the increase of population, the suppression of illicit manufacture and smuggling and the development of communications, though, of course, owing to the area supplied with Madras salt, which competes with that of Bombay, having under the ordinary conditions of trade changed from time to time, the figures above given for different years will have to be corrected to admit of their being compared with one another. The development of railways and the fall in the purchasing power of money have also doubtless made the tax less burdensome in proportion to the increase in the money rates of duty than it would otherwise have been in the inland districts. Thus in 1814, when the monopoly price of salt at the coast was 14 annas a maund, Madras sea salt was sold in Bellary at Rs. 2-8-0 per maund; and in 1850 when the Government price was Re. 1, the price in Bellary was a little less than Rs. 2-8-0. The prices in the Cuddapah, Bellary, Kurnool, Coimbatore and Salem districts in 1862, 1873 and 1883 when the monopoly prices at the factories were Rs. 1-8-0, Rs. 2, and Rs. 2-3-0, compare as follows:

—	Seers of 80 tolas per rupee.		
	1862.	1873.	1883.
Cuddapah	16·61	18·2	16·6
Bellary	12·54	17·11	15·5
Kurnool	15·00	16·5	14·2
Coimbatore	14·04	15·95	14·5
Salem	18·86	15·61	16·0

There can, however, be little doubt that the salt tax presses with severity on the poorer classes, especially on the sea coast, where the duty has been enhanced in recent years, and large preventive establishments have at the same time been employed to put down illicit manufacture and smuggling. There has been much discussion as regards the soundness of the policy of taxing a necessary of life like salt. The Duke of Argyle, the Secretary of State for India, said in 1869: "On all grounds of general principle, salt is a perfectly legitimate subject of taxation. It is impossible to reach the masses of the people by direct taxes; if they are to contribute at all to the expenditure of the State, it must be through taxes levied upon some articles of universal consumption. If such taxes are fairly adjusted, a large revenue can thus be raised, not only with less consciousness on the part of the people, but with less real hardship on them than in any other way whatever. There is no other article in India answering this description upon which any tax is levied. It appears to be the only one which at present in that country can occupy the place which is held in our own fiscal system by the great articles of consumption from which a large part of the imperial revenue is derived. I am of opinion that the salt tax in India must continue to be regarded as a legitimate important branch of the public revenue. It is the duty, however, of the Government to see that such taxes are not so heavy as to bear unjustly on the poor by amounting to a large percentage on their necessary expenditure." That the poorer classes should contribute their quota to the revenue of the country may be fully admitted, but the Salt tax is about the worst means which can be employed to draw contributions from them, and nothing but the direst necessity can, in a country like India, justify resort to taxation of this kind. The tax, taking the consumption per head in this Presidency at 16 lb. per annum, amounts to from $2\frac{1}{2}$ to 5 per cent. of the income of a poor family, which is barely sufficient in many cases for subsistence. The diet of the poorer classes is such that they have to use a much larger quantity of salt than the richer classes who use considerable quantities of sugar and of vegetables containing salt. It has been calculated that the quantity of salt required by a labouring man in this Presidency is double the quantity required by a labouring man in Northern India, part of whose diet consists of wheat; and the equalization of the salt duties throughout India has really had the effect of enhancing the duty on salt to persons who require salt to a large extent and of diminishing it to persons who require salt to a much smaller extent. The greatest objection to the salt tax is, however, the large establishments at heavy cost which it is necessary to maintain to protect the revenue. The strength of the Police force employed throughout the Presidency for the prevention and detection of crime against life and property is 22,668 and the cost $36\frac{1}{2}$ lakhs of rupees; while the force employed for the protection of the salt and abkári revenues, that is, for the purpose of preventing people from doing what, but for these taxes, would be innocent and even meritorious, is 8,606, the cost being $13\frac{1}{4}$ lakhs of rupees. This multiplication of Government establishments of a semi-police character with none of the responsibilities of the regular police force is to my mind a serious evil. The tendency[57] of the Salt Department, as indeed of all depart-

[57] The Salt Department has of late years recommended a reversion to the old monopoly system of manufacture and sale on behalf of Government and this view has been urged strongly in the Administration Report of the department for 1890-91.

ments, is naturally enough to strengthen its own hands, irrespective of other considerations, for the purpose of protecting with theoretic completeness the revenue which it is charged with the duty of collecting, and it is, therefore, a matter for particular satisfaction that the Government of Madras in 1889, when the salt law was revised, resisted the attempt made by this department to have it declared by law that any earth in which salt might enter in ever so small quantities was to be regarded as contraband "salt," and any dealing with such earth including mere collection, as "illicit manufacture," even in places where there is likely to be no appreciable danger to the revenue. A further objection to the salt tax is, that it has rendered the suppression of the manufacture of earth salt in various places a necessity, thus preventing the utilization of natural resources, and has interfered with the development of the saltpetre industry and the manufacture of glass, salt being the chief material in alkali, and alkali in glass. In the Ceded Districts and Kurnool alone, manufacture of earth salt amounting to 5 lakhs of maunds or nearly 6 per cent. of the entire salt production in the country was suppressed. The salt manufactured was perfectly wholesome and considerable quantities of it used to be given to cattle. This practice has now entirely ceased. The effect of the tax on public health[58] is very prejudicial.

The chief grounds for the view are, that the slight enhancement in the price of salt to the consumer in recent years is the result of the excise system, that if Government sold the salt to the public they could control the price so as to reduce it to a lower level than that at which it is now, and that it is possible for Government to regulate production with reference to the varying conditions of trade without the help of natural prices to guide itself by. In a note V.-E. (f) appended to this memorandum, I have endeavoured to show that these expectations are illusory and that it would be an error for the Government to undertake the responsibility of regulating production without any adequate means of discharging it and without leaving it to private trade to adjust supplies to demand. The evils of concentrating all power in the hands of a Government department constitute also an important consideration which ought not to be overlooked.

[58] In England in the first quarter of the century a duty of £30 per ton (equal to £1 a maund) was levied on salt and the consumption per head was only 16 lb. The price of salt was then £32 per ton. No duty is now levied and the price is 12s. per ton. The consumption per head is 72 lb., of which it is calculated that 40 lb. are consumed for cooking and condiment, the rest being used for chemicals, manure, &c. Mr. Mulhall states that reduced death-rate and higher efficiency of workmen are the results of the greater consumption of salt. As regards the Indian *salt tax*, it must be remembered that the poorer classes, who purchase salt required for consumption for a pie or two every day, really pay for the article twice as much (if not more) as the rich who purchase in much larger quantities. The following remarks of the Duke of Argyle must also be borne in mind. He said, "I observe that several of those officers whose opinions on this question have been given in the papers before me, found that opinion upon what they have heard, in the way of complaint among the native population; but this is a very unsafe ground of judgment; it is one of the great advantages of indirect taxation that it is so mixed up with the other elements of price that it is paid without observation by the consumers. Even at home, where the people are so much more generally educated, and more accustomed to political reasoning, the heavy indirect taxes formerly levied upon the great articles of consumption were seldom complained

and it seems to me to be a matter for serious consideration whether this tax should be maintained at its present high level, when so much attention is now being devoted to the improvement of the sanitation of the country and the health of the population. I would therefore venture respectfully to suggest that the gradual reduction and eventual abolition of this tax should be pressed on the attention of the Government of India, a tax on the consumption of tobacco being if necessary imposed as a substitute. A tax on tobacco managed under a system like that in force in France will be liable to none of the objections urged against the tax on salt. The plant can grow only on particular soils and requires careful cultivation; and it will not therefore be necessary to employ as costly preventive establishments for the protection of a tax on tobacco as it is in the case of salt which forms spontaneously in many places on the coast. Any quantity of excellent tobacco might be grown on the lunkas or islands in the Godávari and Kistna rivers which are at the disposal of Government and leased out annually for cultivation. Tobacco is not a bulky article like salt, does not waste in being carried inland or cost much for carriage. According to one estimate the value of the tobacco produced and consumed in the country is 6 millions Rx. and according to another it is $2\frac{1}{2}$ millions. Taking the lower figure, a tax amounting to 300 per cent.[59] on the cost price of the tobacco consumed will yield the revenue now derived from salt. Tobacco is not a necessary of life, at all events to such an extent as salt, and a large proportion of the tax will be contributed by the poorest classes, who it is considered should be called upon to bear their share of the public burdens.

Excise on spirits and drugs.

52. The receipts from this source consist of the revenue derived from (1) country spirits; (2) toddy or fermented palm juice; (3) spirits and fermented liquors imported or made in the country according to the European methods; and (4) opium. The abkári or revenue derived from intoxicating liquors is an ancient one in this Presidency. Tavernier mentions that the King of Golgonda derived a very large revenue from the

of by the poor; they were not themselves conscious how severely they were affected by those taxes, and how much more of the articles they would consume if the duties were lower. But while this peculiarity of indirect taxation makes it a most convenient instrument of finance, it throws additional responsibility upon all Governments which resort to it to bring the most enlightened consideration to bear upon the adjustment of taxes, which may really be very heavy and unjust, without the fact being perceived or understood by those on whom they fall."

[59] In France the cost price of 1 lb. of tobacco appears to be 6*d*. and the tax levied is 44*d*. or more than 700 per cent. of the cost price.

consumption of toddy (fermented palm juice), notwithstanding that the use of liquors was strictly forbidden by the Muhammadan religion. Among the Hindus, drinking appears to have been general among the lower classes of the population and especially the aboriginal tribes from the earliest times. In a letter, written in 1683, by Father John DeBritto, of the Madura Jesuit Mission, to the General of the Society at Rome, he states: "The King of Marava encamped with his army, offered the wonted sacrifice to the mother of the gods and did not fail, according to his custom, to satisfy his devotion heartily with the liquor of the palm, which he styled piously the milk of the goddess. It must be observed that the Maravars do not think themselves bound to keep the law which so sternly forbids the nobler castes the use of intoxicating liquor. So they have taken care to dignify in name this liquor which the other castes call the devil's drink (petannir)." Tippu Sultan endeavoured to carry out the injunctions of the Muhammadan religion by issuing an order to the effect that all the palm trees within his dominions should be cut down. The order was obeyed only in the neighbourhood of his capital. No special measures were taken by the English Government until about 1870 to check the consumption of liquors beyond farming out places of sale. Since then the liquor traffic has been brought under regulation, and consumption checked by the gradual enhancement of duty levied both on liquors manufactured in the country and imported from abroad. A detailed account of the various measures adopted for this purpose and of the success which has attended them is given in a note printed as appendix V.-E. (g) to this memorandum, and it is unnecessary to repeat here what is there fully stated. The facts and statistics given in the note will show beyond doubt that the allegations, sometimes made, to the effect that drunkenness is spreading both among the higher and the lower classes, and that the Government is directly interested in extending the consumption and not in checking it, are entirely untrue, so far at all events as this Presidency is concerned. As a matter of fact, the quantity of country liquor now consumed is about 5 per cent. more than what it was in 1875 as shown by the returns of liquor which has paid excise duty, while the population has increased by about 10 per cent. The real diminution in consumption is very much more than this, for there was no special preventive agency employed prior to 1884 to check illicit consumption which was then very prevalent. In Malabar, for instance, which is full of palm groves, the consumption of liquor was formerly practically unregulated. The stringent measures adopted in recent years for concentrating distillation of liquors in a few central places and for limiting sales to licensed places have increased the price of liquor and reduced the consumption so much, that the complaint is now often made that the poorer classes suffer hardship in being deprived of toddy which, though an intoxicant, is believed, to some extent, to be a substitute for food. The number of licensed places for the sale of liquors, which had to be kept at a high level at the outset with a view to take away the inducements for illicit traffic, has since been enormously reduced. All these measures were inaugurated long before Mr. Caine interested himself in the Indian abkári question, though the credit certainly belongs to him of not allowing the Government to relax its efforts in this direction. That the consumption of liquor can be regulated by increasing or diminishing the duty levied thereon is shown by the fact that it increases in prosperous years and diminishes in years of scarcity. The impression that drunkenness is spreading among the higher classes is also, to a great extent, unfounded. It is true that among the educated classes there is now less religious scruple than formerly in taking liquor under medical advice, when there is absolute necessity for doing so, but drunkenness is not considered among these classes less disgraceful than formerly, and the number of persons addicted to drinking is exceedingly small and has shown no tendency to increase in recent years. The returns of imported liquors show that the imports of spirits and wines have greatly fallen off during the last fifteen or twenty years. The imports of beer have, on the other hand, very considerably increased. Beer, however, is drunk by Europeans and Eurasians, and by the lower classes of natives on the Nílgiri hills, where it is superseding country spirit, the price of which has very much risen on account of the heavy duty levied on it. The duty on imported and country-made beer in proportion to its alcoholic strength is much lighter than that on spirits or even toddy, and it is very desirable that it should be [60] raised. Mr. Caine would do a real service if he could induce the Home Government to consent to an enhancement of the import duty on beer, and the enhancement of the excise duty will follow as a matter of course.

---

[60] The excise duty on beer in England is 6*s*. 3*d*. a barrel or a little over 2*d*. a gallon. The excise and import duty on beer in India is 1 anna a gallon. Beer contains about 8 per cent. alcohol, and, if it were taxed at the same rate as spirit, viz., Rs. 6 per gallon of proof spirit, the duty would be nearly 1 rupee. A duty of 4 annas to begin with will not be unsuitable. Toddy, under the tree tax system, pays a higher duty than beer.

The sale of opium was, till 1880, unregulated, chiefly because it was not generally consumed except for medicinal purposes in the greater portion of the Presidency. Its use, however, was all along pretty general in the hill tracts of the four northern districts and on the Nílgiris, the drug being considered to be a prophylactic against malarial fever. The poppy plant used to be cultivated, to a small extent, in the hill tracts, but the cultivation has been prohibited since 1880. As now a duty is levied on the transport and retail sale of opium in addition to the excise duty, the price of the drug has been considerably enhanced and its consumption has been much restricted. The total quantity consumed throughout the Presidency is only 77,000 lb., of which 68,000 lb. forms the consumption of the four northern districts. Of the total number of shops licensed, viz., 1,050, no less than 716 are situated within these districts.

The total revenue from the excise on spirits and drugs since the beginning of the century has been as follows:

				Million Rx.
Average of ten years ending		1809-10	...	·06
Do.	do.	1819-20	...	·12
Do.	do.	1829-30	...	·15
Do.	do.	1839-40	...	·17
Do.	do.	1849-50	...	·22
Do.	do.	1859-60	...	·26
Do.	do.	1869-70	...	·42
Do.	do.	1879-80	...	·59
Do.	do.	1889-90	...	·83
In 1889-90 ...	...	... ...	...	1·14

It will be seen that the revenue has risen enormously especially during the last decade, the causes for the increase being, as already explained, not any extension of consumption but the enhancement of taxation. The excise on intoxicating liquors and drugs, from an economic point of view, is a very desirable form of taxation, for whereas all taxes are objectionable, because they restrict production and consumption, the objection does not apply to this tax, the restriction of consumption being the very object aimed at in regulating the traffic and the revenue derived being obtained, as it were, incidentally and not being in itself the object. To some extent,[61] the increase in the revenue is an index to the

[61] The total revenue in this Presidency from excise is 1·2 million Rx. and the total expenditure on drinking may be taken at about twice that sum or 2·4 million Rx. In England the expenditure on drink is enormous, being estimated at 180 millions sterling. The consumption per head is ·96 gallon of spirit, ·36 gallon of wines and 26·80 gallon of beer. In this Presidency the consumption per head may be roughly estimated as follows: Spirit ·044 gallon; wines ·0001 gallon; toddy ·25 gallon; beer ·025 gallon. In the estimate given above imported liquors are assumed to have been consumed within the Presidency, whereas large quantities of them are exported to Native States.

improved means, though not the improved education, of the working classes, from which it is almost entirely drawn. It seems to me, therefore, that it is right and proper that this revenue should be entirely at the disposal of the local Government in view to its being devoted to the amelioration of the moral and intellectual condition of the classes to whose ignorance and improvidence it owes its existence. Under present arrangements, three-fourths of the revenue is taken by the Government of India for imperial purposes, and this, I venture to submit, is not as it should be.

Customs revenue.

53. The fluctuations in the Customs revenue of the Presidency since the beginning of the century have been as follows:

				Rx. millions.
Average of ten years ending		1809-10	...	·34
Do.	do.	1819-20	...	·49
Do.	do.	1829-30	...	·58
Do.	do.	1839-40	...	·43
Do.	do.	1849-50	...	·25
Do.	do.	1859-60	...	·14
Do.	do.	1869-70	...	·24
Do.	do.	1879-80	...	·28
Do.	do.	1889-90	...	·15
In 1889-90	...	... ...	...	·18

The decline in the revenue of the later years as compared with the revenue of the earlier years of the century is the result of the policy of freeing trade and industries from all obstacles calculated to impede their natural growth and of leaving them to their unfettered development, which, under the impulse of the free trade principles adopted in England, has been maintained in this country during the last 40 years. The abolition of the Sayer or inland transit duties which had given rise to frightful abuses and had weighed upon the springs of industry like a dead weight has already been referred to. In 1844, the year in which the Sayer duties were abolished, the trade between ports within British India was declared free, the revenue relinquished on both accounts being 36 lakhs of rupees. The tariff as regards foreign trade was at the same time remodelled, but the old principle of differential and discriminating duties in regard to articles imported from and exported to British territories and similar articles exported to and imported from other countries, as well as in regard to merchandise carried in British and foreign ships was still maintained. Thus the rate on metals, wrought and unwrought, the produce of the United Kingdom, or any British possession, if brought in British ships, paid a duty of 3 per cent., and if brought in ships of other countries paid 6 per cent. Metals, the produce of foreign countries, if brought in British ships, paid 6 per cent., and if brought in ships of other countries paid 12 per cent. On cotton goods manufactured in the United Kingdom or any British possession the duty was 3½ per cent. if brought in British ships and double that rate if brought in foreign ships. Similar discriminating duties were imposed on articles of export merchandise also. Cotton shipped to Europe, the United States of America and any British possession in America paid no duty, if the article was taken in British ships, and 9 annas a maund if taken in foreign ships. The export duty on cotton taken to other countries in foreign ships was Rs. 1-2-0 a maund. These injurious restrictions, the relics of the old Colonial system, which must have prevented the development of a trade between India and foreign countries, were done away with in 1858-59, but as the necessities of Government on account of the Indian mutiny and the consequent increase of public expenditure were very great, the Customs duties were generally raised from 5 to 20 per cent. Since 1860, the reforms of the tariff, with some notable exceptions, have consisted in the reduction and subsequent abolition of the duties on most articles of merchandize. The only articles on which an import duty is now levied are: (1) arms and ammunition and military stores, (2) liquors, (3) salt, and (4) petroleum; and the export list of dutiable articles consists of (1) paddy and rice, and (2) opium. The import duty on arms and ammunition is necessitated by political, and that on liquors by moral, considerations, the object in both cases being to prevent and not to promote their unrestricted use. The import duty on salt is necessitated by the excise duty on the same commodity, and I have already given my reasons for considering this tax to be in the highest degree objectionable. The import duty on petroleum, which is "the light of the poor," is also open to objection, but the tax is a light one, and its collection does not involve any special hardship, or additional machinery, as owing to the explosive nature of the article, its import and storage can, under any circumstances, be allowed only subject to special restrictions imposed for ensuring public safety. Among the dutiable articles of export tariff the duty on opium is, of course, unobjectionable, at all events from the point of view of the anti-opium society whose object is to restrict the consumption of Indian opium in China. Sir Evelyn Baring in his financial statement for 1882-83 made the following remarks in connection with the economic objections to the Government monopoly of the drug and the moral aspects of the traffic in it,

"The economic objections to the manner in which the opium revenue is raised, whether in Bengal or Bombay, may be admitted to be considerable. In the former case, the Government itself engages in private trade—a course which is open to obvious objections. In the second case, a heavy export duty is imposed. In both cases the course adopted interferes with, and restricts the free production of, and the trade in, opium. It cannot be doubted that it would be profitable to any trader to pay for crude opium a much higher sum than is now paid by Government to cultivators of Bengal. If, therefore, supposing such a thing to be possible, no restriction were placed on the cultivation of the poppy, and if at the same time the export duty were taken off, it is certain that an immense stimulus would be given to the production of opium, and that China would be flooded with the Indian drug. Thus in direct proportion to the removal of the economic objections, the moral objections would be intensified in degree. So long, therefore, as the plea of the anti-opium society is confined to the contention that the Indian Government should cease its direct connection with the opium trade, it may be said, with perfect truth, that their policy is based purely on theory. Not only can it effect no practical good, but it almost certainly would do a great deal of harm. It would increase the consumption of opium in China. It would, by cheapening the price of the Indian drug, cause the poorer classes of the population who now smoke native opium, to substitute Indian opium in its place. It would, moreover, encourage the use of opium amongst the native population of India, some of whom, notably the Sikhs, are already addicted to the practice; and it would result in a diminution of the food supply of India, by reason of the cultivation of the poppy over land on which cereals are now grown. If, therefore, the policy is not merely to be theoretical, but is to be productive of some practical good, it must aim not only at the disconnection of the Indian Government with the manufacture and sale of opium, but at the total suppression of the cultivation of the poppy." To us in Madras where the cultivation of the poppy is entirely prohibited, the interest in the opium question arises from the fact that the abolition of the export duty on the drug and the relaxation of the restrictions placed on its transport will have the effect of flooding Southern India with a noxious article and of creating a taste for it among its population, which is not now addicted to the practice of consuming opium. Further the relinquishment of the large revenue derived from the opium duty would also render the imposition of additional objectionable taxation necessary, while what is wanted is that the salt duty should be either removed or reduced. The export duty on rice violates every principle, and is most injurious in practice. It used to be defended on the ground that India enjoyed a monopoly of the production of rice, but this argument, as has been repeatedly pointed out by Mr. O'Conor in his trade reviews, is not, and was never, fairly sustainable. Indian rice is used (1) for distillation, (2) for starch, and (3) for food, and in these various uses rice has to compete with several other products, and India with several other countries. The countries that enter into competition with India are Siam, Cochin-China, Japan, Java, Northern Italy, and the productions which enter into competition with rice are maize, barley, rye, potatoes, Mohwa flower, and even wheat and sugar, many kinds of which are being sold in the English market as cheaply as rice, and even more cheaply. The rice used for food has to compete with European rice (that of Lombardy in particular) and with the rice of the Asiatic countries as well as with Madagascar rice and the rice produced in the Southern States of the Union. Mr. O'Conor points out that whereas 20 years ago we did a large business with China, that trade has almost ceased to exist, Cochin-China as well as Siam having driven our rice out of the market. The export duty on rice, 3 annas a maund, which amounts to 7 per cent. on the value, is a heavy one, and its retention in the tariff, while duties far less injurious in their effects have been abolished, gives occasion for valid complaint.[62]

---

[62] The objections to the export duty on rice were very forcibly stated by the Honorable Mr. Steel in the Legislative Council of India in 1885. He said: "I must protest in the strongest terms against any budget which does not redress this crying evil of our financial system. I refer to the export duty on rice. To my mind it seems inconceivable that such an objectionable impost should be preserved in any civilized country. An export duty on raw produce and that produce the food of the people! With all our study of economics, can we do no better than this? It is as hurtful in practice as vicious in principle. Who would dream of an export duty on wheat? In principle there is no difference. Let us consider its effect. An export duty of 10*s*. per ton is equal to a tax of 5 to 10 per cent. upon its value. It absolutely shuts out the grain from important consumption for distilling and sizing purposes. It reduces the foreign consumption of rice for food when it comes into competition with other articles of food. It thus limits the production of the principal agricultural product of Bengal and Burma at the cost of the agricultural and labouring classes. By checking the production of rice, it diminishes the reserves to which we must look in case of scarcity and famine. I look upon this rice-tax as the very worst possible source of revenue which could be devised, and cannot approve of any budget which does not get rid of it even at the risk of fresh taxation. I have been informed that of the abundant harvest of 1882, much rice was actually allowed to rot on the ground, because not worth the cost of saving, which but for this duty might have been saved and shipped." Sir Evelyn Baring, when examined before the Royal Commission on the value of the precious metals, admitted that it was a fair criticism that the export duty on rice should have gone first, that is, before the cotton duties, because the abolition of the export duties would have been extremely beneficial to India, more especially in view of the difficulty regarding the rate of exchange. He added: "I look upon this as the most important fiscal reform in India, and I always immensely regret that while I was in India, I was not able to crown the free trade edifice by abolishing the export duties."

Stamps. 54. The growth of the stamp revenue will be seen from the following figures:

				Rx. millions.
Average of 10	years ending	1819-20	...	·04
Do.	do.	1829-30	...	·06
Do.	do.	1839-40	...	·04
Do.	do.	1849-50	...	·04
Do.	do.	1859-60	...	·07
Do.	do.	1869-70	...	·29
Do.	do.	1879-80	...	·47
Do.	do.	1889-90	...	·58
In 1889-90	... ...	...	...	·65

This revenue has developed rapidly since 1859 when the Code of Civil Procedure was passed, and the system of levying court fees by means of stamps on civil suits instituted was introduced. Of the sum of 65 lakhs of rupees, which is the revenue now derived from stamps, 40 lakhs are obtained from judicial stamps and 25 lakhs from general stamps. The institution fee levied on civil suits is 7½ per cent. on the value of the property in litigation when it does not exceed Rs. 1,000, and the rate is reduced for higher values, the maximum fee being limited to Rs. 3,000. On criminal complaints a fee of 8 annas is levied. Apart from the abstract question of the propriety of taxing justice, there is little to complain of in regard to the stamp duties on judicial proceedings. The growth of the revenue is entirely due to the increase in litigation consequent on the general progress of the country and the great increase in value of moveable and immoveable property, more especially the latter. The number of civil suits instituted in 1850 was 81,392, the value of the property involved being 55 lakhs. In 1889 the number of suits had increased to 255,006 and the value of the property to 3·75 crores of rupees. The average value of a suit, which in 1850 was Rs. 70, is now Rs. 146. Recently the Government of India had the question of the extent to which the expenditure on the maintenance of Civil Courts was recouped by the stamp duties paid by the litigants, investigated. The result as regards the Madras Presidency was that the receipts were found to be very slightly in excess of the expenditure. If the scheme which appears to be under the contemplation of Government for further improving the position and status of the District Munsiffs and Sub-Judges be carried out, there will be no profit to Government, but on the other hand a slight loss. The court fees levied on suits doubtless bear hard on the poorer litigants to some extent; but the remedy for this, however, is not the abolition of the fees, but the provision of popular and inexpensive tribunals for the settlement of petty litigation.

The duties levied under the general stamp law are not very onerous as the rate for transfers of land[63] on sales and mortgages, which form the bulk of the transactions in regard to which duties have to be paid, is only one per cent. The provisions of the stamp law, which are based mainly on those of the corresponding English Act, are not intelligible in many respects, and this obscurity and the stringency of the provisions made for ensuring compliance with the requirements of the law sometimes work considerable hardship to ignorant and unlettered peasants who cannot afford to obtain competent legal advice when they have documents to execute. Much of this hardship has, however, been since removed by the orders issued by Government making it obligatory on officers of the Registration department to advise persons consulting them as to the stamp duty payable on documents. At present the opinion of the Registration officer is not conclusive and does not relieve the person who has acted upon it from responsibility for insufficient stamping. An alteration of the law relieving from responsibility persons whose documents have been accepted as sufficiently stamped and acted on for registration purposes by an officer of the Registration department will remove all room for complaint. I do not believe that the revenue will be in the least affected by this change of procedure, as the proceedings of the subordinate officers of the Registration department are being very closely scrutinized by the District Registrars in this respect and any laxity observed is promptly taken notice of.

Registration fees.

55. The system of registration and authentication of documents is one of recent introduction and the fees collected are, to a great extent, devoted to the maintenance of the establishments required for the purpose. The present revenue is about 11 lakhs of rupees, of which about 8 lakhs of rupees are annually expended. Further improvements in contemplation will reduce the surplus, out of which have to be met the pensionary liabilities as regards the officers employed in the department The registration fee amounts to ·63 per cent. of the value of the transaction in the case of sales and ·60 per cent. in the case of mortgages and is therefore very moderate. On

[63] In France the value of immoveable property which changes hands by transfer is estimated at 80 millions sterling and that which changes hands by succession 60 millions sterling. The duties charged on both amount to 8 millions or 5·7 per cent. on the value of the property.

transactions of small values, viz., those not exceeding Rs. 100 in value, the fee is comparatively high, but the minimum fee cannot well be fixed lower than 8 annas the present limit, having regard to the cost of stationery and the charges incurred for transcribing the documents in the registers. In this Presidency the convenience of the general public has been consulted by the establishment of registration offices in large numbers; and the time has arrived for making the registration of all documents relating to immoveable property, even where the value is less than Rs. 100, compulsory. Under the present law, documents of this kind, except sales and gifts, are not required to be registered, but it is provided that unregistered transactions as regards such properties, even if prior in point of time, are to have no effect as against registered transactions. This leaves a considerable loop-hole for fraud. If this is remedied, the registration system will be capable of considerable development in directions which will admit of a complete record of transactions connected with landed properties being maintained in a readily accessible form.

Incidence of taxation.

56. In the appendix V.–E. (i) will be found a statement showing the incidence of the taxes levied in 1852-53, 1872-73, and 1889-90 per head of the population. In 1852-53, the incidence was Rs. 1-14-6, in 1872-73 Rs. 2-10-8, and in 1889-90 Rs. 2-14-3 per head, or, in other words, the rate of incidence has increased since 1852 by 51 per cent., while the purchasing power of money has fallen by 60 per cent. There can be no doubt also that of the taxes collected more is spent in promoting the public safety, health and convenience and education in this Presidency than formerly as will be seen from the following figures: Expenditure on irrigation works 45·7 lakhs of rupees in 1889-90 against 9·7 lakhs in 1849-50; buildings and roads not including railways 58 lakhs against 7·2 lakhs; judicial establishments 41·3 lakhs against 23·6 lakhs; police 39·8 lakhs against 9·8 lakhs; education 22·9 lakhs against 1·1 lakh; medical relief 33·3 lakhs against 1·2 lakhs; and the postal service 13·9 lakhs against 4·3 lakhs. The development of the resources of the country by the construction and maintenance of irrigation works, canals, railways and roads has already been noticed. In 1852-53 there were three public schools with an attendance of 448 pupils; in 1889-90, there were 16,226 public institutions with 517,055 pupils and 4,286 private institutions with 83,496 pupils. In 1850 there were 130 post offices con-

trolled by 30 postmasters; at the close of 1889-90 [64] there were 1,691 imperial post offices, 1,412 letter boxes, 985 postmen, and 893 village postmen, besides 68 district post offices and 748 village postmen. The telegraph offices have of course been all established since 1850. The number of letters posted in 1853-54 was 3·66 millions and newspapers 0·29 millions; in 1889-90 the numbers were 48 and 3·8 millions respectively. I have no exact statistics as regards the number of hospitals and dispensaries in 1850; these institutions were maintained only at the head-quarter stations of the several districts and the rural tracts had not the advantage of them. In 1889 there were 393 institutions, in which 2½ millions of persons were treated, the daily average attendance being 17,000.

57. *The standard of living and the general condition of the different classes of the population.*—For purposes of this enquiry, the general population may roughly be divided into four main divisions; viz., I, the agricultural classes, comprising landowners, tenants and agricultural labourers;

---

[64] The following extracts from the petition presented by the Madras Native Association to Parliament in 1852 complaining of the insufficiency and unsatisfactory character of the postal arrangements at that time will be read with interest:

"That your petitioners will now advert to some other subjects requiring redress, such as the Post Office, which, besides being very tardily and slovenly conducted, acts, by the exorbitance of its charges, like a dead weight upon commercial correspondence and the circulation of knowledge; and which weight would be considerably lightened, were the conveyance of official papers, which form three-fourths of the mail conveyed by tappal, placed to the expense of the Government: this would make the Post Office revenue four times the amount now credited, and of course would permit of a corresponding reduction in the cost for carriage; a letter or package which now is taxed at 1*s.* might then reach its destination for the cost of 3*d.*; and still the returns of the department would more than cover the expenditure, even without an increase of correspondence, which, however, would certainly take place to a considerable extent, as a consequence of a diminution in the rates of postage.

"That a necessary auxiliary to the increase of correspondence is a thorough reform in the management of the Post Office departments, beginning at the capital, and extending to the most remote boundaries of the Presidency, which, although containing an area of upwards of 140,000 square miles, has no more than 130 post offices, controlled by 30 Postmasters, a number totally inadequate to the wants of the public, to meet which efficiently your petitioners suggest that there should be at least one or more offices in every taluk, according to its size, so that no inhabited part of the country should be more than 10 miles from a post office. At present, the arrangements for distributing the letters among the native population, even at the stations where the offices are situated, are most defective and imperfect; the agents employed are of an inferior description, who frequently retain the delivery for days, till the parties to whom the letters are addressed submit to some unauthorized demand; while, as regards places at a distance from the post stations, the evil is much greater; enormous delay extending not unfrequently to weeks, is incurred and a heavy charge besides; while after all, the delivery of letters is uncertain, and wrong parties are sometimes permitted to obtain their possession.

"That these combined circumstances, the paucity of offices and their inefficient supervision, the delays, exactions and uncertainties, cause the post office to be greatly less trusted, than it would otherwise be by the Native public, who, in very many instances, have established dawk transit at their own expense, thereby depriving the State of a part of its income, to an extent necessarily unknown, but as necessarily of no trivial importance; and your petitioners, therefore, request that there may be a thorough reform in this department, reaching to the whole of its branches; and that every paper or package passing through it shall be made subject to the same uniform rate of charge."

II, labourers not connected with land; III, the professional, mercantile and other classes owning capital other than land; IV, the artizan classes and small traders. The divisions here referred to have been very roughly made, and, in some instances, they overlap one another. A landlord is often a money-lender or trader, and an artizan frequently owns a piece of land; and a peasant proprietor ekes out his small income from land by non-agricultural labour, *e.g.*, by spinning or working on the roads during the non-agricultural season. The prosperity or the reverse of large sections of the population must also re-act on the condition of other classes, for instance, traders prosper when the agricultural classes thrive and so on. Nevertheless, there is a convenience in considering the condition of different sections of the population separately, and the main divisions above given are sufficiently accurate for the purpose in view. For the most recent information regarding the number of persons falling under each of the main divisions, we must wait till the detailed tables connected with the census taken in 1891 are published. I have given in the appendix V.–F. (a) a table extracted from the census report of 1881, showing the number of persons engaged in the several occupations in 1881 as compared with the number in 1871, but, owing to the dissimilar methods adopted in classifying occupations at the two censuses, the results shown cannot be fully relied on. Statistics as regards persons engaged in the several occupations according to the census of 1891 are not yet available.

The land-owning classes.

58. There is a pretty general impression that in this Presidency land is held in small properties by pauper ryots. There is truth in this, but not to the extent that is often supposed. Out of the 90 millions of acres forming the area of this Presidency, 27½ millions, or between one-third and one-fourth, are held by 849 zemindars; 15 of these zemindars hold 6¾ million acres, or nearly half a million each, paying to Government a peshcush of 2 lakhs of rupees on an average; 128 zemindars hold 9½ millions of acres and pay to Government an average peshcush of 18,100 rupees; and 706 zemindars and mittadars hold 2¾ million acres and pay a peshcush which averages 1,300 rupees. The peshcush of the zemindaris was fixed at two-thirds of the rental in the case of ancient estates, and 90 per cent. of the rental in the case of estates newly created at the time of the permanent settlement. A few large estates, which were held as military jaghirs, pay a quit-rent. The rental of all these estates amounts to 161 lakhs of rupees, while the peshcush amounts

to 50 lakhs, or, in other words, the rental is now more than three times the peshcush, and the zemindars have consequently enormously benefited. Between 1830 and 1850, owing to the low prices of grain which prevailed, several zemindars in the Kistna and Godávari districts were unable to meet their engagements with Government and their estates were consequently sequestered, sold by auction and purchased by Government and incorporated with ryotwar lands. But for this circumstance, nearly the whole of the rich delta of the Godávari and Kistna would, at this day, have consisted of zemindari lands. The estates, which escaped this process, yield a very large revenue to their owners, who, with some exceptions, squander it in litigation and dissipation, and the benefits, which, it was expected, would accrue from the permanent settlement, have not so far been realized. Education, however, has been forcing its way latterly even among zemindars, and it may be hoped that they will, within another generation, utilize their wealth and resources in improving the condition of their tenantry and in aiding the general progress of the country.

The next class of landowners are the inamdars who number 438,659 and hold between them 8·2 millions of acres or 19 acres each on an average. Out of this area, a little more than 3 millions of acres are comprised in entire inam villages and the remainder consists of petty holdings originally held on service tenure in ryotwar villages and recently enfranchised. The position of the latter does not differ materially from that of the ryotwar puttadars. The holders of whole inam villages, who generally belong to the sacerdotal and non-cultivating classes, are in an impoverished condition, their property having got sub-divided into minute portions. The revenue paid by these estates amounts to 16 per cent. of the rental. Originally inam properties were not transferable by sale and were liable to be resumed by Government on failure of direct heirs of the holders. All these properties, with a few insignificant exceptions, have, as already observed, been freed from these restrictions and declared heritable and transferable property, subject to the payment of a light quit-rent imposed by way of compensation to the State for the reversionary right relinquished by it.

The third-class of landowners are those numbering 550, who have redeemed the land-tax by making a lump payment to Government. These properties consist of parcels of land forming house-sites or gardens attached to house-sites.

The fourth-class consists of purchasers of waste lands in hill tracts for the formation of plantations. The area held under this tenure is small, and the land-tax imposed is not liable to enhancement.

The fifth and by far the most numerous class comprises the ryotwar puttadars or peasant proprietors. The total number of estates on this tenure is 2,850,000 and the number of owners including shareholders is 4,600,000. The total area of ryotwar villages is 59·3 million acres, from which 31 million acres must be deducted on account of unculturable waste and lands held on inam tenure and lying interspersed with ryotwar holdings, leaving 28·3 millions which, at present, are considered fit for cultivation. Of this area 21·2 million acres, paying a revenue to Government including cesses of a little more than Rs. 2 per acre, are comprised within ryotwar holdings, the remainder being unoccupied. The marginally-noted statement [65] shows the distribution of the ryot-war puttadars into several grades, with reference to the amount of tax paid by them. The revenue statistics of this Presidency do not show the distribution according to the areas, but the revenue paid is a better index to the status of a ryot than the area of holding, and the area can be roughly deduced from the revenue, by assuming that each acre pays Rs. 2 as land-tax.

Class.	Percentage of ryots to total number.	Percentage of revenue to total revenue.	Average revenue paid by a putta.
			RS.
Ryots paying below Rs. 10 as land tax ...	65·6	17·5	4
Ryots paying land-tax between Rs. 10 and Rs. 30 ...	23·5	27·7	17
Ryots paying land-tax between Rs. 30 and Rs. 50 ...	5·7	14·9	37
Ryots paying land-tax between Rs. 50 and Rs. 100 ...	3·5	16·5	67
Ryots paying land-tax between Rs. 100 and Rs. 250 ...	1·4	13·7	143
Ryots paying land-tax between Rs. 250 and Rs. 500 ...	0·2	5·3	324
Ryots paying land-tax between Rs. 500 and Rs. 1,000.	0·06	2·8	646
Ryots paying land-tax above Rs. 1,000 ...	0·02	1·6	1,542
Total ...	100	100	14

[65] It would be interesting to compare these results with the distribution of land among several grades of proprietors in France which is as follows:

——	Number of proprietors (thousands).	Percentage to total.	Acreage (millions).	Percentages of acreage to total.
Under 5 acres	10,426	74·1	13·0	10·5
5 to 15 acres	2,174	15·1	18·9	15·3
15 to 125 acres	1,352	9·6	48·0	38·9
125 to 500 acres	105	0·7	23·9	19·1
Over 500	18	0·1	20·	16·2

If settlement calculations can be relied on, one acre of ordinary dry land, which is assessed at Rs. 1-12-0,[66] gives an outturn of Rs. 17 taking good and bad seasons together, and 8 acres of such land would give Rs. 136. Deducting Rs. 14, the Government tax, which is a little more than 10 per cent. of the gross outturn, there is left about Rs. 122 for the subsistence of the family of the ryot and for defraying the cultivation expenses, which are estimated at Rs. 5 per acre. Out of this, wages of labour amount to about Rs. 3, and what the ryot will have to expend in cash or grain is Rs. 2 per acre or Rs. 16 for 8 acres, when he cultivates the land himself and does not employ hired labour. There is,[67] therefore, left for subsistence about Rs. 106 or Rs. 9 a month, and this sum will enable a ryot's family to subsist according to the standard of living in force among the ryot population. Probably, the family will make also something by growing vegetables, keeping a cow for raising dairy produce for consumption, &c., all of which will leave a margin above the cost of subsistence, but this may be neglected. Eight acres, therefore, of ordinary dry land, paying Rs. 14, or a proportionately larger area of inferior land, paying the

---

An acre cultivated in France produces much more than an acre here; but the standard of living there is higher in proportion than here. In France, about 90 per cent. of the proprietors have 2½ acres each. Here 90 per cent. pay Rs. 7-8-0 each, which gives an average holding of rather more than 3½ acres. The number of landed estates held directly under Government in this Presidency is about 3·3 millions and the number of holders including shareholders is 5·4 millions (*vide* statement of Varieties of Tenure given in the appendix V.-F. (b). The last number does not include the holdings of ryots in zemindari and inam villages, which may be estimated at about another million. The total number of families having landed property may roughly be taken to be about 6·5 millions out of a total number of families of, say, 7 millions forming the population of the whole Presidency; or in other words, upwards of 90 per cent. of the families in the Presidency have landed properties, however small. There is no information as regards the extent to which ryotwar proprietors possess zemindari and inam lands. In the dry districts many ryotwar proprietors possess inam lands; and allowing for this, the number of families possessing landed property may safely be estimated at, say, 80 per cent. In the South Arcot district, the number of ryotwar proprietors alone is 83 per cent. of the total number of families in the district, taking 5 persons to a family. In European countries the extent to which landed property is diffused among the population will be seen from the following figures, which represent the percentage of the number of possessors of land to the total number of families taking 5 persons to a family: United Kingdom 2·5; France 45; Germany 25; Russia 70; Austria 45; Italy 35; and the United States 40.

[66] I have taken an acre of land of ordinary quality for illustration, and, in some districts, land of very poor quality predominates; but there the area of holding is considerably larger. The average area of holding varies in each district, with reference to the quality of land and the standard of living in force among the agricultural population.

[67] As some objections have been taken to the estimate of income given in this paragraph, the following remarks are made to explain clearly what is meant. The object is to find the distribution of the *agricultural income* among four classes of ryots, viz., 1*st*, those who chiefly live by wages of labour but have also small holdings to supplement their earnings from this source; 2*ndly*, those who can subsist entirely by cultivating their holdings, provided they do all the work themselves and do not employ hired labour; 3*rdly*, those who can subsist partly by cultivating their lands and partly by employing hired labour; and 4*thly*, those who can live entirely on rent. Now it is useless to classify

same amount of tax, may be taken as the area, which a ryot family must cultivate by means of the labour of its members to procure subsistence, and that, where the area of holding is less, the ryot must supplement his earnings from cultivation of his own holdings by labouring for others to procure a subsistence. Similarly, owners of land, who hold 50 acres of ordinary wet and dry land, paying to Government about Rs. 100 as land-tax, will be able just to maintain their families on the rent of the lands obtained by letting them to tenants. These are the minimum limits for obtaining a subsistence, by working in the fields in the one case, and by letting the lands in the other, without other resources. Ryots holding lands, which are between 8 and 50 acres in extent, may be taken as belonging to the class of persons who cannot afford to let their lands to tenants and live solely on the rent, but will be able to hire labour for cultivation, themselves doing a portion of the work of cultivation, or, at all events, superintending its details. Their larger holdings will, of course, enable them to keep a larger number of cattle, and, provided that the families are of the average size, to save some money. Now, bearing these limits of area in mind, it will be seen

---

the ryots under these four heads simply with reference to the average area held by each class, and moreover statistics of areas are not available for this purpose. Lands are of all degrees of fertility, and unirrigated lands differ so enormously in value from irrigated lands that the revenue assessment per acre varies from 4 annas to 12 rupees in the case of single crop and to 18 rupees in the case of double crop lands. It is for this reason that I have taken the assessment as a better test for determining the *status* of each ryot. It is found that about 27·7 per cent. or about one-third of the land revenue is paid by ryots who pay on an average Rs. 17 per head. As the average assessment per acre, taking wet and dry land together, is about Rs. 2, and the average assessment for dry land alone Re. 1 per acre, a man who pays Rs. 17 as revenue can hold 8 acres assessed at Rs. 2 each or 17 acres assessed at Re. 1 each. The income of a ryot of this class including the wages of his own labour and that of his family, I calculated at Rs. 9 per mensem, when he and the members of his family cultivate the holding themselves. It has been objected that according to settlement calculations the income comes out as only Rs. 5 per mensem. The objection overlooks the fact that the settlement calculations are based on certain assumed commutation rates for valuing produce, which are much below the actual market rates, while what is required is the *present* income of the family. Moreover it has been found in connection with the enquiries instituted by the Agricultural department as to the condition of the Pariah population in the Chingleput district that a *padial* or land-less agricultural labourer, and his wife earn more than Rs. 5 per mensem besides obtaining presents on occasions of marriages, feasts, &c., from their employers; and the income of a ryot cultivating 8 acres of land assessed at Rs. 1-12-0 or Rs. 2 each or 17 acres assessed at 1 rupee per acre is surely not over-estimated, but much under-estimated by being put down at Rs. 9 *per mensem* when it is remembered that such income includes the wages of the members of the ryot's family. Similar considerations apply to the other classes of the ryots referred to in the text. The calculations are based on the assumption that the agricultural income is proportional to the revenue assessment which is true only as a very rough approximation; and this is sufficient for my purpose which is to indicate the manner in which the question should be regarded from the point of view of general distribution of agricultural income and not to decide the exact percentage of income of each class. It has been contended that the great majority of the agriculturists have very small holdings. This is true, but it is the case all the world over in countries where peasant properties prevail; and it must be remembered that where large farms prevail, the vast majority of the agricultural population owns *no* land whatever.

that out of the total revenue of ryotwar holdings, 17·5 per cent., or, say, roughly, one-fifth, is contributed by agricultural labourers who must eke out a living by working for others, the small extent of land held by them being in the nature of agricultural allotments, the produce of which merely goes to supplement their earnings by labour. Another 27·7 per cent., or, roughly, one-third, is contributed by peasant proprietors who cannot afford to employ hired labour, except during the time of harvest. Another 31·4 per cent., or about one-third, is contributed by proprietors who must farm their own lands, but who can employ hired labour for carrying on some or all the manual work connected with the farm. The remainder is paid by the class who can afford to, but need not, let their lands, and subsist, not certainly in plenty, but, as I have already stated, in accordance with the standard of living usual among their class in this country. If this class were sufficiently educated, and cultivated the holdings without sub-letting them, they would be able to adopt, not indeed very expensive improvements, but such as those which small proprietors in European countries might be expected to undertake.

The number of ryots in zemindaris may be estimated at about a million, but no particulars as regards the quantity of land held are available. It may, however, be presumed that the distribution among the several classes of zemindari ryots is much the same as with Government ryots with the reservation that as the incidence of the land assessment, whether paid in money or in kind, is higher in zemindari tracts than in Government taluks, the average extent of land to be cultivated for subsistence must be larger and the number of ryots smaller in the former case than in the latter. In countries in which lands are held by a small number of proprietors there is a very large section of the population dependent solely on daily labour for subsistence, while in countries where small properties predominate the capitalist classes capable of initiating and carrying out agricultural improvements do not exist; but the labouring classes have, for the most part, the income derived from a small piece of land to supplement their earnings from daily labour. In this Presidency, it will be seen from the facts stated above that while the bulk of the area is held in small properties averaging 8 acres in extent, there are nearly 1,000 landed proprietors, some of them with princely incomes. The reason for the absence of agricultural enterprise must, therefore, be sought not so much in the predominance of peasant properties as in the absence of conditions which make high farming a necessity.

59. It is extremely difficult to obtain reliable information regarding the wages of agricultural labour or to put it in a shape which will admit of the condition of the labourers in different parts of the country being compared or of a decisive opinion being formed as to the extent to which their position has improved in recent years. Wages are generally stated to be paid in grain and the rates of wages are believed[68] not to have varied materially since the beginning of the century. This view of the matter, however, entirely overlooks the fact that a considerable portion of the wages has always been disbursed in the shape of perquisites or other advantages such as huts and small allotments of land for cultivation free of rent, &c., and these additional allowances have been adjusted from time to time with reference to the demand for labour, the prices of food-grains, the efficiency of the labourer, the constancy of employment and opportunities afforded to the labourer as well as those dependent on him for making extra gains, &c. For the old years the only systematic enquiries on this subject were those of Dr. Buchanan made in 1800. It is really surprising that he should have been able, within the short period of a few months, to collect and collate the large amount of minute information regarding the agricultural condition of the several districts which is contained in the two volumes, entitled, *Journey through Mysore, Canara, and Malabar.* Generally accurate as the information is, it was obtained chiefly from the landholders who would naturally be anxious to exaggerate the expenses of cultivation, and the rates of wages given have, therefore, to be somewhat discounted on this account. In fact, Buchanan himself was fully aware of this and has mentioned several instances in which he had reason to suspect

Wages of agricultural labourers.

---

[68] The following instances of enhancement of grain wages have been reported by the Sub-Registrar of Karúr. In 1829 at *Selappallayaputtur*, *Trichinopoly* district, the wages of a reaper varied between 2½ and 3 Tanjore small padis. Now 6 small padis are paid, and if the crop has to be reaped and brought from a distance to the threshing ground, 8 padis. At *Merathur*, *Tanjore* district, in 1832 and 1833, the daily wages paid to a labourer was 4 small measures. Now 5 small measures are given. At *Sanaparathi*, *Coimbatore* district, the wages of a labourer, which was 4 small measures formerly, has increased to 6. The above particulars have been obtained from the accounts kept by landholders. In reply to enquiries made by the Board of Revenue recently the following Collectors have reported a rise in grain wages in recent years. *Godávari*, an increase of *one-eighth* ; *Kistna*, an increase the extent of which is not ascertainable ; *Kurnool*, a tendency to rise ; *Madura*, in *Periyakulam* and *Tirumangalam* taluks, a rise of 25 and 20 per cent. respectively ; and *Tinnevelly*, a rise in the northern part.

that the information furnished to him was exaggerated. Moreover, large portions of the country had been almost entirely depopulated by the Mysore wars, shortly before Buchanan visited the tracts which he has described, and consequently, there was great scarcity of labour in these places at the time. Further, agricultural labourers had to pay in those days the moturpha tax, which was practically levied from their masters. For later years we have absolutely no information beyond vague statements in the settlement reports which are worse than useless, no systematic enquiry having ever been made on the subject ; and it is a matter for regret that the services of the settlement-officers who have for years been working in the rural tracts and who have had exceptionally favorable opportunities for enquiries of this kind should not have been utilized for the purpose of collecting information regarding matters connected with agricultural economy. The Board of Revenue some time ago, at the instance of Government, called for reports from Collectors regarding agricultural wages in considerable detail; the results have not yet been published, but I have had the advantage of reading the reports received. I have also obtained some information from the officers of the Registration department regarding the wages now prevailing in some of the places visited by Buchanan in 1800. The following imperfect account is based on the information obtained from the sources above indicated :

Agricultural labourers are of all grades from the casual daily labourer to the metayer tenant who divides the produce of the land he cultivates with the landlord in defined proportions. This class of labourers, however, may be divided into three main divisions, viz., *first*, farm-servants more or less permanently employed and remunerated by payments in money or grain; *secondly*, casual labourers employed on agricultural work at the time of the harvest or as occasion arises and not permanently attached to the farm ; and, *thirdly*, labourers on the varum or sharing system.

Of the permanent farm-servants, those who live in the master's house and partake of the meals cooked for him are the most efficient and the best remunerated. They are, comparatively speaking, generally well off, being well fed and clothed and receiving, at the end of the year, as much as their feeding and clothing would cost or a little more. The servants employed are of the same or corresponding castes as the masters and sometimes their relations. It is stated in a report on cotton cultivation in the Tinnevelly district published by the Agricultural department that "It is noteworthy that labourers receiving part of their wages in the shape of food do more earnest and willing work than labourers who get their wages in cash or kind. The Brahmins and the Pillays are not so successful in farming, because they, unlike the Naickmars and Reddis, find it inconvenient to feed their servants at home. The latter recognizing the truth of the adage 'he who feeds well, works well' allow their servants to consume as much as they want, and make no difference between themselves and their servants as regards the service of meals." The remuneration of a ploughman is Rs. 30 in addition to his food which, at the high prices of food grains prevailing in the Tinnevelly district, may be valued at Rs. 30. In Bellary the remuneration of a farm-servant varies from Rs. 24 to Rs. 40 per annum, or Rs. 10 to Rs. 20 *plus* the feeding and clothing, estimated to cost Rs. 25. The food given amounts to 1½ seers or more than 3 lb. of cholum a day (a high rate) and condiments worth Rs. 3 a year. The clothing consists of cloths, a cumbli, a turban, a pair of drawers and a pair of slippers worth in all Rs. 4. These servants are not solely attached to the farm, but are expected to look after all kinds of household work. They are sometimes allowed by their employers, for marriage purposes, &c., loans ranging from Rs. 50 to Rs. 100, which are liquidated by deductions from the salary. In the Anantapur district (Gooty division), the servant is given food and cloths, the food comprising three meals a day, together with betel and tobacco, and an annual sum, ranging from Rs. 5 to Rs. 16, according to the nature and urgency of the work, character of the season and the capabilities of the labourer. Single men are preferred, and, if married, their wives are temporarily employed. In some cases, instead of an annual cash payment, a daily allowance of 1 seer (2 lb.) of grain is made in addition to food and clothing. In the Coimbatore district, this class of servants is not employed to any great extent. The servant is always an unmarried man and is provided with food stated to cost between Rs. 15 and Rs. 30, and with sandals, cloths, and occasionally blankets, costing Rs. 2. At the end of the year, he receives a present in money of from Re. 1 to Rs. 3. In Salem, unmarried labourers, if Sudras, are fed by the ryot and are given a cloth valued at 1 rupee, a blanket worth 14 annas, and Rs. 4 or Rs. 5 at the end of the year in cash. They are allowed loans, ranging from Rs. 20 to Rs. 50, without interest, at the commencement of service, or at the time of marriage. In the Nellore district, labourers, employed on the cultivation of garden land, are fed and clothed and receive annually from Rs. 6 to Rs. 24, the food consisting of three meals a day and betel and tobacco. In Vizagapatam, farm-servants are not given meals, except in some places in the northern taluks, where the custom obtains of giving them two or three meals a day: where two meals are given, the annual wages are cut down by one-third, and if three meals are given by one-half. In the first case one meal consisting of a quarter of a seer of boiled rice and cunji is given in the morning at about 8 or 9 o'clock, and the second meal consisting of a quarter of a seer (½ lb.) of ragi or other flour boiled, at about 4 P.M. In the other case, the servant is fed in the morning, noon and evening, the meals given being the same as those of a member of the employer's family. In Cuddapah the servant gets one local seer of food daily (1·7 Madras seers) worth Rs. 14 annually, clothes worth Rs. 4-8-0 and cash Rs. 3. Higher money wages are paid if the ryot is a woman who cannot herself superintend the cultivation. In a few cases, presents amounting to Rs. 4 or Rs. 5 are allowed on occasions of marriages, &c.; sometimes the servant is allowed loans, without interest, amounting to Rs. 50 or Rs. 60. But these do not form part of the service contract. If the servant has a child above five and below twelve years of age, the latter is given wages from Rs. 3 to Rs. 4-8-0 with three meals a day and clothes. No deduction is made in the wages for the temporary absence of labourers on account of illness and other unavoidable reasons. In North Arcot, servants in the Chittoor taluk are given three meals estimated to cost Rs. 36 a year, Rs. 6 in cash and cloth worth 1 rupee. Their presents and perquisites may amount to about Rs. 5 or Rs. 6. The examples given above will sufficiently show how difficult it is, amidst the wide variety of form, which the remuneration assumes in different parts of the country, to state in money values the earnings of the labourers. The following general deductions may, however, I think, be drawn from the facts stated; viz., (1) permanent servants are employed only by the well-to-do ryots and, when they are fed at the master's house, get as much food as they can possibly take; (2) the quantity of food is variously given from 3 lb. in Bellary to 1½ lb. in Vizagapatam, and 2 lb. of dry grain per diem and 1½ lb. of rice may, on an average, be taken as ample allowance for an adult doing full work; (3) the value of the meal is estimated at from Rs. 14 to Rs. 36, per annum, the differences being due to the variation in the prices of grain in the several districts and to the money value of the grain consumed being calculated with reference to the average prices ruling at the cusba stations instead of the prices ruling in the rural tracts. The general average money value of the feeding charges of an adult labourer may be taken for the Presidency at Rs. 20 per annum; and (4) the remuneration of a permanent farm-servant may, on an average, be taken as twice the cost of his feeding and clothing expenses. The practice in the northern parts of the Vizagapatam district, where, in the case of permanent servants fed in the master's house, the remuneration is cut down to one-half, clearly shows this.

The next class of agricultural labourers consists of those who are engaged by the month or for the cultivation season. In Coimbatore, labourers are employed by the month by ryots who have dry or garden land to cultivate. These are called padials and receive from 16 to 20 bullahs of grain, if men, and 12 to 15, if boys, the money value being Rs. 2 to Rs. 2-8-0, in the case of a man, and from 10 annas to Rs. 1-8-0 in the case of a boy. The padial is bound to give the whole of his time to his master. The grain given is cumbu, ragi or samai. A bullah is equal to two Madras measures and a man's ration is ½ to ¾ Madras measure or 1½ to 2¼ lb. If a ryot has a large farm the head padial is sometimes paid 25 bullahs—value Rs. 3. At the end of the term of hiring the padial receives Rs. 2 or two cloths. The daily wages of the labourer are thus between two and two-and-half times the daily ration. The perquisites of a padial consist of a basketful of corn at the time of cutting, which may consist of 8 bullahs of grain valued at 1 rupee and a portion of any other crops, the value amounting in all to Rs. 2. The wife of a padial, if she works at the picking of cotton or harvesting of a crop, gets a little more than ordinary women, who get one-eighth of the pickings of cotton or a bullah of grain equivalent to from 2 annas to 2½ annas. In Salem main division, the monthly wages of an adult labourer vary from 18 to 24 vullums (each vullum measuring 3½ seers of 80 tolas each) with a cash payment varying from Rs. 2½ to Rs. 3 at the end of the year. In the Sub-division, the yearly wages vary between 3 and 4 kandagams (187 seers of 80 tolas per kandagam) and Rs. 4 or 5 at the end of the year. In the Head Assistant's division, 112 seers of 80 tolas of cumbu or varagu together with 5 annas per mensem are given. Taking the quantity of grain required for each adult at 2 lb., the grain wages are between two and two-and-half times an adult's ration in the first case, and between three and four times in the second and third cases. In the Nellore district, Gúdúr taluk, labourers are paid 2½ tooms of paddy per month or 4⅔ seers or 6¾ lb. per day, 2 tooms in addition to one meal a day, or $\frac{1}{2}$ toom of cumbu or ragi or jonna or 1 toom of paddy per month in addition to two meals a day. The labourers are further allowed straw for fodder and for roofing purposes, some land free of rent for cultivation, loans without interest, presents in grain or money on festive occasions, and advance of pay on occasions of marriage or death in addition to other gratuitous help. In the Kávali taluk, Nellore district, farm-servants are paid $2\frac{5}{8}$ seers of paddy or $1\frac{3}{4}$ seers of ragi or cholum daily. Such labourers get—besides gleanings of the threshing ground, which are estimated to amount to 15 tooms a year, worth Rs. 24-6-0 to Rs. 30 according as the grain is paddy or ragi and cholam, one cumbli worth Rs. 1-8-0, and a pair of slippers. They also take, with the permission of their masters, some bundles of hay or straw. The total income is estimated as high as Rs. 60 per annum. In Cuddapah, the yearly wages amount to 336 Madras measures, or nearly twice the daily ration.

The wages, above referred to, relate mostly to cases in which the servants employed are of the Sudra castes. Where the degraded castes, such as Pariars and Pullers, are employed, especially in wet cultivation, the wages are considerably lower. These castes were, till 1843, hereditary slaves sold with the land or mortgaged. In Malabar, according to Buchanan, Churmars were, in 1800, the absolute property of their masters and could be employed on any work the masters pleased, the only restriction being that a husband and wife could not be sold separately. Buchanan adds, "The master is considered as bound to give the slave a certain allowance of provisions; a man or woman, while capable of labour, receives 2 edangallies (equivalent to $1\frac{1}{2}$ seers of 80 tolas) of rice in the husk weekly, or two-seventh of the allowance, which I consider as reasonable for persons of all ages included. Children and old persons past labour get one-half only of this pittance, and no allowance is made whatever for infants. This would be totally inadequate to support them; but the slaves on each estate get one twenty-first part of the gross produce in order to encourage them to care and industry. A male slave annually gets 7 cubits of cloth and a woman 14 cubits. They erect for themselves huts that are little better than large baskets." Both Messrs. Buchanan and Warden, the Collector of the district, in the beginning of the century, remark that, owing to ill-treatment and insufficient nourishment for generations, the Churmars have become very diminutive in size. Churmars are no longer slaves, but are treated like other ordinary coolies. They receive 2 seers of 80 tolas of paddy *daily* when they work for their masters, but when there is no work on the farms they are not maintained by the masters and they are allowed to seek work elsewhere. During the time of harvest fixed wages cease and the reapers —men and women—are paid a share of the grain, generally one-tenth; in the southern part of the district it is stated that as much as one-sixth is paid. The amount earned varies according to the strength of the labourers, and is stated not to exceed one or two rupees. They are allowed, however, presents on special occasions and receive 2 parahs (7⅔ seers) of paddy yearly, if they continue in the service of the masters. On occasions of marriages and deaths, small presents are made, and, during confinement of women, a small quantity of oil and paddy, in addition to a daily subsistence allowance for a period of 28 days, is granted. Their position, as regards wages for subsistence, has, therefore, distinctly improved, though they cannot be said to have, to an appreciable extent, emerged from the position of social degradation which they have occupied for ages. In South Canara, farm-servants (who were originally slaves), if men, get from 1 to 2 seers of clean rice, (80 tolas each) with condiments, the average rate being 1½ seer with condiments; and women and children get less; the labourers are generally given a midday meal by the masters. In addition to the daily wages, they receive annual perquisites consisting of cloths and blankets, presents of rice and other eatables at important festivals and for marriage purposes, and they are given an allotment of rent free land from ⅛ to ⅓ acre in extent, except on the coast of the Mangalore taluk. In the Malayalam portion of the district, the allowances to the farm-labourers do not appear to be so liberal, but, on the whole, it seems to be clear that the farm-servants are in good seasons well off in the sense that their food is not insufficient for subsistence. Mr. Sturrock, who made careful enquiries on the subject, estimates the annual income of a labourer's family at Rs. 107 and the expenditure at Rs. 76, the greater portion of the balance being expended in toddy. Buchanan, writing in 1801, stated that a male slave was allowed daily 1½ hanies (2 seers) of rice or three-fourths of the allowance for a hired servant. With reference to this statement, Mr. Sturrock observes, "These rates correspond rather with my maximum rates than with those I have adopted as typical; but Dr. Buchanan seems to have got his information from the masters who would naturally mention the highest rates allowed. In the preceding paragraph, he remarks that the amount said to be paid in wages for transplanting rice seems to be exaggerated. With regard to hired servants, whose wages are said to be higher than those of the slaves, Dr. Buchanan remarks, these wages are very high and may enable the hired servants to keep the family in the greatest abundance." In Tanjore the pannial, who is the descendant of the old hereditary slave, was paid, according to the account given by Mr. Ramaiyangar in 1872 (see appendix IV.–F), one Madras measure of paddy per diem. The present rate, from recent reports, appears to be 1½ Madras measures per diem and in the Kumbakónam taluk it is even 1¾ Madras measures. Mr. Pennington, in 1885, estimated the whole earnings of a pannial at about 30 to 36 kalams of paddy per annum, worth as many rupees; and stated that the earnings of the whole family did not exceed Rs. 50, of which Rs. 7-8-0 must be spent on drink or the enormous toddy revenue of the Tanjore district (6½ lakhs of rupees) could not be accounted for. In many of the taluks of the district, they are allowed 40 gulis (·132 acre) for house-site and 60 gulis (·198 acre) more, as yermanium or plough allotment, for cultivation, the produce of which they enjoy rent free. Mr. Pennington adds, "The comparative poverty of the pannial class is attributed to their fondness for drink and a want of prudence and forethought in storing up paddy to provide against a rainy day. They are in fact the most barbarous part of the community, and live precisely like animals, being to all intents and purposes serfs attached to the soil and generally of the Pariah caste, few being Sudras." These remarks are, to a great extent, true, though their condition, so far as mere physical subsistence is concerned, has somewhat improved in recent years. Mr. Clerk, who has made special inquiries into the condition of this class of labourers, writes, "In former times, the pannials were the slaves of the mirasidars, on whom they depended solely for livelihood. They were paid then as now in paddy and, during the cultivation season, were well fed, but they suffered considerably in the off-season from insufficiency of food. Their position has greatly improved during the last forty years, and, at the present time, they are as independent of the mirasidars as the porakudis. It is beyond doubt that wages have considerably risen during recent years. For transplanting and harvesting, wages are double what they were twenty years ago, and there has been an increase in the price paid for cooly labour of every description. . . . Many causes have tended to improve the condition of both tenants and labourers within the last forty years, but the facilities placed within their reach for emigrating have done more for them than anything else. Both classes emigrate, though chiefly the labourers, and all return with considerable savings, by means of which the porakudi becomes a landholder and the labourer sets up as a tenant. The returns show that, during the last ten years, 118,000 emigrants embarked from Negapatam for the Straits Settlements, the average number per annum during the last six years being 15,000. In addition to this, the poorer classes in the south of the district emigrate in large numbers to Ceylon, but no statistics are available to show their approximate number. As proof, however, of considerable savings remitted by emigrants from this part of the district, I am informed that the money order transactions at the Post Office at Arantángi, Patukóta taluk, are larger than at the head office in Tanjore." In the South Arcot and Chingleput districts, pannials do not seem to be as well off as in Tanjore. In the Chingleput district, from Mr. Place's report, written in 1799, it appears that the earnings of a pannial and his wife averaged about 2½ kalams of paddy or 105 pucka seers of 80 tolas. Now their earnings amount to 45 measures or 67½ pucka seers, and very little is given in the shape of perquisites or extra allowances. This is rather surprising as one would have expected that the vicinity of the town of Madras and the demand for labour there would have forced up wages. Further inquiries [69] might show that the present rate of wages assumed is under-estimated. In Tinnevelly, Mr. Brandt, the Sub-Collector, in 1872, estimated the income of a Pullan and his wife at Rs. 42 per annum and inferred from this that, for a considerable part of the year, they could not take a full meal at all. Mr. Puckle, the Collector, who had much greater experience of the district was, however, of opinion that the position of the pullars and free labourers of the district was remarkably good; they were better fed and clothed than similar classes in any of the districts south of Madras, and their houses, as a rule, were superior to, and very different from, the squalid huts that were to be found elsewhere.

---

[69] The Madras Board of Revenue has, since the above was written, instituted, in connection with the condition of the Pariahs in the Chingleput district, enquiries into the wages paid to a Pariah agricultural labourer, and found that, including the harvest perquisites, his average wages per mensem amounted to 8 merkals or 64 Madras measures, or 96 pucka seers of paddy, against 105 seers in 1800; but the Board state that from the latter figure a small deduction has to be made on account of the fees of artificers, which were included in the original calculations. On this account the Board made a deduction of 10 Madras merkals, and stated that the allowance in 1800 amounted to 95 merkals a year, or about the quantity now earned. It further appears that the 8 Madras merkals above referred to are the lowest wages now paid, and that it is difficult to get the labourers to accept them; and that, owing to dearness of labour, the mirasidars are compelled to be liberal in the matter of perquisites. The wages of the labourer and his wife are estimated at more than Rs. 5 per mensem, exclusive of presents on occasions of marriages, feasts, &c.

Casual labourers, who are employed as occasion arises, are paid at higher rates than regular farm-servants, and, notwithstanding the irregularity of employment, they appear to be better off than the pannial class. In Coimbatore, according to Mr. Nicholson, casual wages are from 1 to 3 measures daily (3 to 9 lb.), varying with reference to season and demand—quite high wages being paid at harvest. Women find work for many months in the year on wet lands, from the collection of green manure to the work of harvest. There is less to be done by them in gardens and still less on dry lands except at harvest, especially that of cotton, the cost of picking which is estimated at from one-twelfth to one-eighth of the crop. Since the last famine, there has been a decided increase in the money price of work in this district; the labouring class was largely affected by the famine and consequently there is competition for labour especially in the towns where labourers are hard to get. Mr. Nicholson states that Wo Iders have even struck work on being refused the rate of 12 cubic yards of easy earth-work, 20 being a nominal rate. From 2 to 2½ annas per day for ordinary unskilled male labourers and 1½ to 2 annas to females is about the average. Hence a man and his wife can earn at least 3½ annas per day or the equivalent of 12 to 15 lb. of dry grain in husk or 8 to 10 lb. without husk. When paid in grain, the wages would amount to this quantity. For well-digging, it is usual to pay the labourers chiefly in grain, with an occasional sheep for the Wodders, money being seldom paid by the regular ryot. Mr. Benson says of Kurnool, that the supply of labour is usually adequate to all rural demands, but of late years the construction of the Bellary-Kistna Railway has largely drawn on the supply and forced up rates near the places through which it runs. Of Bellary, Mr. Sabapathy Mudaliar (see appendix V.-F. (1 5)) says: "This year (1890) the cotton and cholum crops having been exceptionally favourable and cotton crops having ripened simultaneously in almost every place, the labouring classes were benefited thereby to an enormous extent. The wages which were paid were three times as high as those ordinarily paid before the current year." He adds that the increase in the number of cotton presses has been the cause of giving technical knowledge to numbers of male and female labourers who are now able to earn exceptionally high wages, *i.e.*, Rs. 10 to Rs. 15 per mensem for a man and Rs. 6 to Rs. 10 for a woman, who do work on the piece-work system. The same remark applies more or less to the Tinnevelly district also. In Tanjore temporary coolies are employed by the landholders whenever they have more work than can be done by their own servants, especially in times of reaping, digging and levelling the fields. They are mostly employed by contractors in road works and their daily wages are much higher than those of Pannials—often double.

Among agricultural labourers, the highest class consists of those who cultivate lands on the sharing system. These labourers must be men of some means; they must ordinarily have at least ploughing cattle. The sharing system does not prevail to any great extent in the dry districts, for instance, in Anantapur. In the few places of this district in which it prevails, the cultivator gets half the produce for mere labour and when he contributes cattle, a still larger share. In Bellary, the varum or cultivator's share is one-half ordinarily and two-thirds where cultivation is expensive, as when water has to be baled or land overgrown with long grass has to be broken up. The cultivation expenses are borne by the tenant and the landowner pays the assessment. In both cases village servants' fees and the harvesting expenses are deducted from the produce before division. If the landowner contributes half the seed, he takes half the straw. In the Salem district the conditions are very similar. In some cases where labour is not easily procurable, the produce is equally divided after the cultivation expenses are deducted. The cultivator also pays sometimes half the assessment, getting three-fourths, or three-fifths of the produce, the landlord paying the full assessment. Sometimes, again, the arrangement is that the cultivator should take one-fourth or one-fifth of the net produce *plus* a fixed quantity of grain. In the case of irrigation by baling, the landlord's and cultivator's shares are two-fifths and three-fifths, respectively; the cost of seed and harvesting is shared equally. In the Cuddapah sub-division and in the Kanigiri taluk of the Nellore district, labourers who do not contribute anything for cultivation expenses are given, what is called, half a "bullock's share," that is, if the ryot has four bullocks, he employs four servants and gives each servant one-eighth share of the produce. The "pungal" system in the Polláchi taluk of the Coimbatore district is somewhat similar. Buchanan describes the system as it existed in 1800 as follows. The pungals go to a rich farmer and for a share of the crop undertake to cultivate his lands. The farmer lends the cattle, implements, seed and money or grain that may be required for the subsistence of the *pungals*. He also gives each family a house. He takes no share in the labour which is all performed by the pungals and their wives and children; but he pays the rent out of his share on the division of the crop which takes place when it is ripe. If a ryot employs six pungals to cultivate his land, the produce is divided into 15 portions which are distributed as follows: to the ryot for Government assessment, seed, &c., 6; to the ryot for profit 1; to the ryot for interest on money advanced 2; to the pungals 6; total 15. Out of their share, the pungals must repay the ryot the money advanced for their subsistence. The system as now practised is stated to be the following: If the ryot employs a pungal to cultivate his fields, it is only when the latter is able to contribute plough-bullocks to some extent. The produce is divided into two portions, of which one-half goes to the ryot as *Nilavaram.* The remaining half is divided between the ryot and the pungal according to the number of plough-bullocks contributed by each.

In Tanjore, the varum or porakudi system is extensively prevalent. From Mr. Wallace's report, written in 1805, it appears that in this district in 1,012 villages lands were cultivated directly by the mirasidars, in 1898, lands were cultivated on the sharing system and in the remaining 1,923 villages the cultivation was conducted under both systems. The varum or share given to the porakudi varied from 22 to 30 per cent. of the gross produce. Under the Mahratta Government, which took 60 per cent. of the gross produce leaving only 40 per cent. to be divided between the mirasidar and the porakudi, the share of the latter was as low as 15 per cent. The porakudi varum now varies between 20 and 50 per cent., the lower rates prevailing in the delta taluks where crop is abundant and more or less assured, and the higher rates in the upland taluks where the crop is precarious. There can be no doubt that the position of the porakudis has very considerably improved, several of them having become landholders. Mr. Clerk observes "they are beginning to realize the fact that they are masters of the situation and can dictate their own terms to the mirasidars. Of late years some of the porakudis have refused to cultivate on the varum system, which gives to the mirasidar 75 per cent. of the gross produce and have demanded a five or ten years' lease at a fixed money rent. These terms have been conceded by the mirasidars in favour of the tenants inasmuch as the rents have been fixed on a basis of something like 65 per cent. of the gross produce instead of 75." The records of the Registration Department show that grain and money leases are rapidly superseding cultivation on the sharing system, and this proves that the porakudis are becoming substantial farmers able to carry on cultivation without much help from the landlords and to pay the stipulated rent in all seasons. They are also enabled to enjoy the fruits of additional labour bestowed on the cultivation of the lands without having to share them with the landlords as under the porakudi system. The same improvement, it will be seen from the note of the District Registrar of Tinnevelly on the agricultural classes, printed in the appendix, V.–F. (l 6), is observable in the condition of the corresponding cultivating class in that district also, many of whom have saved money and bought landed properties; the general result being that, while the rent receiving class is somewhat going down, the cultivating class is rising gradually in importance. In the Coimbatore district, where the sharing system obtains to a considerable extent, the share of the landlord on dry lands is now one-half the gross produce instead of as in 1839 one-half of the net produce after deducting the expenses of cultivation. In the South Canara and Malabar districts, the varum system does not obtain, lands being leased out to tenants on fixed money and produce rents.

II. Labourers, other than agricultural.

60. Labourers, other than agricultural, are chiefly employed in towns, and their condition has distinctly improved. The rates of wages per diem for unskilled labour, according to the official returns, vary from 1 anna 9 pies in Vizagapatam to 7 annas 4 pies in Kurnool. The average rate in towns for the whole Presidency is 3 annas 9 pies, while that in rural tracts is 2 annas 9 pies. The rate for Madras town is, however, only 4 annas, and the high rate in Kurnool is evidently due to the recent opening of the Bellary-Kistna railway. Employment is fairly constant and an unskilled labourer in towns may be taken on an average to earn 3 annas per diem throughout the year, while the labourer in rural tracts earns about 2 annas. The establishment of mills, the extension of railways, the increase of trade and the large expenditure, by Government on roads and irrigation works, and by private individuals on buildings, have forced up wages both in inland and sea-port towns, as labour is much in demand at these places. Among the higher classes, it is a well-known fact that domestic servants, especially cooks and water-carriers, are hard to get, and their wages, in addition to food, have increased to three times of what they were thirty or forty years ago.

61. In the preceding paragraphs I have endeavoured to give such particulars as I have been able to obtain regarding the wages of agricultural and other labour.[70] It would, of course, be hopeless to attempt to state in exact numerical proportions the improvement in wages for the reasons already explained. Money values are fallacious guides in this respect, and it is impossible to assign money values to perquisites which are allowed on special and not regularly recurring occasions, and are regulated by customary usages and the good understanding between the employers and the employed, rather than by contract. If it is necessary to sum up, in a single statement, the remuneration that is allowed in such a wide variety of forms, I should say that 2 annas

In what directions the labouring classes have improved.

---

[70] Since the memorandum was written, above 7,000 service agreements, both for agricultural and non-agricultural labour, registered in the several registration offices of the Presidency, were examined and enquiries made as to the changes which have occurred in grain-wages. It was found that there has been nowhere any reduction in the customary wages paid for agricultural labour. The labourers generally receive advances from their employers varying from Rs. 10 to upwards of Rs. 100, and agree to serve for some definite period or till the loan is re-paid. No interest is charged, except in special cases, on the loans. The loans are to be liquidated either by means of small deductions from the wages, or at the end of the period of service by a lump payment.

For agricultural labour, the wages are given in money, in kind, or in food and clothing with a small cash payment at the end of the year. The money payment ranges from Rs. 18 to Rs. 60 a year. The average may be taken at from Rs. 30 to Rs. 36. The quantity paid in grain varies from 20 to 60 Madras measures a month, according to the age and efficiency of the labourer, a midday meal being generally provided by the employer; the average quantity may be taken at about 36 or 37 Madras measures a month, or 1¼ Madras measures a day. When food is given the labourers are paid from Rs. 3 to Rs. 30 at the end of the year.

For non-agricultural labour, the wages of goldsmiths, blacksmiths and carpenters vary from Rs. 4 to Rs. 30 a month.

For tanning, which is a large industry in this Presidency, and in which, from religious scruples, none but the Pariahs are engaged, the wages are nowhere less than Rs. 5 per mensem. If paid daily the wages are 3¾ annas. The maximum wages are Rs. 10 a month.

Brahmin cooks receive from Rs. 4 to 7 a month in addition to food.

Shop-boys are paid from Rs. 4 to Rs. 15 a month.

The tendency everywhere appears to be for an increase in grain wages, and the complaints often made are that it is difficult to obtain labourers for the due customary rates of wages or to make them work with zeal or full time as in the old days for these wages. There is, of course, great reluctance on the part of the employers to alter the customary rates; but perquisites and presents and the amounts of loans given without interest are generally increased. The grain wages given for casual labourer, *e.g.*, additional labour employed during harvest, appear to have generally increased, and in some cases doubled. The tendency towards increase in the rates of daily grain-wages allowed to field hands permanently employed is less marked, though there are a number of instances in which there has been an increase even as regards these. This shows that custom is gradually giving way to competition, and that the tendency on the whole is towards an increase in the earnings of labourers as estimated in food-grains.

Since the memorandum was written, H. Subbaraya Aiyar, Esq., Deputy Collector, Coimbatore district, has made personal enquiries into the condition of the labouring classes in parts of the Coimbatore district, and the conclusion he has arrived at is, that their condition "is not what it was thirty or forty years ago, but has materially improved in several respects. . . . . Those who have once formed the landless class, the petty traders, the artizans and the weavers, who have chosen to work in the fields and elsewhere, have now acquired landed property to some extent. . . . . . ." *Vide* appendix V.-F. (1 8).

per diem all through the year, or a little more than twice the value of his daily ration in grain, may be taken as the average wages of an adult labourer. Servants of the degraded castes, such as Pariahs and Pallars, probably get 25 per cent. less, as they are not allowed to enter the houses of the ryots and attend to cattle and other household work, while other servants, to whom the objection does not apply, probably get 25 per cent. more. Taking the labouring classes as a whole, the improvement in their condition in recent years is manifested, not in any clearly visible rise in the standard of living of the lowest grades or in the comforts that they enjoy, but in the fact of a considerable proportion of the labourers, who, under the old conditions, would have remained in the lowest grade, having been drafted into the next higher grade, while a portion of the latter has gone into the grade which is next higher, and so on. Thus, a percentage of labourers of the pannial class, as will be seen from Mr. Clerk's account, has gone into the grade of porakudies, and a considerable percentage of porakudies has gone into the class of tenants, paying definite rents in cash or kind, while a portion of the latter has acquired landed property and become puttadars. Confining our attention to the lowest classes—the Pariahs and the Pallars—one would hardly be inclined to believe that their condition could, at any time, have possibly been worse than it is at present, but there is no doubt that this was the case. The statistics, compiled in the Census office and kindly furnished to me by Mr. H. A. Stuart, show that, in the three districts of Tanjore, Chingleput and South Arcot, in which these classes are found in large numbers, a considerable proportion possesses landed property. In Tanjore, the Pallar and Pariah population, according to the recent census, comprises 567,700 persons; of these, 24,600 persons, or 6 per cent. of the families, taking 5 persons to a family, possess land. In the Chingleput and South Arcot districts, the Pallar population is altogether insignificant. In the former district, of the Pariah population amounting to 310,000, 38,900 persons, or 12 per cent. of the families possess land. In the South Arcot district the number of possessors of landed property is very considerable, being 196,600 out of a population of 583,000, or 33 per cent. of the families. As regards the landless labourers, all the measures of Government during the last forty or fifty years have tended to ameliorate the condition of the lowest down-trodden classes so far as it is in the power of laws or administrative arrangements to do so; and in this respect the policy pursued by the Indian Government has been more liberal than that in force in [71] England itself till within very recent times. Agricultural slavery, which, in this country, originated mostly in voluntary contract, was abolished in 1844, and labourers declared to be free to carry their labour where they pleased or to emigrate without being subjected to any harassing restrictions, such as those in force in Russia, for instance, where no peasant is allowed to travel 30 miles from his own *commune* without observing irksome formalities and paying from 7*s*. to 10*s*. for a passport. Labourers freely emigrate to Burma, the Straits Settlements, Ceylon, Mauritius and the West Indies, and as Mr. Clerk, the Settlement Officer in Tanjore, points out, very often labourers who have received advances or loans from landholders "do take their departure without payment." The labourers are now quite aware that the higher classes dare not molest them, and the abolition of the system of *corvée* or compulsory labour on Government works has taken away all excuse for doing so. The abolition of torture, as one of the recognised methods of enforcing discipline, of collecting the revenue or detecting crime, and the severity with which violations of the law in this respect have been punished, have clearly demonstrated to the landholders that the employment of the old coercive methods in the exaction of work will not be tolerated by Government, and that labourers might be coaxed to remain in their service, but not compelled to do so. The non-recognition of class distinctions and the special privileges claimed by mirasidars to keep the lower classes out of the occupation of land, and the uniform treatment accorded to all puttadars, whether recent occupants or ancient mirasidars, in all administrative arrangements have raised the position of the lower classes, if they have somewhat depressed that of the higher classes. Numbers among the Pariah population have enlisted as sepoys, and several have found employment in the domestic establishments of Europeans as cooks, nurses, horsekeepers, gardeners, &c., and also in factories, plantations and railways. Missionary agencies have also done this class invaluable service by establishing schools and by teaching them to live, whenever their circumstances would permit of it, in a more respectable manner than they have been accustomed to do for ages, and by interceding for their protection and advocating their cause whenever there is any real or fancied danger of their being oppressed by the classes above them.

---

[71] The statute of labourers, the statute of apprentices and a multitude of laws against combinations of workmen were all enacted in England in the interest of capitalists. The last remnants of combination laws were abolished only in 1875, and they were enforced with considerable severity so recently as 1844.

I am informed that forty or fifty years ago, in some parts of the country, landholders used to have two measures, one of the usual capacity for ordinary transactions, and the other, a somewhat smaller one, for measuring out wages to the labourers who were thus cheated out of a part of their customary dues. This infamous practice has now, I believe, been completely discontinued. Further amelioration of the condition of this class must be the outcome of educational agencies employed in connection with missionary enterprise; and indeed, the best thing that can happen to them is conversion to either the Christian or the Muhammadan religion, for there is no hope for them within the pale [72] of Hinduism, the ordinances of which originated in a state of things in which it was necessary for a small minority of colonists of a superior race, with a view to prevent their civilization from becoming swamped by the surrounding barbarism, to construct "moral barriers," which would absolutely prevent fusion of races. The lower classes themselves are finding out this and the work of conversion is proceeding apace in some parts of the Presidency, for instance, in Tinnevelly, Nellore, Kistna and Malabar. Mr. McIver, in the census report of 1881, writes: "The extensive conversion to Muhammadanism of the lower castes of Hindus in Malabar has, for some years, been a matter of notoriety. The social distinctions created by caste are very marked in parts of the West Coast districts, and some of the lower castes occupy a very degraded position. The advantages which Moplahs or Hindu-sprung Mussulmans enjoy in this respect are obvious enough, and this seems at last to have dawned on the lower caste Hindus. The Moplahs were willing to receive them, and the work has of late years thriven." The increase of the Muhammadan population of Malabar in the decade ending 1881 was 12·3, while the increase in the total population was only 3·4 per cent. The Anglican missionaries in Tinnevelly, and the Baptists in Kistna and Nellore, made large additions to their followers in the ten years ending 1881, the increase in the Christian population in the three districts in that decade being 37·4, 371·9 and 590·4 per cent., respectively, while there was an increase in the total population of Tinnevelly and Kistna of only 0·34 and 6·62 per cent., respectively, and a decrease in Nellore of 11·4 per cent. on

[72] An attempt was made by certain philanthropic Hindu gentlemen in Mysore, under the inspiration of the late Mr. C. Runga Charlu, to organize a system of teaching for the Pariah population, in order that some impression might be made on the dense ignorance and grovelling superstition of this class. The attempt, however, altogether failed.

account of the famine of 1876–78. As soon as a person of the lowest classes of the Hindu population is converted either to the Christian or the Muhammadan religion, he emerges at a bound from his position of social degradation, and is acknowledged by persons belonging to the higher classes to have done so; and he often turns the tables against the latter by calling them "Kafirs" or "Heathens." It is also noteworthy to what extent the removal of the social stigma of degradation stimulates the industrial activity of the classes who have been relieved of it. The Moplahs of Malabar, for instance, are far more active, enterprising and well to do than the classes of the Hindus from whom they have seceded. The work of conversion, however, can only proceed *pari passu* with the improvement in the material condition of the lower classes of which it is both a consequence and a cause; for, conversion implies a desire to live a more respectable life on the part of the degraded classes than what they have been accustomed to, and the means for doing so must be within reach before the desire is felt. As regards the further amelioration of the condition of the Pariah population, which has recently excited so much public attention, it seems to me that it would be erroneous to assume that they are worse off now than they were fifty years ago, or that they are oppressed by the landholders. On the contrary, they are distinctly better off than before in the sense that they have a great many more opportunities of bettering their condition than were available under the old régime, and of which an appreciable percentage of the class has actually availed itself. There is, however, still a large class which, though somewhat better than before, is in a deplorably miserable and degraded condition, and its amelioration must, as already observed, be brought about by educational agencies; and it is in this direction that the efforts of Government should be directed, and not, as is sometimes advocated, to the procuring of benefits to the labouring classes at the expense of the land-owning classes which can only have the effect of introducing among the two classes, so necessary to one another, a spirit of mutual hostility similar to what is growing up in England to the injury of both. There is one hopeful feature in the situation, viz., that the Pariahs, notwithstanding centuries of social degradation, are singularly docile, attached to their masters, amenable to instruction and not unintelligent; and there can be little doubt but that a great deal may be made of them and that their improvement is not such a difficult or hopeless undertaking as one might be inclined to think when one sees their present degraded condition in the rural parts,

When we compare the smart intelligent looking servant in an Anglo-Indian household with the "Pannial" who, in point of intelligence, does not, to all appearance, compare very favorably with the cattle he tends, we should be hardly inclined to suspect that the two belong to the same class of the population. Pariahs who serve as sepoys in the Indian army have the reputation of being the best of the recruits from the population of Southern India.

III. Propertied classes other than landholders, mercantile and professional classes.

62. Among the propertied classes, the military classes, and more especially the Poligars who used to lead plundering expeditions, have become peaceful landholders, and, as such, while they have benefited by the rise in the profits of landed property, they have lost their old power and influence. Referring to the Poligars and the robber castes of the Tinnevelly District, Bishop Caldwell says: "Of the many beneficial changes that have taken place, one of the most remarkable is that which we see in the Poligars themselves. The Poligar has become a Zemindar, and has changed his nature as well as his name. One can scarcely believe it possible that the peaceful Nayaka and Marava Zemindars of the present day are the lineal descendants of those turbulent and apparently untameable chiefs, of whose deeds of violence and daring the history of the last century is so full. One asks also, can it really be true that the peaceful Nayaka ryots of the present day are the lineal descendants of those fierce retainers of the Poligars who were so ready, at the merest word of their chief, to shed either their own blood or that of their chiefs' enemies? The change wrought amongst the poorer classes is not perhaps so complete, but many of them have merged their traditional occupation of watchmen in the safer and more reputable occupation of husbandmen, and it may fairly be said of the majority of the members of the caste that though once the terror of the country, they are now as amenable to law and reason as any other classes." The only question is whether, under the Roman peace established by the British Raj, the transformation above described is not too complete, and whether, while the suppression of the power of lawless chiefs and their retainers was, at the outset, undoubtedly the first condition of civilized government and general progress, the time has not now arrived for finding some means of utilizing the waning martial spirit of these classes, before it is completely crushed out, for purposes of the defence of the country in the hour of trial, when every available resource may have to be strained to the utmost. The problem is certainly a difficult

one, but it cannot be that British statesmanship will be unable to find a solution, more especially as steps have been already taken for rendering the armies maintained by Native States effective for purposes of Imperial defence. Whether it might not be possible to introduce some plan by which the bigger Zemindars, whose estates are as large as small kingdoms, might be entrusted with the duty of training a certain number of militia-men to be kept as a kind of reserve for purposes of Police and internal defence in times of danger, under strict supervision and adequate guarantees for good behaviour, it is not competent for lay men to decide; they can only note the necessity for something being done in this direction. Meanwhile, the entire closure of the military career to the junior members of Hindu and Muhammadan families of high rank and military reputation, and the necessity imposed on all of them to obtain a living entirely out of the landed estates of the heads of their families which do not grow with the growth in their numbers, or to enter a civil profession for which they may have no special aptitudes, is a serious drawback from the point of view of that many-sided development which is an essential condition of the economic progress of the country.

Another class, which has suffered under the present régime, consists of the favourites and minions of Native chiefs who had fattened on the substance of the poor and are now no longer allowed to do so. It is the existence of this class, to some extent, that gives the capital cities of Native States an appearance of greater wealth and prosperity than is the case in the cities of British territory, where wealth is more diffused and less concentrated in particular localities. The town of Tanjore is an instance. Though the Rajah of Tanjore was relieved of the administration of that province in the beginning of the century, he was paid annually for over half a century one-fifth of its revenues for the maintenance of his court besides a fixed allowance of three and a half lakhs, and all this money was spent within that single town. Thousands of families lived on his bounty; palatial buildings sprang up in various parts of the town, and music and painting and other arts, which minister to the pleasures of a luxurious court, flourished. When the Raj became extinct, misfortune overtook the thousands of families of unproductive consumers who had not been bred in any useful occupation, and the town has not yet recovered from the blow, while the other towns in the district have greatly increased in size and wealth. The ruined buildings in the Tanjore town no doubt attest its former magnificence, and place in strong relief its present decayed condition as a centre of wealth; but in point of fact, industrially speaking, the town is not now, probably, in a less flourishing condition than it was ever before.

A third class, which has increased in numbers, but has lost in individual share of the wealth of the country, consists of the Native bankers, sowkars and banias. Formerly, there was no security for property except in the capital cities and their vicinity, and all the wealth was found concentrated there. A few men, who were in favour with the chiefs, monopolised all the banking business of the country, issued bills of exchange (or hundis), and cashed them, and thus made colossal fortunes like the "Navakoti Naraina Chetti" of the Hindu tales. Their association with the ruling chiefs, whose necessities they fed, gave them immense power, and though they were themselves sometimes plundered, as for instance, when Hyder levied a contribution of 70 lakhs of rupees from the bankers of Mysore, they had great opportunities of enriching themselves by altering the rates of exchange for coins, of which large numbers were current. According to Mr. Grant (1787), Zemindars and others had to offer as security "teeps" or promissory notes of sowkars, or other moneyed men, for about two-thirds of the revenue of the tracts of country farmed out by Government to them. Mr. White, a member of the Council of the Governor of Fort St. George, in 1793, mentions that, by the low value fixed on copper currency and the tricks of the sowkars in altering the rate of exchange, the poor cultivators were defrauded of a great part of the wages of their daily labour, that the shroffs used to raise or lower, in a few days, by combination, the rates of exchange by 10 or 15 per cent., and that the evil had operated, in a material degree, to depopulate the country during the famine which had then occurred.[73] The account given by Tavernier as to the rates of discount on bills of

[73] Mr. Warden, the Collector of Malabar, mentions a curious arrangement about the farming of *kaas* (copper coins) which was in force at Pálghat in 1801. He says, "The person farming the coinage fixes his own particular stamp upon the new kaas, which he intends coining and circulating for the period of his lease which is limited to one year. The introduction of the new kaas takes place in the Malabar month of Chingum (part of August and September), at which time it is sold for 22 kaas the Veray fanam, and continues at this price till the month of Makaram (January and February), in which month, there being a fair in one of the villages of the country (at which an immense concourse of people assemble), the farmer attends it with his kaas and disposes of them at the rate of 24 to the fanam, after which the price decreases in proportion to the demand there might be in the bazaar, till the latter end of Khumbum (beginning of March), in which month another fair happens, when the farmer disposes of his kaas at 26 or 28 the fanam. The sale or exchange of kaas, after the conclusion of this fair, becomes free and common to all, and the new and old kaas

exchange issued by Indian bankers will show how their gains were made up. The rates of exchange for goods payable at Surat within two months were at Lahore on Surat, $6\frac{1}{4}$ per cent.; Agra 1 to $1\frac{1}{2}$ per cent.; Sironj 3 per cent.; Burhanpore $2\frac{1}{2}$ to 3 per cent.; Dacca 10 per cent.; Patna 7 to 8 per cent.; Benares 6 per cent.; Golconda from 4 to 5 per cent.; Goa from 4 to 5 per cent.; Deccan 3 per cent.; Bijapur 3 per cent.; and Dowlatabad 1 to $1\frac{1}{2}$ per cent. Tavernier adds "In some years the exchange rises 1 to 2 per cent., where there are Rajahs or petty tributary princes, who interfere with trade, each claiming that the goods ought to traverse his territory and pay him custom. There are two in particular between Agra and Ahmedabad, one of whom is the Rajah of Antawar (Danta or Dantewar), and the other the Rajah of Bergam (possibly Wungaón), who disturb the merchants much in reference to this matter. One may, however, avoid passing the territories of these two princes by taking another route, from Agra and Surat by way of Sironj and Burhanpore; but these are fertile lands, intersected by several rivers, the greater number of which are without bridges and without boats, and it is impossible to pass until two months after the rainy season. It is for this reason that the merchants, who have to be at Surat in the season for going to sea, generally take their way through the country of these two Rajahs, because they are able to traverse it at all seasons, even in the time of the rains, which consolidate the sand with which the whole country is covered. Besides, it is not to be wondered at that the exchange is so high, for those who lend the money run, for their part, the risk that if the goods are stolen the money is lost to them." Tavernier's remarks illustrate the difficulties which trade had to contend with owing to the general insecurity of property in the country and the absence of easy communications, and they further show how it was possible for a few merchants and bankers to accumulate enormous wealth at the

---

indiscriminately pass at one and the same value. During the period that the restraint continues, viz., from Chingum to Khumbum (seven months), every person wishing to exchange a fanam in the bazaar is required to receive it from the farmer at the price at which his kaas might be current at the time. His own kaas is to be the only one current at the bazaar during the above period; and all the old kaas (those coined in the years preceding, although their intrinsic value is the same with, and *often better* than, that of the new) are bought up by the farmer at the rate of 150 old to 100 new, and he is at liberty to take them wherever he can find them passing in the bazaar, and give his own kaas in exchange at the above rate. These old kaas he either recoins anew or reserves them till the month of Khumbum, when old and new passing without distinction he disposes of the former, which he got before at 50 per cent. discount, at their *real* or what may be their current value in the bazaar, which is from 36 to 38 to a fanam. Besides the above privileges, he has that of levying a kaas daily from every shop that may be open in the bazaar. This is an institution which has been of very old standing and not one of late introduction."

expense of the general community. We thus learn that the banking firm of Jaggat Sait, of Moorshedabad, was plundered, during the Mahratta invasion of 1742 of specie to the amount of $2\frac{1}{2}$ millions sterling. Trade in the old days was, in fact, one of peril and adventure and restricted to a few individuals, who reaped enormous profits, which were sometimes expended in the construction of alms-houses and temples, caravansaries, roads and bridges. All this is now changed. The extension of the security of property to all parts of the country, the adoption of a uniform currency, the introduction of the money order system and of currency notes and State banks and the creation of a public stock in which money can be invested with perfect security, have rendered it now impossible for the money-lending classes to make the enormous gains which they did in former times. Their loss, in this respect, however, is as nothing compared with the immense gain to the public resulting from the decentralization of money and capital, increased conveniences for the transfer of money, and the more secure investment of savings. The value of the money orders now issued at trifling cost amounts annually to 12 millions Rx for the whole of India, and 1·3 million Rx for the Madras Presidency; the bank notes in circulation amount to 16 millions and 2 millions respectively. The deposits in the savings banks have also increased from 0·4 millions Rx in 1857-58 to 6·9 millions Rx in 1889-90 for the whole of India. There can be no doubt, however, that with the increase of trade and the growth of a money economy, money-lending classes have increased in large numbers and spread all through the country instead of being confined to the towns. According to the returns of income-tax for the year 1890-91, there were in this Presidency 14,621 money-lenders with incomes exceeding Rs. 500 per annum. There is no means of forming an estimate of petty money-lenders with less income than Rs. 500. The tax paid by the former class amounted to nearly Rs. 3,59,000, and the income assessed may be estimated at 1·6 millions Rx. The income is not large as compared with incomes in European countries, but it is much larger than was the case formerly in this country, and, being made up of smaller profits than before, denotes increased activity of trade.

Other mercantile and trading classes have increased largely in numbers and are in a prosperous condition, owing to the development of trade of which a full account has already been given. As in the case of money-lenders, the income of this class is made up of small gains in a large number of transactions and not by large profits in a small number of transactions. This is a wholesome change, for, as has been pertinently observed, the advantages of trade can no more be measured by the gains of individual traders than the advantages of learning by the salaries of schoolmasters. The gains of traders represent the sacrifice incurred for securing the advantages of trade, and the less the sacrifice and the more the volume of trade, the greater the advantage to the general community.

Among the learned professions, the official classes have also increased in numbers, owing especially to the increased activity of Local Fund administration. Barristers, vakils and other legal practitioners are rising into importance. According to the income-tax returns the income assessed, that is, of legal practitioners who get not less than Rs. 500 per annum is about 26 lakhs of rupees. 1,034 persons get an income of nearly 10 lakhs of rupees and 267 persons an income of 16 lakhs of rupees. Of the latter, 47 persons, with an income of about 6 lakhs, reside in the Presidency town, and 220 persons, with an income of 10 lakhs, reside in the mofussil stations.

IV. Artizans.

63. Among the artizan classes, the decline of hand-loom weavers has already been referred to. All handicrafts patronized by native courts, such as painting, manufacture of articles of luxury, pith-work, &c., have disappeared with those courts. This change is due not so much to the competition of European manufactures as to revolution in taste. The decline of indigenous arts is certainly a matter for regret, but it is a small factor in the present economic condition of the country. As regards cotton hand-loom manufactures, Mr. T. N. Mukharji, in his *Art Manufactures of India*, says: " Notwithstanding the extent of their present production, cotton manufactures in the old style are in their last gasp. The few small pieces of wood and bamboo tied with shreds of twine and thread, which the weaver calls his loom, and which he can as easily make himself as buy from his neighbour, the village carpenter, can no more compete with the powerful machinery than a village cart of Western Bengal can run a race with the 'Flying Scotchman.' Yet the wonder is that cotton fabrics can still be manufactured with the old primitive loom all over the country. In one sense, it is a misfortune that it should be so; for it shows the low value of human labour in India. Machinery, with all its modern improvements, seems to contend in vain with a moribund industry, that must linger on as long as the worker in it has nothing more to do than to produce from

it 4*d.* a day as the joint earnings of himself, his wife, a boy and a girl. Those that wield the machinery should lay their heads together and devise means to teach the people how better to employ their hands in other crafts. Another reason why Indian looms can still compete with Lancashire goods is that the European process of manufacture has not yet been able to give the fabrics that strengh for which native manufactures have a reputation. Nor has machinery yet been able to make those gossamer fabrics for which a wealthy Indian always paid a fabulous price." In the present stage of industrial development it is the useful and not the artistic and ornamental that is likely to be sought after in this country, and it is perhaps right that this should be so. When the whole community was divided into two sections, one consisting of a few individuals enormously rich and living entirely on the produce of the labour of the other consisting of an immense mass of the population in abject poverty whose property and even life were completely at their mercy, there was room for the existence of a class of handicraftsmen who could obtain a living by manufacturing articles of luxury. Now the greater diffusion of wealth and the decline of the classes who patronized them have rendered it necessary that these artizans should turn their attention to the manufacture of such articles as are in general demand among the population. When wealth increases and a class of merchant princes such as mark a high and not a low stage of industrial and commercial development springs up, there will again arise a demand for articles of luxury, though not necessarily of the old type.

The condition of black-smiths, brass-smiths, gold-smiths, carpenters and masons is very prosperous, owing to the demand for jewels, for substantial houses and for metal vessels which are coming into general use. The cheapened cost of metal including gold and silver, has created the demand for metal vessels and jewels. Since 1850, about 140 millions sterling worth of gold and a still larger value of silver have been imported into the country, and this great influx of the precious metals provides sufficient occupation for gold-smiths. The wages of artizans generally, as will be seen from the statement of wages printed in the appendix V.-F. (h), have greatly risen. Of the Coimbatore District, Mr. Nicholson remarks that town wages are very high; higher indeed, considering the efficiency of the workman, than in England. Irrespective of the quantity of work, the food purchasing power of the wages of skilled labour in towns is quite equal to that of similar wages in England, where money is much cheaper and the artizan's wants much more numerous, owing to the cold and damp climate and other demands. Ordinary carpenters can, with their daily wages, buy about 20 or 22 lb. of dry grain free of all husk (30 to 33 lb. with the husk). As the artizan's sons work with him, and as work is plentiful and the caste a small one, he is well off. Tables and chairs, which are coming into use among the educated classes, have afforded increased employment to carpenters, while they have affected prejudicially the carpet-weaving industry. Another noticeable feature in the present situation is the gradual rise of the capital artizan who, to some extent, turns out finished products in his factory and sells them, instead of merely fashioning the materials supplied to him by persons in need of the articles and receiving the wages of labour.

The standard of living.

64. The best means of finding out whether the economic condition of the country has improved or not is to enquire whether the standard of living has risen or not among all but the lowest classes of labourers who practically live from hand-to-mouth. There is ample evidence that this has been the case.[74] On this point I have obtained the opinions of a number of gentlemen who have had exceptional opportunities of forming an intelligent and trustworthy opinion as to the condition of landowners in different parts of the country at the present time as compared with their condition in the old days. The facts stated in the previous portions of this memorandum place it beyond doubt that the vast majority of landowners were in a state of abject poverty amounting to almost destitution fifty years ago. In this connection refer-

---

[74] The following extract from a recent report of the Commissioners of Public Debt on the condition of European Turkey (written by Mr. Vincent Caillard, the English Commissioner), will show what are the symptoms of a real deterioration in the economic condition of the masses of the population. "The peasant, in the interior, has reduced his wants to their simplest expression, and signs are to hand which show him to be less and less able to purchase the few necessaries he requires. For instance, a few years ago in many decent peasant households copper cooking utensils were to be seen. Now they are scarcely to be found, and they have been sold to meet the pressing needs of the moment. Their place has been taken by clay utensils, and, in the case of the more affluent, by iron. The peasant's chief expenses lie in his women folk, who require print stuffs for their dresses and linen for their under-clothing, but of these he gets as little as possible, since as often as not, he cannot pay for them. This smallness of margin is one of the reasons why the amount of importation increases so slowly. The peasant hardly ever pays for his purchases in cash; what little he has goes in taxes. He effects his purchases by barter. Another significant sign is the increase of brigandage which has taken place. New bands of brigands are continually springing up; reports from the interior are ever bringing to our knowledge some fresh acts of violent robbery. This simply means that men, desperately poor and refusing to starve, take to brigandage as a means of living." It will be observed that in Southern India, so far as the conditions of the present differ from the past, the change has taken place in exactly the reverse direction to what has occurred in European Turkey.

ence should be made in particular to the description of the income and the ways of living of even the richer ryots given by Mr. Bourdillon, whose account is printed in the appendix III.-B. It is true that there is a considerable portion of the ryot class which still answers to Mr. Bourdillon's description, but it is also true that there is a class—a daily increasing one—which seeks and enjoys more comforts. This is evidenced in various ways. The number of houses as shown by the last census has increased in a greater ratio than the population; and tiled and terraced houses are superseding the old thatched cottages. Better clothing, especially of elegant and costly kinds for women, has come into ordinary use among the higher classes in most districts, and in the Southern districts women of the present day will not, as Mr. Seshaiyar, Professor of the Kumbakónam College, observes,[75] even look at the coarse clothing which their grandmothers wore. In the richer families servants for doing the menial work are being more largely employed than before. Much larger quantities of gold and silver jewels are now worn. Metal vessels have, to a very large extent, taken the place of earthen vessels, even among the lower classes, and rice is becoming a part of the ordinary diet of the classes which, in former days, would have used it as a luxury on special festive occasions. A great deal of money is being spent on the education of children. The money expended in school-fees for a single boy would formerly have sufficed to maintain two adults. It is true, at the same time, that everybody feels that his means are inadequate to the satisfaction of his wants, but this is not because his means have not increased, but because his wants have increased in a greater ratio. Formerly, none but the richest would have dreamt of giving collegiate education to their children. Now persons with very small means wish to educate their sons and make great sacrifices for this purpose. Sometimes the sons turn out well, but occasionally they do not, and, in the latter case, great is the suffering inflicted on the parents. Nevertheless, the general effect, both on the parents and the sons, of this state of things, is very beneficial. Formerly, the father would have pinched himself and saved to leave his children property for subsistence. Now he saves to give them education leaving them to earn their living. Indeed, the benefits of education are so much appreciated that even if the father be not willing to educate his children, the mother insists on its being done. Lads who have been educated and who have passed University examinations are so much

---

[75] *Vide* appendix V,-F. (1 2).

sought after by parents as suitable husbands for their daughters that they command a high price in the matrimonial market. The following extracts from the report of the Bengal Salaries Commission, 1886, describing the rise in the standard of living among the official and other classes in that province, might almost, word for word, be taken as accurately portraying the condition of things in the more advanced districts in this Presidency:

"We find it quite impossible to arrive at any definite conclusion as to the actual cost of marriages, because our informants' statements vary so much one from the other. It seems, however, that the marriage of a son does not, as a rule, cost so very much more than it did in old days; indeed, some people tell us that a father may even gain by his son's marriage. It is a strange but undoubted fact that academical distinctions command a very high price in the matrimonial market, a youth who has several '*University passes*' being regarded as a very desirable *parti* and having to be highly paid to induce him to bestow his hand in marriage. It would also seem that 'Kulinism,' or the practice of marrying a daughter to a man of the very highest section of one's caste, and paying a large sum for the honour of having so exalted a son-in-law, is dying out in proportion as academical honours and the success in life to which they lead are more and more valued. In either case, however, the cost of getting a daughter married is very heavy, and at times is even ruinous, to men of limited means, such as are most of the ministerial officers; and the spread of education, so far from having led to more reasonable practices, seems rather to have exercised a contrary influence. . . . . . .

"Native ladies and children also now wear more cloths than formerly. Although, for obvious reasons, we cannot go deeply into this delicate subject, we have ample evidence to show that both in material, fashion, and ornamentation, female clothing is more costly than before. Children also, who even in respectable families wore no cloths at all during their early years, are now often clothed in expensive garments. It must not, however, be forgotten that some articles of clothing are cheaper than formerly, such as those made of English piece-goods and the like. It is doubtful how far this cheapness counterbalances the increased outlay caused by a love of finery.

"Under the head of dress comes the important question of jewelry. This also, we think, must always have formed a serious item in Indian domestic economy, because, in days when life and property were unsafe, a man usually invested his gains and savings in jewelry and gold and silver ornaments for his women. These could be buried in the ground in time of danger or sold to procure funds in time of distress. It seems therefore probable that the increase of expenditure under this head will be found rather in more exquisite workmanship, the greater use of precious stones, and more valuable materials generally, than in the greater number of articles worn by native ladies. On this subject, one of the gentlemen, already quoted, writes as follows: 'It would be tedious to enumerate the different items of jewelry; simple gold is now despised and a profusion of precious stones is considered indispensable. A lady in the class of society to which I belong would be considered poorly adorned on three thousand rupees. Five thousand would be nearer the mark.' . . . .

"With the progress of knowledge and science the old system of native medicine with its charms, incantations and other superstitions is fast dying out, and resort is freely had to the European method of treatment. The good derived from this change is great and palpable, and no man begrudges even heavy expenditure to save the lives of himself or his family. Many, however, look back, with some regret, to the native system, which, whatever its failings, was remarkably cheap. There was no such thing as the settled daily fee of a physician, much less a fee for each visit. The remuneration of a native physician (kabiraj) generally depended on the pecuniary means of the patient. For ordinary cases requiring three or four days' treatment, a fee of a couple of rupees, including the price of medicine, was considered fair for a family man whose income was Rs. 20 or Rs. 30 per mensem; at the present time and under the altered system, four times the sum would meet the requirements of such a case. In mofussil stations the *amla* class suffer great distress owing to their inability, for want of means, to obtain good medical advice and medicine for their family and children."

There can be no doubt that the higher and middle classes live much more respectably than in the old days, and, as there is nothing in the present *régime* to specially favour these classes, and, as there are no such sharp differences in wealth between the several grades of society as exist in European countries, the rise in the standard of living above noticed may be taken as an index of general prosperity. The rise in the standard of living is sometimes very erroneously attributed to the diffusion of habits of extravagance. A sudden increase of prosperity before a taste for rational modes of enjoyment is developed, no doubt, gives rise to extravagant unproductive expenditure in particular directions, as was the case during the years of the cotton famine when the ryots, especially in the Bombay Presidency, reaped enormous profits which were spent on marriages and festivals with the result that, when the profits ceased, the inevitable crash soon followed. Then the ryots learnt a lesson which will not soon be forgotten. I know that in the Tanjore district there has been a wholesome change in recent years in this respect, less being now spent on marriages and show on special occasions and more on education and substantial comforts. The slow rise in the standard of living, such as has been observable of late years, cannot be the result of formation of habits of extravagance, for large sections of society cannot continue to live well, unless they have the means to do so. "An interesting German writer," says Professor Cliffe Leslie, "has reproduced one of the popular theories of Elizabeth's reign —that luxury, ostentation, and expensive habits among all classes are the causes of the modern dearness of living, and not the abundance of money. There cannot, however, be more money spent, if people have no more to spend than before. A mere change in the ideas and desires of society would add nothing to the number of pieces of money, and could not affect the sum total of the pieces. If more money were spent upon houses, furniture, and show, less would remain, if pecuniary means were not increased, to be spent upon labour and food, and the substantial necessaries of life; and if the former became dearer, the latter would at the same time become cheaper. But, when people have really more money than formerly to spend, they naturally spend more than they formerly did, and their unaccustomed expenditure is considered excessive and extravagant. And, when an increase in the pecuniary incomes of large classes arises from, or accompanies, greater commercial activity and general progress, there commonly is a general taste for a better or more costly style of living than there was at a lower stage of society. There is always, it is true, much folly and vanity in human expenditure; and masses of men do not become philosophers of a sudden because they are making more money. But their state is improving on the whole when their trade is increasing, and the value of their produce rising to a level with that of the most forward communities, and when the lowest classes are breaking the shackles of barbarous custom, and furnishing life with better accommodation than servile and ignorant boors could appreciate." These remarks are, to a great extent, applicable to the transformation that is taking place in this country among the higher classes and to some slight degree among the lower classes of the population also. The desire to live in a respectable manner, to give a good education to their sons, to procure greater comforts, and it may be more expensive jewels for their wives, and to marry their daughters to young men who have received an English education and who will not treat them merely in the light of household drudges have compelled many men, who, under the old conditions, would never have thought of leaving the neighbourhood of their villages, to proceed to distant parts of the Presidency in search of a competence. Even the mania for making jewels is not without its good side. It is quite as legitimate, if less refined, a mode of enjoyment as costly furniture, dress equipage, horses and dogs. The difference between the two methods of enjoyment lies in the fact that in the latter case the superfluities which constitute articles of luxury bear a smaller proportion to the capital devoted to production than in the former. Though the standard of living among the higher and middle classes in this country has risen, it is as yet nothing like what it is in European countries, and it ought to rise much higher if India is to attain to the same rank as European nations in industrial development. What is it that makes a ryot in the Ceded Districts or in Ganjam so liable to suffer distress when there is even a partial failure of crops? In the former district it is the capriciousness of the seasons and the low standard of living, and in the latter, isclation from the other parts of the country by want of communications and the low standard of living, that is the cause of the ryot's poverty and helpless condition. In countries in which people have very few wants and can live cheaply, the population increases up to the limits of bare subsistence, and, when a failure of seasons or other causes diminish in the least degree their resources, they are deprived of food and die off in large numbers.

Pressure of population.

65. Notwithstanding the great increase in population during the last decade, there is no reason to suppose that the population has as yet begun to press on the land in any part of the Presidency to such an extent as to cause any deterioration in the standard of living to which any class has hitherto been accustomed. The districts in which population is the densest are also districts in which all classes of the population, not excepting even the lowest, are, comparatively

speaking, the most prosperous, while districts in which population is sparse are those in which the major part of it lives from hand-to-mouth. Tanjore, with a population as dense as 600 persons to the square mile, is a typical instance of districts of the former class, and Anantapur and Kurnool, with 134 and 109 persons, respectively, are examples of the latter. In Tanjore, as we have already seen, the real wages of agricultural labourers have considerably risen, and their condition has distinctly improved. The rate of increase of population in this district during the last decade, viz., 4·5 per cent., is no doubt very low as compared with the general rate for the whole Presidency, amounting to 15·5 per cent., but the reason for this is to be found not in insufficiency of the means of subsistence, but in emigration caused by the higher remuneration for labour obtainable in Ceylon, the Straits Settlements, Burma, West Indies, &c. From the emigration returns it appears that the loss of population due to emigration, from 18th February 1881 to 26th February 1891, amounts to 97,237 persons, and if this number be added to the population as ascertained by the census of 1891, the real rate of increase in the Tanjore district will come out as 9·1 per cent., or double the rate shown by the census. It must also be remembered that, as emigrants are generally male adults, the effect of emigration on the birth-rates, calculated with reference to the whole population, is to depress the rates, while the effect of famine mortality, which falls heaviest on the old and the young, sparing mostly adults of the productive ages, is exactly the reverse. Thus the 97,000 emigrants, though forming only 4·5 per cent. of the total population, bear the proportion of 18 per cent. to the adult male population between the ages of 15 and 50, or, in other words, the reduction in the birth-rate due to emigration, assuming it to have operated throughout the ten years, may be taken at nearly one-fifth. The death-rates must also show an apparent increase in consequence of the larger proportion of the juvenile and aged persons left in the population, among whom the mortality, even under normal conditions, is heavy. In no district, so far as is known, is there any marked redundancy of labour in normal years, and, since the last famine, there is a deficiency of it in several districts. Even in a densely-peopled district like Vizagapatam, with 452 persons to the square mile, it has been found necessary to import thousands of labourers from such a great distance as the Punjab, for the construction of the East Coast Railway, local labour not being procurable at anything like reasonable rates. The same difficulty was felt in the

Kurnool and Kistna districts when the Bellary-Kistna Railway was under construction, large numbers of labourers having had to be imported from Poona in the Bombay Presidency. In Tanjore difficulty is now felt in finding labour for the construction of the Máyavaram-Mutupet Railway. There are many tracts, even in the river-irrigated parts of the Nellore and Kistna districts, where the extension of irrigation is held in check, owing to the paucity of labourers for carrying on cultivation. On the whole, therefore, it seems clear that it is not so much the pressure of population as the precariousness of the seasons, which keeps down the economic condition of the ryots, especially in the districts situated on the tableland between the Eastern and the Western Ghâts. The Kurnool district contains a population of about 818,000 persons. The area of ryotwar land under occupation is about 1,135,000 acres, and the extent of inam lands is 906,000 acres or 2 millions in all. This gives on an average $2\frac{1}{2}$ acres per head of the population. The average assessment of ryotwar land is nearly 1 rupee per acre corresponding to an outturn in dry grains, after deducting 25 per cent. on account of vicissitudes of seasons, of 600 lb. or 10 bushels according to the settlement calculations. Allowing even as much as $1\frac{1}{2}$ lb. per head of men, women and children—a very high all-round-rate—the produce of one acre per head ought to be sufficient to feed the entire population, leaving $1\frac{1}{2}$ acre per head for seed, for fallows, for purchasing the other necessaries of life such as clothing and condiments and for payment of Government revenue. There is besides an additional acre per head of inferior land assessed at 8 annas 10 pies available for occupation, and there is very great scope for extension of irrigation under the Cuddapah-Kurnool canal, should intensive cultivation in the form of application of irrigation in those sparsely-populated tracts become necessary. The Anantapur district, which is the driest and the poorest in the Presidency, contains a population of 708,000 persons. The area of ryotwar land under occupation is 933,000 acres, besides inam lands 608,000 acres, or about $1\frac{1}{2}$ million acres in all, which gives rather more than 2 acres per head. The poverty of the soil is shown by the fact that the average assessment is only 10 annas, while the average for the whole Presidency is 1 rupee. The ryot's condition is consequently more precarious in this district than in Kurnool. Nevertheless, even here the outturn in all normal years is more than sufficient to feed the population. There is a large area of unoccupied land amounting to 1 acre per head of the population, available for cultivation. The average assessment of this land is 11 annas 6 pies, and it is therefore presumably not inferior in quality to the land now under occupation. This shows that the poverty of the district and the low condition of the population are due to the precariousness of the seasons and sterile soil, and that the state of things was just the same or even worse when the population was only one-half of what it is now. It must at the same time be admitted that, while it is undoubtedly true that the population has not so far trenched upon the means of subsistence, it is equally true that if the population increases in anything like the rate at which it has been doing during the last ten years without not only a corresponding increase in the productive powers of lands but also in habits of thrift and prudence among the ryots themselves, every effort to ameliorate the condition of the masses must sisyphus-like end where it began. During the last ten years, there is no doubt that production has increased in a greater ratio than the population by the extension of irrigation as is evidenced by the fact that, while the land revenue demand prior to 1876 was about 450 lakhs, it is now 490 lakhs, or 40 lakhs in excess, inclusive of allowances to Hindu religious institutions deducted from the beriz or the demand. Of these 40 lakhs, only about 5 lakhs represent the increase due to enhancement of the settlement rates, the remainder being due either to extension of irrigation or to cultivation of superior soils which has become profitable owing to the opening up of remote tracts by means of communications. The land revenue is also collected with the greatest ease; the area of land sold for arrears of revenue is hardly 1 per cent. of the total area of holdings, and the greater portion of such lands as are sold are generally those on the margin of cultivation, which are taken up by the ryots or relinquished at their pleasure. Till before the last two years the ryots of the greater portion of the Presidency had a run of good seasons, and the creditable self-reliance which they have shown under the adverse circumstances of the last two years affords satisfactory proof of the fact that their position has materially improved. Their resources, however, have been already strained a great deal, and another bad season next year may bring them down, and we can only hope that this may not occur. The Government has already now done nearly all that it is possible for it to do in the way of extending irrigational facilities and opening up the country by the extension of railways and other communications. When the Periyar project is completed, more than 100,000 acres in the Madura district will be efficiently irrigated, and the Melúr taluk, notoriously the poorest taluk in the district containing a predatory population, which derives its subsistence more from other tracts than from its own soil, will be protected to a considerable extent from droughts which now occur almost every second year. The Rushikulya irrigation project will add another 100,000 acres of permanently-irrigated land to the food-producing area of the country. The tank restoration scheme which is under execution, and which has almost removed the chronic complaint about the neglect of irrigation works will improve the yield of lands now under cultivation. The large numbers of wells for irrigation, which have been excavated with advances granted by Government under the Land Improvement Loans Acts on very favorable terms, have also been the means of protecting arid tracts from partial droughts. The East Coast Railway will bring the very fertile and sparse-populated country of Jeypore within reach of the crowded parts of the Presidency to the advantage of both and be the means of lightening the pressure of population on the latter. It is sometimes asked, how can railways prevent famines? The answer is simple. Railways, by distributing the produce of tracts where the harvest has been abundant in tracts where it has been scanty, give value to produce which would have been wasted or been allowed to rot for want of an outlet and thus mitigate the effects of scarcity; and they bring fertile regions shut off from the rest of the country by want of communications within easy reach of congested tracts. The idea of bringing labourers from Poona to work on the Bellary-Kistna Railway and from the Punjab to work on the East Coast Railway would, for instance, have been scouted as absurd by even the wildest visionary in the pre-railway period. Above all, railways by equalizing prices and by preventing sudden and violent alternations in the condition of the masses, who are at one time gorged with plentiful means of subsistence and soon after suffer the direst distress—a state of things most fatal to self-reliance—have rendered the creation of the habits of forethought and prudence possible. Life has been made somewhat harder than before to the poorest landless classes in times of plenty when the pressure is not severe, while, to the cultivating and landowning classes who form the bulk of the population, the means are made available of accumulating savings; and, in times of scarcity, when the pressure on the landless classes might be expected to be severe, the burden is lightened. Doubtless, when parts of the country, which have hitherto been isolated from other tracts, are suddenly placed in communication with the latter, the result often is a feeling that they are denuded of food supplies which are required for their own use. This feeling soon wears away, and when these parts suffer in their turn from scarcity, the effects of which are mitigated by supplies derived from other regions, the advantages of communications become at once manifest. I suppose this has been the case with Kurnool, where the season of 1890 was excellent, but the surplus produce was drawn off by the surrounding distressed tracts, the new railway assisting in the transport of grain. In 1891, when the crop failed in the Kurnool district itself, there were no stores of grain to fall back upon, and the result was that the population was taken by surprise. I believe the recent distress and riots must have, in a great measure, been due to this cause. As regards the moral benefits conferred by railways, it is sufficient to say that they are of even greater importance in stimulating the intelligence of a hitherto inert and stay-at-home population and removing provincial prejudices, than schools and Universities. A great deal, then, has been done by Government indirectly to improve the position of the agricultural classes. What remains to be done is, as Mr. Nicholson has put it in his excellent report on the economic condition of the Anantapur district, "to attack the ryot himself directly and to bring to bear on him the force of education in agriculture and rural economy." The situation is not a hopeless one; and Sir James Caird, a Member of the Famine Commission, who devoted considerable attention to the investigation of the agricultural conditions of the Presidency, has told us, "it is possible to obtain such a gradual increase of production in India as would meet the present rate of increase of population for a considerable time. One bushel per acre gained gradually in a period of ten years, in addition to a moderate reclamation of cultivable land, would meet the demand of the present growth of population. Considering the generally fertile nature of the soil, and that in most parts of India two crops can be got in the year, this would seem to be a possible result. By these two methods, wisely combined, the increase of population may be safely provided for several generations. The attainment of this will be vastly increased by committing to each province the responsibility of the operations necessary for its own success and of enlisting the active assistance of the most capable native officials, municipalities and landowners in the work." The increase of production has, however, its limits, and for a permanent marked improvement in the standard of living and the general condition of the masses, a change in the national habits in regard to early marriages is a necessary requisite. I have already in my remarks on the increase of population alluded to the difficulties in this respect. We can only hope that, as institutions and practices, which not very long ago appeared as immovable as the everlasting hills, have been undergoing transformation, the difficulties referred to will, in the course of the next half a century, disappear. Meanwhile, the lower classes, to whom the difficulties are not applicable, will have an advantage over the higher classes.

Does a large proportion of the population live on insufficient food in ordinary seasons ?

66. After what has been stated above, it is hardly necessary to say much on the question which engaged the attention of the Government of India two years ago, viz., "whether the greater proportion of the population suffer from a daily insufficiency of food." It is exceedingly difficult to give a categorical answer to a question of this kind without having a definite idea as to what is meant by insufficiency of food. As to certain broad facts, however, there can be no doubt. The population is mainly agricultural and a considerable portion miserably poor, not in the sense of wanting the means of subsistence in ordinary seasons according to the standard which the conditions of climate and resulting national habits formed in the course of ages have established, but in the sense of being without resources to fall back upon when adverse seasons appear in succession. That standard includes little more than the barest necessaries of life, the secondary wants being few; and, when adverse seasons occur, there is a section of the population which has to reduce its rations and live partly on wild fruits and such other inexpensive food as can be picked up on the way side. This class forms the lowest stratum of the population and its condition has been described by Mr. Turner, the Collector of Vizagapatam, in the following terms. He says that the people of this class "require very little tamarind and curry powder, as they live mainly on cunji. This requires much salt to make it palatable. They use, as relish, onions and green chillies, which they procure from the farm or otherwise without buying. They generally consume ragi or cumbu or such other inferior grains as their employers disburse to them as wages. During the season when the palmyra bears fruit, they for the most part live on these fruits which they can, to a large extent, get gratis. In the mango fruit season they collect the wind-fallen young fruit and boil and use it for one substantial meal at least. At other times they live on sweet potatoes. They buy no fuel. The female members and children pick up here and there the droppings of cattle and dry twigs and leaves of trees and utilize the same as

firewood." This class can tide over one or two bad seasons, provided the failure of crop is not general. In all ordinary seasons deaths by starvation are almost unknown, and there is no lack of work to the labouring classes. The old and infirm are supported by their kinsmen or by spontaneous charity and not left to starve, a striking contrast to the state of things in England, where recent inquiries into the condition of the poor have brought to light the fact that of men and women above the age of 65 years not less than 40 per cent. have to choose between starvation and resort to the poor-house. Curiously enough too, it is not in the districts in which famine is unknown, as for instance Malabar and Tanjore, that the lower classes of the population have the strongest physique, but in districts like Kurnool and Anantapur. Whether this is due to the dry climate of the latter districts or to the superiority of dry grains which form the staple food in these districts over rice, it is difficult to say. It is noteworthy, however, that these districts contain many malarious tracts, and rice in popular estimation is richer food than dry grains. Inferences based on calculations of money values of earnings of labourers and cost of food in rural tracts are apt to be very fallacious. In his analysis of the agricultural statistics of the Kurnool district, Mr. Benson remarks that "the whole aspect of the figures is that a vast majority of the ryots in most parts of the district lead a life of poverty, and must, at all times, be but little removed from a state of 'short commons.' Nevertheless, whilst observation confirms the general aspect of poverty, still it also shows that the people do not in their appearance record any signs of being in a chronic state of semi-starvation." Again, after describing the dwellings of the poorer classes of ryots as ill-lighted, undrained, unventilated, dirty and uncleaned, and not water-tight—furnaces in the hot weather and stifling blackholes in the cold,—he goes on to state that "it is wonderful how the people manage to exist in them, *and develope a large proportion of fine men.*" Mr. Nicholson says much the same as regards the lowest class of labourers in the Anantapur district. According to him the people are not of weak physique. They are sturdy and well set up, the poorest classes, viz., Boyas, being particularly "lusty." The ordinary ryot is a favourable specimen of a man physically, and the general impression given by the appearance of the people is that of a good physique and ability to bear toil. Rickety children are scarce, and deformed and idiotic children are especially few. The last census shows a notable decrease in the number of blind and insane persons and of those suffering from leprosy. In seasons where there is only a partial failure of crops, the classes who suffer and who are inured to privation show a strong dislike to avail themselves of the relief afforded by Government works. When there is a failure of crops for two or three seasons in succession over large areas of country simultaneously, the resources of even the better classes of labourers and ryots become exhausted, and in the dry districts almost half the population may succumb to the calamity as was the case in 1876 and 1877. The conclusions then may be stated as follows: (1) The great majority of the population is very poor when judged by a European standard; (2) compared with the condition of the people fifty years ago, as shown by the accounts given by Sir Thomas Munro, Mr. Russel, Sir Henry Montgomery, Mr. Bourdillon and others, whose statements have been referred to in a previous portion of this memorandum, there has certainly been improvement in the material condition of the population, the advance consisting mainly in a rise in the standard of living of the upper strata of society, and a reduction in the percentage which the lowest grades bear to the total population; (3) the very lowest classes still live a hand-to-mouth existence, but not being congregated in towns, they have a better physique than one would expect to find in them, considering their resourcelessness and the frequency of crop failures on which occasions they have to pick up a scanty subsistence as best they can; and (4) the economic condition of the country, as a whole, though improving, is at best a low one, and is such as to tax the energies and statesmanship of government to the utmost in devising suitable remedies for its amelioration.

Comparison of the economic condition of India with that of European countries.

67. As comparisons are often instituted between the value of trade, average income, &c., per head of the population in India and European countries, and inferences are drawn therefrom as to the relative condition of the masses of the population in these countries, it may be worth while to enquire how far these comparisons are legitimate, and subject to what qualifications the inferences based on them may be accepted.

First, as regards the value of trade: The foreign trade of India in 1890-91 amounted to 6·8 rupees, or, say, less than 14*s*. per head of the population. The trade of England in 1884 was £19 and even of Russia £1·3 per head. That as a commercial country England is immensely ahead of India or any other country goes without saying, but the relative importance of any two countries cannot be gauged simply by comparing the values of foreign trade per head of the population, without taking the size of the countries and the omitted factor of their internal trade into account. For instance, Holland has a trade of £34 per head, or nearly double the rate for England, and from this it does not follow that its maritime greatness is twice that of England. India in point of size is as big as Europe without Russia, and if Europe *minus* Russia were treated as one country and its foreign trade were alone considered, that is to say, if the trade of Russia with other European countries and the trade of European countries other than Russia with non-European countries were alone taken into account, the value of trade per head of the population would come out very small. The Madras Presidency by itself is one-sixth larger in point of size than the United Kingdom, and its external trade by sea amounts to 18*s*. per head of the population. There is besides a large land trade with other provinces, including Native States. The distinction, in fact, between foreign and domestic trade is itself an artificial and accidental one. For instance, the trade of Tuticorin with Ceylon or Pondicherry is foreign trade; its trade with Calcutta or Rangoon is domestic trade; and for commercial purposes, England itself is, or at all events was until railways were constructed, more accessible than the Punjab. This being so, it is the aggregate of foreign and domestic trade, and not the foreign trade considered by itself, that is important for the purpose for which comparisons of this kind are instituted. Another fact to be borne in mind in judging of the increase of prosperity of a country from the increase in the money-value of trade is the change in the purchasing power of money. So far as India is concerned, the purchasing power of money has fallen, and, therefore, the increase in the money-value of trade does not represent a proportionate increase in the volume of the commodities exchanged. Nevertheless, as already pointed out, the producer in India now realizes for his produce a larger value than he did in 1850 and obtains his imported articles much cheaper, that is, by giving a smaller quantity of his own articles in exchange, and consequently his gain has probably not been less than what it would have been if the volume had increased in proportion to the money-value of trade, the purchasing power of money itself remaining stationary.

Secondly, as regards the total income of the country and the share of it per head of the population: The total income of the United Kingdom has been estimated at 1,247 million £, of France at 965 millions, of Russia at 848 millions and of Spain at 218 millions, the share per head of the population being £35·2, 25·7, 10·1 and 11·5, respectively. I have made no attempt to estimate the income of India, as I do not believe that there are data for doing this with any approach to accuracy. Sir Evelyn Baring some years ago estimated the income of India at 540 millions Rx. and the rate per head at Rs. 27. The Famine Commissioners estimated the average value of agricultural production in the Madras Presidency at 50 millions, and taking the income from other sources at half of that from land, the rate per head comes out as Rs. 25. In France the non-agricultural income is stated to bear the proportion of 122 per cent. to the agricultural, in Russia 75 per cent., and in Spain 64 per cent. The 50 per cent. assumed for India is, therefore, probably not far from the mark, but the income from land itself is estimated on very uncertain data, and it is quite as likely that the total income amounts to Rs. 30 per head as that it is Rs. 25 per head. The difference, small as it looks, is 20 per cent., and will really amount to a large percentage of error. In England the savings annually made, that is, the additions to the capital, amount to 150 millions sterling out of a total income of 1,247 millions or only 12 per cent.[76] I

[76] It is sometimes asserted that taking the income of India at Rs. 27 per head of the population and the expenditure at nearly the same amount, there is no margin for saving at all. In these calculations the assumed cost of living of an adult male labourer is taken as the average cost of living per head of the population. This is of course quite erroneous. In England the cost of living of men, women and children is estimated to be in the ratio of 20, 16 and 8. Of the population in this Presidency 35 per cent. or more than one-third is under 15 years of age, and assuming that the proportions as to the relative cost of living of men, women and children to be the same as in England, the cost per individual of the population will be, roughly speaking, less than half of that of a male adult labourer. This leaves a considerable margin for saving, though not of course any thing like what it is in England. At least 10 millions a year are saved in the shape of coin and bullion, and there is a considerable quantity of property added to the capital in the shape of new houses, furniture, wells, &c. The growth of capital is of course much slower here than in England, but even in that country it is only during the last three centuries that capital has grown rapidly as will be seen from the following estimates of capital in England at different periods given by Mr. Giffen:

—	Years.	Population. Millions.	Capital. Million.	Capital. Per head.
			£	£
England	1600	4·5	100	22
	1720	6·5	370	57
	1800	9·0	1,500	167
United Kingdom ..	1812	17·0	2,700	160
	1845	28·0	4,000	143
	1885	37·0	9,600	270

In 1600 the *capital* per head in England was only two-thirds of the annual *income* per head now.

do not therefore attach much value to the estimate put forward as regards the total income of India, but assuming it to be correct, it will be seen that India shows very poorly in comparison with European countries. There can be no doubt that India is really very poor, but this is not seen so much in the hard struggle for existence of the lowest classes as in the comparatively small number of wealthy persons. This will be evident when we take into account the distribution of incomes among the different classes of society. In England and Scotland, out of a total number of 14½ million persons who make earnings, 1·4 millions or nearly 10 per cent. pay income-tax, *i.e.*, have an income of not less than £150 per annum. The average income of this class is £411 per head. It is estimated that 1½ million persons or another 10 per cent. of the upper and middle classes have incomes less than £150 earn £71 each. Manual labourers (11·6 millions) or 80 per cent. get £44 each. In Ireland, on the other hand, out of 2 millions of persons who make earnings, 0·1 million persons or 5 per cent. have an income of £260 each; ·3 million persons or 15 per cent. have £37 each; and 1·6 million manual labourers or 80 per cent. earn £22 each. In France, out of 17·7 million persons who get incomes, 3·7 million persons or 20 per cent. earn £113 each, another 3·7 million persons or 20 per cent. earn £43; and the remaining 10·3 million persons or 60 per cent. earn £29. For the Madras Presidency we have no means of making any estimate which can at all be compared with those given above. The following figures, however, will serve to show how poor the greatest portion of the population here is. Out of a population of nearly 35 millions there are 7 millions of heads of families allowing 5 persons to a family. The number of persons assessed to the income-tax, *i.e.*, having non-agricultural incomes of not less than Rs. 500 per annum, is 56,809. The number of Government ryots paying not less than Rs. 250 revenue to Government, and their income from land may be estimated at twice the assessment they pay, is 8,869. Including Zemindars and inamdars and ryots in zemindaries having large landed properties, the number of persons with incomes from land and other sources exceeding Rs. 500 per annum cannot be higher than 70,000, which is 1 per cent. of the total number of families. As there is more than one person earning income or wages in a family, it is obvious that the persons earning more than Rs. 500 cannot be even so high as 1 per cent.

Thirdly, in considering the question, whether the low money income of this country means greater hardships to the lowest classes of the population than in European countries, the bare necessaries of life, both as regards quantity and money-value, required in the countries compared must be taken into account. To begin with, the quantity of food required or assimilated in this country is less than in colder climates, as shown by the fact that whereas in England a British soldier's weekly rations are fixed at 25·7 lb., the allowance for the same soldier here is 20 lb. only. Many things which are absolutely necessary in a cold climate are either not necessary here, or nature gives them gratis. House-room, clothing and fuel for protection from cold and damp are required to a much smaller extent here than in colder climates. Thus taking the family of an English labourer with an income of £60 a year, the cost of food and groceries amounts to only £30 or 50 per cent., while £6 or 10 per cent. goes for rent and £24 or 40 per cent. for clothing, &c. In this country labourers in villages pay no house-rent; their clothing does not cost them more than Rs. 4 or Rs. 5 a year for all the members of the family. They buy no fuel and hardly require any light or fire except for cooking purposes at nights. From inquiries I have made I find that the cost of food in this country in ordinary times in the case of an adult labourer in rural tracts amounts to about Rs. 1-12-0 per mensem [77] or 1 anna per diem; for Brahmins and higher castes the cost is Rs. 3-8-0 per mensem or 2 annas per diem. In towns the cost of living may be taken at 50 per cent. more including house-rent and cost of fuel. The weekly earnings of a town labourer and of the other members of his family (say 2*s*. 6*d*.) will thus maintain the family in ordinary times comfortably according to the standard of living to which it is accustomed. In London, on

---

[77] I have given in the appendix V.–F. (m 5, 6 & 9) the particulars of the cost of living of a labourer in this country and in European countries. The scales of diet prescribed in jails for Europeans and natives are also given for comparison, appendix V.–F. (m 8 & 10). There can be no doubt that the jail diet is much more liberal than that in use among ordinary labourers in the lower classes of the population. The latter certainly do not get meat three times a week with curds on non-meat days, and skilled medical attendance in case of sickness. The grain given is cholum, cumbu, or ragi, but a considerable portion of the lowest classes use *varagu*, a much inferior grain, the price of which is only two-thirds of that of the other grains. In England it was three centuries ago that wheat became a common article of diet in substitution of rye, barley and oats, and the consumption of meat has increased within the last 40 years. It is estimated that the cost of meat and of wheat containing equal quantities of nourishment are in the ratio of 7 to 1. In the case of the English labourer in times of pressure there is scope for the reduction of the secondary wants of life and of the cost of food by the substitution of cheaper for more costly food forming part of the ordinary diet. In India to some extent wheat and rice have taken the place of the cheaper dry grains, and this change is very beneficial.

the contrary, 10*s*. a week would mean almost starvation; for the same money wages represent far less real wages in England than here. About 1850, or 40 years ago, the price of wheat was 60*s*. per quarter in England and not more than 6*s*. a quarter in India. Now the price of wheat has heavily fallen in England owing to extensive importations, stimulated by the development of railways in America and the cheapness of ocean freights, and is now between 30*s*. and 35*s*. a quarter, while the price of wheat in India has risen to about 18*s*. a quarter, but still the price of wheat in England is nearly double that of India. On the whole, there is greater uniformity of conditions as regards wealth, or rather poverty, in India than in England, while, on the other hand, in the latter country, in spite of its immense wealth, the intensity of suffering and distress is greater among the lowest classes, owing partly to the inclemency of the climate and partly to the conditions of social and industrial life. In ordinary seasons, as already stated, the poor in this country have no difficulty in finding a subsistence, and the infirm and old are supported by relations or voluntary charity; and deaths by starvation are unknown; and in years of famine, nearly all suffer alike and people die in thousands. In England, though there is incomparably greater wealth, 1,800,000 or 6·3 per cent. of the population receives State relief, and of the persons above 65 years of age, nearly 40 per cent. are dependent for subsistence on the State, having no provision to fall back upon or relations able and willing to support them. "In England," says Mr. Hobson in his *Problems of Poverty*, "the recorded deaths from starvation are vastly more numerous than in any other country. In 1880 the number for England is given as 101. In 1879, the number for London alone is 27. This is, of course, no adequate measure of the facts. For every recorded case there will be a hundred unrecorded cases where starvation is the practical, immediate cause of death. The death-rate of children in the poorer districts of London is found to be nearly three times that which obtains in the richer neighbourhoods. Contemporary history has no darker page than that which records not the death-rate of children, but the conditions of child-life in our great cities. In setting down such facts and figures as may assist readers to adequately realize the nature and extent of poverty, it has seemed best to deal exclusively with the material aspects of poverty, which admit of some exactitude of measurement; the ugly and degrading surroundings of a life of poverty, the brutalizing influences of the unceasing struggle for a bare subsistence, the utter absence of a reasonable hope of improvement, in short, the whole subjective side of poverty is not less terrible because it defies statistics." On the other hand, periodic famines and wholesale destruction of life of the kind frequent in India are unknown.[78]

Fourthly.—It is when we consider vital statistics that the low condition of this country, as compared with European countries, becomes most apparent. The expectation of life or the number of years which every person born may, on an average, be expected to live is less than twenty-three years in this country, while it is nearly 43 years in England. The number that die before reaching five years is 50 out of 100 here, and 25 out of 100 in England. The number of persons dying between the ages of ten and twenty, the period in which they may industrially be expected to become most efficient, is 8 out of 50 in this country, and 3 out of 73 in England. The registration of births and deaths is very imperfect; still the rate of recorded deaths is as high as 29·3 per 1,000 of the population in the 55 municipal towns, and

---

[78] I have given in the appendix V. (m 2) particulars of the ratios which the taxation in some European countries bears to the assumed national income, to compare with similar ratio in this country. It will be seen that the ratio is not higher here (Rs. 2-14-3 out of say Rs. 27 or 11 per cent. including local taxes) than in European countries with the exception of England, whose wealth is enormous, and where much of public business is performed by voluntary unpaid agency. Of course in a country like India, where by far the larger portion of the national income is expended on the bare necessaries of life, a certain percentage of the national income taken by way of taxation may, in point of fact, be heavier than a higher percentage in a wealthy country. On the other hand, in a country where the people are unenterprizing and indolent, the Government has to assume functions which elsewhere are performed by the people themselves in order that they may reach a higher stage of industrial development than they would do if left to themselves. The conflicting considerations bearing on this subject have thus been forcibly stated by Professor Walker with special reference to India.

"By raising money as other money is raised, by taxes (the amount of which is taken by individuals out of their expenditure on the score of maintenance), Government has it in its power to accelerate to an unexampled degree the augmentation of the mass of real wealth. Such is the claim in behalf of Government expenditure. What is to be said of it? Let us proceed by way of an example. Let us take a large population spread over a vast extent of country, like India, which possesses almost illimitable facilities for the improvement of the soil through irrigation, and whose broad spaces demand numerous and extensive lines of artificial communication, by canal or railway. Let it be supposed that the people occupying this country are what the people of India now are, in numbers, in character, in habits of living and working. Alike under the influence of sexual passion and of religious superstition, they continually tend to increase up to the limits of subsistence, even to the verge of famine; not only accumulating no capital, but laying by no store for future wants; having neither the genius for organization nor the capacity of self-denial which would be required to initiate the simplest local improvements. Now, we may imagine such a population ruled by a benevolent, disinterested despot of the highest order of intelligence, a Napolean devoted to the arts of peace. We may imagine this ruler, by a system of taxation that shall be as just between individuals and as judicious in its seasons and methods as human wisdom can make it, first, drawing from the crops of good years a store against the occurrence of bad harvests; then, by a gradually increasing stringency of exaction, adding to the cost of living in such a way as to discourage the growth of population, while applying the proceeds to great public improvements which enable the food-supply of the empire to be readily equalized in the event of local scarcity; which guard the crops against the

22·9 per 1,000 in rural parts, while the rate in such a large city as London is only 21 per mille. High as the mortality is in this country, there is little doubt that it is much lower than what it was formerly. Surgeon-General Sir W. J. Moore, in his address, read before the Congress of Hygiene and Demography, held recently in London, pointed out that death-rate in the army in India had been reduced from 69 to less than 14 per 1,000; European residents were so healthy that the best insurance offices were willing to issue policies to them without exacting extra premium, and, although the system of registration was still defective, the official reports of recent years showed that the average death-rates among the native population had decreased in a few years from 35 or more to 26·67 per 1,000; many diseases were diminishing, some had been extirpated. Even in the town of Madras where the high mortality in recent years has attracted public attention, elephantiasis, a loathsome disease which was once very prevalent, has now gone out almost completely. There is still a great deal to be done by means of greater

---

effects of periodical drought; which afford rapid and cheap passage to the products of inland districts. And as the productive power of the country increased under such an administration, we can imagine the high-minded ruler, intent on his benevolent object, still drawing away from the people, by taxation, all the surplus above the necessary cost of subsistence for the present population, which might otherwise be applied to the increase of population, and with the means thus acquired, providing capital in its various forms for the use of the frugal and temperate, perfecting communications, protecting the health and lives of his subjects by sanitary arrangements, and, at last, undertaking the elementary education of the whole body of the people.

"All this, it is clear, an absolute ruler of the character indicated might do for his people; and not a little of this many a benevolent and able ruler has done for his people. 'The forced frugality,' to use Bentham's phrase, which his taxes have imposed, has at once repressed population and stimulated industry among the existing body of labourers. His wise expenditure upon public works, and in public education has sown the seed from which has sprung many a golden harvest.

"But while we see, thus, what an ideal monarch might do for a people indolent, unambitious, sensual, by applying a portion of the wealth they created to ends more useful, elevating and satisfying, than their individual tastes and appetites would have selected, we are forced also to remember how a large part of the wealth raised by taxation has, in all ages, been spent in war, pomp and folly; how strong is the tendency to extravagance and even to corruption in Government expenditure; how much of what the people pay the treasury does not receive; how much of what the treasury disburses does not reach its intended object. These considerations are strong enough to justify in a large degree, if not wholly, that unwillingness to entrust to Government, the consumption of the wealth of the community, much beyond what is necessary to secure domestic tranquillity and the administration of justice between man and man, which is so peculiarly American.

"Yet it is possible that this feeling may be carried too far. When one contrasts the highways, the bridges, the streets, the harbours, the breakwaters, the light-houses, and other aids to transportation and commerce, which Government provides, with the best that could be reasonably looked for from individual or associated effort, without the taxing power; when one contrasts our system of public education with the best that voluntary contributions or private munificence ever supplied; when one contrasts the sanitary arrangement for supplying pure air and pure water to our crowded cities with the condition of things which exists where these matters are left to un-official action; he will find occasion to qualify in no small degree his assent to the proposition that, under a well ordered constitution, Government is only a police man, to keep people from breaking each others heads or picking each others pockets."

attention to sanitation and water-supply to improve the public health of this Presidency; but, on the whole, there is no reason to suppose that public health is worse now than in times past. Destructive as fever is, it is much less destructive now than formerly, and it is noteworthy that fever is most prevalent, not in bad, but in good agricultural seasons when the rainfall is abundant. Of all the Provinces of India, the Central Provinces, which are exceptionally favoured by the comparative fertility of a large portion of the land, show the greatest mortality. These Provinces are taxed the lightest, the revenue assessed per acre being between 5 and 8 annas and reaching 9 annas in only one district.

Lastly, if we wish to find a parallel in European countries to the state in which this country was 50 years ago, we must go back to the England of 400 years ago or at the end of the fifteenth century, which has been described by Dr. Cunningham in his *Growth of English Industry and Commerce* as follows: "Unless the statements of the chroniclers are grossly exaggerated, England suffered severely during the fifteenth century from two scourges which are now entirely unknown—famine and pestilence. The population was dependent on the seasons for the food-supply, and though this might be plentiful in good years, there was often a general scarcity which was intensified in particular districts into a local famine. At such times men were driven to use acorns and roots for food and had recourse to the flesh of dogs and horses: some cases of cannibalism are reported. It was only rarely that starving people were reduced to such extremities; but there is some reason to believe that they habitually used diseased and unwholesome food, and that they were thus rendered a ready prey to the ravages of pestilence. The Black death was specially terrible, but we read of many other visitations, the accounts of which are sufficiently appalling. A century during which more than twenty outbreaks of plague occurred, and have been recorded by the chroniclers, can hardly be regarded by us except as one long unbroken period of pestilence. Besides these occasional outbreaks there was chronic typhoid in the towns, and leprosy all over the country. The undrained and neglected soil; the shallow stagnant waters which lay upon the surface of the ground, the narrow unhealthy homes of all classes of the people; the filthy neglected streets of the towns; the abundance of stale fish which was eaten; the scanty variety of vegetables which were consumed; predisposed the agricultural and town population alike to typhoid diseases and left them little chance of recovery when stricken down with pestilence." The small money incomes of those days may be judged from the fact that the bailiff in husbandry, who was a superior servant, got yearly 26*s*. 8*d*. and 5*s*. for clothing, besides meat and drink, which may be estimated at 2*d*. a day; the ordinary artisan had 3*d*. or 4*d*. a day and the reaper 3*d*. a day, with meat and drink; so that in 22 weeks of continuous work, the ordinary artisan would earn as much as the bailiff did in a year. No sufficient data as regards regularity of employment in those days are available. The common servant in husbandry was paid 20*s*. 8*d*. and his wife 14*s*. per annum besides their food, according to the highest statutable rate in the fifteenth century; so that their united earnings would provide a little more than half the usual allowance for an adult's food, and out of this sum they had to feed their family, pay for fuel, rent and clothing. Even if they could eke out a living in the common waste, says Dr. Cunningham, it is most unlikely that they had a larger free income than the agricultural labourer at the present day; we could not institute an accurate comparison unless we knew not only the prices of the articles they used, but also the quality of the goods they were able to procure. It is not easy to obtain such information in the present day and we cannot hope to get sufficient data for judging certainly about the distant past. So far as regularity of employment and short hours are a test of the well-being of the workman, the fifteenth century day labourer was badly off; his summer hours lasted from five in the morning till half-past seven at night with breaks which amounted to two or two and a half hours in all. The conditions of the banking business in the fourteenth century were such that banking operations were very circumscribed. The most striking difference between their times and ours is the entire absence of commercial credits; there were no bank-notes or cheques, or other instruments of credit except a few foreign bills. Dealing for credit was little developed and dealing in credit was unknown.

The sufferings of the people have probably never been as severe in this country as is described above in consequence of a less inclement climate and a more fruitful soil, but the wonderful improvement which has taken place in England during the last three centuries might well inspire the hope that similar improvement here is not unattainable.

SECTION VI.—*Certain alleged evils in the present economic position and remedial measures considered.*

Alleged evils in the present economic position.

68. In this section, I propose to make a few remarks on certain special evils which are alleged to retard, to a greater or less extent, the improvement of the condition of the masses of the population. These are, first, periodical revisions of land assessment; second, the uncertainty of the tenure of ryots in zemindaries; third, the increasing dependence of ryots on professional money lenders, the stringency and inelasticity of methods of revenue collection, and the absence of a developed system of credit; fourth, the decay of domestic industries, the absence of diversity of occupations, and the dense ignorance of, and want of enterprise among, the agricultural and industrial classes; fifth, the excessive cost of litigation; and sixth, the disintegration of village communities and the decay of the spirit of co-operation so necessary in a poor country for the purpose of carrying out large undertakings and for providing safeguards against common dangers, and the absence of a machinery which would serve as a safe and trustworthy gauge to Government of the necessity for undertaking legislation in matters affecting the laws of inheritance and domestic relations of the people, corresponding to the rapid changes that are taking place in their economic condition. I shall endeavour to state to what extent the evils enumerated exist and are the outcome of the present *régime*, what measures have been taken by Government to remove them or mitigate their effects, and what further remedial measures are practicable.

I. PERIODICAL REVISIONS OF LAND SETTLEMENT.

The circumstances under which the Settlement department was organized and the general principles laid down for its guidance.

69. The Settlement department in this Presidency was organized in 1856, that is, at a time when it was just beginning to recover from the effects of an acute agricultural depression. The old assessments had been excessive and far beyond what the ryots could pay regularly in all seasons, and their incidence, notwithstanding the reductions made from time to time, had, owing to the great fall in the prices of produce, become oppressive. A large extent of land, often of superior quality, had fallen out of cultivation in consequence of the unequal pressure of assessments on the different classes of soil; and cultivators who were unable or unwilling to cultivate lands were forced to do so.

Persons who possessed inam or tax free lands were prohibited from cultivating such lands, unless they cultivated at the same time an equal quantity of lands paying full tax to Government; and torture was freely resorted to for collecting the revenue. It was to put an end to this state of things, so repressive of the prosperity of the agricultural classes, and to promote agricultural enterprise, that Government undertook the survey and re-assessment of the cultivable lands throughout the Presidency. The object in view was two-fold, viz., first, to reduce heavy assessments and to fix a moderate tax on lands; and, secondly, to remove anomalies and inequalities in the assessments and to adjust, to some extent, the tax levied on lands of different qualities with reference to their relative productive powers. It was acknowledged that the classification of soils in relation to their productive capabilities and the ascertainment of their values for purposes of assessment was a task of enormous magnitude and difficulty, but it was expected that by fixing the assessments in a liberal manner, after making large allowances for all possible errors and miscalculations, a fair assessment could be arrived at. The spirit in which the operations connected with the revision of settlement were intended to be carried out will be seen from the following extract from the despatch sent by the Madras Government to the Court of Directors in 1856. "An exact and scientifically accurate classification, distinguishing all the minute variations of composition, quality and fertility of soil, is an operation of extreme difficulty in any country, even with all the aids that can be supplied by a high degree of scientific knowledge, accurate and practised observation, and a trustworthy agency. In this country, all these helps must in a great degree be wanting, and it is the more necessary that the Government should enter on the undertaking in a liberal spirit; and if so entered on, the difficulties will almost wholly disappear. It must be remembered that the right of the Government is not a *rent* which consists of all the surplus produce, after paying the costs of cultivation and the profits of agricultural stock; but a *land revenue only* which ought, if possible, to be so lightly assessed as to leave a surplus or rent to the occupier, whether he in fact let the land to others or retain it in his own hands. Nor is this simply an abstract question of right; it is certain that the course here advocated is that which will give the highest land revenue, because it holds out the greatest inducements to the extended occupation of the land. It must be remembered that this Presidency contains a vast extent of unoccupied land, liable to pay revenue if cultivated, but heretofore waste, greatly in consequence of the exorbitant assessment fixed or liable to be fixed on it; and it is certain that this land will be increasingly brought under the plough if moderately assessed. If the settlement be undertaken in this liberal and comprehensive spirit, the preliminary classification of the soil will not be difficult. Under a moderate assessment exact accuracy is immaterial, because the greatest difference of assessment which could be caused by the want of it would not be such as to render the land an unprofitable holding, or to prevent its occupation; at the utmost, it would only render such land somewhat less profitable than other land." These principles were approved in their entirety by the Home Government who went even further than the Madras Government in insisting that the agricultural classes should be treated with the utmost liberality with a view to ensure their prosperity. The Madras Government had proposed in accordance with ancient customary usage to fix the land revenue at a certain share, viz., 30 per cent. of the *gross* produce. The Home Government, however, ruled that the land revenue should represent a fixed proportion of the *net* produce. They pointed out that the proposal to take a proportion of the gross produce was inconsistent with the principle that the right of Government was not even to the *whole rent*, but only to a *share* of it; for, while as regards lands of a high degree of fertility, possessing every means of communication and in the neighbourhood of good markets, 30 per cent. of the gross produce might fall short of the share of the rent Government was entitled to, the same percentage of the gross produce might, in the case of lands less fertile and less favorably situated, considerably exceed the whole rent and trench on the profits of cultivation and wages of labour. The natural and inevitable consequence of such a procedure would be to favour the most fertile lands and to press with increasing severity on the poorer lands. They further pointed out that the fact that the holdings in this country were of small extent, that the labour was in most cases performed by the ryot and his family, and that the agricultural capital employed was small, did not interfere in any way with the principle laid down, "as the produce of the land must at least be sufficient to feed and clothe the labourer and his family and to replace the cattle and agricultural implements as they become worn out; and besides this, a surplus must remain for the payment of the assessment imposed by the State." In 1858 again, Lord Stanley, the first Secretary of State for India, re-affirmed the same principle. He remarked, "I am satisfied that it is quite impossible to ascertain, with any approach to minute accuracy, either the gross or the net produce of each field; but I am at the same time convinced that, if either or both of these objects could be accomplished, the right course would be to take a fixed proportion of the *net* and not of the *gross* produce. The expenses of cultivation vary greatly in areas of land of different qualities, yielding the same quantities of gross produce; and the net produce will, of course, vary inversely in the same degree. I do not desire that the Director of Revenue Settlement should endeavour to ascertain with precision the actual net produce of each field; but that, in determining the rates of assessment for the different qualities of land, the principle which was laid down should be carefully borne in mind." In other words, a share of the net produce was to be considered as the *maximum* State charge, and having regard to the difficulty of calculating it accurately and to the injurious consequences of over-assessment, the tax was to be so fixed as to leave a liberal margin for miscalculations. This share of the net produce was eventually fixed at one-half. It was further ruled that the grain assessment should be commuted into money-value with reference to the average prices at which grain had been sold by the ryots for a sufficiently long period of years, in view to taking account of the fluctuations in prices which usually occur, and that the money rates imposed should not be liable to alteration for thirty years. Another important consideration to be taken note of and allowed for in the conversion of land revenue payable in kind into a money assessment is the fact that payment in kind with reference to each year's produce, however inconvenient in other respects, has the merit of calling upon the ryot to pay a small tax in years of deficient produce when the ryot is straitened in his means of payment, and a proportionately higher tax when he has reaped an abundant produce and can afford to pay with ease a larger revenue.

The elaborate methods of Madras settlement compared with the simpler method of Bombay; the two do not substantially differ.

70. These are the cardinal principles of the settlement, and they are as applicable to the Bombay as to the Madras Presidency. The instructions issued to the Madras Settlement officers for carrying out these principles require that the net produce of every variety of soil should be ascertained by a very large number of actual experiments, and the procedure prescribed for this purpose is most elaborate. The first process is to divide the soil into certain main classes according to the mechanical composition and chemical properties of the lands dealt with; there are 14 such classes recognized by the Settlement

department. Each class of soil is then subdivided into, some 3 and others 5, "sorts," with reference to their degrees of fertility as ascertained by an examination of the constituents of the surface soil and sub-soil, the total varieties of soils dealt with being 66. All lands, whether irrigated or unirrigated, are classed under these 66 varieties of soil. But for irrigated lands the classification is still more elaborate, because these lands are again divided into a number of groups according to the nature and efficiency of the sources of irrigation from which the lands derive their supply of water, and lands falling under each of these groups are classified under the 66 "sorts" of soil already referred to. The second process is to ascertain the grain outturn of the lands irrigated and unirrigated classified as above shown. For this purpose, certain prevailing dry crops in the case of dry lands, and paddy in the case of irrigated lands, are taken as standards, and the average outturn, in terms of these crops, of every variety of soil, is to be ascertained by actual harvest experiments conducted for a series of years. From the average outturn thus ascertained a deduction of from 15 to 25 per cent. is made on account of extraordinary vicissitudes of season and barren patches unavoidably measured with fields. The third process is to find the money value of the grain outturn. For this purpose, the average of the market prices of standard crops in the months in which the ryots sell their produce for a number of years, generally twenty, is ascertained, and deducting from it 8 to 20 per cent. for cartage and merchant's profits, the remainder is taken to represent the ryot's prices and adopted as the commutation rate; and the grain outturn is converted into money at this rate. The fourth process is to ascertain by actual enquiries the expenses of cultivation for each kind of soil. The difference between the money value of the grain and the cultivation expenses is taken as the net value of each kind of soil of which a moiety represents the land tax; and a table of rates is accordingly framed. To correct inequalities arising (1) from the adoption of a single commutation rate for an entire district or other large tract of country comprising a number of taluks, while the prices of grain often differ from village to village according to facilities of communication and proximity to markets, and (2) from the adoption of the same grain values for similar soils whose fertility may be affected by local circumstances, such as, vicinity to the sea, rivers or hills, the villages are grouped together into separate groups, and the money rates applicable to the lands classified in each group are raised or lowered according to circumstances. Minor differences in the value of lands due to the same causes are allowed for by modifying the classification under "sorts" in each group. Thus fair land in a good situation immediately adjoining the inhabited portion of the village would be classed in the first sort "good," while good land at a great distance would be classed as "moderate." In the case of irrigated lands their classification into "sorts" also is adjusted with reference to their facilities for irrigation owing to their proximity or otherwise to the irrigation source.

The procedure prescribed in the Bombay Presidency for the valuation of soils is, on the other hand, much simpler. Lands in each village are divided into 10 classes, and their relative values are ascertained by noting their advantages in respect of irrigation, and their defects, such as (1) admixture of nodules of limestone, (2) admixture of sand, (3) sloping surface, (4) want of cohesion, (5) impermeability to water, (6) exposure to scouring from flow of water in the rains, and (7) excessive moisture from springs, each of the defects being held to lower the soil one class. The rate for the highest class of soil in each village is fixed by the Superintendent of Survey with reference to general considerations, such as climate, facilities for market communications, average prices and the prosperity or deterioration of the village under previous settlements; and the rates to be imposed on the lands of the other classes are determined by a mere arithmetical process.

The Madras settlement operations, however, though conducted under elaborate rules resolve themselves in the final result into the simple method adopted in Bombay, firstly, because, the minute and extended enquiries which they involve are in most cases impossible to carry out and have frequently been dispensed with; secondly, because, none of the data on which reliance has to be placed, such as prices of food-grains in former years, are perfectly trustworthy, and in some cases information regarding the quotations of prices in the ryot's selling months for the old years are entirely wanting; and thirdly, because, the determination of the rates of assessment with reference to a large number of factors, slight errors in regard to which might seriously vitiate the total result, is apt to make the assessments excessive. The late Mr. Pedder, Revenue Secretary in the India Office, has pointed this out very clearly.[79] After describing the procedure prescribed for the Madras settlements by "the instruc-

---

[79] *Vide* Statement of Moral and Material Progress and Condition of India for 1882-83, part i., page 115.

tions," he goes on to say, "Such is the *theory* of the Madras settlement. In practice, however, it has been found impossible or dangerous to adhere to it strictly. In the first place, the difficulty of determining with accuracy the average yield of land is great; next, the only way of finding the average cost of cultivation is to ascertain what it would cost to cultivate a given holding by hired labour, and, as this labour would be needed for only a certain number of weeks or months, it is obvious that nothing would be allowed as wage for the subsistence of the cultivator and his family during the rest of the year. Hence, the first step in a Madras settlement practically is to determine, on general considerations (such as those described under Bombay), whether the tract coming under settlement requires a decrease or will bear an enhancement of its land revenue, and to what extent. The total amount of assessment to be imposed having thus been decided on, the results of the process above described are adjusted so as to yield it. The estimates of average yield are reduced to allow for error, or for exceptionally bad seasons, and the commutation rate is lowered to cover possible fluctuations of prices in the future. In practice, therefore, the elaborate process above described determines rather the relative than the absolute assessments of different classes of land, and the Madras method does not really differ very widely from that of Bombay."

In Madras, as in Bombay, valuation of soil dependant greatly on judgment and discretion of individual assessors and has no claim to scientific accuracy.

71. An idea may be formed as to how greatly the rates imposed by the Settlement department must depend upon the discretion and judgment of individual officers and how little upon demonstrable calculated results, from the following instance taken from the Salem settlement. The calculated dry rates for black loam are in the first group Rs. 3, Rs. 2-8-0 and Re. 1 per acre, respectively, according as the land is placed under the sorts "*good*," "*middling*" or "*bad or indifferent*." The classification under these "sorts" depends not only upon the quality of the soil but also upon the distance of the land from the village site and other circumstances, some of which affect the gross produce of the land and others the net produce or rent value, by increasing or diminishing the cultivation expenses or the cost of bringing the produce to market. It can be readily conceived what great difference it would make to the ryot whether his land is classified under class 4, sort 3 or class 4, sort 2, the assessment in the latter case being 150 per cent. greater than in the former; and yet in many cases it would be difficult to say whether

classification under sort 2 or sort 3 was the more correct. In later settlements, the difference in the rates appertaining to consecutive sorts of land has been reduced by increasing the number of "sorts" from 3 to 5; but it is obvious that even a difference of 50 or 25 per cent. in the money rates must affect the ryot to a considerable extent.

Hence the necessity to allow a large margin for error in fixing land assessments. Mr. Goodrich's remarks regarding "excessive allowances" ignore this fact.

72. It is important to bear in mind these considerations which illustrate the inherent difficulties in all land valuations, as proposals are often made for increasing or diminishing the land tax, more often the former, on the supposition that the hypothetical data assumed in settlement calculations, whose main object may be stated to be (1) to systematize the classification made by the subordinate officers for purposes of easy check by the higher officers, and (2) to regulate the relative incidence of the tax imposed upon lands of different soils in small tracts of country whose conditions as regards climate, facilities for irrigation, access to markets and supply of labour are fairly homogeneous, have any pretensions to scientific accuracy. Thus, Mr. Goodrich, late of the Madras Civil Service, in an article entitled "Land Revenue in Madras," published in the *Economic Journal* for September 1891, states that the grain valuations and their money-equivalents fixed by the Madras Settlement department are unduly low, the estimates being "whittled down by excessive allowances, or by making a fair allowance several times over in the course of the calculation." Mr. Goodrich in making these remarks entirely ignores the original instructions issued to the Settlement department when it was organized, viz., that having regard to the extreme difficulty of valuing soils, the variability of the seasons and the precariousness of the crops, the poverty of the agricultural classes and the injurious consequences of over-assessment, the assessment imposed should be extremely moderate, and that a very liberal margin should be allowed for errors and miscalculations. I agree with Mr. Goodrich in considering that on the whole the estimates of average outturn of soils adopted by the Settlement department are below rather than above the mark, though one cannot be very certain about this in the case of the poorer soils, large areas of which obtain a catch-crop when they can. As regards the "*excessive*" allowances, it seems to me that the allowances, so far from being excessive, are barely sufficient. The deduction of from 15 to 25 per cent. from the average outturn for vicissitudes of season and unprofitable areas measured with holdings is, in many cases, less than

the percentage of dry lands under occupation, which though not cultivated is charged with assessment annually.[80] This percentage for the Godávari district is 48·5, for Tinnevelly 31·5, for Nellore 27·3, for Chingleput 26·6 and for the whole Presidency 16·9. In some of the districts, the lands are left uncropped for pasture, but this is only in a small number of cases. Then again, in fixing the commutation rate, from 8 to 20 per cent. is deducted from the average prices for cartage and merchant's profits. The average prices are prices for the entire district, while the price in one taluk station often differs from that in another by as much as 30 per cent. To the ryots who have lands in the vicinity of the taluk stations, where prices rule high, the rate is favorable, but, to the ryots in out-of-the-way parts, the commutation rates are unfavorable, and relief has to be given by reducing the rates under the system of "*grouping*" already alluded to. Moreover, the settlement calculations do not, ostensibly at all events, make allowances for the liability of the ryot to pay a fixed cash assessment in all seasons whether the crop he reaps is abundant, or so scanty as to be hardly sufficient for his subsistence. It is well known that poor ryots who borrow grain from sowkars or the richer ryots in the cultivation season have to repay at the harvest, *i.e.*, in 6 or 8 months, the quantity borrowed together with an additional amount varying from 25 to 50 per cent. When the crop fails and payment has to be postponed to the next harvest the additional quantity payable is, of course, proportionately increased. Again, as remarked by Sir Thomas Munro, "it is in the nature of assessment, proceeding from single fields to whole districts, and taking each field at its supposed average produce, to make the aggregate sum greater than what can be easily realized," and in view of this, he used to lower the estimates of the assessors from 5 to 15 per cent. When it is remembered that a margin has to be provided on account of all these sources of error as well as weather-chances, Mr. Goodrich's complaint as regards "excessive allowances" will be seen not to have much foundation. In this connection, it may be worth while noting that Mr. Puckle had obtained the sanction of Government to the lands of the Salem district being assessed at rates favorable to the ryots. Mr. Goodrich,

---

[80] This applies, of course, to the poorer soils. As regards soils of the higher qualities, the allowances are probably more than sufficient. The result of applying a uniform scale of deduction to all soils is to make the incidence of assessment heavy on the soils of the poorer qualities and light on the better soils. As regards the high percentage of dry lands left waste, the Board of Revenue have, it appears, been instituting enquiries and the results must be awaited.

who was entrusted with the duty of introducing the settlement rates, succeeded soon after in getting Government to reconsider its decision and consent to impose higher rates. Whether Mr. Goodrich or Mr. Puckle was right may be judged from the fact that, in the famine of 1876–78, the mortality was the heaviest in the Salem district, next after Kurnool and Bellary, amounting to 18·7 per cent. of the population. The Salem district is one of the poorest in the Presidency, and in fixing the land tax it is necessary that the actual conditions of the case should not be lost sight of and that the scheme should not be based on mere theoretic considerations. In the above remarks, I have assumed that the data made use of in settlement calculations are fairly trustworthy, but for forming an idea of how extremely difficult it is to obtain even approximately correct data, and with what imperfect materials Settlement officers have to deal, some further particulars given in the appendix[81] may be referred to. There is, however, a curious proposal in Mr. Goodrich's article which completely neutralizes his suggestion that the land assessments should be considerably enhanced at each revision of settlement. It is this, viz., that in settlement calculations allowance should be made for the interest on the purchase value of the ryot's holding, which he estimates as being generally thirty times its assessment. The purchase money is, of course, the capitalized annual value of the holding at the current rate of interest, and if the annual value of the holding prior to the revision of the settlement is to be secured to the ryot under all circumstances, it is obvious that the land-tax cannot be enhanced at all. Though the interest on the purchase money of the ryot's holding cannot be taken into account, there is one important item which is omitted from the estimates of expenses of cultivation framed by the Settlement department, but which ought, properly speaking, to find a place in them, viz., *farming profits* as distinguished from *rent* properly so

---

[81] *Vide* Section VI.-A. (1). Compare also Mr. Benson's remarks on settlement calculations in his *Analysis of the Agricultural Statistics of the Kurnool District.* He says, as regards the commutation rate, "it is doubtful whether full allowance has been made in considering this matter for all the deductions made to arrive at the commutation rate and to compare that with the prices at which the ryot may be forced to dispose of his produce. *If therefore the estimated outturn and the calculations of the cost of cultivation are accurate,* the commutation rate for Pattikonda should be lowered at least to that adopted for Kurnool proper, and that followed in Koilkuntla to not more than Rs. 125 per garce. Nevertheless, it does not appear that the assessments are more than the land can in general be made to bear, nor more than the people will pay as is evidenced by the great recovery of the holdings since the famine; but, though the people may exist under such a burden, it must prevent their making any accumulations, such as would enable the ryots to form a reserve store on which to support themselves during an unfavorable season."

called. The original instructions prescribing the procedure for determining the land revenue rates, already quoted, make it clear that the right of Government is to a land revenue which "ought to be so lightly assessed as to leave a surplus or *rent* to the occupier, whether he in fact let the land to others or retain it in his own hands." Now, ryots are of three classes, viz., first, land-owners, who do not farm their lands but lease them to farmers; second, ryots, who farm their own lands employing hired labour for performing the manual operations of cultivation; and third, peasant proprietors, who cultivate their lands themselves with the aid of the members of their families without employing hired labour. In the first case, the *rent* is the payment made by the farmer to the land-owner *minus* the cultivation expenses borne by the latter and the return for such permanent improvements to the land as might have been made by him. In the second and third cases, the *rent* would be what the land would fetch annually, had the land been let to a tenant instead of being cultivated by the owner. Where the rent is not ascertainable in this way, it must be taken to be the surplus produce left after paying the cost of hired labour, other expenses of cultivation, interest on stock and farming profits, which last must at least be sufficient for the subsistence of the farmer's family, according to the standard of comfort prevailing in the class to which it belongs. In this Presidency, owing to the prevalence of peasant properties, the letting value of lands is not in the majority of cases ascertainable, and consequently the distribution of the gross produce into its three components, viz., rent, farmer's profits and expenses of cultivation, has to be arrived at by estimating separately the several items of cost. In doing this, the settlement calculations make no special allowance for farming profits.

The enhancement of revenue in districts settled moderate. Hence the success of the settlements, growth of the value of landed property and rise in the standard of living among the agricultural classes.

73. In a previous portion of this memorandum, I have adduced evidence to show that, notwithstanding the difficulties above alluded to in making even approximately correct land valuations, the assessments imposed by the Settlement department have not been excessive, but on the contrary have been such as to admit of the large increase which has actually taken place in the money value of landed property—an increase which is considerably higher than the increase in the prices of agricultural produce. This result is due to the fact that the Government has in all settlements hitherto made taken care to see that the aggregate revenue of the

tracts settled is not enhanced by more than a very moderate[82] percentage. With the exception of Nellore and Vizagapatam in which the increase of revenue was 11 per cent. and 15 per cent., respectively, and the Nilgiris and the Wynaad taluk of the Malabar district in which a peppercorn rent has been imposed on a large area of waste land included in private holdings, which, under the previously existing revenue system, was charged for only when cultivated, the increase of revenue has in no case exceeded 10 per cent.; and in most cases it has fallen far short of the percentage of increase in the area of holdings brought to light by the new survey as compared with the area entered in the old accounts.[83] The Godávari district and the Masulipatam portion of the Kistna district are really no exceptions to the above statement, because the large apparent increase in the revenue of those districts, shown as due to the revised rates of settlement in the accounts, is really due to extension of irrigation under the anicut works recently constructed and to the fact that the water-rate levied on lands irrigated with anicut water, which had been tentatively fixed at Rs. 3 an acre, was raised to Rs. 4 per acre at the time the settlement rates were introduced and to some extent also to the land assessment itself having been raised in view to the increased value conferred on them by the construction of the anicut works. The statistics collected as regards leases registered in the Coimbatore district in 1889 and referred to in para. 48 of this memorandum show that the rental for which wet lands are leased out are between 4 and 5 times the Government assessment; in the case of dry lands the rental is between 3 and 4 times the assessment and as regards garden lands, or lands irrigated by means of wells, between 5 and 6 times. Of course the lands leased out under registered leases are mostly

---

[82] *Vide* statement printed as appendix (2) to section VI.-A. Sir George Campbell, in his minute on certain proposals, submitted by Lord Hobart's Government in 1874, in connection with the Madras Settlements (*vide* Notes on Indian Land Revenue, pages 134, &c., in Appendix I. to the Famine Commission Report, 1881), has remarked "According to the Governor they (the Settlement department) are supposed to be elaborately carrying out, under explicit instructions from Home, a system of valuation and assessment, on the basis of half net profits, but practically the rate of assessment is decided by very different and simpler considerations, the most important of which is that no cultivator is to pay more than he paid before, *plus* a very small percentage." This circumstance is referred to in a spirit of depreciation by Sir G. Campbell and other persons not acquainted with the objects and methods of Madras settlements and the previous history of the question, but there can be no doubt that it is precisely this moderation so frequently and emphatically enjoined by the Home Government that has ensured the success of the settlements and the improvement of the agricultural classes.

[83] The excess in the area of holdings brought to light by the survey is not in all cases due to waste land encroached upon by ryots and held without payment of tax. In many cases they were due to the fact that areas expressed in native land measures were converted into acres in the old revenue accounts at rates which were below the truth.

of superior qualities and form only a small proportion of the total lands under cultivation, and the whole of the rent is not realized in adverse seasons, and consequently it would be erroneous to accept the ratios, ascertained as regards them, as applicable to all lands leased out, much less to all lands generally. From inquiries I have made, I find that in most districts, and more especially in Coimbatore and Tinnevelly, the rental of wet lands taken as a whole is a little less than 3 times the Government assessment, and that of dry lands is about twice. The land-owner has to bear a portion of the cultivation expenses in connection with farm repairs and pays the Government assessment and local cesses out of the rental. Roughly speaking, the net profit of the owner of wet lands may be stated to be half as much again as the Government assessment and that the owner of dry lands makes as much as the Government assessment. Lands in the vicinity of towns, on which market garden produce can be grown give an enormous profit, but, on the other hand, there is a large extent of land of very poor quality on which chance crops are grown. These lands which are on the margin of cultivation pay no rent, and the land tax imposed on them is not a share of the *rent* but a *tax* on the earnings of labour. Individual districts have, of course, been dealt with, more or less liberally, according to the circumstances of the period during which the new settlement rates were introduced and the views entertained by the officers who had a predominant influence in the decision of the question of the extent to which the tracts settled could bear increased taxation. Thus in the Trichinopoly district, which was settled by Mr. Puckle at a time when the country had just begun to recover from the prolonged depression from which it had suffered and when the enormous rise in prices which soon after took place could hardly be foreseen, the assessments were reduced by 25 per cent., notwithstanding that the survey disclosed an increase in the area to the extent of 18 per cent. Salem, Nellore and Chingleput, settled at the end of the period of high prices, were treated less liberally, this being the result of the re-action of the lenient assessments of the earlier period. The enhancement of the revenue in Nellore, especially, viz., 11 per cent., must be considered heavy when it is remembered that the survey, so far from disclosing any excess in the area of holdings, showed a slight deficiency. Taking all the districts in which the settlements have been completed, as a whole, the increase in the revenue due to the enhanced settlement rates does not exceed 5 per cent., which cannot be considered excessive. In special tracts and as regards individual holdings, the increase of assessment has been much higher and has caused occasional hardship, and it is open to question whether sufficient consideration has been paid by the Settlement department in settling districts to the hardship in individual cases. The question came up for discussion in connection with the settlement of the Nellore district, and the rule was then laid down that, where the revised rates exceeded the old rates by 25 per cent., the difference should not be levied at once but by gradual increments. This is undoubtedly a great boon to the ryots and mitigates, so far as it goes, the hardship caused by a sudden and large increase of assessment, but it is obvious that in years of deficient produce, the revised assessment, even though imposed in this manner, must bear hardly on the ryots and possibly cause a deterioration in the standard of living, if the enhancements be great and general. This danger has to be guarded against even if the settlement calculations are so thoroughly reliable as to justify the confidence that the true "half-net" has been found. To quote Mr. Pedder again. "The conclusion with which Mr. Knight's writings (Editor of the *Indian Economist*) have made us all familiar—that the rates of Government assessment should increase in proportion to a general and permanent rise in the prices of agricultural produce—is based on the assumption that Government tax is or should be a fixed and definite proportion of the gross or net produce. Granting the assumption, the argument cannot be refuted. If the assessment in 1840 averaged in a particular district Re. 1 per acre, and this was equivalent to one-tenth the produce with the grain at Re. 1 a maund, it being assumed that one-tenth produce is a fair assessment, it is perfectly clear that when, in 1870, grain has risen to Rs. 3 a maund, the assessment should be raised to Rs. 3 an acre. Differences in rates of wages, &c., have nothing to do with the question; if the one-tenth produce is fair assessment, it is equally fair whatever the price of grain may be. But the case is entirely altered if we consider the assessment, not as a tax of a certain proportion of the produce, but as a [84] rent regulated and determined by the ordinary standard of comfort

---

[84] In this connection, it should be mentioned that in the Bombay Presidency the Government has all along been considered as the sole landlord and the occupancy right of the ryot as a recent concession and it is known by the name "Survey tenure." Waste lands are treated as the property of Government and sold to applicants for cultivation. In this Presidency, on the other hand, the ryot has all along been considered joint proprietor with Government and in the case of waste lands, they are granted to strangers only in cases in which the resident ryots refuse to cultivate them and pay the revenue assessed thereon. The land tax, according to the instructions laid down by the Home Government, is or should be in this Presidency not a "competitive" rent, but a *moiety* of the surplus produce "regulated and determined by the ordinary standard of comfort of the peasantry at a particular time."

among the peasantry at a particular time. If, in 1840, the ordinary subsistence of a peasant was then represented by the then equivalent of 10 maunds of grain, but in 1870 it is represented by the equivalent of 20 maunds, it is evident that (assuming the efficiency of cultivation to have remained the same), the assessment of Re. 1 an acre with grain at Re. 1 a maund can only rise to an assessment of Rs. 1-8-0 with grain at Rs. 3, unless the standard of comfort is to be lowered." It is in view of these considerations that the Bengal Tenancy Act of 1886 provides that the rent of an occupancy ryot shall not be enhanced by the landlord even with the consent of the ryot by more than 2 annas in the rupee or 12½ per cent. and that the rent once fixed by contract shall not be liable to enhancement during a period of 15 years from the date of such contract.

Districts in which settlements are in progress. Those which remain to be settled, the wealthiest and the most prosperous. Necessity for applying the principle of "moderation" to these districts also, to prevent impairment of the standard of living.

74. The land assessments in 16 out of the 22 districts have been revised in accordance with the principles above referred to, and settlement operations are in progress in the remaining 6, viz., South Arcot, Bellary, Anantapur, Tanjore, Malabar and South Canara. In South Arcot, the settlement rates have been introduced into the two most important taluks, viz., Cuddalore and Villupuram. The revenue from wet lands has been increased by 8 per cent., and that from dry lands diminished by 1 per cent., the net increase on the whole being 3 per cent., while the excess area discovered by the Survey is 8 and 9 per cent., respectively, in the two classes of lands. The Bellary and Anantapur districts are, as recently remarked by Government, "the poorest and most backward in the Presidency, the most sterile and the most subject to drought;" and for this reason, the Government declined to sanction a scheme for the settlement of these districts which would have raised the revenue by 12·5 per cent. After prolonged correspondence, the Government has accepted a modified scheme which will have the effect of increasing the revenue in five taluks in these two districts by 8 per cent., while the increase in the area is only 4 per cent. There is to be practically no increase in the case of wet lands, but on dry lands the revenue is to be increased by 9 per cent. In the Tadpatri taluk, the increase is to be as much as 15 per cent. in the case of dry lands, while the increase in the area is hardly 2 per cent. I venture to think that, having regard to the general poverty of the districts and the unsatisfactory nature of the data on which settlement rates are based, which fact was fully brought out in

the correspondence, even the modified scheme finally sanctioned is not as liberal as the circumstances of the case require. It is true that the taluks to which the scheme sanctioned relates are the best taluks in these districts, and it may be that in the remaining taluks considerable relief from taxation will be afforded; but there is obviously great necessity for caution in enhancing the revenue even in the favorably circumstanced taluks of these backward districts. As these two districts are the poorest in the Presidency, so Tanjore, Malabar and South Canara are reputed to be the wealthiest and the most prosperous. The manner in which these latter districts are dealt with by the Settlement department will form a precedent for adoption in revising settlements in the case of other progressive districts, and the question, therefore, demands, and will doubtless receive, the most careful consideration. In view of the importance of the subject and of the extent to which any decision that is arrived at is likely to influence the prosperity of the agricultural classes, I beg to be permitted to make the following remarks. The Settlement department was, as will have been seen from the account already given, organized to reduce assessments in backward districts, to correct inequalities in the assessments, to promote the growth of the value of landed property and to secure the prosperity of the agricultural classes. To attain these objects, in the early settlements taxation had to be largely reduced. The methods of the Settlement department were acknowledged to be necessarily rough, but any nice adjustment of the rates of land tax on lands of different qualities was not then a matter of great consequence as the question before Government was one of *relief* from taxation and not the imposition of fresh burdens. No ryot could, under the new settlement, be placed in a worse position than he was in previously, though in the adjustment of glaring inequalities found in the old assessments and the merging of the innumerable rates then existing in a few broad classes, one ryot might receive more or less relief than another. The enormous rise in prices which subsequently took place in the decade ending 1870 rendered a large reduction in revenue unnecessary and made it possible to enhance taxation to a reasonable extent, to meet the growing cost of administrative improvements, which the progress of the country and the ever widening duties and responsibilities of Government necessarily entail. The additional taxation imposed has, on the whole, been moderate, and though in individual cases here and there, hardship was caused by heavy enhancements, in the general result the reduction in incomes was probably not much in excess of what is met with in the ordinary fluctuations of fortune and certainly not such as to cause any deterioration in the standard of living of the agricultural classes. The aspect of the question as regards the districts which remain to be settled is, however, quite different. These districts are believed to be lightly taxed,[85] and whether this is so or not, they

---

[85] I have based the above remarks on the assumption that the Tanjore, Malabar and South Canara districts are very leniently assessed as compared with other districts already settled by the Settlement department. My belief, however, is that as regards Tanjore at all events, this impression is, in the main, unfounded. Quality for quality, I do not think that irrigated lands in Tanjore pay a much lower tax than lands in other districts. The settlement scheme for Tanjore, now under consideration, will, doubtless, undergo extensive modifications before it is finally sanctioned, but for the purposes of the present argument, the average outturn per acre of irrigated land in the Cauvery delta may be accepted at 24½ kalams or say 33 bushels of paddy. In the previous settlements (Mr. Kindersley's and Mr. Ramiengar's) the outturn had been assumed to be a little less than 24 kalams, and Mr. Venkasami Rao in his *Manual of the Tanjore District* calculates the average outturn, with reference to the average rate of assessment and the recognized proportion of the gross produce which the assessment is intended to represent, at 22 kalams. Since the earlier estimates were framed, the area of cultivation of lands of necessarily poorer qualities has largely increased; and this must have reduced the average outturn per acre, both because a larger proportion of poor lands than formerly is cultivated, and because the quantity of water available has had to be distributed over a larger area, thus diminishing the supply of water per acre and of the fertilizing silt which it brings. On the other hand, the irrigation of the district has been materially improved by the construction of the Colleroon anicut and the Cauvery regulating works, and there is probably much less wastage of water now than before. Lands also are believed to be much more carefully cultivated now than in the old days. It is, therefore, impossible to say at what figure the average outturn should be taken. But assuming simply for the sake of argument the settlement average in round figures, viz., 25 kalams per acre, the cultivation expenses and rent may be calculated roughly as follows. The customary charges for reaping are about 5 and for threshing 3 per cent., or 8 per cent. of the produce harvested on the whole; after deducting these charges, 25 per cent. is paid as porakudivaram or the cultivator's share. Other sundry charges, such as farm repairs, manure, and artisans' fees, amount to about 5 per cent. The total cost of cultivation, not including the landlord's wages for superintendence, comes to about 36 per cent. If the land be rented out for fixed rent, the landlord's net rent amounts, on an average, to only 60 per cent. of the gross produce, and it must be remembered that, when there is deficiency in the outturn of produce, reductions are allowed in the stipulated rents. Under the principles of the existing settlement, the Government assessment is the commuted money value of 47 per cent. of the gross produce, of which roughly 45 per cent. represents land revenue proper and 2 per cent. is set apart for the remuneration of village servants. 40 per cent. being, as above shown, absorbed by cultivation expenses, the remaining 13 per cent. represents the land-owner's profit. Applying these percentages to the average produce per acre, the distribution of 25 kalams will stand thus: 10 kalams cost of cultivation, 11¼ kalams land revenue, ½ kalam village officer's remuneration, and 3¼ kalams landlord's net rent. The average price of a kalam of paddy in Tanjore may be taken to be about 1 rupee. I have examined a large number of registered leases and found that this rate is the one most frequently adopted. Out of 556 leases examined in villages belonging to the Tanjore and Kumbakónam taluks the price of paddy mentioned is 1 rupee and less per kalam in 279 and more than 1 rupee in 277 cases for the years 1889 and 1890. On account of the favorable commutation rate fixed for the district, the land-owner, instead of paying for the Government share of the produce made over to him at 1 rupee per kalam, pays only at the rate of 8 annas, or more correctly, 7 annas 8⅜ pies. The Government, therefore, instead of getting Rs. 11-12-0 on account of land revenue and village officer's remuneration, gets only Rs. 5, both because the Government share is commuted at a rate which is only half the market price, and because the gross produce has been under-estimated. The landlord's rent which should be Rs. 3-4-0 is, on the other hand, increased to Rs. 10, or in other words, the landlord's rent is double the Government assessment. This estimate I believe to be above and not below the mark. Now in revising the settlement of the district, three courses may be adopted. The first is to retain the principle of the old settlement and to recalculate the assessment with reference to existing conditions as regards gross produce and market prices. If this were done, the assessment would be increased from Rs. 5 to Rs. 11-12-0 or by 135

are comparatively more favoured by nature than most other parts of the Presidency with the exception of the Godávari and Kistna districts. The unfailing south-west monsoon rains, the ancient anicut works and facilities of sea communication had given these districts an early start in the career of prosperity. Ryots in these districts have had a valuable pro-

---

per cent. This will be simply tantamount to giving up all enlightened principles of administration and reverting to the old native system of rack-renting the land by taking a moiety of the *gross* produce. Such a proposal, it is unnecessary to say, Government will not for a moment entertain. The second course is to exact in full half the *net* produce which, as shown by me, is the *maximum* assessment leviable under the principles laid down for regulating the revision of assessment by the Settlement department. If this be done, the rate per acre would come out as Rs. 7-8-0 and the present revenue increased by 50 per cent. The third course is to treat the lands in the Tanjore district in the manner in which lands of the same quality and irrigational advantages in other districts dealt with by the Settlement department have been treated. I have already shown that irrigated lands in other districts pay a net-rent to the landlord equal to about half as much again as the assessment, or, in other words, that the land-tax is not much lighter, if at all, in Tanjore than elsewhere. One test of this is the value of the lands. For the Coimbatore district Mr. Nicholson, whose estimate is as accurate as any that can be framed, gives the average selling price of wet land at Rs. 250 per acre. Land-owners on an average get a return from investments in lands of not more than 5 per cent. At this rate the landlord's profit amounts to Rs. 12-8-0 per acre, which is two-thirds as much again as the average assessment per acre, viz., Rs. 7-8-0. In reasoning from averages, of course, large allowance must be made for possible error, and the calculations above given merely serve to illustrate the considerations to be taken into account in arriving at a decision on the question. The calculations themselves will have to be verified with reference to statistics as regards rental and prices of land taken from the records of the Registration department which are far more trustworthy for these purposes than conjectural estimates. To prevent possible misapprehension, I wish once more explicitly to state that the figures assumed here are hypothetical and are put forward for the purpose of illustrating the considerations applicable to the question and not as in themselves even approximately correct. The average outturn per acre especially might be anything, for ought we know, between 20 and 25 kalams per acre, and I have taken the higher limit for purposes of argument. It is in view of this uncertainty that the settlement calculations make a reduction for "vicissitudes of season" and this I have not taken into account in my calculations, though the Settlement department will have to do so, to avoid the danger of cutting the ryot's profit too close. On the whole I think it may be stated that the wealth and prosperity of the Tanjore district are due, not so much to the undue leniency, as compared with other districts, of the assessment of lands of the several varieties of soil enjoying similar irrigational advantages, as to the fact that the bulk of the lands in the former district is irrigated, or, in other words, consists of lands which yield a large net return. In the case of Malabar and South Canara, data for forming an opinion as to the weight of assessment are not available, and the conditions of agriculture are in these districts so different from those of the districts on the East Coast that it would be erroneous to argue from the one to the other. While, on the one hand, these districts enjoy the advantage of never failing south-west monsoon rains, on the other hand, cultivation is very expensive, in that cattle are scarce and the soil is very porous and the expense of levelling lands which become constantly cut up by torrents is specially heavy. Owing to the hilly nature of the country, to prevent the soil in the uplands from being washed off by the rains and impoverished, banks of great breadth and thickness have to be constructed round fields and the soil collected at the lower end of the sloping fields has now and again to be redistributed over the whole surface. The holding of landed properties by joint families consisting of members belonging to several generations under the Marumakkatayam and Alayasantana systems, the impartibility of these properties except with the consent of all the members of the families, the existence of complicated tenures and customs regarding payment of rent and of compensation for improvements and the fact of the country being covered with plantations which have been formed by the expenditure of much capital and labour both by land-owners and tenants in the course of generations render the revision of the assessment of these districts an undertaking of very great difficulty; and the hardships likely to result by a revision of settlement can be minimized only by making the enhancement of revenue extremely moderate at the outset at all events.

perty in land from time immemorial, while in other places the bulk of the land has only recently acquired value. In wealth, intelligence and enterprise these districts stand ahead of all others and the standard of living is much higher there than elsewhere. It is also true that, if the necessities of Government require extraordinary sacrifices to be made in grave emergencies, these districts are in a better position to make them than other parts of the Presidency. But the question is whether, in ordinary times, it is desirable that the principle of "moderation," referred to by Mr. Pedder, which has been the guiding principle in all settlements hitherto made, should be laid aside and that Government should impose additional burdens amounting, say, to 50 or 100 per cent. of the present revenue, simply in order to level up taxation so as to reach the "half-net," which the Madras Board of Revenue in 1870 pronounced to be "indeterminate," thereby causing depreciation of landed property and disturbance of the relations between land-owners and mortgagees and tenants, at the imminent risk of lowering the standard of living, the raising of which within the last 40 years has been the best proof of the undoubted beneficence of British rule in this Presidency. I do not think that the question can admit of any but one answer. Irrespective of all abstract questions of right, it is obvious that the transference to the public exchequer of a moderate percentage of incomes of the agricultural classes, though it may cause temporary inconvenience, is not likely to leave permanently injurious effects; it may, on the contrary, even call forth energy and forethought and engender habits of prudence among these classes. The augmented resources of Government will also enable it to undertake the many reforms in administrative arrangements and in other directions which the country stands sorely in need of, and a moderate increase of taxation will doubtless, while leaving the margin available for maintaining undiminished, and even increasing the standard of comfort interpose a salutary check to an inordinate increase of population. A sudden and great reduction of incomes must, however, paralyze energy and bring discontent and despair; and when a large portion of the population is subjected to this operation, its injurious consequences can be readily conceived. A landholder's income which has been, say, Rs. 2,000, Rs. 500 or Rs. 100 for 30 years may, without causing permanent hardship, be reduced perhaps to Rs. 1,800, Rs. 450, and Rs. 90, respectively, by additional taxation. The deficiency in the income, which is not much in excess of what one must be prepared for in the natural course of things, whether caused by changes in the prices of commodities or in the value of money, may be met by effecting little economies in various directions and may even act as an incentive to exertion without compelling the persons affected to forego substantial comforts and conveniences. If the income be suddenly reduced to Rs. 1,000, Rs. 250 and Rs. 50, not in individual cases but in the case of the majority of the population which derives its subsistence from land, whether in the capacity of landlords and rent-receivers, farmers or agricultural labourers, the result cannot but be a great check to the growing prosperity of the country.

The question of permanent settlement of land revenue, the several phases it has passed through.

75. The obvious remedy for the evils of periodical revisions of assessment is, of course, the permanent settlement of the land tax, a settlement, so far as the Madras Presidency is concerned, not of the kind made with middle-men in the early years of the century to the injury of the rights of cultivating ryots, but one with the ryot proprietors themselves. This question, as might be expected, has been much discussed during the last 30 years and a full account of the several phases which the discussion went through will be found in Sir Auckland Colvin's "Memorandum on the Land Settlements of the North-West Provinces." In 1862, the Secretary of State for India sent out orders directing that "a full, fair and equitable rent must be imposed on all lands under a temporary settlement," and that wherever this had been done a permanent settlement of the revenue might be made. The measure was considered to be calculated to accelerate the development of the resources of India and to ensure in the highest degree the welfare and contentment of all classes of Her Majesty's subjects. These advantages were believed to be sufficiently important to justify incurring the risk of some prospective loss of revenue in order to attain them. The probable effect of rail-roads, the construction of which was then being vigorously pushed on, it was anticipated, would be towards the equalization of prices in different parts of India and a general improvement in the wealth of the country, rather than to give any peculiar advantage to the land-holders; and the apprehension of a fall in the value of money was considered as not being of sufficient importance to influence judgment, to any material extent, on the question. The Madras Board of Revenue in 1868 also advocated strongly a settlement in perpetuity of the land tax imposed on ryotwar holdings. The Board pointed out that "the ryot is owner of his land in a very limited and uncertain sense so long as Government

retains the right of raising his assessment without his concurrence. It may, and doubtless will be, that the Government will exercise this right with prudence and forbearance, but the uncertainty necessarily lessens the value of the land and affects the ryot's relations with his sub-tenants. The ryot will naturally be debarred from freely investing his capital in the improvement of his estate, because its value is liable to deterioration whenever Government may order, or the public may apprehend; an enhancement of the assessment, and, while deprived himself of a secure title, the ryot can give his sub-tenants no more than leases which must terminate or vary with his own, and must reserve the power of raising his rents, if and when Government raise their assessment. The growth of large estates and the creation of a class like the tenant farmers of England cannot but be impeded by such a policy." The Board accordingly recommended that the land assessments should be declared permanent, while reserving to Government the right to alter, according to circumstances, the water rate levied on lands supplied with water for purposes of irrigation from Government works. The enormous rise in the prices of agricultural produce which took place in the succeeding years, and the influence of the agitation, which was started in England about this time for the appropriation for national purposes of the "unearned increment" in the rent value of lands, had worked a great change in the views of Government, and in 1869 the Secretary of State negatived a proposal made by the Madras Government to declare the grain valuations imposed by the Settlement department to be permanent, remarking that Her Majesty's Government felt themselves precluded from "sanctioning the surrender of such a legitimate source of revenue as the Government share of the increased value which has been conferred on the land by improved administration, the construction of public works, especially works of irrigation and railways, together with the improved prices of produce." In 1871 again, the Government of India directed that the permanent settlement of estates in the North-West Provinces should not be proceeded with, the previous orders on the subject being held in abeyance. They remarked "when the question of the permanent settlement was formerly under discussion, the magnitude of the economic revolution through which India is passing was less obvious than it is now. It may be doubted whether any parallel could be found in any country of the world to the changes which have taken place during the last 10 or 15 years in India; to the diminution in the value of the precious metals and the enormous increase in the prices of agricultural produce." Sir Auckland Colvin sums up the several stages of the discussion as follows: "With the aspect of the day, the aspect in which the assessment of land revenue is regarded has changed. '*Increased security of fixed property*' has given way to the '*just rights of the State.*' '*Freedom from the interference of the fiscal officers of Government*' is now thought of little account, when compared with '*a sacrifice of any portion of that rental of the land to which the State is entitled.*' The fiscal side of the question is the one chiefly regarded in these days of peace and apparent security." Since Sir Auckland Colvin wrote, the views of the Government of India have once more, owing to the famine of 1876–78 and the distress suffered by the agricultural classes during that catastrophe and the fall in the prices of produce notwithstanding the fall in the value of silver, veered round, not indeed to the position occupied in 1862, but to a point midway between it and that of 1871 when the theory of "unearned increment" was in the ascendant and had taken possession of the public mind. The orders at present in force, regulating the procedure to be adopted in revising land settlements, which will be described at length later on, are based on an attempt to reconcile the claims of the State to share in the unearned increment in the value of property accruing from natural causes with the necessity for seeing that the interference with, and consequent depreciation of, landed property, which the ascertainment of the Government share must entail, is not carried to such an extent as to discourage the investment of capital in effecting improvements to land.

Arguments for a permanent settlement.

76. The question of the permanent settlement of the land tax on ryotwar holdings is one in regard to which the arguments *pro* and *con* may be said to be nearly equally balanced. The arguments in its favour may be thus succinctly stated. The *first* is, that the theory of "unearned increment" in the value of land and of the advantage of making it available for meeting public expenditure, with a view to avoid the imposition of *taxation* properly so called, can have but a limited application in this country. The "true rent" of land, that is the rent due to the inherent qualities of soil and advantages of situation, as contradistinguished from value imparted to it by the application of capital or labour, is extremely difficult to discover and is subject to constant fluctuations. There is no certain measure of the fertility of lands, as the rent of the same land varies according to the crops grown and the systems of cultivation practised. There is further great difficulty in deciding what is "normal cultivation," "normal harvests" and "normal prices." As Professor Marshall has pointed out,

good and bad seasons come so much in cycles that many years are required to afford a trustworthy average of harvests and prices; and in those many years, the industrial environment, *e.g.*, the local demand for the produce, the facilities for selling it in distant markets, and for competitors from a distance to compete in local markets, may have all changed. Facilities of communication especially, by equalizing prices, decrease the advantages enjoyed by such districts as Tanjore, Malabar and South Canara, and enhance the values of rich soils in the districts which had been less favorably circumstanced owing to the difficulty of access to markets. *Secondly* the possibility of determining the "economic rent" presupposes the existence of alternative occupations and the possibility of movement of farming capital and labour to them to admit of the ascertainment of the "normal farming profits" and "normal wages." These conditions are almost entirely absent in this country, both because land can be worked as a practical monopoly in the hands of Government which has the power of enhancing the land assessments at its will, and because the manufacturing industries in this country are, relatively to agriculture, of little importance.[86] *Thirdly*, the question as to whether the funds required for public purposes are taken out of rent or raised by taxation is of far less importance here than in England. In England, the bulk of the land is owned by a comparatively small number of persons who have benefited by the enormous[87] rise in rent at the expense of the

---

[86] It is the absence of alternative occupations that makes it necessary that a liberal margin should be allowed in settlement calculations for farming profits and labourer's subsistence. Professor Marshall observes: "In the greater part of India the cultivator holds lands directly from the Government under a lease the terms of which can be revised at intervals. And the principle on which these leases are arranged, especially in the North-West and North-East where new land is being settled, is to adjust the annual payments due for it to the probable surplus produce of the land after deducting the cultivator's necessaries and his little luxuries, according to the customary standard of the place, on the supposition that he cultivates with the energy and skill that are normal in the place. Thus as between man and man in the same place the charge is of the nature of economic rent. But, since unequal charges will be levied in two districts of equal fertility, of which one is cultivated by a vigorous and the other by a feeble population, its method of adjustment as between different districts is rather that of *tax*, than a *rent*. For, *taxes* are supposed to be apportioned to the net income which actually is earned, and *rent* to that which would be earned by an individual of normal ability; a successful trader will pay on ten times as large an actual income ten times as large a tax as his neighbour who lives in equally advantageous premises and pays equal rents." As holdings consist of lands of different qualities, it is not by any means easy to adjust the land assessment on the principle above stated, and moreover, over and above the cost of subsistence of the peasants, a margin for profit with a view to accumulate savings to tide over bad seasons has to be allowed for.

[87] It has been estimated by Sir James Caird that the rental of land in England, owing to the increased competition of foreign corn due to improvements in ocean transport, fell from 1876 to 1886 by 20 millions sterling. If, therefore, the proposal of the Land Tenure Association in 1870 of buying up the land-lord's rights and of nationalizing land with a view to secure for the State the future "unearned increment" had been carried out, the loss to the country would have been 20 millions sterling annually, which capitalized at 33 years' purchase would have amounted to 660 millions, a sum nearly equal to the national debt of the United Kingdom.

general community. In this country, on the contrary, property in land is diffused throughout the population almost to an inconvenient extent, so much so that landed properties consist mostly of "five-acre farms" and there are nearly as many properties as there are families. The rent of land, therefore, instead of going to swell the fortunes of a few is distributed over the whole population and the objection to raising the funds required for the purposes of Government by taxation of earnings instead of by appropriating the "unearned rent" is deprived of much of its force. The right of Government to increased revenue from waste lands brought under cultivation will, under the ryotwar system in force in this Presidency, of course remain intact. *Fourthly*, the limitation of the land-tax will allow large scope for the development of taxation [88] for local and provincial purposes on lines determined with reference to the wants and requirements of the several provinces or districts, and will, subject to the condition of contributing to the common expenses of the Empire according to actual needs, enable Local Governments to devote their energies to the improvement of the provinces committed to their care in the way best calculated to secure it, without being subjected to external interference. In this connection it must be remembered that, when the principle regulating the share of the net produce which was to represent the land tax was settled in 1856, it was intended that the charges for the maintenance of roads and of village establishments should be met out of the Government assessment, and accordingly it was declared that the assessment included a percentage set apart for these purposes. The original principle has since so far been departed from by the development of the system of local taxation that, as regards the local land-cess at all events, the charges which it was intended should be met from the Government share of the produce are now practically met out of the ryot's share. Various proposals on an extensive scale, such as, the improvement of village sanitation and water-supply, extension of elementary education, relief of the poor and distressed not merely in times of famine but in years of partial failure of crops, are being pressed on the attention of Local Governments, and the work and responsibilities of these Governments are being enormously increased in various directions; and if these responsibilities are to be adequately discharged, it can be done only by widening the basis of local

---

[88] In this connection the remarks of Mr. Giffen on the development of local rates in England in his "Essay on Taxes on Land" (see *Essays on Finance*, 1st Series) are so apposite that I have ventured to extract them in the appendix VI.-A. (3).

administration and, with it, of local taxation. The development of local taxation will also enable Government to call upon Zemindars who have largely benefited by the increase in the value of landed property throughout the country to contribute towards the performance of duties to their tenantry which, it was intended at the time of the permanent settlement, they should discharge, but which have now practically devolved on Government. The funds raised by local taxes will probably in no way fall short of the additional revenue obtainable from periodical revisions of assessment at long intervals, while the taxes themselves would be imposed according to the exigencies of each case after full discussion.

Arguments against a permanent settlement.

77. I will now proceed to state the arguments telling against a permanent settlement. When the scheme for introducing a permanent settlement throughout the whole of India under the orders of the Secretary of State issued in 1862 was abandoned in 1871, the Government of India was influenced chiefly by the consideration that the enormous rise in prices and the consequent increase in the rents of the landholders which had taken place in the decade ending 1870 would continue. During that period, while the silver prices of commodities had risen in India, there was no appreciable change in the relative values of gold and silver. After 1870 there was a re-action and prices fell considerably. More than 20 years have since elapsed and prices which now rule are still 15 per cent. below the average of the decade ending 1870, notwithstanding that the price of silver in terms of gold has fallen by more than one-third. If it were not for the de-monetization of silver in Europe, prices would probably have been 50 per cent. below the average of the decade ending 1870. This shows that the anticipation of continued increase in the rental owing to the general progress of the country has not so far been realized, and, that but for the fall in the price of silver, owing to causes specially affecting that metal in its relation to gold, the land-tax would have had to be considerably reduced. The objection to a permanent settlement on the ground that it involves a needless sacrifice of certain increase of future revenue has not therefore much weight; and, as already shown, the additional funds found necessary for meeting the increased cost of administration can be raised by developing the system of local taxation. The real objection is that a permanent settlement of the land revenue will be altogether one-sided The future as regards the value of silver is entirely uncertain

and a permanent settlement, while debarring Government from increasing the assessments if there should be a further great fall in the value of silver leading to a corresponding rise in the silver value of produce in this country, would in no way obviate the necessity for granting remissions of revenue if the price of silver should rise to its old level of 2*s*. per rupee; for, land assessments even though permanently fixed would then have become very heavy in their incidence and unrealizable except at the cost of a permanent deterioration in the condition of the agricultural classes. Another objection is that there is difficulty in fixing permanently the assessment of lands irrigated by works constructed by Government from borrowed capital. The outlay on these works is regulated by commercial principles and it would be an injustice to the general tax-payer, if the money assessment leviable on the lands irrigated be permanently fixed and made independent of the changes in the value of money instead of the payments made, by the land-holders specially benefited by the works being adjusted from time to time according to circumstances with reference to the value of the benefits received. It is possible to separate the charge[89] for water from land assessment *proper*, and to fix the latter permanently while the former may continue liable to alteration. As, however, the charge for water forms in the case of irrigated land the larger portion of the payment made to Government, the land-holder gains little or nothing by a permanent settlement of this kind. A *third* objection is that to tracts which are liable to frequent droughts a permanent settlement is unsuited. In these tracts it is not the amount of assessment that presses, but the collection of any assessment in adverse seasons when the ryot has reaped either no produce or only such short produce as hardly suffices for his subsistence. In tracts of this kind subject to extreme vicissitudes of season, the introduction of the old native system of sharing the crop, which is really an annual settlement, has been frequently advocated. Even in the case of irrigated lands, the duty of maintaining irrigation works

---

89 This is the plan adopted in the case of lands irrigated by the Godávari and Kistna anicut works. The plan has been found to work badly and has not been adopted in the case of other irrigation works recently constructed. The separation of land assessment from charge for water is entirely artificial. Lands unfit for unirrigated cultivation may be eminently fitted for irrigated cultivation. The levy of a charge for water at a uniform rate unduly lowers the land revenue imposable on some soils and enhances that of others and causes great inequalities in the assessments. The system of levying a water-rate on lands permanently irrigated from productive irrigation works has therefore been abandoned and the profit from the works is now roughly arrived at by taking the difference between the entire assessment of the lands irrigated and the highest dry rate which would have been imposed had the lands remained unirrigated, as the charge for water.

devolves on Government and the Government assessment is remitted when there is a failure of supply of water for irrigation. These considerations, however, important as they are, only limit, it seems to me, the scope of a permanent settlement, but do not show that its application to the bulk of unirrigated lands in the country is impracticable. The advantages of a permanent settlement of land revenue are so great, that I am inclined to think that it should be introduced, wherever practicable. I must, however, at the same time admit that, considering the extreme uncertainty in regard to the future value of silver and the instability of the opium revenue, the present time is very inopportune for Government to commit itself to any irrevocable decision on this question.

Government of India scheme for minimizing the evils of periodical revisions of assessment.

78. Barring a permanent settlement, the scheme of the Government of India propounded in 1883 for minimizing the evils incidental to periodical revisions of assessment, is undoubtedly the best that can be devised. As these orders are not as well known as they deserve to be, a summary of them will be given here. In these orders the Government of India announce that the policy of a permanent settlement, pure and simple, proposed in Sir Charles Wood's despatch in 1862, has been definitely abandoned as involving an unjustifiable sacrifice of the future resources of the State. The evils of periodical revisions of assessment are at the same time admitted in the most unreserved manner. The most prominent among them are "the uneasiness arising from uncertainty, the harassment of the agricultural classes, the discontent engendered by mistaken assessments, the check to expenditure on improvements, the positive deterioration of agriculture in the last years of the term of settlement, and the heavy cost and great delay involved in the operations." In calling attention to these evils, the Government of India is careful to point out that it is not intended to disparage or under-value in any way the work done by the Settlement department. That department has had a gigantic task to perform and has done it in a creditable manner. It has demarcated the boundaries of every property, and provided a map of every field; and in the face of almost insurmountable difficulties has effected an official valuation of land which is as approximately correct as it is possible for an official valuation to be; and indeed without an initial valuation of this kind it would be impossible to introduce any reforms whatever in the system of settlement. The problem for solution is how best to secure to the land-holding classes a

diminution from the vexations incidental to a settlement without a complete sacrifice by the State of its right to a reasonable share in the increase of agricultural wealth due to causes independent of the exertions of the agriculturists. One thing is quite clear, viz., that the object in view cannot be secured so long as the valuation of the various classes of soil forms the main part of the work of a settlement officer; for, such a valuation cannot in the nature of things be effected without enquiries of a minute and prolonged, and therefore of a troublesome and vexatious, character; and attempts to arrive at a valuation by rough methods and hasty generalizations have only too frequently resulted in uncertainty and inequality of assessment to the injury of the agricultural classes. An absolutely equal assessment of land is, in any case, impossible, both on account of the imperfection of the data on which the valuation has to be based, and the constant variation, in the natural course of things, of the conditions which affect the valuation. The Government of India has accordingly declared that, when once the soil has been carefully classified, there should be no re-valuation when the assessment has to be revised, and that the revision of the assessment should be effected under such principles and based on such data as will enable any person investing money in landed property or in improvements to land, to forecast, with tolerable precision and without official aid, the enhancement of revenue to which he will in future be subject, in order that "certainty of assessment might become one of the inherent attributes of agricultural property." The procedure prescribed for effecting this object, so far as it is applicable to the conditions of this Presidency, is as follows. The causes which contribute to an enhancement of the value of estates are: 1st, increased area brought under cultivation; 2nd, increased produce due to improvements to land, and the adoption of improved methods of cultivation; 3rd, rise in the prices of produce; and 4th, diminished expenses of cultivation or diminished cost of bringing the produce to market. In this Presidency, the question of increase of revenue due to extension of cultivation does not, so far at least as the East Coast districts are concerned, arise at periodical revisions of assessment, as, under the system of field assessments in force, every new field taken up for cultivation is made to pay the prescribed assessment at once. In the case, however, of estates in the Wynaad taluk of the Malabar district a large area of waste lands has been assessed at nominal rates, because to assess them at full rates while they remain uncultivated will enhance the assessment on the holding far beyond its present capabilities; and it will be a question whether, when the term of the present settlement expires, these lands will be allowed to pay pepper corn assessments, if they should, in the meanwhile, have been brought under cultivation. The same considerations will apply to large estates containing waste lands brought under the settlement now in progress in the South Canara and Malabar districts. Under the 2nd head, increased produce due to improvements effected by Government, such as the construction of irrigation works, will be charged for by the imposition of a water-rate. The increased produce arising from the improvements effected by the land-owners at their own expense is, of course, to be left entirely untaxed. These improvements consist chiefly of wells and other works for irrigation, and the rule of freedom from taxation as regards these, has indeed been scrupulously observed in this Presidency since 1850; and reductions of assessment amounting to several lakhs of rupees have been granted on lands irrigated by works constructed prior to that date. In Upper India and Bombay, however, a less liberal policy appears to have prevailed till a very recent date. It further appears that in Upper India, the gradual enhancement of value of land effected by improvement in the system of cultivation and increased application of labour and skill to the operations of tillage by the agricultural classes had formed an important item in the increment of revenue obtained by new assessments. The Government of India has relinquished the right to tax improvements of this kind, being convinced that it is false economy to discourage in any way the employment of such increased skill and labour. It is under the 3rd head, viz., the rise in prices, that an enhancement of assessments at periodical revisions of settlement is to be mainly looked for. Even here it is not every rise of prices, however small, that is to form a ground for enhancement; nor is the assessment to be enhanced in full proportion to the rise in prices. There should be a substantial rise in prices to justify an enhancement, and the Government of India has also directed that at each periodical revision a margin, say 15 per cent., of the profits arising from increase of prices, should be left untouched "with the view both of raising the standard of living among the agricultural classes, and of meeting the increasing cost of labour, stock and implements." In cases in which there is a fall in prices and the assessments fixed become on this account really oppressive, remissions or suspensions of revenue are to be granted at the discretion of Government, as the circumstances of the case might require. Under the 4th head, the most important consideration is the saving in the cost of carriage of produce to market and consequent enhanced value of produce by provision of increased facilities of communication by the construction of railways or canals. The Government is of opinion that it would be best to leave these advantages untaxed with a view to avoid the minute enquiries that would otherwise be necessary. The saving in cost of cultivation by labour-saving appliances, such as improved water-lifts, will, of course, in like manner with increase of produce due to the adoption of superior methods of cultivation be left untaxed. The assessments once fixed are not to be liable to variation for 20 years. In the case of prices, an initial schedule is to be prepared with reference to which future adjustments of the revenue are to be made. This initial schedule, according to the instructions of the Government of India, is to be based, not on the prices of any one year, but on the average prices of a period of years, say ten, immediately preceding the year which is taken as the commencement of the settlement, excluding years of famine or severe scarcity. The staples which are to be taken into consideration, the markets at which prices are to be registered, the period for which the average is to be calculated and such like matters, are to be decided after full discussion with the Local Governments. The Government of India further directs that in those cases in which there are interests subordinate to those of the land-holders to be safe-guarded (*e.g.*, tenants in South Canara and Malabar holding at fixed rates), arrangements should be made for the limitation of future enhancements of assessments according to well-recognized principles easy of application, being accompanied by similar limitation of the rents payable by tenants to land-holders. The principles enunciated by the Government of India have been accepted by the Madras Government with modifications on two points and are to be applied to revisions of assessments in all districts which have been settled by the Settlement department. The modifications are : *first*, that as regards the calculation of average prices, a period of 10 years being too small to give a fair average, a longer period should be taken, the precise period being left for consideration when the time for a revision of settlement approaches; *secondly*, that when a substantial rise in the value of agricultural produce justifies an augmentation of the State demand, a limit to the increase to be made at any one time should be laid down. The second condition added by the Madras Government is most important and is calculated to protect agricultural classes from the hardship of large and sudden enhancements, to whatever cause they may be due.

79. It will be seen from the scheme described above, that it would be impossible to have rules regarding revisions of assessment conceived in a more liberal spirit or more calculated to minimize the annoyances to land-holders arising from the operations connected with revisions of assessment and to remove the uncertainty in the value of landed property resulting therefrom. These rules, however, are not generally known, and unless the widest publicity be given to them, it is obvious that the object in view, viz., to enable persons desirous of investing money in the purchase of land or in improvements to it to forecast with reasonable certainty the changes in its value likely to result from the enhancement of Government assessment, apart from changes arising from natural causes, cannot be attained. I beg to suggest, therefore, that the rules should be embodied in a legislative enactment, or if this is considered undesirable, that they should be notified in the Official Gazettes. Before this is done, certain preliminary questions will have to be settled. The *first* is the initial schedule of prices which is to be taken as the standard and with reference to which future revisions of assessment are to be regulated. The commutation prices adopted for the existing settlements cannot be taken as the standards for reasons which will be apparent from the account already given in regard to the manner in which the calculations as to the land valuations made for purposes of settlement are adjusted with a view to see that the enhancements of revenue resulting therefrom do not exceed what the tracts settled may be expected from their general condition to be called upon to pay with ease. Moreover, the principle adopted in fixing the commutation rates has not been uniform in all districts. In the earlier settlements, the commutation rates were based on the average prices of as many years as there were accounts for. In connection with the Salem settlement, this rule was altered and it was laid down that the commutation rates should be based on the average prices of 20 years ending 1864. Then again, in connection with the settlement of the Madura district, the latter rule was modified, and it was enjoined that the commutation rates should be the average prices for the 20 years preceding the year of revision of settlement *minus* a percentage allowance for cartage and merchant's profits, subject to the condition that, where the rate thus deduced was higher than the lowest price which had obtained during the period of 20 years, the latter should be taken as the commutation rate. This latter condition has since 1887 been dispensed with. In the earlier

Suggestions as to measures to be adopted for making the Government of India scheme effective for the purpose intended.

settlements the prices taken were the prices of ryot's selling months. In recent settlements the average prices of whole years are taken subject to the deductions above referred to. In view of these differences, it seems to me, that the commutation prices should be discarded and that the average prices of 20 years prior to the existing settlements or such other period as may be considered sufficiently long for arriving at a fair average should be taken as the initial standard and compared with a similar average of the period immediately preceding the year in which the revision of settlement is undertaken. This evidently is the course enjoined by the Government of India, and it is the fairest under the circumstances. The price lists on which future enhancements of assessment are to be based should also be published in the Official Gazettes under arrangements similar to those prescribed in section 39 of the Bengal Tenancy Act.[90] The deduction to be made from prices for cartage and merchant's profits in order to find the producer's prices and the margin to be left untouched in the increased value of produce—whether 15 per cent. as mentioned by the Government of India or other proportion—should be definitely fixed. The limit to the enhancement of assessment at any one time, suggested by the Madras Government, should likewise be laid down. When these provisions are embodied in definite rules and promulgated, the object aimed at by the Government of India in propounding the scheme above referred to will be fully secured.

II. The uncertainty of the Tenure of Ryots in Zemindaries.

The condition of Zemindari ryots not improved to the extent that the condition of Government ryots has.

80. Before the commencement of the present century the ryots in Zemindari tracts, as well as the ryots who paid revenue direct to Government, were rack-rented and oppressed. During the last 90 years, however, the latter class of ryots have prospered in consequence of the measures adopted from time to time

---

[90] The provisions of this section are based on the principles adopted in the English Tithe Commutation Acts. For finding the average prices arrangements will have to be made for the selection of markets for the several descriptions of produce with reference to their relative importance. Allowances will have to be made for the fact that the average is unduly raised (1) because the average is struck on quotations of prices merely, without taking into account the quantity sold at each price, quantities sold at higher prices being smaller than quantities sold at lower prices ; and (2) because the grain sold by ryots is of superior qualities while that consumed by them is of inferior quality. The average varies also according as the quotations are in terms of varying amount of money for a definite quantity of the article sold or in terms of varying quantity of the article for a definite sum of money. It is the former that is *price* properly so called, but in practice retail prices are quoted at so many seers per rupee. These and other details will, of course, have to be carefully considered when revisions of land assessments are made to depend solely on changes in prices.

for the amelioration of their condition, as detailed in the foregoing pages, while the former have remained in most parts of the country in much the same condition as before. The Zemindari ryots form nearly one-fourth of the total agricultural population of the Presidency, and as the question of improving their status is now engaging the attention of Government, the following remarks are offered for consideration.

The rights of the cultivating classes to the lands held by them under the Hindu and Muhammadan systems.

81. For a proper understanding of the relations of Zemindars and ryots, it is necessary briefly to glance at the state of the case before the permanent settlement was carried out in the beginning of the century, and to form some idea as to how far the relations then subsisting have been affected by subsequent legislation and judicial decisions. Ancient Hindu law recognized only two beneficial interests in land, viz., (1) that of the sovereign or his representative, and (2) that of the cultivators holding the land either individually or as members of a joint family or a joint village community. Neither the sovereign nor the cultivators had unlimited proprietary right or full ownership in the modern sense. The sovereign's right consisted in his power to collect a share of the produce of the cultivated lands, known by the name *Melvaram* in the southern districts of the Presidency; and this *Melvaram* is not *rent* in the strict signification of the term. The share of the ryots or cultivators is known by the name *Kudivaram;* and by ryots [91] is to be understood "the cultivators who employ, superintend and assist the labourer, and who are everywhere the farmers of the country, the creators and payers of the land revenue." The ryot's right to land arises from mere occupation; [92] and is not derived from the sovereign in the manner in which the right of an English tenant is, under modern English law, derived from his landlord. The relation between the Government and the ryot may perhaps be described as one of co-partnership,[93] but it is certainly not that of landlord and tenant. The ancient Hindu law-books clearly establish this position. The Hindu law-giver Menu declares [94] cultivated land "to be the property of him who

---

[91] See definition given by the Madras Board of Revenue in Proceedings, dated 5th January 1818, page 370 of the "Papers on Mirasi Right."

[92] *Vide* Judgment of the Madras High Court in Sivasubramanya *versus* the Secretary of State for India: I.L.R., IX, Madras, page 285. Also decision in the Attapadi valley case: I.L.R., IX, Madras, page 175.

[93] See para. 45 of this memorandum and the authorities quoted in the note at its foot.

[94] See minute of Sir Charles Turner, late Chief Justice of Madras, on the draft Bill relating to Malabar Land Tenures.

cut away the wood and who cleared and tilled it." Another Hindu sage, Jaimuni, states that the expressions magnifying the power and glory of the king, such as that he is "lord of all," ought not to be understood as placing all property at his unrestricted disposal. His kingly power is for government of the realm and extirpation of wrong, and for that purpose he receives taxes from husbandmen and levies fines from offenders. But right of property is not thereby vested in him; else he would have property in house and land appertaining to the subjects abiding in his dominions. The earth is not the king's, but is common to all beings enjoying the fruit of their labour. "It belongs to all alike; therefore, although the gift of a piece of ground to any individual does take place, the whole land cannot be given by a monarch; nor a province by a subordinate prince; but houses and fields acquired by purchase and similar means are liable to gift." Again, "the revenue only is to be taken by the prince; therefore, in a gift or other alienation by him of such lands as aforesaid, gift of lands is not effected; it is only a provision of income; but in purchase from the land-holder, ownership does accrue in the houses, land or other property purchased; and through ownership thus acquired and such objects given, the benefits to the donor of the gift of land may really be obtained." On the other hand, the property of the ryot did not necessarily carry with it power to dispose of it in any manner he thought fit; and this for several reasons. One is that the right of individual ownership had not in most parts of the country been developed, as lands were held in joint-ownership by members of joint families and village communities and regarded as constituting "an estate dedicated equally to the support of sacrifices to the deceased members, as to the sustenance of those living, and still to come into life."[95] Ancient Hindu Law accordingly required that the deed of sale of land should be attested by the "heir, kinsmen, neighbours, villagers, an officer of the sovereign and scribe." Dr. Burnell in his *South Indian Palæography* gives the results of his examination of ancient documents and inscriptions relating to transfers of property as follows: "Down to recent times the land in South India was held by village communities, and thus the greatest number of existing private deeds are of grants by Sabhaiyar (from Sanscrit Sabha), the heads of the community acting on its behalf. The earliest documents of this kind, which are now in exist-

---

[95] *Vide* decision of the Bombay High Court in Bhaskarappa *versus* the Collector of North-Canara: I.L.R., III, Bombay, page 452.

ence, indicate that the earliest form of communal property (in which the common land was cultivated by all the owners in common who divided the produce) had already become uncommon; for though townships exist where this system is followed,—and there are traces of it,—yet the inscriptions indicate that the system which still exists to a great extent in South India, viz., communal lands with shifting lots exchanged periodically, was already widely practised. Under this system the rights of ownership in a township are divided into a number of shares, and these again subdivided to a great extent. The township land is divided into *kattalais* which answer to fields. And these are sub-divided into lots which answer to the shares (*pangu*) or fractions of shares owned by the several members of the community. But the township land consisted only of the arable land; the ground on which the houses of the community were built (*úrnattum*), that on which the serfs or artizans resided (*paraseri nattam, &c.*), the village burning ground (*Súdúkadú*), water courses and tanks, temples, waste land (*irayili nilam* = land without owner) were private property or reserved for the public use in general, and over which the members of the community had merely the right of use. What could be transferred was, therefore, a certain extent of land corresponding to a share or shares together with the undefined rights over the public property which attached to every member of the community, but which were not, and seldom are, mentioned in deeds, or to the separate property of the individual member of the family. There can be no doubt that all such transfers of either kind were illegal and void without the sanction of the community, and the Sanscrit lawyers clearly recognized this principle. . . . . The numerous attestations to transfers of property are intended to represent the co-proprietors' assent and ratification, rather than evidence of execution of the document." Even where the communal and joint family systems had given way to individual property, land might still not be transferable, both because, by heavy taxation the value of the interest of the cultivator might have been reduced to little or nothing, and because owing to the sparseness of the population and abundance of waste lands the difficulty might be not in finding lands but in finding men to cultivate them. The fact that the ascertainment of the share of the sovereign and its valuation were left to his officers led to continual encroachments on the cultivator's share and thus rendered his property an uncertain one, is an objection applicable to all forms of property which were exposed to inroads of this kind. All rights were in former times based on the authority of custom, and the ruling power professed to respect custom, even though it might violate it on special occasions. The Muhammadan rule did not alter the internal constitution of villages and the rights of landed property, except by increasing the tax and diminishing the value of the ryot's interest by collecting the revenue by means of farmers. The limitation of the share of the sovereign applied of course to lands newly reclaimed from waste as well as to lands previously under cultivation. In parts of the country where joint village communities were in existence—and this was generally in tracts where lands were irrigated under great systems of irrigation—these communities claimed the right to cultivate the waste within their villages to the exclusion of strangers. In the portions of the country exposed to the ravages of frequent wars, droughts and famines, village communities would constantly tend to disappear almost as rapidly as they were formed; and the rights in cultivated land would consequently be of small value; and there would be no assertion of any right to cultivate waste lands because there was no necessity to do so. Even here, when waste land was cultivated, the right of Government was limited to taking the share recognized as its due in the case of lands already under cultivation. On this point, Sir G. Campbell in his *Essay on Indian Land Tenures* observes, "In no part of India and under no form of Government did the State undertake the latter functions (of letting lands at competitive rents) or any others analogous to those of an English landlord. Except in the assignment of waste land to be cultivated on the *customary tenure*, there never was any system of interference with the immediate possession of the soil; no letting it by competition or anything of that kind."

Melvaram and Kudivaram rights independent rights and other interests derived from these.

82. The melvaram and kudivaram rights are thus the two principal independent interests in land, and all other interests are derived from, or are subordinate to, either the one or the other. The ryot or *ulkudi* or mirassidar was the receiver of the kudivaram, and he might cultivate the land himself or have it cultivated by tenants in cases in which the Government share of the produce left him a kudivaram which had a margin above the cost of the cultivator's subsistence. The tenant put in by the ryot was called a *porakudi* or stranger cultivator. In exceptional cases, the *porakudi* was permitted to acquire a beneficial interest in land and the status of an *ul-porakudi*, but this was not recognized as a part of the general common

law of the country.[96] At the other end of the scale, there were the Zemindars, Jaghirdars, and Inamdars, who derived their rights from the sovereign with jurisdiction over portions of the country which would not, under the Hindu law, affect the kudivaram right vested in the ryots. The Zemindars were of very various origin. Some of them were the descendants of ancient chiefs, holding the territories assigned to them on condition of paying tribute and rendering military service. Others were revenue officers and farmers of revenue employed by the Hindu and Muhammadan Governments, who had acquired power and influence which led to their being recognized as Zemindars. Others, again, were originally heads of villages or ryots or even kavalgars, taliaries, or watchmen who had collected round them armed bands of robbers and levied blackmail from the surrounding villages, and by the assistance rendered to sovereigns during troublous times got themselves recognized as Poligars. In all cases, the Zemindar's right extended only to the melvaram, except in the case of *Khamar*, *Pannai* or home-farm lands which were kept distinct from lands cultivated by ryots. This was the common law of the country, but in practice, of course, owing to the absence of settled authority, the ryots were grievously oppressed by the levy of illegal cesses. In a few cases, where the "sist" or regular assessment was a fixed sum of money, the extra assessments represented the additional value of the Government share due to the rise in the value of produce, and as such was legitimate enough; but in most cases the extra assessments were purely arbitrary. In the Northern Circars, as we have already seen, the ryot's share of the produce which was originally not less than one-half was, by the additional imposts levied on various pretexts, reduced to one-fourth or one-fifth. Mr. Stratton has given a full account of the revenue system prevailing in the Chittoor polliems in his report, dated 14th July 1801. His report shows that, besides the mamool teerva which was in itself sufficiently onerous, imposts were being levied in the Venkatagiri and Kálahasti Zemindaries under the denomination of *katnams*, and that most of these were arbitrary exactions which had originated within the previous 35 years. In the Ramnad Zemindari also, additional cesses over and above the mamool teerva were levied, among which may be mentioned *Nilavari* (land-tax), *Vakkalvari* (the straw tax), *Pádakánikkai* (a present placed at the feet of the Zemindar), *palam katchi* (a present made to the Zemindar when the glad

[96] See decision of the Madras High Court: I.L.R., VII, Madras, page 374.

tidings of the ripening of dry crops was conveyed to him), grain fees for the maintenance of an English writer in the establishment of the Zemindar, &c. Venkatagiri and Kálahasti Zemindaries are instances of Zemindaries in which the existence of a kudivaram right in the ryot is denied: in the Ramnad Zemindari, on the other hand, the right is fully admitted and transfers of lands by sale or mortgage are quite as common as in the Government ryotwar taluks.[97]

Permanent settlement with Zemindars in 1802.

83. The rights of the Zemindars to hold their estates were, before the permanent settlement, much more uncertain than those of the ryots, and the object of the permanent settlement was to place the rights of the former on a secure basis by limiting the demands of the Government on Zemindars on account of the revenue, in order that the demands of the latter on the ryots might be equally defined and limited. On the occasion of introducing the permanent settlement in Bengal in 1792, the Court of Directors remarked as regards the tenure of Zemindars as follows: "On the fullest consideration, we are inclined to think that whatever doubt may exist, with respect to their

---

[97] The nature of the ryot's right was everywhere the same, though its saleable value varied in different places and in most was nothing. This is clear from the following extract from Board's Proceedings, dated 5th January 1818, in which the Board stated the results of their enquiries into the nature of the ryot's right in different parts of the Presidency. "The universally distinguishing character as well as the chief privilege of this class is their exclusive right to the hereditary possession and usufruct of the soil, so long as they render a certain portion of the produce of the land, in kind or money, as public revenue; for whether rendered in service, in money, or in kind, and whether paid to Rajahs, Jaghirdars, Zemindars, Poligars, Mootahdars, Shrotriemdars, Maniemdars or to Government officers, such as Tahsildars, Amuldars, Ameens, or Thanadars, the payments which have always been made are universally termed the dues of the Government.

"The hereditary right of the ryot above described, though everywhere the same or at least of a similar nature, is in value different in different districts. After discharging the wages of his hired labourers, and defraying the subsistence of his slaves or other immediate expenses of cultivation, if the public assessment payable by him is so moderate as to leave him a considerable surplus, his interest in the soil is that of a landlord, and his land yields a clear land rent and is, of course, a saleable and transferable property; but where the revenue payable by him is so high as to absorb the whole of the landlord's rent, and to leave him a bare and precarious subsistence only, his interest in the land dwindles into mere occupancy, and from a *landlord* he is reduced to a *landholder* still indeed clinging to the soil and subsisting by tilling it, but no longer possessing any saleable interest.

"The value of the ryot's right, therefore, varies with the weight of the public assessment on the land, which is generally found to be heavy in proportion to the length of the time that the country may have been subjected to the Muhammadan Government. On the West Coast of the Peninsula, where the Mussalman power was both of most recent introduction and short duration, this right constitutes property of great value, which is vested in each individual ryot. In the Tamil country, it is vested more frequently in all the ryots of a village collectively than in each individually; and is of less value than in Canara and Malabar, and sometimes of little or no value as a saleable property. In the Ceded Districts and Northern Circars, which were the longest under Muhammadan rule, though the Coombees, Reddies, Naidoos and other Kadeem inhabitants assert their hereditary right to a priority and preference of occupancy, they do not now appear to possess any saleable right in the soil."

original character, whether as proprietors of land or collectors of revenue, or with respect to the changes which may in process of time have taken place in their situation, there can at least be little difference of opinion as to the *actual* condition of the Zemindars under the Moghul Government. Custom generally gave them a certain species of hereditary occupancy, but the sovereign appears nowhere to have bound himself by any law or compact not to deprive them of it; and the rents to be paid by them remained always to be fixed by his arbitrary will and pleasure, which were constantly exercised upon this object. If considered, therefore, as a right of property it was very imperfect and very precarious, having not at all, or but in a very small degree those qualities that confer independence and value upon the landed property of Europe. Though such be our ultimate view of this question, our originating a system of fixed equitable taxation will sufficiently show that our intention has not been to act upon the high claims of Asiatic despotism; we are, on the contrary, for establishing real permanent valuable landed rights in our provinces, and for conferring that right upon the Zemindars, but it is just that the motive of this concession should be known and that our subjects should see that they receive from the enlightened principles of a British Government what they never enjoyed under the happiest of their own." The authors of the permanent settlement inappropriately called the rights conferred on the Zemindars, "proprietary rights," being influenced by the notion fostered by modern English law, that there should be full ownership vested in some one person, and all other rights should be considered as derived from or through him. This view of the case placed the rights of the ryots at a disadvantage in that they were regarded as a sort of inferior, derivative, possessory rights. The existence of the latter rights was, however, fully acknowledged and the Government reserved to itself the fullest power to legislate, when necessary, for the protection of the ryot's rights. The Court of Directors specially cautioned the Governor-General "to so express himself as to leave no ambiguity as to their right to interfere from time to time, as it might be necessary, for the protection of the ryots and subordinate landlords, it being their intention in the whole of this measure effectually to limit their own demands, but not to depart from their inherent right as sovereigns of being the guardians and protectors of every class of persons living under their Government;" and the Governor-General in accordance with the Court's injunctions issued, in 1793, a proclamation containing, among other things, the following declarations addressed to the "Zemindars, independent Talukdars and other actual proprietors of lands," viz., "It being the duty of the ruling power to protect all classes of people, and more particularly those, who from their situation, are most helpless, the Governor-General in Council will, whenever he may deem fit and proper, enact such regulations as he may think necessary for the protection and welfare of the dependent Talukdars, ryots and other cultivators of the soil. No Zemindar, independent Talukdar or other actual proprietor of land, shall be entitled on this account to make any objection to the discharge of the fixed assessment which they have respectively agreed to pay." It was further declared "that implicit obedience be shown by the proprietors to all regulations which had been or might be prescribed by Government, concerning the rents of the ryots and the collections from under-tenants and agents of every description as well as from all other persons whatever." In the Madras Presidency the permanent settlement was made on the same principles as in Bengal. The instructions issued to Collectors for the purpose of carrying out the permanent settlement acknowledge that "distinct from these (Zemindar's and Talukdar's) claims are the rights and privileges of the cultivating ryots, who, though they have no positive property in the soil, have a right of occupancy as long as they cultivate to the extent of their usual means, and give to the Sircar or proprietor, whether in money or kind, the *accustomed* portion of the produce." Laws were to be made for the protection of the ryots and under-tenants on the one hand, and for enabling Zemindars on the other, to recover the rents due to them. In order that the Courts might easily determine the rents payable, the Zemindars were to enter into specific engagements, called puttahs, with the ryots. The rents to be paid, by whatever rule or custom regulated, were to be given in specific money amounts, wherever possible. In cases where the rate only could be specified, such as when the rents were adjusted upon a measurement of the lands after cultivation, or on survey of the crop, or when they were made payable in kind, the rate and terms of payment and proportion of the crop to be delivered, with every other necessary condition, were to be clearly specified. Every Zemindar was to be required to prepare a form of a puttah or puttahs, adapted to the circumstances and usages of his Zemindari and after obtaining the Collector's signature to it in token of his approbation, to register a copy of it in the Civil Court of the district and deposit copies also in the principal Cutcherries of the

Zemindari. Every ryot was also to be entitled to receive a copy on application and no puttahs which were not in the prescribed form were to be held valid. Refusal on the part of a Zemindar to grant a puttah to a ryot was to be punishable by a fine "proportioned to the expense and trouble of the ryot in consequence of such refusal." Receipts were to be granted for all rents paid, and a refusal to grant a receipt was similarly to be punished with fine equal to double the amount of the rent paid by the ryot. The instalments in which the rents were payable were to be fixed with reference to time of reaping and selling the produce and a Zemindar violating this rule was liable to be sued for damages. It was hoped that in course of time, Zemindars and ryots would find it to their mutual advantage to enter into agreements in every instance for a specific sum fixed on a certain quantity of land, leaving it to the option of the latter to grow whatever crops they might consider most profitable to them. In the meantime, the ryots were to be protected from the levy of any new taxes "under any pretence whatever," and any Zemindar who imposed such taxes was to be made liable to a heavy penalty. The attention of the Collectors was drawn to the taxes which were already being levied, and which it was apprehended had already become oppressive and too intricate to adjust; and the hope was expressed that the Zemindars would revise the same in concert with the ryots and consolidate the whole into one specific sum, by which the rents would be much simplified, and much inconvenience to both parties be thereby obviated in future. The Government was prepared to relinquish its right to derive any revenue from the cultivation of waste lands which were "to be given up in perpetuity to the Zemindars, free of any additional assessment, with such encouragement to every proprietor to improve his estate to the utmost extent of his means, as was held out by the limitation of the public demand for ever, and the institution of regular judicial Courts to support him in all his just rights, whether against individuals or the officers of Government, who might attempt in any respect to encroach upon them." The advantages expected to accrue from the improvement of these lands were stated to be "to put the Zemindar upon such respectable footing as to enable him with the greatest readiness to discharge the public demand, to secure to himself and family every necessary comfort and to have, besides, a surplus to answer any possible contingency."

These instructions formed the basis of the series of regulations passed in 1802 defining the rights and liabilities of Zemindars with whom a permanent settlement was entered into, both as regards Government and the ryots who were placed under them. The Zemindars were, of course, in accordance with the erroneous ideas as to the rights of ryots prevailing at the time, declared to be "proprietors of the soil" (section 2 of Regulation 25 of 1802). The safe-guards provided for the *protection* of the ryots were these: First, it was made imperative on the part of the Zemindar to offer puttahs to his ryots (and to exchange muchilikas with them) clearly specifying the rent demandable from them, within six months from the date of the permanent settlement. These puttahs and muchilikas were to be signed and registered, not by the Collector as originally contemplated, but by the kurnam of the village who, by another regulation passed at this time, was made independent of the Zemindar on the one hand, and the Collector on the other (section 14 of Regulation 25 of 1802 and section 3 of Regulation 30 of 1802). The expectation was that by insisting on the terms as regards rent, &c., being reduced to writing with the mutual consent of the parties interested, and registered in the office of a village officer who was supposed to be placed in a position in which he would not be amenable to the influence of the Zemindar, the rights of the ryot would be secured and the Courts would be furnished with the means of deciding readily disputes regarding rates of rent between Zemindars and ryots; secondly, Zemindars were required to consolidate rents and imposts of all kinds customarily levied from ryots into one specific sum within two years from the date of the permanent settlement and enter it in the puttah; and if the Zemindars neglected to do so, the rents and cesses were not to be enforceable in a Court of Law (section 6 of Regulation 30 of 1802); thirdly, Zemindars were forbidden to impose any new cesses or taxes on the ryots, under any name or pretence, and the levy of any sums other than those included in the consolidated amount entered in the puttah was made punishable with fine equal to three times the amount levied unauthorizedly (section 7 of Regulation 30 of 1802); fourthly, it was laid down that if disputes arose between Zemindars and ryots regarding rates of assessment, in money, or of division in kind, the rates were to be determined according to the rates prevailing in the cultivated lands in the year preceding the permanent settlement of the revenue of the estate; and where these rates might not be ascertainable, according to the rates established for lands of the same description and quality as those respecting which the dispute arose (section 9 of Regulation 30 of 1802). By these provisions it was thought that, though cesses which previous to the permanent settlement had been unauthorizedly imposed might be perpetuated, the imposition of any further cesses subsequently would be prevented and that the adoption of the rates levied in the year previous to the year of the permanent settlement, would in most cases obviate the necessity for enquiry into difficult questions of vague and undefined usage as regards rates of rent. On the other hand, the *powers* conferred on the Zemindars for the recovery of their rents were the following: first, they were authorized to distrain for rent the moveable property of the ryots, with the exception of lands, houses, articles of trade or manufacture, and also ploughs, implements of husbandry, ploughing cattle or seed grain so long as other property might be forthcoming (sections 2, 3 and 4 of Regulation 28 of 1802); secondly, they had power to eject from their lands the ryots who refused to accept the puttahs offered to them in the presence of witnesses, and to grant the lands to other persons (section 10 of Regulation 30 of 1802); thirdly, where a person who made default in the payment of rent had by grant or established usage of the country a transferable right in the land, the Zemindar might apply to the Court to sell such right in satisfaction of the rent due; and where the defaulter was a lease-holder or other tenant having a right of occupancy only so long as he paid the rent, without right of property or possession, the Zemindar could eject him of his own authority (Regulation 28 of 1802, section 34, clause 7); fourthly, Zemindars were empowered to summon, and, if necessary, compel the attendance of ryots for the adjustment of their rents, or for measuring lands, or for "any other lawful purpose." These powers were exerciseable without any previous application to the Courts, but for abuse of these powers the Zemindars were liable to fine and damages (section 34, clause 8 of Regulation 28 of 1802). Zemindars were prohibited from confining or inflicting corporal punishment on ryots on pain of prosecution in a Criminal Court (section 29 of Regulation 28 of 1802).

Mr. Webbe, the Chief Secretary to the Madras Government in 1802, was appointed Special Commissioner for carrying out the permanent settlement in this Presidency, and the duty of drafting the regulations passed in connection with the settlement devolved on him. In a communication made to Mr. Webbe by Messrs. Hodgson and Greenway, the latter gentlemen strongly urged the desirability of inserting in Regulation 30 of 1802 certain provisions which would have had the effect of placing the rights of ryots on a secure basis. The section suggested was to the following effect: "No Zemindar, proprietor (or whatever name be given to these persons) was entitled by custom, law or usage to make his demands for rent according to his convenience, or in other words, that the cultivators of the soil had the solid right from time immemorial of paying a defined rent and no more for the land they cultivated." Mr. Hodgson pointed out that "the first principle of the permanent settlement was to confirm and secure these rights" and that "the proprietary right of the Zemindars was no more than the right to collect from the cultivators that rent which custom has established as the right of Government; and the benefit arising from this right was confined, first, to an extension of the *amount*, not the *rate*, of the customary rent by an increase of cultivation; secondly, to a profit in dealings in grain, where the rent may be rendered in kind; thirdly, to a change from an inferior to a superior kind of culture, arising out of a mutual understanding of their interest between the cultivator and proprietor." Mr. Webbe, however, did not think it necessary to adopt Mr. Hodgson's suggestion on the grounds that the rights of the ryots would be best *developed* in the Courts, then for the first time to be established, and that to suppose knowledge of them would be suppressed by the acts of the Zemindars was "contrary to the whole course of human experience." [98]

The safe-guards provided for the protection of the ryot's rights nugatory and further measures taken in 1822.

84. As might be expected the safe-guards provided by the permanent settlement regulations for the protection of the rights of the ryots proved entirely unavailing. No steps were taken to see that in accordance with these regulations, puttahs and muchilikas were exchanged between the Zemindars and their ryots and that all cesses levied under various denominations were consolidated into a single specific sum within two years from the date of the permanent settlement. The ryots were mostly illiterate peasants who could not understand written agreements containing stipulations regarding rates of rent; and the kurnams who were supposed to be the guardians of their rights were in the pay of the Zemindars and had no motive to help the ryots, even if they dared to do so. The ryots themselves had for long periods of time been subjected to the arbitrary power of the Zemindars and could not be expected to become bold enough to try conclusions with them, by a mere legislative declaration that they were free to do so. The Courts, then for the first time established, and in which the rights of the ryots were to be "developed," were also far

[98] *Vide* Proceedings of the Board of Revenue, dated 2nd December 1864, No. 7843.

too distant and inaccessible to be of any use to persons who had never left their villages, nor known any other judicatory than their own caste punchayets. The powers possessed and arbitrarily exercised by the Zemindars of forcibly procuring the attendance of the ryots and of ejecting them for not accepting puttahs offered had been distinctly legalized. The only course open in the circumstances for affording effectual protection to the ryots was for Government itself to have settled the rents payable by the ryots and recorded them carefully. The Government of the day had, however, too much of other urgent work on hand to enter on this laborious and difficult enquiry. It was therefore not at all surprising that the Board of Revenue reported in 1820 on the condition of the Zemindari ryots as follows:

"The Board are assured, not only from the reports of officers deputed to enquire into complaints in the Provinces, but from other unquestionable sources of information, that the great body of ryots is not in that state of ease and security in which the justice and policy of the British Government mean to place them. In general, the ryots submit to oppression and pay what is demanded from them by any person in power rather than have recourse to the tedious, expensive and uncertain process of a law-suit. The cases in which they are sufferers are so numerous, various, intricate and technical, —they and their witnesses are so far from the seats of the Courts of Judicature—delays are so ruinous to them—they are so poor, so averse to forms, new institutions and intricate modes of procedure—they are so timid and so simple a race, that it is necessary for the Government to endeavour to protect them by a summary and efficacious judicial procedure; and it is evident that the officer entrusted with the general government of the Province, as having the greatest and most immediate interest in the welfare of those under his government, and as the only officer having a free and full intercourse with them, should be vested with the duty of conducting these summary proceedings. It is necessary, therefore, in the opinion of the Board to provide by regulation, first, for the protection of the ryots, the great object of all our provincial institutions, and indeed of civil government in the country, but one most difficult of attainment; and for that purpose the Collector or other officer entrusted with the general government of the Province, his assistants when he delegates his authority to them, and the native officers acting by his orders should have primary and summary jurisdiction in all disputes between Zemindars and their under-farmers and ryots regarding rates of assessment, occupancy of land, and payment of revenue, and that they should hold a revenue Court for the investigation and settlement in the first instance of such disputes, custom or special agreement and should regulate the demand of the Zemindar against the ryot. The Zemindar should not eject the ryot from his land, unless the ryot should refuse to pay the stipulated rent as soon after the beginning of the season for the settling for the cultivation of the year, as may be reasonable and customary; nor should the Zemindar demand more than the customary or stipulated waram or rent."

In accordance with the Board's recommendations, Regulation 4 of 1822 was passed which *inter alia* provided (1) that Collectors should summarily enquire into all disputes between Zemindars and ryots regarding rates of rent; (2) that no property attached for arrears of rent could be sold unless puttahs had been granted, tendered or refused, nor until notice had been given to the Collector and leave obtained for the sale; (3) that no ryot could be ejected from his land without the Collector's permission on the ground that he refused to accept a puttah offered to him; (4) that if the Collector found on examination that the puttah tendered by the Zemindar was *just and correct*, the ryot might be ejected, unless he assented to the terms; but if the rate should exceed the *just rate prescribed*, an order should be issued prohibiting the ejectment and requiring the issue of a proper puttah within one month, under penalty; (5) that suits preferred in the Zillah Courts for arrears of rent were to be rejected where no puttah had been granted unless it were proved that a puttah had been offered and rejected, or that both parties had agreed to dispense with the use of puttah and muchilika; and (6) that Collectors might refer disputes relating to rates of rent or to occupancy of land to village or district Punchayets for decision. The designation in the permanent settlement regulations of the right of Zemindars as "proprietary right" being calculated to prejudice the rights of the ryots, it was declared by Regulation 4 of 1822 that in passing the former regulations Government had no intention of authorizing any infringement or limitation of any established rights of any classes of its subjects.

Sir Thomas Munro, in his famous minute on "The condition of the Country" in 1824, has described the condition of the ryots in Zemindaries in the Northern Circars at this time as follows:

"When these districts came into our possession, one part of them was in the hands of Zemindars and the other and most valuable part was in the hands of Government, and has since, by the permanent settlement, been made over to new Zemindars of our own creation. As in these provinces no fixed assessment has been introduced, nor the rights of the ryots been defined, the ryots can never become land-holders nor their lands acquire such a value as to make them saleable. It may be said that they have a right to be assessed only according to ancient usage, and that this right will secure them from undue exaction, and give them the same facilities as the ryots of the Government districts of rendering their land a valuable property; but many causes combine to prevent this. The ancient usage was different in every little district or even village. It is *not* recorded or defined, and is very little known to us. It is, I believe, in the Northern Circars very generally so high as to leave the ryot no more than the bare recompense of his labour and stock, and thus to preclude his ever obtaining any portion of a land-lord's rent. Even supposing that usage did leave to the ryot some surplus as land-lord's rent, the Zemindar might not permit him to enjoy it. He might raise the assessment. If he were an old Zemindar or hill Rajah, the fear of violence would deter him (the ryot) from complaining. If he were a new Zemindar, the ryot would, nine times in ten, submit quietly to the loss, not from fear of personal injury, but from the well founded fear of losing his cause in Court. He knows that the influence of the Zemindar would easily procure witnesses to swear falsely on the question of ancient usage, and that they would be supported by the fabricated accounts of the kurnam, who is entirely under the authority of the Zemindar, and that if he even gained his cause, it would be of no advantage to him, as the Zemindar, without transgressing any law, would be able to harass him in many ways and make his situation uncomfortable."

Notwithstanding these drawbacks, the rights of the ryots in this Presidency, do not appear to have suffered quite to the same extent as in Bengal for three reasons; viz., first, that it was all along acknowledged here that the rights of the ryots were distinct from and independent of those of the Zemindars; secondly, that the maximum rent demandable by the Zemindar was limited to the rent paid in the year preceding that in which the settlement was made, instead of being regulated by the indefinite pergunah rates as in Bengal; and thirdly, the maintenance of a record by kurnams or village accountants facilitated to some extent the ascertainment of the proper rates of rent. Even before the enactment of the Regulations 4 and 5 of 1822, the Sudder Court (of which Mr. Greenway was one of the judges) had in several decisions declared that Zemindars had no power to alter the *rate* of division of crop obtaining in the year preceding the permanent settlement, although the money value of the Zemindar's share of the crop was a matter to be settled by mutual agreement by the Zemindars and ryots and to be entered in the puttahs issued to the latter, and that by the Act of permanent settlement, the government transferred to Zemindars "the proprietary right exercised by itself" and that "it could not do more without infringing the rights of others."[99]

Rent legislation in 1865.

85. The enactments passed in 1822 continued to regulate the relations between Zemindars and ryots until 1865 when they were superseded by Act VIII of 1865. The immediate occasion for amending the old law was the necessity for the provision of summary remedies to enable Inamdars to recover their rents from their tenants, as the procedure prescribed by the old regulations was understood not to be applicable to estates which did not pay revenue to Government. The reduction of assessments granted by Government in the case of ryotwar lands and the great rise which had also taken place in the value of the ryot's interest in land had brought into existence a class of sub-tenants under ryotwar holders, and it became necessary to provide for the recovery of the rent due by such sub-tenants. While the proposed legislation was under the consideration of the Madras Legislative Council, Mr. Carmichael, the Collector of Vizagapatam, brought to the notice of the Board of Revenue a decision which had been passed by Mr. Collett, the District Judge, and which raised very important questions respecting the right of the Zemindar to enhance the rents payable by his ryots. A Zemindar of a permanently settled estate had applied to the Collector for the issue of an order for ejecting certain ryots who had refused to accept puttahs providing for the payment of enhanced rent. The Collector rejected the claim on the grounds that the Zemindar's demands on the ryots were absolutely limited by the Regulations 28 and 30 of 1802, and that rent could not be enhanced beyond the sums entered in the puttahs issued in accordance with the provisions of those regulations. Mr. Collett reversed the Collector's decision holding that sections 8 and 9 of Regulation 30 of 1802, which provided a limit of time for the issue of puttahs on demand and prescribed the

[99] See decisions quoted by the Board of Revenue in their Proceedings of 2nd December 1864, No. 7843.

mode of adjusting disputes regarding rates of assessment, were intended to apply only to the first occasion of issuing a puttah after the permanent settlement of an estate, that there was nothing in the regulation to preclude an enhancement of the demand in future years, that, on the contrary, such changes were contemplated was shown by the fact that the regulation provided for puttahs being renewable every year, that the terms "just and correct rate" and the "just rate prescribed" used in Regulation 5 of 1822 were equivalent to "fair and equitable" rate, and that to suppose that rents were intended to be limited by the Regulations of 1802 was incompatible with the declaration in Regulation 4 of 1822, viz., that those regulations were not intended to define, infringe, or destroy the rights of any parties.

Mr. Collett's decision left it in doubt whether he objected to the *money value* of the share of the produce representing the Zemindar's rent being considered as limited, or to the share of the produce itself being limited; and also whether the "fair and equitable rate" referred to by him had reference to rents payable according to customary usage, or to rents determined by the application of the principle of competition. In the latter case, the value of the ryot's interest in the land would, of course, be destroyed. A similar case had arisen in Bengal about the same time and it was decided that the principle of competition was to be appealed to in settling rates of rent and it was only in 1865 that this decision was overruled by the Calcutta High Court in what is known as the "Great Rent case." The Madras Board of Revenue, justly apprehending that the rights of the ryots were imperilled by Mr. Collett's decision, exhaustively reviewed the whole question and communicated their views to the Select Committee of the Legislative Council appointed to settle the lines of the proposed legislation.[100] In the report submitted by the Committee they stated that they unanimously agreed with the Board that the Regulations of 1802 were intended to protect the occupants of land under Zemindars by fixing the maximum rent demandable from them and forbidding their ejectment so long as the rent was paid, and that Regulations 4 and 5 of 1822 were passed for the increased protection of such occupants of land, in consequence of passages in the Regulations of 1802, which made mention of a *proprietary* right having been conferred on Zemindars, having led to doubt and misapprehension as to the rights of the

---

[100] The conclusions arrived at by the Board in their Proceedings, dated 2nd December 1864, No. 7843, are printed as appendix VI.-B. (1).

ryots. Experience, however, having shown that even these regulations were not free from ambiguity, the Committee was of opinion that the main principles on which disputes regarding rent should be decided should be clearly laid down as follows:—first, ryots who held in their own right hereditarily or by custom of the country, at a fixed or long established rent, were to be protected; secondly, a division of the crop between the land-holder and the tenant formed the ancient basis of rent, and the local rate of this division was to be referred to in cases of dispute, when other means of settling the rate of rent to the satisfaction of both parties proved unsuccessful; thirdly, land-holders were to be at liberty to arrange their own terms for rent in the case of unoccupied lands. The Committee was further of opinion that voluntary engagements regarding rent between the land-lord and tenant should be respected and that any other course would lead to great confusion and wrong. As regards the terms on which the occupation of waste lands was to be allowed, the Committee remarked, "While it is essential to protect the rights of old tenants, it would injure the due rights of the land-holder and oppose the advancement of the country to declare that he cannot let out unoccupied land to the best advantage. By introduction of valuable new products, such as indigo, silk, coffee, oil-seeds, &c., and by improved means of communication in some parts of the country, lands have attained an enhanced value, and as a land-holder can refuse application for waste lands, it would be anomalous and injurious to declare that he can only arrange for their cultivation by cultivating them himself or leasing them out on inadequate rent founded on an ordinary and obsolete grain crop. The Committee, therefore, proposed to enact the following rules, viz., (1) all contracts for rent, express or implied, shall be respected; (2) where no express contract exists, the payment of rent continuously at the same rate for 12 years is to be considered an implied contract to hold permanently at that rate; (3) in districts or villages which have been surveyed by the British Government and in which a money assessment has been fixed on the fields, such assessment is to be considered the proper rent, where no contract for rent, express or implied, exists; (4) where no express or implied contract has been made between the land-lord and tenant, and where no money assessment has been fixed on the fields, the rates of rent shall be determined according to usage, and where such usage is not clearly ascertainable, then according to the rates established or paid for neighbouring lands of similar description and quality; provided that if either party be dissatisfied with the rate so determined, he may claim that the rent be discharged in kind according to the *Waram, i.e.* according to the established rate of the village for dividing the crop between the Government or the land-lord and the cultivator; (5) in the case of immemorial waste or of lands left unoccupied either through default or voluntary resignation, it shall be lawful for land-holders to arrange their own terms of rent. As regards the question of ejectment, the Committee provided that tenants of Zemindars were not to be ejected except by an order of the Collector or the decree of a Court. This provision, however, they explained in their report to be intended "to protect ryots who had land in their own right hereditarily or by the custom of the country against sudden ejectment" and that "the case of temporary tenants who refused to vacate land or who resisted the land-holder's entry when the term of their tenancy had expired did not belong to this bill" but was to be dealt by the Civil and Criminal Courts.

When the Bill was passed into law, the provision to the effect that payment of rent at a certain rate for a period of 12 years should be taken to import an implied contract to pay at that rate for ever was omitted, but the reasons for the omission have not been stated. On the other hand, the absolute right intended to be conceded to land-holders to arrange their terms of rent in the case of waste lands was qualified by the proviso that this provision was not to affect any special rights which, by law or usage having the force of law, are held by any class of persons in such waste or unoccupied lands.

Failure of Act VIII of 1865 to protect the rights of Zemindari ryots.

86. Act VIII of 1865, instead of clearing up the ambiguities in the law of land-lord and tenant and placing the rights of the ryots on a well understood basis, has had the effect of involving the relations of Zemindars and ryots in greater confusion than they were in before. By declaring that all contracts "express" or "implied" are to be enforced, it has opened a wide door for doubts and contentions of all kinds. It has entirely missed its object which was to accord legislative recognition to the principle that was understood to be part of the common law of the country, viz., that the ryots were entitled to hold the lands in their occupation as long as they paid the customary rent according to the established rates. As regards immemorial waste and lands left unoccupied by default or voluntary resignation, it has established a presumption in favour of the Zemindar's

right to let it on any terms he pleased, by throwing on persons contesting this right the burden of proving that they had special rights recognized by law or usage having the force of law which derogated from the Zemindar's right. The decisions of the High Court have also not tended to clear up the obscurities and supply the deficiencies in the law, and the frequent fluctuations in the views entertained by the courts as regards the rights of the ryots have, if anything, rendered the law more uncertain. In some of their earliest decisions, the High Court had upheld the view that a ryot was entitled to retain possession of the land as long as he paid the customary rent or share of the produce. Subsequently a change came over the views of the High Court and they ruled that a ryot "holding" as it is called "under a puttah" was not entitled to hold the land for a longer period than that during which the puttah was in force, unless he could prove a special contract, custom or usage to the contrary. This decision was arrived at in the case of lands paying revenue direct to Government and the express declarations of Government to the contrary in their Standing Orders were set aside as not "constituting rights enforceable at law." In recent decisions there has been a tendency to take a more favorable view of the rights of ryots in the case of ryots paying revenue direct to Government by regarding the ryot's right as arising from occupation of the land and not the puttah which simply defines the demand for rent on the ryot for the period specified therein, and not the duration of the occupancy. But still it is impossible to say what view the courts would take as regards the right of a Zemindari ryot to hold the land at the end of the term of any subsisting puttah.[101] If the Zemindar sued for ejectment on the ground that the ryot would not pay enhanced rent, the suit would probably go against him unless he showed that the demand for enhanced rent was justified on the score of the rent-value of the lands having been enhanced by improvements effected by him. If, on other land, the ryot were turned out of the holding on the ground that he had no right to hold the land beyond the term of the puttah, he would have to show either that he derived his title from some one who had occupancy right in the land prior to the permanent settlement of the estate—manifestly almost an impossibility,—or that the circumstances of the case were such as to "imply" a contract to allow him to hold the land, and this is a hardship, as there is no certain criterion to determine what circumstances will be accepted by the courts as leading to

---

[101] *Vide* note on the decisions regarding the rights of the ryots; appendix VI.-B. (2).

the inference that there was an "implied" contract. This state of the law is an incentive to violent proceedings and places at a disadvantage land-holders who are willing to allow ryots to retain their holdings on payment of enhanced rents. In some respects, the decisions of the court have disallowed the just rights of the Zemindars to enhance money rents with reference to the increase in the prices of produce, while the Government itself exercises such a right in the case of the ryots it directly deals with. The law as regards the rights of the Zemindar to regulate the mode of cultivation or the nature of the crops grown, and of the tenants to make improvements and obtain compensation therefor when they are evicted, is unsettled. In two other respects, the landlord is placed at a disadvantage. He cannot sue for rent either in a Revenue court or in an ordinary Civil court, unless he offers to the tenant such a puttah, as he is bound to accept. It often happens that there is a dispute about the terms of the puttah leading to litigation extending over several years, as to whether the puttah offered by the landlord was a proper one or not. If it is decided by a court that any condition in a puttah offered was an improper one, to whatever extent the claims of the tenant might be disallowed in other respects, the landlord forfeits the rent for the whole period of litigation. Again, under the existing law, the landlord's claim for rent is not recognized as giving him a lien on the land in the hands of the stranger to whom the occupancy right might be transferred. This acts as an incentive to fraudulent conduct on the part of the tenant and, by rendering the recovery of rent difficult in cases in which a transferable occupancy right exists, makes it the interest of the landlord to endeavour to destroy it. There are, besides, various other flaws and omissions in the Act which promote disputes between landlords and tenants and embitter their relations, and the Act itself has been so carelessly drawn up that Mr. Justice Holloway once declared judicially that he did not in the least profess to understand its provisions.

Present unsatisfactory condition of the Zemindari ryots.

87. The result is what might be expected, and there can be no doubt that the present condition of the Zemindari ryots is very unsatisfactory. In the Southern districts where the occupancy rights of ryots have all along been conceded, the ryots hold their own against the Zemindar and often defy them. In the Northern districts, the ryots are in a miserable condition and the Zemindars have everything their own way. There is abundant testimony to this effect. Mr. Forbes, the Col-

lector of[102] Ganjam, shortly after the famine of 1866 wrote, "The thirteen Oorya Zemindars of Ganjam are, with few exceptions, the most grasping landholders and the least enlightened proprietors in the world; they take 50 per cent. of the crops and lay out little or nothing in improving or in maintaining irrigation works. They lease their villages to middle-men, and the under-tenants are consequently deprived of all chance of accumulating capital and are little better than serfs of the soil; the bulk of the ryots in Zemindari estates would hail a change to Government management with joy." We have more recent information as regards the condition of the ryots in the Nuzvid Zemindari in the Kistna delta. The estate was placed under the management of the Court of Wards and the manager of the estate, Mr. Singarazu Venkata Subbarayudu, a Vakil of the High Court, reported in 1879 in the following terms of the manner in which the rents of the ryots had been screwed up by the previous Zemindars. "Once every 5 years it is usual to fix a certain amount of sist upon every village, taking into account the circumstances then existing, the nature of the soil and the quality of the crops, and to take joint muchilikas with 6 dry or 3 wet kists from the pettanadars (Headmen) and kurnums, &c., of every village with conditions following :— (1) the lands shall not be relinquished before the prescribed term; (2) for losses arising from excess or failure of rains, they shall hold themselves responsible and the prescribed rent shall be paid whether the land be cultivated or not; (3) payments made after time shall be charged interest at 1 per cent. per mensem; (4) no cultivation shall be carried on without obtaining a puttah after the termination of the prescribed time; (5) individual muchilikas shall be presented apportioning the total amount of the muchilikas on the different descriptions of land, viz., best, middling, and inferior; (6) all shall jointly and severally be responsible for the whole rent. . . . . The tarams are subject to alteration when the villages are re-rented at the end of the cowle in the same manner as they are fixed at the beginning. . . . . Some villages have the same rate for the best and worst sort of lands, while others have the least rate for the best land and the highest rate for inferior land. These rates are now in force. The best lands are possessed by kurnums, pettanadars and rich inhabitants. It is most irregular that there should be hundreds of rates in every taluk, and that rates should be different for the same kind of land according to the caste, loyalty and otherwise

---

[102] *Vide* appendix VI.-B. (3).

of the landholder." In forwarding this report to the Court of Wards Mr. Horsfall, the Collector, noted by way of comment: "The system is profitable, no doubt, to the Zemindar, but faulty and oppressive in the extreme. No tenant is secure of his tenure for more than the period of his lease, and any improvements that he may have effected during the period of tenure are turned against him and made the reason for raising his rent; should he not agree, his lands are given to another, and he is ousted. Besides this, under the system of joint liability, he was held responsible for land with which he had really nothing to do. It is by a system like this that the rents have been doubled during the past 10 years. Should no one be willing to pay the price demanded, the lands were included under Kamatam or home farm lands. The conditions speak for themselves." Mr. Wynch who was also in charge of this estate writes in 1890: "No remissions are granted for lands left waste or for loss of crop (*vide* condition of puttah); if the tenant does not pay the rent in full, it remains in the accounts as an arrear against him; and this system of never writing arrears off the accounts is productive of the greatest oppression. Payments are credited to arrears, in order that the right to distrain for the current arrears may be kept alive. If this is not done and if the tenant cannot obviously pay the arrears accumulated against him,—for it is observed that they run on from generation to generation—and supposing that one tenant dies or deserts his holding, the incoming tenant is made to bind himself to pay the arrears due against the holding; then a bond will be taken from the tenant, conditioned for the repayment of the whole debt, with interest, by instalments within perhaps 12 or 20 years or more, as the circumstances require; if default is made in payment of any two consecutive instalments the whole amount of the bond immediately becomes due." As regards the relative condition of Government and Zemindari ryots, Mr. Subbarayudu writes in 1879: "There is no doubt that the estate ryot is poorer than the Government ryot. The reason is to be found in the difference of sist and the difference of administration. Before the expiry of the cowle there can be no alteration of sist, but after it the Zemindar is at liberty to enhance it. Under Government besides occasional remissions, arrears are written off as irrecoverable after lapse of some time; and the ryot is annually allowed to relinquish lands which he cannot pay for. These privileges are not conceded to the Zemindari tenant. Unless the agreement is executed for the rich and poor lands together, no fresh lease is granted on the expiry of a lease. The poor lands cannot be set aside. The ryot is always indebted to the Zemindar. . . . . Money is recovered according to his produce; he is always fettered." The report, printed as appendix VI.-B. (4), of Mr. Cotton who was employed as a relief officer during the famine of 1876 shows the miserable condition of the ryots in the Kalahasti Zemindari. In the Southern districts the condition of the Zemindari ryots is not, as already observed, so bad as in the Northern districts. Nevertheless even here, it seems to be the case that Zemindari ryots are worse off than Government ryots, taking tracts of similar climatic conditions for comparison. As regards the Ramnad Zemindari, Mr. Rajaram Rao, who was for several years the manager of the Zemindari, states that the condition of the ryots in this estate is not as good as that of the Government ryots and that this is due partly to natural disadvantages and partly to the evils incidental to the system of sharing the crop which is in force. He remarks, "the evils of 'Waraput' or sharing system are too obvious to need comment. Under this system, a ryot, with whatever good and efficient arrangements made, is necessarily left at the mercy of the village and taluk officials for getting his crop home. He is not at liberty to reap his crops, harvest them and take his produce of his own accord, but must obtain the permission of the estate officials for every one of those purposes. . . . . Attention was not paid to the proper supervision of harvest, &c., and to the punctual collection of rents. The result was that the ryots contracted a habit of dishonesty and unpunctuality in their dealings and the officers were habituated to corruption and foul play."[103] There are, of course, estates like Ettiyapuram in which the condition of the ryots is nearly as good as in the Government taluks, but this is mostly due to the fact of these estates having had the benefit of several years of careful administration by the Court of Wards during the minority of the owners. The Ettiyapuram estate was surveyed, and money assessment was introduced in lieu of the sharing system to the great advantage of both the Zemindar and the ryots.

Suggestions as to amendment of the law of landlord and tenant.

88. An amendment of the law regulating the relations between Zemindars and tenants is therefore urgently necessary to prevent further injury to the ryot's rights, and a bill based on the lines of the recent legislation in Bengal is now under the consideration of Government. I have mentioned in a

[103] For a graphic description of the evils of the sharing system by Mr. A. Seshayya Sastriar, C.S.I., Dewan of Pudukota, see appendix VI.-B. (5).

note printed as appendix VI.-B. (6) the points in regard to which provision should be made in the new law. The history of the previous legislation, which I have attempted briefly to sketch in the preceding paragraphs, will, I trust, have shown the defects in the present law and the causes of its failure. The main cause seems to me to be the idea of the legislature that any attempt on its part to define, in an unequivocal manner, the relative rights of Zemindars and ryots might necessitate interference with "rights of property" and "freedom of contract" and that if it were made imperative that all contracts between landlords and tenants should be reduced to writing, and machinery provided for summarily deciding disputes between them, matters would adjust themselves in the manner best calculated to secure the public interests. This view of the case assumes that the Zemindar is the full owner of the lands in the Zemindari and that the rights of the ryot are derived through him. The assumption, as will be seen from the account already given of the origin of the ryot's property, is unfounded. The share of the produce which the Government was entitled to take was always limited in lands occupied as well as waste reclaimed, and the rights conferred on Zemindars were no higher than the rights possessed by the Government itself. Any doubts which the inaccurate language of the permanent settlement regulations might have given rise to in this respect were fully cleared up by the legislation of 1822. The ryot's interest in land had, however, no saleable value in most parts of the presidency at the time of the permanent settlement. The Zemindar's interest was likewise of small value as he had to pay the major portion of his receipts to Government. Now, owing to improved administration and the general progress of the country, and more especially owing to the great rise in the value of agricultural produce consequent on the expansion of foreign trade which has taken place during the last 40 years, the value of both the Zemindar's and ryot's interests has greatly increased. The question involved in according legislative protection to ryots is therefore not what shall be taken away from the Zemindar and given to the ryot, but how shall the Zemindar, while being allowed to enjoy to the fullest extent the enhanced value of his share of the produce, be prevented from appropriating, as far as legislation can do so, the enhanced value of the ryot's share. The experiment of allowing the ryots to establish their rights in the courts has been tried, and it has grievously failed. In the first place, the courts can act only on the evidence produced before them, and in a contest between a rich and powerful Zemindar and a poor ignorant ryot, the odds are, of course, immensely in favour of the former. The rights too, whose origin has to be referred [104] back to times when there was no settled Government or regular administration of law, are not capable of easy proof or even of exact definition. In this state of things, the natural result is that whatever is not proved to belong to the ryot is taken to belong to the Zemindar. The only effectual way of protecting the ryot, then, is to define his rights precisely by legislation and to allow him freedom to contract himself out of them only to a limited extent, seeing that in the case of cultivators cultivating for subsistence, with no alternative occupation to fall back upon or education or means to hold their own in a contest with their landlords, there can be no real freedom of action. Bearing these considerations in mind, the principles on which the legislation should be based may be thus stated :—According to the common law of the country, there are two distinct interests in land recognized, viz., the *Melvaram* and *Kudivaram*. Melvaram belongs to the Government or its assignee the Zemindar; and the Kudivaram to the ryot. There are also two distinct classes of land, viz., one Pannai, Kamar, home farm or private lands, and the other Aiyan, Jeroyati, or peasant lands. In the first class of lands both the Melvaram and Kudivaram rights belong to the Zemindar; and in the second, the Melvaram right alone. The bulk of the lands belong to the latter class, and so the presumption must be that land not proved to be private land is peasant land. This rule should be applied to cultivated land as well as the waste. As regards waste, the Zemindar should be entitled to apply to a Civil Court for permission to enclose waste lands and treat the enclosed lands as " private " in view to forming plantations, establishing factories, growing jungles, &c. The Court should in such cases give notice to the ryots to state any objections they may have to the enclosure and, after hearing their objections and making such arrangements as may be found necessary to reserve sufficient area of waste land to meet the requirements of the ryots as regards *boná fide* increase of cultivation and pasturage, it may grant the application. In regard to the grant of unenclosed waste lands,[105] the

---

[104] *Vide* extract (appendix VI.–B. (7)) from Sir H. S. Maine's speech in the Legislative Council of India for a full explanation of the difficulty of ascertaining the rights of ryots when there is no settled Government. See also extracts from Sir Frederick Pollock's " Land Laws " regarding the manner in which the rights of tenants became gradually abridged (appendix VI.–B. (8)).

[105] As to the discussions in the case of Government waste lands and the final settlement of the question—*vide* note printed as appendix VI.–B. (9).

Zemindar's powers to grant them for cultivation must be assimilated to those exercised by Government. It would certainly be difficult to control the Zemindar's discretion in granting waste lands for cultivation or to prevent his making a profit out of them, but the recognition of the principle that the waste lands are not at the Zemindar's unrestricted disposal is necessary to prevent the lands being rack-rented and lands resigned being added as a matter of course to "private lands;" otherwise all peasant lands as they become vacant will be converted into private lands. The ryot should have the right to adopt such modes of cultivation and raise such crops as he finds profitable, and to make improvements to land, provided he pays the customary rent determined with reference to the standard crop of the village. As regards the rents, though these have been pushed up in the Northern districts so as to absorb nearly the whole of the increase in the value of the ryot's share of the produce that has resulted from the general progress of the country in recent years, still a sudden reduction of them would cause hardship to the Zemindars. Existing rents must, therefore, be recognized, and the efforts of legislation directed towards securing to the ryot the enjoyment of any increase in the value of his share of the produce which may accrue to him in the future. As regards the detailed provisions to be made for this purpose, the note printed as appendix VI.–B. (6) should be referred to. The most noteworthy point in connection with this question is the rule laid down to the effect that rents shall not be enhanced even with the consent of the ryot to a greater extent than 12½ per cent. at a time, and that rent once enhanced shall not be liable to alteration for 15 years. Zemindari ryots should be conceded the right to transfer their holdings after giving due notice to the Zemindars. This right is possessed by the ryots in the Southern districts, and though it is disputed by the Zemindars of the Northern districts, it should be recognized by legislation as it is the necessary consequence of the limitation of the demand of the Zemindar and the creation of a saleable interest for the ryot in the land. Public interests require that there should be no obstacles interposed to the consolidation of holdings for purposes of profitable cultivation; and the Zemindar himself may have to purchase ryot's holdings for such purposes. He loses nothing by conceding the right, more especially when he is not allowed to annex lands vacated to his "private lands." His interest will be amply protected by making him retain a lien for the rent due on the land in the hands of the purchaser. To prevent the Zemindar from allowing rent to accumulate by withholding remissions when due, it should be ruled that not more than three years' rent shall be recovered by the sale of the ryot's interest in the land. As regards "private lands" the Zemindar is to have full liberty to deal with them as he likes. It seems to me that provisions of the kind above referred to will, without injuring the rights of the Zemindars, prevent, at all events, further encroachments on the rights of the ryots in the future. These provisions are based on principles recognized by the common law of the country and they do not ignore existing facts and conditions. The present unsatisfactory state of the law is injurious in some cases both to the Zemindars and tenants; and [106] every day's delay must add greatly to the difficulty of dealing with the question. This is especially the case in the Northern districts where lands have within the last two or three years greatly increased in value by the opening of the Hyderabad Railway; and when the East Coast Railway is completed the value of lands is likely to increase still further. If steps are not taken betimes to secure a share of this increase of value for the improvement of the condition of the Zemindari ryots, the growth of vested interests will make it difficult or impossible to do this in the future. Another measure which would effectually protect the rights of the ryots without injuring those of the Zemindars is the survey of Zemindaries. This should be encouraged as much as possible, and the survey should be carried out in all estates under the charge of the Court of Wards. The Court of Wards now naturally hesitate to carry out the survey in the Zemindari estates in the Northern districts, as the rights of the ryots are still undefined. When the new law is passed, this will no longer be the case.

Legislation to arrest the rapid dismemberment of large Zemindari estates.

89. There is also for consideration the question of protecting by legislation large Zemindari estates in this Presidency from dismemberment. Out of a total number of 849 permanently settled estates covering an area of 27½ million acres, there are 135 estates covering an area of 15½ million acres, which are supposed to be held under the law of primogeniture and to be impartible. Some years ago it was believed that the holders of these estates had only a life interest in them, and that they could not alienate or encumber the properties so as to have effect beyond

---

[106] As regards the necessity for legislative interference to regulate the relations between landlords and tenants in view of the rapid changes that are taking place in the economic condition of the country—*vide* Extract from a speech of Mr. Ilbert on the Bengal Tenancy Bill before the Legislative Council of India in 1886 (appendix VI.-B (10)).

their own lifetime. Subsequently the courts discovered that the powers of a Zemindar were the same as those of a manager of a Hindu family holding property in co-parcenary under the ordinary law, with the exception that partition could not be claimed by the junior members of the family who were only entitled to maintenance out of the income of the estate. The Zemindar, it was declared, could, like the manager of an ordinary Hindu family, alienate the property in satisfaction of debts incurred for necessary family purposes, and that where there were no junior members, the powers of alienation of the Zemindar were unrestricted. Next, the Courts ruled that where the junior members of the co-parcenary family were sons, the latter were bound by the alienations made by the father even for debts not incurred for family purposes, it being the pious duty of sons under the Hindu Law to pay the debts of the father, provided they were not incurred for immoral or illegal purposes. The rule of primogeniture and impartibility was also declared not to attach necessarily to the property on grounds of public policy but was to be treated as a family custom liable to be annulled with the mutual consent of the members of the family. The question whether an estate was governed by the law of primogeniture or the ordinary law of equal division was thus made to depend upon the facts of each case and the conduct of the parties, there being no certain criterion laid down to determine the point in any particular case without resort to protracted litigation. Lastly, in a recent decision the Privy Council has ruled that the Zemindar of an ancient and impartible estate is absolute owner and can dispose of it as he pleases, the property being impartible only in the sense that it is not divisible among the members of the family; there is thus nothing to prevent the Zemindar cutting it up into any number of portions and alienating them at his will and pleasure to the prejudice of the rights of succession of the junior members of his family. These rapid changes in the law, or at all events, in what was believed to be such by all the parties interested in the question in this presidency, have led to a great amount of litigation, the junior members in the case of several estates which had hitherto been supposed to be impartible having instituted suits for partition. The Zemindars themselves are apprehensive that the unrestricted powers of alienation conceded to them will lead to the rapid extinction of their estates and the decay of the influence and importance of their families which it was the intention of the rule of primogeniture to conserve. This apprehension seems well founded, for while in the case of ordinary ancestral property the power of alienation by the managing member is restricted only to his fractional share of the property, there is no such limit in the case of an impartible Zemindari; and consequently the dismemberment of impartible estates is likely to be brought about more quickly than the dismemberment of properties to which the ordinary rule of inheritance applies. This result could not have been contemplated, whatever theory is adopted in regard to the origin of the rule of primogeniture, *i.e.*, whether the object of the rule is taken to be the maintenance of the dignity and influence of a certain official position, or the maintenance of the dignity and influence of certain ancient families; for to secure the object in view, the estate must be inalienable from the office in the one case, and from the family in the other. The means adopted by the English landed aristocracy to preserve the integrity of estates, viz., successive settlements voluntarily made by the owner of the reversion of the estate for the time being, as soon as he attains majority, are not available to the Zemindars, as the Hindu Law does not permit of the settlement of estates on 'unborn' persons. In fact, the ancient Hindu Law, as already observed, regarded land as constituting 'an estate dedicated equally to the support of sacrifices to deceased members, as to the sustenance of those living, and still to come into life;' and powers of alienation are a modern development. It seems to me, therefore, desirable that with a view to prevent litigation and dissipation of properties it should be declared by legislation, after due enquiry by a commission, (1) which estates are ancient Zemindaries subject to the rule of primogeniture and of impartibility, and whether the rule attaches to the estate or to the family which holds it at present; and (2) that the powers of the holder of the estate for the time being shall be those of the managing member of a Hindu family governed by the ordinary law of succession as they were understood to be before the recent Privy Council decision. The modern Hindu Law seems to steer clear of the evils of the strict entails of the English system as well as of the restrictions on the powers of bequest of self-acquired landed property imposed by the French Law on the one hand, and on the other of unrestricted powers of disposition of ancestral property in a purely agricultural country where the vast majority of the population has to subsist by the cultivation of land. The powers of the managing member in family property to deal with it for the purposes of its improvement are, under the Hindu Law, unrestricted; but at the same time he is prevented from alienating the means of subsistence of the junior members of his family including his own sons, while parental control is, to some extent, preserved by the liability of the sons to pay the debts of the father except in certain contingencies; and as regards self-acquired property, the acquirer can do what he likes with it. In making the above remarks, I have assumed that the preservation of these large estates, which are found scattered in the midst of a vast multitude of peasant properties, is a desirable object. I do not propose to discuss the much vexed question whether the system of landholding in large estates or in peasant properties is the more conducive to the general prosperity of the country. Each system has its special advantages and disadvantages, and as Dr. Walker in his book on *Land and its Rent* points out, the most wholesome of national and economical organizations is perhaps that which admits of an admixture of large, medium sized and small properties, those of medium size predominating. It is true that the Zemindars as a body have as yet done nothing to assume their proper position as leaders of social and industrial movements; but in fairness to them, it must also be remembered that to a great extent circumstances have been against them. They were most of them in possession of unrestrained power in the beginning of the century, and the necessities of orderly and civilized government in the then existing state of the country required that they should be deprived of all power and influence and relegated to the position of landholders. The conditions also of farming in this country, so dissimilar to those which existed in England in the latter half of the last century, were not such as to render high cultivation profitable. Brought up in the old traditions, with no sphere of public usefulness open to them to develop their better qualities or enlarge their minds, they have hitherto, with some notable exceptions, formed an idle and dissipated class. Recently, however, a change has become perceptible. Several of them are being educated, and the proceedings of the Landholders' Association recently organized distinctly show that they are beginning to realize their duties and responsibilities and to feel that if they do not rise to the requirements of the present *régime*, they will lose all social influence and importance and be doomed finally to disappear. With the great increase in population and expansion of an export trade, the necessity for better methods of cultivation, such as those which only rich landlords have it in their power to adopt, will become greater and greater, and a sphere of usefulness will be opened out to them in this direction as well as in the management of industrial enterprizes which peasant proprietors cannot be expected to undertake. It would, therefore, not be right to judge of the future usefulness of this class from what they have done in the past; and if they could be assisted to maintain their ground without the aid of legislation of any drastic character involving violent interference with private rights and weakening motives of self-help or personal independence, it would, it seems to me, be good policy on the part of Government to afford that assistance. The Government might also encourage in an indirect way, by the grant of titles and honors, such of the Zemindars as take interest in the welfare of their tenantry and prove useful auxiliaries to Government in its efforts to introduce agricultural knowledge and improvement in the country. This is now done to some extent, but in a spasmodic, isolated manner. What is required is more systematic and continuous action in this direction. It might be made a rule that all the more considerable Zemindars are to be invited to meet the head of the Government and the representative of the Queen-Empress on or about the New Year's day, when they would be expected to give in an informal way an account of the management of their estates. This will give them an opportunity of becoming personally acquainted with the head of the Government and with other Zemindars, and may be trusted to engender in them a spirit of emulation in works of public usefulness. The head of the Government will also have an opportunity of showing his appreciation of the more public spirited Zemindars by calling them to his council and treating them as the trusted advisers of Government; while those who neglected their duties and responsibilities would receive due warning that they would be incurring the displeasure of Government if they persisted in this course of conduct. In many cases, such warnings and indirect influence would prove effectual; and though it may not be possible to make any marked and immediate impression on the older Zemindars, the effect on the ambition for distinction in works of public usefulness of the younger generation cannot be otherwise than beneficial.

III.—Agricultural Indebtedness, its Causes and Remedies.

Extent of agricultural indebtedness.

90. The next group of questions we have to consider relates to the extent of the agricultural indebtedness prevalent in this presidency, its causes and the measures which it is possible for Government to take to mitigate the evil.

Without a minute inquiry extending over all parts of the country, it would not be possible to form an entirely trustworthy idea of the extent of agricultural indebtedness, as the conditions of different tracts vary widely. The following general account is based on inquiries made and information furnished on the subject by the officers of the Registration Department within the limited time allowed to them for the purpose.

The aggregate value of the documents registered in the registration offices of this presidency in 1891-92 amounted to about 15·68 crores of rupees; but it would, of course, be a mistake to take the aggregate value of registered transactions as a measure of agricultural indebtedness. Registered transactions are not all loans, but, on the contrary include a large number of cases of cancellation of debts, such as reconveyances of mortgaged property, releases and discharges of debts, receipts, &c., besides gifts, sales, leases, and partitions of immoveable property. Of the aggregate amount shown above, 14·45 crores related to immoveable and 1·23 crores to moveable property and simple bonds. The value of gifts of immoveable property amounted to 20 lakhs of rupees; of sales of immoveable property 4·29 crores, and of mortgages of immoveable property 6·67 crores. The annual rents of leases registered aggregated 48 lakhs and the amount of fine or premium paid therefor was 10 lakhs. Among documents not relating to immoveable property, the value of sales was 3 lakhs and of simple bonds 60 lakhs.

The total extent of debts registered—mortgages and bonds—therefore amounted to 7·27 crores of rupees. There is no means of finding out how much of this amount relates to debts renewed and how much to debts newly contracted. A rough analysis of a large number of mortgage deeds in the several districts shows that nearly 75 per cent. of the mortgages executed are for terms not exceeding three years, that in nearly 50 per cent. of cases there is either no term stipulated or the term is less than one year, and the average term stipulated for all mortgages is about three and-half years.[107] Mortgages for short terms might, of course, occasionally be permitted to run for the full period allowed by the law of limitation, but the practice appears to be to renew the mortgages as frequently as possible. 66,396 mortgage deeds and 12,720 bonds[108] registered in the registration offices of nine districts were examined, and it was

---

[107] **For particulars *vide* statement printed as appendix VI.-C. (1).**

[108] **Do. do. VI.-C. (2).**

found that in 27,845 cases the purposes for which debts were contracted were not stated; and that in 28,206 cases the documents were executed either in renewal of subsisting mortgages or for obtaining loans to discharge other debts. In the remaining 23,065 cases, the purposes for which the debts were contracted were as follow:—To discharge court decrees 568; for purchasing lands and houses 3,873; for purposes of trade 836; for purchase of cattle and for cultivation expenses and payment of Government assessment 2,973; for sinking wells and defraying the expenses of garden cultivation 569; for marriage expenses 3,502; for funeral expenses 155; for other household expenses 5,194; for court expenses 298; and for various other purposes 5,097. The above figures relate only to a small number of transactions registered in a few districts, but a similar analysis of the statistics for all the offices in the presidency would entail an enormous amount of labour and take up considerable time.

The aggregate amount of debt may, perhaps, be guessed at four times the annual value of mortgages and bonds registered, viz., 29 crores of rupees for the whole presidency. The unregistered debts are mostly temporary loans which are either repaid in a few months or converted into debts secured by registered documents. Of the above sum of 29 crores, a considerable portion is secured on house property in towns. There is no means of estimating how much is so secured, but there is no doubt that the amount is considerable. In the Madras town, where the properties mortgaged are mostly house properties, the total value of the mortgages amounts to 26 lakhs of rupees a year.

We have also no information in regard to the total value of landed property and the extent to which it is encumbered, but there is no reason to think that, high as the figures relating to indebtedness look, they bear anything like the proportion to the total value of landed property that obtains in European [109] countries.

---

[109] Mr. Jenkins, Assistant Commissioner, who reported on the state of agriculture in France to the British Royal Commission on Agriculture in 1881, remarks as follows on the indebtedness of the peasantry in France:

"A report on the agriculture of any portion of France without a mention of that spoilt child of the doctrinaires, the 'peasant proprietor,' would appear to many persons like the play of Hamlet without the impersonation of the Prince of Denmark. Therefore I feel constrained to say a few words on the subject, although, as a matter of fact, I have very little to add to what has already been reported by my colleague Mr. Sutherland. I quite agree with everything that Mr. Sutherland had stated in his report, and also with the views on the same subject expressed by my late friend Mr. Gibson Richardson in his well known work on the *Corn and Cattle Producing Districts of France*. But it seems necessary to draw attention to one remarkable omission by Mr. Sutherland, namely, the extent to which peasant properties in France are mortgaged. Mr. Richardson states that 'the mortgage debt is put at 480 millions sterling, which is one-sixth

In this country, there being no artificial obstacles interposed to the free transfer of properties, the extent to which property is annually transferred by private sale, taken in conjunction with the average term of mortgages, may, in some measure, serve as an index to the extent of indebtedness of the agricultural classes. In the year 1890–91, out of an extent of ryotwar holdings amounting to a little more than 21 million acres, the extent returned as transferred by private sale was a little over 366,000 acres or 1·7 per cent. The irrigated land transferred was 87,000 acres out of 4·1 million acres or 2·1 per cent.; and the unirrigated land 279,000 acres out of 17 million acres or 1·6 per cent. The assessment of lands transferred under each class to the total assessment of lands under occupation bore the following proportions; irrigated land, 2·2 per cent.; unirrigated 1·7; both classes 2 per cent. In his *Manual of the Coimbatore District*, Mr. Nicholson has given interesting calculations as regards the extent of land transferred, based on the registration statistics for the three years ending 1882–83. Mr. Nicholson estimated the value of land as follows: Irrigated lands, 90,000 acres at Rs. 255 per acre, 2·25 crores; unirrigated lands, 1,800,000 acres at Rs. 12 per acre, 2·15 crores; garden lands, 410,000 acres at Rs. 46 per acre, 1·9 crores; total 6·3 crores. He observes, "The actual

---

of the estimated value of the land, borrowed at a high rate of interest, as much, including costs, as 7 per cent. calling for a yearly payment, mostly from the smallest owners, of 34 millions sterling.' The same writer states that small plots of land, when purchased, 'do not pay 2½ per cent. to let, and they can be sold when conveniently placed for division at a price which bears no proportion to the letting value.' Again, referring to the rights of heirs to their share of each kind of property, he remarks 'the consequence of this is a continual division and sub-division of plots of land, until at last no cultivation is possible, except with a spade, and in some cases that must not be a full sized one; and a tree cannot be planted in an estate, because it is illegal to plant one within two yards of your neighbour's boundary, and your neighbour on each side is within that distance.' These quotations from Mr. Richardson bring into relief the three vices of the French land system as it affects the peasant proprietor; these are (1) an excessive sub-division of the land which used to be called in France '*morcellement*' until the progress of facts rendered the word too feeble to express the reality, and so of late years, it has been replaced by the term '*pulverisation*'; (2) the 'demon of property' which is the curse of the French peasant, which causes him to beg, borrow, and almost to steal, to starve himself and his family, and in fact to do anything in order to obtain possession of a piece of land; and (3) the recklessness with which the peasants borrow money at even ruinous rates of interest to complete their purchases."

The following facts as regards agricultural indebtedness in European countries have been taken from Mr. Mulhall's *Dictionary of Statistics*:

United Kingdom.—Lord Reay estimates the mortgages at 58 per cent. in England of the value of real estate; in Ireland, according to Commissioner Greene, they amount to 40 per cent., say 120 millions sterling. *Germany*.—In 1870, the mortgages in Prussia reached 190, and in all Germany 273 millions sterling. Professor Meitzen, however, considers that 41 per cent. of all real estate in the Empire is mortgaged. An official return for 1883 shows that the houses of Berlin were mortgaged for 105 millions sterling, being 67 per cent. of their assessed value. *Russia*.—Mortgages of land are known to reach 148 millions sterling, but probably amount to much more. *Belgium*.—The registration of mortgages was as follows:—1860, 3·4 millions; 1870, 4·4 millions; and 1886, 8·2 millions sterling. *Spain*.—Mortgages are estimated to amount to 172 millions sterling; annual average of new mortgages, 8·5 millions. *Egypt*.—New mortgages average 1·3 millions per annum.

sales for the three years ending 1882–83 averaged about $12\frac{2}{5}$ lakhs per annum, or less than one-fourth of the transactions, and about one-fiftieth of the capital value. In 1882–83 the total of land transactions was 24,765, of which mortgages were 11,400 or 46·2 per cent., and sales 10,610 or 43 per cent. The ratio of all transactions to the kinds of land has not been ascertained, but in 1880–83 sales averaged as follows: wet lands 1,567 acres or $\frac{1}{55}$ of the total occupied area; dry lands 35,726 acres or about $\frac{1}{50}$ of the total occupied dry area excluding gardens; and gardens 3,462 acres or about $\frac{1}{118}$ of the nominal garden area of 408,326 acres and $\frac{1}{72}$ of the area (251,275 acres) actually irrigated. Of the prices realized, nearly $\frac{8}{24}$ are credited to the small area of wet land; $\frac{13}{24}$ to dry land; and $\frac{3}{24}$ to gardens. Acre for acre, wet lands as sold were worth Rs. 255 or $13\frac{1}{2}$ times as much as dry land and $5\frac{1}{2}$ times as much as gardens, while gardens were worth Rs. 46 or $2\frac{1}{2}$ times as much as dry land, which averaged Rs. 19 per acre. The low garden rate is due to the fact that much nominal garden in a given field is only dry land, a 6-acre field having probably only 3 to 4 acres of actual garden, the total area actually irrigated being only 251,275 acres out of a field area of 408,326 acres; hence the actually irrigated area is probably worth about Rs. 60 per acre. The average value of the dry lands (Rs. 19) must not be taken as a gauge of the value of poor lands, such as VII 4, 5 and VIII 3, 4, 5; a vast area has little or no sale value, being so unproductive; an examination of the tables from 1878 to 1883 shows that sales are much larger where the generality of dry lands are most valuable; in Polláchi, where the soil is generally rich and the south-west monsoon abundant, and in Udamalpet, with its high-priced black cotton lands, the sales averaged in five years almost $\frac{5}{12}$ths of the total district sales, though the occupied area of these two taluks, including poliputs, is two-twelfths of the district occupied area. The number of professional money-lenders in these taluks possibly accounts for the large sales and the value of the lands for the money-lenders. Since, therefore, the average price of Rs. 19 has been struck upon the sale of an unduly large proportion of the valuable lands of the district, a lower rate (Rs. 12) has been taken in roughly estimating the capital value of the *total* occupied dry lands. The sales of garden lands in the Palladam taluk, including Avanáshi, were very heavy, totalling 8,563 acres out of 16,448 acres sold from 1878 to 1883 or above one-half, whereas the garden area of the taluk is above two-elevenths of the district garden area, and the dry sales were only about one-eleventh of the total dry sales." Information is not available in a readily accessible form to make a similar analysis of statistics for later years. The agricultural returns published by the Board of Revenue show that in 1890-91, the area transferred by private sale was 58,000 acres in the Coimbatore district or 2·4 per cent. of the total area of ryotwar holdings, which pretty closely accords with the estimate arrived at by Mr. Nicholson. There is no reason to think that the percentage is higher in other districts.

It is also a noteworthy fact that land transactions take place mostly between the ryots themselves, and that money-lenders in not less than 80 per cent. of the cases belong to the agricultural classes. Information furnished by the officers of the Registration Department clearly establishes this point.[110] This fact explains the reason why the evils of agricultural indebtedness do not appear to have developed in this presidency to the extent they appear to have in the Bombay-Deccan. There the money-lenders are stated to be foreigners, different in religion from their clients; entirely out of sympathy with them; and accustomed to retire with their profits after a sufficiently long course of business to their homes in Rajputana. The money-lenders in this presidency may roughly be divided into four classes, viz., 1st, the richer ryots; 2ndly, the Komaties or Banya traders in the Telugu districts; 3rdly, the Lingayet traders in the tracts of country bordering on the Mysore territory; and, 4thly, the Muhammadan Lubbay traders on the East Coast and Moplahs in North Malabar, and the Nattukottai Chetties in the southern districts. As already stated, taking the presidency as a whole, not less than 80 per cent. of the money-lenders belong to the agricultural classes, who are of all castes. The Komaties or Banyas form a small class, and as they have been for generations permanently established in their several places of business, their terms are generally moderate, and harmonious relations prevail between them and their clients. In the Cuddapah and Nellore districts, where this class is numerous, the rates of interest are generally lower than in other parts of the presidency. The Moplahs are usurious money-lenders, and as they are keen men of business placed in the midst of an indolent population, alien to them in religion, they are more than usually hard in their dealings. The Moplahs do not, however, except in North Malabar, practise money-lending to any great extent and they are more often borrowers. The Nattukottai Chetties are the Marwadies of this presidency; but they are established only in a few trading centres

---

[110] For particulars *vide* statement printed as appendix VI.-C. (2).

and lend money to the poorer classes to a small extent, though the terms exacted by them are harder than those exacted by other classes of money-lenders. They do a large business in the way of lending large sums to zemindars and other big landholders and make an enormous profit.

The terms and conditions of money loans differ in different districts. 12 per cent. is the usual rate of interest for loans amounting to between Rs. 100 and Rs. 500; for loans between Rs. 500 and Rs. 1,000 it varies from 12 to 9 per cent., and for loans above Rs. 1,000 between 9 and 6 per cent., the rate of interest diminishing as the amount of the loan increases. On the other hand, for loans below Rs. 100 the rate of interest ranges between 12 and 18 per cent., the rate increasing as the amount of the loan diminishes. These are the most usual rates,[111] but in exceptional cases and for large amounts the rate of interest is occasionally less than 6 per cent. In the case of small sums when the security offered is insufficient and the risk in recovering the loan great, the rate of interest is even higher than 18 per cent. Sometimes it is stipulated that when there is failure in payment of the loan together with the usual interest at the appointed time, and the solvency of the debtor becomes doubtful, a higher rate of interest shall be paid from the date of default. This condition is not, however, generally enforced except when the money has to be recovered by resort to the courts. Loans on mortgages of value of Rs. 100 and upwards amounted in 1891-92 to 5·85 crores of rupees and loans on mortgages of value less than Rs. 100 to 82 lakhs or about one-seventh of the former, the average amount[112] of a loan in the first case being Rs. 313, and in the second, Rs. 44. Loans on simple bonds registered averaged in value Rs. 200. Taking all transactions together, the average rate of interest may, therefore, roughly speaking, be estimated at 12 per cent.

The transactions between money-lenders and ryots, especially in the districts subject to drought, are usually of the following description. The poorer ryots open an account with a money-lender who is generally a well-to-do ryot or Komati trader, and obtain from him small sums of money or food grain or seed grain during the cultivation season, June or July, on condition that the advance is to be repaid in grain after the next harvest with an addition which varies from 12½ to 50 per cent., the most usual rate being 25 per cent.

---

[111] For particulars *vide* statement printed as appendix VI.-C. (2).
[112] Do. do. VI.-C. (3).

As long as the ryots repay regularly what they have borrowed, they are allowed further advances on the same conditions. If there is failure in repayment, a bond or mortgage deed is taken. In the case of hypothecation of property the amount of the loan is about half, and in the case of mortgage with possession about three-fourths, of the value of property offered as security. Money on mortgages of land with possession is rarely lent except by persons belonging to the agricultural classes. Money is sometimes lent to ryots by persons who have no lands of their own with a view to secure food grains for their household consumption, the stipulation being that the borrower shall pay grain in lieu of interest at the harvest at a rate which is below the then market rate. In some cases grain merchants and dealers in commercial produce make advances to ryots stipulating for delivery of produce at certain fixed rates or at the rate prevailing at the time of repayment *minus* a deduction in the price on account of interest or at the lowest rate at which grain was sold soon after harvest. Sometimes the ryots deal directly with merchants, but in some cases, especially in the dry parts of the country, brokers are employed. In several cases, advances are made by landholders to agricultural labourers on the condition that they are not to pay interest so long as they work under them for the customary wages, and that, on default, the amount advanced should be repaid with interest at 18 or 24 per cent. Money is also borrowed by the industrial classes, viz., weavers, artizans, &c., under what is called "Kandu labha" system. An artizan, for instance, borrows Rs. 300 to make his wares and sell them daily. The interest for the whole amount is taken at Rs. 60 per annum and added to the principal and the whole amount is made repayable in daily instalments throughout one year at the rate of one rupee a day by the sale of his goods.

It would, however, be a great mistake to suppose that the rates of interest above referred to, high as they appear, are necessarily usurious. The gross profits derived from the use of capital consist, as is well known, of three parts, viz., (1) the remuneration for the labour of managing the capital, (2) the insurance against the risks involved in the particular use of it; and (3) the interest proper. Taking the case of a ryot borrowing a quantity of grain on condition of repaying at the end of six months the whole of it *plus* an additional 25 per cent., it might seem as if the interest paid were 50 per cent. per annum, a most exorbitant rate; but this is really not so. The price of the grain during the cultivation season is usually 15 or 20 per cent. higher than the price at the time of the harvest, and occasionally even as much as 25 per cent. This difference in price is due no doubt partly to the inability of the majority of the ryots to wait for a price; but even if they waited they would not be able to profit by the whole difference, for that difference consists, to a considerable extent, of the wastage and dryage of grain during the intervening period and the charges for storing. The gains of the money or grain lenders are, taking one year with another, and allowing for losses, not more than what keen men of business can reasonably expect for the time they give to the business and the risks they undergo. And in the case of the poorest ryots, the money lenders are almost a necessity, seeing to what extent, under the conditions of climate, the outturn of harvests in this country differs from year to year. The late Rajah Sir T. Madhava Rao has explained the useful service this class renders to the ryots with reference to the state of things in the Baroda State. He states ." The ryot can never, as a rule, altogether dispense with the services of the sowkar; for the seasons are not so regular, nor are the means of irrigation so extensive as to ensure equality or constancy of production. Again, the land tax is, in most cases, fixed, and absorbs a considerable proportion of the produce; and again, prices of produce fluctuate, changing the incidence of tax from year to year. In other words, while the outturn of the land is necessarily varying, the ryot has to pay a fixed and considerable tax which must come from the land. In other words, again, the exchequer has to draw a constant and continuous stream out of a fitful supply. The sowkar by his interposition meets the mechanical necessity of the problem. He is the receiver of the fitful supply, and makes the ryot pay the sirkar equably. He often performs another useful function, namely, he enables the ryot also to draw from that fitful supply an equable subsistence for himself and his family. It is thus to him that the sirkar and the ryot are indebted for equalizing the annual receipts from a fluctuating source. He, therefore, fulfils beneficial duties and deserves to be conserved as an almost indispensable part of the rural organization. At the same time we are bound to see that he does not over-ride the interests of the ryot. Let the Civil Courts enable the sowkar to recover his just claims from the ryots. But the Courts should not permit the sowkars to press the ryots to the point of crushing." The speculators in commercial produce perform equally useful functions. By watching the state of the market for different kinds of produce in different parts of the world, and entering into contracts to take the produce which is likely to be in demand, they enable the ryots to realize a larger value for their produce than they would have done if they had been left to their own devices. In the case of the *Kandu labha* system, instanced above, the risks undergone by the lender are probably not very great, and the greater portion of the high interest charged represents the remuneration due for the trouble of collecting small sums at short intervals from a number of persons and lending them out again.[113] The true interest is what is obtained for loans of fairly large amounts on adequate security for considerable periods of time. Transactions of a genuine usurious type appear, however, to be common in Malabar. Traders sometimes combine money-lending with trade operations whenever they have money lying idle on their hands, but in such cases the terms allowed are very short and repayment is punctually and sometimes harshly enforced. The Moplahs, it is stated, expect to make as much profit by money-lending as they would do if the amount were employed in trade. From inquiries I have made it appears that, taking one year with another, the profits of trade amount to about 25 per cent., of which about 15 per cent. goes to defray the charges including the trader's subsistence and 10 per cent. forms interest on the capital invested. An interesting account of the methods of dealing practised by the firms of Nattukottai Chetties settled at Karúr is printed as appendix VI.-C. (4).

Has agricultural indebtedness increased in recent years.

91. As regards the question whether agricultural indebtedness as measured in money value has increased in recent years, the answer must certainly be in the affirmative; first, because of the great rise which has taken place in the value of property of all descriptions and of the facilities available, owing to fixed laws and security of property, for raising money required for various purposes; and, secondly, because of the abundance of money and the growth of a money economy. If, on the other hand, the question be asked, whether the agricultural classes generally are more in the hands of sowkars or professional money-lenders than before, the answer must as decidedly be in the negative.

---

[113] Professor Marshall points out, "A pawnbroker's business involves next to no risk; but his loans are generally made at the rate of 25 per cent. per annum or more, the greater part of which is really earnings of management of a troublesome business. Or to take a more extreme case: there are men in London and Paris, and probably elsewhere, who make a living by lending to costermongers. The money is often lent at the beginning of the day for the purchase of fruit and returned at the end of the day at a profit of 10 per cent.; there is little risk in the trade; the money so lent is seldom lost. Now a farthing invested at 10 per cent. a day would amount to a billion of pounds at the end of a year. But no man can become rich by lending to costermongers, because no one can lend much in this way."

The evidence of Mr. Grant, Sir Thomas Munro, Messrs. Mellor, Bourdillon and Pelly, referred to in previous portions of this Memorandum, will show the extent to which the ryots in the Northern Circars and the Ceded Districts were dependent on the sowkars in former days for their means of subsistence. The extracts, printed as appendix VI.–C. (5 and 6), from Mr. Warden's report and Buchanan's *Journey in Mysore, Canara and Malabar* furnish particulars as regards the state of things in Malabar. There can be no doubt that agriculturists as a class have gradually been emancipating themselves from the thraldom in which they had been held by the money-lending classes formerly, and that the monopoly[114] and the tremendous power and influence exercised by the latter classes have been breaking down. In the Godávari and the Kistna districts the ryots, it is reported, "instead of being in the hands of sowkars, are becoming sowkars themselves," or in other words, the transactions are getting more and more to be between the agriculturists themselves, the richer ryots lending to the poorer. In Bellary, it is stated that, "whereas about 40 or 50 years ago there used to be only a few important ryots and sowkars scattered here and there in villages and taluks, each having at times a number of families depending on him as so many parasites, the present aspect is that wealth and importance are more generally distributed." The Acting Registrar of the South Arcot district, referring to the condition of things in that district as well as Chingleput, states: "I have experience of two or three districts, and I am able to state that the improvement is marked and is perceptible to all unprejudiced observers. Nearly one-half of the huts that existed 25 years ago have disappeared, and tiled houses have taken their places. Houses which were tiled then have changed their dimensions and appearance now. So in clothing and other comforts. Agriculturists have in their turn become money-lenders and have learnt to dispense with the aid of the professional money-lenders, to a very great extent. The improvement in material prosperity can be easily gauged by

[114] See para. 62 *ante*. Compare the following remarks of Sir Alfred Lyall: "There is much vague talk about the English rule in India being the paradise of money-lenders; but the great bankers of Upper India with one accord look back regretfully from these levelling times of railway and telegraph to the golden days of immense profits upon daring ventures, when swift runners brought early secret news of a decisive battle, or a great military leader offered any terms for a loan which would pay his mutinous troops. In those times a man whose bills were duly cashed in every camp and court of the Northern Provinces had often to remit specie at all hazards, and the best swords of Rajputana were at the service of the longest purse. A tremendous insurance policy was paid to some petty chief or captain of banditti, who undertook, by hook or by crook, to cut his way across the country and deposit the treasure at its appointed place, and who almost always discharged his contract with great daring and fidelity."

the fall in the rate of interest which [115] was then 12 per cent. at least (then called *dharma vaddi, i.e.*, equitable interest) and is now nearly 6 per cent. Time has come when ryots are able to take advantage of any help that may be rendered to them to organize a system of mutual credit. By getting a small loan for a bullock or two, by industry and economy, they become in time proprietors of a plough and a pair of cattle and are able to maintain themselves independently. As farmers they are able to repay their loans, which as servants they were not. By dint of exertion and thrift they are even able to purchase a small piece of land and attain the status of proprietors. Rich landholders, on the other hand, have been losing ground. The sons by partition get only a fraction of their patrimony, while their family and expenditure are in many cases equal to or greater than those of their parents. They involve themselves in debt and have ultimately to part with their lands. They become poor, and by hard necessity understand their position and try to lift themselves with those who were originally poor. The lands are passing from them to vakils and Government officials" (appendix VI.-C. (7)). The District Registrar of Tinnevelly remarks "the higher classes, who were sole landholders before, have become impoverished and have given up their land little by little, whereas the poor labouring classes have acquired land by dint of their economical savings. As agricultural profession is found to be more safe and secure by the lower classes, they lay out their earnings on landed property." The Honorable P. Chentsal Rao in discussing the question which forms the subject of this Memorandum observes, "You may ask, why is it that, in spite of all the improve-

---

115 The inscriptions in the famous temple at Tanjore show that loans made to individuals or village assemblies in the eleventh and twelfth centuries out of temple funds paid interest at the rate of 12½ per cent. per annum. Even now, the usual rate of interest cannot be said to be so low as 6 per cent. It must, however, be remembered that most of the transactions in former days having been carried on by barter, the demand for money must have been much less than at the present day. Leaving out of account usurious transactions, the ordinary transactions were between persons belonging to the same community, thoroughly known to each other, generally kinsmen or co-religionists. Money was lent not for the sake of profit, but with a view to relieve the necessity of the borrowers. The interest taken was small, and no security was demanded, the only witnesses to the transaction being the "sun and moon"; such transactions were necessarily few. When lending becomes general, and the dealings are between strangers, greater security is demanded and the rates of interest are determined with reference to mercantile considerations; and the rates thus established are applied also to loans to persons who as kinsmen or friends of the lenders would formerly have been granted easy terms. This change is due to the extension of the system of credit and not to any loss of "confidence" as between borrowers and lenders as is sometimes supposed. Another circumstance which has possibly tended to keep up the rate of interest is the diminishing purchasing power of money. If the principal sum be not expected to be worth as much when returned as when lent, the difference must be made good by the rise in the interest. It may be doubted whether the lender is consciously influenced by this consideration, but these matters have a tendency to adjust themselves automatically.

ments I have mentioned, there is such a cry as that we are becoming poor. I fancy that this is due to three causes. One is, it is a fact that we now fail to see those 'big men' in the country who once existed with enormous wealth and great influence over the people. My grandfather once told me that when he was a Tahsildar, the Collector having on one occasion called upon him to expedite the revenue collections and intimated to him that if he did not remit at least Rs. 50,000 within a week, he would be dismissed, a single ryot in his taluk paid all the money in advance and received it afterwards from the ryots in his taluk, almost all of whom were dependent on him. Such men of wealth and influence over the ryots do not now exist. This change has taken place, because the lower classes of ryots have slightly recovered from their extreme poverty and dependence upon the bigger men. I myself knew that in some villages of the taluks of which I was the Tahsildar, there were one or two big men who paid all the taxes of the ryots of those villages and took possession of all the produce raised by them, lending them again small quantities of produce for their subsistence. Now such men have diminished in number, because the ryots are able to pay their own taxes and keep to themselves the little they could save, instead of sending it to the pockets of the rich men. Thus, wealth is now more spread than it was, and this change is mistaken by some of us to be a sign of poverty. I do not mean to say that the disappearance of large capitalists is not a misfortune in itself, for I know that Rs. 1,000 in the hands of a single individual may often do more [116] good than Rs. 2,000 distributed among 1,000 persons; but all that I mean to say is that the aggregate wealth of the country has by no means diminished. Another cause of the feeling that we are getting poorer is that the intelligence of the people having improved, the educated men compare themselves with the more wealthy and civilized nations, whose habits and tastes they have imbibed, and feel their poverty more keenly than their ancestors did. The third and most important cause is, that although we are on the whole undoubtedly better off than we were fifty years ago, still the masses are extremely poor and most of them are

---

[116] It is for the reasons stated here by Mr. Chentsal Rao that his proposal to legislate in view to arresting the too rapid decay of the landed aristocracy of the country has commanded general approval. As a return for protection thus afforded, greater public services than hitherto rendered will be expected from the great landed proprietors, and, if need be, will have to be enforced. Another important means of counteracting the evils of diffusion of capital amongst innumerable persons, instead of its being concentrated in the hands of a few individuals in a form readily available for industrial enterprises, is the provision of facilities for the establishment of banks and joint stock companies all over the country.

half-starving—a condition which is enough to induce an ordinary observer to think that we could not have been worse before." The growth of a money economy and the new wants created by it have not only deprived the classes, which had hitherto benefited at the expense of the working classes, of much profit which they had formerly enjoyed, but also by placing temptations in their way to adopt a more expensive style of living than they had been accustomed to, have diminished a large portion of their accumulated wealth which has been distributed among the earning classes. The condition of the working classes has improved to some extent by means having been placed within their reach of engaging in occupations for which they may be qualified, while the creation of new wants and the easy means available of satisfying them have to some extent improved the standard of living. So far as land is concerned, the tendency has been to transfer it to actual cultivators or to persons who, in addition to capital, have sufficient education and intelligence to adopt improved methods of cultivation when they are found to be profitable. The changes which have taken place, so far as this presidency is concerned, have, therefore, on the whole, been beneficial, though possibly it may be that the diminution of dependence of the lower on the higher classes has to some extent had the natural result of diminishing the protection afforded by the latter to the former.

Some remedies suggested for mitigating the evils of agricultural indebtedness retrogressive and inapplicable to this presidency.

92. Various measures were suggested for remedying the evils of agricultural indebtedness, some of them of a drastic character, in connection with the inquiries instituted by the Famine Commission of 1878. The late Sir James Caird, a member of the commission, recommended a reversion to the old system of dividing the produce of land in defined proportions between the ryot and the Government, which he considered to be sound in principle, suited to the circumstances of small cultivators, and calculated to make them independent of the money-lenders, by taking from them a large quantity of produce by way of tax in years of abundance and a small quantity in years of scanty produce. The proposal was rejected by the Famine Commission as altogether impracticable. The "Fifth Report" of the Parliamentary Committee on Indian Affairs, 1812, shows that even under the old native governments, the principle of collecting the Government tax in kind by taking a share of the produce was adopted only in the case of lands irrigated by river channels and tanks. The lands cultivated with unirrigated

crops, of which there are a great many varieties, as well as those on which garden produce was raised, always paid money assessments. It is obvious that the application of a uniform rate in fixing the Government share of the gross produce must unduly benefit lands of the better qualities, while rendering the incidence of the tax very heavy on the poorer soils; and if the rates are to be graduated with reference to the qualities of the soil, situation of the lands and the nature of the crops raised, the number of rates must be so large as to entirely preclude the supervision necessary for securing the due share of Government. In the case of irrigated lands there was in former days a single rate for a whole village, and the ryots who held the lands jointly were left to adjust the differences in the produce of lands of different qualities in the same village by private arrangement. This was generally effected by giving to each ryot a share in the lands of every quality situated in every part of the village and by periodically redistributing the parcels so as to remedy any inequalities which may have arisen owing to changes in the conditions of the several parcels brought about by natural causes. The waste of labour involved in cultivating innumerable small plots of land situated in different parts of a village can be readily conceived. There can, moreover, be no incentive to make any improvements to land or to adopt superior methods of cultivation or raise valuable commercial crops under the sharing system, because all such improvements would be taxed by Government. The difficulties in securing the Government share of the produce and of disposing of it for a money price would also be enormous. To ensure even a fair amount of success in the application of the system, it would require minute and constant supervision on the part of the superior officers of Government and the cost of the establishments, if the officers employed were to be paid *bonâ fide* salaries and not be expected to make a living by colluding with the ryots to cheat the State and divide the gains with them, must be prohibitive. The graphic description given by Mr. A. Seshiah Sastriar (appendix VI.–B. (5)) of the evils of the system when it prevailed in the small State of Pudukóta and of the demoralization it caused has already been referred to. When the Government directly collects its share of the produce, it practically combines in itself the three-fold functions of a Government, a landlord and a sowkar or trader; an army of watchers, inspectors, estimators and measurers of produce will have to be let loose on the people, interfering with the ryots at every stage of production and the harvesting and storage of the produce.

The result must be oppression and peculation on the one hand, and fraud, evasion and concealment on the other. If the Government share is farmed out to renters, who must be armed with the necessary powers to collect the tax, such an arrangement must equally be disastrous to the ryot's rights which have been slowly built up by half a century of good government and fairly just administration of the laws; and the oppressions and exactions of the renters, must be far more difficult to be borne than the exactions of sowkars under the present system. In zemindaries where the sharing system prevails, the ryots are anxious for the introduction of a system of money assessments. There is, however, one fact to be remembered in the conversion of assessments in kind into assessments in money, viz., that under the former system the Government is practically both a landlord and a sowkar, and that it has in seasons of scanty produce not only to remit the assessment, but also to advance to the ryot the necessaries of life and the means of carrying on cultivation. When, however, money assessments are introduced and the Government divests itself of the functions of a landlord, the ryot being expected to shift for himself in all seasons except those of dire famine, the assessments must represent a tax pure and simple, and care should be taken to see that it does not include any portion of the landlord's and merchant's profits realized under the old system.

Another proposal of Sir James Caird was that the ryot should be deprived of the right of transferring his land by sale or of raising money on it by mortgaging it. The Famine Commission did not support this proposal either. So far as this presidency is concerned, it will have been seen that land is not being transferred from the agricultural to the non-agricultural classes to any injurious extent. Land is sought after as an investment to some extent by the labouring classes, and to throw any impediments in the way of transfer will arrest the beneficial process of land passing into the hands of those who can make the best use of it. Moreover, in all countries where peasant properties are the rule, France for instance, freedom of transfer of land has been found to have the effect of counteracting in some degree the minute subdivision of holdings which results from the law of equal division of patrimony among the children.

The Famine Commission suggested that restrictions should be placed on the power of a ryot to sub-let his lands. This proposal was negatived by the Madras Government, as no evil consequences, such as those apprehended by the Famine Commission, have been experienced in this presidency.

In the vast majority of cases the lands owned by the ryots are farmed by them, either by themselves working on the fields or by employing farm servants monthly or yearly or on the sharing system known in the southern districts as the *porakudi* system. In the last case it is often erroneously supposed that the land is leased out and that the porakudi is a tenant,[117] but the fact is that the land is farmed on the co-operative principle, the labourer being remunerated by a share of the crop instead of being paid daily wages, on condition of his furnishing the stock, the labour and the seed required, and the owner bearing the expenses of farm repairs, of the clearance of irrigation channels and of manures. The arrangement is highly advantageous to the labourer and is sought after by such of the labourers as have the means to purchase a pair of cattle and engage in cultivation. It is in fact the system of *metayage* prevalent in European countries in regard to which Professor Marshall remarks that it "makes a man who has next to no capital of his own to obtain the use of it at a lower charge than he could in any other way and to have more freedom and responsibility than he could as a hired labourer; and thus, the plan has many of the advantages of the three modern systems of co-operation, profit-sharing and payment of piece-work." The leasing out of land for fixed rent in kind or money marks the next higher stage in the status of a labourer. He attains to a

---

[117] There is much misconception as to the part taken by the Mirassidars of Tanjore and corresponding classes in the other districts in the farming of lands. The true state of the case was pointed out by Mr. John Wallace, the Collector of Tanjore, in 1805. He said: "Although the Mirassidars, in employing either class of porakudis, renounce all interference in the business of tillage, it is not to be considered that they neglect the management of their lands. On the contrary, they superintend and direct the labours of the porakudis in all the particulars of rural economy. Their engagements with porakudis are not for a fixed quantity of grain or a determinate sum of money. The porakudis have an active interest in cultivating the lands of the mirassidars in the most beneficial manner possible, as a fixed proportion of the produce is the only remuneration they have to look to for their labour. This proportion varies in different villages. It is not anywhere less than 22 per cent. of the gross produce nor more than 30." The remuneration of the labourer is, of course, determined by the standard of living of his class, which, as pointed out in a previous portion of this Memorandum, has to some extent risen and certainly not deteriorated. It must also be remembered that, 1st, where the land-tax is so high as to leave to the landholder nothing more than the barest means of subsistence, the State has to perform the functions of a landlord by supplying him with the means of cultivation and often of subsistence; 2ndly, where the tax is so moderate as to leave a sufficient margin to meet both the expenses of cultivation and of subsistence, the State is relieved of the functions of a landlord, but the ryot has to resort to the money-lender on account of the vicissitudes of the seasons to obtain the wherewithal to live and carry on cultivation in years of scanty produce, the advances made being repaid from the surplus of years of abundant produce; and, 3rdly, where the tax is still more moderate so as to leave a margin sufficient to meet not only the cost of cultivation and subsistence, but also to enable him to lay by savings which would help him to tide over bad seasons, resort to a money-lender can be dispensed with. At this stage, however, the landholder in many places no longer consents to be a mere peasant actually working in the fields, but he becomes a farmer, with skill, intelligence and capital sufficient to adopt improved methods of cultivation *provided it is found to pay.*

position somewhat analogous to that of an English farmer, and during the term of the lease is enabled to enjoy the full benefit of the extra labour bestowed by him on the land without having to share it with the land-owner. There is no object in compelling the owner by prohibition of sub-letting to cultivate the lands by means of hired labourers under his own superintendence or that of paid agents, and the measure is likely to have mischievous effects in the case of owners who, because they are minors or women or for other reasons, are unable to look after the lands themselves. It will also injuriously affect labourers who, though they may not have the means to purchase lands themselves, have sufficient means to take lands on lease, and by farming them properly make a profit and gradually raise themselves in the social scale as has happened in several districts. The value of land is so great that it hardly pays 5 per cent. as an investment, and it is clearly more advantageous to a farmer or labourer with small means to take as much land as he can farm on lease, pay 5 per cent. of the value of land to the owner as rent, and make a profit by cultivation, than to hire himself out as a day labourer or buy with his slender means a small parcel of land, the cultivation of which will not give him sufficient occupation.

Other remedies suggested for mitigating the evils of agricultural indebtedness are the placing of restrictions on the sale of immoveable property for simple debts and the grant of power to courts to disallow usurious contracts where the creditor is shown to have taken undue advantage of the simplicity and ignorance of the debtor. Sections 320-327 of the Civil Procedure Code contain provisions for transferring to the Collector for execution decrees directing that immoveable property shall be sold for debts in tracts of country where the Government deems it expedient that the usual judicial processes should not be allowed full operation; but in this presidency it has not been found necessary to take action under these provisions. In 1889-90, the area of permanently settled estates transferred by court decrees was 36,571 acres or 1 in 800; of ryotwar holdings 7,409 acres or 1 in 3,000; and of inam holdings 1,334 acres or 1 in 3,000. The enactment of a usury law, however suitable to a condition of society where almost all transactions are carried on by barter and money payment is the exception, is entirely inapplicable to present conditions in which the old *régime* of barter has been superseded by one of cash payments and an active internal and external trade has been developed by the extension of communications. As regards manifestly extortionate and inequitable contracts, the High Court of Allahabad has held that Courts of Justice in India as courts of equity and good conscience have, notwithstanding the repeal of usury laws, power to set aside contracts, where the extortionate character of the terms imposed on the debtor, taken in conjunction with his helplessness and ignorance, lead to the presumption that undue influence, amounting to fraud, has been exercised upon him. This seems all the remedy that the nature of the case requires in this presidency.[118]

The measures suggested all retrogressive.

93. All the plans mentioned above had special reference to the condition of the ryots in the Bombay-Deccan and were based on the supposition that certainty of tenure, fixity of the Government tax, and freedom to the ryot to raise on the land such crops as he finds most profitable and to deal with his possessions, in the way of transfer or mortgage, according to his necessities and requirements without being subjected to constant official interference, had worked to the disadvantage not merely of the idle and improvident who are found more or less in every community, but of the agricultural classes as a whole who are not fitted by education and hereditary training to receive the boons conferred on them, and that the remedy lies in reverting to the old systems of administration under which these classes were maintained in a state of serfdom.[119] I have no know-

---

[118] The Allahabad case referred to is Lalli *versus* Ram Prasad decided in 1886 (Indian Law Reports, IX, Allahabad, pp. 74–85). In that case an extortionate bond under which an original debt of Rs. 97 due by an agriculturist to a Mahajan had grown in ten years to Rs. 991, after Rs. 157 had been paid, was set aside. Mr. Justice Mahmood said: "I am aware that a general notion prevails in the mofussil that ever since the repeal of the usury laws, the Courts of Justice are bound to enforce contracts as to interest regardless of the circumstances of the case, the relative conditions of the parties, and irrespective of the unconscionableness of the bargain. Courts of Justice in India exercise the mixed jurisdiction of the Courts of Law and Equity, and in the exercise of that jurisdiction, whilst bound to respect the integrity of private contracts, they must not forget that cases which furnish adequate grounds for equitable interference must be so dealt with, not because such a course involves any the least contravention of the law, but because by reason of undue advantage having been taken of the weak and ignorant, the contract itself is tainted with *fraud* in the broad sense in which that term is understood in the Courts of Equity in England and America—a remark which seems to me fully justified by the rule of justice, equity and good conscience, which we are bound to administer in such cases." No case of a similar kind has come before the High Court of Madras, and, therefore, it is difficult to say whether the Allahabad decision will be followed in this presidency; but if it is, it will fully meet cases of a really usurious and extortionate type. The large powers given to the Courts to set aside contracts deliberately entered into would need to be exercised with great discrimination and discretion, but as there has been of late years very great improvement in the moral tone and legal knowledge of the Native Judges before whom the cases are likely to come in the first instance, there is considerable security for the powers being properly exercised.

[119] The ryots in the Bombay-Deccan must indeed be a remarkably idle, ignorant and unthrifty race, for otherwise it is difficult to account for the fact that in some of the writings of Native politicians on the Bombay side the "culture system" adopted by the Dutch in Java is recommended as a model for imitation by the British Government. A description of the system is printed as appendix VI.-C. (8), and it will be seen from it

ledge of the condition of the ryots in the Bombay Presidency, but as far as the Madras Presidency is concerned I have no doubt that there is no necessity for taking such a desponding view. That a very large class of ryots, especially in the Ceded districts which are subject to frequent droughts, are still in a very low economic condition, does not admit of doubt, but as already pointed out their condition is steadily, if slowly, improving. Lands which had little or no value before have acquired value, and the ryots having better security to offer for the repayment of advances made to them are able to obtain the advances on easier terms than before. The extension of communications, chiefly railways, has mitigated the violent fluctuations in prices which used to occur, and thus to some extent, has relieved the poorer ryots from the necessity of placing themselves entirely in the hands of sowkars and the richer ryots in regard to the disposal of their produce. What has to be done in this presidency for the amelioration of the condition of the ryots is, therefore, not to reverse the policy which has been pursued for the last fifty years, and which, so far as it has gone, has been fruitful of good results, but to adopt such administrative measures as will, without increasing the dependence of the ryots on Government, afford to them facilities for exerting themselves to better their condition and stimulate a spirit of self-help and enterprize among them.

Practicable measures.

94. I will now mention some of the measures which can with advantage be adopted by Government with a view to still further diminish the necessity for the dependence of the poorer ryots on money-lenders. One of these is the reform of the kistbundy by fixing the time for the payment of instalments of land revenue due to Government in such a manner that the ryots may not be put to the necessity of selling their produce prematurely. A great deal has already been done in this direction during the last five years, but there is still considerable room for further improvement. Under the old native system, as the land itself had in most places little or

---

that it is neither more nor less than a system under which the fertile island of Java famed for its spices is worked as a farm for the benefit of the Dutch Home treasury by means of compulsory servile labour. The Dutch do not make even a pretence of acknowledging their obligation to educate the Javanese and to raise them in the scale of civilization. They used to make an enormous profit from the colony which was obtained mostly by treating all the lands as the property of the State and the tenants as serfs liable to render compulsory service to the Dutch Government. Latterly the Government, under pressure of public opinion, has been obliged to adopt a more liberal policy towards the natives, with the result that the enormous gains formerly made have disappeared, and State industries, which paid under a system of compulsory labour, were found to be losing concerns when carried on under a sysem of free labour This shows clearly how the profits under the former system were derived.

no value, the crop raised was regarded as the security for the Government revenue, and the instalments of revenue payable were so timed that a considerable portion of it might be collected before the crop could be removed from the field or the threshing ground. As lands became more and more valuable, the necessity for regarding the standing crops as security for the revenue ceased, and the tendency has been to advance the kists so as not to compel the ryots to borrow money for the payment of Government revenue and to enable them to pay the revenue by the sale of their produce. The relief afforded to the ryots by the changes made has been considerable; but the scope of the reform had to be restricted in consequence of objections raised by the Government of India on the score of difficulties likely to be felt by the reduction of cash balances at particular periods of the year. It is possible to introduce the change gradually so as to obviate these objections which ought not to be allowed to stand permanently in the way of a much needed reform of this kind. Thus, for instance, in his "Preliminary Note" submitted by Mr. Nicholson to the Madras Agricultural Committee, 1889, he remarks as regards the former kistbundy of the Tinnevelly district, "A kistbundy demanded from December to May, three-quarters being payable by the 15th March, must be wrong when the crop is sown in October-November and picked only in March to May, and that in fact the kists were actually paid by the broker whose terms of advance were said to be Rs. 10 to Rs. 12 per podi of cotton deliverable on, say, 15th May, the real market price being then Rs. 16 or 16½, besides penalties for non-delivery on due date. This kistbundy has now been altered to one beginning in February, to the great relief of the ryot." The present kistbundy for the Tinnevelly district consists of four equal instalments beginning in February, and it is obvious that if the produce could be delivered only in the middle of May, three-fourths of the Government assessment is being demanded, even under the altered kistbundy, at a time when the ryot could not sell his crops to advantage. It is true the ryot does not take advances for the delivery of crops solely with a view to raise money to pay the Government assessment, but there can be no doubt, that if the kists were put forward, he would be able to make better terms with the merchant than he does at present. In the case of the southern taluks of Coimbatore where, as in Tinnevelly, cotton is an important article of produce, the kistbundy consists of four equal instalments beginning with January so that almost the entire revenue becomes due before the ryot could sell his produce. In many districts the ryot pays the Government assessment by the sale of commercial produce, reserving the grain produce for his own consumption. A kistbundy fixed with reference to the actual conditions of the several tracts of country in regard to the time at which ryots deliver their produce to middlemen is therefore still a *desideratum*. The crops grown and the times for harvesting and selling them vary so much in different tracts, that considerations of uniformity should not be allowed any great weight in fixing the kistbundy. A properly regulated kistbundy would undoubtedly be a great boon to the ryots, and I believe I am within the mark when I say that the relief afforded to the poorer ryots by such a kistbundy would be tantamount to a remission of 5 per cent. of the Government revenue, while, taking the presidency as a whole, the enhancement made by the Settlement Department in taxation does not amount to more than 5 per cent.

Another measure which can be adopted for the relief of the ryot in backward districts like Anantapur, where the climate is dry, soil barren, and crop failures frequent, is to fix the annual revenue on the area actually cultivated and not on the entire area of the holding. This will enable the ryots to leave a portion of their holdings fallow in the arid tracts where the chances of introducing improved methods of cultivation are considerably remote. In the Anantapur district, for instance, about 14 per cent. of the holdings is left waste annually owing to want of rains at the proper season. The assessment of the lower classes of soils might be fixed somewhat higher than it is at present, when this privilege is conceded. The ascertainment of the area left waste, especially when the district has been surveyed, is an easy process and need not entail on the superior officers of Government great labour, while the necessity for careful inspections for this purpose will keep the officers well posted up in the agricultural conditions of the tracts under their charge. Tahsildars have recently been relieved of their magisterial duties and additional Revenue Inspectors have been appointed to assist them; and the plan suggested is now much more practicable than it was before, without risk of oppression.

Agricultural banks.

95. The most effective way, however, in which Government can assist the rural population to extricate itself from indebtedness and enable it to obtain loans on reasonable terms for land improvements and other purposes is by providing facilities for

the establishment of agricultural banks. The question has already been taken up by the Madras Government which has appointed Mr. F. A. Nicholson, C.S., to investigate the subject and to report upon it. Mr. Nicholson is peculiarly qualified for the task both by his study of the working of agricultural credit institutions in European countries and by his intimate knowledge of agricultural practice and the conditions of rural life in this country, and his report is being awaited with interest. Believing, as I do, that Government has in its power, by the establishment of these banks, to accelerate the prosperity of the agricultural classes in a marked degree, I wish to make in this place a few general remarks on the subject, more especially with a view to show that the objections urged by the Secretary of State against certain proposals made in 1883 for starting agricultural banks in Bombay ought not to be allowed to prejudice the consideration of the question at the present time, and that it is possible to work these institutions successfully in this presidency under conditions which will render the objections inapplicable.

In connection with the Bombay proposals Lord Kimberley admitted that it was a serious misfortune that the landholders in India, even when comparatively prosperous and able to give good security, were usually unable to obtain the temporary accommodation they required except at a ruinous rate of interest, and that it would be of the greatest possible benefit to the agricultural community if the place of the present greedy and extortionate money-lenders were supplied by banks and other institutions possessing sufficient capital and honestly managed. The two chief objections urged by him to the scheme proposed in Bombay were: 1st, that it was doubtful whether any ingenuity could provide an effectual substitute for the operation of the ordinary laws of trading between the ryots and those, whether sowkars or banks, from whom they obtain advances; whether without the stimulus of risk of loss as a result of neglect and want of proper precaution on its part, any bank could carry on its business with success; and whether Government could do directly much more for the relief of agricultural debtors than enact laws enabling the courts to see that their poverty or ignorance was not taken undue advantage of, and that they were not oppressed or defrauded by their creditors; secondly, that the sowkars were not merely money-lenders, but also purchased the ryots' produce and thus supplied them with a market, and as the banks established under the auspices of Government could hardly be expected to undertake this function, it followed that the sowkars' assistance could not be wholly dispensed with, and the latter must, especially when the banks' claims were made to take precedence of their own, for self-protection necessarily impose harder conditions than before on their debtors.

As regards the first objection, it must be remembered that in all European countries where peasant properties prevail and where the agricultural classes are far ahead of the Indian ryots in point of education, enterprize and habits of thrift, it has been found necessary and practicable for the State to mitigate the evils of agricultural indebtedness by giving facilities for the establishment of land credit banks. It is true that the Government cannot usefully undertake and effectually perform the functions of a bank in the way of discounting the bills of traders in need of loans for short terms when they have no other security to offer than their own personal credit, but the case is entirely different as regards loans on the security of immoveable property, the value of which is capable of being ascertained with a considerable amount of precision by official estimators aided by information obtainable from the records of the Registration Department. Professor Sidgwick has pointed out that this is a work which can be performed efficiently by official agency. He states "Experience has shown that peasant cultivators are liable to become loaded with debt to money-lenders who, either through the absence of effective competition—partly in consequence of a certain discredit that attaches to their business—or perhaps sometimes through unavowed combination, are enabled to exact very onerous interest. This condition of debt tends to paralyse the productive energies as well as to cause distress; accordingly, under these circumstances, Governments may operate for the benefit of production, no less of distribution, by encouraging with special privileges the formation of commercial companies for the purpose of lending money on easier terms. Indeed, as was before said, the business of lending on the security of land seems to be of a kind which might be undertaken by Government itself, under certain conditions, without the kind of risk that is involved in ordinary banking business. So too, where the pawn-broker is the normal resort in an emergency of poor labourers, Government by undertaking the business of lending money at a moderate interest may give sensible relief without offering any material encouragement to unthrift. These encouragements would tend to strengthen on the whole, rather than weaken, habits of energetic industry, thrift and self-help in the individuals assisted." In this country the considerations above referred to are applicable with all the greater force for two reasons, viz., first, that the agricultural classes being less intelligent and self-reliant than the corresponding classes in European countries require to be taken in hand by Government to a greater extent than in the latter; and, secondly, that Government being a sort of co-proprietor with the ryot, the relations between the two are more intimate. The relations and responsibilities of Government may be briefly described as follows:—The country is, and must for a long time continue to be, agricultural. The returns from agriculture are precarious in considerable portions of the country owing to frequent droughts; and this very uncertainty weakens the inducements to thrift and provident foresight, and the ryot is consequently very poor. Former Governments took all that they could from the agricultural classes, leaving them but the barest means of subsistence. During partial droughts, they gave the ryots the wherewithal to carry on the cultivation on which their own revenue depended, but when a really great famine came on the land, owing to the failure of several seasons in succession, the people were left to die, and did so in large numbers. The British Government, on the other hand, has limited the demand for revenue, and left the ryot to shift for himself in ordinary seasons, but has undertaken the duty of saving life to the extent of its power and resources, when extraordinary calamities occur. Further, by the extension of communications and the creation of a foreign trade, it has imparted additional value to the ryot's produce and mitigated the violent fluctuations in the prices of food stuffs forming the chief articles of internal trade. The ryot has thus been freed from a state of bondage or serfdom, and is allowed to enjoy the full benefit of what he earns by his industry, enterprise or skill; and the result is that many ryots have accordingly benefited. The present system, however, bears hard on the incapable, the unfortunate and the unenterprising. No laws or institutions can, except in an indirect way by educational agencies, help those who will not help themselves, but whenever it is in the power of Government to do so, means ought to be provided for those who are merely unfortunate,—*i.e.*, those who for no causes which human foresight can prevent are reduced to distress—obtaining, on reasonable terms and not as an eleemosynary grant, the help which would enable them to tide over a brief season of distress or carry out improvements which the lands they cultivate stand in need of. This class is a numerous one in this country, as the population is mainly agricultural, the holdings of lands of small size and the seasons variable. Indeed, the duty and responsibilities in this respect are amply acknowledged by Government, and there can be no clearer proof of this than the fact that during the last season of drought the Government assisted the landed classes with loans to the extent of nearly 30 lakhs of rupees for the purpose of digging wells and effecting land improvements, in the spirit of true charity "which blesseth him that gives and him that takes." The establishment of agricultural banks will, as will be shown further on, enable aid of this kind to be rendered to the landed classes in even a more effectual and a more desirable form.

The second objection urged by Lord Kimberley had reference to the special circumstances of the tract of country in the Bombay-Deccan in which it was proposed to establish an agricultural bank, and to the special privileges and concessions asked for by the projectors to render the scheme workable. The ryots in the tract of country referred to were admittedly in such a state of hopeless insolvency that it was considered that the first thing to be done to enable them to deal with the bank was to rescue them from the clutches of the sowkars by paying off their dues, as it was apprehended that so long as it was in the power of the sowkars to harass their debtors, the latter could not be expected to take advantage of the facilities provided for obtaining loans on easy terms. A scheme of liquidation of this kind would, doubtless, be a gigantic undertaking, and it might well be questioned whether the properties of these insolvent ryots would be adequate security for the sums advanced on their behalf, and whether in the case of the poorest classes, the assistance of the sowkars could, under any circumstances, be dispensed with. The projectors had also asked that the claims of the bank should have precedence over all other claims, even though the latter might be prior in point of time to the former. Happily, the ryots in this presidency are not in the hands of sowkars to such an extent as to render it necessary to undertake the liquidation of the debts of the entire body of the peasantry in order to clear the field for the operations of banks. The ryots here do not find any difficulty in disposing of their produce. In the case of commercial produce, in regard to which the fluctuations in the demand in foreign markets have to be watched, middlemen and brokers are doubtless a necessity, but even in these cases, if the ryots can obtain money on easier terms than heretofore, they will be able to obtain better terms from brokers and merchants whose gains will be limited to a fair mercantile profit, instead of consisting, as they do at present, of these high profits, as well as of a high rate of interest on the money laid out by them in trade. The objection, however, that the grant of special privileges declaring that the claims of the banks protected by Government shall have preference over all other claims is likely to render the terms on which the sowkars would be willing to lend money to such of the poorer ryots as could not obtain loans from the banks harder than before, is quite valid. And, accordingly, when, in 1884, a proposal was made by an association designated the Land Mortgage and Commercial Association, Cuddalore, to establish a bank on the condition that privileges similar to those above referred to were to be granted, the Government very properly declined to comply with the request on the ground that the grant of such privileges to a particular bank was likely to render the terms obtainable from ordinary bankers and merchants harder than ever, by rendering the security offered of uncertain value. It would, however, be quite possible to establish agricultural banks which could be successfully worked, even though no special privileges of the kind were granted.

The nature and constitution of the proposed Agricultural Banks.

96. Agricultural banks, which are likely to be successful in this country, are land credit institutions like the Swiss Land Credit Banks, a description of which is given in the paper printed as appendix VI.–C. (9). The management and control of these banks should be vested in a directorate composed partly of Government officials and partly of non-official persons. The two essential conditions for success are, first, the provision of securities for the stability of the institutions and for good faith in their management and command of the requisite capital on easy terms; and, secondly, fairly accurate knowledge of the solvency and other circumstances of the applicants for loans and of the adequacy of the security offered to admit of applications being complied with the utmost promptitude. Official supervision and the use of Government credit are necessary to secure the first, and the association of non-official agency possessed of local knowledge with official agency in the transaction of business is necessary to secure the second of these conditions. The arrangements may, after the model of the constitution of the Swiss Land Credit Banks above referred to, be somewhat as follows: A bank might be established at a taluk station, Karúr for instance, where, as we have already seen, several firms of Nattukottai Chetties lend money at exorbitant rates of interest to ryots. The capital required might be subscribed in shares of, say, Rs. 50 each, the Government undertaking

to find half the capital required to work the concern. The Government obtains its loans at about 3½ per cent. interest, and it might well be content with an interest of 4 per cent. on the capital subscribed by it, especially when a guarantee fund is constituted to meet losses. It should guarantee the capital subscribed by private individuals, together with 4 per cent. interest. Loans should be granted to applicants on the security of immovable property. As it is not desirable to make loans obtainable on too easy conditions at the commencement, thereby tempting people to borrow money unnecessarily, the rate of interest charged for loans granted by the bank might be fixed at 9 per cent. and gradually reduced to 6 per cent. in course of time. The dividend payable to private shareholders might be limited to 6 per cent., any excess above it being credited to a guarantee fund. Any excess above 4 per cent. falling to the shares subscribed by Government might, likewise, be credited to the guarantee fund. In course of time it would be possible to find funds by issuing debentures in amounts as small as Rs. 50 and thereby reduce both the interest guaranteed to private shareholders and the interest charged to applicants for loans; but at the outset a reasonably high rate is necessary in both cases. The control and management of the bank should be vested in a council of 20 or 30 persons, of whom one-third might be nominated by Government and the remaining two-thirds elected by the shareholders, the Tahsildar of the taluk being *ex-officio* President. The council might meet half yearly to settle the scheme of business for the ensuing half year and fix the rates of interest to be charged, &c., and the transaction of business might be entrusted to a committee composed of about half a dozen persons, of whom one-half might be Government officials and the remainder non-official persons, with the Sub-Registrar at the taluk station as Secretary. The Sub-Registrar is peculiarly qualified for this duty, as he has command of the official registers of transactions affecting immovable property and the means for acquainting himself with the market value of lands offered as security for loans applied for. The loans might be made repayable by instalments or by a sinking fund so adjusted as to extinguish the debt in 10, 15 or 20 years, the longer period being allowed in the case of loans for substantial improvements to land, such as wells and other works of irrigation or drainage. There would be no enquiry as to the purposes for which the loan was required; but if the improvement has actually been made, the borrower should be allowed, on furnishing proof thereof, to convert a loan for a short period into one for a longer period.

Loans might be made up to two-thirds or three-fourths of the value of the property offered as security, and in the case of property in which several members of a family have interest, the consent of all the members of the family or those representing them should be required. This is the rule adopted by the several "funds" or "benefit societies" in Madras, and no difficulty has been experienced in working it. In the Mylapore Permanent Fund, for instance, which has been in existence for over 20 years, the losses incurred on account of defective title as regards property offered as security have been very small. It is in making these enquiries that the assistance of non-official members of the committee is likely to be of the greatest value. The funds of the bank should be lodged in the Government treasury; and the committee might be allowed to search the registration books without payment to ascertain whether and to what extent properties offered as security for loans are encumbered. I do not think that any special privileges should be conferred on the bank in regard to the recovery of debts, for such privileges might, as already remarked, be taken advantage of by dishonest borrowers to defeat the claims of persons having prior encumbrances on the properties mortgaged to the bank, and the additional risks thus introduced might have the effect of raising the rate of interest for loans not obtainable from the bank. The necessity for such special privileges arises from the fact that, owing to the imperfect record of transactions connected with landed properties maintained in registration offices, and the enormous labour and expense involved in obtaining the necessary information, the risks in granting loans on the security of immovable property are now considerable. I have in my official capacity made proposals [120] for combining the registers kept in Revenue offices for the purpose of showing the particulars of lands held by every individual assessed for the land revenue with the

---

[120] It would not be proper to enter into a discussion in detail, in this place, of the improvements to be carried out in the registration system for the purpose of facilitating the ascertainment of encumbrances on landed properties. The importance of this question has been fully recognized by the Secretary of State for India, who, in his despatch, dated 23rd October 1884, on the proposal to establish agricultural banks in the Bombay Presidency, has observed: "It is possible that the adoption of an "improved system of registration of titles to land might tend to give such further "security and greater facility to the business of agricultural banking as would render it "practicable for private capitalists to embark thereon with a fair prospect of success, "on terms which should not be so onerous to the cultivating classes as those to which "the latter are now compelled to submit when borrowing from the village sowkars. "It is, I am informed, in reliance on effectual registry of titles that the land banks of "Europe and the British colonies have been carried on, and although I am conscious of "the very different conditions under which an Indian agricultural community exists, "yet, I recommend this suggestion to the consideration of your Excellency's Government as possibly affording some opening in the desired direction."

registers maintained in registration offices in such a manner as to allow of the encumbrances existing on the lands being readily ascertained; and if this scheme be sanctioned, the operations of the banks will be immensely facilitated. The accounts of the bank should be audited every year, and for this purpose the services of District Registrars might be availed of. The success of the banks would, in a great measure, depend upon the promptitude with which applications for loans are disposed of, in order that persons in need of loans might obtain the loans at the time they are in need of funds; and it will be seen from the methods of dealing of the Nattukottai Chetties at Karúr that their success is due mainly to the quickness with which they transact their business. There is, however, no reason why, under proper supervision, the business of the bank should not be done with equal expedition. When the usefulness of the bank develops, it may be possible to have branches at each Sub-Registrar's station within the taluk. The managing committee should have power to grant further time for payment of instalments on due cause shown, and the general council should, likewise, have power to postpone the collection of instalments in very bad seasons by a general order, and also to arrange for sales of properties pledged for the loans in such a manner that they might not be thrown on the market at one and the same time. The above sketch is intended simply to show the manner in which an institution of this kind can be worked, and there can be no difficulty in modifying the details so as to suit the circumstances of particular localities in which the institutions are established.

Provision of funds for Agricultural Banks.

97. The most important question in connection with these land credit banks is, of course, the question of provision of funds. I have made some enquiries on the subject, and the results tend to show that abundant funds will be forthcoming if the solvency of the institutions be guaranteed by Government, and the management be such as to inspire confidence. It is quite certain, on the other hand, that, without a Government guarantee, the banks cannot be expected to be successful. Centuries of misgovernment have made the people in the rural tracts very suspicious and averse to letting their money go out of their sight, and though this feeling is wearing away, occasional failures of banking firms, through fraud or mismanagement, have helped to retard the growth of confidence in private banking institutions. Lawyers and Government officials—the latter of whom have been practically debarred from investing their savings in landed properties by

the rules promulgated by Government—will undoubtedly invest money in the banks if they can be sure of getting the principal back with 4 per cent. interest, with the further chance of the interest being increased to 6 per cent. The people in the rural tracts, who are solely guided by popular report and tradition, will, there is little reason to doubt, likewise commence to invest in these banks, and, if once their natural timidity is overcome, and they are made to see that the principal, at least, is quite safe, the investments are likely to increase very rapidly. There are indications in the development of what are called 'funds' or benefit societies, that the people in many parts of the country are feeling the necessity for the establishment of such associations. There are 123 such associations with a nominal capital of 2·204 crores of rupees and a paid up capital of 78·2 lakhs registered under the Joint Stock Companies' Act in this presidency. Besides these, there are large numbers of 'chit funds,' which are registered under the Registration Act without being registered under the Joint Stock Companies' Act, and a great many others which are not registered under either enactment. In the Sub-Registrar's office at Kásargód, in the district of South Canara, I found that the agreements of 16 such associations were registered in a single year, viz., 1891, the total number of members being 204. The arrangements made are generally of the following description. A number of persons, say 16, agree to contribute annually Rs. 100 each, on a fixed date, and the sum collected in the first year, Rs. 1,600, is made over to one of them, who is appointed manager of the concern and is required to give security for the due accounting of the moneys received by him and for ensuring payment of his contributions regularly during the remaining 15 years. As regards the money collected in the second year, lots are drawn as to which of the remaining 15 persons is to have it, and the process is repeated every succeeding year till every one of the members has obtained a full year's contribution. The members who get the use of the money during the early years of the period for which the agreement is to last are, of course, the most lucky, and the man who gets it last gets back barely the sum subscribed by him without any interest. Nevertheless, these arrangements are extensively resorted to, as it makes people subscribe from time to time small sums, which, if retained by themselves, might be frittered away, in the hope that they may receive a lump sum after an interval, even though the interval should be one of 16 years. Another method of managing this business is to put up the sum collected annually to Dutch auction, and hand over to the lowest bidder among the members the amount bid. Thus, one of the members in want of money might consent to receive Rs. 1,400 in lieu of the sum of Rs. 1,600 he is entitled to receive. The difference of Rs. 200 is divided among the other members, and the process is repeated year after year during the whole period of the agreement. The aggregate annual amount payable under the 16 agreements registered in Kásargód Sub-Registrar's office was Rs. 15,000, and the periods for which the agreements were to be in force varied from 9 to 20 years. Members who fail to pay a particular instalment are charged interest at 24 per cent., which is debited to the contributions already made by them. Similar 'chit' or 'kuri' agreements are very common in Malabar, Tinnevelly and Madura districts. The arrangement is a cumbrous one and difficult to work owing to failures and casualties. Nevertheless, the fact that people enter into such arrangements shows how sorely they stand in need of banking facilities.

As regards funds to be provided by Government, I do not think that a very large sum will be necessary at the outset, as the scheme will have to be experimentally introduced in a few places, and it seems to me that Government will really incur no risk whatever in connection with the scheme. The Government might safely place at the disposal of the banks a portion of the Savings Bank deposits, which will thus earn interest for Government, instead of lying idle as at present. The balance on 1st April 1892 to the credit of depositors in Post Office Savings Banks throughout India was upwards of 7 crores of rupees, the amount appertaining to the Madras Presidency alone being above 63 lakhs of rupees. The balance on hand of these deposits is likely to grow rapidly from year to year. In fact, the limits of yearly deposits in the Post Office Banks, which were originally fixed at Rs. 500, were reduced to Rs. 200 in 1889, because the amount deposited was so large that it was considered that Government was likely to suffer loss by keeping so much money idle in their hands, while paying interest to the depositors.

The utility of Land Credit Banks.

98. Of the great utility of land credit banks in furnishing, on reasonably easy terms, the capital required for agricultural improvement, it is not necessary to write at any length. It is obvious that if peasant proprietors have to borrow money at 12 or 18 per cent. interest, the only improvements that can be carried out without loss are those which will cost

little and yet afford abundant returns; and cases of this kind must, of course, be very few. For instance, take the case of irrigation by wells. A well, costing say Rs. 300, will irrigate about 4 acres, and to work the well by means of bullock-power would require probably about Rs. 100 more, including cost of wages of labour and depreciation of live and dead stock. It makes to the ryot an enormous difference, whether the sum of Rs. 400 can be borrowed at 6 per cent. interest or at 12 or 18 per cent. In the first case, the annual charge for interest amounts to Rs. 6 an acre, and in the second and third cases to Rs. 12 and Rs. 18, respectively. If the produce of the 4 acres of unirrigated land be taken at 40 bushels of grain at the rate of 10 bushels an acre and valued at Rs. 40 at the rate of Re. 1 a bushel, it would not pay the ryot to irrigate the lands, unless the produce is tripled, in other words unless the produce per acre increases to 30 bushels, if the interest on the outlay is 12 per cent. If, however, the interest is only 6 per cent., the cultivation might pay if the produce is doubled, or, in other words, is at the rate of 20 bushels an acre. Of course, if money has to be borrowed at the rate of 18 per cent., cultivation by wells may be stated to be well nigh impossible. Irrigation in this country increases the produce enormously; and in the case of application of expensive manures, there is comparatively much less scope for increase of produce. In the latter case, the increase of produce per acre should be such as to pay not only the interest on the outlay on manures, but also such portion of the cost of the manures as will allow of its being recouped during the period in which the manures are exhausted. Further, when the risks in well-construction, owing to uncertainty of finding water at a reasonable depth, and the liability of the country to suffer from droughts, are borne in mind, it can be readily conceived how much the hard terms on which capital required has to be obtained must retard agricultural improvements in this country. The Government, no doubt, has been anxious to lend money for land improvements at low rates of interest, and owing to the prevalence of drought during the last two years, the Government rules, in this respect, have been largely availed of by the ryot population. In ordinary seasons, however, the ryot has to fall back upon the assistance of the sowkar when he needs funds for purposes other than land improvement, and what is required is, that the rate of interest for money needed by him for all purposes should be reduced. The present arrangement, under which all prior claims are postponed to the claim of Government to recover the loan granted by it for agricultural improvement by the sale of the land to be improved, has the effect of impairing his credit with the sowkar in emergencies which, under the conditions of rural life in this country, are very common, and it is not, therefore, surprising that the ryot should hesitate to avail himself of Government help except in seasons when he is unable to obtain assistance from the sowkar. Another reason for the ryots not readily availing themselves of Government help is the stringency of the rules made with a view to ensure that loans are granted on adequate security and the instalments are punctually collected as they fall due. These inconveniences will be greatly minimized when a bank, which is managed by a directorate composed partly of official and partly of non-official agency, with full power to grant extension of time for the payment of instalments on due cause shown, lends money for all purposes, and not merely for land improvements.

Land credit banks will not, of course, directly benefit either the landless classes or cultivators who have not security of tenure in the lands they cultivate, as for instance, tenants in Malabar, and in some of the northern zemindaries. Indirectly, however, the establishment of these banks will benefit them by reducing the rates of interest, inasmuch as persons who are able to offer proper security for loans to be obtained on easy terms from these banks will be enabled to compete for the custom of lending to poor agriculturists to a greater extent than hitherto. For the landless artisan classes and day labourers, it might be considered whether institutions, like *montes de piete* established in European continental countries, for carrying on pawn-broking on a small scale could be established under the guarantee and superintendence of municipal corporations in large towns. There are, however, great difficulties in the way of working such institutions, and in this country the goods pawned will consist mostly of jewels and trinkets of inferior materials difficult to value. The interest also except for loans for very short periods is not so exorbitantly high as to make the interference of Government necessary to check it. In England itself, the legal rate of interest for loans not exceeding £2 obtained from pawn-brokers is 25 per cent. per annum.

Savings Banks.

99. Schemes for promoting habits of thrift depend for their success on the facilities afforded to people to take advantage of trivial occasions to save small sums of money, which, if they retained in their own hands, they would be under a great temptation to spend unprofitably. The post office savings banks' scheme introduced a few years ago by the Government of India is a step in the right direction, and it has evidently a great

future before it. In 1890–91, there were open 6,455 post office savings banks in the whole of India, and 981 such banks in the Madras Presidency, with a balance to the credit of depositors of 6·35 crores and 61 lakhs of rupees, respectively. Of these sums, the amounts to the credit of native depositors were 5·57 crores and 49 lakhs of rupees respectively. The deposits would have been much larger but for the reduction made in 1889 in the maximum limits of sums that can be deposited by a single person. Considering the importance of giving all possible encouragement to persons wishing to deposit money in savings banks, I venture to think that the reduction was a mistake. The average amount deposited by each depositor during the year 1891–92 was in this Presidency only Rs. 30, and the average balance at the end of the year only Rs. 90, and this shows that the banks are being made use of only by the poorer classes and do not compete with the larger banking institutions to an appreciable extent. The reason given for the reduction was that facilities had been afforded to persons residing in the interior for investing money in Government securities through post office savings banks and also to deposit them for safe custody, and it was accordingly unnecessary and undesirable to maintain high limits for deposits. The classes that deposit money in post office savings banks are, however, too poor to buy Government securities. The facilities afforded by the post office savings banks have so far been availed of mainly by Government servants, servants of local bodies and Railway companies, pleaders and other professional classes of the community. The commercial classes and domestic servants have also made deposits, but the agricultural classes have scarcely as yet taken advantage of the banks. In England, considerable impetus appears to have been recently given to the formation of penny savings banks by the issue of a circular from the educational department, calling the attention of schoolmasters and school managers to the importance of inculcating thrift upon children under their care, and pointing out the desirability of establishing a bank in every school. It might be desirable to issue a similar circular in this Presidency though in this as in other schemes newly introduced no very great results can be expected at the outset. The formation of benefit societies should be encouraged as much as possible ; there is a great demand for such societies in this Presidency, and some years ago, some persons taking advantage of this started 'bubble' companies which soon collapsed. An amendment of the law insisting on the registration of such societies, giving power to Registrars to refuse sanction for the establishment of such as are proposed to be worked obviously on an unsound basis and providing for a careful official audit of their accounts, would have a most beneficial effect. There should also be Registrars appointed for various places in the mofussil, in order that persons may not be compelled to proceed to Madras for the registration of such societies. Whenever there was a necessity for extraordinary expenditure on account of marriages or deaths in a family, it was formerly the custom for kinsmen and clansmen to subscribe towards the expenses, each according to his means, the understanding being that persons who had received this benefit were, in their turn, expected to assist when similar occurrences took place among the other members of the community. This custom still lingers in the rural parts, but owing to the dispersion of the members of communities consequent on facilities for free locomotion, the custom is rapidly disappearing, and the necessity for making provision for contingencies of the kind by means of benefit societies and such like institutions is being increasingly felt. The country has not yet arrived at a stage at which it would be possible to work general schemes of insurance successfully, but the scheme introduced by the Government of India in the case of post office servants is a step in the right direction, and it is desirable that it should be extended to other departments of the Government service. Though confined to the official classes, the educative effect of such measures on the general population will be considerable.[121]

Further remarks on the advantages of banking facilities.

100. In former days, as we have seen, the farming out of taxes, the want of checks on the rapacity of officials, and the monopoly privileges possessed by bankers and special classes of traders, though detrimental to general welfare, were favorable to the concentration of a large amount of

---

[121] The violent fluctuations in condition due to the uncertainty of seasons and other causes is a great hindrance to the formation of habits of provident foresight, and the only remedy is to minimize the injurious effects of such irregularities by schemes of insurance whereby "aggregate regularity" is availed of to counteract the effects of "individual irregularity", or "accidents." From a report on "Rice cultivation in Italy" published as a "bulletin" by the Madras Agricultural department, it appears that there are societies in Italy, which insure cultivators against losses by hail. The report states, "Hail is one of the inflictions most feared by rice cultivators. If it falls after the ear is formed and is long continued, it may destroy the whole crop over a large area. Insurance against hail is universal. The following figures show the amount of this business done by the Mutual Assurance Society in Milan in the six years 1881–1886. Value insured, 81·74 million francs; premiums received, 5·51 million francs; damages paid, 4·01 million francs. The premiums paid vary from 6 to 9 per cent. on the gross value of the crops, or about 14 to 21 francs per acre. The three principal societies, which have nearly all the business of the country in their hands, insure annually against hail to the value of about 50 millions of francs." It might be worth while to enquire how the damages are assessed and fraudulent claims prevented. It may not be possible to introduce similar institutions *at present*, but I allude to the matter to show in what direction improvements in the future may proceed.

wealth among a small number of persons. I have already alluded to the tendency of the present *régime* to diffuse wealth among the masses of the population, and this tendency, while improving the condition of the lower classes to a certain extent, dissipates the wealth, which might be otherwise available for being devoted to productive purposes. The corrective of this tendency is, of course, the provision of banking facilities whereby the wealth diffused can be collected again in one mass in a form readily available to those who are in need of capital for carrying on industrial undertakings. As Mr. Bagehot has pointed out "a million in the hands of a single banker is a great power; he can at once lend where he will, and borrowers can come to him, because they know or believe that he has it. But the same sum scattered in tens and fifties through a whole nation is no power at all; no one knows where to find it, or whom to ask for it." There are various classes of the community in possession of capital who, for want of ability, opportunities, or inclination, do not employ it directly in industrial enterprises; these are, first, persons who, by age, sex, or infirmity, are disabled from active occupations; secondly, zemindars and rajahs, who, from a sense of dignity or love of leisure, do not care to engage in undertakings requiring constant attention to business; and thirdly, persons engaged in Government service or in professional occupations whose work is of too engrossing a character to permit of their being constantly on the look-out for opportunities for the employment of their savings. Even of those who venture on business undertakings, success is confined to those who have special aptitudes, and this deters many men from incurring the risks. Banking facilities would furnish persons with special aptitudes for industrial enterprises with the capital needed by them, while giving those who have capital without special aptitudes for business, opportunities for earning an income by lending it. Owing to want of banking facilities in this country, with the exception of trading classes with hereditary aptitudes and connections, the modes of investment hitherto known and practised have been—first, investment in lands; second, investment in jewels and houses; third, hoarding; and fourth, investment in Government securities. With the growth of security of tenure and the gradual diminution of undefined exactions, land has come to be regarded as a "safe investment," and the competition for it has raised its value to such an extent, that in the more populous districts of the Presidency, investments in land do not yield a larger return than investments in Government securities, except to the cultivating classes. Latterly, how-over, in view of the small returns and the risks[122] and trouble in the management, landed property has been somewhat losing its attractions as a field for investment; and if banking institutions under the guarantee of the State are established, many persons, who invest money in land, would take shares in banks, thus still further lightening the pressure on land to the manifest advantage of the cultivating classes who will be enabled to obtain lands for cultivation on easier terms than heretofore. There can be no doubt that, in this country, an immense quantity of money is either hoarded or converted into ornaments. The net imports of gold into India between 1565 to 1835 or during a period of 270 years was 112 millions sterling, while the net imports in the 56 years from 1835 to 1891 was 140 millions. The net imports of silver from 1850 to 1891 was 302 millions Rx. $317\frac{1}{4}$ millions Rx. of silver were coined in the Indian mints from 1835, being nearly 15 rupees per head of the population; but of this quantity, Mr. Harrison (in his article in the *Economic Journal* for June 1892) estimates that only 166 millions Rx. or 5·8 rupees per head is now in circulation, the remainder being either hoarded or converted into ornaments. The practice of hoarding is gradually going out except in rural tracts, but that of investing money in jewels is probably on the increase. Sir David Barbour collected information in regard to the quantity of gold and silver hoarded, more especially in Upper India, for the use of the Royal Commission on the value of precious metals. He estimated the quantity of gold and silver hoarded since 1835 at something like 300

[122] The same tendency has been noted as being observable among the small proprietors in France whose one passion was the acquisition of land. Guyot, in his *Principles of Social Economy*, observes: "The *bourgeois* proprietor is beginning to see that, if the land which serves him as an investment has its advantages, it has also grave disadvantages for a man who looks for a return without troubling himself about it. The pride he once took in treading his own soil is beginning to disappear. The rail roads are making him a traveller and breaking up his attachment to a particular spot. He finds personal property far more convenient than land, which involves draining and planting and legal proceedings; or houses which he must look after and keep in repair, and with the tenants of which he cannot always keep on good terms. So he goes to the stock-broker, instead of the notary, and takes in a Railway Company or mine, or buys into the *rentes fonciere*, a company based on the observation of this very psychological fact to which I have been drawing attention." Mr. Jenkins, in his *Report on the Agriculture of France*, writes of peasant proprietors: "It must, nevertheless, be admitted that the French peasant has, for some years past, been learning to look for an investment of his capital elsewhere than in land. The national loan, after the termination of the Franco-German war, was to him the alphabet of the language of investment in anything but land. The hoards of thousands of farmers were dug up from the ground, hoisted from the well, cut out of the mattress, pulled down the chimney, and in fact, brought to light from all sorts of secret places to enable M. Thiers to get rid of the hated Prussians. A considerable proportion of the peasants, I am assured, looked upon the subscription to the national loan as a patriotic act for which their only reward would be the disappearance of the invader. In course of time, they found that this 'subscription' brought them an annual interest, that the principal sum had a fluctuating value, and that they had the right to sell their own investment and buy their neighbours.' They thus learnt to speculate and now the French peasants are among the most eager speculators in the world in a small way."

millions Rx. It was found on enquiry that the people living in Simla and the hills had absorbed in 25 years 6·6 crores of rupees worth of silver. The Maharajah of Burdwan had a large hoard, out of which £230,000 were brought out, and the Gwalior regency invested 3 millions sterling in Government securities, out of the hoard which was left by the late Maharajah. A native prince was found to be hoarding at the rate of £40,000 or £50,000 a year. Sir David Barbour was of opinion that the introduction of banking facilities would not affect the habits of the people very much in this respect; the European banks took deposits from any body, but the hoarding, as a rule, was by men who hoarded so little individually that no bank would accept their deposits; nor would they themselves be willing to deposit money in a bank. It is obvious, however, that if small banks were established under Government guarantee, like the Swiss land credit banks, small deposits would be received and the reluctance of the people to make deposits would be gradually overcome. The practice of hoarding makes an immense amount of wealth practically useless for industrial purposes, and if even a third part of the wealth thus remaining unutilized were invested in industrial undertakings, it would bring about a great revolution in commerce. Of the entire amount of debt of the Government of India, viz., 218 millions Rx, only 25 millions are held by the natives of the country. 100 millions Rx. invested in the rupee debt would pay it off almost entirely, and save the country from an annual remittance of 4 millions Rx. on account of interest. The great utility of small banks as contradistinguished from large central banks in this respect has thus been explained by Mr. Bagehot: "A single monopolist issuer of notes, like the bank of France, advertises banking slowly. On the other hand, the Swiss banks, where there is always one or more in every canton, diffuse banking rapidly. The reason is that a central bank which is governed in the capital and descends to a country district has much fewer modes of lending money safely than a bank, of which the partners belong to that district and know the men and things in it. . . . . . . But the mass of loans in a rural district are of small amount; the bills to be discounted are trifling; the persons borrowing are of small means and only local repute; the value of any property they wish to pledge depends upon local changes and circumstances. A lender who lives in the district, who has always lived there, whose whole mind is a history of the district and its changes, is easily able to lend money safely there. But a manager deputed by a single central establishment does so with difficulty. The worst people will come to him and ask for loans.

His ignorance is a mark for all the shrewd and crafty people thereabouts. He will have endless difficulties in establishing the circulation of the distant bank, because he has not the knowledge, which alone can teach him how to issue that circulation with safety." It is from this point of view that it is important that the banks established in the rural tracts should have in its directorate non-official members with local experience. The existence of such banks will also, to some extent, diminish the practice of investing money in jewels. So long as money is kept idle, pressure is put upon the head of the household by the female members of the family to lay out the money in the purchase of jewels; when it is lodged in a bank and earns interest, the pressure and the temptation to yield to it would be considerably less. There are, of course, reasons founded on social necessities, which contribute to the maintenance of the practice of purchasing jewels for women over and above those arising from a desire for their personal adornment. These are, first, that, as jewels are under the personal control of the female members of the family to a greater extent than any other form of property would be, and less subject to the interference of their husbands, sons, or other relations, provision intended for them takes this form; and secondly, as the Hindu law does not give a share in the father's property to the daughters, social usages founded on natural sentiment supplement the deficiencies of the law in this manner.

Another great advantage likely to result from the provision of banking facilities is the extension of the use of credit instruments, and the saving affected by the economizing of the use of coin. There has been a considerable extension of the circulation of bank notes during the last two years, the value of circulation amounting to 24 crores of rupees against a value of 6 crores of rupees in 1864. The circulation of bank notes not covered by coin or bullion has been increased to 7 crores of rupees. This represents a saving in interest at 4 per cent. of nearly 28 lakhs of rupees. The precious metals needed for currency purposes have to be purchased for value like any other commodity, and if coin could be economized [123] by extension of other forms of credit, the necessity for enlarging the metallic currency with the growing needs of trade and commerce would be partly at least counteracted, and this would be a very great benefit.

---

[123] It has been calculated that the average value of daily transactions in the London clearing house is 20,000 millions sterling. Mr. Jevons estimated that if all this business were transacted by the actual payment of coin, the weight to be carried would be 157 tons of gold requiring 80 horses to carry the metal. If in silver, the weight would be more than 2,500 tons. The actual metallic coinage of England (in 1878) was 100 millions of gold, 15 millions worth of bullion in the bank of England, 15 millions silver and 1⅛ of bronze—total 131⅛ millions sterling.

IV.—Absence of Diversity of Occupations and Necessity for encouraging General and Technical Education.

The facts connected with pressure of the population recapitulated.

101. The next group of questions has reference to the necessity for providing sufficient safeguards to prevent the increase of population pressing on the land to such an extent as to cause a deterioration in the standard of living of the masses. The principal dangers of the present economic position in this respect have been described to be (1) the absence of diversity of occupations and the crowding of the population on a single resource, viz., agriculture; (2) the necessity, as population increases, for bringing under cultivation the poorer soils which are peculiarly liable to the effects of droughts and yield a very precarious subsistence to the cultivators; (3) the large exports of agricultural produce to foreign countries tending to impoverish the soil and diminish its yield; and (4) the lack of a spirit of enterprise, of technical knowledge, and of means among the agricultural classes to repair the waste caused by the export of agricultural produce, by the adoption of improved methods of cultivation, or by opening out new paths of industry with the aid of wealth obtained in return for the produce exported.

I have in the last section examined the actual position as regards the pressure of population on the means of subsistence. The conclusions arrived at may be here briefly recapitulated. During the last forty years there has been great increase of production owing to (1) the extension of the area of cultivation of food-crops; (2) the extension of the area irrigated by large works constructed by Government, and by small works, such as wells, constructed by the cultivators at their own expense; (3) the extension of the area grown with valuable commercial crops; and (4) improvement in the methods of cultivation in places where there is a fairly constant remunerative market for the produce grown. Of this increase of production a very large portion has been absorbed in the increase of population which has taken place, and the remainder in improving the standard of living of all classes. The improvement that has taken place among the higher and middle classes is evidenced by the higher and more costly style of living which has undoubtedly come into vogue among these classes. It is, however, the case of the landless labouring classes that is always one for anxiety whenever there is a large increase in population; and, as regards these classes, it has been shown that their condition has not in any way deteriorated, but on the contrary has to some extent improved.

All legal impediments in the way of these classes bettering their condition have been removed; employment is procurable in all normal seasons; and an appreciable number of persons belonging to these classes have been able to save money, purchase landed property and rise in the social scale, thus setting a stimulating example to the bulk of their brethren who, owing to want of means, ability or opportunities, still continue in the old state of degradation. The complaint that one often hears in most places is that labourers are difficult to get for the old customary rates of wages, and that it is necessary either to pay them higher rates of grain wages or larger allowances in the shape of perquisites to make them work willingly or with zeal. This shows that a struggle is going on to adjust the old customary rates of wages to the new conditions under which there is increasing mobility of labour.[124] The signs of improvement in the condition of these classes must, of course, be comparatively less marked, but it is none the less certain. We have also seen to what extent the complaint that the expansion of foreign trade has destroyed the indigenous industries other than agriculture is well-founded. The spinning and weaving industries have, undoubtedly, suffered severely, the former having dwindled to very small proportions indeed. The weaving industry has not, however, suffered to the extent generally believed for two reasons; viz., first, the working population in the rural tracts in the inland districts, where the cold in the winter months is severer than elsewhere, still use the durable and warm clothing woven out of country thread; and secondly, while, on the one hand, imported machine-made cloths have, to a great extent, superseded country cloth used by the higher and middle classes for male attire, there has been considerable extension of demand for female colored cloths of the finer varieties woven in the country owing to reduc-

---

[124] As regards the manner in which economic customs are modified, Mr. Marshall remarks: "To say that any arrangement is due to custom is little more than to say that we do not know its cause. I believe that very many economic customs could be traced, if we only had knowledge enough, to the slow equilibration of measurable motives: that even in such a country as India, no custom retains its hold long after the relative positions of the motives of demand and supply have so changed, that the values, which would bring them into stable equilibrium, are far removed from those which the custom sanctions. Where economic conditions change but little in one generation, the relative values of different things may keep very near what modern economists would call their normal position, and yet appear scarcely to move at all: just as, if one looks only for a short time at the hour-hand of a watch, it seems not to move. But if the preponderance of economic motive is strong in one direction, the custom, even while retaining its form, will change its substance and really give way." As regards the influence of custom on prices of articles of general consumption, Mr. Marshall says, "After examining in detail the prices of chief purchases made by the peasants in some parts of India, I have come to the conclusion that custom has less to do with them than is the case with the agricultural laborer in the south of England."

tion in their price on account of the cheapness of imported thread. As a set-off against the decadence of spinning industry, we have the outturn of the spinning mills, which is daily increasing, and which bids fair to enable the country to recover the ground lost under the stress of Manchester competition. So far, however, as the spinning and weaving classes are concerned, the extension of the mills will, of course, accelerate their decline. The iron smelting industry has nearly ceased, but this is due to the scarcity of fuel. The cheapness of imported iron and other metals, and the gradual introduction of metal vessels among classes of the population which were formerly using earthen vessels have given extended employment to the workers in metals. The artisan classes—masons, carpenters, &c.,—are well off and find employment at remunerative wages both on Government and Railway works, and in the construction of substantial buildings, which are springing up in all parts of the country. The native shipping industry has declined, but this simply means that the old expensive modes of carriage by native craft have been superseded by cheaper carriage by ocean steamers, the producers of the export articles profiting by the difference in the cost. It is the reduction in the cost of freight that has enabled the mill-manufactured yarns and cloths of Bombay to enter into competition with Manchester for the markets of China and Japan. New fields of employment have been opened in connection with coffee, tea, cinchona and indigo industries, cotton mills and presses. The railways, roads and canals which have come into existence afford increased employment to the surplus population during the non-cultivation season to a greater extent than was the case in the past. The expansion of the tanning industry has specially benefited the lowest classes of the population in particular places, the wages given for tanning being higher than for other kinds of work, as owing to religious prejudices the ordinary labourers do not compete for employment on tanning works. I have not alluded to the decay of the Indian art industries and of the classes engaged in them. The proportion of the population affected is numerically small, and though on other grounds the decay of Indian art may be a matter for regret, it can only be assigned a subordinate place in an enquiry referring to the economic condition of the general population.

The increase of population, then, has not, so far, pressed on the means of subsistence to such an extent as to cause a deterioration in the standard of living of the population as a whole, and this is conclusively shown by the fact that the prices of food-grains during recent normal years have not been higher than the average prices of years prior to the famine of 1876–78, notwithstanding that in the intervening period there has been a great fall in the value of silver. In this connection it must be remembered that the tendency of increase of population accompanied by a more than corresponding increase of wealth is generally not to augment the share of wealth of the different classes in a uniform ratio, but to improve the condition of such sections of the society as are able to profit by the opportunities afforded by the new *régime* in a marked degree, while benefiting in a less degree other sections of the community, and in some cases even rendering the condition of the very lowest landless classes of the population harder than before. The following illustration, in which the figures assumed are entirely hypothetical, will show what is meant. If the average income per head of the population were, twenty years ago, Rs. 30 per annum, and if wealth has since increased by 30 per cent. while the population has increased by 15 per cent., the income per head of the population at present would be a little less than Rs. 34 per annum. The income of all classes, however, would not have increased in the ratio of 34 to 30, but that of the higher and more intelligent classes would have increased in a greater ratio, while that of the less intelligent and helpless classes in a smaller ratio or even diminished. The peculiarly satisfactory feature of the present position is that the condition of the lowest classes has not in any way deteriorated, but, on the contrary, in so far as these classes have been able to take advantage of the opportunities for employment opened out to them, has improved for three reasons, viz., the prices of food-grains, which rose enormously between the years 1860 and 1870 owing to special causes, declined afterwards, while the money wages which had risen at the same time remained steady or even increased; the prices of imported articles, chiefly clothing and metals, declined; and the abolition of slavery and serfdom, and the discouragement by Government in administrative arrangements of all social rules and usages tending to depress the condition of the lower classes have ensured to these classes greater opportunities for employment and greater security in the enjoyment of their earnings.[125]

---

[125] I have dwelt at greater length on the question of the pressure of population during the last twenty years in a reply published by me in the *Madras Mail* to certain criticisms which appeared in an article in the *Calcutta Review* of January 1893. I have given in appendix VI.-D. (1) extracts from my reply omitting all matter of a controversial nature not possessing any but very temporary interest.

102. We have further seen that production cannot go on continually increasing as fast as the population, unless there is a continual improvement in the intelligence, spirit of enterprise and habits of thrift of all classes, and that to secure this end, it is of the utmost importance that education should be diffused as widely as possible. It will therefore be interesting to glance briefly at what has been done and what remains to do in this direction.

Progress of general education.

I have printed as appendix VI.–D. (2) a brief account of the progress of education during the last 20 years kindly furnished me by Mr. S. Seshaiyar, Professor in the Kumbakónam College. Considering the short period during which educational measures have been at work, the advance made has been astonishingly rapid. During the last 20 years the number of collegiate institutions for higher education have increased from 12 to 35, and the attendance of scholars from 385 to 3,200. The number of candidates who appeared for the Bachelor of Arts degree examination in 1891 was 548 against 65 in 1871. The total number of persons who had passed the examination since the Madras University was established up to 1871 was only 197, but the number up to 1891 increased to 2,679. The number of persons who had passed the First Examination in Arts was 852 up to 1871, and 7,866 up to 1891.

In secondary education also there has been similar advance. The number of candidates who appeared for the Matriculation examination has increased from 1,358 in 1871 to 7,002 in 1891. It has been calculated that 75 per cent. of the pupils who pass the Matriculation examination read for the First Examination in Arts and that 90 per cent. of the pupils who pass the latter read for the B.A. examination. The number of pupils receiving secondary instruction in schools was 32,000 in 1891.

Primary education has advanced still more rapidly. In 1871, there were 1,606 primary schools for boys registered in the official returns with an attendance of 43,000 pupils. In 1891 the number of primary schools registered was 21,000 with an attendance of 560,000. The figures for the latter year include pupils in indigenous *pial* schools which have been improved and brought under the inspection and superintendence of the Educational Department subsequent to 1871; but making allowance for this circumstance, the progress made will still be seen to be very remarkable. The number of candidates who appeared for the Primary school examination in 1891 was 16,000, of whom 12,000 were declared to have passed. The recent orders issued by Government making it obligatory on candidates for village offices to pass this examination have given a great impetus to the extension of primary education which will progress even more rapidly than it has done hitherto. Night-schools have been established in several places for the education of the labouring classes. There were 802 such schools in 1892 with an attendance of 14,771 pupils. Special measures are now being taken for the instruction of Pariahs and other degraded classes of the population.

Schools for the education of girls aided by Government may be said to have almost come into existence since 1871. In 1891 there were 1,021 schools with an attendance of 48,090 pupils. Including the girls attending boys' schools the total number of girls under instruction was 87,715. Female candidates appeared for the Matriculation examination of the Madras University for the first time in 1877. Since then 314 candidates have been examined up to 1892, of whom 171 were declared to have passed, 34 in the first class. Of the number passed, however, 26 were Native Christians, 57 East Indians and 84 Europeans and 3 Parsees.

Great as has been the advance made since 1871 as compared with the past, there is almost unlimited scope for further progress, when it is remembered that education, in however elementary a form, has touched the merest fringe of the population, and that there is a dense mass beneath which has yet to be brought under its influence. This has been clearly shown by Dr. Duncan in his very interesting report on public instruction for the year 1891-92. He points out that out of every 1,000 boys between the ages of 5 and 9 years who ought to be under instruction, 230 or between one-fourth and one-fifth are receiving instruction, the remaining three-fourths being allowed to grow up absolutely illiterate. Again out of every 1,000 boys between the ages of 10 and 14 years who might be expected to be in the 'lower secondary stage' as regards instruction, only 12 receive such instruction. And out of 1,000 boys between the ages of 15 and 19 who might, if circumstances permitted, be expected to be in the 'upper-secondary' stage, only six reach that standard. Lastly, only 26 out of every 10,000 young men between the ages of 20 and 24 enjoy the benefits of collegiate education. Dr. Duncan's remarks in regard to higher education are specially worth quoting, as considerable misapprehension prevails on the question of collegiate instruction having overpassed its due limits. He observes: "These figures show how little reason there is for the not uncommon opinion that collegiate education is advancing too rapidly and extending itself too widely. The growing cost of living, especially in large towns, the comparatively poor prospects of a successful career after graduating, owing to the very keen competition that exists for employment in almost all the branches of the public or the private service—these and other similiar considerations will tend to deter all except young men favorably circumstanced as regards means or possessed of exceptionally good natural ability, from entering on a collegiate course of instruction." The results of the higher education too, so far as they have gone, have been, on the whole, most beneficial. There has been a distinct improvement in both the public and private morality of all those who have come under its influence. Many unreasonable prejudices which stand in the way of the progress of the country are being silently transformed into practices more in consonance with the spirit of the present times and less injurious to the welfare of the community, and the way is being gradually prepared for still greater social changes. Brahmin young men, who would never have dreamed of working in a dissecting room in a medical laboratory or of crossing the sea to serve in Burma, have little scruple now in taking up work of either kind. These results are entirely due to the forces which have been set in motion by the British Government, among which the system of education introduced by it is undoubtedly the most potent; and as the Government is precluded by differences of race and religion from actively interfering to help on or regulate these changes, it is all the more incumbent on it to afford indirect encouragement by concentrating all its efforts for the advance of education. In all poor countries the persons who first come under the influence of education are not the scions of the aristocracy, but scholars [126] sprung from the poorer classes, who from religious motives devote themselves to the pursuit of knowledge; and this was the case in England itself 500 years ago, when the English universities swarmed with thousands of poor scholars who

---

[126] In Scotland even in the present day a considerable portion of the scholars educated in the universities belong to the labouring class. Sir Lyon Playfair in his essays on subjects of Social Welfare remarks: "It is believed that 500 working men or sons of working men are in attendance in these Scottish Universities. Many that I have personally known have worked hard during the summer as ploughmen, fishermen, masons, carpenters—in one or two cases which I happen to know as gillies to young English University Students during grouse shooting—in order that they might have enough to pay their moderate fees and live on porridge and milk during the winter sessions of the universities."

were fed at alms-houses or who literally begged their bread from door to door. The education of these poor scholars was provided out of the income of religious endowments founded both by sovereigns and private individuals. The dissociation of education from religion in this country under the British Government has rendered this resource unavailable, and unless the State supports higher education in a liberal manner the progress of the country will be seriously arrested. The outlay on higher education will prove in the long run to be a most profitable investment even from a commercial point of view. As observed by Mr. Marshall: "The wisdom of expending public and private funds on education is not to be measured by its direct fruits alone. It will be profitable as a mere investment to give the masses of the people much greater opportunities than they can generally avail themselves of. For by this, many who would have died unknown get the start that is required to bring out their latent abilities. And the economical value of one great industrial genius is sufficient to cover the expenses of the education of a whole town. One new idea, such as Bessemer's chief invention, adds as much to England's productive power as the labour of a hundred thousand men. Less direct, but not less in importance is the aid given to production by such medical discoveries as those of Jenner or Pasteur which increase our health and working power, and again by scientific work, such as that of mathematics or biology, even though many generations may pass away before it bears visible fruit in greater material well-being. All that is spent during many years in opening the means of higher education to the masses would be well paid for, if it called out one more Newton or Darwin, Shakespeare or Beethoven." It may be that the chances of the appearance of such great benefactors of the human race who widen the bounds of knowledge are too remote to justify a large outlay on higher education in a poor country, but the urgent necessity that exists for effecting reforms in practices which retard the material well-being of the nation, and the extreme improbability of the occurrence in this country of any religious upheaval which, under favourable conditions, often has the effect of imbuing whole peoples with a new spirit and by a sudden impulse of lifting them high in the scale of civilization, render the rapid advance of secular education almost the only available resource for social regeneration and progress; and no amount of money expended by the State would be ill-spent in perfecting this instrument. This being so, there need be no fear that higher education is being pushed on too rapidly, for, as observed by Dr. Duncan, the growing cost of living and the difficulty of obtaining entrance into the liberal professions will, of themselves, fix the saturation point beyond which a literary education will not be absorbed in the existing circumstances of the country. These considerations apply with even greater force in the case of female education, which is still in its infancy, for whereas 20 per cent. of boys between the ages of 5 and 9 years are under instruction, only 4 per cent. of girls of the same ages are taught even the three R's. The enormous disproportion in the advance in education of Indian men and women is recognised on all hands to be one of the most serious dfficulties in the way of social progress.

While higher and secondary education are required for the higher and the middle classes who must lead industrial movements and promote social progress, the salvation of the lower classes lies in the diffusion of elementary education. Owing to the bulk of the land in the country being held in small farms by a poor peasantry, the adoption of improved methods of cultivation with a view to raise food for a growing population will be possible only if there is a general quickening of intelligence among them sufficient to overcome the spirit of routine and the tenacious hold which traditional practices have over a proverbially conservative class. Moreover, the only effectual check to overpopulation is the improvement of the standard of comfort by the multiplication of innocuous secondary wants and diffusion of a feeling of self-respect among the masses which prevents this standard of comfort being lowered—a result which can be brought about by education alone. Elementary instruction must, therefore, be pushed on as fast as funds and teachers can be provided. It would doubtless be a mistake to adopt any scheme of compulsory State education, as is sometimes advocated, because the margin of the earnings of a poor family in this country over and above what is required for mere subsistence is so small that it cannot afford to dispense with the wages of labour earned by the juvenile members of the family. In fact, no compulsory measures undertaken by the State for the benefit of a large population can be successful unless a very large majority of the population acquiesce in and feel the necessity for such measures, and the aid of the State is invoked for the purpose of enforcing the performance by recusant individuals of duties recognised by public opinion. But there cannot be the slightest doubt that the extension of elementary education should be recognized as being of prime necessity in the existing situation, and as an essential pre-requisite for carrying out improvements of every kind, and that its continued rapid advance should be provided for.

Another most pleasing feature in connection with the progress of education is the extent to which the taste for field sports and manly exercises is spreading among the school-going population and the youth of the country. The advance made in this direction during the last ten years has been remarkable and is calculated to dispel the fears which were once entertained in regard to the danger of the mental strain caused by the new exotic education resulting in stunted growth and deteriorated physique.

Agricultural education.

103. Agricultural education is, of course, of the greatest importance in this country, where 90 per cent. of the population is either engaged in agriculture or in subsidiary operations connected with this industry, and this question has much occupied the attention of the Madras Government since 1871, when the Saidápet Agricultural Farm and School were established. There cannot be the slightest doubt as to the duties and responsibilities of Government in the direction of improving agricultural methods both on account of the intimate association of it with land, the revenue derived from which forms the mainstay of Indian finance, and because the bulk of the land is held in small farms by peasant proprietors who are too poor and dispirited to depart from established routine and adopt new processes without aid and encouragement from Government. The results from the point of view of improved processes and scientific agriculture have not perhaps been commensurate with the efforts made, though there is not much reason for disappointment when the economic conditions applicable to the case are taken into account. In all countries improvements in agriculture are made slowly and by insensible degrees, and as Mr. Thorold Rogers has pointed out, even in England it took a hundred years to naturalize turnip culture, and nearly as long to diffuse the principle of artificial selection in cattle. The conditions under which agriculture has to be practised in this country differ so totally from those of England that it can hardly be expected that the development of this industry will follow the same lines in the two countries. The two most important respects in which the conditions differ are—first, that whereas in England one of the main problems of agriculture is getting rid of excessive moisture, in this country the difficulty lies in obtaining and retaining moisture for the growth of crops, the former being, of course, much more capable of regulation and much less dependent upon fortuitous circumstances not

modifiable by human action than the latter; and, secondly, that the breeding and fattening of cattle in England for meat make it remunerative to retain the greater portion of cultivable lands for purposes of pasture, thereby contracting the area available for being put under corn crops, providing cattle manure for these crops, and enabling the farmer to diversify corn crops with restorative crops which are useful as food for cattle—conditions favorable to intensive farming which, owing to the poverty of the cultivators and religious prohibition as regards the consumption of cattle meat, are absent in this country.[127] Hitherto the increased production required to meet increase of population has been met by extension of cultivation of lands of all except the poorest descriptions, by the extension of large irrigation works constructed by Government and of small works, such as wells, constructed by the ryots themselves, and by the stimulus given to production in backward and hitherto inaccessible tracts by the extension of communication and the cheapening of the cost of carriage. As these resources are becoming, to a great extent, exhausted, the two dangers now apprehended are first, the necessity to bring under cultivation the poorer classes of soil peculiarly liable to the effects of droughts, and secondly, the impoverishment of the soil, owing to the growing exports of agricultural produce—chiefly oil-seeds. The first danger is, to some extent, guarded against by imposing pretty high assessments on lands of the lowest classes and by enclosing poor soils for fuel and fodder reserves and thus preventing their being taken up for cultivation. These measures have, however, to be adopted very cautiously to prevent hardship to the agricultural classes by unduly enhancing the assessment of holdings containing poor lands and by depriving them of grazing grounds for cattle. As regards deterioration of the soil, the opinions of scientific experts who have examined

---

[127] I have in my reply to the article in the *Calcutta Review*, extracts from which are printed as appendix VI.-D. (1), alluded briefly to the circumstances which favored the consolidation and enclosure of farms and the adoption of *intensive* farming in England. Sometimes violent measures are suggested with a view to bring about consolidation of farms and improved cultivation, but all such measures are calculated to strike at the root of security of property which is the first condition of agricultural improvement, unless the Government itself undertakes the functions of a landlord—functions which it can never properly discharge. With reference to a similar proposal, Mr. Thorold Rogers puts the evils of State landlordism in a clear light: "The cultivator of the soil would have exchanged a landlord, who is, after all, a human being, with sympathy and consideration, at least at times, with some desire to live at peace and good-will among his neighbours, for a Government office the servants of which, by a very natural impulse, would manipulate the whole estate by a set of hard inelastic rules. They would, by the very nature of their duties, be unaffected by all sympathetic influences. Their first object would be to earn the interest on the purchase-money, and to insist on its punctual payment, come what would. The business of the office would be enormous and prodigiously costly."

the subject, as already stated, go to show that there is no proof as yet of any deterioration having taken place, but that there is reason to apprehend such deterioration in the future should the exports of agricultural produce—chiefly seeds—increase at the rate they have, and manurial substances, such as bones, should continue to be exported in increasing quantities. The exports of agricultural produce, however, bear now but a small proportion to the total agricultural production of the country, and bones have been ascertained not to be exported to any appreciable extent from this presidency. Nevertheless, the dangers referred to should be provided against, and this can be done only by the diffusion of knowledge of improved agricultural principles and practices among the ryots and by the establishment of agricultural banks already referred to, which will enable the ryots to adopt agricultural improvements when the conditions of the market admit of their adoption with advantage. The efforts of agricultural officers for bringing about agricultural improvement were not successful at the outset, because there was a disposition among them to condemn native methods of cultivation wholesale without stopping to inquire whether the conditions of the case admitted of European methods being adopted. The failure of the Saidápet Farm itself to yield profitable results has since produced a re-action, and the tendency has perhaps been to go to the other extreme and hold that the ryot has nothing to learn in this direction. The fact is that in this as in other things the ryot is neither so stupid as not to be alive to his interests when the desirability of adopting an improvement is demonstrated to him in the only way in which he can understand, viz., by showing that it will pay under the conditions under which he has to work; nor is he so enterprising and watchful as to dispense with skilled assistance and guidance. For the purpose of furnishing him with this assistance and guidance, agricultural experiments have to be tried under as diverse conditions as possible in a great many parts of the country when the requisite agency for conducting the experiments can be provided. The Government Agricultural College should be able to provide the necessary subordinate agency which should be made to work under local committees, and the co-ordination and tabulation of results obtained should be conducted under the advice and superintendence of a skilled scientific expert trained in England. To attain this object, the Agricultural Committee appointed by Lord Connemara's government suggested the establishment of agricultural schools and farms in half a dozen stations to start with, but though three years have since elapsed, no action has as yet been taken on the committee's suggestions, because the Government of India has taken up the question and has not been able to arrive at any final decision regarding it. The matter, however, seems to be entirely one for the local Government to deal with, and it is undesirable that further delay should be permitted in taking action in the matter. It would not, of course, do to look for any immediate visible results from the establishment of these schools, but they would undoubtedly be the means of diffusing knowledge which will render cultivation, according to existing methods, more careful, thereby increasing the produce by almost insensible increments and prepare the way for the introduction of new methods when the time is ripe for it.

Technical education.

104. Some attention has been paid by Government of late years to the promotion of technical education in arts and industries though in this, as in the case of agricultural education, the results attained have as yet been small. Leaving out of account colleges and schools for law, medicine and engineering, the principal institutions aided by Government giving instruction in arts and industries are the School of Arts at Madras with an attendance of 426 pupils, Chengalvaraya Naicker's Commercial School at Madras with 123 pupils, and 18 other industrial schools with an attendance of 997 pupils not including special classes attached to a few schools aided by Government. There are 91 teachers in these institutions, of whom 11 are men educated in Europe, America or Australia. In 1891, 80 pupils passed the technical examinations in industries. The articles manufactured in these institutions during 1891 have been valued at Rs. 40,826 and the profits realized at Rs. 10,184. The Victoria Technical Institute has been organized for the promotion of technical education, and its secretary, Mr. John Adam, has, after inspecting a considerable number of technical institutions in England, recently written a memorandum containing suggestions for the development of education in arts and industries. His main proposals are (1) that systematic attempts should be made by Government to collect information about industries; (2) that an Upper Secondary technical school should be established at Madras; (3) that evening and morning classes for the instruction of artizans should be instituted; (4) that peripatetic lecturers should be employed to lecture and exhibit products, processes and tools of manufactures; and (5) that Inspectors should be appointed to inspect and advise mofussil institutions. Mr. Havell, the Superintendent of the School of Arts, in an article

contributed by him to the *Industrial Review*, has pointed out that the only effectual means of fostering technical education is to take the industries which exist and endeavour to improve them or lead them into new developments. This is a work which requires patient and prolonged investigation, and for carrying it out the requisite staff should be provided by Government, as the funds of the Victoria Technical Institute are altogether insufficient for such an undertaking. It is of course futile to expect that by establishing technical institutions new industries, which will absorb a considerable amount of labour now devoted to agriculture, can be brought at once into existence, thereby lessening the pressure on agriculture and providing employment unaffected by the vicissitudes of agricultural seasons. The artizans and handicraftsmen have to depend upon the local market for the sale of their wares, and if a succession of bad seasons brings distress on the agriculturists who are their customers, they themselves suffer along with the latter.[128] The best mode in which special industries can be encouraged is to introduce cottage industries which can be carried on by agricultural peasants or their womenfolk during the non-cultivation season in places where there are special facilities for carrying on such industries and to make the articles produced as widely known as possible so as to create a demand for them. All this requires time and expenditure of money which would, however, in the long run, be repaid manifold. As regards the introduction of improved tools, Mr. Havell remarks that the native workman is not too slow in adopting superior tools or simple and effective mechanical contrivances when they are placed before him. In large towns carpenters and brasssmiths are found using English or American lathes worked by a treadle, and imported tools for turning the thread of screws, drawing wire, &c., are commonly used by goldsmiths and brassmiths. Mr. Havell observes that even in the remotest villages carpenters use English saws, planes, chisels, &c., and he suggests the employment of a few commercial travellers to demonstrate the advantages of using such tools to the artizans in the mofussil. It is desirable that some decisive action should be taken by Government in the directions pointed out by the gentlemen above named, or that the Victoria Technical Institute should be sufficiently subsidized

---

[128] The primitive handicraftsman, observes Mr. Marshall, "was far from enjoying unbroken prosperity; war and scarcity were constantly pressing on him and his neighbours hindering his work and stopping their demand for his wares. But he was inclined to take good and evil fortune, like sunshine and rain, as things beyond his control: his fingers worked on, but his brain was seldom weary."

so as to enable it to undertake this duty. The Government has from time to time employed specialists to conduct investigations in particular directions for developing the resources of the country, *e.g.*, in connection with the investigation of mineral resources, sericulture, curing of tobacco, &c., but the investigations made have been on too small a scale to lead to any practical results. The two chief difficulties in the way of such enquiries are to ensure that adequate return is obtained for the money expended and that the officers employed show good work during the time they are under employment. These difficulties are very real, but as no particular time can be fixed for showing adequate results, the expenditure must be incurred in the belief that it will sooner or later be amply repaid. The mineral resources of the presidency, more especially as regards iron and coal, are stated by experts to be of sufficient importance to justify the institution of a special department of mines and minerals for the systematic investigation of these resources. The Salem District, for instance, has long been known to contain some of the richest iron ores in the world. The tanning industry has grown in importance in this Presidency, and investigations as to whether methods of tanning superior to those now in use might be profitably introduced and could be suggested to the manufacturers might be undertaken. It is believed that the introduction of improved methods of fish-curing which is a very important industry on the West Coast might lead to further development of this industry which is in the hands of the poorest classes who are without the knowledge and the means to improve the processes now employed. The establishment of fish-curing yards under the supervision of Government and the supply of salt at cost price furnish Government officers with the necessary opportunities and powers of control for this purpose. Experiments in cattle-breeding can be tried by the Forest Department in connection with the fuel and fodder reserves maintained by it. In these various ways there is considerable scope for Government paving the way by precept and example for the development of industries. All these experiments will doubtless cost money, but the State must, from an educative point of view, be prepared to expend and even waste money, within certain limits, in these directions, without looking for an immediate return for the money thus expended, the local Government being allowed to do what it thinks best subject to the conditions laid down as to the limits of expenditure. For instance, the revenue derived by the State from land including local cesses exceeds 5 crores of rupees, and the expenditure of 1 per cent. of this revenue, viz., 5 lakhs of rupees for the purpose of agricultural improvement cannot be considered extravagant, and the whole of this amount will not be required at the outset. Again, during the last fifteen years, the revenue from excise on country spirits and drugs has risen by nearly 60 lakhs of rupees, and this revenue is drawn from the poorest classes of the population. The object in maintaining the excise duty is not so much a fiscal as a moral one. In these circumstances it is right and proper that a fixed percentage of this revenue should be devoted to the mental, moral and physical improvement of the classes who contribute it and be expended in the promotion of elementary and technical education and the improvement of sanitation. So far as education is concerned, the expenditure from Provincial funds has increased within the last five years from 12 to 18 lakhs of rupees and this is so far satisfactory. But in view of the rapid increase of population and the necessity for improving the intelligence of the people and the standard of comfort amongst them, the further advance of education should be recognised as pressing and provided for in the manner above pointed out.

Encouragement of industries by the imposition of protective duties.

105. A question that is frequently discussed in connection with the encouragement of diversity of occupations is the fostering of manufacturing industries by the imposition of protective duties. This measure has often been recommended more especially in connection with the depression of the handloom industry which has seriously suffered by the competition to which for several years it has been exposed from the machine-made goods of Manchester. I do not wish to enter into any elaborate discussion regarding this question, but will briefly state whether, and to what extent, the arguments usually advanced in favour of a policy of protection are applicable to the circumstances of this country. It is acknowledged on all hands that from the point of view of individual consumers, protective duties, if they are to serve their intended object, must enhance the cost of the protected product to such consumers, but it is contended that it may be to the interest of a nation to incur this sacrifice temporarily with a view to enable a struggling industry to establish itself on a firm basis, and that when this has been accomplished, the artificial support afforded can and should be withdrawn. The sacrifices incurred during the period referred to would, in fact, be tantamount to an outlay on an industrial undertaking made by the nation, for which an adequate return would be received in due time. Among other arguments for protection, the most cogent,

which alone need be considered here, is the desirability—nay necessity—for maintaining in the interests of the well-being of the nation, a due balance between agricultural and manufacturing industries. This necessity applies to both agricultural and manufacturing countries—agricultural countries, because, agriculture being mainly dependent upon the seasons is in its nature precarious and dooms the countries to a low economic position, and because exports of agricultural produce to foreign countries tend to impoverish the soils in which they are grown; and manufacturing countries, because, it is dangerous for any country to rely entirely on foreign sources for food-supplies which might fail in times of war. From a mere theoretical point of view, the validity of the first argument must be admitted, but the case is entirely an hypothetical one, which cannot be realized in practice. No government will be able to determine in any particular case in which protection is demanded whether the conditions laid down have been satisfied, and if it is a case in which the eventual success of the industry is beyond all reasonable doubt, it will either be undertaken by private individuals without the aid of protection, or, if there is not sufficient private enterprize for the purpose, the government itself should pioneer the industry and lead the way. The only way to determine whether the industry will succeed is actually to carry it on without the aid of protection. Moreover, when once protective duties are imposed, it would be extremely difficult to take them off, or know when to take them off, because, the withdrawal must cause suffering to the protected classes by destroying that portion of the industry brought into existence which could not be carried on without protection, and by diminishing the profits derivable from the remainder. The harm done by inducements held out to capital and labour to flow into other than their natural channels would also be considerable, though not easily calculable. In this country, if a protective policy were adopted, it is the influential classes that would benefit by it, and the industries carried on by the less influential classes, who have not the means to make their voices heard, would suffer. Taking the depressed hand-loom industry already referred to, it would be wrong to induce people to cling to a doomed industry or occupation and to bring up their children in it, though in view of the sufferings undergone by them it might be legitimate and proper for government to give them special aid and enable them to betake themselves to more profitable occupations. Moreover, the imposition of protective duties, by calling into existence an increased number of factories and mills within the country, will instead of protecting the handloom weavers precipitate their decline and increase their sufferings. Ordinarily when human labour is displaced by machinery, there ensues considerable impoverishment and suffering to the labourers employed in the industry, but as machinery comes into use by slow degrees, there is generally time for the labourers to adapt themselves to the new conditions until the impetus given to increased production by the introduction of labour-saving appliances eventually gives employment to the displaced labour. While, on the one hand, it would be wrong in the general interests of the community to prevent the introduction of machinery and other agents tending to increase the efficiency of production, it would, on the other hand, be cruel to accelerate the decline of the labouring classes and tax them indirectly at the same time by means of protective duties.

Turning to the argument, based on the necessity for maintaining a due balance between agricultural and manufacturing industries, it is doubtless true that purely agricultural countries are generally found to be in a low economic position, but the only way in which such countries can be economically raised is by giving an opening for and increasing foreign trade; and protective duties by diminishing that trade would hinder and not help their progress, the professed object of protective duties being to diminish imports and consequently exports also, as all imports must in the long run be paid for by exports. It was pointed out by Mr. Mill forty-five years ago in his work on Political Economy, that the expansion of foreign trade was the only means by which a backward country like India could be economically elevated. He observed that it was the deficiency of town population which limited the productiveness of the industry of this country in which agriculture was conducted entirely on a system of small holdings. There was a considerable amount of combination of labour, but on a limited scale, and village institutions and customs which were the real frame-work of society made provision for joint action in cases in which it was seen to be necessary; or when they failed to do so, the government, when tolerably well administered, stepped in, and by an outlay from the revenue executed by combined labour the tanks, embankments and works of irrigation which were indispensable. The implements and processes of agriculture were so rude that the produce of the soil, in spite of great natural fertility, was miserably small. Mr. Mill was, at the same time, of opinion that the land might be made to yield food in abundance for many more than the present number of inhabitants without departing from the system of small holdings; but to this the stimulus was wanting which a large town population connected with the rural districts by easy and inexpensive means of communication would afford. That town population did not grow up, because the few wants and unaspiring spirit of the cultivators, joined, until lately, with great insecurity of property from military and fiscal rapacity, prevented them from attempting to become consumers of town produce. In these circumstances, Mr. Mill considered that the best chance of an early development of the productive resources of India consisted in the rapid growth of the export of its agricultural produce, cotton, indigo, sugar, coffee, &c., to the markets of Europe. The producers of these articles would be consumers of food supplied by their fellow-agriculturists in this country; and the market thus opened for surplus-food would, accompanied by good government, raise up by degrees extended wants and desires towards European commodities or towards things which would require for their production in this country a larger manufacturing population.

Since Mr. Mill wrote, it is exactly by means of the expansion of foreign trade that the country has made the progress it has made; that communications have been and are being developed; that internal trade has been fostered, and a re-arrangement of industries with reference to the natural advantages and productive resources of the several localities is being effected; that factory industries are being brought into existence; that the standard of living of the various classes has improved; and that these classes have been enabled to benefit to some extent by the example, skill, and enterprise of European nations and the cheap capital furnished by them. If it be said that factory industries have as yet been introduced on a limited scale, the answer is that the influences of foreign trade have hardly had thirty years' time to work, and that it would be distinctly mischievous to adopt any measures which would retard the rate of its expansion and prevent the only chance the country has of having established within it industries carried on under modern conditions and worked on an economical basis. As regards the argument that the soils of the country are being impoverished, I have already pointed out that the evil has not been as yet felt to an appreciable degree, that the extension of foreign demand for agricultural produce is the only means available for the introduction of improved methods of cultivation, because it furnishes the incentive for the adoption of such improved methods and the means to adopt them, the former by the necessity it imposes on the people for keeping up the fertility of the soil, and the latter by the additional value received for the produce exported. It is with a view to enable the cultivators to take advantage of the opportunities and openings presented by foreign trade that the diffusion of education—general and technical—has to be provided for by the State. From the point of view of the interests of the country, a policy of protection would, therefore, be injurious. The above remarks refer, of course, to a policy of protection as such and does not apply to duties imposed for purposes of revenue. The cotton duties which were repealed in 1878 and 1882 belonged to the latter class. The duties were only 5 per cent. on the value of the articles; and a special investigation made as to the character of the duties showed that they operated in a protective manner to a small extent on an insignificant portion of the trade affected. From the point of view of the interests of India they were far less injurious than the salt duties or the export duties, the former of which were enhanced soon after the cotton duties were removed.[129]

V.—Costliness of Justice.

The machinery provided for the decision of petty litigation.

106. Another evil which is frequently complained of as tending to the impoverishment of the agricultural classes is the costliness of litigation, the uncertainty of the law, and the insufficiency of the judicial machinery. There seems to be a pretty general impression among those who have given attention to the working of the courts that, while on the one hand the machinery provided for the settlement of petty litigation is much more costly and complicated than is necessary or desirable, that dealing with the more important litigation is weak both in numbers and quality. Out of a total number of about 260,000 suits for

---

[129] Even the German economists who have laid so much emphasis on the necessity for securing many-sided development of the industries of a nation by means of protective duties recognise that a purely agricultural country like India should begin with free trade, stimulating and improving its agriculture by intercourse with richer and more cultivated nations, importing foreign manufactures and exporting raw produce. On the other hand, uncompromising free trade economists like Mr. Fawcett admit that in the choice of modes of raising revenue a government cannot be guided solely by economic considerations and duties operating protectively may sometimes have to be tolerated as the least objectionable of the modes available of raising revenue required for purposes of government.

claims valued at about 4 crores of rupees, 58,000 petty suits are disposed of by the village munsifs and 92,000 small cause suits by the district munsifs. Of the latter, 20,000 suits are for personal claims of value not exceeding Rs. 10; 23,000 for claims of values above Rs. 10, and not exceeding Rs. 20; and 41,000 for claims of values ranging between Rs. 20 and Rs. 50; the total number of suits for claims of values not exceeding Rs. 50 being thus 84,000 or 92 per cent. of the total number of small cause suits instituted in the courts of district munsifs. The cost incurred by both plaintiffs and defendants in suits of this kind is out of all proportion to the value of the claims, and the successful litigant cannot recover under process of court a considerable portion of the expenses actually incurred by him. I have printed as appendix VI.-E. a statement prepared by a judicial officer who has had experience of litigation in the Tanjore, Trichinopoly and Tinnevelly districts, where the courts are numerous and the distances to be travelled by suitors and witnesses from their homes to get to the courts are not very great. From this statement, it will appear that, at a moderate computation, the cost incurred by a litigant for enforcing a claim of value of Rs. 50 through all its stages in the original court is Rs. 34, out of which he cannot recover Rs. 12. As the value of the claim rises, the cost incurred bears a more reasonable proportion to it, but it is obvious that where the value of the claim is only Rs. 10 or Rs. 20, the irrecoverable portion of the costs must often exceed such value, and this is one of the reasons which make it impossible for the poor peasantry to obtain small loans at anything like reasonable rates of interest, even when the security offered is good and sufficient.[130] Lord Kimberley, Secretary of State for India, has in his despatch on the proposals for the establishment of agricultural banks already referred to, remarked that "notwithstanding the immense improvement which has of late years been effected in the efficiency and integrity of the administration of civil justice generally, much remains to be done towards making it cheap and speedy. Everything which adds to the expense, delay and difficulty of recovering just debts increases the price at which the money-lender gives his help to the land-owner." Some steps have already been taken in this presidency in the direction pointed out by Lord Kimberley by the passing of the Madras Village Courts' Act I of 1889, under which the pecu-

---

[130] It is in view of the cost of recovering by resort to litigation money lent, it is generally stipulated in bonds that the loan shall bear a higher rate of interest from the date on which default is made in repayment.

niary limit of jurisdiction of village munsifs has been raised from Rs. 10 to Rs. 20, and power has been taken to constitute benches of village courts with the village munsifs as presidents. Rules have recently been framed for the preparation of lists of persons who are liable at the election of the suitors to serve on the benches, the qualifications prescribed for such persons being that they should pay land revenue or income-tax of not less than Rs. 10 to Government, or hold revenue free lands capable of being assessed at not less than Rs. 10 per annum; and benches have been directed to be constituted, wherever possible. It remains to be seen to what extent the orders issued will have the effect of substituting the inexpensive machinery of popular tribunals for the regular courts for the settlement of petty litigation. The greatest obstacle to the rapid extension of the scheme is the ignorance of village munsifs in the backward districts and the low estimation in which they are held in the more advanced districts, on account of their liability to be called upon to do somewhat degrading duties in connection with revenue administration—a state of things handed down from a period when village servants were subjected to personal chastisement for remissness—real or supposed—in the collection of revenue. In many zemindaries the office of village munsif has not been maintained. The whole subject of placing the village officers in zemindaries on an efficient footing is now under the consideration of Government, and legislation is contemplated for the purpose. Recently the Government has also issued rules making it obligatory on village officers to pass certain educational tests. These measures will, doubtless, improve the efficiency of village munsifs as a class. Meanwhile, village court benches may be organised in all large villages or groups of villages where official or non-official persons of sufficient education and intelligence may be available for presiding over the benches. The sub-registrars in most of the stations in the Ceded Districts and Kurnool and in the zemindaries of the Northern Circars have very light work to do, and they might be entrusted with judicial duties under the Village Courts' Act without prejudice to their duties as registration officers. The law should be amended so as to make it compulsory on suitors to institute their suits in the village courts in all villages or groups of villages where a village court bench has been established, when the value of the claim does not exceed Rs. 20. It ought not to be in the power of a plaintiff who wishes to annoy a defendant to compel him to appear before a district munsif to answer a claim and subject him to all the vexation and expense incidental to being called away from his village and his work, when there is a village court at a convenient distance. The constitution of a bench, of which one of the judges is chosen by the defendant and another by the plaintiff is a reasonable guarantee for securing the impartiality of the tribunal, and in special cases the district munsif has the power of withdrawing, for reasons shown, a suit from a village court for trial before himself. As regards suits involving claims exceeding Rs. 20 and not exceeding Rs. 50, the plaintiff may be given the option of instituting them either in the village or the district munsif's court, but in such cases, if a suit is instituted unnecessarily in a district munsif's court, the munsif should have the power of refusing costs to the plaintiff or of allowing only such costs as he would have incurred if he had instituted the suit in the village court. This appears to be the rule in England as regards suits which are instituted in the High Court of Justice in Westminster when they might have been instituted in one of the county courts. Similar provisions have been enacted in this country in the Presidency Small Cause Act and in the City Civil Court's Act to check the institution of suits in the High Court that might be instituted in courts of lower grade possessing concurrent jurisdiction as regards the entertainment of such suits. Eventually, I think the pecuniary limits as regards suits to be instituted compulsorily in the village courts might be considerably enhanced. In this connection it should be remembered that the recent enhancement of the pecuniary jurisdiction of village munsifs from Rs. 10 to Rs. 20 is no real enhancement, as the purchasing power of money has fallen by more than 50 per cent. since 1816 when the lower limit was fixed. To ensure the successful working of the whole scheme, it will, of course, be necessary to inspect the records of the village courts from time to time, giving the presiding judges the needful advice in regard to working the provisions of the Act and clearing up difficulties. This work can be done by Revenue Officers not below the rank of Tahsildars.

Higher litigation.

107. The extensive utilization of the agency of village courts' benches for the settlement of petty litigation is the means by which the superior courts, from the district munsifs upwards, can be relieved of work, which can, with advantage, be done by inexpensive popular bodies in view to the former being set free to devote their attention exclusively to the higher litigation. The mere quantity of litigation in the superior

courts, and more especially in those of district munsifs, has been fast increasing, while owing to the multiplicity of laws, the growing legal consciousness of the people and complexity of social relations, the rise of a class of legal practitioners with high educational qualifications, and the necessity for justifying every decision given by such elaborate arguments as will commend themselves to appellate tribunals, the old rough methods of arriving at decisions are no longer available. To meet the growing work the Government had recently to appoint additional district munsifs, but the relief thus afforded has hardly been appreciable; and as judicial officers cannot be indefinitely multiplied, except at enormous cost and consequent increase of taxation, the expediency of leaving petty litigation to be dealt with by popular tribunals becomes obvious. The present system of administration of civil justice is felt to be faulty also in other important respects. The necessity for ensuring full consideration of the facts and of the legal aspects of each case as well as rectitude of decision, by tribunals in the rural tracts presided over by single paid judges not amenable to the influence of public opinion, has led to the provision of an elaborate system of appeals; and this has in its turn given rise to serious evils. The chances of error in the ascertainment of facts even by native judges, conversant with the language of the country, and the customs, habits and idiosyncracies of the people, in accordance with artificial tests borrowed from a foreign jurisprudence, are considerable; and these chances are greatly multiplied when appellate courts presided over, for the most part, by European judges have to decide from recorded evidence on the credibility of witnesses and the truth of the story told by them, without having an opportunity of watching their demeanour at first hand when they tell the story. Added to this, there is the inconvenience arising from the absence of opportunities for legal training on the part of the European officers who are liable under administrative necessities to be transferred from executive to judicial appointments, even when they have no special aptitude for judicial work, while the native judges in the lower courts are mostly men who have had a legal training. These circumstances enhance greatly the uncertainty to which litigation must always be more or less subject and, I believe, I am expressing the opinion of persons who have had special opportunities of watching the working of the courts, when I say that these circumstances have led to the growth of much unwholesome litigation. The following remarks of the Honorable Mr. Chentsal Rao extracted from a paper written by him some years ago show to what extent the uncertainty of law promotes litigation: "I think that the character of our courts is a cause of our poverty. The law charges are enormous and the law administered is too refined for the country, and the uncertainties of law are so great that resort to courts has almost all the characteristics of gambling. . . . . . Apart from the enormous cost, the general ignorance of the English judges of the manners, customs and habits of our people has made the results of a suit extremely uncertain, and has encouraged the people to resort to courts upon the slightest grounds. I will give you one small instance of the uncertainty of the law. In a certain case of Hindu adoption, a man from the mofussil, with whom I was acquainted and against whom the District Judge had passed an adverse decision, came to me and asked my advice as to whether he should appeal against the decision. I told him that he had no good grounds and so said an eminent vakil whom he consulted. He, however, ventured to appeal and try a chance. He had the decree of the lower court upset against the convictions of the vakil whom he employed. There was an appeal to the Privy council, and the decree of the High court was upset. Such instances are not few. It is not so much the cost of the courts and the uncertainties of law that I so much regret as the enormous amount of time, energy and attention that is lost in the courts."

Reforms suggested by Mr. Strange.

108. The remedy for this state of things appears to be the adoption of some scheme similar to that advocated by Mr. T. L. Strange, one of the judges of the late Sudder Court, in his letter written to Government so long ago as 1860 on the subject of judicial reform.[131] The main features of Mr. Strange's scheme were as follows. For the settlement of petty litigation, he proposed panchayets constituted somewhat like the Village Court benches above described; and he expected that these panchayets would relieve the regular tribunals of nearly half the litigation of the country. For the settlement of higher litigation, he proposed to have two sets of courts, viz., first, District Courts, 50 in number; and secondly, ten appellate or Provincial Courts with a High Court in the Presidency Town. The District Courts were to be presided over by two judges of which one was generally to be an European and the other a native. The object in associating

---

[131] Mr. Strange's letter seems to me to be admirable and one that deserves to be carefully read by every one who is interested in reforming the administration of justice.

40

natives with Europeans in the district courts was four-fold; viz., firstly, to secure correct appreciation of the evidence given before the court by a native judge familiar with the language, turns of thought and devices of native witnesses; secondly, to secure impartiality of decision; thirdly, to limit the number of appeals; and fourthly to afford opportunities for legal training to European officers, who may be called upon to fill high judicial offices. As regards the necessity for a plurality of judges to form a court, Mr. Strange observed: "The assistance and check which one judge provides to another when working together on the same bench, even when the one is inferior to the other, few, I imagine, will fail to recognize. As respects the number of the judges to form the bench, I have been in the habit of sitting in a court consisting, sometimes of two judges, and sometimes of three. I much prefer the court of two judges for working purposes. Two judges can literally put their heads together. The presence of a third, dividing the other two from each other, produces a physical impediment to close consultation. I believe, moreover, that a case is apt to receive greater consideration on a difference of opinion arising, when two judges form the court than when there are three. The one has to persuade the other, but if a third be present and prematurely interposes an expression of opinion, a majority may be formed and the case terminated without proper discussion." For the Provincial courts Mr. Strange proposed to have only a single judge—a covenanted civilian. As regards appeals, where the judges of the District courts differed on any point of fact in any suit a reference was to be made to the Provincial judge, who, in this way, would stand as a third judge or referee to each such court. The reference was to be made without expense to the parties who were, however, to be at liberty to be present and conduct the case in the superior court. Where the judges of the District court liffered on a point of law the reference was to be made to the High court. The decision of the Provincial court was to be final on the facts of the case, but if that court differed from the District court on a point of law in a case thus referred for decision of fact, the Provincial court was to refer the point of law for adjudication by the Presidency court. By a question of fact, Mr. Strange meant the question of the credibility of testimony, oral and documentary; and the points of law on which Mr. Strange would allow an appeal, he defined to be, first, the refusal to admit to hearing any material evidence; second, the misconstruction of any material document; third, the subsidiary facts found not warranting the main fact derived therefrom, or the facts ascertained not warranting the judgment founded on them. The above are the main outlines of the scheme propounded by Mr. Strange, and doubtless it would require modifications in detail, more especially in regard to the definition of matters of law and matters of fact, but the broad principles on which the scheme is based are, I believe, quite sound and as applicable to the litigation of the present day as they were to litigation thirty years ago. The principal changes which have occurred since Mr. Strange wrote are the immense improvement, owing to advance of education, in the learning, efficiency and probity of the native judges, and the substitution for the old corrupt, inefficient race of petition writers, of a class of intelligent native legal practitioners, who have mostly received a university education and whose moral tone and general probity are daily advancing. It is not my object to do more than draw attention to the necessity for reform in the directions pointed out by Mr. Strange, and I have, therefore, refrained from suggesting any detailed scheme. It is, however, my impression that though more courts will have to be established than were contemplated by Mr. Strange, and the Provincial courts will have to consist of two judges in like manner with District courts, the needful reform can be carried out without entailing on Government any appreciable additional cost. The extension of communications in recent times has diminished the inconvenience to suitors in having to proceed to the stations in which the courts are held, and this inconvenience might be still further minimized by the courts holding sessions in different stations within their territorial jurisdiction in different periods of the year. The despatch of business might also be expedited by allowing one judge to take the evidence of witnesses, both the judges, however, hearing the cases argued before them. Arrangements, it seems to me, can easily be made for all European and native officers in the Civil Service being made to serve as judges in these courts.

Criminal Justice.

109. The administration of criminal justice is believed to be even less satisfactory than that of civil justice on account of the inferior character of the agency which has to be employed, though latterly there has been some improvement. Petty cases are disposed of by village magistrates under Regulation XI of 1816, but this agency is not as efficient as it ought to be, and it is desirable that steps should be taken to secure the

services of really influential men for these posts under arrangements similar to those contemplated for the appointment of village munsifs in the Village Courts' Act. This object will, to a considerable extent, be secured if the appointments are made on the recommendation of Taluk Boards, or union panchayets constituted under the Local Boards' Act. The village magistrates selected should receive a commission under the seal of the Governor in Council in view to enhancing the importance of the office in the eyes of the general public and making it one to be sought after by the more respectable class of land-holders. For the disposal of petty nuisance cases benches of magistrates have been constituted in all large towns under the Criminal Procedure Code, and this is a step in the right direction, and capable of considerable extension. The bulk of the work of the mofussil magistracy is, however, done by Sub-Magistrates paid Rs. 100 and Rs. 120, who generally exercise second class powers, and are empowered to pass sentences of 6 months' rigorous imprisonment and of fine to the extent of Rs. 200. Till recently they were paid such low salaries as Rs. 60 and Rs. 70 and the recent enhancement of pay to Rs. 100 and Rs. 120 is so far an improvement. Nevertheless, even the enhanced pay is inadequate considering the enormous powers and responsibilities of the magistrates. Moreover, Tahsildars who are paid higher salaries have recently been relieved of all magisterial work and the whole of the work done by the subordinate magistracy has now devolved on Deputy Tahsildars. It is, of course, out of the question enhancing the salaries of the latter class of officers still further, and the only feasible course for improving the administration of criminal justice appears to be to constitute benches of Magistrates under the presidency of Tahsildars for the disposal summarily of all offences specified in section 261 of the Code of Criminal Procedure. The graver cases should be tried by the District courts already referred to. It is not desirable to deprive Tahsildars altogether of all magisterial powers, more especially as in case of emergencies, such as imminent danger of a breach of the peace, their influence will have to be availed of for the purpose of preserving or restoring order; and accordingly the Government has withdrawn from them only the power of entertaining complaints and of committing cases to the Sessions courts for trial; they retain the preventive powers under Part IV of the Code of Criminal Procedure for the dispersion of unlawful assemblies, &c. Tahsildars might arrange to preside over benches at different stations during their tours. It may not be feasible to introduce these arrangements at the outset in all parts of the country. They should be introduced in all districts in which litigation is very heavy and gradually extended throughout the presidency.

Merits and demerits of British system of justice as applied to this country.

110. In making the above remarks, I do not wish to be understood as in the least undervaluing the immense advantage resulting to the country from the introduction of the liberal principles of English law breathing the spirit of free institutions. The most important of these principles are, first, that nobody is punishable for anything done, spoken or written by him, except according to the known conditions of the laws and by regularly-constituted tribunals, the accused being given the benefit of the doubt in all cases in which the act complained of is not clearly shown to have been committed or clearly shown to be an offence; secondly, that nobody, however highly placed he may be, is above the law or held to be unaccountable for infractions of law; and thirdly, that private individuals have the same remedies against Government for injuries caused to them by acts authorized by it in excess of the powers conferred by law, as they would have if the acts had been committed by other private individuals. The conscientious spirit in which these principles have, on the whole, been carried out, notwithstanding the adverse conditions under which they have to be worked, is truly wonderful; and the result is the diffusion throughout the country of a sense of security of person and property, which is above all price and which was formerly altogether unknown. Nor is the complaint often made that the Indian legislature has been over-active well-founded. This charge has been effectually disposed of by Sir Henry Maine, who pointed out that if the legislature had not provided intelligible codes of laws for the guidance of courts of justice, judicial legislation would have imported into India whole masses of English law with all its technicalities, and that all really important influence in the direction of law-making would have fallen "into the hands of a very small minority of lawyers trained in England, whose knowledge must have seemed to the millions affected by it hardly less mysterious and hardly more explicable than the inspired utterances of Mahomet or Menu." The law in any case having to be derived from exotic sources instead of being developed gradually according to social necessities, it is a great advantage to have it authoritatively embodied in codes of manageable

dimensions, capable of being studied and understood instead of having to be fished out in thousands of volumes of the English law reports. The real evil arises from the fact of the law, and criminal law especially, being far too refined[132] for the people for whom it is intended, and its administration having to be entrusted to judges who have no intimate acquaintance with the usages and customs and modes of thought of the people to whom it is applied, or to low-paid native magistrates who are clothed with enormous powers. The complicated procedure and the machinery of appeals prescribed to ensure correct decisions multiply the chances of error and add to the delay, vexation and expense of litigation. It is in view

---

[132] The late Mr. Runga Charlu, Dewan of Mysore, made the following remarks on the working of the Penal Code: "It is impossible not to feel some surprise at the complacency and even admiration with which the working of this theoretic code is usually regarded without considering its effects on the interests of the people at large. Theoretical minds carried away by the logical perfection of the code forget the evil effects of its artificial definitions, which are not altogether based on the popular train of ideas. Popular definitions admit of natural expansion to meet every new circumstance, while artificial ones perpetually stand under the necessity of artificial expansions which serve only to remove them further from popular thought. It is undeniable that the code is not understood without great effort even by the educated officers, and much less carried in their daily train of thoughts. What must be the effect upon the illiterate population of such legislation bearing on their daily concerns! Popular experience can only describe the code as a cruel piece of legislation which, in its anxiety that no description of offence might possibly be left out, has framed such wide and comprehensive definitions as to mingle serious crimes and mere civil injuries in the same category, and in order that all aggravated cases might be adequately met, has provided for offences exorbitant and often unlimited fines and imprisonment. It has thus placed the peaceful citizen equally with the professional dacoit perpetually under the tender mercies of a not immaculate official hierarchy. No one can be sure that any momentary indiscreet act of his might not bring him under the grasp of the Penal Code, and in so bringing him, consign him to a punishment, which, to him, may be a social death under the prevailing ideas of religion and custom. . . . . Where there is such unlimited latitude of punishment, it is vain to expect that it will be properly exercised. . . . A simpler code keeping to popular ideas, with certainty rather than severity of punishment in all ordinary cases, with exceptional powers confined to special courts, is the want of the country." This was written within 6 or 7 years after the introduction of the Penal Code and it reflects the popular feeling at the time. I myself remember the vague undefined feeling of terror with which the Penal Code was regarded by the rural population soon after it was introduced. Sir Henry Maine also refers to the same feeling in the following remarks: "I have had described to me a collection of street songs sung in the streets of the city which is commonly supposed to be the most impatient of British rule by persons who never so much dreamed of having their words repeated to an Englishman. They were not altogether friendly to the foreign rulers of the country, but it may be broadly laid down that they complained of nothing which might naturally have been expected to be the theme of complaint. And without exception, they declare that life in India had become intolerable since the English criminal laws had begun to treat women and children as if they were men." During the last 30 years the experience of the working of the code has led to its provisions being better understood, and it does not inspire the terror that it once did. Even now, however, as regards the punishments prescribed for some offences, the provisions as to certain offences being non-bailable and the compulsory enforcement of the attendance of women without distinction of caste or rank, the Penal Code and the Code of Criminal Procedure are unsuited to the prevailing ideas of the people and their social and religious usages. The consequence of refusing bail to many a Hindu charged with a non-bailable offence is, in some parts of the country, excommunication, a punishment far in excess of the requirements of the offence of which he may or may not be convicted. The fear of compulsory personal attendance in courts of respectable women as parties or witnesses is an encouragement to false or vexatious criminal proceedings. And the purchase of immunity from this disgrace by pecuniary payments is a not unlooked-for result in the institution of such proceedings.

to adapt the abstract propositions laid down in the law to the customs, usages and sentiments of the people in their practical application, that it is necessary that all petty offences which can be left to be dealt with by popular tribunals should be so left, while the graver offences, on the suppression and punishment of which the well-being and safety of the State depend, should be enquired into by single judges with the aid of juries, or where the conditions of the country preclude the employment of juries, by benches of judges containing a due admixture of the native element.

VI.—Local Fund and Municipal Administration and Legislation affecting Social Usages.

Disintegration of village communities.

111. The last group of questions we have to consider relates to the disintegration of village communities and the decay of the spirit of co-operation among the villagers for the purpose of carrying out large undertakings and warding off common dangers; and also to the evils arising from the absence of a trustworthy machinery for ascertaining when Government can safely undertake legislation affecting laws of inheritance or social usages corresponding to changes which are taking place in the economic condition of the people.

Causes of the decay of communal spirit.

112. It is commonly believed that the solidarity of the village communities was undermined by the ryotwar system introduced by Sir Thomas Munro. The fact, however, is that village communities, which were originally composed of kinsmen, were, at the beginning of the century, becoming disintegrated by the introduction of strangers even in those parts of the country where they still retained their original form; common holdings were in process of transformation into individual holdings, and the intermediate stage of holding lands of whole villages in defined shares subject to the condition that each sharer was to cultivate the lands allotted to him for a period of years had been reached. Thus we find in the Tanjore district, where village communities flourished in an unimpaired condition down to recent times, the Collector, Mr. John Wallace reported in 1805 that, out of 5,063 villages, 1,087 villages were owned by single owners or families, that 2,202 villages were owned by mirassidars who held their lands in severalty in distinct plots and that 1,774 villages were held in common by the mirassidars. The

extent to which in the natural course of things strangers had been introduced into the mirassi bodies will be seen from the fact that, out of 62,048 mirassidars in the district, 17,149 were Brahmins, 43,442 were Sudras or Native Christians, and 1,457 were Muhammadans. That the ryotwar system brought into force in the beginning of the century by Sir Thomas Munro hastened the decay of the village communities does not, however, admit of doubt; for, as pointed out by Sir Henry Maine, in a state of society where the rights of individual members are determined by custom more or less vague, the question as to whom the government makes responsible for the payment of its dues practically determines what type the society and the tenure of lands by its members shall assume. If the government, for instance, makes the head of a village the person responsible for its revenue, the interest of such head in the lands becomes the predominant one, and other persons having interests in the lands become his tenants unless the process is arrested by positive legislation. Similarly, if the whole body of proprietors in the village be made jointly responsible for the government revenue, the natural evolution of individual property is arrested. Again, if the government decides to deal with each individual cultivator as regards the payment of revenue, the tendency is to break up the village communities. The most potent cause, however, of the disintegration of village communities was the establishment of orderly government and internal tranquillity and the suppression of external aggression. So long as there was lawlessness in the country, the village communities were kept in a state of cohesion for purposes of self-defence, the successful repulsion of attacks from without which might otherwise sweep whole communities away being of far greater importance than the prevention of petty tyranny within the communities themselves. When the external blows by which these communities are kept in a state of kinetic equilibrium are removed, the internal rivalries and jealousies come into play, and the result is that the inconveniences and injustices of common holding of land are felt to be great hardships; and the improvements in production which a settled condition of things brings about create a preference for individual holdings. This transformation of common into individual property is a most beneficial process, and one which is an essential factor in the industrial progress of a country. Similar considerations apply to the joint family system. Under this system personal comforts, personal feelings and personal advantage must be sacrificed by each member in the pursuit of the common good of the family, and the result is that, while the earning and non-earning members are placed on a par, thereby preventing extreme hardships to the latter, the incentive to exertion among the earning members is weakened to the extent to which their earnings have to be shared with members who have not in any way contributed their quota of labour towards such earnings. So long as mere numbers give strength to a family by enabling it either to cultivate a larger extent of waste lands or to fight other communities with greater chances of success, there is every inducement to the members of the joint family to hold together, notwithstanding the restrictions imposed on the personal independence and comfort of the several members. When, however, these cohesive forces are removed, the family breaks up. This tendency is, as already stated, a beneficial one, notwithstanding that thereby the chances of co-operation for the purpose of carrying out large undertakings are made more difficult in the same way as it is more difficult to raise a large pile of buildings by means of free labour than by means of slave labour.

Progress of local administration.

113. The obvious remedy for the evils incidental to this situation is the promotion among the people of habits of voluntary co-operation for carrying out public objects, and it is this object that education obtained by taking part in the administration of local and municipal affairs is intended to secure.

The policy of entrusting the management of affairs connected with the well-being of towns to bodies composed partly of official and partly of non-official members was, for the first time, inaugurated in 1865. In 1871, similar bodies were created for the management of public matters affecting the well-being of rural tracts. In 1884, the scheme of municipal and local administration was placed on a somewhat wider popular basis, and the principle of allowing the inhabitants of towns and rural tracts to elect their representatives to serve on the boards was to some extent recognized. The elective system is in force in 32 out of the 55 towns constituted municipalities, the former containing a population of 1,200,000. The extent to which non-official persons take part in the administration of affairs connected with municipalities will be seen from the following figures. There were, on 31st March 1892, 871 municipal councillors, of whom 473 were nominated by Government and 398 elected by the townspeople. The number of official members was 207 and of non-official members 664. Of the total number 158 were Europeans or Eurasians and the remainder natives. For the administration of local affairs of rural tracts there are 270 Union Panchayats, 86 Taluk Boards and 21 District Boards. There are 654 members serving on the District Boards, 277 being elected by the people and the remainder nominated by Government. 118 of them are Europeans or Eurasians and 536 are natives. In the Taluk Boards there are 1,141 members, of whom 317 are officials and 824 non-official persons. 65 among these are Europeans or Eurasians and 1,076 natives. In the Union Panchayats there are 2,511 members, of whom 865 are officials including 622 village officers and 1,646 non-official persons. Thus the total number of persons taking part in municipal and local administration is 5,177, of whom 3,562 are non-official persons.

Difficulties of local administration and success attained therein.

114. The figures given above show that there is a considerable number of non-official persons who are being trained in the performance of public duties; and, as the number of Local Fund Union Panchayats increases, still larger numbers of such persons will, in course of time, be entrusted with such duties. Since 1884 the Government has paid unremitting attention to Municipal and Local Fund administration, and by close scrutiny of the work done, and of the attitude of Government officers towards it, has sought to awaken in non-official bodies an adequate sense of their duties and responsibilities. The success that has attended these efforts will be seen to be considerable when it is remembered how entirely new the idea of combination for public purposes of persons not organized in castes, or guilds under natural leaders, is in this country. In reviewing the results of Local Fund administration for 1889–90, the Madras Government remarked: "These results are, to a great extent, "due to the exertions of the Taluk Boards and Union Panchayats, which worked, on the whole, with considerable "success and energy and has thus amply justified the action "which called them into existence. His Excellency the Governor in Council trusts that, in course of time, all these local "bodies will become still more efficient and that their individual members will devote more and more of their attention "to the interests of the administration. The advancement "of primary education, the extension of medical relief and vaccination, the improvement of village communications, and "the utilization of sanitary allotments are subjects calling for

"their earliest and most careful consideration." The Government review of the work done by local bodies in 1891–92 shows still greater progress. On the other hand, in municipalities, the administration has been less successful, owing to the lack of interest in their duties displayed by the majority of the councillors. There is, in these councils, a tendency to split up into factions, and moreover the duties of the chairmen of municipalities, especially in large towns, are so heavy as to require four or five hours' work from them daily, an amount of time which very few non-official persons, who have their own business to attend to, can afford to give to the performance of public duties. The regulations laid down for the guidance of the councils in the various departments of work entrusted to them are also so numerous and complicated as to require special study. It has, therefore, been found necessary in several of the larger municipalities to employ a salaried chairman. If arrangements can be made for lending to municipalities the services of Government officers of the rank of Tahsildars, Deputy Collectors or District Munsifs for carrying on the duties of chairmen there can be no doubt that it will much improve the efficiency of municipal administration, and while giving to non-official members full scope for scrutinizing the work will prevent the danger of municipal councils being split up into factions. The chairmen too will be persons trained in public business, who, if they neglected their duties, would forfeit their prospects of promotion in the Government service. It would, of course, be easy to point out in the conduct of local administration instances of apathy and ignorance on the part of some members and factious conduct on the part of others, but it must be remembered that the whole scheme has had to be worked on entirely new lines unfamiliar to the traditional habits and feelings of the people. The old organic groups of castes, village communities and guilds were broken up and new bodies composed of members belonging to different creeds with divers interests created. The duties entrusted to these bodies at the outset were also not of a kind calculated to appeal to their sympathies. These duties had nothing to do with the care and superintendence of places of religious worship and of charitable endowments which are generally more or less connected with religion, with the relief of the poor, with the assessment of taxes, with the maintenance of the police, and with the administration of justice—matters affecting closely the inner life of the villagers and in which they might be supposed to be primarily interested. The construction of roads and bridges is best attended to by the central government, and ideas of sanitation are too refined and modern to be popular in a poor and backward country; and education, by being dissociated from religion, has lost one of its strongest supports. The creation of municipalities and Union Panchayats has also been generally accompanied by the imposition of additional taxation, a circumstance calculated to render the bodies unpopular. The funds at the disposal of the local bodies have been much too limited to admit of anything very substantial being effected in the way of improvements and the recurrence of scarcities in several parts of the country frequently throws the finances of the local bodies out of gear and impairs their usefulness. When these difficulties are borne in mind, it will be readily seen why greater success has not been attained in Local and Municipal administration.

On what lines local administration should be worked to ensure greater success.

115. Further advance in this direction can be looked for only by entrusting to local bodies more and more of the work of real administration. The measures recommended by me for the settlement of petty litigation—civil and criminal—by means of popular bodies will, to some extent, have the effect of creating greater interest in public affairs than has been displayed hitherto. The assessment of taxes like the income-tax might, in rural tracts, be entrusted in course of time to Local Fund Panchayats who might be assessed at a lump sum which would be distributed by them according to the means of the individuals liable to assessment. The obligation to maintain village forests, agricultural experimental farms, technical schools may, wherever possible, be imposed on them. In the matter of the dispensation of relief in times of distress the assistance of Local Fund Union Panchayats might be made use of more than it has been. Under the influence of a watchful public opinion the duties and responsibilities of Government in this respect have greatly widened of late years, as the Government is made responsible for ensuring that, in times of failure of crops, no deaths by starvation ensue. This is a duty which it is very difficult for any government to discharge satisfactorily. The Government has to act according to fixed rules to prevent public money being wasted or misappropriated, and this makes it difficult to adapt the forms of relief to the circumstances and needs of the different localities. While, on the one hand, it would be in the highest degree demoralizing by a too liberal dispensation of relief to teach the people to look for Government assistance, whenever they feel pinched, instead of

teaching them to provide in prosperous seasons against contingencies of this kind, it would, on the other hand, be inhuman to refuse help to the suffering population when large tracts are distressed. It is, therefore, an extremely difficult and delicate task to determine in any particular case at what stage of the distress the Government ought to intervene and provide relief at the expense of public funds instead of leaving cases of distress to be dealt with as in ordinary years by voluntary private charity. Whenever, therefore, distress owing to failure of crops is apprehended, large establishments have accordingly to be employed to be in readiness to start measures of relief in case the distress, that is beginning to be felt, should grow in intensity. The officers employed are generally men who know little about the circumstances of the localities in which distress prevails, and, often, a favorable turn in the season renders any measures of relief unnecessary. For instance, during the last drought a considerable portion of the expenditure on famine relief represented the cost of the additional establishments employed to watch and report on the state of the country. In spite of all precautions it would be futile to expect to ensure that all cases requiring relief in all parts of the country had been sought out and provided for and deaths by starvation were completely prevented. It seems to me that this is a duty which should be performed by local unpaid non-official agency and that, instead of Government being made responsible for deaths by starvation, the Local Fund Union Panchayats should be made responsible and placed in funds in order that they might be enabled to discharge this duty efficiently except in times of dire famine, when the whole power of the State will, of course, have to be applied to it in grappling with so serious a crisis. A certain percentage of the land revenue might be assigned for this purpose, and to ensure its economical administration, the Local Boards should be asked to supplement it with funds at their disposal. The administration of relief should also be regulated by rules laid down by Government, and questions as to the circumstances under which, and the persons to whom it should be dispensed should be determined by Local Fund Union Panchayats.

Necessity for utilizing Local Boards as initiating and advising bodies in legislation affecting social usages, &c.

116. There is another important direction in which the usefulness of local bodies might be developed, viz., in ascertaining by their means when legislation affecting social usages and laws of inheritance can and should be undertaken for the benefit

of the people; and the necessity for utilizing these bodies in this manner is all the greater, now that under the scheme for enlarged legislative councils just introduced, the local bodies have been conceded the privilege of nominating members to these councils. One of the effects of the introduction of the British system of administration of justice by fixed laws and regular courts is to suppress the indigenous agencies, whether caste assemblies or guilds, by which the customary usages regulating the conduct and rights of the members of the communities were constantly though unconsciously modified to suit change of circumstances. Even now in the rural tracts, the headmen of certain castes enquire into and dispose of disputes among the members of the castes regarding offences relating to marriage, partition of family property, breaches of caste observances, &c., the decisions being enforced either by the imposition of fines which are paid to the village temple, or to a common fund, or by excommunication of the delinquents by depriving them of their social privileges, such as the "taking of fire and water" from their neighbours, entering the village temple for purposes of worship, attending at marriages and funerals, and availing themselves of the assistance of the village barber, washerman, &c. These caste assemblies, which are not now recognized by law, have lost much of their vitality and will, in course of time, disappear altogether. This is from one point of view a necessary and beneficial process, as it is desirable in the interests of the country that the endless differentiations of customary law in small communities should be removed, and a fairly homogeneous law applicable to large communities evolved. This result has been brought about in most civilized countries by judicial legislation which, while reducing the law to a uniform type introduces at the same time, such modifications in it as the progress of society requires. But as justice is administered in this country mostly by judges who belong to a different nationality from that of the litigants, and who would incur blame if they, instead of administering Hindu law of the strictest type, modified it according to their own ideas of the fitness of things and of the necessities of individual cases, the tendency is to stereotype the ancient law and arrest the changes which it would have undergone in its natural course of evolution. This curious and unexpected result of English judges being greater conservators of ancient ritual law than native judges even of the most orthodox type would be, has been noticed both by Mr. J. D. Mayne and Sir Henry Maine. "The pundit," writes Mr. J. D. Mayne in his work on Hindu Law, "however bigoted he might be, "was at all events a Hindu, living amongst Hindus and "advising upon a law which actually governed the every day "lives of himself and his family and his friends. He would "torture a sacred text into an authority for his opinion, "but his opinion would probably be right though unsustained "by, or even opposed to, his text. With the English judge "there was no such restraining influence. He was sworn to "administer Hindu law to the Hindus and he was determined "to do so however strange or unreasonable it might appear." As regards the arrested development of the Hindu law as administered in South India, Mr. Mayne goes on to remark: "The fact really was that the law had outgrown the authori-"ties. Native judges would have recognised the fact; English "judges were unable to do so, or else remarked (to use a "phrase I have often heard from the Bench) 'that they were "'bound to maintain the integrity of the law.' This was a "matter of less importance in Bengal, where Jimuta Vahana "had already burst the fetters. But in Southern India, "it came to be accepted, that the Mitakshara was the last "word that could be listened to on Hindu law. The conse-"quence was a state of arrested progress in which no voices "were heard except those which came from the tomb. It "was as if a German was to administer English law from the "resources of a library furnished with Fleta, Glanville and "Bracton and terminating with Lord Coke." Judicial legislation to adapt the law to changing circumstances being then not possible, the only alternative is positive legislation. But how is the Government to know when legislation can be safely undertaken and when it ought to be avoided on the ground that it will run counter to the sentiments of the people affected by it? On the one hand, if the Government were to refuse altogether to legislate in matters affecting social usages, domestic life and laws of inheritance, it would injure the community in two ways, viz., first by setting in motion strong forces which have the effect of unsettling the old state of society and disturbing the relations which subsisted; and secondly, by depriving the society of its capacity for adjusting its institutions to its requirements and refusing to do what is necessary by positive legislation. This state of things must seriously arrest the progress of the community. "Social necessities and social opinion," observes Sir H. Maine, "are more or less in advance of law. We may "go indefinitely near to the closing of the gap between them, "but it has a perpetual tendency to re-open. Law is stable; "the societies we are speaking of, progressive. The greater "or less happiness of a people depends on the degree of "promptitude with which the gulf is narrowed." On the other hand, a foreign legislature has to be extremely cautious in interfering by legislation with cherished institutions affecting the every day domestic life of the people, as any hasty or ill-judged action in this direction is likely to cause great discontent and suffering. The only way in which the Government can ascertain whether it can legislate with safety in matters of this kind is by making it a necessary condition for legislative action that the demand for legislation should come from local bodies more or less representative of the classes of the community whose interests are affected by such legislation.

Difficulties in dealing with legislation affecting social usages illustrated by projects for legislation before the Madras Legislative Council.

117. That the above remarks are not merely theoretical will be seen from a consideration of the circumstances connected with the three bills affecting the laws relating to Marriage and inheritance now before the Madras Legislative Council. One of these bills is intended to provide a legal form of marriage to the Hindus in the Malabar country who follow the Marumakkatayam or nepotismal rule of succession as regards inheritance. The second has, for its object, the settlement of the law regulating the succession of self-acquired property under the general Hindu law and of moot questions as to the circumstances under which the earnings of a member of joint Hindu family shall be considered his self-acquisition and when they shall be regarded as family property. The third bill is intended to give to the sister and sister's son a higher place in the line of succession prescribed by the general Hindu law as understood to prevail in this presidency than they at present occupy. I do not wish to express any final or decisive opinion in regard to the necessity for the legislation proposed, but will explain the great difficulty which the Government has in dealing with questions of this kind.

On the question of prescribing a legal form of marriage to the community governed by the Marumakkatayam law, no stranger to the community, which is to be affected by the proposed legislation, has any right to dogmatise. "There "is no subject," remarks Sir Henry Maine, "on which it is "harder to obtain trustworthy information than the relations "of the sexes in communities very unlike that to which the "enquirer belongs. The statements made to him are apt to "be affected by two very powerful feelings, the sense of shame "and the sense of the ludicrous, and he himself nearly always "sees the facts in a wrong perspective. Almost innumerable delusions are current in England as to the social condition, in regard to this subject, of a country so near to us in situation and civilization as France." These remarks are profoundly true of Malabar, and if I allude to this subject at all, it is not because I am not conscious of my unfitness to pronounce any opinion on the question, but merely to show how extremely difficult and delicate it is for Government to deal with such questions. In the Malabar country, the Marumakkatayam law does not recognize the institution of marriage, though the unions of men and women are practically permanent, being regulated by social opinion; and a high state of civilization has been found compatible with this condition of things. The inheritance of property descends in the female line. Property is held jointly by families consisting of members belonging to several generations despotically governed by the eldest male among them, the junior members being entitled to a bare maintenance. This archaic type of society has subsisted so long, because Malabar was till within recent times shut off from the other parts of the continent of India by the difficulty of communication; women especially were strictly forbidden to cross the frontiers of the country, and even the boundaries of recognised sub-divisions of it. Facilities of locomotion and free intercourse with the people on the East Coast and the ideas of personal liberty and independence engendered by the operation of the British system of law and the diffusion of English education are, however, now rapidly undermining the foundations on which the fabric of society rests. The implicit obedience paid by the junior members to the head of the family is diminishing in force every day. The junior members themselves, who, under the old conditions, would never have left their *tarwads*, go for education to distant places like Madras, or even England in a few cases, or are employed in Government service or as Vakeels, and while so employed, take their wives from their *tarwad* homes to live with them. The result is a closer feeling of sympathy and affection for their wives and children, and a correspondingly diminished regard for the interests of their sisters and their children, both on the part of the head of the family, and on the part of the junior members. A strong feeling is also growing up among those who have had the benefit of English education, that the non-recognition by law of the relationship of wife and children and of the claims to support and education founded on such relationship when voluntary provision for such purposes fails owing to accidents, and other means of support are not available, is a great social injustice. The class that feels in this manner, though numerically small, is an influential one growing in intelligence and importance day by day. The fact of the laws of devolution of property running counter to natural sentiment must necessarily lead to the adoption of devices to counterwork it, giving rise to litigation among members belonging to the same family, and to dissipation of the family property which it is the object of the *tarwad* system to preserve intact. The State is also interested in seeing that the institutions of society are so modified as to ensure that the care, nurture and education of the young, according to modern requirements—matters in which it is deeply interested—are entrusted to those who may be trusted under the impulse of natural sentiment to discharge the duties with the greatest fidelity and to be likely to submit to great personal sacrifices in the attainment of this object and not to those who in the majority of cases will be content to do the minimum that they are bound legally or by social opinion to do. This is one side of the case. On the other side, it has to be remembered that the existing institutions have struck their roots so deep in the past, affect so many relations of life and the subsistence of such large numbers of persons, that any sudden modification of them is likely to give rise to many unexpected evils, disappoint many just expectations and cause suffering and widespread discontent. The Government cannot possibly, by enquiries by means of commissions and such like bodies improvised for the time, be able to determine in projects for legislation of this kind, having such wide-reaching issues, whether after balancing the conflicting considerations, the gain to the community is sufficiently great to justify legislation and if legislation is resolved on, what precautions shall be taken to minimize the evils of the change. Even where the gain is beyond question, the feeling of the community itself as to the necessity for legislation is a factor which must necessarily be taken into account.

Legislation, then, in such cases can only be carried out in a spirit of compromise and should provide for a gradual modification of the institutions found unsuitable without causing any violent breach of social continuity. For work of this kind, the provincial legislature composed, as it must be, of members, the majority of whom are of different habits and ways of thinking from those whom the proposed legislation is to affect, must be entirely unsuited, unless it is aided in its deliberations by other bodies constituted by law and composed in the main of members belonging to the community which is affected by the legislation. In the case immediately under discussion, the Hindu members of the Local Fund Boards in the Malabar district might be regarded as a legally constituted standing committee for the consideration of questions as to the expediency of undertaking legislation of this character. Members of the community who feel keenly the evils of the present state of the law as regards marital relations and wish for a reform should be at liberty to bring the question before the committee. If they did not succeed in getting a majority of the committee to pass a resolution, making a demand on the legislature for legislation, that would be proof of the fact that the time was not ripe for carrying out the contemplated reform. Those interested in the reform would not, however, be discouraged by a single unsuccessful effort; they would try to educate public opinion on the subject, and endeavour to get persons elected as members of Local Fund Boards who would support the cause of reform, and they would bring the question again and again before the committee. In course of time if the reform was a desirable one, the good sense of the community would prevail even over deep-rooted prejudices and the reform party would doubtless be able to get a majority of the committee to make a demand on the legislature. If the majority was a narrow one, the Government might still consider it unsafe to undertake legislation until the will of the more enlightened and influential portion of the community had more unmistakably declared itself. If after further lapse of time the demand was made by a large majority of the committee, the Government would be in a position to undertake legislation with confidence. It is true that there is nothing to prevent voluntary associations formed with a view to promote particular objects, petitioning Government for legislation for carrying out those objects, but such associations cannot command the same confidence as Local Fund Boards having a legal status, and further it would be impossible to gauge the relative strength of rival voluntary associations and determine how far each represented the feelings and wishes of the community. In matters affecting the community as a whole, the whole Board would represent the community, and in cases where the interests of particular sections of the community were concerned, the committee composed of members belonging to such sections would have these powers. The right conferred on these Boards of discussing such questions would infuse life and spirit into them, and they can, if necessary, be enlarged so as to secure adequate representation of different sections of the community. A very great advantage of this system would be that a legal machinery would be provided for educating local public opinion in favour of legislation affecting social [133] relations.

Further remarks regarding legislation on social matters, &c.

118. In the above remarks I do not by any means wish to ignore the unequal advance in knowledge and intelligence of the population of different parts of the Presidency and of the consequent improbability of the Local Fund Boards in some parts being able to discuss questions as regards legislation with intelligence and to arrive at a correct opinion regarding them. I can only reply that what I have stated is the ideal to be aimed at and gradually worked up to, and that the arrangements made at the outset should be such as will allow of Boards which are sufficiently advanced to deal with such questions. The more advanced parts of the country ought to be allowed their legitimate influence in raising up the less advanced parts and not be compulsorily kept at the level of the latter. And after all, the arrangements are intended merely to enable Government to determine whether legislation on matters affecting social usages can be undertaken with safety; the final responsibility for undertaking or refusing legislation will still rest with Government. The Local Fund Boards will in fact be constituted bodies which have limited executive powers in certain directions to act of their own authority, but possessing unlimited powers for making representations on all other matters of general administration, the final decision of which is vested in the central Government.

Unsatisfactory state of the law relating to native religious endowments.

119. There is one other subject which may be appropriately noticed here, viz., the unsatisfactory state of the law regarding the management and supervision of religious endowments and the urgent necessity for reform in this direction. There is here an immense national property which, in course of time, might be devoted to many beneficial purposes, such as provision of religious instruction, of art education, &c., and which is now largely misappropriated. One of the most popular acts of Government would be to provide for the efficient supervision of the management of these properties to ensure their being devoted in the main to the uses for which they were intended, by means of responsible committees which, without doing violence to public feeling, would be able gradually and insensibly to introduce such changes as would tend to

---

[133] The second and third bills relate to complicated questions of Hindu Law, a discussion of which will take up more space than can be afforded here, and I have therefore merely contented myself with alluding to them.

the removal of abuses which have grown up around religious institutions and to afford education to the people in directions which Government arrangements cannot reach. The annual income of the religious endowments has been estimated to amount to 75 lakhs of rupees, a sum higher than the income of the Local Fund Boards and Municipalities in the Presidency, and a considerable portion of the income is contributed by the State. That this income should be misappropriated to private uses is a melancholy waste of resources; and it is futile to expect that the worshippers at the shrines, scattered as they are throughout the Presidency, would come forward and embark in expensive litigation with trustees of endowments who have command of trust money. The enactment of a law which will provide an efficient control of these public trusts will be welcomed as a great [134] boon by the general public.

CONCLUDING REMARKS.

120. I have endeavoured in the foregoing pages to point out the directions in which the country has progressed during the last forty years, the special evils which the transition from the old to the new state of things has given rise to, and some of the measures which might be taken by Government to remedy or mitigate the effects of these evils and secure unfettered economic development. I will now close my long review with a few general remarks in regard to the considerations to be borne in mind in estimating the value of the results achieved.

The *first* point to be noted is the disordered state of the country which had to be reduced to order and fitted with the appliances of civilization and regular administration, and the low economic condition from which the great mass of the population had to be elevated. We saw how, in the beginning of the century, Southern India had been devastated by wars, famines and bands of plunderers; the cultivating classes were

---

134 The question of the duty of the State to make adequate provision for the supervision of the management of *public* endowments whether devoted to secular or religious uses is too intricate to be usefully discussed here, and I have therefore made a few brief remarks as to the public feeling on the subject. I have given in the appendix VI.-F. extracts from the remarks of Sir Alfred Lyall in regard to the political inexpediency of Government relinquishing its right to provide for the election of the heads and managers of religious endowments, and to declare in case of dispute who shall be regarded as properly elected as such heads and managers, referring, if need be, persons who contest the decision to establish their contention in the courts. In the same way, the Government should have the right to license new places of public worship and regulate religious processions to prevent the rival religious communities coming into collision with each other. The state of the law on this subject is vague and uncertain and leads to collisions which might be prevented. The exercise by Government of powers vested in it with a view to ensure rival religious communities living in peace without coming into dangerous collisions with one another is no breach of the principle of religious neutrality.

ground down by oppressive taxation, by the illegal exactions of the officers of Government, of the renters employed to collect the Government dues, and of the sowkars without whose assistance the ryots could not subsist and carry on their calling and who kept them in a state little removed from that of perpetual bondage; trade was hampered by insecurity of property, defective communications and onerous transit duties; the vast majority of the population suffered extreme hardships when there was even a partial failure of crops in small tracts, owing to the great difficulty and cost of obtaining supplies of grain from more favored regions; the peasantry and even possessors of considerable landed property when not holding offices under Government themselves were cowering before the pettiest Government officer and submitting to tortures and degrading personal ill-treatment inflicted on the slightest pretext; persons who had chanced to acquire wealth, if they belonged to the lower classes, dared not openly use it for purposes of enjoyment or display for fear of being plundered by the classes above them; the agricultural classes as a whole had few wants beyond those imposed by the necessity for bare subsistence, no ambition or enterprize to try untrodden ways, and no example to stimulate them to endeavour to better their condition, while the rigid rules and usages of castes and communities in which society was organized repressed all freedom of action and restricted the scope for individual initiative. To understand the full significance of the change which has come over the country one has to contrast what he sees at present, unsatisfactory as it may appear from some points of view, with the state of things described above.

Secondly, it must be remembered that considerable portions of the country are liable to frequent droughts and occasional famines, which no human foresight can prevent, and that the results of several decades of good administration are liable to be suddenly swept away by the occurrence of one of these terrible visitations. The famine of 1876–77 is a case in point. It was the severest in magnitude and duration of any known during the present century; but it is satisfactory to find that the districts affected by it have recovered more rapidly than those affected by the famine of 1833, which prevailed in a smaller tract of country and was of shorter duration. The development of communications since 1877 has also greatly mitigated the effects of temporary scarcities. This is illustrated in a remarkable manner by what has happened during the last two years. The railway from Chittoor to Váyalpád and Dharmavaram was opened in February and March 1892. There was a great drought and failure of crops in those places at the time, and prices of food-grains were ruling very high; but as soon as the railway was opened prices fell at once largely. The last season was a splendid one in most parts of the Ceded districts and ryots had a bumper crop, while in the southern districts, viz., Madura and Tinnevelly, there was failure of harvests. Large quantities of rice from Dharmavaram were exported to Tinnevelly for the first time within the memory of the ryots of the former place, bringing them a large profit. If a famine, such as that of 1876–77, should again unfortunately occur, its effects will not be as disastrous as on the last occasion, though in any case it would cause great suffering. If, however, by some unfortunate combination of circumstances famines should occur in quick succession, no amount of good administration could make head against such calamities. On the other hand, if there is no famine of a very severe type for the next half a century, the measures in progress would have had time to produce their effect and the suffering caused by failure of crops over large areas in consecutive years would not probably be much greater than in European countries.

Thirdly, we have to take into account the limitation to the action of Government imposed by the necessities of the situation, in considering the *rate* of progress. The zemindars and poligars were most of them the terror of the country in the beginning of the century, and they were with difficulty reduced to submission. To have utilized them for purposes of government would have been dangerous and would have indefinitely postponed all chance of introducing regular and orderly government. They were accordingly relegated to the position of mere landholders with no part or lot in the government of the country. The recognition of caste and village assemblies for purposes of administration of justice was likewise impossible, as owing to the innumerable subdivisions of castes it would have been a matter of extreme difficulty to decide as to the persons over whom the assemblies had jurisdiction, and moreover this plan would not answer in cases in which the contending litigants belonged to different castes and would have perpetuated the feuds between them. The decision of disputes by punchayets when the litigants were willing to abide by their decisions was provided for, but this arrangement was seldom availed of and the law on the subject was practically a dead letter. The whole work of Government had, therefore, to be conducted by a hierarchy of officials. At the same time, owing to wide differences in religion, civilization and social usages between the rulers and the ruled, all institutions having living connection with matters which are intimately bound up with the daily life of the people had to be rigidly excluded from official cognizance. The Government could not, as it were, take the people by the hand and by intimate association with them lead them on in the path of progress. It had to stand aloof, contenting itself with providing the material appliances of civilization and with clearing away all obstructions to progress trusting to the influence of education to work out such changes as the healthy progress of the society might require.

Fourthly, we saw that some of the evils which have been felt under the new *régime*, "the tares," as they are called, "which have grown up with the wheat," are either not new or are sacrifices without incurring which the benefits could not be secured. For instance, take the case of the growth of agricultural indebtedness. As a matter of fact, the ryots were formerly much more in the hands of sowkars than now, though their indebtedness as expressed in money value appears to be greater now than before. The dependence of the ryots on sowkars is greatest in tracts of country in which the seasons are very uncertain. Formerly when lands had no value, the ryot's credit was limited to the value of the year's crop, and if the crop failed for two or three years and the sowkar stopped supplies, there was nothing between the ryot and starvation. Now the increased credit of the ryot enables him to obtain better terms and hold out longer. The more prudent among the ryots have now a chance of making use of their credit for their own advantage, and even those who recklessly pledged it would be in no worse condition than they would have been under the old conditions. Again, the tendency of a *régime* favoring industrial improvement is to prevent the military, official and sacerdotal classes from intercepting the earnings of the laboring classes. The result is that the production of articles of luxury or art which ministered to the gratification of persons who were maintained in great opulence at the expense of the general community suffers and must necessarily do so until the industrial classes themselves become sufficiently rich and acquire a taste for such luxuries. Similar considerations apply to economic redistribution of productive powers and resources. The introduction of railways, for instance, by superseding less efficient means of conveyance must cause suffering to the classes who make a living by rendering services in connection with the latter. We thus hear that the extension of the railways in the Punjab has caused distress to camel drivers. A diversion of trade is also often caused, from particular localities or tracts of country, and places which were once prosperous decay and new places spring up in their stead. Wallajahnugger, for instance, which was once a place of great importance as an emporium of trade is now much decayed. The facilities of intercommunication between different parts of the country, and the rapid diffusion of information as to the conditions of the market as regards demand and supply of commodities by means of telegraph render the maintenance of central depôts to some extent unnecessary, the dealers in commodities being enabled to communicate directly with the producers in the rural tracts. There is thus increase of trade in the country as a whole, while there may be a diminution in some of the centres. And, generally, in gauging the extent of improvement it would not be right to confine our attention exclusively to special localities or classes, but the entire industrial field should be taken as a whole.

Fifthly, it must be borne in mind that by improvement here referred to must be understood the development of an industrial *régime*, and that the motive power under it being the multiplication of wants and the stimulus given to exertion by the necessity for gratifying them, the dissatisfaction with one's lot that is beginning to be generally felt is in this case a sign of progress and not of deterioration. There is, undoubtedly, increasing pressure felt by the community as a whole, because wants have been increasing faster than the means of satisfying them. At the same time the wants could not increase unless the means increased also. It is this increasing pressure that makes it difficult for people in general to believe that they are making headway, but the real fact is that they are somewhat richer in life from an industrial point of view and their ideal of comfortable existence, is gradually expanding though they may be poorer in contentment. A landholder who would have lived in a simple contented way 40 years ago, giving his boys no education, and marrying his daughters to village boors provided they had a sufficiency to live upon, requires better house accommodation and more comforts, wishes to give his boys an expensive English education and to marry his daughters to educated husbands and finds it a hard pull to arrange for all this; and the very pressure impels him to make increased efforts to increase his means. This result is seen in a district like Tanjore where of brothers in a family who would formerly have lived in their villages in their poor contented way on their patrimony, several leave the villages and seek employment in other distant districts. It is true that the wants developed are not always of a wholesome kind, and this is generally the case when means increase faster than education and taste for rational modes of enjoyment. But the first condition necessary for progress is the increase of wants and when once the desire for improvement is excited, the wants can be regulated by education. For instance when in the sixties, owing to the cotton famine in England and other causes, the ryots in several districts realized large profits, they increased their style of living and spent large sums of money on marriages and festivals. When prices fell, however, they had to cut down expenditure on purposes of mere show, retaining what was necessary for substantial comforts. It is doubtless true that in European countries the evils of the industrial *régime* in the form of undue concentration of wealth making "the rich grow richer and the poor poorer" and of the exploitation of labour by capital have been forcing themselves on public attention, but in this country the conditions are altogether different. Though the old *régime* of status is now being replaced by a *régime* of competition, the transition has been rendered gradual and easy by the tenderness shown to the rights and interests of the lowest classes under the influence of the humanitarian sentiment which is the characteristic feature of the nineteenth century and to which the essentially just and beneficent policy of the British Government in India owes its origin. As we have already seen, the tendency till now in this country has been towards not so much undue concentration of wealth as its diffusion exhibiting itself in the gradual formation of a middle class between the small class of persons who were once immensely rich and who find their hereditary influence and wealth fail them when not supported by individual worth and personal exertions, and the great mass of the population which has always been in a state of great poverty; and owing to this, while perhaps the increase of wealth may go on at a slower rate, it may be that we shall never have to feel the evils of unequal distribution of wealth in the acute form in which they have appeared in European countries.

Bearing, then, these considerations in mind and remembering that methods of progress calculated to evoke national feeling and religious enthusiasm are unavailable under the conditions of the case, the progress that has been made under the new *régime* during the short time that it has been in force —fifty years is a brief interval in the life of a people— is little short of marvellous. Some of the evils which have appeared and the remedies for them we have already noted,

What has been accomplished has been effected chiefly by providing the country with the material appliances of civilization, by clearing the ground of all obstructions to progress and by making it possible for people to take interest in public affairs outside the narrow limits of castes and creeds into which they are divided. What requires to be done is gradually to widen the foundations of local government and make it strike deeper roots into society, so as to enable it to adjust its institutions to its needs as they arise, without weakening in any way the power of the central Government for maintaining the due balance between rival interests and creeds and for interfering effectually when there is danger of such balance being disturbed. And this work will need even greater foresight and statemanship for its successful accomplishment than in the past. There is, however, no reason whatever to suppose that either the Government or the people will fall short of requirements in this respect. As regards the Government, the work already accomplished under enormous difficulties, as narrated in the foregoing pages is a standing testimony in its favour. The quickness with which the people have adapted themselves to the new *régime* affords also every ground for hope that they might be trusted to assimilate the elements of progress even more rapidly in the future. I remember that twenty years ago, complaints were very general that laws were being passed with bewildering rapidity, that society was being shaken to its foundations and that social relations were being loosened to an undesirable degree. Now the feeling among the educated classes, daily growing in importance and numbers, is that progress does not proceed fast enough, just in the same way as persons who were content to travel two miles an hour by country carts thirty or forty years ago consider it a hardship now to travel by slow railway trains moving at the rate of 15 miles an hour.

Whatever might be the feeling of persons who forgetting the evil side of the old type of society and its injustice to the lowest classes, shutting out all prospect of improvement from them, are fascinated by its stationary civilization, ordered relations, and freedom from worry, those who believe in the modern principle of progress and in the necessity for giving free play to individual energy have no reason to look on the future in a spirit other than that of thankfulness and hope. To those again who are inclined to under-value the progress made under the mistaken idea that thereby they would be calling attention pointedly to the evils that now exist in order that great exertions might be put forth to uproot them, I would reply in the following words of Mr. Marshall from whose invaluable work I have so often quoted:

"There is a strong temptation to overstate the economic evils of our own age, and to ignore the existence of similar and worse evils in earlier ages; for by so doing we may for the time stimulate others, as well as ourselves, to a more intense resolve that the present evils shall no longer be allowed to exist. But it is not less wrong and generally it is much more foolish to palter with truth for a good than for a selfish cause. And the pessimist descriptions of our own age, combined with romantic exaggerations of the happiness of past ages, must tend to the setting aside of methods of progress, the work of which, if slow, is yet solid; and to the hasty adoption of others of greater promise, but which resemble the potent medicines of a charlatan, and while quickly effecting a little good, sow the seeds of wide-spread and lasting decay. This impatient insincerity is an evil only less great than that moral torpor which can endure that we, with our modern resources and knowledge, should submit patiently to the continued destruction of all that is worth having in multitudes of human lives, and solace ourselves with the reflection that anyhow the evils of our own age are less than those of the past."

To the considerations pointed out by Mr. Marshall may be added as regards this country the mental distance owing to differences of race, of social usages and civilization between the Government and the people and the necessity for the Government understanding rightly the difficulties of the people, and for the people appreciating the good work done by Government so as to secure their cordial co-operation in measures tending to the advancement and welfare of the country. Full knowledge of either of the difficulties of the other can only arise from sympathy, while sympathy must in its turn result from knowledge. The object I have proposed to myself in writing this humble work of mine is to contribute in some measure to the bringing about of such a mutual understanding.

APPENDICES.

SECTION I.—THE STATE OF THE COUNTRY AND THE CONDITION OF THE PEOPLE IN FORMER CENTURIES.

(A.)—*Sketch of the Dynasties of Southern India extracted from "Lists of Antiquities, Madras," by Mr. R. Sewell, M.C.S.*

In the earliest days of which we have any knowledge as to the sovereignties ruling the Continent of India, it appears that the great Maurya dynasty held the north, while the south was divided amongst the Pāndiyans of Madura, who governed the extreme south, the Cholas, who held the country to their north and east, and the Cheras (Keralas), who ruled over the tracts to their north and west. This was in the fourth century B.C. I say "it appears" because, although we are certain of the Mauryas (probably B.C. 325—188) and the Pāndiyans as existent in the time of Megasthenes (B.C. 302), we have only the fact of the Cholas and Keralas (or Cheras) being mentioned in the inscriptions of Asoka (B.C. 250) to verify their existence at that still earlier period. But tradition mentions no earlier kingdoms than those of Pandiya, Chola and Chera in the south of India, and always speaks of them as contemporary. As we are certain of the Pandiyan, therefore, in B.C. 302, we may safely place the Cholas and Cheras as far back as that date. The Keralas appear to have occupied the whole Western Coast under the ghāts, and it is probable that the Eastern Coast was also inhabited almost throughout its entire length; but there is no evidence of any kingdom having been in existence throughout the Dakhan, and it is quite possible that almost the whole of its entire area was waste (the *Dandakaranya*) or inhabited only by a few half-wild tribes under their own chiefs, such as those so often mentioned in the *Puranas*. It is necessary for students of history to remember that very large areas now cultivated and populated were absolutely waste—mere barren tracts of rock, forest, and wild plains—till comparatively modern times, and this seems especially to have been the case with the Dakhan country. It must not be forgotten, however, that the earliest Buddhist legends speak of the Kingdom of Kalingā as then in existence.

At some period subsequent to that of Asoka, the Pallavas appear to have grown into importance on the Eastern Coast, and they gradually increased in power till they constituted themselves a great kingdom, with extensive foreign trade, and proved a source of danger to the Cholas and their other neighbours. They appear to have held the entire Eastern Coast from Conjeeveram to the borders of Orissa. At present there is no evidence as to when they arose from obscurity into the dignity of a kingdom, but they seem to have been one of the principal southern powers when the first Chālukyas immigrated from Northern India about the fifth century A.D.

To the Mauryas in the north succeeded the Sanga dynasty (B.C. 188—76) and this was followed by the short Kanva dynasty (B.C. 76—31). The last of these kings being murdered, the Andhra or Andhrabritya dynasty succeeded, and ruled from B.C. 31 to A.D. 436. They were Buddhists, and it was by them that the magnificent marble *stupa* at Amarāvatī was erected. About this period, *i.e.*, the fifth century A.D., began to grow into importance the Chālukyan sovereignty of the Western Dakhan, and it is in connection with the early Chālukyas that we hear of the Nalas (probably a Western Coast tribe), the Mauryas (possibly descendants of the earlier Mauryas) who inhabited part of the Konkana, the Sendrakas, Mâtangas (apparently a barbarous tribe, perhaps aboriginal), the Katachchuris, the Gangas of Maisūr, and the Ālupas or Āluvas, a tribe or dynasty apparently living to the south or south-west of the present Bombay Presidency. Early Chālukyan grants mention a number of other tribes, such as the Lātas (of *Latadesa* in the north of Bombay), Mâlavas (of Mâlwa), Gurjaras (of Guzerât), &c.

The Chālukyas divided into two branches in the beginning of the seventh century, an eastern branch conquering the Pallava kings of the Vengī country, or tract between the Krishnā and Godāvāri rivers, and settling in that locality which they governed till A.D. 1023, the western remaining in their original home in the Western Dakhan.

The Chinese pilgrim Hiouen Thsang, who visited India, A.D. 629 to 645, gives a graphic account of the state of the country in his time.

The Kadambas now began to grow into importance, and they fought with and defeated the Pallavas of Kañchī and were perpetually at feud with the Chālukyas and their other neighbours. Their territory was in the south-west Dakhan and north Maisūr. About the same period we find the Rāshtrakūtas giving great trouble to the Chālukyas. It is as yet uncertain whether these Rāshtrakūtas were "an Aryan Kshatriya, *i.e.*, Rājput, race which immigrated into the Dakhan from the north like the Chālukyas or a Drāvidiyan family which was received into the Aryan community after the conquest of the Dakhan" (*Dr. Buhler*). The wars with the Rāshtrakūtas seem to have resulted in the complete downfall for two centuries (A.D. 757—58 to 973—74) of the Western Chālukyas and the consequent accretion of great power to the Rāshtrakūtas. The latter do not appear, however, to have attempted any conquests in the south. They were completely overthrown by the Western Chālukyas in A.D. 973—74, when the latter once more rose to great eminence. The overthrow of the Rāshtrakūtas, too, enabled the Ratta *Máhāmandalésvaras* to assert themselves, and their dynasty lasted till about A.D. 1253. About the same period we find the Śilāhāras and Sindas rising into importance, and, like the Rattas, establishing independent dynasties which lasted for several centuries. The Śilāhāras were overthrown by the Yādavas of Devagiri about A.D. 1220, and the Sindas ceased to be heard of about A.D. 1182—83.

Little is known of the history of Southern India for two or three centuries immediately preceding the sudden rise of the Cholas to great power, which took place in the middle of the eleventh century. At the beginning of that century the Eastern Chālukyas held all the country along the Eastern Coast from the borders of Orissa as far south as the borders of the Pallava country. The Pallava kingdom was a powerful one, possessing the coast from its junction with the Chālukyas down to the northern border of the Chola territories, *i.e.*, just south of Kañchī. The Cholas remained within their own borders and the Pāndiyans in theirs, while the Kongu kings, who governed (apparently) the old Chera country east of the Malayālam tracts along the coast, although they were still independent and powerful, were beginning to feel the effect of the attacks of the little kingdom of the Hoysāla Ballālas, then rising into power and destined to subvert many of the surrounding monarchies.

In A.D. 1023, by an intermarriage between the two dynasties, the Chola sovereign acquired possession of the whole of the Eastern Chālukyan dominions. This was followed, apparently at the beginning of the reign of his successor, Rājendra Kulottunga Chola (1064—1113), by the complete subversion of the Pallavas by the Cholas, and the annexation to the latter kingdom of their possessions. Rājendra also conquered the Pāndiyans, and established a short dynasty of "Chola-Pandiyan" kings at Madura. A little later the Hoysāla Ballālas entirely overthrew the Kongu kings and seized their territories, so that the whole of the south of India passed at that time through a period of great political disturbance, which resulted in the Cholas obtaining almost universal sovereignty for a short period, checked, however, by the power of the Hoysāla Ballālas above the ghāts in Maisūr.

This latter power was increased in importance by its conquest of the Kādambas and Kālachuris to its immediate north about the beginning of the thirteenth century, and by the downfall of the great Western Chālukyan dynasty about A.D. 1184, which was caused partly by its wars with the Kadambas and partly by the rise of the Ballālas. A little later the Cholas lost their northern possessions, which were seized by the Ganapatis of Orangal.

We now find ourselves in the thirteenth century, the three great southern powers being the Cholas and Pāndiyans—both seemingly losing strength—and the Hoysāla Ballālas, rapidly growing in power. What might have occurred it is needless to enquire, though imagination readily depicts the impetuous Ballālas sweeping down from the ghāts and succeeding in subverting the ancient dynasties of the plains; but a new power now appears on the scene, which was destined to acquire universal dominion in course of time—the power of the Musalmáns.

Delhi had been captured by the Ghazni Ghōrians in 1193, and a dynasty established there which lasted till A.D. 1288. The Khiljis succeeded (1288—1321), and Alaū-d-din Khilji despatched the first Muhammadan expedition into the Dakhan in A.D. 1306. Four years later the Musalmán armies under Malik Kāfur swept like a torrent over the peninsula.

Devagiri and Orangal were both reduced to subjection, the capital of the Hoysāla Ballālas was taken and sacked, and the kingdoms both of the Cholas and Pāndiyans were overthrown. Anarchy followed over the whole south—Musalmán Governors, representatives of the old royal families, and local chiefs being apparently engaged for years in violent internecine struggles for supremacy. The Ballālas disappeared from the scene, and the kingdoms of Devagiri and Orangal were subverted. A slight check was given to the spread of the Muhammadan arms when a confederation of Hindu chiefs, led by the gallant young Ganapati Rāja, withstood and defeated a large Muhammadan army; and the aspect of affairs was altered by the revolt of the Dakhānī Musalmáns against their sovereign in A.D. 1347, which resulted in the establishment of the Bāhmani kingdom of the Dakhan. But the whole of Southern India was convulsed by this sudden aggression of the Muhammadans, and all the old kingdoms fell to pieces.

This period, then, about the year A.D. 1310, is to be noted as the second great landmark in South Indian history, the first being about the period 1023—1070, when the Cholas became almost supreme over the south.

While the Bāhmani rebels were consolidating their kingdom in the Dakhan, another great power was being formed south of the Krishnā. This was the kingdom of Vijayanagar. Established on the ruins of the Hoysāla Ballālas and the other Hindu sovereignties, it speedily rose to a height of power such as no southern kingdom had yet aspired to, and it held the Muhammadans in check for two centuries. From 1336 till 1564 A.D. we have merely to consider, roughly speaking, two great powers—that of the Musalmáns north of the Krishnā and that of Vijayanagar to the south.

The Bāhmani kingdom fell to pieces at the close of the fifteenth century, being succeeded by five separate kingdoms founded by rival Musalmán leaders. Their jealousies aided the Vijayanagar sovereigns in their acquisition of power. In 1487 Narasimha of Vijayanagar completely subverted the Pāndiyan country, Chola having fallen long before, and by the close of the fifteenth century the power of Vijayanagar was acknowledged as paramount through the entire peninsula. Small principalities existed, such as that of Maisūr, the Reddi chieftainship of Kondavīdu south of the Krishnā (which lasted from 1328 till 1427), and the always independent principality of Travancore, but Vijayanagar was supreme. At the beginning of the sixteenth century Krishnadeva Rāya of Vijayanagar further extended the power of his house by the reduction of refractory chiefs far and wide, till his dynasty arose in his day to its greatest height of glory.

In 1564 (the third landmark) all this collapsed. The Muhammadan sovereigns of the Dakhan combined, and in one grand effort swept over Vijayanagar, sacked the capital, put to death the powerful chief who had ruled over the destinies of the empire, and for ever crushed out all semblance of independent Hindu power from the south of India. Even the very family that governed Vijayanagar divided, so that it becomes almost impossible to trace their history, and for a second time the whole of the peninsula was thrown into confusion.

Naturally the minor chiefs seized this opportunity for throwing off all fealty to their sovereign, and throughout the peninsula arose a large number of petty Poligars and small chieftains, whose quarrels and wars and struggles for supremacy kept the whole country in confusion for two and a half centuries. The only chiefs that attained to real power were the Madura Nāyakkas, formerly Viceroys of

Vijayanagar, who speedily became independent and reduced to subjection almost the whole of the old Pāndiyan kingdom, their compatriots, the Nāyakkas of Tanjore, holding sway over *Choladēsa*. The Rājahs of Maisūr, too, became independent, and established a kingdom, though not a very powerful one.

Over all this distracted country the Muhammadans gradually pressed downwards, securing the dominion of the countries south of the Tungabadrā, and eastwards to the sea, and encroaching southwards till they had reached the southern confines of the Telugu country, by the middle of the seventeenth century, and by the beginning of the eighteenth were in power far south. The Mahrattas had established themselves in Tanjore in 1674 and remained there till the English supremacy. In 1736 the Musalmáns obtained possession of Madura.

The English, settled at Madras since 1639, now began to acquire more and more territory and power, and in the course of the century had conquered almost the whole of the south of India, the defeat of the Maisūr Musalmáns under Tīpū Sultān in 1799 finally laying the peninsula at their feet.

(B.)—*Orissa under Hindu and British Administrations.*

Practically, the revenue-paying parts of Orissa under the Gangetic dynasty stretched from the Hugli to the Chilka, and from the sea to the Tributary States; a compact territorial entity of twenty-four thousand square miles. The province continues the same size to this day, having lost three thousand square miles on the north, towards the Hugli, and gained about an equal extent on the west, towards Central India. In the twelfth century, when the Gangetic Line obtained the kingdom, it yielded a revenue of £406,250 [326] a year. Besides the doubtful southern strip, they added 12,000 square miles of unproductive hill territory; and when in the sixteenth century they sank beneath the Musalmáns, the revenue remained about £435,000. An early Muhammadan Geographer of the sixteenth century gives the income of the parts of Orissa already subjugated by the Musalmán arms at £368,333 [327]; and the official survey made by Abkar's Minister, *Circ*, 1580, gives the entire revenue of the province, including the tribute from the Hill States, at £435,319 [328]. As the Muhammadans more firmly established their power, they gradually increased the taxation, and in the seventeenth century a detailed list of the Orissa fiscal

---

[326] 1,500,000 Márhas of gold. See note 309, p. 316. That is to say at the close of the Sivaite Dynasty. The area was only 11,000 square miles; but of the territory since added to it to make up the present province, about 12,000 square miles are Hill States paying a tribute of only about £6,000 a year. The few hundred square miles added on the north in Balasor are more productive, and the total revenue of the province may now be put down at £450,000.

[327] Sicca Rs. 3,400,000, or Company's Rs. 3,683,333. *Haft Iklim*, a Persian MS., *apud* Professor Blochmann.

[328] 160,733,237 dáms, which, at the official rates of conversion under Akbar, equal Sicca Rs. 4,018,330, or Company's Rs. 4,353,191. Prinsep's Tables; Thomas' Pathán Kings; As. Res. XV.

divisions shows a revenue of £537,495 [329] However the revenues might be deranged from year to year by tumult or rebellion, the nominal demand remained the same in the Imperial account books; and the Père Thieffenthaler, amid the Mahratta anarchy of the eighteenth century, was still informed that the province yielded £570,750 [330]

The revenue under the Gangetic line (1132—1532 A.D.), its last independent dynasty, may therefore be set down at £435,000 a year from the twenty-four thousand square miles of Orissa Proper. The southern strip had long ceased to yield any income to the Orissa kings. The present province, comprising an equal area, yields to the British Government, in round numbers, £450,000 [331]. But while the actual revenue remains about the same, its purchasing power has completely altered. Under the native dynasty, it sufficed to maintain a gorgeous court, a vast army, innumerable trains of priests, and to defray the magnificent public works of the Gangetic kings. Under the English it barely pays the cost of administering the province. The charges for collecting the revenue and protecting person and property amount to £339,696; the interest on one of the local public works, the Orissa canals, comes to £65,000 a year [332]; a single native regiment at Cuttack costs £17,000; and a petty balance of £28,000 is all that remains over after paying the merely local charges of holding the Province. Orissa contributes scarcely anything to the general expenses of Government. It does not pay its share of interest on the public debt; it contributes nothing to the cost of defending the Empire; and hardly does more than support the charges of the local administration. Under the native dynasty, the same revenue sufficed to support an administration infinitely more minute, and, as regards its higher officials, infinitely higher paid. None of the English governing body in Orissa ever hopes to make a fortune; under the Hindu princes, Government employ was synonymous with assured opulence. Sixteen great ministers regulated the kingdom, with seventy-two deputies, and thirty-six separate departments of State. Under the English, the revenue of Orissa with difficulty maintains seven hundred sepoys; under the Hindu princes it supported, besides a peasant militia of 300,000 men, a regular army of 50,000 foot, 10,000 horse, and 2,500 elephants. About a vast militia being attached to the soil there can be no doubt; and if Hindu chroniclers have magnified the number of the regular troops, we know from the Musalmán annalists, that the Orissa king could at a moment's warning take the field with 18,000 horse and foot. But the public works of the Hindu dynasty attest the magnitude of their resources in a way that admits of no dispute. Thirty or forty-thousand pounds were not considered extravagant for an ordinary temple.

---

[329] Sicca Rs. 4,961,497, or Company's Rs. 5,374,955, under Sháh Jahán, 1627—1658; As. Res. XV. 213.

[330] *Selon Manouchi*, As. Res. XV. 212. This sum may possibly have included outstanding arrears. Mr. Stirling, without stating any grounds, conjectures that it included also the revenue of the Northern Circars; but such a conjecture is opposed to the historical facts of the time, and to the recorded statistics about the Orissa revenue.

[331] The area is 23,907 square miles, but it has lost the fertile tracts towards the Hugli and received in place of it an addition to its hill territory. In 1870 the total revenue was £464,861, but this included the extraordinary income-tax. £450,000 is a fair average in round numbers.

[332] 1½ millions sterling had already been spent on 31st March 1871.

The accumulations of one monarch [333] are stated at £1,296,750 [334] and from this he set apart £406,250 [335] for the holy edifice of Jagannáth. A similar magnificence surrounded the private life of the Orissa kings. Their five royal residences (*Kataks*) still live in popular tradition; and although the story of the prince [336] who died just as he had married his sixty-thousandth wife is doubtless a fable, yet it is a fable that could only be told of a great and luxurious court.

How came it that the same amount of revenue which made the Orissa kings so rich, now leaves the English Governors of the province so poor? I have already shown that the great influx of silver, which European trade poured into India, so decreased the value of that metal that it sank from $\frac{1}{10}$th the value of gold in the twelfth century, to $\frac{1}{14}$th or $\frac{1}{15}$th six hundred years later. But even this decrease would not explain the affluence of the Hindu rulers of Orissa as compared with the poverty of the English. It is when we consider the value of silver as expressed, not in gold, but in food, that the explanation becomes clear. Nothing like a regular record of prices under the Gangetic dynasty (1132—1532) exists. But fortunately the maximum prices of food during the great famines, which in almost each generation decimated Orissa, have come down to us, with the proportion which those prices bore to the ordinary rates. In the famine at the beginning of the fourteenth century, unhusked paddy rose to sixty times its average rate, and sold from six shillings and eightpence to nine shillings per hundredweight [337]. In the next century, under King Kapilendra (1452—1479 A.D.), paddy rose to 62½ times the ordinary price, and fetched from 6*s*. 11½*d*. to 9*s*. 11*d*. per hundredweight [338] Stirling, one of our first Commissioners in Orissa, obtained an ancient paper showing the exact rates under the Gangetic dynasty. According to it, unhusked paddy sold from just under a penny to

---

333 Rájá Anang Bhim Deo.

334 4,788,000 Márhas of gold.

335 1,500,000 Márhas of gold. Purushottama Chandriká, As. Res. XV.

336 Purushottama, in the Solar List of Kings, described on a previous page.

337 The following calculation, the first of the kind in Lower Bengal history, is submitted with diffidence to Indian statisticians. While I believe that the data here collected are absolutely correct, it will be seen that several elements of uncertainty exist. In the famine at the beginning of the fourteenth century, paddy rose to 120 *kahans* per *bharan*. The Orissa bharan will be found fully explained in my Stat. Acc. of Puri, App. 1, p. 16. The paddy bharan contains nominally about 9½, but practically 9 cwt. A káhan is 1,280 cowries, and 4 káhans or 5,120 cowries, were taken as the official rate of exchange per rupee when we first obtained Orissa (in 1803). Afterwards this rate was complained of, on the ground that a rupee cost 6 or 7 káhans instead of 4; and this formed one of the alleged causes of the Khurdha rebellion in 1817. (Mr. Commissioner Ewer's Report to Chief Secretary to Government, dated Cuttack, 13th May 1818, para. 95, O.R.). At present the rate is 3,584 cowries to the rupee, the great difference being due to the fall in the value of silver which has rapidly gone on since we obtained Orissa; and so far as I can judge, the rate officially fixed in 1804 of 5,120 cowries per rupee was considerably under the actual rate of exchange. 120 káhans per bharan of 9 cwt. would be 6*s*. 8*d*. per cwt. at the rate of 4 káhans or 5,120 cowries per rupee, thus: 120 káhans = 30 rupees or 60 shillings; and if 60 shillings buy 9 cwt., the price of 1 cwt. will be 6*s*. 8*d*. On the other hand, if we take the lower or present rate of exchange at 3,584 cowries per rupee, 120 káhans per bharan will equal 9*s*. 6*d*. per cwt. If we take the exchange at the alleged old rate of 6 káhans or 7,680 cowries to the rupee, which I believe to be nearer the truth, the price would be reduced to 4*s*. 6*d*. per cwt. But in this and the following calculations I have taken the rates of exchange which would give the highest possible prices in the fourteenth century, so as to avoid the risk of overstating the rise in prices since then.

338 125 káhans per bharan of 9 cwt., *i.e.*, 6*s*. 11½*d*. at 4 káhans or 5,120 cowries per rupee; and 9*s*. 11*d*. at the lower rate of exchange of 3,584 cowries per rupee.

$1\frac{7}{8}$ of a penny per hundredweight [339], husked rice at $2\frac{1}{8}d.$ to $3d.$ per hundredweight [340], and cotton at from $2s.\ 1\frac{1}{4}d.$ to $3s.\ 0\frac{1}{4}d.$ per hundredweight [341].

From the above calculations we cannot take the price of paddy under the Gangetic line (1132—1532 A.D.) at above $1\frac{1}{2}d.$ per hundredweight. It was probably less. Paddy now costs on the field in Orissa a shilling per hundredweight, or at least eight times its ancient price. An almost equal depreciation in the value of silver has gone on in other parts of India. Thus, in Upper Hindustan, under Alá-ud-din (1303—1315 A.D.), the officially fixed rate of barley was a little under sixpence per hundredweight [342], and of peas fourpence half-penny a hundredweight [343]. In the latter part of the century, under Féroz Sháh (1351—1388 A.D.), the price of barley remained exactly the same, viz., sixpence per hundredweight [344]. But no sooner did the tide of European trade set in, than the value of silver fell, and at the time of Akbar (1556—1605 A.D.) the price of barley rose to $9\frac{1}{2}d.$ per hundredweight [345]. The price of barley in the same localities is now, on an average, about three shillings and sixpence per hundredweight retail, or seven times what it was throughout the fourteenth century.

We may therefore fairly assume that, as estimated in the staple food of the country, the value of silver in Orissa has fallen to $\frac{1}{8}$th of its purchasing power. Wages were regulated then, as now, by the price of rice, and in fact were mostly paid in grain. The Gangetic dynasty of Orissa (1132—1532 A.D.), with a revenue nominally the same as our own [346], were therefore, as regards the home products of the country, and their ability to keep up armies and pompous retinues, eight times richer than we are. The reason clearly appears why a revenue which now barely defrays the charge of collection and the cost of protecting person and property, with one or two absolutely necessary public works, formerly supported a great standing army, a wealthy hierarchy of priests and ministers of State, and a magnificent royal court. As the native dynasty had practically eight times more revenue

---

339 Two káhans per bharan of 9 cwt., *i.e.*, just under a penny, at 6 káhans per rupee; $1\frac{1}{3}d.$ at 4 káhans; and $1\frac{7}{8}$ of a penny at 3,584 cowries per rupee.

340 Ten cowries per Cuttack seer of 105 tolas.

341 One *pan* and 10 *gandas* per seer. If, as seems possible, the rate in ancient times was at six or seven instead of 4 káhans to the rupee, these prices would be a full third less; and the depreciation in the value of silver would be about one-twelfth instead of one-eighth of its former purchasing power.

342 Four *jítals* per *man*. The jítal was $\frac{1}{64}$ of the silver Tanká of 175 grains; or say $\frac{1}{64}$ of the present rupee, or a farthing and a half. The *man* of that *period* contained 28·8 lb. avoirdupois. As barley cost 4 jítals or six farthings per 28·8 lb., the price was a little under six pence per cwt. For a full discussion of these weights, see Mr. Thomas' Pathán Kings of Delhi, p. 161, ed. 1871.

343 Three jítals per *man*.

344 Four jítals per *man*.

345 8 dáms per *man*. The dám was officially reckoned at $\frac{1}{40}$ of a rupee; the *man* then contained 55·467 lb. avoirdupois.

346 The revenue under the Gangetic line may in round numbers be set down at £435,000, and under the English at £450,000 a year. With regard to the present price of paddy, the people consider eight annas a cheap rate for a Cuttack *man*, containing 107 lb. avoirdupois; or as nearly as may be, a shilling a hundredweight. This is the rate on the field; and as will be seen in my Statistical Accounts (Appendices I, II, and IV), the retail price varies in different localities. In Puri district I found that an ordinary rate in good seasons was 210 lb. for two shillings. In Balasor town the price has varied from 240 lb. per rupee in 1850, to 140 in 1870. These are the prices of the common sort of unhusked paddy, the staple food of the people.

to spend than we have, so they practically took eight times more from the people. That is to say, their revenue represented eight times the quantity of the staple food of the province which our own revenue represents.

The truth is, that a whole series of intermediate rights has grown up between the ruling power and the soil. I shall show in the next volume how the native kings of Orissa enjoyed the undivided ownership of the land. Instead of a long line of part-proprietors stretching from the Crown to the cultivator, as at present, and each with a separate degree of interest in the soil, the *plenum dominium* was firmly bound up and centred in the hands of the Prince. The growth of these intermediate rights forms the most conspicuous phenomenon in the history of Orissa under its foreign conquerors. For centuries, under the Musalmáns and Mahrattas, the unhappy province knew no Government but that of the sword; yet the very roughness of the public administration allowed private rights to spring up unperceived, and to harden into permanent charges upon the soil—charges which its native Princes would never have tolerated. Thus from long anarchy and misery a fair growth of rights has blossomed forth, and the magnificence, which the Hindu Princes of Orissa concentrated upon themselves, is now distributed in the form of moderate prosperity among a long-descending chain of proprietors, each with his own set of rights in the land.

* * * *

It is to such miscellaneous imposts as the stamp revenue and salt tax that the British Government of India has to look for the means of carrying on the administration. The native dynasties trusted almost entirely to the land revenue. They managed to raise an annual income variously stated at from £406,250 to £570,750, or say £450,000 a year, between the twelfth and the eighteenth centuries. This almost exactly corresponds, in figures, to the total revenue which, by a great machinery of miscellaneous imposts, we now collect from the province. In actual purchasing power, it amounted to seven times our present revenue, and supported the magnificence of a Hindu Court, with a standing army, an opulent hierarchy, and a costly civil list. Under British rule, the Orissa revenue barely suffices for the charges of the local administration.

Had we dealt with the land as the Native rulers did, and considered it the inalienable property of the State, the land-tax might possibly still have sufficed. But under our more liberal policy of developing private rights in the soil at the expense of the public burdens upon it, the land-tax has become wholly inadequate to the cost of Government. In 1829—30, the land revenue of Orissa amounted to £158,965. In 1836—37, the Government leased out the province for thirty years; and in 1867 the Legislature renewed that settlement for another period of thirty years. It now amounts to £168,286, and no further increase can be hoped for till the end of the century. Meanwhile, the bare cost of Local Government amounts to £422,000 a year; and before the end of the century it will in all probability exceed half a million. Before the expiry of the present leases, the land-tax will yield less than one-third of the merely local expenditure.

If, therefore, the province is to pay its way, Government will be under a constant necessity of raising additional revenue by means of the miscellaneous imposts which are so distasteful to an Indian people.

This difficulty was partly inevitable. No materials have come down showing the precise proportion of the produce of the soil which the ancient Orissa Dynasties took. Many conflicting traditions exist on the subject, and doubtless the proportion varied in different parts of the country. The rich delta of Orissa could afford to pay a larger share to the Prince than less productive arid tracts; and, as a matter of fact, the Rájáh of Parikud, who still maintains his fiscal independence, takes exactly three-fifths of the crop. He, however, like other Hindu Princes, dealt with the cultivators direct. We, on the other hand, have allowed a whole series of intermediate holders, each with his own set of rights, to grow up between the State and the actual husbandmen; and practically not one-tenth of the harvest reaches the public treasury. The following figures will, I think, establish this fact. The three Orissa districts contain 7,723 square miles, or 4,942,720 acres. At least one-half of this, or say two million and a half of acres, are under cultivation. The value of the ordinary crops varies from 10*s*. to £1 16*s*. Taking the low average of 15*s*., the total value of two million and a half of acres would amount to £1,875,000; and a land-tax of ten per cent. would yield £187,500. Now the actual land-tax from all sources amounts to £168,286. While, therefore, a Hindu Prince like the Rájáh of Parikud takes three-fifths as his share of the annual produce of the soil, the British Government obtains not one-tenth of it.

This difference is partly due to the liberality of our land settlement, partly to the growth of intermediate holders; but it is also in a large degree due to the fact that we take our rent in money and not in kind. The rent-roll of an Orissa estate, when offered for sale in the market, is now found, as a rule, to be double its Government land-tax. Of course, extreme instances occur on both sides, but native gentlemen and native officers have alike assured me that this is below rather than above the average. In settling with the landholders in 1837, the Company allowed gross reductions to about one-third of the rent for the charges and risks of collection [347]. The extension of cultivation, with the natural rise in rents, has doubled the landholder's profits during the past thirty-three years; so that, as above stated, the proprietor now generally realizes at least as much again as he pays to Government. The landholder, in his turn, collects from the cultivator as rent from one-half to one-quarter of the actual yield of the land, or say one-third. Government, therefore, as it only receives at most one-half of the landholder's collections, cannot get more than one-sixth of the net yield of the soil. In reality it receives much less. For it takes its share, not in grain, but in silver, which is constantly depreciating in value. This circumstance further decreases by nearly one-half the share which the State actually obtains, and reduces its one-sixth to one-tenth or one-twelfth of the produce of the land. I have shown, on what I believe to be irrefragable evidence, that the purchasing power

---

[347] The theoretical allowance was ten per cent., but the various extra allowances raise it to between thirty and forty per cent. in Orissa—*vide* Vol. I, p. 53.

of silver in India has fallen during the last five hundred years to one-seventh of what it was in the thirteenth century. I propose, very briefly, to prove that this decline, at least in Orissa, is still going on, that it has proceeded at a rapid rate during the present century, and that at the present moment it continues unchecked.

The period of anarchy which preceded our accession in Orissa in 1803 has left few memorials behind it. But I have brought together, from the archives of the adjoining district of Ganjam, a series of papers which illustrate the state of prices a hundred years ago. My materials commence with the year 1778, and they show the average price of unhusked rice, except in years of famine, to have been about 8*d.* a hundredweight, and the price of husked rice 1*s.* 4½*d.* [348]. In Orissa the cost was always about one-third less, and indeed Ganjam imported a large portion of its rice-supply from Puri and Cuttack. This would show the price of paddy in Orissa to have been under 6*d.* a hundredweight; and when we obtained the province in 1803, 6*d.* a hundredweight was considered rather a high price. A shilling per hundredweight is now reckoned a cheap rate for paddy bought on the field at harvest time. In 1771 a bullock sold for 10*s.* which would now cost at least 24*s.*, and a sheep from 1*s.* to 1*s.* 3*d.* whose present price would be at least 4*s.* The whole evidence to be derived from the official records shows that the average price of staple commodities towards the end of the last century was less than one-half their present rates. The wages of laborers bore the same proportion, and palanquin-bearers cost 4*s.* a month who now receive 8*s.*

We have, however, another means of ascertaining the decline in the purchasing power of silver. From time immemorial Orissa, like some other parts of India, has used a local currency of *cowrie*. When the province passed into our hands in 1803, the public accounts were kept and the revenue was paid in these little shells. In granting liberal leases to the landholders, however, we stipulated that they should henceforth pay their land-tax in silver, and fixed the rate of exchange at 5,120 *cowries* to the rupee. For many years after our accession the proprietors bitterly complained that the rupee was worth much more than this rate, and that, in order to make up their revenue in silver, they had to pay the village banker from 6,400 to 7,680 *cowries* per rupee. This was alleged as one of the causes of the Khurdhá rebellion in 1817; and although the hardships may have been exaggerated, the common rate seems to have been from 6,000 to 7,000 *cowries* per rupee. But during the last seventy years the value of silver has steadily declined, and a rupee now only purchases 3,584 of these little

---

[348] In 1778 the price of paddy in Ganjam varied from 7*d.* to 7¾*d.* per cwt.;
,, 1779 .. .. 7*d.* to 7¾*d.*;
,, 1780 .. .. 7¾*d.* to 8¾*d.*;
,, 1781 (a year of scarcity) it rose to 8½*d.*;
,, 1782 .. .. 9¼*d.*;
,, 1783 from .. .. 9¼*d.* to 9¾*d.*;
,, 1784 (a year of famine) it sold at the almost nominal rate of 11*d.*;
,, 1785 it fell to 8*d.*;
,, 1786 .. .. 8¾*d.*;
,, 1787 .. .. 8¾*d.* to 9¾*d.* After that year followed a series of famines and disturbances, which completely disorganized prices, and for a time put a stop to importations. The years from 1789 to 1792 are still spoken of as the period of the first Ganjam famine under our rule.

shells[349]. In 1804 the official exchange was 5,120, and the practical rate of exchange from 6,460 to 7,680.

The purchasing power of silver in Orissa has, therefore, declined to one-half during the last seventy years, whether estimated in the local currency or in the staple food of the province. The depreciation has of late been accelerated by the vast amount of specie expended upon the irrigation enterprises, and by the large payments in silver which have been made to Orissa for rice and other products since the canals opened up the seaboard. These great works practically date from the year 1860, and during the twenty years between 1850 and 1870 prices have risen from one-third to one-half. Thus to take the town of Balasor, which exhibits the rise in its extreme degree. In 1850 the best unhusked paddy sold at 168 pounds per rupee; in 1870 at 84 pounds, or just one-half. Fine cleaned rice was 100 pounds per rupee in 1850; 80 pounds in 1860; and 40 pounds in 1870. Common rice has not risen quite so much, as the cultivation has in the meanwhile extended. It was reported at 120 pounds per rupee in 1850; 100 pounds in 1860; and 70 pounds in 1870. Wheat sold at 33 pounds per rupee in 1850; 29 in 1860; and 18 in 1870.

The rate of wages has risen in proportion. In Balasor, unskilled laborers earned a penny halfpenny a day in 1850; they now get from twopence halfpenny to threepence. Carpenters' wages were in 1850 threepence a day; they are now fivepence farthing. Smiths and bricklayers could be had at threepence three farthings in 1850; they now earn sixpence. If we take the two other large cities in Orissa, Cuttack and Puri, the same results appear. In Cuttack, day-laborers received twopence farthing in 1850; they now obtain threepence three farthings. Smiths got fourpence halfpenny in 1850; they now earn sixpence. Bricklayers' wages have risen more rapidly, or, from twopence farthing in 1850, to sixpence in 1870. In Puri, the money wages are officially returned at the following rates; unskilled laborers in Puri town, fourpence a day; in the rural parts twopence halfpenny. Their wages twelve years ago were twopence halfpenny in the town, and three halfpence in the country. In 1860, smiths and carpenters got threepence three farthings in the town, and twopence in the country; they now get sixpence a day in the town and threepence three farthings in the country. Bricklayers, who used to get fourpence halfpenny in the town twelve years ago, now get sevenpence halfpenny.

Within the last twenty years, therefore, the price of food in the large city of Balasor has almost doubled; and throughout the whole province, so far as statistics exist, it has risen by about one-third. The rates of wages have also increased by upwards of one-third during the same period. That these results are due, not to any altered degree of pressure of the population on the land, or in their demands on the food of the province, is clear from the following fact. While town wages, which are paid in money, have thus risen, agricultural wages, which are paid in kind, have remained absolutely the same. The field-laborer has always earned a lower wage than unskilled workmen in the towns. In 1850 he received from twelve to fifteen pounds of unhusked

---

[349] The rate, of course, varies, but I am informed that 14 *gandas* or 56 cowries per pice has of late been the ruling exchange in the larger marts. This gives 3,584 to the rupee.

paddy per diem according to the locality; and at the present day he receives exactly twelve to fifteen pounds according to the locality. *All wages that are paid in money have risen by more than one-third; all wages that are paid in kind remain the same.*

These, it should be remembered, are the results of only twenty years. During this brief period, silver has lost more than a third of its purchasing power, whether expressed in wages, or in the staple food of the people. Indeed, one District officer reports to me that the price of food has doubled within twelve years. The public revenues have been depreciated to at least one-third of their former purchasing power, whether expressed in wages or in grain. I have already shown that the value of silver, as estimated in the popular or cowrie currency, has fallen thirty per cent.[350] since 1804, even calculated at the rate of exchange which Government then arbitrarily fixed in its own favour. If computed according to the actual rate of exchange then current, it has decreased by one-half. Had our first administrators contented themselves with taking payment in silver at the current rate of the cowrie exchange, the Orissa land-tax would now have been double what it is at present. But had they resolved to collect it at a grain valuation, according to Akbar's wise policy, it would now be more than double; for the prices of food have rather more than doubled since 1804. The system of paying the land-tax by a grain valuation appears to me to be the best means of giving stability to the Indian revenues. In Orissa, it would have enabled us to reduce the salt duty to the easy Madras rate; it would have saved the necessity of an income-tax altogether; and by shorter leases, it would now yield as large an income as the total which we extract by a variety of vexatious burdens.

The experience of the past few years shows that the fall in value of silver still continues. Every morning the Government of India wakes up poorer than when it went to bed the night before. A lakh of rupees in 1850 represented a great deal more in actual purchasing power than a lakh of rupees in 1860; and a lakh of rupees in 1860 represented a great deal more than it did in 1870. Apart, therefore, from the cost of increased efficiency in the administration, the English in India must inevitably go on increasing the miscellaneous public burdens so obnoxious to the people, as long as the land-tax is calculated in silver. The one remedy is a grain valuation, either struck annually or revised at intervals of about five years. It might be possible to suggest several sources of revenue, such as a duty on *Pān*, the aromatic leaf that the people chew instead of tobacco, which would be less unpopular than the income-tax. But miscellaneous imposts, however unobjectionable in themselves, are mere makeshifts and stop-gaps in a fiscal system like that of Bengal. The secret of making India pay is the due conservation of the land-tax; and in order to conserve the land-tax, it must be estimated, not, as in Orissa, upon the so-called rent of the landholder, but upon the actual produce of the soil. Until this necessity is realized and acted upon, every few years will bring a fresh set of financial embarrassments. Under the present system, without adding a single Judge, or Magistrate, or officer of any sort to the Civil List; without granting one of the administrative improvements

---

[350] *I.e.*, $\frac{3,584}{5,120}$ = 70 per cent., showing a decrease of 30 per cent.

which India's rapid advance in civilisation suggests; without undertaking any of the rural public works which a tropical country so urgently requires; without allowing a rupee for bringing our materiel of war up to the modern European standard; the Indian Government will find at the end of each ten years the revenue which sufficed at the beginning of the decade altogether insufficient at the close of it.—*Hunter's "Orissa."*

(C.)—*Extract from the Article on "India" in Hunter's "Gazetteer of India."*

Revenues of the Moghul Emperors at thirteen various periods, from 1593 to 1761,[1] from a smaller area and population than those of *British* India.

Moghul Emperors.	Authority.	Land revenue.	Revenue from all sources.
		£	£
1. Akbar, A.D. 1593.	Nizám-ud-dín; not for all India.	..	32,000,000
Do. ,, ,, ..	Allowance for Provincial Troops [2] (*bumi*) .	..	[2] 10,000,000
			Net 42,000,000
2. Akbar, A.D. 1594..	Abdul Fazl, MSS.; not for all India.	Net 16,574,388	..
3. Do. ,, ,, ..	Official documents; not for all India.	,, 16,582,440	..
4. Do. ,, 1605..	Indian authorities quoted by DeLáet.	,, 17,450,000	..
5. Jehángír, A.D. 1609—11.	Captain Hawkins ..	..	Net 50,000,000
6. Do. ,, 1628	Abdul Hamíd Láhorí ..	Net 17,500,000	..
7. Sháh Jehán, A.D. 1648–49.	Do. ..	,, 22,000,000	..
8. Aurangzeb, A.D. 1655.	Official documents ..	Gross 26,743,970 Net 24,056,114	..
9. Do. A.D. 1670 (?)	Later official documents.	Gross 35,641,431 Net 34,505,890	..
10. Do. A.D. 1695.	Gemelli Careri ..	..	Net 80,000,000
11. Do. A.D. 1697.	Manucci Catrou ..	Net 38,719,400	,, 77,438,800
12. Do. A.D. 1707.	Ramusis	,, 30,179,692	..
13. Sháh Alum A.D, 1761.	Official statement presented to Ahmad Sháh Abdali on his entering Delhi.	,, 34,506,640	..

[1] The above table is reproduced from Mr. Edward Thomas' *Revenue Resources of the Moghul Empire,* published in 1871, and has been revised by him from materials which he has collected since that date.—I insert the words *net* and *gross* by his direction.

[2] This is the lowest estimate at which the *Bumi* or Landwehr, in contradiction to the Royal Army, can be reckoned.—Mr. Thomas' *Revenue Resources of the Moghul Empire,* page 12.

The following statement shows the revenues from the provinces of the Delhi Empire under Emperor Sháh Jehán, 1648-49 :—

In India.

Provinces.	Land-tax.
	RS.
1. Delhi	25,000,000
2. Agra	22,500,000
3. Lahore	22,500,000
4. Ajmere	15,000,000
5. Daulatabad	13,750,000
6. Berar	13,750,000
7. Ahmedabad	13,250,000
8. Bengal	12,500,000
9. Allahabad	10,000,000
10. Behar	10,000,000
11. Malwa	10,000,000
12. Khandeish	10,000,000
13. Oudh	7,500,000
14. Telingana	7,500,000
15. Multan	7,000,000
16. Orissa	5,000,000
17. Tatta (Sind)	2,000,000
18. Baglanah	500,000
Total for all India ...	207,750,000
19. Kashmere	3,750,000
20. Kabul	4,000,000
21. Balkh	2,000,000
22. Kandahar	1,500,000
23. Badakhshan	1,000,000
Total ...	220,000,000

Aurangzeb.—All Northern India except Assam and the greater part of Southern India paid revenue to Aurangzeb. His Indian Provinces covered nearly as large an area as the British Empire at the present day, although their dependence on the central Government was less direct. From these provinces his net land revenue demand is returned at 30 to 38 millions sterling, a sum which represented at least three times the purchasing power of the land revenue of British India at the present day. But it is doubtful whether the enormous demand of 38 millions was fully realized during any series of years, even at the height of Aurangzeb's power, before he left Delhi for his long southern wars. It was estimated at only 30 millions in the last year of his reign, after his absence of a quarter of a century in the Deccan. Fiscal oppressions led to evasions and revolts, while some or other of the provinces were always in open war against the Emperor. The table given below exhibits the Moghul empire in its final development in 1697, just before it began to break up. The standard return of Aurangzeb's land revenue was *net* £34,505,890; and this remained the nominal demand in the accounts of the central exchequer during the next half century, notwithstanding that the Empire had fallen to pieces. When the Afghan invader, Ahmad Sháh Duráni, entered Delhi in 1761, the Treasury officers presented him with a statement showing the land revenue of the Empire at £34,506,640. The highest land revenue of Aurangzeb, after his annexations in Southern India and before his final reverses, was 38½ millions sterling; of which close on 38 millions were from Indian Provinces. The total revenue of Aurangzeb was estimated in 1695 at 80 millions and in 1697 at 77½ millions sterling. The gross taxation levied from British India, deducting the opium excise, which is paid by the Chinese consumer, averaged 35⅓ millions sterling during the ten years ending 1879.

Land revenue of Aurangzeb in 1697 (according to Manucci).		Land revenue of Aurangzeb in 1707 (according to Ramusis).	
	RS.		RS.
1. Delhi	12,550,000	1. Delhi	30,548,753
2. Agra	22,203,550	2. Agra	28,669,003
3. Lahore	23,305,000	3. Ajmere	16,308,634
4. Ajmere	21,900,002	4. Allahabad	11,413,581
5. Guzerat	23,395,000	5. Punjab	20,653,302
6. Malwa	9,906,250	6. Oudh	8,058,195
7. Behar	12,150,000	7. Multan	5,361,073
8. Multan	5,025,000	8. Guzerat	15,196,228
9. Tatta (Sind)	6,002,000	9. Behar	10,179,025
10. Bakar	2,400,000	10. Sind	2,295,420
11. Orissa	5,707,500	11. Doulatabad	25,873,627
12. Allahabad	7,738,000	12. Malwa	10,097,541
13. Deccan	16,204,750	13. Berar	15,350,625
14. Berar	15,807,500	14. Khandeish	11,215,750
15. Khandeish	11,105,000	15. Bedur	9,324,359
16. Baglanah	6,885,000	16. Bengal	13,115,906
17. Nande (Nandair) ..	7,200,000	17. Orissa	3,570,500
18. Bengal	40,000,000	18. Hyderabad	27,834,000
19. Ujain	20,000,000	19. Bijapur	26,957,625
20. Rajmahal	10,050,000		
21. Bijapur	50,000,000		
22. Golconda	50,000,000		
Total ..	379,534,552	Total ..	292,023,147
23. Kashmere	3,505,000	20. Kashmere	5,747,734
24. Kabul	3,207,250	21. Kabul	4,025,983
Grand Total ..	386,246,802 or £38,624,680	Grand Total ..	301,796,364 or £30,179,686

The above lists have been taken from Edward Thomas' Resources of the Moghul Empire, pages 46 and 50.

(D.)—*Extract from the Journal of the Archæological Survey of India, Vol. IV.*

Translation of a copper-plate grant, dated the 23rd year of Rajendra Chola (probably A.D. 1046).

Hail to Kōvirājakēsaripanma, the *Chakravartī* Śri Kulōttungaśōḷadēva, swaying his sceptre over all the directions of the west sea of Vikkḷar and Siṅgaḷar (Ceylon). He, in the twentieth year of his reign, while graciously seated on *Kāliṅgarāyaṉ*, the temple throne placed in the *Tirumañjanaśālai*[1] inside the temple of the town of Ahavamallakulakaralpuram otherwise called Ayirattaḷi, was requested by the king of

[1] The apartment in the temple where water is stored for bathing the idol.

Kiḍāra to exempt the villages belonging to the temple of Rājēndraśōḻaperumballi and Rājarājaperumballi which were built in Sōḻakulavaḻḻipaṭṭaṉa, situated in Paṭṭaṉakkūṟṟu division of the fertile country of Keyamāṇikkavaḷanāḍu from the taxes of *antarāya*,[2] *vīraśīshai*,[3] *panmaipaṇḍaveṭṭi*[4] and *kundāli*[5] and to permit the exchange of the possession of lands from the old inhabitants to the temple. Thus at the request of the king of Kiḍāra which was reported by his messengers, we graciously issue this order to our agent, Rājarājamūvēndavēḷāṉ, to execute copper plate document to this effect. The lands and produce belonging to the temple of Rājarājaperumbaḻḻi, which was built in Sōḻakulavaḻḻipaṭṭaṉa in the division of Paṭṭaṉakkūṟṟu of the fertile country of Keyamāṇikkavaḷanāḍu; ninety-seven and three-eightieths and a-hundred-and sixtieth[6] (*vēlis*[7]) of land in Ānaimaṅgalam of Paṭṭaṉakkūṟṟu are now fixed in the possession of the temple in exchange of the owners with the calculated[8] paddy produce of 8,943 *kalams*, 2 *tūṇis*, 1 *kuruṇi*, and 3 *nāḻis*, and the settled[9] paddy produce of 4,506 *kalams;* 12¾ (velis) of lands given to Brāhmans of Ānaimaṅgalam with the calculated produce of 400 *kalams* and the settled paddy produce of 560 *kalams ;* 27¾ and $\frac{3}{80}$ and $\frac{1}{160}$ (velis) of land in Muñjikkuḍi of this country with the calculated paddy produce of 2,779 *kalams,* 1 *tūni* and 4 *nāḻis* and the settled paddy produce of 1,806 *kalams ;* 106 $\frac{1}{16}$ (velis) of land in Āmūr of Tiruvārūr division, with the calculated paddy produce of 10,606 *kalams,* 2 *tūnis* and 2 *kuruṇis* and settled produce of 5,850 *kalams,* 70¾ and $\frac{9}{40}$ (velis) of land in Ṇāṇalūr, otherwise called Vaḍakudi of the country of Alanādu, with the calculated paddy produce of 6,514 *kalams,* 5 *kuruṇis* and 1 *nāli* and the settled paddy produce of 2,840 *kalams.* 10 $\frac{2}{20}$ and $\frac{1}{80}$ and $\frac{1}{160}$ and $\frac{1}{320}$ and $\frac{3}{1280}$ (velis) of land of Kīḻachandirappādi of this country with the calculated paddy produce of 1,012 *kalams* and 5 *kuruṇis ;* 60¾ (velis) of land given as donations to the Brahmans of Pālaiyūr of this country with the calculated paddy produce of 1,000 *kalams* and the settled paddy produce of 1,500 *kalams.* 87¼ (velis) of land in Puttakkudi of Kurumbūr division of the fertile country of Jayaṅkondaśōḻavaḷanādu with the calculated paddy produce of 8,720 *kalams* and the settled paddy produce of 6,107 *kalams;* 3$\frac{3}{20}$ (velis) of land in Udayamārṭṭāṇḍanallūr of Idaikkaḻinādu of the fertile country of Vijāyarājēndrāśōḻavaḷanāḍu with the calculated paddy produce of 12 *kalams* and 5 *kurunis* and the settled paddy produce of 135 *kalams,* 3 *kurunis* and the settled dry land paddy produce of 78 *kalams* and 5 *kurunis* as favorably fixed during the settlement of taxes. Half of this the above stated lands and produce shall be in the enjoyment of this temple and the other half shall cover the several expenses of *antarāya,*

---

[2] It may possibly be interpreted import duties.

[3] Fees given to the temple at marriages—a practice which in all Hindu societies continues to this day.

[4] Fee for the use of old paths.

[5] *Kundāli* is an axe for cutting wood (generally fuel wood for use in the houses). It is not plain whether by this the ancient Chōḻa kings also levied a tax on the use of arms, or whether it is a tax on cutting firewood in forests.

[6] The Tamil way of expressing fractions. The mode of expression would be lost if it were translated 97$\frac{7}{160}$ instead of 97$\frac{3}{80}$ and $\frac{1}{160}$.

[7] The measurement of land is not given. The grant being in the Tañjore district, according to the way of calculation there we may roughly translate *velis.*

[8] and [9] Calculated and settled paddy produce. Even now the lands have these two systems, the former calculated produce having been fixed in past times.

panmaipandavetti, and other taxes incurred in money or paddy by this village. Thus for the exemption from taxation and for the exchange of the lands from the former owners to the temple we issue this order.

Thus $31\frac{3}{4}$ and $\frac{2}{20}$ and $\frac{1}{320}$ (velis) of land within the four boundaries with all the taxes of *antarāya* and *panmaipandavetti* and others exempted we give to the temple.

Note.—The terms "calculated produce" and "settled produce" in the above inscription probably refer to the gross produce and the portion of it representing Government share. If this surmise be correct, the Government share, it will be seen, exceeded a half in some cases. In one or two cases there must be a mistake in the transcription of the inscription as the "settled produce" given exceeds the "calculated produce." It is assumed that the figures representing the superficial contents of lands denote "velis"—a veli being equivalent to $6\frac{2}{3}$ acres. "Veli" is an ancient measure and there is no tradition current in the Tanjore district showing that either the extent of a veli has been altered or that any other land measure was at any time in use.

The following extract from a grant, dated A.D. 1084 by Kulothunga-cholà shows the taxes and seigniora l dues levied in the times *of the Cholas* in the Tanjore district.

* * * *

may you enjoy the several trees and the enjoyment and cultivation of mango trees; may you have the privilege of opening up big oil-presses; may you enjoy the upper irrigation and straining in the channels that, passing through this village, irrigate other villages; may you enjoy the upper irrigation and straining in the channels that, passing from other villages, come to this village. The cocoa and palmyra trees cultivated in this village shall not be climbed up by the *Īlavar* [10]; may you enjoy the privilege of the planting of (pillars for) *toraṇas* [11] as befitting your position. For the enjoyment of the above rights; may you enjoy also the *nāḍāṭchi*, the *ñirāṭchi*, one *nāli* (of rice collection) for every *vatti* (platter), one *nāli* (of rice collection) on (the days sacred to) the manes, the tax on weddings, the (tax on) washer-men's stones, the tax on potters, the rent on water, the leaves collection, [12] a cloth for (every) loom, the brokerage, the taxes on gold-smiths, the tax on neatherds, the tax on sheep, the good cow, the good bull, the watch of the country, the guana, tortoise, frog and others of the kind in the common embankments inside (the village); may you enjoy the right of sowing *Kār*, the supreme management, the *ikudi* petitions and other rights even without the exception of the lands used for raising good crops. For the enjoyment of the above rights, may you enjoy also the right of irrigating by obstructing the water by embankments, of straining and allowing the flow of the current. May

---

[10] Literally the polluted, by which term is meant the *nádars* or *sānārs*, commonly called the toddy-tree climbers.

[11] The gate of a house in Sanskrit, but it also means festoons strung of green leaves, generally mango leaves.

[12] For manure or to be used as dishes for eating in taking meals.

you enjoy the right of the upper irrigation and straining in the channels irrigating this land; in these channels none (else) shall enjoy the right of cutting up branch channels, of obstructing the water, of shutting up the lower sluices, of raising up the water by obstructions, and of lifting up water by baskets. Let none obstruct the common running water or use that water for purposes of irrigation by obstructing its course. Let none raise round-about storeyed houses and mansions or sink unwalled wells or enjoy the proceeds of the cocoanut trees yielding (cocoanuts), *damanakam* [13], *marū* [14], *iruvēli* [15], *senpaka*, the blue lily, mango, jack, areca-nut, palmyra.

(E.)—*The following abstract shows the revenue in paddy which a number of villages in the Chola and other countries assigned to the temple at Tanjore by the Chola King Rajaraja deva in the 29th year of his reign (end of the tenth century) had to pay to the Tanjore temple as recorded in the inscriptions on the walls of the temple.*

Names of villages.	Extent of tax-paying lands.	Revenue payable in paddy.
	VELIS.	KALAMS.
1. Palaiyur (Inganadu)	125½	12,530
2. Arappar do.	107½	10,745
3. Kirandevankudi in Inganadu	41	4,070
4. —— do.	21¾	2,183
5. —— do.	115	11,526
6. Tannirkunram do.	34	3,378
7. Kirvadugakkudi do.	26½	2,600
8. —— do.	6¾	674
9. Usikkannangudi do.	5½	518
10. Vadaviraiyanpallam do.	23¾	2,393
11. Arakkankudi (Tirunaraiyurnadu)	6¾	656
12. Pidaraseri do.	5½	535
13. Nerkuppai (Tiramunadu)	37	3,722
14. Maruttuvakkudi (Innambarnadu)	29¾	2,967
15. Tiruttevankudi (Tiruvalinadu)	29¾	2,900
16. Anpanur (Mipalaru)	75¾	5,850
17. Ingaiyur (Kilpalaru)	42¾	4,278
18. Panamangalam (Kilpalaru)	40¾	4,072
19. Sattanpadi do.	18¾	1,883
20. —— do.	4½	469
21. Mandottam do.	14½	1,456
22. Iraiyanseri do.	11¾	1,169
23. Venkonkudi do.	48	4,784
24. Maganikudi do.	23	2,315
25. Siru Semburai do.	6	612
26. Turaiyur do.	149½	14,888
27. Karimangalam do.	11	1,083

Note.—The denomination in which the extent of lands mentioned in the inscriptions is given, has not been specifically stated, but it is assumed to be "Velis" (1 veli = 6⅔ acres) the local land measure in use in the Tanjore district from time immemorial. The "kalam" grain measure referred to is equivalent to 12 adavallan merkals. An adavallan is a somewhat smaller merkal than that now in use. The old merkal was reported in the beginning of the century to contain 192 tolas of rice. The present merkal contains 240 tolas.

---

[13] and [14] Fragrant shrubs.

[15] *Iruvēli* is a shrub, the roots of which are very fragrant.

SECTION II.—THE CONDITION OF THE PRESIDENCY AT THE END OF THE 18TH CENTURY WHEN MOST OF THE PROVINCES OF SOUTHERN INDIA WERE ACQUIRED BY THE BRITISH.

(A.)—*Extracts from official reports showing the condition of the several districts at the time they came under British administration.*

Northern Circars—Ganjam, Vizagapatam, Godávari (*acquired from the Nizam in* 1766), *Kistna* (*acquired from the Nizam in* 1759 *and* 1768), *Palnad* (*acquired from the Nabob of Carnatic in* 1801).—The zemindari lands are situated in the hill country of the western frontier, and in the plains between the hills and the sea. The hill zemindars, secure in the woody and unwholesome heights which they inhabited, and encouraged by the hope of an eventual asylum in the dominions of the Nizam or of the Rajah of Berar, had often furnished examples of successful depredation and unpunished revolt. They were surrounded by military tenants, whose lands were held on stipulations of personal service, and whose attachment to their chiefs was increased by the bond of family connection. These zemindars consisted of three classes: First, the *Velmas* of Tellinga origin, who were driven from the Carnatic in the year 1652 by the Muhammadan arms, and who established themselves on the borders of the Kistna. Second, the *Rachewars*, of the race of ancient sovereigns of Orissa, who were also compelled by the Muhammadans to relinquish the plains of the Circars, and retired to the highland woods that formed their western frontier. Their possessions are principally situated to the north of the Godávari. Third, the *Wooriars* being petty chieftains of the military tribe, who, after the overthrow of the empire of Orissa by the Muhammadans, were enabled, from their local situation, to acquire an independent jurisdiction. Their possessions are chiefly situated in the highlands in the northern division of Chicacole.

The zemindars in the plains could boast of no higher extraction than being descended from the officers and revenue agents of the sovereigns of Orissa, who were employed by the Musalmán conquerors in the management of their new acquisitions, and who appear to have first acquired lands and influence, after the conquest of Aurangzeb, and during the distracted administration of his children.

The military force of the zemindars, like that maintained by the Poligars in the modern possessions under the Madras Government, consisted of three descriptions. First, the *Common* peons, who were paid in money and whose constant attendance was expected. Secondly, the *Mocassa* peons, who were paid by grants of land, subject to a quit-rent only. Thirdly, the *Mannoverty* peons, who consisted of military tenants of a higher order, and who were bound to bring their adherents with them to the field. At the time the Circars came into the hands of the Company, the zemindars were, for the most part, in a very irregular state of subjection to Nizam Ally. During the weakness of his Government and that of his predecessors, they had embraced every opportunity to extend their power, and to assume a degree of independence incompatible with any other character than that of tributary chiefs. In the pursuit of these views, they were assisted by the successive wars and contentions for empire, which followed the death of Aurangzeb in 1707. Amidst these convulsions arose a dispute for the succession to the soubahship of the Deccan, in which Nizam-ul-Mulk, by maintaining himself in opposition to the orders of the Moghul, excited the zemindars to disregard an authority, which then possessed not the means of enforcing their obedience. During the period of Nizam-ul-Mulk's usurpation, little progress was made in reducing these countries to a state of order; and a second contest for the Government of the Deccan arising upon his death in 1749, the confusion of the internal Government was continued and increased. Such was the state of the Northern Circars when obtained by the French. At the commencement of their administration, they made the Zemindars feel the weight of their power; but being called upon to march their troops into different parts of the country, for the purpose of supporting Salabut Jung, before their authority was established, they were soon driven to the necessity of temporizing with those they had attempted to subdue, and disorders ensued, which prevailed from the time the French were expelled the Circars. They reverted to the Government of the Nizam, under whom they continued to the period when they were transferred to the English East India Company. In that interval, the whole system of internal management had become disorganized. Not only the forms, but even the remembrance of civil authority, seemed to be wholly lost

*   *   *   *

By the custom of the Hindoo Government, the cultivators were entitled to one-half of the paddy produced (that is, grain in the husk) depending upon the periodical rains. Of the crops from the dry grain lands, watered by artificial means, the share of the cultivator was about two-thirds. These were the proportions which generally obtained; but particular castes were allowed a larger share, as well as strangers, that is, those ryots who were not fixed residents in the villages. Before the harvest commenced the quantity of the crop was ascertained in the presence of the inhabitants and village servants, by the survey of persons unconnected with the village, who, from habit, were particularly skilful and expert in judging of the amount of the produce, and who, in the adjustment of this business, were materially aided by a reference to the produce of former years, as recorded by the accountants of the villages. The cultivators were at liberty, if they thought it necessary, to make another survey by people of their own; and if any material difference appeared in the two estimates, a third account was taken, under the orders of the village officers. The quantity which belonged to the Government being thus ascertained, it was received in kind or in money. Before the division took place, certain deductions were made from the gross produce, which the Committee will hereafter explain.

Of the plantation or garden culture, which was of greater value than the other descriptions of produce, no larger portion was demanded from the ryots than one-fourth to one-eighth of the entire yearly crop, according to the additional expense, trouble and time required in bringing such articles to maturity, and the distance and hazard of carrying them to market. The rule with respect to these superior articles, as well as small grains, was to assess them with a fixed money-rent, not liable to fluctuation, as the produce might be more or less.

Such were the rights of the ryots according to the ancient usage of the country. In consequence, however, of the changes introduced by the Muhammadan conquest, and the many abuses, which later times had established, the share really enjoyed by the ryots was often reduced to a sixth, and but seldom exceeded a fifth; for instead of the former usage, the expedient of an impost originally founded on a measurement of the arable land, and of additional assessments in proportion to that impost, was generally adopted, and the amount of such additional assessments had no bounds, but those which limited the supposed ability of the husbandman. In those parts of the country where the practice of receiving rents in kind, or by a monied valuation of the actual produce, still obtained, the cultivators were reduced to an equally unfavorable situation by the arbitrary demands and contributions to which they were subjected beyond the stipulated rent. The effects of this unjust system were considerably augmented by the custom which had become common with the zemindars, and to which your Committee have already alluded, of sub-renting their lands to farmers, whom they armed with unrestricted powers of collection, and who were thus enabled to disregard, whenever it suited their purpose, the engagements they entered into with the ryots, besides practising every species of oppression, which an unfeeling motive of self-interest could suggest. If they agreed with the cultivators at the commencement of the year for a rent in money, and the season proved an abundant one, they then insisted on receiving their dues in kind. When they did take their rents in specie, they hardly ever failed to collect a part of them before the harvest time had arrived and the crops were cut, which reduced the ryots to the necessity of borrowing from money-lenders at a heavy interest of 3, 4 and 5 per cent. per month, the sums requisite to make good the anticipated payments that were demanded of them. If from calamity or other cause the ryots were the least remiss in the discharge of their rents, the officers of the renters were instantly quartered upon them, and these officers they were obliged to maintain until they might be recalled on the demand being satisfied. It was also a frequent practice with the renters to remove the inhabitants from fertile lands, in order to bestow them on their friends and favourites; and to oblige the ryots to assist them, when they happened to be farmers, in the tilling of their lands, and to furnish them gratuitously with laborers, bullocks, carts and straw.

In addition to the assessment on the lands, or the shares of their produce received from the inhabitants, they were subject to the duties levied on the inland trade, which were collected by the renters under the zemindars. These duties, which went by the name of Sayer, as they extended to grain, to cattle, to salt and all the other necessaries of life passing through the country, and were collected by corrupt, partial, and extortionate agents, produced the worst effects on the state of society, by not only checking the progress of industry, oppressing the manufacturer, and causing him to debase his manufacture, but also by clogging the beneficial operations of commerce in general, and abridging the comforts of the people at large. This latter description of imposts was originally considered as a branch of revenue too much exposed to abuses to be entrusted to persons not liable to restraint and punishment. It was, therefore, retained under the immediate management of the Government. The first rates were easy, and the custom-houses few; but in the general relaxation of authority prevailing in the Circars, this mode of raising revenue for the support of Government was scandalously abused. In the course of a little time, new duties were introduced under the pretence of charitable and religious donations, as fees to the chokedars or account-keepers, guards and other officers at the stations; as protection money to a zemindar, or as a present to those who farmed the duties. Not only had the duties been from time to time raised in their amount, and multiplied in their number, at the discretion of the zemindars and the renters under them, but they were at length levied at almost every stage, and on every successive transfer of property. Uniformity in the principles of collection was completely wanting; a different mode of taxation prevailing in every district, in respect of all the varieties of goods and other articles subject to impost. This consuming system of oppression had, in some instances, been aggravated by the Company's Government, which, when possessed of a few factories, with a small extent of territory around them, adopted the measure of placing chokies or custom stations in the vicinity of each, for the purpose of ascertaining the state of trade within their own limits, as well as to afford them a source of revenue Under the head of Sayer revenue was also included a variety of taxes indefinite in their amount, and vexatious in their nature, called *moturpha;* they consisted of imposts on houses, on the implements of agriculture, on looms, on merchants, on artificers, and other professions and castes.—(*Extract from the Fifth Report of the Parliamentary Committee for East India affairs*, 1813.)

Nellore District (*acquired from the Nabob of Carnatic in* 1801).—The district of Nellore did not suffer much in comparison with the rest of the Carnatic in the wars which took place in the latter half of the 18th century; and being exempt from the presence of armies, was saved from the devastation and drain on the population inseparable therefrom. Its proximity to the seat of Government, however, exposed it in a peculiar degree to the abuse and mis-government which characterised the Nabob's durbar. The mass of the people were cultivators who were ground down by the renters and left nothing but their ploughs and cattle. There was no monied class. The head inhabitants who had been sub-renters had amassed some wealth, which they hoarded. Persons who lived by trade were few. . . . . . Roads, properly so called, there were none and the lines of traffic were infested by robbers and dacoits. The trade of the district was unimportant and the only outlet for it was by the sea. The chief commodities were grain and tobacco and some cloth, while cattle were exported in some quantity principally to Hyderabad. The trade in cloth was the most considerable at one time. There were a number of Moghul merchants who bought for the market in Bassora and the Persian Gulf, but the English obtained access to those markets about 1800; and the Indian merchandise being undersold, the trade declined. The grain traffic was not great. The demand was chiefly in the southern districts and the only means of transport by sea, on native craft; and the winds prevailing at the harvest season being contrary, the transport was precarious and the trade small. The enormous expense of land carriage was prohibitive. Carts were not obtainable. All goods were conveyed on bullocks (the cost of transporting 1 putti of grain was 1 star pagoda and 5 fanams for every 8 miles in 1805. This is about one-third of the average price of that quantity ruling throughout the district). These difficulties, combined with oppressive customs and other taxation and the insecurity of the roads, completely paralysed trade. The confusion and uncertainty of the revenue system; the oppression of the renters, themselves the victims of the rapacity of the Nabobs and compelled to recoup themselves by exactions from their people; the fraud and venality which had infected all ranks; the poverty of the cultivators who were nine-tenths of the community; their ignorance and apathetic indifference to their own improvement; the stagnation of trade and manufacture consequent on restrictive taxation and general insecurity; the depredations of Poligars and Kavalgars, the supposed guardians of the public security; the total want of a system of judicature; all these combined to produce a state of things wretched in the extreme, and from which it would be vain to hope for sudden or rapid improvement.—(*The Nellore District Manual.*)

Ceded Districts—Bellary and Cuddapah (*acquired from the Nizam in* 1800).—The state of the districts in 1800, when they were ceded by the Nizam, has been thus described: Probably no part of Southern India was in a more unsettled state or less acquainted either by experience or by tradition with the blessings of settled Government, the collection of the revenue being entirely entrusted to zemindars. Poligars and potails each of these became the leader of a little army and carried on destructive feuds with the villages immediately contiguous to him. Bands of robbers wandered through the country, plundering and murdering such travellers as refused to submit to their exactions, while the Government, conscious of its weakness, scarcely attempted to interfere. It is computed that in the year 1800, when the Ceded districts were transferred to the Company's rule, there were scattered through them, exclusive of the Nizam's troops, 30,000 armed peons; the whole of them, under the command of 80 Poligars, subsisted by rapine and committed everywhere the greatest excesses.

Kurnool (*acquired from the Nabob of Kurnool,* 1838).—It is impossible to draw out any history of the revenue management of the country during the time of the Nabobs. There were no laws between the governing and the governed, the taxer and the taxed, except the ruler's own will. The little that we can learn of the internal economy of the country, before the immediate rule of the British, shows us that the manner of imposition of the revenue was most arbitrary and the collection most iniquitous. The whole known history, with the honorable exception of Manauwar Khan's rule, is but a series of acts of oppression and violence on the part of the Nabob, and passive resistance or flight on the part of the people. Mr. Blane, the Commissioner, on the assumption of the country, constantly mentions these facts and shows that the population was about one-half in proportion to that of the surrounding districts. There are, however, now few records of those times extant. The story of their destruction is amusing. The British soldiers who were employed in installing Manauwar Khan on the throne took a fancy to the cloths in which the records were wrapt and pilfered them, throwing the records into inextricable confusion. When Manauwar Khan was fairly seated on the throne, he tried to re-arrange them; but finding the trouble too great, he employed all his elephants and camels for some days to throw them into the river. That flowing tide carried down in its bosom the evidence of many a deed of oppression and many a by-gone story of woe! This act of Manauwar Khan the Mild has effectually thrown the cloak of oblivion over the doings of his ancestors. In this oblivion we perforce must leave them.

It will be, however, as well to record a few of the acts of the last Nabob, to show the state of the country when it was first assumed. The revenue administration was in the greatest disorder and was carried on without any system whatever. No public accounts were kept except by the village officers, and the amount of remittances was carried straight into the Nabob's zenana, that being his only treasury. The amount to be paid by each village was changed according to the caprice of the Nabob, and he would increase his demand without any ostensible reason. When his demands passed all bounds, the people would fly. Then the Nabob would allure them back with promises, and give them a cowle to re-assure them, but as soon as the crops were ready to be cut, he would seize the produce, breaking through his word without scruple. In Nandyál, where there is some valuable cultivation under a fine tank, he played the people this trick for two or three years, until at last they threw up the land, leaving the pariah servants of the village to carry on the cultivation as best they could for the Nabob. In another village, Nannur, he added Rs. 5,000 to the demand, because a horse of that value died there. The inhabitants fled and left the Nabob to continue the cultivation with his own servants and bullocks. —(*Mr. Morris' Report on the settlement of the Kurnool district.*)

Chingleput (*acquired in* 1765 *and* 1801).—The Jaghire was twice invaded by Hyder Ali; in 1768, and in the war of 1780, when he entered it with fire and sword. On the termination of the latter war, in 1784, hardly any other signs were left in many parts of the country of its having been inhabited by human beings, than the bones of the bodies that had been massacred, or the naked walls of the houses, choultries, and temples, which had been burnt. To the havoc of war succeeded the affliction of famine; and the emigrations arising from these successive calamities nearly depopulated the district.

The system of management in the Jaghire, while it was rented by the Nabob, was of the same oppressive and unjust character which marked the administration of affairs in his own territory, the Carnatic. It exhibited throughout a scene of boundless exaction and rapacity on the part of the Government and its officers; of evasion on that of the inhabitants; or of collusion between them and the public servants; while the revenue diminished every year with the cultivation. The husbandman was entitled to a certain standard share of the crop, but a considerable proportion of it was extorted from him under the varied devices of *usual assessment, fixed assessment and additional assessment, durbar khirch*, and by private contributions levied by the revenue officers for their own use.—(*Extract from the Fifth Report of the Parliamentary Committee for the East India affairs*, 1813.)

Trichinopoly (*acquired in* 1792).—Under the Nabob's Government, the revenue had been collected in the irrigated taluks by a division of the produce with the ryots. As a general rule, the crops were equally divided between the Government and the cultivators, after a deduction of 5 per cent. of the gross produce had been made for reaping expenses. This was the ordinary rate of division (*váram*), but in lands irrigated from tanks and also in those which, from their position, were liable to have the crops damaged by inundations, the ryots were allowed to take 55 to 58 per cent. of the gross produce. In newly formed wet lands the cultivator's share (*kudivaram*) was 60 per cent. and in those irrigated by picottahs and other mechanical contrivances, it varied from 65 to 68¾ per cent. The allowances (*sutantrams*) paid to the village artificers, karnams, watchers, cultivating slaves (*Pallars*), and others varied from 23 to 28 per cent. of the gross produce, and were paid by the inhabitants alone out of their share.

In the dry portions of the country, the revenues were collected in some villages according to the sorts of grains cultivated, while in others the assessment varied according to the nature of the soil. The demands were, however, made in a most arbitrary manner, and were invariably increased if the outturn of the crops happened to be better than usual. The collections in these villages were made in money, and not in kind, as in the wet villages.

The sale of grain was a strict monopoly, the price being fixed by the manager. All importation was forbidden, and it was an offence, punishable by exorbitant fines, even to lend a neighbour such small quantities of grain as he might require for his immediate support. The grain was taken from the cultivators at the rate of 7 and 8 fanams [1] per kalam [2], and sold back to them from Government granaries kept up in different parts of the district at 9 and 10 fanams per kalam.

In some remarks that he makes on the system of government prevailing in Trichinopoly before the English got possession of the country, Mr. Wallace remarks that, under the system then in force, the people never knew when the demands on them would cease. The so-called fixed assessments seemed to have been imposed merely with the view of inducing the ryots to cultivate, in the hope that nothing beyond the settled amount in money or grain would be exacted from them. In this hope they were, however, invariably disappointed, and he asserts that, if in any one year the revenues were actually collected according to the fixed rates, this was done merely with the view of inducing the ryots, by this apparent moderation, to increase the extent of their cultivation in the succeeding year, and thus give the managers or their sub-renters an opportunity of doubling their exactions.—(*Trichinopoly District Manual.*)

Tinnevelly (*acquired in* 1d92 *and* 1801).—Colonel Fullerton in 1783 wrote:—"The last, but not the least, considerable of your southern

---

[1] There were 30 fanams to the pagoda, so that one fanam equalled 1 anna 10½ pies of our present currency.

[2] The kalam contained 39 measures of 100 cubic inches.

territories is Tinnevelly. It is a hundred and fifteen miles in length and seventy miles in breadth. A ridge of inaccessible mountains divides it on the north from the wild valleys of Watrap and Outumpollam, belonging to Tippoo Sultan. It stretches to the confines of Madura and Ramnad on the north-east and east, reaches to the sea upon the south, and borders on the west with the Rajahship of Travancore, both terminating near Cape Comorin. Nature has been bountiful to this province. Its surface is generally flat, from the sea-coast till it approaches the mountains on its northern boundary. The rivers by which it is intersected ensure luxuriant crops of rice, and the driest parts yield cotton in abundance. The productions of the neighbouring island of Ceylon would flourish here, and thus render us the rivals of the Dutch in the cinnamon trade; but the peculiar tenure under which the country has been held, the convulsions it has endured from the first intrusions of the Mussalmans in the course of this century, and the depravity of its rulers, have counteracted the benefits of nature. Even when a native Rajah governed Tinnevelly, the flat and open country only was reduced. This was let for specific sums to great renters, who were invested with despotic powers and harassed the peaceful subjects, while various leaders who possessed considerable territory maintained armed forces and withheld their stipulated tribute on the first appearance of disturbance. These chiefs, as well as their subjects, are called Poligars; they amount at present to 32, capable of bringing 30,000 brave, though undisciplined, troops into the field. They have also fortified towns and strongholds in the mountains, whither they retire in cases of emergency. Besides the territory that these Poligars possess under the range of hills that form the northern boundary of Tinnevelly, many of them hold ample tracts in the flat and cultivated country. Adverse to industry, they suffer their own possessions to remain waste, while they invade each other and plunder their industrious neighbours. Such is the dread of these ravagers, that every district in the province has been forced to purchase their forbearance by enormous contributions."

Of the renters employed to collect the revenue, Colonel Fullerton gives the following account:—

"It was not possible for the English Government entirely to repress the misconduct of inferior instruments who are eager to perpetuate oppression and to enforce unusual measures by unprecedented means. The situation of the country rendered it necessary to continue the practice of renting extensive districts to the highest bidder; although every precaution was adopted to prevent the abuse of power, still the collections could not be enforced unless an unrestrained authority were vested in the renter. His object, too, frequently is to ransack and embezzle that he may go off at last enriched with the spoils of his province. The fact is, that in every part of India where the renters are established, not only the ryot and the husbandman, but the manufacturer, the artificer, and every other Indian inhabitant, is wholly at the mercy of those ministers of public exaction.

"The established practice throughout this part of the peninsula has for ages been to allow the farmer one-half of the produce of his crop for the maintenance of his family and the recultivation of the land, while the other half is appropriated to the sircar. In the richest soils, under the cowle of Hyder, producing three annual crops, it is hardly known that less than 40 per cent. of the crop produced has been allotted to the husbandman. Yet renters on the coast have not scrupled to imprison reputable farmers, and to inflict on them extreme severities of punishment, for refusing to accept of sixteen in the hundred, as the proportion out of which they were to maintain a family, to furnish stock and implements of husbandry, cattle, seed and all expenses incident to the cultivation of their lands. But should the unfortunate ryot be forced to submit to such conditions, he has still a long list of cruel impositions to endure. He must labour week after week at the repair of water-courses, tanks, and embankments of rivers. His cattle, sheep and every other portion of his property are at the disposal of the renter and his life might pay the forfeit of refusal. Should he presume to reap his harvest when ripe, without a mandate from the renter, whose peons, canakapillays and retainers attend on the occasion, nothing short of bodily torture and a confiscation of the little that is left him could expiate the offence. Would he sell any part of his scanty portion, he cannot be permitted while the sircar had any to dispose of; would he convey anything to a distant market, he is stopped at every village by the collectors of sunkum or Gabella (transit duties), who exact a duty for every article exported, imported, or disposed of. So unsupportable is this evil, that between Negapatam and Palghautcherry, not more than 300 miles, there are about 30 places of collection, or in other words, a tax is levied every ten miles upon the produce of the country; thus manufacture and commerce are exposed to disasters hardly less severe than those which have occasioned the decline of cultivation.

"But these form only a small proportion of the powers with which the renter is invested. He may sink or raise the exchange of specie at his own discretion; he may prevent the sale of grain, or sell it at the most exorbitant rates; thus, at any time he may, and frequently does, occasion general famine. Besides maintaining a useless rabble, whom he employs under the appellation of peons, at the public expense, he may require any military force he finds necessary for the business of oppression, and few inferior officers would have weight enough to justify their refusal of such aid. Should any one, however, dispute those powers, should the military officers refuse to prostitute military service to the distress of wretched individuals, or should the Civil Superintendent (the 'Superintendent of Assigned Revenues', the Collector of that time), remonstrate against such abuse, nothing could be more pleasing to the renter; he derives from thence innumerable arguments for non-performance of engagements, and for a long list of defalcations. But there are still some other not less extraordinary constituents in the complex endowments of a renter. He unites, in his own person, all the branches of judicial or civil authority, and if he happens to be a Brahmin, he may also be termed the representative of ecclesiastical jurisdiction. I will not enlarge on the consequences of thus huddling into the person of one wretched mercenary of those powers that ought to constitute the dignity and lustre of supreme executive authority."—(*History of Tinnevelly by Bishop Caldwell.*)

Salem (*acquired in* 1792 *from Tippu Sultan*).—That the generality of the peasants who inhabit the Bauramahl are extremely indigent is a truth of which daily experience convinces us. The system of oppression, which obtained in the last Government, and the frequency of destructive wars, have entailed upon them a state of poverty from which nothing but the operation of time, under the fostering influence of moderate taxation, mild laws and the impartial distribution of justice, can relieve them. Far removed from the seat of Government and seldom obtaining substantial redress, even though their complaints should reach the throne, patient of injury because hopeless of relief, and rarely possessing the means by which the venal award might be procured, they were subjected to the unrestrained hand of oppression, which, insatiable in its grasp, preyed indiscriminately on their property, palsied the very nerve of industry, and implanted in their minds a distrust of the intentions of their rulers, which better treatment and more attention to their circumstances have scarcely been able to eradicate. The undistinguishing ravages of war, ever fatal to the industrious husbandman, brought with them an accumulation of distress. Exposed from their centrical situation to the incursions of contending armies and the depredations of unprincipled Poligars, equally mistrusting the power that invaded and the friends who ought to protect them from violence, they had no safety but in flight, no security but what was afforded by inaccessible mountains, from the tops of which they beheld the destruction of their former habitations.—(*Mr. Graham, Assistant Collector, Salem District*—1797.)

* * * *

Malabar (*acquired in* 1792 *from Tippu Sultan*).—"Malabar," says Mr. Brown, Commercial Resident, "when Hyder invaded it, was divided into a number of petty Rajahships, the government of which being perfectly feudal, neither laws nor a system of revenue were known amongst its inhabitants. Owing to the quarrels between the different rajahs and the turbulent spirit of the Nair chiefs, who were frequently in arms against each other, the state of the country was little favorable to the introduction of order or good government. Malabar, however, was then a country very rich in money. For ages the inhabitants have been accumulating the precious metals that had been given them for the produce of their gardens. Hyder's only object, in the countries that he conquered, was to acquire money, and, provided he got plenty of that, he was very indifferent as to the means which his officers took to obtain it. Immediately after the conquest of Malabar, vast sums were extorted from its inhabitants by the military officers and by the Canarese Brahmins placed over the revenues. Of these extortions Hyder received a share; and no want of a system of revenue was felt until these sources began to fail. When he found the assets from Malabar fall short of its charges, he listened to proposals from the rajahs to become tributaries. An estimate of the revenue was made by the abovementioned Brahmins, who, as many of them were to remain with the rajahs as spies on their actions, took care that the estimate should be so formed as to leave a large sum to be divided between them and the rajahs. By this new order of things, these latter were vested with despotic authority over the other inhabitants, instead of the very limited prerogatives that they had enjoyed by the feudal system, under which they could neither exact revenue from the lands of their vassals, nor exercise any direct authority in their districts. Thus the ancient constitution of government (which, although defective in many points, was favorable to agriculture from the lands being unburthened with revenue) was in a great measure destroyed, without any other being substituted in its room. The rajah was no longer, what he had been, the head of a feudal aristocracy with limited authority, but the all-powerful deputy of a despotic prince, whose military force was always at his command, to curb or chastise any of the chieftans who were inclined to dispute or disobey his mandates. The condition of the inhabitants under the rajahs thus reinstated in their governments was worse than it had been under the Canarese Brahmins, for the rajahs were better informed of the substance of individuals and knew the methods of getting at it. In short, the precarious tenures by which the rajahs held their station, joined to the uncontrolled authority with which they were vested, rendered them to the utmost degree rapacious; and not even a pretence was set up for exacting money from all such as were known to have any. There were no laws; money insured immunity to criminals; and innocent blood was often shed by the rajahs' own hands under the pretence of justice. In the space of a few years many of them amassed treasure to an amount unknown to their ancestors; and had it not been for the dread that they entertained of Hyder's calling them to an account of their ill-gotten wealth, their situation under them was better than that which they held before the invasion. The country, however, was daily declining in produce and population, insomuch so that, at the accession of Tippoo, I have reason to conclude, from my own observations, and from the inquiries which I then made, that they were reduced to one-half of what they had been at the time of Hyder's conquest. But still greater calamities were reserved for the unfortunate inhabitants of this country in the reign of the Sultan. During the government of his father, the Hindus continued unmolested in the exercise of their religion, the customs and observances of which, in many very essential points, supply the place of laws. To them it was owing that some degree of order had been preserved in society during the changes that had taken place. Tippoo, on the contrary, early undertook to render Islamism the sole religion of Malabar. In this cruel and impolitic undertaking he was warmly seconded by the Moplahs, men possessed of a strong zeal and of a large share of that spirit of violence and depredation which appears to have invariably been an ingredient in the character of the professors of their religion in every part of the world where it has spread. All the confidence of Sultan was bestowed on Moplahs, and in every place they became the officers and instruments of government. The Hindus were everywhere persecuted and plundered of their riches, of their women, and of their children. All such as could flee to other countries did so; those who could not escape took refuge in the forests, from whence they waged a constant predatory war against their oppressors. To trace the progress of these evils would carry me too far. I mention them only for the purpose of showing how the ancient government of this country was at last completely destroyed, and anarchy was introduced. The Moplahs never had any laws nor any authority except in the small district of Cannanore, even over their own sect, but were entirely subject to the Hindu chiefs, in whose dominions they resided. Tippoo's code was never known beyond the limits of Calicut. During this period of total anarchy, the number of Moplahs was greatly increased, multitudes of Hindus were circumcised by force, and many of the lower orders were converted. By these means, at the breaking out of the war conducted by Lord Cornwallis, the Hindu population was reduced to a very inconsiderable number. The descendants of the rajahs were then invited to join the Company's forces; and, when Tippoo's army had been expelled from Malabar, many Nairs returned from their exile in Travancore; but their number was trifling compared with what it had been at the commencement of the Sultan's reign.

"From this short sketch it is evident that this province, at the time it was ceded, had really no form of government, and required a new system to be framed for its use. The feudal system was broken; and no other kind of administration was known to the rajahs who laid claim to their respective districts than that which they had exercised or witnessed under Hyder, and which was a compound of corruption and extortion. To these men, however, the most unfit that could have been selected, was the whole authority of government over the natives entrusted. Two evils of great magnitude were the consequence of this measure; the extortions and corruptions of the preceding administrations were continued, while the ancient feudal institutions of military service were revived, and all the Nairs thereby attached to the different chieftains, and these again to the rajahs. Nothing could exceed the despotic rapaciousness of these men to oppose which there was no barrier; for it is well known that none of the inhabitants dare complain against a rajah, whatever injuries they may have sustained, assassination being a certain follower of complaint. It is not surprising that under such rulers agriculture did not flourish, and that the fields now cultivated (which in some districts bear but a small proportion to those that are waste) should yield but very indifferent crops."

South Canara (acquired from Tippoo Sultan in 1799).—Canara has, however, now completely fallen from this state of prosperity. The evils which have been continually accumulating upon it since it became a province of Mysore have destroyed a great part of its former population, and rendered its remaining inhabitants as poor as those of the neighbouring countries. Its lands, which are now saleable, are reduced to a very small portion and lie chiefly between the Kundapur and Chandragiri rivers, and within five or six miles of the sea. It is not to be supposed, however, that the whole of this tract can be sold, but only that saleable lands are scattered throughout every part of it, thinner in some places, and thicker in others, particularly in the Mangalore district. There is scarcely any saleable land, even on the sea-coast, anywhere to the northward of Kundapur or anywhere inland from one end of Canara to the other, excepting on the banks of the Mangalore and some of the other great rivers. In the vicinity of the ghâts, the lands are not only unsaleable, but the greater part of them is waste and overgrown with wood. It is reckoned that the population of the country has been diminished one-third within the last forty years; and there can be little doubt but that its property has suffered a much greater reduction. Garisappa, Ankola, and Kundapur, formerly flourishing places, contain now only a few beggarly inhabitants; Honawar, once the second town in trade after Mangalore, has not a single house; and Mangalore itself is greatly decayed.

It may be said that this change has been brought about by the invasion of Hyder; by the four wars which have happened since that event; by Tippoo himself destroying many of the principal towns upon the coast and forcing their inhabitants to remove to Jamalabad and other unhealthy situations near the hills; by his seizing in one night all the Christians, men, women and children, amounting to above sixty thousand, and sending them into captivity to Mysore, from whence one-tenth of them never returned; by the prohibition of foreign trade; and by the general corruption and disorder of his government in all its departments. These circumstances certainly accelerated the change, but taken altogether, they probably did not contribute to it so much as the extraordinary augmentation of the land rent.

A moderate land rent carries in itself such an active principle of prosperity that it enables a country to resist for a long time all the evils attending a bad government, and also to recover quickly from the calamities of war. When it is fixed and light, the farmer sees that he will reap the reward of his own industry; the cheerful prospect of improving his situation animates his labours, and enables him to replace in a short time the losses he may have sustained from adverse seasons, the devastations of war and other accidents. But when an oppressive rent is superadded to all the other mischiefs of a tyrannical Government, the country, however flourishing it may ever have been, must sink under them at last, and must hasten to ruin at a more rapid pace every succeeding year.

Hyder ruined Canara, a highly improved country, filled with industrious inhabitants enjoying a greater proportion of the produce of the soil and being more comfortable than those of any province under any native power in India; but instead of observing the wise and temperate conduct which would have secured to it the enjoyment of these advantages, he regarded it as a fund from which he might draw, without limit, for the expenses of his military operations in other quarters. The whole course of the administration of his deputies seems to have been nothing but a series of experiments made for the purpose of discovering the utmost extent to which the land rent could be carried, or how much it was possible to extort from the farmer without diminishing cultivation. The savings accumulated in better times enabled the country to support for some years the pressure of continually increasing demands, but they could not do so for ever; failures and outstanding balances became frequent before his death.

The same demand and worse management increased them in the beginning of Tippoo's reign. He was determined to relinquish no part of his father's revenue. He knew no way of making up for failures, but by compelling one part of the ryots to pay for the deficiencies of the other; he made them pay not only for those which arose upon the cultivation of the current year, but also for those which arose from the waste lands of dead and deserted ryots which were annually increasing. Severity and a certain degree of vigilance and control in the early part of his government kept the collections for sometime nearly at their former standard, but it was impossible that they could remain so long, for the amount of land left unoccupied from the flight or death of its cultivators became at last so great that it could not be discharged by the remaining part of the inhabitants;

and the collections before the end of his reign fell short of the assessment from ten to sixty per cent. The measure which he adopted for preserving his revenue was that which most effectually destroyed it; he forced the ryots, who were present, to cultivate the lands of the dead and absent; but as the increased rent of their own lands required all their care and labour, by turning a part of it to these new lands the produce of their own was diminished, and they became incapable of paying the rent of either. The effect of this violent regulation was to hasten the extinction of the class of ancient proprietors or landlords; for, many, who might still have contrived to have held that rank, had they been permitted to confine their stock to the cultivation of their own lands, when they were obliged to employ it in the cultivation of those of other people, and when the consequent decrease of the produce left no surplus after paying the rent of Government, sank to the state of laborers. Nothing can more strongly indicate the poverty of a country than when its lands, so far from being saleable, must be forced upon the cultivators, but this practice prevails more or less throughout Canara, and is very general everywhere to the northward of Kundapur.—(*Sir Thomas Munro.*)

(B.)—*A list of moturpha taxes levied in the village of Singanallur in the Coimbatore district taken from the records kept by the kurnam of the village.—The tax was levied on all persons with the exception of land-holders. The following are the rates at which some of the moturpha taxes were levied.—*

	RS.	A.	P.
Salt-tax on each kavali or pot	1	7	6
Tax on cloth-bazaars, first-class, 40 fanams ...	11	12	0
„ on „ second-class, 20 fanams.	5	14	0
„ on „ third-class, 10 fanams ...	2	15	0
„ on barbers, 8 fanams	2	5	8
„ on blacksmiths, 8 fanams	2	5	8
„ on carpenters, 8 fanams	2	5	8
„ on double bullock carts, 8 fanams	2	5	8
„ on weavers, 6 fanams	1	12	3
„ on pack-bullocks, 4 fanams	1	2	10
„ on shanars (toddy drawers), 2 fanams ...	0	9	5
„ on kurumbas (weavers in wool), 2 fanams.	0	9	5
„ on washermen, 8 fanams	2	5	8
„ on pariahs, 3 fanams	0	14	2
„ on neeladuppu (indigo vat), 8 fanams ...	2	5	8
„ on chucklers, 8 fanams	2	5	8
„ on oil-mills, 10 fanams	2	15	0

SECTION III.—THE CONDITION OF THE AGRICULTURAL CLASSES UNDER BRITISH ADMINISTRATION DURING THE 1st HALF OF THE PRESENT CENTURY.

(A.)—*Extract from the "Indian Economist."*

LAND REVENUE: PAYMENT IN KIND, OR IN MONEY.

The causes of the remarkable fall in prices which has almost invariably followed the transfer of territory from Native to British rule, have nowhere, we think, received so satisfactory an exposition as in a paper that appeared in the April number of the old Bombay Quarterly Journal in 1857. We shall make no attempt to recast what was there so well stated, but devote our present space to the reproduction of a part of that paper :—

"It seems to us that there are certain prominent characters by which the British system of revenue and finance is broadly marked and distinguished from that of all the Native Governments which have preceded it, and that in their peculiarities we shall find an adequate explanation of the remarkable phenomenon which we are now considering. The Anglo-Indian financial system differs from that of the Native Governments in the following most important particulars :—

"*1stly.*—The payment of the army, police and other public establishments in cash.

"*2ndly.*—The collection of the land tax in money instead of wholly or partially in kind.

"*3rdly.*—The transfer of a portion of the Indian revenues to England, for the payment of the Home charges, usually and correctly styled—"The Indian Tribute."

"*4thly.*—The creation of a funded public debt, of which the interest has to be paid in cash.

"The charges to be defrayed out of the Indian revenue, being of an inflexible character, could only be met in years of deficient collections by borrowing, and hence they involved the creation of a funded public debt. But they brought about more important consequences still; for, the payment of troops and establishments and the interest of the public debt in cash, of necessity, involved the collection of the revenue in cash too, and the latter measure, however little thought of at the time of its introduction by our Indian Land Revenue Collectors and Financiers, has produced a momentous revolution in the value of property and bearing of taxation in India far exceeding in degree, but similar in kind to that effected in England by the return to cash payments in 1819.

"Under Native rule the land tax was the chief source of revenue and was in great part either levied in kind, or assigned for the support of troops and establishments. There was only a small portion of the whole collected in money, and transferred from the local to the central treasuries. The standing military force kept and regularly paid by the Government was small. The bulk of the troops consisted of a kind of militia furnished by jaghirdars and other landlords, to whom the collection of the taxes was assigned for the support of these levies and for conducting the civil administration of the districts placed under their jurisdiction. The troops or retainers of these feudatories were in great measure maintained on the grain, forage and other supplies furnished by the districts in which they were located. The land tax was in consequence either wholly or partially taken in kind and what was collected in money was generally paid away to parties on the spot, and thus quickly returned into circulation. The hereditary revenue and police officials were generally paid by grants of land on tenure of service. Wages of farm servants and agricultural laborers were paid in grain. Grain also was the common medium of exchange for effecting petty purchases in country towns. The farmer's or laborer's wife took a basketful of grain on her head to market instead of a purse of money, and therewith purchased her week's supplies. The people lived in a rude and simple fashion, having few wants, and knowing little of luxuries. In inland districts the chief imports were salt, metals, and a few luxuries for the better classes; but the value of the whole was inconsiderable and the exports with which these were purchased were, of course, correspondingly limited. In this state of things money was hardly wanted at all, and a small supply of coin sufficed for the realization of the public revenue and the settlement of commercial transactions. But while the quantity of coin in circulation was small, the prices of agricultural produce were well sustained, owing to the limited extent of land in cultivation and the large demand for food by the numerous body of the people employed unproductively as soldiers, retainers, and public officers of all kinds, and the difficulty of supplementing deficient harvests by importations from more favored districts, through the want of good roads or other facilities for the transport of bulky produce. The foreign commerce of the country at large was necessarily confined within very narrow limits. It was only the products of the coast districts and the more valuable commodities of the interior, such as indigo and manufactured goods, that could bear the expense of carriage to the ports of shipment so as to admit of being exported. India, at that time, coveted few of the productions of foreign countries and her most important imports were the precious and common metals, broad-cloths, jewels, and other luxuries for the wealthy.

"The innovations made in the revenue and financial system by the British have, however, effected the most sweeping changes in all of these particulars, and we shall now endeavour to trace their operation on the territory of a native prince passing under the sway of the Company. The first steps taken were to substitute regularly-paid and disciplined troops, located in military stations, for the rural militia of the native feudatories, and a staff of European and native officials receiving fixed salaries, in place of the former mamlutdars and revenue farmers with their followers, who paid themselves by perquisites and other indirect gains, but received very trifling emoluments from the treasury of the State. The next and an all-important step in Anglo-Indian administration was to collect the land tax in money instead of realizing it in kind, according to the practice which had virtually, if not nominally, obtained to a great extent under native rule. The immediate and inevitable consequence of this general enforcement of money assessments was, that the amount of coin, previously circulating and sufficient for the adjustment of the limited transactions connected with revenue and commerce under the native system, proved quite inadequate for the settlement without a derangement of prices of the greatly enlarged transactions resulting from the British system. Under the native system, the sale for cash of a small part of the agricultural produce of a district sufficed to provide for all its liabilities connected with taxation and commerce. Under the British system, on the contrary, twice or, perhaps, three times the quantity of produce had to be so sold in order to provide for the same objects, owing to the whole amount of the land tax being demanded in coin. But the supply of coin remaining as before, the effect of this increased demand for it was of course to enhance its price. The coin in circulation had to perform double or treble the work it had accomplished before. The ryot requiring more cash to pay his money assessment had, of course, to bring more produce to market, which occasioned a glut and brought down prices. And this state of things was aggravated by the demand for grain and forage in the country markets being less than before, owing to the disbanding of the irregular force which had been kept up by the native jaghirdars and other functionaries of the former Governments and to the increased production due to an extension of cultivation by means of these disbanded levies. Prices fell more and more until, in many cases, our Collectors found it to be wholly impossible to collect the full land assessment, and large remissions had to be annually made. The village grain merchants, who are also the village bankers, deprived of a sufficient market at their own doors, were compelled, in order to find money to supply their constituents with, to seek more distant markets for the disposal of the produce left upon their hands in liquidation of advances previously made by them to the ryots. This awakened a spirit of greater enterprise and activity among the commercial classes, which was gradually communicated to the ryots, and laid the germ of that active foreign trade which now advances with gigantic strides, and has already penetrated into the remotest recesses of the interior. This collateral benefit, conferred by the British plan of administration, has fairly set free the spirit of progress long spell-bound in the native mind under the iron fetters of Asiatic customs, far more than compensates India for the period of suffering in which it originated.

"The sufferings of the rural population during this transition period were, without doubt, very severe. The revenue reports of our Collectors in newly-acquired territories abound with harassing descriptions of the depressed condition of the agricultural classes, and with representations of the difficulties they experienced in collecting the land assessment, owing to the great fall in the prices of all descriptions of agricultural produce. The assessments of Sir Thomas Munro in the Madras districts failed from this cause. So did the early Revenue settlement of the Bombay territories, and also the permanent settlement of Bengal, which occasioned the ruin of the first proprietors. And quite recently we have had a striking example of the same phenomenon in the case of the Punjab. It is stated in the report of the Board of Administration for the years 1849-50 and 1850-51, printed for the Court of Directors, that fixed money assessments were substituted in 1847 for the system we found in existence, and that in the whole of the Punjab a reduction of the land tax, equal to 25 per cent., has been effected. The demand for food has not decreased; it has probably increased; for although the army of the late Government has been disbanded, there are not, between the Sutlej and the Khyber, less than 60,000 fighting men with, perhaps, five times that number of camp followers. Hence there is a larger demand than before for food over the country generally, though the market round about Lahore is more limited. The labour employed on canals, roads, cantonments, and other public works must cause the circulation of large sums of money, and increase the demand for food. The pay of our army within the limits (of the Punjab) has been estimated to be equal to one million six hundred and fifty thousand pounds. The expenditure by the various civil establishments, the Commissariat and Executive departments, and the different works in progress under the Board, are probably equal to another million; so that nearly double the Punjab revenues are at present spent in the country. In despite, however, of large reductions (of assessment), the complaints during the past year on the part of the agriculturists have been loud and general. Prices (in many villages) have fallen a half. The cry of over-assessment is loud and general. There has been a very general demand among the agriculturists for a return to grain payments, and to a division or appraisement of the crops every season.

"It is clear from these statements of the Board of Administration that the specie in the Punjab must have been largely increased under our rule, even if we make the most ample allowance for the re-export of a portion of it, remitted by our sepoys and camp followers to their homes in the older provinces. And yet, in the face of this large increase of coin in circulation, prices have fallen nearly 50 per cent. The Board, following the example of our early Collectors, attribute this decline of prices to abundant harvest and extension of cultivation; but it may well be doubted whether the increase of production in the Punjab, up to the time referred to in the Board's report, had more than kept pace with the increased consumption due to the presence of our army, numbering with its camp followers nearly four hundred thousand souls. The phenomenon of a great and sudden fall of prices is not singular, or confined to the Punjab, but was equally observable in other parts of India when they first passed under the rule of the British Government. The fall in the former, as in the latter case, will be of a lasting character, and an explanation for it must be sought in some cause of wider and more enduring action than the casual state of the harvest, or the extension of land under tillage. These circumstances may have contributed to the effect, as already pointed out, but only to a very limited extent. It would also seem to be capable of demonstration that the cause in question cannot be a drain of bullion to meet the tribute paid by India to England, for in this particular instance of the Punjab, bullion was fast flowing into the country when prices were falling, and so of India at large. The tribute has been paid by means of exports of produce, without requiring the transmission of bullion to England, excepting on rare occasions; and the imports of bullion into India have, as already noticed, been, on the whole, very large; so that the metallic currency of all British India must have been rapidly increasing for many years past.

"This remarkable fall of prices, which has almost invariably followed the transfer of territory from Native to British rule, while neither capable of being accounted for by the state of the crops and extent of cultivation, nor by the annual tribute remitted to England, may yet be clearly traced to the extraordinary demand for money occasioned by our collecting the land assessment in cash, and conveying it away from the agricultural district to our large military stations for the payment of the troops located there. A much larger currency than before would clearly have been required under this change of system, in order to sustain prices at the old standard. It was, however, impossible to enlarge the currency so as fully to meet the change, and no attempt to do so was made, or apparently ever thought of. The consequence was, that in order to obtain money for the payment of his assessment, the ryot brought more produce to market than before; but as there was no corresponding enhancement of the demand for it, prices necessarily fell."

(B.)—*Description of the Madras ryot by Mr. Bourdillon in* 1853.

The ryots may be divided into two principal classes—those who are comparatively well-off, the few, and those who are poor, the many. The former in general are either those whose villages or lands were from any cause favorably assessed at the first; or those who have inam or rent-free land in addition to their rent-paying land; or those who have more extensive holdings than common, all of whom have good land and have more or less inam. Individuals of the favored classes, as they are called, who hold their land on easier terms than usual, because belonging to certain castes, are also necessarily better off than others; and, lastly, personal character has its own influence here as elsewhere; the careful and frugal will get rich, and so will the crafty and subtle, skilful to gain the favour of the tahsildar or to supplant a rival.

2. Even among this more wealthy class of agriculturists, the number of those who possess any considerable amount of property is very small. It is difficult to form or to convey an exact idea of their real means, but I will attempt it. I should say that if a man of this class is able to spend 15 or 20 rupees a month, or rather if he can command a value equal to that, for he will rarely see so much money, such a man, I say, may be accounted to be very well off; and that a net income from all sources to the value of from 30 to 50 rupees a month

is very rare among the agricultural classes. Such an income, indeed, is far more in this country than the money amount indicates to English ears. The actual purchasing power of money in this country is sometimes estimated at four times what it is in England, sometimes at six times. Assuming the intermediate proportion of five to one, an income of 20 rupees a month will be equal to one of £120 a year in England; and 30 rupees and 50 rupees a month in this country will be the respective equivalents of £180 and £300 a year in England. In point of fact, indeed, the difference is greater, both because from the nature of the climate, the range of absolute necessaries is here much abridged, and also because the general scale of incomes and style of living throughout all grades of society are so much lower here than they are in our own country. But though the incomes above specified undoubtedly raise their possessors far above want, still they appear small in extreme when regarded as the highest incomes from the possession of land in a very extensive country, and the largest of them certainly confined to an extremely limited number of instances.

3. The dwellings of this class certainly do not indicate much wealth; tiled houses are rarely seen, and masonry walls are still much more rare. The almost universal habitation has mud walls and a thatched roof; the latter of a very flimsy order, and both often much dilapidated: and both walls and roof are the same within as without; the rooms have no ceiling, and their walls no sort of ornament or decoration; rarely even whitewash, and the floor is of simple earth beaten hard. The value of the residence of a ryot of the more wealthy class, of whom I am now speaking, probably rarely exceeds 200 rupees or £20. It may be urged that the habits of the people do not incline them to spend money on improving their dwellings, but that they rather invest savings in jewels or rich cloths for great occasions, or in cattle, or expend them on marriages and other family occasions. There is some truth in this; but though every family above actual poverty possesses some jewels, yet probably very few agricultural families possess to so large a value as 1,000 rupees or £100 for both jewels and clothes; and even supposing an equal value in agricultural stock (and so much would very rarely be met with), the whole aggregate value, £220, equal to £1,100 in England, is extremely small to represent the whole property (exclusive of land) of one of the most wealthy members of the land-holding class; and it is the most wealthy only who possess as much as this.

4. And if we look within their houses, we still find few evidences of wealth, or even of what we should consider comfort. I have already described the interior of the house itself; and as to its contents, there is nothing of what is commonly called furniture. There are no chairs, or tables, or couches, or beds; sometimes there is seen a single rude cot which would be dear at 2 rupees. The inmates for the most part sleep on the earthen floor, with nothing else below them but a mat or a small cotton carpet. They sit on the floor, and from it take their food, which is served in a few brass dishes, or perhaps by preference and not from poverty on a simple plantain leaf. Their usual clothes are simply of cotton, and cost little; and when going

a distance to the Tahsildar's or Collector's cutcherry, for example, they generally travel on foot or, in exceptional cases, usually of age or infirmity, on a pony not worth above 7 or 8 rupees.

5. It may, perhaps, be replied to all this that such are the simple habits of the country, and that the people are satisfied, and require no more. This is no doubt true as a fact, to this extent at least that, in the absence of sufficient promise of success, these people abstain from active effort to better their circumstances. But if it be meant that they choose to be poor when they might be rich; that they are satisfied with the necessaries of life when they might command some of the comforts and luxuries; that they are content to have only their physical wants supplied when they might rise to the perception and enjoyment of intellectual pleasures; then I deny the truth of the assertion. And I must add that, if true in any degree, it would only prove the ignorance and debasement of the people to whom it relates.

6. The foregoing description refers to the better class of ryots, men who are above the world and well off; but the condition of the great majority is much worse. From the official list of puttahs for the Revenue year 1848-49, it is seen that out of 1,071,588, the total number of puttahs (excluding joint puttahs) in the fourteen principal ryotwar districts,[1] no fewer than 589,932, being considerably more than half, are under 10 rupees each, and in fact average only a small fraction above 4 rupees each; that 201,065 are for amounts ranging from 10 rupees to 20, and in fact averaging less than $14\frac{1}{4}$ rupees each; and that 97,891 are for amounts between 20 rupees and 30, and in fact averaging only $24\frac{1}{3}$ rupees; and thus that 888,888 puttahs, out of a total of 1,071,588, or considerably more than three-fourths, are for amounts under 30 rupees, and in fact averaging less than $8\frac{3}{4}$ rupees.

7. Now it may certainly be said of almost the whole of the ryots paying even the highest of these sums, and even of many holding to a much larger amount, that they are always in poverty and generally in debt. Perhaps one of this class obtains a small sum out of the Government advances for cultivation, but even if he does, the trouble that he has to take and the time he loses in getting it, as well as the deduction to which it is liable, render this a questionable gain. For the rest of his wants he is dependent on the bazaarman. To him his crops are generally hypothecated before they are reaped, and it is he who redeems them from the possession of the village watcher by pledging himself for the payment of the kist. These transactions pass without any written engagements or memoranda between the parties, and the only evidence is the Chetty's own accounts. In general, there is an adjustment of the accounts once a year, but sometimes not for several years. In all these accounts interest is charged on the advances made to the ryot on the balance against him.

---

[1] Chingleput. Salem. Madura. Nellore. North Arcot. South Arcot. Tanjore. Trichinopoly. Tinnevelly. Bellary. Cuddapah. Coimbatore. Canara. Kurnool.

The rate of interest varies with the circumstances of the case and the necessities of the borrower; it is probably seldom or never less than 12 per cent. per annum, and not often above 24 per cent.; of course the poorest and most necessitous ryots have to pay the highest.

8. A ryot of this class of course lives from hand to mouth; he rarely sees money except that obtained from the Chetty to pay his kist; the exchanges in the out-villages are very few and they are usually conducted by barter. His ploughing cattle are wretched animals not worth more than from 3½ to 6 rupees each (7 to 12 shillings) and those perhaps not his own, because not paid for. His rude and feeble plough costs, when new, no more than 2 or 3 shillings; and all the rest of his few agricultural implements are equally primitive and inefficient. His dwelling is a hut of mud walls and thatched roofs, far ruder, smaller, and more dilapidated than those of the better classes of ryots above spoken of, and still more destitute, if possible, of anything that can be called furniture. His food and that of his family is partly their porridge made of the meal of grain boiled in water, and partly boiled rice with a little condiment; and generally the only vessels for cooking and eating from are of the coarsest earthenware, much inferior in grain to a good tile or brick in England, and unglazed; brass vessels, though not wholly unknown among this class, are rare.

9. The scale of the ryots descends to those who possess a small patch of land, cultivated sometimes by the aid of borrowed cattle, but whose chief subsistence is derived from cooly labour, either cutting firewood and carrying it for sale to a neighbouring town, or in field labour. The purely laboring classes are below these again, worse off indeed, but with no very broad distinction in condition. The earnings of a man employed in agricultural labour cannot be quoted at more than 20 rupees a year, including everything; and this is not paid in money, but in commodities. As respects food, houses, and clothing, they are in a worse condition than the class of poor ryots above spoken of. But I will endeavour to describe their circumstances a little more particularly.

10. The regular agricultural laborers are usually engaged at the commencement of the season for the whole year. It is customary to advance them a small sum, about 5 or 10 rupees, as a sort of retainer, which, however, is to be repaid when the connection ceases. Frequently they remain without change for years; when a man desires to engage with another master, as he will rarely have been able to accumulate money to pay off the advance received, the sum advanced by the new master goes to pay off the old one. These yearly laborers receive a certain allowance of grain every month, which is usually fixed by the custom of the locality; and at particular seasons, some regular, others occasional, the master makes the servant a small present, also fixed by the local custom. When the wife or children of the laborer work in the fields at weeding, &c., they receive daily hire in grain; and laborers not engaged for the whole year, but only at particular times, are paid in the same manner. The rates of hire are very low. The daily rate varies in different parts of the country from 8 pies (one penny) to 1 anna (3 half-pence); it

is rarely or never above the latter sum for purely agricultural labour, and this is paid not in money but in grain. The occasional presents to the yearly laborers are partly in money and partly in clothes; the entire earnings of a laborer engaged for a year do not exceed from 16 to 20 rupees for that whole term.

11. It appears from the foregoing detail that the condition of the agricultural laborer in this country is very poor. Taking his earnings at the highest rate, viz., 20 rupees a year, this would be equivalent in real value, using the same standard of comparison as above, to £10 a year in England. The English field laborer earns on the average not less than £28 a year, including his extra grains in harvest time; and thus it appears that the real wages of a field laborer in regular employ, his command of the necessaries and conveniences of life, are in this country little more than a third of what they are in England. It is no doubt true that some things are necessaries there which are not so in so high a degree here; the laborer in this country does not need to spend so much on firing, clothing or shelter from the weather as in England; in other words, an equal amount of physical comfort in those respects may be purchased here at a smaller outlay. But making full allowance for this difference, the labourer here will still be found to be much the worse off. In fact, almost the whole of his earnings must necessarily be consumed in a spare allowance of coarse and unvaried food and a bare sufficiency of clothing. The wretched hut he lives in can hardly be valued at all. As to anything in the way of education or mental culture, he is utterly destitute of it.

SECTION IV.—NARRATIVE OF THE PRINCIPAL FACTS BEARING ON THE CONDITION OF THE AGRICULTURAL CLASSES FROM THE MIDDLE OF THE PRESENT CENTURY TO THE PRESENT TIME.

(A.)—*Statement showing the permanent reductions made in different branches of revenue in all the districts during 15 years from* 1841.

Districts.	Year.	Items.	Head to which the item belongs.	Amount.
				RS.
Ganjam	A.D. 1844-45	Tax on priests	Moturpha	40
	Do.	Tax on shepherds	Do.	38
	Do.	Tax on fishermen	Do.	10
	Do.	Tax on sale of dry fish	Do.	8
	1852-53	Tax on cutting and bringing wood from the Colanpoonjah jungle.	Sundry small farms and licenses.	113
	Do.	Tax on cutting and bringing wood from the Chundanea jungle.	Do.	426
	Do.	Tax on cutting mango and tamarind trees in the Moherry fort.	Do.	59
	1844-45	Land Customs	Land Customs	21,310
	1846-47	Duty upon articles imported from ports within the territory of the Honorable Company.	Sea Customs	1,040
	1847-48	Half of the tonnage duty at 1 anna formerly levied upon the several dhonies and vessels.	Do.	414
	Do.	Duty upon British goods exported and imported	Do.	32,171
	1851-52	One-fourth of the duty upon every ton of the foreign and American vessels.	Do.	63
		Total ..	....	55,692
Godávari	1844	Inland and town duties	Land Customs	90,706
	1848	Monopoly of weighing goods in each village in certain taluks annually rented.	Moturpha	6,880

Statement showing the permanent reductions made in different branches of revenue in all the districts during 15 years from 1841—cont.

Districts.	Year.	Items.	Head to which the item belongs.	Amount.
				RS.
Godávari—*cont.*	1848	Gold dust rent on monopoly of purchasing ashes of the furnaces of goldsmiths.	Moturpha	1,590
	1854	Duties on goods exported from or imported into the Nizam's dominions.	Land Customs	4,317
		Total	....	1,03,493
Kistna	1841-42	Tax on sheep and goats	Moturpha	6,410
	1856-57	Do. on do.	Do.	9,585
	1854-55 and 1855-56	Do. on horned cattle in the Nizampatam Circars	Do.	1,255
	1846-47	Do. on the looms of Pariahs	Do.	810
	1843-44	Bootpooroshee or tax on certain classes	Do.	3,256
	1853-54	Town duty or tax on grain brought for sale at Mangalagiri bazaar.	Do.	124
	Do.	Nuzzerana on looms in the Anomully village	Do.	6
	1854	Tax on washing green	Do.	368
	1856	Do. on shepherds	Do.	4,536
	1843-44	Bootpooroshee levied on the huts of toddy drawers	Sundry small farms and licenses.	250
	1856-57	Tax on dates (small) used for making baskets	Do.	200
	1844	General inland and town duties	Land Customs	56,076
	1854-55	Frontier do. do.	Do.	1,742
	1844	Transit duty	Do.	81,820
	1854	Frontier duty	Do.	43,202
	1847-48	Duty on cotton exported to Nizam's territory	Do.	692
	Do.	Do. on goods exported to and imported from British ports	Sea Customs	1,849
	1853-54	Do. on paddy, &c., imported at any of the ports in the district.	Do.	2,076
	1854	Tax on exports and imports	Do.	11,740

Statement showing the permanent reductions made in different branches of revenue in all the districts during 15 years from 1841—cont.

Districts.	Year.	Items.	Head to which the item belongs.	Amount.
				RS.
Kistna—*cont.*	1855-56 and 1856-57	Poollary or grazing tax	Miscellaneous	76,625
	1856-57	Tax on firewood cut in certain jungles on the coast	Do.	800
	Do.	Reduction of assessment in the Mangalagiri taluk	Do.	29,080
	Do.	Reduction of assessment in certain villages on the sea coast	Do.	22,581
	1855-56	Abolition of Toonga rent in Churala village	Do.	642
	1847-48	Rush and rattan rents paid by basket-makers	Do.	74
	Do.	Rent of fishing creeks	Do.	58
	Do.	Tax on collecting cow-dung in two villages	Do.	6
	Do.	Do. paid by petty shopkeepers during the digging of cheyroot	Do.	8
	Do.	Fee on gathering (barian) leaves for platters in the village of Pedda Lanka.	Do.	8
	1847-48	Toonga, Relloo, Awara—Rents of different kinds of grass	Do.	678
	Do.	Tax on spades for digging cheyroot	Do.	7
	1854-55	Do. on fruit trees grown in ryots' fields (estimated)	Do.	400
	1852 (These are petty exactions originated rather by the subordinate officers of Native Governments than by authority, although acknowledged and maintained as customary payments.)	1. Presents made to zemindars, &c., in the Dasara feast	Land Revenue	816
		2. Presents made to the landlord by the farmers for permission to cut the crop.	Do.	1,688
		3. Proportionate contribution on assessment to zillahdars or petty revenue officers.	Do.	1,304
		4. Charges of a purganah or division of estate	Do.	991
		5. Fees to shroff or money-changer	Do.	140
		6. Village charges	Do.	586
		7. Extra assessment collected by zemindars for palan expenditure.	Do.	2,679
		8. Fees to the writer or accountant	Do.	8
		9. Grain allowance to village goddess	Do.	78
		10. Do. to a person employed to watch the produce	Do.	216
		11. Puttah in the name of village goddess	Do.	68
		12. Two handfuls of grain to village servants	Do.	61
		13. Fees to the revenue accountant	Do.	138

Statement showing the permanent reductions made in different branches of revenue in all the districts during 15 years from 1841—cont.

Districts.	Year.	Items.	Head to which the item belongs.	Amount.
				RS.
Kistna—*cont.*	1852 (These are petty exactions originated rather by the subordinate officers of Native Governments than by authority, although acknowledged and maintained as customary payments.)	14. Increase of the price of the Government share of the produce.	Land Revenue	51
		15. Sundry charges	Do.	71
		16. Fee for measurement	Do.	22
		17. Allowance for reaping or cutting the crop	Do.	2
		18. Grain allowance to Brahmins of Peishcars	Do.	23
		19. Grain to peons who watch the produce	Do.	26
		20. Grain to village-watcher	Do.	68
		21. Fees to zemindars	Do.	10
		22. Pagoda fees	Do.	42
	1853	Jungle tax	Do.	115
	1856	Grain allowance	Do.	430
		Inams	Do.	2,002
		Total	....	3,68,599
Nellore	1855	Tax on goldsmiths' ashes	Moturpha	179
	1844	Inland duties	Land Customs	1,07,109
	1848	Duties on exports and imports	Sea Customs	13,000
	1855	Reduction in Mooloom and Jarib or garden assessment	Land Revenue	50,718
	Do.	Do. dry land assessment	Do.	65,921
		Total	....	2,36,927
Cuddapah	1844-45	Duty levied on articles of consumption	Land Customs	1,90,980
	1848-49	Tax on goldsmiths' ashes	Sundry small farms and licenses.	1,519
	1842-43	Pagoda offerings	Do.	1,601
	1844-45	Loss in the exchange of Canteroy pagodas	Miscellaneous	32,000
	1855-56	Reduction in assessment of waste lands	Land Revenue	7,597
		Total	....	2,33,697

Statement showing the permanent reductions made in different branches of revenue in all the districts during 15 years from 1841—cont.

Districts.	Year.	Items.	Head to which the item belongs.	Amount.
				RS.
Bellary and Anantapur.	1855-56	Reduction of "wet" land rates above Rs. 18 for a single crop and Rs. 27 for two crops to those rates respectively.	Land Revenue	1,131
	1842-43	"Goodivaram" on money collected at the native pagodas	Moturpha	681
	1854-55	Sheep tax levied from other classes than shepherds cultivating land.	Do.	1,311
	1843-44	Town duties	Land Customs	71,387
	Do.	Inland duties	Do.	1,31,817
	Do.	Inland duties on the frontier of Kurnool	Do.	13,567
	1845-46	Inland duties on the Soondoor frontier	Do.	838
	1844-45	Do. on the Mysore do.	Do.	1,01,388
	1844-45	Do. on the Nizam's do.	Do.	6,567
	1854-55	Do. on the do. do.	Do.	5,186
	1848-49	Sundry collections made on small farms and licenses	Sundry small farms and licenses.	599
		Total	....	3,34,472
Kurnool	1850-51	Tax on skins	Moturpha	404
	1852-53	Do. vegetable-sellers	Do.	640
		Do. indigo vats	Do.	174
		Do. skins	Do.	198
		Do. lime-kilns	Do.	40
		Do. butchers	Do.	500
		Do. kabob cooks	Do.	30
		Do. contractors for safe delivery of carts, horses, &c., at Hyderabad.	Do.	85
		Do. cattle-grazers	Do.	37
		Do. measurers	Do.	104

Statement showing the permanent reductions made in different branches of revenue in all the districts during 15 years from 1841—cont.

Districts.	Year.	Items.	Head to which the item belongs.	Amount.
				RS.
Kurnool—*cont.*	1853-54	Tax on Mahomedans' houses	Moturpha	275
	1854-55	Do. butchers	Do.	776
		Do. toddy shops	Do.	1,288
	....	Reduction of assessment	Land Revenue	2,595
	....	Customs	Land Customs	11,257
		Total	....	18,403
Chingleput	1843	Higher rate of ryots' share	Land Revenue	677
		Remissions at $12\frac{1}{2}$ per cent.	Do.	661
		Do. at 11 do.	Do.	114
		Do. at 2 do.	Do.	2
		Do. from the usual fixed assessment	Do.	137
		Permanent cowle	Do.	304
		Dasabandam on remission of a portion of public revenue to those who created sources of irrigation.	Do.	51
		Fixed money cowl	Do.	582
		Total	....	2,528
North Arcot	1848	Tax on persons selling betel in the Chittoor and Kaveripak taluks.	Moturpha	19
	Do.	Daily tax on the bazaars, &c., in Ranipet	Do.	147
	Do.	Tax on catching water-fowls in the Kaveripak tank.	Do.	5
	1841	House-tax on bearers in the Satghur taluk	Do.	32
	1848	Tax collected from the bazaarmen at Tirupati and Trichanoore under the denomination of "Viralum Amavasya Punnoo" or new moon tax.	Do.	34

Statement showing the permanent reductions made in different branches of revenue in all the districts during 15 years from 1841—cont.

Districts.	Year.	Items.	Head to which the item belongs.	Amount.
				RS.
North Arcot—*cont.*	1848	Tax collected from the weavers in Tirupati under the denomination of "Parsay Cutnum."	Moturpha	32
	1849	Tax on houses collected in Tirupati under the denomination of "Illoovaripannoo."	Do.	292
	Do.	Tax on skins in the Chandragiri taluk	Do.	3
	1850	Do. in the Kangundi division	Do.	57
	1844	Tax on Congoos of villages collected under the denomination of "Congoetundagem."	Do.	6
	1850	Tax on iron foundries in the Kangundi division.	Do.	66
	Do.	Tax on shepherds collected under the denomination of "Coorootaree" in the Kangundi division.	Do.	18
	1855	Davastanam obayem (festival) tax in the Chittoor, Tiruvallam and Tirvuttoor taluks.	Do.	209
	1856	Tax on the manufacture of saltpetre in the Tiruvallam taluk.	Do.	37
		Tax on the privilege of collecting fuller's earth	Do.	32
	1848	Tax collected from the Pariahs in the Satghur taluk under the denomination of "Maula Sunkeyalum."	Do.	8
	1849	Tax on the privilege of cutting and selling grass in the Chandragiri taluk collected under the denomination of "Pilloovaree."	Do.	1
	1840	Tax on sellers of vegetables	Do.	25
	1849	Tax for collecting honey and wax	Do.	70
	Do.	Tax on the privilege of digging for pipe clay	Do.	15
	1855	Tax on digging for sandal stone	Do.	40
	1849	Tax on the privilege of cutting wood for building houses	Do.	11
	1844	For the entire district	Land Customs	1,12,221
	1845	Frontier customs	Do.	28,147
	1854	Tax on betel-sellers in Walajapet	Moturpha	39
	Do.	Tax collected from the villages of Dasoor in the Wandiwash taluk under the denomination of "Summarathum" or community of small traders.	Do.	37

Statement showing the permanent reductions made in different branches of revenue in all the districts during 15 years from 1841—cont.

Districts.	Year.	Items.	Head to which the item belongs.	Amount.
				RS.
North Arcot—*cont.*	1854	Caval Cundayem tax in the Wandiwash taluk	Moturpha	42
	Do.	Tax on shepherds collected in the Wandiwash taluk under the denomination of "Golla caurum."	Do.	11
	Do.	Tax on betel-sellers in the town of Chittoor	Do.	22
	....	Temporary remission of assessment in anticipation of remission in progress.	Land Revenue	3,49,900
		Total	....	4,91,578
South Arcot	1st September 1854	Duties on various articles liable to Land Customs.	Land Customs	1,41,735
	Do.	Duties on tobacco, betel-nut, bhang and godauk	Do.	17,062
	July 1848	Fee on stamping weights and measures in Cuddalore town	Do.	327
	....	Frontier customs on various articles	Do.	31,851
	July 1848	Duties on cotton wool	Do.	1,111
	July 1851	Duties on various petty articles of consumption	Do.	3,722
	1848	Equalizing the duty on goods imported and exported on foreign bottoms with that levied on British bottoms.	Sea Customs	2,500
	Do.	Tax on temporary shops	Moturpha	12
	1856	Other petty items	Do.	110
	Do.	Duty on washermen's earth	Sundry small farms and licenses.	22
	Do.	Rattan rent	Do.	221
	1853	Chank rent	Do.	50
	1854	Duty on jungle produce, dyeing bark, bees' wax, honey, &c.	Do.	35
	1854 to 1856	Land-tax assessment, &c., and water-rates	Land Revenue 9,63,723. Sundry small farms and licenses 988.	9,64,711
		Total	....	11,63,469

Statement showing the permanent reductions made in different branches of revenue in all the districts during 15 years from 1841—cont.

Districts.	Year.	Items.	Head to which the item belongs.	Amount.
				RS.
Tanjore	1844	Total	Land Customs.	2,89,112
Trichinopoly	1852-53	Tax on bamboos	Sundry small farms and licenses.	1,402
	1853-54	Taxes on trees	Do.	3,790
	....	Roossooms	Miscellaneous	3,275
	....	Saderwar	Do.	6,183
	....	Cawnyvary	Do.	7,721
	....	Nanyarvuttum	Do.	10,989
	....	Yarymera	Do.	151
	....	Kunemera	Do.	46
	1855-56	Land tax	Land Revenue	2,37,602
	1844-45	Land Customs on cloths and sundries	Land Customs	98,748
		Total	....	3,69,907
Madura	1843-44	Tobacco monopoly	Tobacco	63,660
	Do.	Tax on betel	Do.	96,250
	Do.	Customs on drugs, piece-goods, &c.	Land Customs	1,14,761
	1852-53	Kallar Caval fees	Stamp Revenue	35
	....	Rents of honey and bees' wax	Do.	276
	1854-55	Reduction of assessment on tobacco gardens	Land Revenue	6,432
	Do.	Do. on nunjah gardens	Do.	4,596
	Do.	Do. on punjah gardens under wells	Do.	16,506
	1856-57	Abolition of assessment on wet lands in Settanandel villages in Ramnad.	Do.	156
		Total	..	3,02,672

Statement showing the permanent reductions made in different branches of revenue in all the districts during 15 years from 1841—**cont.**

Districts.	Year.	Items.	Head to which the item belongs.	Amount.
				RS.
Tinnevelly	1851-52	Assessment upon 37 descriptions of trees	Land Revenue	4,454
	1853-54	High level nunjah lands watered by means of picottahs, &c., exempted from payment of a moiety of the usual nunjah tax.	Do.	9,088
	1854-55	Revenue derived from petty hill products	Do.	5,780
	1856-57	Nelavary or grazing tax collected from the Nattamygars and shepherds of a few villages in certain taluks.	Do.	106
	1855-56	Abolition of special assessment on trees in inam and puttah land.	Do.	14,672
	1842-43	Arupoogootah of seeking for jewels, bits of precious metal, &c., dropped on the roads.	Moturpha	65
	1843-44	Land Customs	Land Customs	88,557
	Do.	Betel farm rented	Do.	37,120
	Do.	Tobacco rent	Do.	25,336
	Do.	Rent of the duty on cheyroot	Do.	2,700
	1853	Frontier export duty on piece-goods, rape seed, &c., reduced from 5 to 3 per cent.	Do.	24,555
	Do.	Frontier export duty on cocoanut, &c., reduced from 5 to 3½ per cent.	Do.	622
	1847-48	Frontier export duty on cotton wool exported	Do.	3,996
	1850-51	Do. on sundry articles	Do.	762
	1847-48	Export duty on cotton wool	Sea Customs	44,596
	Do.	Do. on sundry articles	Do.	13,882
		Total	....	2,76,291
Coimbatore	1844 to 1849	Duty on piece-goods, &c.	Land Customs	1,80,164
	1853-54	Calacachadam or tax on persons selling tobacco, betel, &c., in the fields during harvest.	Moturpha	393

Statement showing the permanent reductions made in different branches of revenue in all the districts during 15 years from 1841—cont.

Districts.	Year.	Items.	Head to which the item belongs.	Amount.
				RS.
Coimbatore—*cont.*	1850 and 1851	Mudurcutty or tax on basket-makers and house tax on Pariahs, &c.	Moturpha	1,211
	1850 to 1854	Tax on palmyras	Miscellaneous	22,033
	1850 to 1855	Tax on fruit trees	Do.	3,901
	1851 and 1854	Honey rent, tax on dyeing root, hill-rent	Do.	4,378
	1854 and 1855	Reduction of assessment at 12 and 15 per cent. on old gardens.	Land Revenue	68,067
	Do.	Reduction of assessment at ⅓rd of the fixed assessment	Do.	50,543
	Do.	Reduction of assessment on gardens classed with first-rate punjah.	Do.	38,969
	1856	Reduction of assessment on nunjah lands over-assessed	Do.	3,027
		Total	....	3,72,686
Salem	Board's Proceedings, dated 28th March 1844.	Inland duties on goods Farms of betel and tobacco	Land Customs.	1,15,946
	17th March 1845	Transit duties levied on the Mysore frontier	Do.	17,010
	17th March 1851	Tax on cocoanut trees in putcut lands	Land Revenue	1,284
	2nd October 1854	Tax on other trees in putcut lands	Do.	1,953
	By sanction of Government, dated the 10th July 1854.	Land assessment in the Paramatti taluk	Do.	1,662
	By sanction of Government, dated the 20th December 1855, conveyed in Board's Proceedings, dated 24th January 1856.	Assessment on well garden lands in the Talaghaut taluk	Do.	18,310

Statement showing the permanent reductions made in different branches of revenue in all the districts during 15 years from 1841—cont.

Districts.	Year.	Items.	Head to which the item belongs.	Amount.
				RS.
Salem—*cont.* ..	By order of Government, dated 31st May 1855 (Board's Proceedings, dated 29th October 1855).	Tax on scattered trees in unoccupied lands	Land Revenue ..	2,965
		Total ..	....	1,59,130
Canara	1841-42	Tax levied from blacksmiths, carpenters, and weavers ..	Moturpha ..	450
	April 1844	Duty levied on frontier trade and the Halut duty on betel-nut, pepper and cardamoms.	Land Customs ..	2,55,554
	Do.	Duties (sayer) levied on exports of betel-nut, pepper, cardamoms, &c.	Sea Customs ..	2,37,541
	1852	Government tobacco monopoly	Tobacco ..	2,91,141
	1854-55	Duty levied on the manufacture of jaggery from toddy of palmyra and cocoanut trees.	Moturpha ..	323
	1857-58	Tax fixed by herdsmen	Sundry small farms and licenses.	40
		Total ..	....	7,85,049
Malabar	1852-53	Tax on jungle produce	Sundry small farms and licenses.	1,171
	1853-54	Do.	Do.	803
	1854-55	Do.	Do.	1,814
	1848-49	Addakakally or tax on betel-nut dyers	Moturpha	321
	1846-47 and 1847-48 ..	Tiathora or tax on Tiars	Do.	93
	1848-49 and 1849-50 ..	Vannan Jemmem or tax levied from dhobies or washermen ..	Do.	23
	1851-52	Tax on houses below 1 silver fanam or 3 annas and 2 pies ..	Do.	5,002
	1852-53	Tobacco monopoly	Tobacco	5,66,112

Statement showing the permanent reductions made in different branches of revenue in all the districts during 15 years from 1841—cont.

Districts.	Year.	Items.	Head to which the item belongs.	Amount.
				RS.
Malabar—*cont.*	1843-44	Land customs, except frontier duty	Land Customs	1.02.524
	1846-47	Frontier duty	Do.	4,599
		Total	....	6,82,462
Madras	1852	Quit-rent on certain holdings	Land Revenue	58
	1855	Ground rent on lime-kilns	Do.	756
	Do.	License fee on do.	Do.	72
	1844	Land Customs	Land Customs	5,84,963
	1853	Frontier Customs	Do.	199
		Total	...	5,86,048
		Grand Total	....	68,32,215
		Total for the Presidency	Land Revenue	19,42,806
			Moturpha	50,951
			Sea Customs	3,60,872
			Land Customs	32,23,365
			Sundry farms and licenses.	15,103
			Abolition of tobacco monopoly.	10,17,163
			Miscellaneous	2.21,955
		Grand Total	....	68,32,215

(B.)—*Extracts from Dr. Buchanan's "Journey from Madras through Mysore, Canara and Malabar in* 1800."

Bhavâni, Coimbatore district.—The hinds, or servants hired for the year by the farmers, are here called *Padiyals*, and are on the same footing with the *Batigas* of *Karnata*. They sometimes bind themselves for a number of years, in which case the master advances money for their marriage expenses, and deducts so much from their monthly pay, until he is repaid. Unless tied down by some stipulation of this nature, they may change their service whenever they please. A servant gets from his master a house, and from fifteen to twenty *Gopáláy fanams* or from 5*s.* to 6*s.* 8*d.* a year, with a monthly allowance of twenty *Vullas* or $1\frac{10}{1000}$ bushel of grain. Their wives, when they are able to work, have daily wages. Day laborers at harvest time, whether men or women, get daily one *Bulla* and a half (rather more than $\frac{1}{2}$ bushel) of the grain called *Cumbu*. At weeding the crops, the daily wages are one *Bulla* of *Cumbu*, or about $\frac{10}{32}$ of a bushel. A man working with a hatchet or pickaxe gets one *Gopáláy fanam* (about 4*d.*) a day; carrying earth in baskets, or the like, he gets $\frac{3}{4}$ of a *Gopáláy fanam*, or 3*d.* ; and porters, for carrying a load eight *Urnalivullies*, or *Malabar* hours' journey, get two *Gopáláy fanams* or nearly 8*d.*

On the houses of the Natives in Coimbatore district.—I went ten *Malabar* hours' journey to Navaputty; that is, the nine villages, having formerly been the principal of nine adjacent hamlets. It is a sorry place, containing about 20 houses. The huts of the country, called *Chera*, are like beehives, and consist of a circular mud wall about three feet high, which is covered with a long conical roof of thatch. Contrary to what might have been expected in a hot climate, but agreeably to the custom of almost all *Hindus*, one small door is the only outlet for smoke, and the only inlet for air and light. Each family has a hut for sleeping, another for cooking, and a third for a store-house. Wealthy men add more huts to their premises, but seldom attempt at any innovation in the architecture of the country.

On the condition of the people (Northern division of Coimbatore).—The cultivators and peasantry continue exactly in the same dress, and same houses, that they used in Tippoo's government, and have a prejudice against changes. Major Macleod thinks that their women are beginning to wear more gold and silver ornaments than they formerly did. The merchants and manufacturers are evidently improving in their manner of living, are forsaking their pyramidal or conical huts, and are erecting tiled houses. To enable them to do this, Government, without charging interest, advances money which is repaid by instalments.

On the poverty of the peasantry (Dhárápuram, Coimbatore district).—Mr. Hurdis thinks that the present rents are greatly too high; and no doubt, the peasantry here, as well as in almost every part of India, are miserably poor. I am inclined to think, however, that other causes contribute more to this than the greatness of the rents. Mr. Hurdis says that all the land which is not cultivated is by no means unlet (*Tirsi*); but owing to the want of rain and of stock, the farmers are not able to cultivate the whole of what they rent. This, in my opinion, shows that the fields are by no means over-assessed; and that the farmers, if they would not grasp at more than they have stock to manage, might be in a much more comfortable situation. One great cause indeed of the poverty of the farmers, and consequent poverty of crops in many parts of India, is the custom of forcing land upon people who have no means of cultivating it. Thus all the lands are apparently occupied; but it is in a manner that is worse than if one-half of them were entirely waste. I believe every intelligent farmer in England will say that one acre fully improved will give more profit than two that are half cultivated.

On servants employed in agriculture (Dhárápuram).—The servants employed here in agriculture are hired in the beginning of the year for twelve months. They may change their service when their term expires if they be not in their master's debt; but as he generally advances money for their marriages and other ceremonies, they are seldom at liberty to go away. They get twenty *bullas* of rough rice (*paddy*) a month with four *fanams* and one *siliga* of rough rice yearly, and their master pays their house-rents. The whole is about 31 bushels of rough rice, of which one-half is husk, with two shillings in money, besides the house-rent which will not exceed one or two shillings a year. These servants generally have one wife, who at seed time and harvest works for the master for daily wages. A woman's daily wages are four *puddies* of grain worth about nine-tenths of a penny. A man gets six *puddies* of grain. A servant with these wages can once or twice a month procure a little animal food. Milk is too expensive. His common diet consists of some boiled grain, with a little salt and capsicum, and perhaps some pickles. His drink is the water in which the grain was boiled. He has very little clothing, and that little is extremely dirty; his house is a hovel, and he is commonly overrun with vermin and cutaneous disorders. The women, although not clean, are fully clothed.

On servants and price of labour (Pollâchi, Coimbatore).—There are here two kinds of servants employed by the farmers to cultivate the lands; they are called *padiyals* and *pungals.* The *padiyals* receive yearly 3 *podis* of grain (29 bushels), worth 48 *Vir'-Raya fanams,* with 10 fanams in money, and a house. The 58 fanams are equal to £1 8*s.* 9½*d.* The wife and children of the padiyal are paid for whatever work they perform. He is hired by the year; but if he contracts a debt with his master, he cannot quit the service till that be discharged.

The pungals go to a rich farmer, and for a share of the crop undertake to cultivate his lands. He advances the cattle, implements, seed, and money or grain that is necessary for the subsistence of the pungals. He also gives each family a house. He takes no share in the labour which is all performed by the pungals, and their wives and children; but he pays the rent out of his share on the division of the crop, which takes place when that is ripe. If a farmer employs six pungals to cultivate his land, the produce is divided into 15 portions, which are distributed as follow :—

To the farmer, or punnadi, for rent, seed, &c. ...	6
To do. do. for profit	1
To do. do. for interest of money advanced	2
To the pungals or laborers	6
	15 portions.

Out of their portions the pungals must repay the farmer the money which he has advanced for their subsistence. The farmers prefer employing padiyals, when they can be procured; but among the laborers the condition of the pungals is considered as preferable to that of the padiyals. Six-fifteenths of the whole produce is indeed a very large allowance for the manual labour bestowed on any land, and as the farmer can afford to give it, the rents must be moderate.

Pálghat, Churmars, or Slaves.—By far the greater part of the labour in the field is performed by slaves or churmars. These are the absolute property of their devarus, or lords, and may be employed on any work that their masters please. They are not attached to the soil, but may be sold or transferred in any manner that the master thinks fit; only a husband and wife cannot be sold separately, but children may be separated from their parents, and brothers from their sisters. The slaves are of different castes, such as Parriar, Vullam, Canacun, Erilay, &c., and the differences in the customs by which the marriages of these castes are regulated occasion a considerable variation in the right of the master to the children of his slaves according to the caste to which they belong. The master is considered as bound to give the slave a certain allowance of provisions: a man or woman, while capable of labour, receives two edangallies of rice in the husk weekly, or two-sevenths of the allowance that I consider as reasonable for persons of all ages included. Children and old persons past labour get one-half only of this pittance, and no allowance whatever is made for infants. This would be totally inadequate to support them; but the slaves on each estate get one-twenty first part of the gross produce of the rice in order to encourage them to care and industry. A male slave annually gets 7 cubits of cloth, and a woman 14 cubits. They erect for themselves small temporary huts that are little better than large baskets. These are placed in the rice-fields while the crop is on the ground, and near the stacks while it is thrashing.

There are three modes of transferring the usufruct of slaves. The first is by jenmum, or sale, where the full value of the slave is given, and the property is entirely transferred to a new master, who is, in some measure, bound by his interest to attend to the welfare of his slave. A young man with his wife will sell for from 250 to 300 fanams, or from £6 4*s.* 1½*d.* to £7 8*s.* 11½*d.* Two or three young children will add 100 fanams, or £2 9*s.* 7¾*d.* to the value of the family. Four or five children, two of whom are beginning to work, will make the family worth from 500 to 600 fanams or from £12 8*s.* 3*d.* to £14 17*s.* 11*d.* The second manner of transferring the labour of slaves is by kanom or mortgage. The proprietor receives a loan of money, generally two-thirds of the value of the slaves; he also receives annually a small quantity of rice, to show that his property in the slaves still exists; and he may reassume this property whenever he pleases to repay the money borrowed, for which in the meanwhile he pays no interest. In case of any of the slaves dying, he is held bound to supply another of equal value. The lender maintains the slaves and has their labour for the interest of his money and for their support. The third manner of employing slaves is by letting them for patom, or rent. In this case, for a certain annual sum, the

master gives them to another man; and the borrower commands their labour and provides them with their maintenance. The annual hire is 8 fanams (3*s*. 11½*d*.) for a man and half as much for a woman. These two tenures are utterly abominable; for the person who exacts the labour and furnishes the subsistence of the slave is directly interested to increase the former and diminish the latter as much as possible. In fact, the slaves are very severely treated, and their diminutive stature and squalid appearance show evidently a want of adequate nourishment. There can be no comparison between their condition and that of the slaves in the West India islands, except that in Malabar there are a sufficient number of females who are allowed to marry any person of the same caste with themselves, and whose labour is always exacted by their husband's master, the master of the girl having no authority over her so long as she lives with another man's slave.

Manapuram, Malabar.—At Manapuram a slave, when 30 years old, costs about 100 fanams, or £2 14*s*. 7*d*.; with a wife he costs double. Children sell at from 15 to 40 fanams, or from 8*s*. 2¼*d*. to 21*s*. 10*d*. A working slave gets daily three-tenths of a poray of rough rice, or about 36½ bushels a year. He also gets annually 1 fanam for oil and 1½ fanams for cloth, which is just sufficient to wrap round his waist. If he be active, he gets cloth worth 2 fanams, and at harvest time from 5 to 6 porays of rough rice. Old people and children get from one to two-thirds of the above allowance, according to the work which they can perform.

Támracheri, northern division of Malabar.—The daily allowance here established for slaves is of rough rice—

	Cubical inches.	Bushels.
To able-bodied men, 6 nallis heaped	= 148¼	yearly 25⅕
To able-bodied women, 6 nallis streaked	= 103½	,, 17½
To old persons and children—3 nallis heaped	= 74¼	,, $12\frac{6}{10}$

The average, allowing one child and one old person to every two men and two women in the prime of age, will be $18\frac{4}{10}$ bushels, of which one-half is husk. When the scarcity that usually happens every year prevails, they get part of their allowance in yams (*Dioscoreas*), jacks (*Artocarpus*) or plantains (*Musa*). When harvest is over, they receive each, according to their activity, a present of 3 or 4 porays of rough rice, or from 1 to $1\frac{4}{10}$ bushels, which will make the annual average about 9½ bushels of rice. Their masters give them also some salt, oil and pepper, and they are allowed to keep fowls. Each person has annually three pieces of cloth. The slaves say, what indeed cannot be doubted, that they are much better used by their own masters than when they are let out on mortgage (kanom) or hire (patom).

Tellicherry, Malabar.—The farmers (cudians), whether cultivating rice ground or plantations, according to Mr. Rodriguez, live very poorly, although they get almost four-fifths of the grain, and at least one-third of the produce of the taxable trees. They mostly labour with their own hands, there being few slaves. The hired servants, who are chiefly Tiars, work only from half-past six in the morning until noon, and get as daily wages 2½ edangallies of rough rice. All the afternoon they labour for themselves. The edangally containing 108 cubical inches, a man by half-a-day's work, allowing one-seventh of his time for holidays, can gain 39¼ bushels of grain. Although the cudians may therefore live in a very inferior condition to an English farmer, it is impossible that they should live scantily; while a day laborer by working only half of the day can procure so much grain.

Cherikal, Malabar.—In Cherikal and Cotay-hutty there are slaves, chiefly of the Poliar and Pariar castes; but the greater part of the cultivation is carried on by panicar or hired men, who are Nairs, Moplahs and Tiars. These panicars are at liberty to change their service whenever they please, unless they be indebted to their master; and about one-half of them are in that state. They work from morning to noon, when they are allowed an hour for breakfast. They then work until evening, and all night they watch the crops. The master gives the servant a hut, a piece of cloth twice a year, from 6 to 12 silver fanams (27½ to 55 pence) annually for oil and salt; and a daily allowance of rice, which is larger than that given to the slaves. When the servant is in debt, stoppages from this allowance are made. The panicars are frequently flogged; and as their masters are not bound to provide for them in old age, or during famine, they seem to be in a worse condition than the slaves. Their wives and children, if they do any work for their master, get wages.

Mangalore, South Canara.—The cultivation is chiefly carried on by culialu or hired servants; but there are also some muladalu, bought men or slaves. A hired man gets daily 2 hanies of clean rice or annually 21¾ bushels, together with 1½ rupee's worth of cloth, a pagoda in cash, and a house. A hired woman gets 1⅓ rupees for cloth, and three-fourths of the man's allowance of grain. In the planting season the woman hired by the day gets 2 hanies of rice, or 128½ cubical inches. These wages are very high, and may enable the hired servants to keep a family in the greatest abundance. It is evident from this that the stock required to cultivate eight morays of land was excessively exaggerated by the proprietors. The wages in grain alone would amount to 156½ morays of rice for 8 morays sowing, so that to pay even then would require at least 40 seeds. We may safely allow 6 morays for each plough fully wrought; but the number of ploughs in the whole district amounts to rather less than 1 to 3 morays of rice ground in actual cultivation according to the revenue accounts, owing, probably, to a want of cattle and other stock. At the end of the year, the hired servant may change his service, if he be free from debt; but that is seldom the case. When he gets deeply involved, his master may sell his sister's children to discharge the amount, and his services may be transferred to any other man who chooses to take him and pay his debts to his master. In fact, he differs little from a slave, only his allowance is larger, but then the master is not obliged to provide for him in sickness or in old age.

A male slave is allowed daily 1½ hany of rice, or three-fourths of the allowance of a hired servant; a woman receives 1 hany. The man gets 1½ rupee's worth of cloth and 2 rupees in cash; the woman is allowed only the cloth. They receive also a trifling allowance of oil, salt, and other seasonings. A small allowance is given to children and old people. When a slave wishes to marry, he receives 5 pagodas (2 guineas) to defray the expense. The wife works with the husband's master. On the husband's death, if the wife was a slave, all the children belong to her mother's master; but, if she was formerly free, she and all her children belong to her husband's master. A good slave sells for 10 pagodas, or about 4 guineas. If he has a wife who was formerly free and two or three children, the value is doubled. The slave may be hired out, and the renter both exacts his labor and finds him subsistence. Slaves are also mortgaged; but the mortgagor is not obliged to supply the place of a slave that dies, and in case of accidents the debt becomes extinguished, which is an excellent regulation. Free men of low caste, if they are in debt or trouble, sometimes sell their sisters' children, who are their heirs. They have no authority over their own children who belong to their maternal uncles.

Honavar, in Canara.—In the farms of the Brahmans most of the labor is performed by slaves. These people get daily 1½ hany of rice; a woman receives 1 hany. Each gets yearly 2½ rupees' worth of cloth, and they are allowed time to build a hut for themselves in the cocoa-nut garden. They have no other allowance, and out of this pittance must support their infants and aged people. The woman's share is nearly 15 bushels a year, worth rather less than 14¼ rupees; to this if we add her allowance for cloths, she gets 16¾ rupees a year, equal to £1 16*s.* 8½*d.* The man's allowance is 22¼ bushels, or 23¾ rupees, or £2 3*s.* 0½*d.* A male free servant, hired by the day, gets 2 hanies of rice; both work from seven in the morning until five in the evening; but at noon they are allowed half-an-hour to eat some victuals that are dressed in the family as part of their allowance, and every caste can eat the food which a Brahman has prepared.

Sersi, North Canara.—In this country a few slaves are kept; but most of the labor, even in the grounds of the Brahmans, is performed by the proprietors, or hired servants. The Haiga Brahmans toil on their own ground at every kind of labor, but they never work for hire. The hired servants seldom receive any money in advance, and consequently at the end of the year are free to go away. No warning is necessary, either on the part of the master or of the servants. These eat three times a day in their master's house, and get annually one blanket, one handkerchief, and in money 6 pagodas, or 24 rupees, or £2 8*s.* 4¼*d.* Their wives are hired by the day and get 1½ seers of rough rice and 3 dudus, of which 49½ are equal to 1 rupee. In so poor a country these wages are very high. A male slave gets daily 2 pucka seers of rough rice, with annually one blanket, one handkerchief, a piece of cotton cloth, and some oil, tamarinds, and capsicum. He gets no money, except at marriages; but these cost 16 pagodas, or £6 8*s.* 11½*d.*, for, the woman must be purchased. She and all her children of course become the property of her husband's master. The woman-slave gets daily 1¾ seers of rough rice, a blanket and annually a piece of cotton cloth, and a jacket. Children and old people get some ready-dressed victuals at the house of the master, and are also allowed some clothing. The men work from sunrise till sunset, and at noon are allowed one Hindu hour, or about 24 minutes, for dinner. The women are allowed till about 8 o'clock in the morning to prepare the dinner, which they then carry to the fields and continue to work there with the men until sunset.

Soonda, in Canara.—A farmer who has five ploughs is esteemed a rich man. With these he must keep 6 men and 6 women and 10 laboring cattle, and at seed-time and harvest he must hire additional laborers. Farmers who are not Brahmans, unless their farms be large, work the whole with their own families; but rich men must hire servants, or keep slaves, and to hold their plough Brahmans must always have people of the low castes. This is a kind of work that even a Haiga Brahman will not perform.

A man-slave gets daily 2 seers of rough rice, or yearly about 26 bushels, worth £1 2*s.* 0½*d.*, a handkerchief, a blanket and a piece of cloth worth 2 rupees (4*s.* 0¼*d.*), a pagoda in money (8*s.* 0¾*d.*), 6 candacas of rough rice at harvest (14*s.* 6*d.*); total £2 8*s.* 7½*d.* The women get one piece of cloth annually, and a meal of ready-dressed victuals on the days that they work, which may amount annually to 8*s.* 1*d.* Hired men get four seers of rough rice a day, worth less than three half-pence.

Nagara.—Most of the cultivation is carried on by the families of the cultivators; there are very few hired servants, but a good many slaves, by whom, on the farms of the Brahmans, all the ploughing is performed. A slave gets annually 1½ rupees for a blanket, 3 rupees' worth of cotton cloth, quarter rupee for a handkerchief, 6 candacas of rough rice worth 4 rupees to procure salt, tamarinds, &c., and daily 1½ colaga of rough rice, or annually 27½ candacas (or almost 49 bushels) worth £1 16*s.* 11¾*d.*; add the annual allowances 17*s.* 7¼*d.*, the total expenses of maintaining a male slave one year is £2 14*s.* 7¼*d.* A woman-slave gets as follows: 365 colagas of rough rice, one daily, and 3 candacas at harvest, in all 21¼ candacas or 36¼ bushels, worth $14\frac{1}{16}$ rupees; 2 rupees' worth of cloth, and quarter rupee for a jacket, in all nearly 16⅓ rupees or £1 13*s.* 2*d.* The marriage of a slave costs 10 pagodas, or about 4 guineas. The wife belongs to the husband's master. A master cannot hinder his slave girl from marrying the slave of another man, nor does he get any price for her. The widow and children, after a slave's death, continue with his master. If a slave has no children by his first wife, he is allowed to take another.

Harihar.—The greater number of the farmers here have only one plough each; but all such as have not more than three ploughs are reckoned poor men, and are in general obliged to borrow money to pay the rent, and to carry on the expenses of cultivation. The crop is a security to the lender, who is repaid in produce at a low valuation. Farmers who have 4, 5, or 6 ploughs are able to manage without borrowing, and live in ease. Those who have more stock are reckoned rich men. Each plough requires one man and two oxen, and can cultivate two mars of land, or about 17 acres: In seed-time and

harvest, some additional laborers must be hired. All the farmers, and their children, even those who are richest, Brahmans excepted, work with their own hands, and only hire so many additional people as are necessary to employ their stock of cattle. A servant's wages are from 6 to 9 jimshiry pagodas a year, together with a blanket and a pair of shoes. The jimshiry pagoda is four dudus worse than that of Ikeri, which is rather less than $1\frac{1}{3}$ per cent. The wages are therefore from £2 7*s.* 10*d.* to £3. 11*s.* 9*d.* Out of this they find everything but the shoes and blanket. Men laborers get daily half a fanam or $3\frac{1}{4}$*d.*, and women receive one-half of this hire, which is seldom paid in money, but is given in jola at the market price. The man's wages purchase daily about a quarter of bushel. The people here work from eight in the morning until sunset, and in the middle of the day are allowed 24 minutes to rest and eat. The cattle work from eight in the morning until noon. They are then fed for an hour, and work until about 5 o'clock.

Heriuru (*Mysore.*)—At Heriuru there are no slaves. Most of the labor is performed by the families of the tenants; but a few hire men-servants by the year, and in seed-time and harvest employ women by the week. A man gets from 50 to 70 fanams a year, or from £1 11*s.* $2\frac{1}{2}$*d.* to £2 3*s.* $8\frac{1}{4}$*d.* This is paid entirely in money, without addition, except that for himself and family he generally obtains room in his master's house. Women get 1 fanam, or $7\frac{1}{2}$*d.* a week. Advances to servants are not common, and of course they are entirely free.

The hours of labor in this country are from eight in the morning until noon, and from 2 o'clock till sunset; in all, about eight hours. The laborers get up about sunrise; but an hour is spent in ablutions, prayer, marking their faces with consecrated ashes or clay, and in eating their breakfast. They eat three times a day, their principal meal being at noon.

Bailuru (*Mysore.*)—In the Malayar there are no slaves. Most of the labor is carried on by the farmers and their own families. Servants are hired by the year, month, or day. A man's wages, when hired by the year, are annually 3 pagodas, a pair of sandals, a blanket, and daily a meal of ready-dressed rice, worth altogether about 5 pagodas, or about £2. He eats another time daily, but this is at his own expense. A servant hired by the month gets half a pagoda, or about 4 shillings, without any addition. The daily hire is one-third of a Canterroy fanam or $2\frac{1}{2}$*d.* Hired servants work from eight in the morning until six in the afternoon; but half an hour's intermission is granted to give them time to eat some ready-prepared victuals.

Cancanhully (*Mysore*).—Most of the cultivation is performed by the hands of the farmers and of their own families. A few hired servants, but no slaves, are employed. A man-servant gets annually of ragi 4 candacas of 200 seers of 72 inches, or nearly $26\frac{1}{2}$ bushels, worth at an average 28 fanams, with 12 fanams in money. In all, he receives 40 fanams, or £1 4*s.* $11\frac{1}{2}$*d.* The hours of work are from $6\frac{1}{2}$ in the morning until noon, and from two in the afternoon until sunset. The number of holidays allowed is very small; but the servant occasionally gets four or five days to repair his house. At seed-time and harvest, a day-laborer gets from one-third to one-fourth of a fanam, or from 2½*d.*, to rather more than 1½*d.* a day. Women get daily from one-fourth to one-fifth of a fanam or about 1½*d.*

Killamangalam, Salem District.—Most of the labor is performed by the farmers and their own families. A few rich men hire yearly servants; and at seed-time and harvest additional daily laborers must be procured. There are no slaves. A ploughman gets annually 3½ candacas of ragi (20 bushels), worth 28 fanams, with a hut and 16 fanams in money. His wages, beside a hut, are therefore £1 7*s.* 5½*d.* The additional expense attending a plough is 3½ fanams for implements, and 2 seeds for the hire of day-laborers, or one candaca of grain, worth 8 fanams, for what the plough will cultivate; in all 55¼ fanams. Add 30 fanams for the rent of the dry field, and we have 85¼ fanams of expense, besides the interest of the value of the two oxen, which, however, is a mere trifle. In an ordinary year, the produce, after deducting the seed and the Government's share of rice with the stoppages for village officers, according to the farmers, will be —

	Fanams.
Ragi 45 colagas, worth	22
Avaray 19 colagas	10½
Rice, Hainu crop, 85 colagas	35
Rice, Caru crop, 57½ colagas	23
	90½

This amounts to just about the expense; but I have mentioned that the produce of the dry grains is in this account underrated by at least one-half, and I have not brought into the account the half produce of the 5 colagas which the farmers are compelled to cultivate, and which costs little or no additional expense.

The farmers in general consent to advance money to their servants for marriages and other ceremonies. This money is repaid by instalments out of the wages that are given in cash; for the people here are not anxious to keep their servants in bondage by a debt hanging over them. A day-laborer, whether man or woman, gets daily one-eighth colaga of rough rice or $\frac{356}{1000}$ parts of a bushel. Of this, it must be observed, one-half is composed of husk.

The following is an account of the wages now (1891) prevailing at the places visited by Dr. Buchanan in 1800:—

Bhaváni.—The rates of wages of the agricultural laborers have not much altered since the beginning of the century. There are no slaves now. The wages of the agricultural laborers, who are termed *padiyals* and *pannials*, are 20 *bullahs* in kind per month and from Rs. 2 to Rs. 3 in money. Their wives get wages as other ordinary laborers.

Day-laborers at harvest, whether men or women, get one to one and-a-half bullah of grain according to season and demand. For weeding, transplanting and planting, the laborers are paid from half to three-fourths of a bullah. A laborer working in the field with a hatchet or carrying earth or manure is paid one bullah in kind or As. 2 in cash.

A porter taking a load is paid one bullah of grain or As. 2 for a whole day.

Dhárápuram, Coimbatore District.—Agricultural labourers are hired in the beginning of Chithirai (April) for a year. They change their service when their term expires. They seldom borrow from their masters, but when they do, they repay the loan at the end of their term by the sale-proceeds of their cattle. A male labourer gets 20 *bullahs* of paddy for labour on wet lands in towns, and 16 *bullahs* of dry grain in husk for labour on dry lands in villages as his monthly wages. A labourer on wet lands gets also annually a *salagay* of paddy with a present of one or one and-a-half rupees or cloths of equivalent value for approved service. Where the labourer does not own a house in the village in which he is employed, the master provides for him a thatched hut to live in, to be surrendered to the employer on the termination of the period of service. The labourer's wife works in the master's fields at seed-time and harvest and elsewhere at other times. A woman's daily wages are one *bullah* of dry grain in husk worth about one anna. For reaping, a man gets 6 puddies and a woman 5 puddies a day.

The labourer's diet consists of boiled grain and soup prepared of mochai or avarai (beans) with coriander and capsicum ground into a paste mixed with salt. A rag is his clothing and hut his home. The labourers are strong and hardy and are not overrun with vermin and cutaneous disorders as a class. The women, although untidy, are fully clothed.

Pollúchi.—There are now two kinds of servants, called padiyals, employed by the farmer to cultivate the lands, and pungals. The padiyals are engaged for a year, the year running from Chittirai to Chittirai (April) in some places and Thai to Thai (January) in others. The padiyals invariably receive an advance of money varying from Rs. 10 to Rs. 30, which they have to repay on quitting the master's service. The advance is taken by the padiyals out of necessity and partly in order that they might have a hold on their employers against summary dismissal of their services at the pleasure of the masters. The padiyals are paid monthly in kind. Persons between 12 and 18 years of age are paid from 12 to 16 *bullahs* of grain according to age and nature and efficiency of work. Those over 20 years of age receive 18 *bullahs.* Besides the wages in grain, each padiyal is provided with a cumbli or As. 8 to Rs. 1-8-0 for the purchase of one. He is also supplied with 2 pairs of slippers. The wife and children of the padiyal are paid for whatever work they perform, the wages of a female for transplanting being 8 pies or one bullah of grain. If the padiyals leave their masters' service before the expiry of the term of their service, the masters seize their cattle and sell them and recoup themselves for the money advanced to the laborers. If, on the other hand, the masters dispense with the services of the padiyals, they cannot recover the loans before the full year of engagement expires.

The pungal goes to a rich farmer and for a share of the crop undertakes to cultivate his lands. The farmer advances the cattle, implements, seed and money or grain that is necessary for the subsistence of the pungal. He also gives each family a house. He takes no share in the labour, which is all performed by the pungal and his wife and children, but he pays the rent out of his share on the division of the crop which takes place when that is ripe. If a farmer employs a pungal to cultivate his lands, the produce is divided into two equal portions, one-half going to the share of the farmer as *nilavaram*. Of the remaining half, *i.e.*, yearivaram, in proportion to the number of ploughs owned by the farmer and pungal, the shares are divided at the rate of a share for each plough. For example, if the farmer owns three ploughs and the pungal one plough, half the produce above referred to (yearivaram) will be divided into 4 portions, 3 going to the share of the farmer and the remaining one to the latter. Every pungal should contribute a plough or two or else he will not be considered as such, but will be treated as a mere *padiyal*. The pungal should pay from his share of the produce to the farmer the money which he received for his subsistence. The farmers are better off with *pungals* than with *padiyals*; the greater portion of the responsibility is shoved on the *pungals*, who have equal, if not better, interest in the cultivation of the land. The farmer has therefore less anxiety and greater profit when he employs a *pungal* than when he employs a *padiyal*.

Pálghat, Malabar District.—The greater part of the labour on the field is performed by churmars. Persons of other castes are also engaged for the labour when necessity arises on payment of higher wages. The churmars, who were once slaves, are now ordinary coolies. The tenants and landlords have now no absolute control over them, nor do they maintain the churmars when their services are not required. The churmars are at perfect liberty to proceed wherever they choose and obtain subsistence. They receive 2 parahs of paddy and two pieces of cloth a year so long as they remain in the service of their masters. They also obtain some pecuniary and other assistance when a marriage, death or other contingency occurs in their families. The daily wages of a churmar, both male and female, are 2 edangallies of paddy and one edangally for a boy or girl. The daily wages of labourers other than churmars are 4 edangallies for males, 3 for females, and $1\frac{1}{2}$ for boys and girls.

Támracheri, Malabar District.—The daily wages paid in grain to agricultural labourers in 1891 were much the same as those paid in 1800. The rates generally given are—

	CUB. IN.
To able-bodied men, $1\frac{1}{2}$ dangallis of paddy or 6 nallis heaped	$148\frac{1}{2}$
To able-bodied women, $1\frac{1}{3}$ dangallis of paddy or 6 nallis streaked	$103\frac{1}{2}$
To old persons and children, of paddy, 3 nallis heaped	$74\frac{1}{4}$

They get a present of 3 parahs of paddy during the harvest and 3 or 4 pieces of cloth. In times of scarcity, which generally happens in the months of July and August, their masters give them yams, jacks, plantains, &c. This year when there was a general failure of jacks, yams, &c., the starving populace were driven to the necessity of extracting aliment from fan-palm and date-palm and subsisting upon the cakes formed out of the juice obtained. The rates above given are higher than the rates given for the labourers who receive advances of money and are required to work out the advance by contributing manual labour.

Tellicherry, Malabar District.—The cudians, *i.e.*, tenants, are now worse off than in 1800. They get at the most only one-half of the produce of paddy fields they lease out, and as for plantations, if the trees have not been paid (kuyikanom) price by the jenmies, the tenants get two-thirds of their produce; in other cases they scarcely get one-third, the rest being appropriated by their jenmies. All tenants, whether of paddy flats or of parambas, have the same complaint to make, that they gain little or no profit from tilling or holding lands and parambas under the tenures now obtaining in Malabar.

These tenants are mostly workmen themselves; and all able-bodied men and women of their household work in and for the interest of the farm. But if at all any extra labour is wanted, they hire other men and women at the usual rates of wages. The tenants do not now possess slaves, though it cannot be denied that in remote parts prædial slaves are covertly leased out with the farms. The hired servants are chiefly Tiars, Nairs, Moplahs and Polayars (who were slaves in 1800). Polayars are hired as day-laborers. The working hours are now, as in 1800, almost the same, viz., 7 A.M. to 1 P.M., but the rates of wages are now only 2 edangallies of paddy against 2½ in 1800. All the afternoon the tenants work for themselves.

The edangally in North Malabar, familiarly known as McLeod's seer, contains—

	CUB. IN.
In Cherakal	100·34
In Kóttayam	97·75
In Kurumbranad	97·75

The total earnings, at the present rates, of a day-labourer in Malabar for a whole year may be taken at 626 dangallis of paddy, or Rs. 37½ in money at the present market rates. This gives Rs. 3-2-0 a month for a labourer working half a day.

Cherakal, Malabar District.—The following castes were once slaves in this taluk: (1) Polayars, in the plains near the sea coast and (2) Maviloms, (3) Karimbalans and (4) Vettuvars on the hills. There are now no slaves in the sense that their women and children are not now openly sold, mortgaged or leased with the lands to which they are attached. But the master or jenmi takes particular care that they are not taught to read and write. In remote parts they are even now covertly sold, mortgaged and leased with the lands by word of mouth. In such parts the old allowances are still paid to them, viz., a hut, two pieces of cloth annually and the daily allowance of rice or paddy. The annual money allowance for oil and salt is not now given.

The panicurs or agricultural labourers are generally Nairs, Moplahs and Tiars. Though the master does not now give the servant a hut to live in, yet many have become kuyikanom tenants of the former. They are not bound to render gratuitous service to their masters. For all work done to the masters, they are paid the same wages as are given to non-tenants.

In cases of indebtedness, the debts are not recovered by deductions from wages, but in due course of law. No annual presents are given to the labourers nor are they flogged on any account.

The rates generally given are—

For tilling (work done till 1 P.M).	2	McLeod seers of paddy.
Do. (the whole day)	3	seers with breakfast.
For ploughing (work done till 12 noon).	$1\frac{1}{2}$	seers of paddy.
For weeding (women) whole day.	$1\frac{1}{2}$	nalis or $\frac{3}{5}$ seers of rice.
For reaping (women) ...	10	sheaves for every 100 sheaves brought to the threshing ground.
For turning up parambas (till 1 P.M.).		As. 2-6 in money or 2 seers of paddy.
Cooly work (full day) in urban parts.		As. 4 with 6 pies extra for noon-meal if the latter is not supplied by the employer.

(C.)—*Abstract of the Proceedings of the Board of Revenue, dated 25th November* 1819, *on the subject of agricultural slavery.*

Salem.—There was no vestige whatever of slavery in the district nor had any such practice obtained from the time the district came into the possession of the Company.

Madura and Dindigul.—Slavery had existed during the Muhammadan Government and the slaves were sold at the pleasure of their masters. Since the assumption of the country by the Company, some slaves had continued with their masters; others had left them and even enlisted as sepoys. The Collector could not discover that any Pullan had sold himself as a slave. Indeed slavery seemed gradually disappearing.

Coimbatore.—Slavery existed in the district in but a very few villages and the number of slaves was always inconsiderable.

Tanjore.—Slavery existed in the district, but it was founded in the first instance upon a voluntary contract. The condition of the slaves differed very little from that of the common labourers, and the treatment of both was nearly the same. The system of slaves attached to the soil and transferable by purchase, as appendage to the land, did not obtain in the district.

Tinnevelly.—Slavery existed in the district. It was usual for slaves to be sold or mortgaged, either with the land or separately, at the pleasure of the proprietor. The slaves were afforded subsistence on the lowest scale of allowance, being generally no more than 2 measures of paddy a day on working days. They were also entitled at the time of harvest to a small deduction from the gross produce, which generally amounted to $2\frac{3}{8}$ per cent. It was usual for the masters to assist the slaves with necessary funeral expenses, and to grant them presents on occasions of marriages, births and festivities.

South Arcot.—The system of slavery founded in the first instance on contract existed in the district, the number of slaves amounting to 17,000. The owners were required to provide the slaves with food and clothing, and to defray their wedding expenses and to assist them with presents on the occasion of births of children and to defray funeral charges. The food given was always sufficient for subsistence, but the clothing was very scanty. The owners were bound to protect the slaves in sickness and old age.

Chingleput.—The system of slavery, originally founded on contract, existed in the district. The slaves were given a certain prescribed grain allowance and a proportionate subsistence for each of their children or others of the family. They were also housed and clothed and during the principal festivals certain other allowances were made to them both in money and in articles requisite for their ceremonies; their marriages were also performed at the charge of their masters and when reduced by infirmity they were also supported by their proprietors. The condition of this description of people, composing the chief part of the Pariahs of the district, had, of late, considerably changed, in consequence of the vicinity of the town of Madras where many of them obtained employment and their proprietors found it difficult to reclaim them.

Trichinopoly.—Slavery existed in the district, the number of slaves amounting to 10,600. They were usually sold with the land and sometimes mortgaged. They were supposed to be entirely supported by their masters in sickness and in health. Their marriages were made at the expense of the mirasidars and the expenses of their funerals were also defrayed by them. The slaves enjoyed some little gratuity at every birth and received a certain established sum at the principal Hindu festivals. A list of the yearly emoluments which a slave was properly entitled to receive is noted below. They were not treated harshly.

The quantity of land to be cultivated by a slave is an extent capable of yielding 150 kalams of paddy.

	Kalams.			Gifts.	
Varam of a Pullen ...	8	5⅜			
Do. Pullichi ...	6	6¾			
	15	⅛			
Batta for ploughing ...	2	0		4	
Swatuntrums for sowing ...	0	6		...	
Reaping share at 5 per cent.	7	6		...	
Thrashing	1	0		...	
Pongal feast	1	0		...	
Deepavali	...			⅛	
Gramadavata	...			1½	
Total annual ...	26	⅛		5⅝	fanams.
For a marriage	4	0	8	0	rupees.
Do. birth	0	2		2	fanams.
Do. death	0	2		2	do.
Total ...	30	4⅛	Rs. 9	1⅝	fanams.

Canara.—Slavery existed in the district, the number of slaves amounting to 82,000. The right of sale was the master's exclusive privilege, with or without the land. The slaves could also be let on hire. They were fed and clothed by their masters, who also presented them with a small sum of money on their marriages or on occasions of particular ceremonies. The average quantity of food and clothing given was—

Food.	Clothing.
For a man—	
$1\frac{1}{2}$ Canara seer of coarse rice, 2 rupees' weight of salt, a little betel-nut and leaf.	2 pieces of canthy, 6 cubits in some taluks, a cumbli and a roomal.
For a woman—	
1 seer	1 piece of cloth, 7 cubits.
For a child—	
$\frac{3}{4}$ seer	1 piece of cloth, 4 cubits.

The slaves were not cruelly treated.

Malabar.—There were slaves in the district numbering 100,000. They were frequently transferred by sale, mortgage or hire. The measure of subsistence to be given by the proprietor was fixed, and he was bound by the prescribed customs of the country to see it served out to the slaves daily. The slaves were in more comfortable circumstances than any of the lower and poorer class of natives.

(D.)—*Extracts from the Report of the Commissioners for the investigation of alleged cases of Torture in the Madras Presidency*, 1855.

Many a witness has declared to us that the people would be satisfied if the demands of the Revenue Officers were restricted to the just Government dues; we entertain no doubt but that the extortion, of what are erroneously termed "Bribes," is universal, and that when payment cannot be obtained by fair means, foul will be resorted to. Then is brought into play all that perfect but silent machinery which combines the forces of Revenue demands and Police authority; the most ingenious artifices which the subtlety of the native mind can invent are had recourse to; and it seems highly probable to us that it is a common practice with the native officers to give their own illicit demands precedence, when pecuniary means being more plentiful or easily procurable, the process of extraction is more readily complied with, under hopes and promises of future services, perhaps that of assisting in cheating Government among others, expressly with a view to keep the revenue demand as a *corps de reserve* to fall back upon, the practice of oppression and violence to extract that, being not so apparent an injustice in the eyes of the people as the application of the same measures for mere private personal purposes.[1]

---

[1] Mr. Forbes, Collector of Tanjore, writes as follows:—"The people of India draw a wide distinction between oppressive acts practised with a personal motive, and those, which, however erroneously, they connect with a public duty: they will make complaint upon complaint and appeal upon appeal for the redress of a private wrong, when they will at the same time tacitly submit to a greater injury received in a public act: the motive of the one they see to be personal, and attach no personal motive to the other."

The descriptions of violence commonly in vogue for revenue and private extortion purposes, which have been spoken to in the course of this inquiry, are as follow :—Keeping a man in the sun ; preventing his going to meals or other calls of nature ; confinement ; preventing cattle from going to pasture by shutting them up in the house ; quartering a peon on the defaulter who is obliged to pay him daily wages ; the use of the kittee ; anundal ; squeezing the crossed fingers with the hands ; pinches on the thighs ; slaps ; blows with fist or whip ; running up and down ; twisting the ears ; making a man sit on the soles of his feet with brickbats behind his knees ; putting a low caste man on the back ; striking two defaulters' heads against each other, or tying them together by their back hair ; placing in the stocks ; tying the hair of the head to a donkey's or buffalo's tail ; placing a necklace of bones or other degrading or disgusting materials round the neck ; and, occasionally, though very rarely, more severe discipline still.

Some stress seems to have been laid upon the existence of "instruments" of torture, and many of the gentlemen who have sent in reports to Government state their belief that the kittee has become obsolete in their districts.

That the "anundal" (in Telugu gingeri) or tying a man down in a bent position by means of his own cloth or a rope of coir or straw passed over his neck and under his toes is generally common at the present day, is beyond dispute ; and we see no reason to doubt that the kittee (in Telugu cheerata) is also in frequent use. It is a very simple machine, consisting merely of two sticks tied together at one end, between which the fingers are placed as in a lemon squeezer ; but in our judgment it is of very little importance whether this particular form of compression be the one in ordinary use or not, for an equal amount of bodily pain must be produced by that which has superseded the kittee, if anywhere it has gone out of vogue, the compelling a man to interlace his fingers, the ends being squeezed by the hands of peons, who occasionally introduce the use of sand to gain a firmer gripe ; or making a man place his hand flat upon the ground and then pressing downward at either end a stick placed horizontally over the back of the sufferer's fingers. Independently of the general testimony to its use deposed to before us by the complainants whom we have personally examined, we find its use believed in by Mr. G. Forbes, and admitted by the Sheristadar, who says—"Kittees are sometimes kept in both taluks and villages ; if they are not forthcoming in places where they are required for use, the village carpenter is immediately ordered to procure the required number of kittees, which order is implicitly obeyed ;" and in the case of Akki-nary Appana, we find a Tahsildar tried and sentenced to six months' hard labour in irons and a fine of Rs. 200 for having applied this instrument known in Telugu districts by the name of cheerata to the fingers of the complainant so lately as the middle of the last year.

It is quite certain that the practice of torture prevails in a much more aggravated degree in Police cases than for realizing the revenue. The modes resorted to in the former appear to be more acute and cruel, though we doubt if anything like an equal number of persons is annually subjected to violence on criminal charges as for default of payment of revenue.

*   *   *   *

We have instances of torture being freely practised in every relation of domestic life. Servants are thus treated by their masters and fellow servants; children by their parents and schoolmasters for the most trifling offences; the very plays of the populace (and the point of a rude people's drama is its satire) excite the laughter of many a rural audience by the exhibition of revenue squeezed out of a defaulter coin by coin through the appliance of familiar "provacatives" under the superintendence of a caricatured Tahsildar; it seems a "time-honored" institution, and we cannot be astonished if the practice is still widely prevalent among the ignorant uneducated class of native public servants.

* * * *

Among the principal tortures in vogue in Police cases we find the following: twisting a rope tightly round the entire arm or leg so as to impede circulation; lifting up by the moustache; suspending by the arms while tied behind the back; searing with hot iron; placing scratching insects such as the carpenter beetle, on the navel, scrotum and other sensitive parts; dipping in wells and rivers till the party is half suffocated; squeezing the testicles; beating with sticks; prevention of sleep; nipping the flesh with pincers; putting pepper or red chillies in the eyes; these cruelties occasionally persevered in until death sooner or later ensues.

* * * *

In the course of this investigation there is one thing which has impressed us even more painfully than the conviction that torture exists; it is difficulty of obtaining redress which confronts the injured parties.

In stating this melancholy fact we are very far from seeking to cast any unfounded imputation upon either the Government or its European officers. We think that the service is entitled to the fullest credit for its disclaimer of all countenance of the cruel practices which prevail in the Revenue as well as in the Police department. We see no reason to doubt that the native officials from the highest to the lowest are well aware of the disposition of their European superiors; and although very many of the parties, who have appeared before us in reply to our inquiry why they have not made an earlier complaint, have asked what is the use of appealing to the Collector, we have seen nothing to impress us with the belief that the people at large entertain an idea that their maltreatment is countenanced or tolerated by the European officers of Government. On the contrary all they seem to desire is that the Europeans in their respective districts should themselves take up and investigate complaints brought before them. The distances which the natives will often travel at great personal loss and inconvenience to make complaints even of a very petty nature to the Collector or Sub-Collector is of itself a proof of the confidence which they place generally in those officers. The abstinence of the native officials from such practices in or near stations where Europeans, be they civilians, surgeons, commissariat or other officers, reside, and the prevalence of torture increasing in proportion as the taluk appears less exposed to European scrutiny, are strong arguments in favor of a consciousness on the part of the native officials that they cannot with impunity resort to illegal and personal violence when it admits of easy and speedy substantiation before the European authorities of the district; and the whole cry of the people which has come up before us is to save them from the cruelties of their fellow natives, not from the effects of unkindness or indifference on the part of the European officers of Government.

What then, it may be asked, are the reasons on which we found our opinion that while the natives have confidence in their European superiors, they do not promptly seek redress at their hands in every instance of abuse of authority? They are as follows: In the first place the infliction of such descriptions of ill-treatment in the collection of the revenue as we have above specified has, in the course of centuries, come to be looked upon as "Mamool," customary, a thing of course to be submitted to as an every day unavoidable necessity.[2] It is generally practised probably only on the lower order of ryots, whose circumstances least permit of their making any complaints on the one hand, whilst their ignorance and timidity render them more submissive on the other; such is the native character that very often those able and ready to pay their dues will not do so unless some degree of force be resorted to. "I brought 14 rupees from my house," says a ryot, in a deposition referred to by Mr. Lushington, "but only paid 6. I brought the said money to pay, but as no violence was used towards me, I did not do so. Had I been compelled, I would have paid them." * And in all these cases, it is probable that a sense of the justness of the claim operates in their minds against seeking redress for ill-treatment, which, but for their own stubbornness, they might have avoided. The violence ordinarily used is not of such a character as to leave those marks upon the person which might be appealed to in incontestable corroboration of the truth of the sufferer's story, and we cannot abstain from reiterating our opinion that the great proportion of the acquittals and the lightness of the punishments consequent upon such cases as appear to have been substantiated to the satisfaction of the magistracy, may have had a serious effect in deterring the ryots from bringing forward more numerous complaints.

* * * *

The distances which those who wish to make complaints personally to the Collector have to travel; the fear that their applications by letter if permitted to reach head-quarters unadulterated by misinterpretation will be returned with the ordinary endorsement of a reference to the Tahsildars; the expense and loss of time which a visit to, and more or less prolonged attendance upon, the Collector's office entail; the utter hopelessness, after all is said and done, of the European authorities personally investigating the case, generally speaking; the persuasion that a reference of the petition to the Tahsildar is likely to end in a nullity; the immense power wielded by the native servants in the districts and those in the Collector's office, who work together in concert to render all complaints to the superior European officials nugatory; the probability that if any trial takes place before the Tahsildar the complainant's witnesses will either be bribed and bought off or intimidated, or, if they appear, that their statements will not be

[2] Mr. Forbes, Collector of Tanjore, writes as follows:—"The ryot will often appear at the cutcherry with his full liabilities in his possession, tied up in small sums about his person, to be doled out, rupee by rupee, according to the urgency of the demand, and will sometimes return to his village having left a balance undischarged, not because he could not pay it, but simply because he was not forced to do so."

believed, or will be garbled, and an unfavourable report upon them returned to the Collector; above all perhaps, the conviction that he who seeks redress at the hands of the European is thenceforth a marked man amongst the native officials; that his whole future peace and safety are jeopardized by this attempt, and that every means of annoyance and of oppression, even to false accusations of felony, will be brought into play against him, until his own ruin and that of his family are sooner or later consummated; some or all of these circumstances unite in every case, in more or less forcible combination to render redress not only difficult, but in many instances almost impossible; at the same time it is to be remarked that the authority of the Tahsildar must be supported by his European superiors against the numerous false charges which are unsparingly preferred by the intriguing ryots.

* * * *

The character of the Native Police has been drawn by more than one writer in the reports furnished to Government.

Mr. Mackenzie writes as follows:—"I have no hesitation in stating that the so-called Police of the mofussil is little better than delusion. It is a terror to well disposed and peaceable people, none whatever to thieves and rogues, and that if it was abolished *in toto* the saving of expense to Government would be great, and property would be not a whit less secure than it now is."

Mr. Saalfelt says:—"The Police establishment has become the bane and pest of society, the terror of the community, and the origin of half the misery and discontent that exist among the subjects of Government. Corruption and bribery reign paramount throughout the whole establishment; violence, torture and cruelty are their chief instruments for detecting crime, implicating innocence or extorting money. Robberies are daily and nightly committed, and not unfrequently with their connivance. Certain suspicious characters are taken up and conveyed to some secluded spot far out of the reach of witnesses; every species of cruelty is exercised upon them; if guilty, the crime is invariably confessed and stolen property discovered; but a tempting bribe soon releases them from custody. Should they persist in avowing their innocence, relief from suffering is promised by criminating some wealthy individual, and in the agony of despair he is pointed to as the receiver of stolen goods. In his turn he is compelled to part with his hard earned coin to avert the impending danger. Even the party robbed does not escape the clutching grasp of the heartless peon and duffadar; he is threatened with being torn from his home, dragged to the cutcherry and detained there for days or weeks to the actual detriment of his trade or livelihood, unless he point out the supposed thieves. The dread of, or aversion to, the cutcherry is so great that the owner would sooner disavow the stolen article and disclaim all knowledge of the property, though his name be found written upon it in broad characters; while such is the actual state of things, and while the people entertain such a lively horror of the Police, it is not possible to expect a single victim of torture to come forward and arraign his tormentors; or to bring the charge home to any one of them after the deed has been perpetrated in some ruined fort or deep ravine situated miles away from the town or village."

* * * *

Mr. J. Mackenzie, merchant of Bimlipatam, gives the following account:—"Since the receipt of your communication, however, I have made it my duty to inquire into the subject as far as my opportunities permitted, and the result of my inquiries leads me to the conclusion that the charge has been greatly exaggerated, and that although the use of torture or coercion in the collection of the revenue cannot be denied, its practice is of very rare occurrence, and not at all of the deep and atrocious nature alleged, and I can confidently state, that it is not had recourse to in order to collect an immoderate kist, or, as some writers in the *Athenæum* assert, to screw out of the ryot, over and above his kist, a further sum for the benefit of the revenue servants. I am convinced that this charge is quite unfounded at least as regards the district of Vizagapatam. It is not in this way that the revenue servants make money. I believe I can explain when torture is made use of. There is a class of ryots known as nadars, (paupers) whom a faulty revenue system has taken out of their proper position and converted into ryots, whereas they were never intended for any other position than that of laborers or servants to Mootabar ryots. Now these nadars are compelled to undertake the cultivation of lands which the Mootabar ryots are not disposed to take up. It is unsafe to make them such advances as would give them the means of well cultivating their lands; they cannot be trusted; they are not to be made honest or respectable; their lands are consequently badly cultivated and their crops scanty, and scanty as they are, they generally endeavour to make away with them and to evade the payment of their kist, as they really live by what they can pilfer. Now it is in such cases that punishment, or, as it is called torture, is had recourse to. The Tahsildar knows that crop has been made away with, and that the ryot has the proceeds concealed on his person; he refuses to pay. What is the Tahsildar to do? Sell his property? He has no tangible property. Send him to jail to be well lodged and fed at the expense of Government? He does neither; he flogs him or coerces him in some other way, and rupee by rupee, anna by anna, drop out of unexpected places. One such case is noised about, and the example serves for a long time. This I believe to be the true statement of the torture used in this district. I need not say that it is difficult to prove. The Tahsildar takes good care that no witnesses who are likely to give evidence against him are present. No laws can eradicate it, it has been the practice of the country from time immemorial; the natives in general think it all right; the very nature of the people must first be changed."

(E.)—*The Madras Ryot by Mr. R. A. Dalyell in* 1866.

During the ten years preceding 1866, the price of all agricultural produce has nearly doubled, and that consequently the agricultural proprietor was much better off at the beginning of 1866 than he was at the beginning of 1856, and that there was a still greater improvement in his position as compared to what it had been in 1846. As nearly the whole of his outgoings, whether for food or wages, are mere deductions from the gross produce of the land as his family subsists on the grain raised and wages are paid in the same commodity, his surplus produce has remained nearly the same in quantity during the twenty years, whereas the market value of that surplus has increased threefold, if no allowance be made for the depreciation of the value of the precious metals which has taken place during this period.

In order to the better understanding of the extraordinary improvement that has taken place in the position of the agricultural interest, it will be advisable to consider the nature of the tenures on which land is held in the Madras Presidency. As already stated, a very large proportion of the cultivated area is held direct from Government by peasant proprietors termed Government ryots. According to the statistical returns, there were no less than a million and three-quarters of these persons entered in the registers as land-holders, and their holdings are usually infinitesimally small. Only 420 paid £100 and upwards as Government land-tax, which is supposed to represent half the net produce of the land. Upwards of a million and a half paid less than Rs. 31 or £3-2-0, and of these latter, upwards of a million paid less than Rs. 10 or £1. As has been already shown, the cultivated land held by the registered ryots is about 18 million acres, the average extent of the holdings is therefore 9 acres, but if the million sub-tenants who are entered in the returns as holding under these registered ryots be taken into account, the average size of the holdings will be reduced to 6 acres, supposing, of course, that every registered ryot who sub-lets land retains an equal quantity for his own use. This minute sub-division of the land into small holdings has often been advanced as the great objection to ryotwari system of tenure, but after all it should be remembered that this objection applies equally to the zemindari system, and that, notwithstanding the difference in the value of money, only a few years back there were nearly two millions of small landed proprietors in France whose holdings in no case exceeded 5 acres; that in the present Kingdom of Prussia, out of a population of nine millions dependent on agriculture, there are upwards of two million proprietors of land, and that upwards of a million of these do not possess more than 3 acres; and that in Ireland, in 1861, there were 39,210 persons holding land less than an acre in extent as proprietors or tenants, 75,141 holding between 1 and 2 acres, and 164,000 from 5 to 15 acres.

* * * *

Unfortunately the share of Government was generally fixed too high, and the result of this over-assessment, increased as its pressure has been by the fall in the value of produce since the settlement was made, has never allowed the system a fair trial. Various restrictive rules also led to much interference with the ryots, though they were far from being a necessary consequence of the system. These restrictions are now being removed and the reductions recently made, or in progress, and the correct survey, classification and re-assessment of the land now in contemplation, will do away with these disadvantages, and it may be expected that the superiority of a system which encourages industry and enterprise, by being based on individual proprietorship, will be more clearly evinced.

* * * *

The position of every description of landholder, whether ryot, zemindar, or inamdar, must have improved very materially during the last 15 years. So far as the first class was concerned, the fall in prices, which had taken place between the early part of the century, when the money rates of land-tax payable to Government were fixed, and the year 1850, had had such a serious effect upon their resources, that very liberal reductions were then made in the assessment of all the ryotwari lands in those districts where the rates pressed with severity upon the ryots or where they were so high as to keep land out of cultivation altogether. A special department for the re-assessment of all districts on liberal and scientific principles was also organized. The position of the Government ryot was consequently at once much improved and the steady rise in prices, which has taken place since that period, has, of course, still further benefited him, but this latter benefit has also been obtained by the holders of land on other tenures, the zemindar and the inamdar, and their respective tenants. It has been already shown that an acre of unirrigated land produces on the average 190 Madras measures, or about 5 cwt. of grain, and that an acre of irrigated land produces 370 Madras measures or 10 cwt of rice. The Government ryot, therefore, who held, say, 6 acres of "dry" land and 2 acres of "wet," for which he paid, say, Rs. 20 per annum to Government as land-tax, obtained for the produce Rs. 105 in 1856 and Rs. 209 in 1866 as noted in the margin. On the other hand, the ryot holding the same extent of land under a zemindar or inamdar, after giving half the produce to his landlord, obtained in 1856 only Rs. 52-8-0, the price of 15 cwt. of dry grain and 10 cwt. of rice in 1856, and in 1866 Rs. 104-8-0, the price of the same quantity of grain in that year, the zemindar, or inamdar, in this case, taking the balance of advantage obtained by the Government ryot. This improvement in the position of the agriculturist has manifested itself in the very large increase in the area of land under cultivation, for, whereas, even in 1856, there were less than 10 millions of acres held by registered Government ryots, there were upwards of 16 millions of acres so held in 1865.

1856—	RS.
Value of the produce of 6 acres of dry land ..	50
Do. do. of 2 acres of wet land ..	55
	105
Deduct tax (say) ..	20
	85

1866—	RS.
Value of the produce of 6 acres of dry land ..	104
Do. do. of 2 acres of wet land ..	105
	209
Deduct tax (say) ..	20
	189

* * * *

The position of the agricultural laborer and, indeed, of all those dependent upon wages had not, at any rate, seriously deteriorated during the 10 years preceding 1866, though the enormous increase, which has taken place in the price of food, must press hardly upon those trades for which the remuneration is fixed, by custom, at a certain rate in money. When reporting on this subject about three years ago, the Board of Revenue, after communicating with the Collectors of districts, stated that, as a rule, all agricultural labourers were still paid in grain, and that these grain wages had not risen materially during late years. As to other classes of laborers who were paid in coin, they observed that their wages had risen considerably, and that the increase had then kept full pace with the enhanced price of food. Compared with former rates, the wages were stated to be, in some cases, double of what they formerly were, but the general proportion of increase was 50 per cent., and only in a few cases had the increase been as small as 25 per cent. These conclusions are borne out by the increase which has taken place, during the last 15 years, in the pay of all domestic servants in the families of Europeans in India.

The position of that portion of the population whose wealth is derived from mercantile operations has improved, at any rate, in an equal ratio with that of the agriculturist, if we may judge by the progress which has taken place in the trade of the Presidency. The principal portion of this trade is carried on at the port of Madras, that is, about one-half of the export trade and two-thirds of the import trade. The greater part of the balance of the export trade is from the ports of Cocanada, Negapatam and Tuticorin, on the East Coast, and from Calicut, Cochin, and Mangalore, on the Western Coast. Large exports of cotton take place from Cocanada and Tuticorin, and of grain from Negapatam, whereas the principal articles of export from the western ports are coffee and oil-seeds. The principal item of import at most of these ports is piece-goods, though grain is also largely imported into the Malabar district.

On the whole, then, it is impossible to arrive at any other conclusion than that the mass of the population of the Madras Presidency have considerably progressed in wealth during the 10 years previous to the famine of 1866. The whole of the agricultural interest, which includes certainly three-fourths and perhaps four-fifths of the population, were in twice as good a position at the end of this period as they had been at its commencement, and a large number of them had made enormous gains during the cotton famine in England, the ryots of the district of Bellary alone having, it is estimated, obtained an increase to their capital of nearly a million and a-half sterling on this account. The mercantile class, or, at any rate, such portions of them as were interested in the over-sea trade, had doubled their business, and the position of the poorest classes had certainly not deteriorated. Further, while private wealth had increased to this extent, taxation had been augmented by less than 25 per cent., so that, certainly, three-fourths of the increased profits obtained by the population were enjoyed tax free. At the commencement of the distress the people were, consequently, in a better position than they had ever occupied in any previous year of famine.

(F.)—*Results of the enquiries made by the Board of Revenue as to the condition of the labouring classes in* 1872 (*Proceedings of the Board of Revenue, dated* 11*th November* 1872, *No.* 2179).

Board of Revenue—Labourers.—The general opinion was that the condition of the labouring classes was rapidly improving. Mr. Brandt and Mr. Stuart took the opposite view, but they evidently referred to farm labourers, the old prædial slaves. Wages paid in grain, like those of farm labourers, continued almost stationary, and the rapid increase in money wages was to a great extent neutralized by as rapid a rise in prices. The labouring classes had, however, fully shared in the general improvement which was visible everywhere, and in many places large public works, increasing trades, and improved facilities for emigration had made their advance more rapid than that of other classes.

Honorable V. Ramaiyangar.—Tho agricultural labourers in Tanjore called "pannials" were a kind of semi-serfs squatting on the estates to which they were attached. According to the practice of the district, 40 goolies of dry land out of the holdings of a mirasidar were exempted by Government from assessment and made over to each "pannial" working under him. The mirasidar supplemented this with a grant of 60 goolies, of which he himself paid the assessment. He further granted to each labourer 50 goolies of "nunjah" land free of assessment. The 100 goolies of dry land was calculated to yield 7 kalams[1] of ragi, besides vegetables and enough of ground-nut to supply him with oil for the use of the family. The 50 goolies of wet land were computed to yield 5 kalams of paddy. His wages for daily work consisted of a Madras measure of grain per diem and this for about nine working months in the year would give him 9×30 or 270 measures = $11\frac{1}{4}$ Tanjore kalams. His *calavassam* on the threshing floor at the time of harvest gave him about 11 kalams more. The pannial's wife earned, by beating paddy and separating the husk from the grain on the mirasidar's estate, about 6 kalams of grain a year at the rate of 12 measures a month, so that the total earnings, of the family in one year were as below :—

	KALAMS.
Yield of dry land	7
Yield of wet land	5
Daily wages	11
Calavassam	11
Earnings of the labourer's family	6
Total ...	40

which at an average price of one rupee a kalam was equal to about Rs. 40 in money. The labourer generally earned something by working as cooly during three months in the year in which he was not employed in the field, and including this and the presents he got on festival days, the total earnings of the family were Rs. 4 a month. A non-agricultural labourer and his family in the rural parts of the district earned about the same sum at the rate of three annas per diem.

The agricultural labourers in other districts did not earn so much as in Tanjore. In some districts, their wages were, on an average, but two Madras measures of grain per diem, or 60 measures a month, equal to 12×60 or 720 meaures or 90 merkals per annum. This

[1] A Tanjore kalam 3 Madras merkals or 24 measures, each containing 133 tolas of rice.

was worth Rs. 30 or Rs. 2½ per month. Taking the whole Presidency, he was of opinion that it would probably not be much wide of the mark to assume the average earnings of unskilled labourers to be about Rs. 3 a month. There was no doubt that the wages of labour had increased since fasli 1263 (1853-54) though not in proportion to prices, the latter having risen by 100 per cent. while the former rose by about 50 per cent. So far the condition of the labouring classes must be held to have improved.

Mr. P. Chentsal Row.—The money wages of labourers everywhere nearly doubled, but wages to agricultural labourers were paid in grain and continued unaltered. A full grown labourer in Nellore (of which Mr. Chentsal Row was a native and a landholder) got from 1½ to 2 tooms[2] of paddy or one toom of jonna or ragi monthly with a cumbli and a pair of slippers a year. This was all that had been always paid. The condition of the agricultural labourers had not materially or at all improved, excepting in towns and villages in the vicinity of the railway.

Mr. Wedderburn, Collector of Coimbatore.—Wages were good and employment general; in some places skilled labour, such as, that of the carpenter, the mason, &c., was very high owing to the extension of the railway.

There was an increase in money wages; grain wages were the same as to quantity; but more valuable relatively to money. The cultivators or field-hands of the irrigated lands working for the landlords remained in much the same condition; ryots cultivating their own lands, in other words, owners of dry land, had, by the sinking of wells at their own cost, without being charged for the improvement, as was usual under the old native system, advanced in wealth and comfort. The ryot proprietor and his sons worked their well, tended the cattle, and ploughed the fields; all worked who had not the means to be idle; the females also spun.

Unskilled field labour, in cash or kind.

	30 years ago.			At present.		
	RS.	A.	P.	RS.	A.	P.
Per day—						
Man	0	1	4	0	3	6
Woman	0	0	10	0	1	8
Per month—						
Man ..	1	12	0	4	0	0

Next there were the lowest classes in every village who earned their subsistence by cutting grass, weeding fields, &c.; except in unfavorable seasons when grass failed or cultivation was not carried on, they maintained themselves according to their own standard; when there was no thought of the morrow and people multiplied without the restraints which better circumstances or higher standards of living entail, there was no likelihood of much advancement. But though emigration agents were beating up for recruits in every village and bazaar, and promised food, clothing and Rs. 5 per mensem, apparently they met with limited success; 90 in a population of 1¾ millions appeared before him as magistrate, to be attested, in the course of 12 months from November 1871 to November 1872. There was neither fear of the sea nor of distant travel and those that went had usually no local tie.

---

[2] A toom = 37·1 Madras measures; its value in the country was about Rs. 1¾.

Mr. Venkatesiah, Deputy Collector, Chingleput District.—The wages or earnings of the labouring classes were then nearly double of what they were some fifteen years before, owing partly to the rise in the price of grain and partly to the liberal rates at which they were paid by the Railway Company and the Public Works Department. A common labourer working at the roads got as much as three annas a day, while his wife got an anna and-a-half. Thus a family consisting of a wife and a husband made up about Rs. 80 a year exclusive of non-working days; whereas their annual income in former days had not exceeded half the latter sum.

Mr. Chase, Collector of Kurnool.—Agricultural labourers were generally paid in grain and as the rates of payments seldom changed, their condition had been stationary and had made no perceptible improvement. The wages of non-agricultural labourers, however, had considerably increased, owing to the operations of the Irrigation Company and the general rise of prices; but after the completion of these works in 1870 and the fall in prices, especially in that of cotton, the rates of wages had a downward course, and the condition of the labourers at that time was not much better than what it was 15 years before; and any increase in the rate of wages was nearly counterbalanced by the enhancement of prices, so much so that when coolies were wanted for road work at a time when field work was available, they invariably preferred the latter, which was paid for in grain, to the former, which was paid for in money. Their food and clothing were of the same kind as what they were before. They ate the same coarse grain and used as condiments the same *chatney* composed of hemp-leaves or tamarind fruit. They wore the same coarse clothes and slept on the same rope cots. The women put on no more jewels than they did in former days; he mentioned this because it was a well known fact that when a native was improved in condition, the first thing he did was to purchase jewels for his wife and children.

Mr. Sribaliah, Deputy Collector, South Arcot.—The position of the labouring classes had improved. In the South Arcot district indigo cultivation had increased enormously. Indigo vats were found everywhere. The rate of daily wages to labourers in fields had almost doubled in the past years when there had been a rise in prices. There was a demand for labourers in every direction. A labourer in the field got his wages in kind at the time of harvest and in money at other times. In cash it was two annas and in grain a little more than three Madras measures. Labourers working in the indigo vats obtained three annas a day; but they were not employed all the year round. He estimated their monthly income at Rs. $3\frac{1}{2}$ or Rs. 42 per annum. There was another class of labourers who worked for monthly wages in kind. Their monthly wages were 27 Madras measures of paddy or ragi, besides one meal every day. They also got about 7 or 8 per cent. of the outturn at the time of harvest called *calavassam* and also a rupee in cash. If the approximate outturn of a field managed by one servant were 100 kalams, the labourer's income would be—monthly wages = 324 Madras measures, calavassam = 252 Madras measures, and this at a rupee for 30 measures would be Rs. 20; adding to this one rupee in cash and also the money value of one meal every day, which at 6 or 8 pies a day amounted to one rupee in the month or 12 rupees in the year, the total wages would amount to Rs. 33 and it was more or less this sum that the labourer got from his master every year. This did not include the wages of his wife.

Mr. Puckle, Collector of Tinnevelly.—The wages of labour in this district were high. Four annas a day for men coolies had been the general rate for the previous 10 years. At harvest time everywhere and throughout the year in the northern taluks the rate had been as high as six annas a day, but latterly there was a decrease and during the non-cultivation season of 1872 any quantity of labour was procurable at Palamcottah at from three annas to three annas and-a-half per diem. At the cotton screws at Tuticorin men coolies were receiving four annas a day, and in the coffee estates on the hills the same rates prevailed. The agricultural *pullars* attached to the land received their wages in kind as formerly. The position both of the free labourers and the *pullars* in this district was remarkably good; they were better fed and clothed than similar classes in any of the districts south of Madras, and their houses as a rule were superior to and were very different from the squalid huts that were to be found elsewhere.

Mr. Brandt, Sub-Collector of Tinnevelly.—The following was the result of his experience and of enquiries made unofficially among those personally acquainted with the matter, and among some of the labourers and coolies themselves. The hereditary cultivating peasants, *pullars* as they were there called, who not many years previously had been absolute slaves and whose condition was but little above slavery, were invariably paid in grain, whether in zemindaries or lands held by other landowners. The working season was about 8 or 9 months in the year, of which some 60 days they were employed in cultivation and some 40 days in harvesting operations; during the rest of these 8 or 9 months they got some odd work in the way of baling water and so on.

The earnings of a *pullan* and his wife during the working season in the Valliyur division of the Nángunéri taluk were as follows :—

	Kotahs.	Merkals.	Measures.
Two measures of rice a day or for 9 months	3	4	4
Harvest allowances	1	10	4
Gleaning	1	0	0
Special allowances called *swatantrams* or *nallanashtam* (allowances for good or for bad) as in the case of a birth, marriage, maturity of a child or death in the family ...	0	6	0

Calculating the kotah at Rs. 6 in money this was Rs. 36 in the year. The expenditure was as follows :—

	RS.
Value of diet and household expenses...	24
Drink, without which they would not work	6
Clothing	6
Total ...	36

	Kotahs.	Merkals.	Measures.
In Shermádevi in the Ambásamudram taluk, a *pullan* was reckoned to get about a measure and-a-half and his wife a measure a day in the working season or	1	10	3
Allowances at peshanam harvest ...	0	10	4
Do. at kar harvest	0	7	4
Swatantram	0	1	3
By other field labour	2	10	0
Gleaning	0	4	0
Extra jobs	2	0	0
	7	0	0

equivalent to Rs. 42 per annum. The expenditure was fully equivalent to the income. For a considerable part of the year these labourers could not take a full meal at all.

A cooly or day labourer's wages varied from two annas to three annas four pies per diem and his wife's earnings were taken at from one anna four pies to two annas, according to the nature of the work; for mere carrying and light jobs the lower rates were given; for the higher, such work as erecting mud walls, rude building operations and so on, was exacted. The higher rate was that usually paid by the Public Works Department. They were paid sometimes in kind and sometimes in money. Allowing for feast days, days on which religious ceremonies, bathing in oil, &c., were performed, a cooly would not work more than two-thirds of a month and the working season could not be put down at more than 8 months; the earnings of a cooly and his wife might accordingly be taken at between Rs. 48 and Rs. 60 a-year, according to the nature of their work, and taking their expenditure as equivalent to 7 kotahs of paddy (or at Rs. 6 a kotah) equivalent to Rs. 42 or at the higher rate as equivalent to Rs. 55 a year, there was a margin of saving which, however, was actually but seldom put by. There was, however, no doubt that this class was better off than the hereditary farm servants.

The *shanars* or palmyra-climbers simply got a share of the sweet toddy and the jaggery or coarse sugar which they collected, from their employers. One *shanan* could not extract the produce of more than 30 trees in the working season and from this he got a share and sold such of the jaggery as he did not require for consumption. The working season comprised some 8 months and his earnings could not be more than Rs. 3 or Rs. 3-8-0 per mensem, or in other words Rs. 24 or Rs. 28 a-year. They had only one meal a day, consisting of rice or other grain, with some toddy or jaggery during the daytime.

On the whole, the labouring classes could earn little more and often not enough to keep them in the bare necessaries of life; where a man and his wife had children not old enough to contribute their small quota of labour, they were still more hardly pressed; when their children were old enough to labour, their family earnings would be more, while their expenditure was not proportionately increased. There had been no increase in the wages of the hereditary farm labourers nor was their any likelihood of its increase. These people were destitute of any wish, or, at all events, any idea as to how to better themselves; they had no inclination to emigrate, as many of the cooly class did. If they could live and marry in a condition short of absolute destitution, that was enough for them. In the earnings of day labourers there had been a rise as calculated in money as there had been still more markedly in the remuneration of more skilled labour, such as that of carpenters, goldsmiths, ironsmiths, &c.; but these have not been, in the case of the former at all events, more than commensurate with the diminished purchasing power of money.

In the condition of the farm-labourers there had been one decided improvement, of which they themselves were aware, that their employers could not ill-treat them and overwork them with impunity, and they knew that they could have redress and to whom to apply for it; and compulsory labour was at an end. But so strong was the feeling of dependence on their employers and so potent the influence of the latter, that in consideration of a small present, cases of serious ill-usage and violence were even then hushed up. They were, moreover, very often in debt to their employers, for grain advanced for some family ceremony or for necessities in times of want; from this additional enthralment they could hardly ever expect to free themselves.

Mr. C. T. Longley, Collector of Salem.—Labour in the Salem district was of two kinds—ordinary and agricultural. The first represented labour employed on tanks, roads and other public works and the second, labour connected with cultivation.

Ordinary labour.—Both men, women and children of both sexes (above 7 years of age) were employed on ordinary labour. Their wages were as follow:—

	Per diem.
	ANNAS.
A man cooly	2 to 4
A woman cooly	1 to 2
A boy or girl	1 to 1½

The rates of wages varied according to the demand, but the average might be set down as follows:—

	Per diem. AS.	P.
A man cooly	2	6
A woman cooly	1	4
A boy or girl	1	0

The classes chiefly employed on ordinary labour were *Vellalas, Pullies, Pullans, Pariahs* and *Reddies.* Muhammadans were also employed as labourers, but not extensively. The classes employed on ordinary labour were mostly those that had no lands or craft. But the women and children of the ryots were frequently employed on ordinary labour, when they had no work on their own fields. When agricultural operations were extensively carried on, especially at sowing of the wet crop, labourers for ordinary labour were very scarce owing to wages of agricultural labour being much higher.

Agricultural labour.—Agricultural labour may be divided into two kinds, viz., ordinary and extraordinary.

Ordinary agricultural labour.—Every ryot whose holding was larger than he could cultivate with the assistance of members of his own family was obliged to call in the assistance of labourers known as pannials (*panniam* means cultivation and *al*, labourer). These *pannials* were paid in two ways—

(1*st*) by a monthly grain fee varying from 24 to 40 measures of either cholum, cumbu or ragi, besides an annual ready money allowance of Rs. 2 to 5.

(2*ndly*) by a monthly payment in money of Rs. 2½ to 4.

The first mode of payment was the one universally observed in all purely agricultural villages, *i.e.*, those which had no trade, like the Cauvery villages.

Extraordinary agricultural labour.—Extraordinary agricultural labour was chiefly required for irrigated cultivation. The labour consisted of ploughing, sowing, weeding and harvesting. The wages were high. Females as well as children were employed. Men ploughed, made ridges, and levelled fields; the children trod in leaves for manure, whilst women took out the seedlings from their nursery and transplanted them over the field at a distance of about two inches apart. This was at the commencement of the rice cultivation in September and October. A month subsequently females only were employed for transplanting and weeding. They were paid from one-and-a-half to two annas in ready cash. At the harvest time the labourers would not receive payment in money, but demanded it in grain. They were paid from 3 to 4 Madras measures per diem, two annas six pies or three annas four pies at the commutation rate.

Increase in the number of labourers.—The extension of cultivation and the prosecution of works of public and private enterprise had to a great extent increased the number of labourers. Besides the labouring classes already mentioned, there was a third class, the purely cooly, who had no lands or other means of livelihood. They had no houses of their own and they generally emigrated to places where they could get housed as well as earn wages. They were employed chiefly on the Shervaroy hills, where they occupied the cooly lines of the planters and were paid at the rate of a rupee for 6 days' labour.

Condition of the purely cooly class.—The condition of the purely labouring classes had certainly improved during the previous 10 years. They were better clad, wore some ornaments, and sought for more comforts and better living. Their condition, however, depended on the different castes to which they belonged. For instance, the *Vellalan* was frugal and saving in the extreme. His hard-working wife knew no finery and was content to wear for the whole year one, or at the utmost two blue cloths. The husband lived on the cheapest of dry grains and it was only at high festivals that a platter of rice and a little meat were prepared. On the other hand *Pullies* and *Pullars* were the very reverse, especially the latter. They were improvident of the morrow; "sufficient unto the day" was their motto. They spent their money as fast as they got it. They lived upon rice and meat as often as they could and delighted in gay clothes and ornaments.

Mr. J. F. Price, Sub-Collector of Salem.—Artisans were usually paid by the day, but they sometimes did piece-work. The exception was the village blacksmith who was paid sometimes in charcoal, but custom in this respect varied and in all large villages this workman was either paid by the job or by the day. *Wodders,* who did stone and earth work, usually made a contract, and the chief man and his gang united to do the work and divided the sum paid for it among themselves. When they worked for daily hire, their charge was from 4 to 5 annas a day. For ordinary coolies the payment ranged from 3 annas for the best labourer to 9 pies for a small boy of about ten years of age. Women ordinarily got one anna six pies and young girls 6 pies per diem. The customary arrangement as regards farm labourers was that the master gave from 3 to 4 rupees a year, from 3 to 4½ kandagams (130 Madras measures each) of ragi, and if he was a wealthy and liberal man, a couple of coarse cloths at the Pongal. Boys were hired by the year, and the arrangement was that the master gave them their food, a place (usually the stable) to sleep in, an ordinary handkerchief for the head, a small cloth and a cumbli. When Mr. Price first joined that district, the regular rate of hire of farm labourers had been a pagoda for a year, and from one and-a-half to three kandagams of ragi. The terms for boys had not altered, but there was then a tendency to ask for a small money payment, a rupee or so, in addition to food and clothing. The rates for daily coolies, when he first went there, ranged from 2½ annas to 6 pies for males and from one anna to 4 or 5 pies for females. The wages of artisans were on the same scale; a bricklayer who claimed 12 annas a day only got 9 previously and that was the charge for the best class of workmen. The increase in the price of labour dated from the time of the famine, when the cost of the necessaries of life of every kind was so great that the Government officials had to increase the wages paid by them to labourers. Since then though ragi, for instance, had fallen from Rs. 26 (sic) to Rs. 2½ per kandagam, which latter was its price at that time, it was impossible to reduce the rates. Coolies could get work almost everywhere, and in order to be able to retain them during the weeding and harvesting seasons, when the ryots paid the Government rates and added to them a measure or a couple of measures of ragi a day, besides food, the Government was obliged to pay the same price all the year round. Mr. Price once tried to reduce the pay of the coolies, and they nearly all struck and brought his road work to a standstill at the most important part of the season.

There had been a marked improvement in the condition of both the labouring and artisan classes during the previous 5 years. The famine had given them an opportunity for increasing the rates paid to them, and they had never, though there had been a considerable period of cheapness and plenty, allowed these to retrograde. The labourer then received three annas instead of two annas and-a-half and he paid only Rs. 2½ instead of Rs. 26 (sic) a kandagam for ragi, which was his chief article of food. It was manifest, therefore, that if he could have lived on his two annas and-a-half when ragi was sold at Rs. 26 (sic) a kandagam or even Rs. 12 or 15 at which it had stood for some time, he must have either saved or spent something on extra articles or luxuries when he received 3 annas and spent only Rs. 2½ for a kandagam of ragi, which would last for some two months. His personal observation fully bore out this view. The carpenter dressed better than he used to do; occasionally he wore a laced turban instead of the invariable red cloth handkerchief of former days; was sleek and fat; had often land of his own and was careless in his work. The labourer too was to be seen with a decent cloth instead of a dirty rag round his waist; he occasionally went away at cropping time to sow his small patch of land and returned to cooly work when there was no cultivation going on. He was independent and would not be beaten down in his wages; and there were fewer beggars or persons who stole from want, than there used to be. Any able-bodied man or woman cooly got work, and the difficulty was not to select coolies from a large number of applicants, but to get them at all.

Mr. Macgregor, Collector of Malabar.—Except in the neighbourhood of large towns, wages were paid in kind and averaged two Madras measures of rice for a first-class cooly. The women and children earned proportionately less. The great majority of agricultural labourers were permanently entertained by the landowners, and these were paid a measure and-a-half per diem whether they worked or not. This rate of pay was very little more than enough for a bare subsistence. It admitted of an occasional drink. From a report drawn up by his predecessor in 1863, there was little difference perceptible since then in the rate of wages.

There was no marked improvement in the position of the agricultural labourers during the thirteen years he had experience of the district. They were slaves in everything but name and up to no very distant period had invariably been sold with the land. There were abundant opportunities for this class to better themselves by going to work in Wynaad, but comparatively few availed themselves of this, because they preferred the freedom from anxiety which the protection of a landowner afforded.

In the towns there had been a marked increase of the rate of wages, which was four annas. This class was not much better off than it had been previously as the price of food had also increased.

Mr. Foster, Collector of Godávari.—The ordinary labourers in the Godávari district got 3 or 4 annas a day; they were almost entirely paid in money; before the anicut was made, the daily wage of common labourers was one anna and that was sufficient to maintain them. The cultivating labourers were usually kept as private servants by the puttadars and were given food, &c., all the year round and about two *putties* of grain at the harvest, which, if paddy, would be worth about Rs. 40. Many of these labourers had of late years become puttadars themselves, employing in their turn hired labourers. In the Bellary district the practice of hiring labourers to cultivate was not so common as in the Godávari district; the poorer classes there had small holdings and all the members of the family assisted in cultivating the land; but in the delta taluks of this district the landholder and his family seldom took any part in the actual cultivation of the land; they did not let it out so much as cultivate it by their own private servants maintained all the year round, so that the position of these labourers was much better in Godávari than in poorer districts; but this was the case in the years preceding 1872, after the anicut was made. In the food the labouring classes ate and in the clothes and jewellery they wore there had been a great improvement since that time.

Mr. A. J. Stuart, Sub-Collector of Rajahmundry.—The ordinary rate of wages obtained by a labourer was 3 annas a day or Rs. 67½ per annum, if he managed to find employment every day, which probably was rarely possible. The price of rice then was an anna a seer in Rajahmundry and 3 annas would have done little more than feed 4 or 5 people. Occasional expenses, such as a shred of clothing for men and a common cloth for women, would have disposed of any balances and there was always the toddy shop at hand if there was any unusual balance. The farm labourer was paid chiefly in grain; his earnings were less than the above, but more certain, and he had a master to depend upon in case of any unexpected expenses, or for such outlay as was incurred in marriages or funerals; the earnings might be estimated in the delta at about 2 putties of paddy worth Rs. 50. It was paid in various ways, but amounted on the average to about 2 putties, just sufficient for the support of his family. On the whole, by far the greatest part of the population was poor and had little beyond food, clothing and shelter; in no country in the world was the taxation so high in proportion to the income of the people it was raised from; and little or no advance was observable in the condition of the masses and certainly none in that of the labouring classes.

Mr. H. E. Sullivan, Collector of South Arcot.—The full and interesting account furnished by Mr. Sullivan regarding the condition of the labouring classes in the South Arcot district is given below:—

As regards the present condition of the labouring class, there is not the least doubt that it has materially improved during the last twenty years. It is somewhat difficult to estimate the *annual* earnings of a labourer, as the majority are not employed on the same work or remunerated in the same manner all the year round. Agricultural labourers may be divided into two classes: those who form the regular farm staff and who are engaged at the rate of one man per plough and the occasional hands who are taken on when required.

When the first description of labourers is engaged, it is usual for the employer to make him an advance of money, varying from Rs. 7 to Rs. 35, which is known as the "Mothakadan" or first loan, which binds him to the service of his master. Neither this loan nor any subsequent advances, which, on the same principle, he may receive from his employer, bear interest nor is repayment of the capital sum demanded unless the labourer elects to quit the service. This class of labourers, although they are attached to the farm under the system above described, are not employed on it all the year round, and during certain months of the year their services are dispensed with, and they are at liberty to take employment elsewhere, being bound, however, to come back whenever required. Whilst regularly employed on the farm which is generally from June to November they are paid monthly and in kind, never in money. The following are the ordinary rates:—

45 Madras measures of varagu,
11 do. do. of ragi,

or occasionally thirty-four measures of paddy are substituted for the varagu. When taken on again for the harvest, which commences in December, the labourers employed receive as their remuneration 5 per cent. of the grain harvested. This is called calavassam, the labourers receiving five kalams out of every 100 kalams got in.

The extra hands who are taken on when agricultural operations are in full swing are paid daily wages, either in money or kind or both. If in money, the wage is one anna per diem and two meals of cunji; if in kind two Madras measures of paddy, besides the cunji.

Going back again to the permanent farm labourer or as he is known in the south the "padiyal" or "*padiachy*," it would not appear at first sight that his lot was a very prosperous one. The value of the grain which he receives as wages from June to November does not exceed, even at present prices, Rs. 2 per mensem. Twenty years ago, however, it did not represent a rupee, so that although he receives now the same quantity as he formerly did, he is certainly better off (for he cannot consume it all) than he was then. But he makes a great haul at the harvest and in addition he occasionally cultivates a small portion of his employer's estate on his own account. He receives, moreover, at the different festivals small presents from his employer, and on the occasion of a marriage or other ceremony in his own family a loan to meet the necessary expenses is rarely refused. It is true that this system must more or less tend to prevent the labourer from ever emerging from that position, but this is not universally the case. Instances not unfrequently occur of these men setting up as independent farmers, although whether their condition is thereby ultimately benefited may admit of question. One bad season generally suffices to ruin them, and then they go back contentedly to their old place. I use the expression advisedly, for it is within my own tolerably varied experience that a bond of union exists in India between the landholder and his labourers, which prevents the latter, as a rule, from following the example of their brethren at home in striking for higher wages just at the time when their services are most needed. But the laws of supply and demand are inexorable, and though the landholder in India is prudent enough not to create an inconvenient precedent by raising the rate of wages whenever labour is in greater request than usual, he is still sufficiently alive to the requirements of the times by a judicious enhancement of loans and presents during the period of pressure to secure himself against the difficulties which at this moment beset the farmers in England. There is, moreover, in this country a feeling of sympathy between the employer and his men, which is not to be found in European countries, where the latter are regarded as so many machines out of which a certain amount of work is to be got, and that done, the bargain is at end. A mistaken philanthropist might make great capital at a public meeting in England out of the figures which I have given above, but my experience leads me to believe that the "padiyal" in India, with his comparatively scanty wage, is better off than the farm labourer at home with his 9*s*. or 10*s*. a week.

The wages of unskilled labour other than agricultural have advanced about 25 per cent. during the past twenty years, but the price of food has gone up in proportion. It is not, therefore, to this that we must look for the cause of the undoubted amelioration in the condition of this class of the population evinced by their dwelling in better houses, eating more animal food, and indulging in other luxuries (drinking, I am afraid, amongst the number) to a greater extent than formerly. It is due mainly, I think, to the steady and ever-increasing demand for labour throughout the year, so that the man or woman who is willing to work need never want. This is caused partly by the area of cultivation extending year by year, the development of trade and by public and private works of utility being carried out on a large scale throughout the country. In this respect the expenditure of Local Funds plays no unimportant part, and those who contribute them are repaid with interest in an indirect manner. In former days, within my own recollection, it was a very difficult matter for the labouring classes to tide over those months of the year during which agricultural operations were at a standstill. Public works were few and far between, and those who wished to obtain employment on them had often to travel and encamp many miles away from their homes to earn sufficient to save themselves from starvation. Now the work is brought up to their doors, and when the demand for agricultural labour is slack, employment is always to be obtained on imperial or local works. I believe this Presidency to be at present in the most hopeful condition, and no better evidence can, I think, be adduced in support of the position than the undoubted fact that the labouring classes, by whose aid the bulk of the revenue of the State is produced, are in a happy and prosperous condition, although, as before observed, the figures above quoted might provoke an opposite conclusion.

SECTION V.—STATISTICS SHOWING THE IMPROVEMENT IN THE CONDITION OF THE PEOPLE SINCE 1850.

(A.)—*Population.*

(a)—*Statement showing the population of the Madras Presidency*—000 *omitted.*

Districts.	1871.	1881.	1891.	Percentage of increase or decrease of the population of 1881 over that of 1871.	Percentage of increase of the population of 1891 over that of 1881.	Percentage of increase or decrease of the population of 1891 over that of 1871.
Ganjam	1,520	1,750	1,897	15·10	8·4	24·80
Vizagapatam ..	2,159	2,481	2,804	15·09	13·02	29·87
Godávari	[1] 1,621	1,795	2,079	10·73	15·82	28·25
Kistna	1,452	1,548	1,855	6·62	19·83	27·75
Nellore	1,377	1,220	1,464	—11·37	20·00	6·31
Cuddapah	1,351	1,121	1,272	—17·03	13·47	— 6·21
Bellary .. .. } Anantapur .. .. }	1,653	1,326	1,608	—19·77	21·26	— 2·79
Kurnool	915	679	818	—25·79	20·47	—11·85
Madras	398	406	452	2·09	11·33	13·56
Chingleput	938	981	1,137	4·6	15·90	21·21
North Arcot	2,015	1,823	2,180	—9·8	19·58	8·18
South Arcot	1,756	1,816	2,163	3·36	19·10	23·17
Tanjore	1,974	2,131	2,228	7·94	4·55	12·86
Trichinopoly	1,201	1,215	1,373	1·22	13·00	14·32
Madura	2,267	2,169	2,608	—4·32	20·24	15·04
Tinnevelly	1,694	1,700	1,916	0·34	12·70	13·10
Coimbatore	1,763	1,658	2,005	—5·99	20·93	13·72
Nílgiris	[2] 75	91	100	21·33	9·89	33·33
Salem	1,967	1,593	1,963	—18·68	23·22	— 0·20
South Canara ..	918	959	1,056	4·48	10·11	15·03
Malabar	[3] 2,236	2,365	2,653	5·75	12·18	18·64
Total ..	31,250	30,827	35,631	— 1·35	15·58	14·02

[1] Inclusive of the population of the Bhadráchalam and Rékapallé taluks transferred to the Madras Presidency from the Central Provinces in 1874.

[2] Inclusive of the population of the South-East Wynaad transferred from Malabar in 1877.

[3] Exclusive of the population of the South-East Wynaad transferred to the Nílgiris in 1877.

NOTE.—1. The population entered in this statement does not include the population of the Sandúr, Banganapalle and the Pudukota States.

2. The percentage of increase of the population in 1891 was small for the Tanjore district. But if the net loss by emigration between the 18th February 1881 and 26th February 1891, amounting to 97,237 persons, be added to the population, the total increase comes to 9·10 per cent.

(b)—*Statement showing the civil condition of the population of the Madras Presidency, as per census of* 1891.

Ages.	Percentage of the male population at each age period to the total male population.	Number of males (in thousands).				Percentage of the female population at each age period to the total female population.	Number of females (in thousands).				Proportion of males.				Proportion of females.			
		Single.	Married.	Widowed.	Total.		Single.	Married.	Widowed.	Total.	Single.	Married.	Widowed.	Total.	Single.	Married.	Widowed.	Total.
0—14 ..	39·3	6,812	103	3	6,918	37·7	6,100	661	22	6,783	98·5	1·4	0·1	100	90	9·7	0·3	100
15—19 ..	8·2	1,219	226	4	1,449	7·7	312	1,046	42	1,400	84·1	15·6	0·3	100	22	75·	3·	100
20—24 ..	8·1	768	653	13	1,434	9·7	82	1,544	115	1,741	54·0	45	1	100	5	89	6	100
25—34 ..	16·4	481	2,334	68	2,883	17·4	77	2,563	489	3,129	17	81	2	100	2	82	16	100
35—44 ..	12·5	92	2,006	108	2,206	11·6	41	1,277	768	2,086	4	91	5	100	2	61	37	100
45—54 ..	7·9	32	1,217	137	1,386	7·6	22	513	832	1,367	2	88	10	100	1	38	61	100
55—59 ..	1·8	6	259	45	310	1·6	4	75	202	281	2	83	15	100	1	27	72	100
60 and upwards.	5·1	15	664	223	902	6·1	14	117	966	1,097	1	74	25	100	1	11	88	100
Not stated ..	·7	63	57	4	124	·6	51	55	12	118	51	45	4	100	43	47	10	100
Total ..	100	9,488	7,519	605	17,612	100	6,703	7,851	3,448	18,002	54	43	3	100	37	44	19	100

NOTE.—These figures are exclusive of 15,000 persons (7,000 males and 8,000 females) whose civil condition has not been stated.

(b)—*Statement showing the civil condition of the population of England and Wales, as per census of* 1881.

Ages.	Percentage of the male population at each age period to the total male population.	Number of males (in thousands).				Percentage of the female population at each age period to the total female population.	Number of females (in thousands).				Proportion of males.				Proportion of females.			
		Single.	Married.	Widowed.	Total.		Single.	Married.	Widowed.	Total.	Single.	Married.	Widowed.	Total.	Single.	Married.	Widowed.	Total.
0—14 ..	37·4	4,728	..	..	4,728	35·6	4,740	..	..	4,740	100	..	..	100	100	..	..	100
15—19 ..	10·0	1,262	6	..	1,268	9·6	1,246	32	..	1,278	99·3	0·7	..	100	98	2	..	100
20—24 ..	8·8	864	245	2	1,111	9·1	809	402	5	1,216	77·8	22	0·2	100	66·5	33	0·5	100
25—34 ..	14·4	577	1,218	26	1,821	14·8	576	1,344	52	1,972	31·6	67	1·4	100	29	68	3	100
35—44 ..	11·2	195	1,171	52	1,418	11·4	234	1,165	124	1,523	14	83	3	100	15	77	8	100
45—54 ..	8·2	99	860	74	1,033	8·5	136	810	194	1,140	10	83	7	100	12	71	17	100
55—64 ..	5·7	60	563	100	723	6·1	88	471	252	811	8	78	14	100	11	58	31	100
65 and upwards.	4·3	41	314	180	535	4·9	68	213	372	653	7	60	33	100	10	33	57	100
Total ..	100	7,826	4,377	434	12,637	100	7,897	4,437	999	13,333	62	34	4	100	59	33	8	100

(c)—*Statement showing the birth and death-rates in different countries per mille of the population.*

Countries.	Birth-rate.	Death-rate.	Population per square mile.
England and Wales	35·35	21·27	446
France	26·1	23·6	180
Germany	39·8	27·1	217
Austria	39·9	30·8	158 (Austria and Hungary together)
Hungary	42·6	38·9	
Holland	35·4	24·6	312
Belgium	31·7	22·7	480
Denmark	31·2	19·7	127
Sweden	31·2	19·2	27
Italy	37·2	29·9	247
India	..	..	185
Madras Presidency	[*] 50·4	[*] 44·5	221

[*] Estimated by Mr. Hardy—*vide* Census Report of British India, 1881.

(d)—*Table showing the expectation of life and the number of survivors at different ages out of every 100 persons.*

Ages.	Madras Presidency.				Whole of India.				England.			
	Expectation of male life.	Expectation of female life.	Survival of males in every 100.	Survival of females in every 100.	Expectation of male life.	Expectation of female life.	Survival of males in every 100.	Survival of females in every 100.	Expectation of male life.	Expectation of female life.	Survival of males in every 100.	Survival of females in every 100.
	YEARS.	YEARS.	NO.	NO.	YEARS.	YEARS.	NO.	NO.	YEARS.	YEARS.	NO.	NO.
0 years	22·35	24·18	100	100	23·67	25·58	100	100	41·92	45·25	100	100
5 ,, ...	34·65	34·32	55	60	36·01	35·63	57	62	51·47	53·65	74	76
10 ,, ...	32·92	32·39	50	55	34·00	33·42	52	57	48·16	50·32	71	74
15 ,, ...	30·10	29·70	47	51	30·99	30·56	49	53	43·94	46·15	70	73
20 ,, ...	27·86	27·77	42	46	28·55	28·44	45	48	39·86	42·10	68	71
25 ,, ...	25·74	26·05	38	41	26·19	26·50	41	43	36·05	38·36	66	69
35 ,, ...	21·36	22·30	30	31	21·38	22·33	33	34	28·88	31·12	61	64
45 ,, ...	16·69	17·90	23	24	16·41	17·56	25	26	22·34	24·21	53	57
55 ,, ...	11·88	12·73	16	17	11·52	12·32	17	19	16·09	17·37	43	49
65 ,, ...	7·50	7·87	8	10	7·20	7·54	9	11	10·79	11·55	30	36
75 ,, ...	4·12	4·23	2	3	3·99	4·08	2	3	6·52	7·04	15	19
85 and upwards	2·01	2·03	·1	·2	1·94	1·94	·1	·2	3·78	4·15	3	5

NOTE.—The life table for the Madras Presidency and the whole of India has been taken from the Census Report of British India, 1881.

(e)—*Table showing the proportion of population of various countries grouped according to ages per 1,000.*

Countries.		From 0 to 15 years.	From 15 to 60 years.	60 years and upwards.
France		275	617	108
Belgium		302	610	103
Holland		329	591	80
Sweden		333	597	80
Saxony		342	584	69
England		354	573	73
Russia		353	577	70
United States, white population		377	579	44
Do. colored (free)		338	606	56
Slaves		424	541	35
India	Males	402	559	39
	Females	404	552	44
Madras Presidency ..	Males	378	573	49
		396	553	51
	Females	381	560	59
		379	560	61

NOTE.—The particulars relating to European countries have been taken from Guyot's *Social Economy*. The figures against India and the upper set of figures against the Madras Presidency are according to the Census of 1881. The lower set of figures against the Madras Presidency is according to the Census of 1891. The figures for the Madras Presidency do not include the population of the Agency tracts in the Ganjam, Vizagapatam and Godávari districts. The proportion of children under 10 years of age in the Madras Presidency exclusive of the Agency tracts was, males 287 in 1891 against 262 in 1881; and females, 286 against 265.

(B.)—*Cultivation.*

Statement showing the extent of Ryotwar or fully assessed land cultivated in the several districts of the Madras Presidency (South Canara and Malabar excepted)—in thousands of acres.

Districts.	1852-53.			1870-71.			1880-81.			1889-90.		
	Dry.	Wet.	Total.	Dry.	Wet.	Total.	Dry.	Wet.	Total.	Dry.	Wet.	Total.
1	2	3	4	5	6	7	8	9	10	11	12	13
Ganjam	76	124	200	110	181	291	164	149	313	188	157	345
Vizagapatam	10	11	21	53	22	75	53	23	76	63	32	95
Godávari	1,414	272	1,686	269	238	507	241	292	533	238	355	593
Kistna				1,438	153	1,591	1,239	186	1,425	1,294	266	1,560
Nellore	276	99	375	644	181	825	578	172	750	570	174	744
Cuddapah	1,208	83	1,291	1,160	101	1,261	911	101	1,012	1,020	107	1,127
Bellary and Anantapur.	1,839	84	1,923	2,237	146	2,383	1,777	92	1,869	2,118	105	2,223
Kurnool	493	7	500	1,135	26	1,161	866	22	888	1,066	26	1,092
Chingleput	65	173	238	197	238	435	141	288	429	199	306	505
North Arcot	253	156	409	456	193	649	363	192	555	457	230	687
South Arcot	470	165	635	922	270	1,192	822	275	1,097	954	293	1,247
Tanjore	229	708	937	234	705	939	218	711	929	225	752	977
Trichinopoly	305	125	430	808	129	937	666	129	795	686	130	816
Madura	446	85	531	665	131	796	531	128	659	724	151	875
Tinnevelly	618	129	747	818	156	974	794	175	969	856	176	1,032
Coimbatore	1,542	70	1,612	1,849	79	1,928	1,723	81	1,804	1,889	84	1,973
Nilgiris				44	..	44	60	2	62	63	6	69
Salem	667	51	718	1,088	68	1,156	810	84	894	1,028	88	1,116
Total ..	9,911	2,342	12,253	14,127	3,017	17,144	11,957	3,102	15,059	13,638	3,438	17,076

NOTE.—For remarks *vide* page xcix.

Statement showing the extent of Ryotwar or fully assessed land cultivated in the several districts of the Madras Presidency (South Canara and Malabar excepted)—in thousands of acres—continued.

Districts.	Percentage of increase or decrease in 1880-81 over the area cultivated in 1870-71.			Percentage of increase or decrease in 1889-90 over the area cultivated in 1880-81.			Percentage of increase or decrease in 1889-90 over the area cultivated in 1870-71.			Percentage of increase or decrease in 1889-90 over the area cultivated in 1852-53.		
	Dry.	Wet.	Total.	Dry.	Wet.	Total.	Dry.	Wet.	Total.	Dry.	Wet.	Total.
	14	15	16	17	18	19	20	21	22	23	24	25
Ganjam	49	— 17	7	14	5	9	71	— 13	18	147	26	72
Vizagapatam	..	14	1	19	28	20	19	45	26	530	191	352
Godávari	— 10	22	5	— 1	21	11	— 11	50	17	} 5	128	27
Kistna	— 13	23	— 10	4	43	9	— 10	73	— 2	}		
Nellore	— 10	— 5	— 9	— 1	1	— 1	— 14	— 4	— 9	106	85	98
Cuddapah	— 21	..	— 20	12	6	11	— 12	6	— 10	— 15	29	10
Bellary and Anantapur..	— 20	— 37	— 21	19	14	19	— 5	— 28	— 6	15	25	15
Kurnool	— 23	— 15	— 23	23	18	23	— 6	..	— 6	116	271	118
Chingleput	— 28	21	— 1	46	6	18	1	28	16	206	76	112
North Arcot	— 20	— 5	— 14	26	20	24	..	19	6	80	47	68
South Arcot	— 10	2	8	16	4	14	3	9	5	103	77	96
Tanjore	— 7	1	1	3	6	5	— 4	6	4	— 2	6	4
Trichinopoly	— 17	..	— 15	3	1	2	— 15	1	— 14	125	4	90
Madura	— 20	— 2	— 17	36	18	33	9	15	10	62	77	65
Tinnevelly	— 3	12	— 5	8	5	6	4	13	8	38	36	38
Coimbatore	— 7	2	— 6	9	3	9	2	6	2	} 26	28	26
Nilgiris	36	..	41	5	..	11	43	200	71	}		
Salem	— 26	23	— 23	27	5	25	— 6	29	— 3	54	72	55
Total ..	— 15	2	— 12	14	10	13	— 3	14	— 4	37	47	39

NOTE.—For remarks *vide* page xcix.

REMARKS.—In comparing the figures given in the above statement for different years, the following facts should be borne in mind :—

1. The taluks of Cumbum, Markapur and Koilkuntla were transferred from the Cuddapah to the Kurnool district in 1857-58.

2. Ninety-seven villages were transferred from the Kurnool to the Nellore district in 1863.

3. Forty-nine villages were transferred from the Chingleput to the Nellore district in 1863.

4. A portion of the Sattiavedu division was transferred from the North Arcot to the Chingleput district in 1860.

5. Several of the districts were surveyed since 1852-53, and the survey showed that the areas entered in the old accounts were below what they ought to be. The percentage of the excess area discovered by the survey to the area entered in the old accounts was as follows :—

Districts.	Year in which the settlement was introduced.	Area in thousands of acres.		Percentage of increase.
		Old accounts.	By survey.	
Ganjam	1878-79, 1879-80 and 1883-84 ...	281	336	20
Godavari	1862-63 and 1866-67	Not available.		
Kistna	1866-67 and 1873-74	1,683	1,794	7
Nellore	1873-74 and 1874-75	910	910	...
Cuddapah	1874-75 and 1877-83	1,162	1,259	8
Kurnool	1864-69, 1872-73, 1874-75 and 1877-78.	1,122	1,226	9
Chingleput	1875-76 and 1877-78	489	544	11
North Arcot	1883-86	627	706	13
Trichinopoly	1864-65	647	764	18
Madura (3 taluks)	1885-88	503	544	8
Tinnevelly	1873-78	1,299	1,397	7
Coimbatore	1878-82	2,193	2,336	7
Salem	1870-71 to 1873-74	1,048	1,209	15
	Total ...	11,964	13,025	8

Applying the rates given above to the areas under cultivation in 1852-53, the correct area is found to be 13,231 thousands of acres. Up to a recent period, the area under cultivation included portions of fields left waste and the extent on this account may on a rough calculation be taken to be 2 per cent. of the cultivated area. The net area, after deducting the area of portions of fields left waste, under cultivation, is thus 12,967 thousands of acres, or about ¾ of a million of acres in excess of the area entered in the statement.

6. In the column headed "Dry" is included the area of lands irrigated by private sources of irrigation, such as wells, &c. The areas thus irrigated in each district for the years 1852-53 and 1889-90 are in thousands of acres :—

Districts.	1852-53.	1889-90.	Districts.	1852-53.	1889-90.
Ganjam	21	...	North Arcot	3	105
Vizagapatam	... } 15	... } 2	South Arcot	2	54
Godavari			Tanjore	42	2
Kistna			Trichinopoly	31	39
Nellore	17	48	Madura	6	92
Cuddapah	46	71	Tinnevelly	9	89
Bellary and Anantapur ...	25	50	Coimbatore	} 175	357
Kurnool	3	15	Nilgiris		
Chingleput	2	6	Salem	10	77
			Total ...	407	1,007

7. The extent of lands (in thousands of acres) irrigated under the principal systems of irrigation are as under :—

Irrigation systems.	Old irrigation.	1888-89.	Percentage of increase.
Godavari delta system	28	302	978
Kistna delta system	19	246	1,195
Penner anicut	28	48	72
Sangam project	41	45	9
Cauvery delta	622	790	27
Srivaikuntham anicut	13	21	61
Palar anicut	37	59	60
Chembrambakam tank	2	11	450
Kurnool-Cuddapah canal	...	35	...
Pelandorai anicut	1	4	300
Madras water-supply and irrigation project	4	6	50
Tota ...	795	1,567	97

(C.)—*Prices.*

(a)—*Table showing the prices of second sort rice in terms of seers of 80 tolas per rupee (averages for quinquennial periods excluding famine years).*

Districts.	Average of 5 years from						
	1809 to 1813.	1819 to 1823.	1828 to 1832.	1849 to 1853.	1861 to 1865.	1870 to 1874.	1883-84 to 1887-88.
1. Ganjam	43·9	39·5	49·1	54·1	18·3	20·9	17·2
2. Vizagapatam ..	35·6	32·4	41·4	46·8	15·7	17·3	15·0
3. Godávari (Rajahmundry) ..	25·6	25·8	34·2	39·7	16·9	20·0	15·4
4. Kistna (Masulipatam) ..	21·0	23·1	31·3	29·7	13·6	15·9	14·7
Guntúr	20·5	19·4	25·6	..			
5. Nellore	22·1	24·7	28·6	35·0	13·8	17·6	15·0
6. Cuddapah	..	19·6	24·1	30·2	10·8	16·0	15·3
7. Anantapur	22·2	20·1	25·3	31·6	11·0	15·6	15·2
8. Bellary							13·6
9. Kurnool	..	..	..	27·9	11·1	13·7	13·3
10. Madras	22·6	26·5	26·3	32·4	13·3	15·1	14·1
11. Chingleput ..		26·4				17·6	16·2
12. North Arcot ..	22·1	21·4	21·9	39·8	13·7	18·8	16·3
13. South Arcot ..	22·9	25·7	26·2	34·5	14·1	18·5	16·2
14. Tanjore	28·9	31·3	31·2	38·7	14·8	16·9	16·0
15. Trichinopoly ..	28·6	29·5	30·3	35·3	12·8	16·5	14·9
16. Madura	26·4	27·6	26·1	30·4	11·6	14·5	15·0
17. Tinnevelly ..	31·4	25·7	28·4	28·1	11·5	13·1	13·4
18. Coimbatore ..	23·4	22·5	24·7	31·8	11·2	14·3	14·7
19. Nílgiris	..	..	..	..	..	10·2	11·8
20. Salem	24·1	24·5	27·2	35·0	11·4	17·0	15·7
21. South Canara ..	24·5	26·2	30·0	30·7	13·8	14·7	14·6
22. Malabar	43·6	30·1	36·6	31·6	12·3	13·7	14·1
Average for the Presidency	27·2	26·0	29·9	34·9	13·2	16·1	14·9
Index numbers representing average prices, taking the average for the years 1849 to 1853 = 100.	128	134	117	100	264	216	234

(b)—*Table showing the prices of cholum in terms of seers of 80 tolas per rupee.*

Districts.	Average of 5 years from						
	1809 to 1813.	1819 to 1823.	1828 to 1832.	1849 to 1853.	1861 to 1865.	1870 to 1874.	1883-84 to 1887-88.
1. Ganjam	..	..	..	..	28·5	30·1	27·8
2. Vizagapatam ..	45·5	40·6	56·5	58·7	28·3	30·1	26·5
3. Godávari (Rajahmundry) ..	40·9	37·0	50·2	62·0	27·8	33·9	26·5
4. Kistna (Masulipatam)	31·6	25·7	37·1 }	38·4	23·1	24·1	22·6
Guntúr	40·8	27·4	33·2 }				
5. Nellore	33·2	35·1	43·3	49·2	23·5	28·3	24·8
6. Cuddapah	39·5	29·4	42·6	43·7	18·1	27·2	28·9
7. Anantapur	} 36·1	32·1	51·1	45·3	18·6	30·2	{ 30·8
8. Bellary	}						{ 30·0
9. Kurnool	..	..	..	47·1	19·4	26·5	28·8
10. Madras	} 30·9	{ 30·5	} 35·3	44·6	21·1	{ 24·1	21·8
11. Chingleput ..	}	{ 32·7	}			{ 22·6	22·8
12. North Arcot ..	33·0	31·2	36·9	52·3	21·1	31·3	28·6
13. South Arcot ..	33·1	38·4	42·3	49·8	26·6	36·2	31·9
14. Tanjore	30·8	32·7	38·3	48·2	25·0	28·3	26·7
15. Trichinopoly ..	38·3	37·2	36·8	52·2	22·6	32·7	40·6
16. Madura	50·5	51·6	55·1	73·9	21·9	33·0	32·7
17. Tinnevelly ..	..	51·1	55·6	51·2	18·1	24·5	25·0
18. Coimbatore ..	49·6	40·3	44·5	54·8	19·7	24·8	23·8
19. Nílgiris	..	..	..	..	..	18·3	20·9
20. Salem	45·8	50·7	51·9	57·7	24·3	33·4	28·7
21. South Canara ..	..	..	..	..	..	..	..
22. Malabar	..	..	..	..	..	..	24·8
Average for the Presidency	38·6	36·6	44·4	51·8	22·8	28·4	27·4
Index numbers representing average prices, taking the average for the years 1849 to 1853 = 100.	135	141	118	100	227	182	189

(c)—*Table showing the prices of ragi in terms of seers of 80 tolas per rupee.*

Districts.	Average of 5 years from						
	1809 to 1813.	1819 to 1823.	1828 to 1832.	1849 to 1853.	1861 to 1865.	1870 to 1874.	1883-84 to 1887-88.
1. Ganjam	48·8	52·6	67·2	75·5	32·8	35·4	31·8
2. Vizagapatam ..	49·2	46·0	63·6	71·1	28·8	31·1	28·7
3. Godávari (Rajahmundry) ..	38·4	38·1	54·5	70·6	29·4	35·7	29·0
4. Kistna (Masulipatam)	34·1	35·0	47·0	47·5	25·8	29·9	29·7
Guntúr	47·3	32·8	41·7				
5. Nellore	33·7	38·5	46·6	51·3	25·7	32·0	29·0
6. Cuddapah	35·2	30·6	43·6	46·3	19·1	29·9	32·9
7 Anantapur ..	45·3	35·4	53·4	50·2	20·3	35·0	33·7
8. Bellary							34·4
9. Kurnool	..	..	..	28·7	20·2	27·8	29·3
10. Madras	31·5	30·1	32·0	41·8	20·1	28·5	27·2
11. Chingleput ..							27·3
12. North Arcot ..	32·2	30·7	34·3	53·9	22·4	34·1	31·6
13. South Arcot ..	37·3	39·7	44·2	49·1	25·6	34·7	30·3
14. Tanjore	35·0	43·3	52·0	63·9	27·9	33·0	29·2
15. Trichinopoly ..	40·5	39·0	48·7	58·4	24·6	33·5	30·3
16. Madura	45·0	48·3	49·6	65·5	22·5	31·7	30·7
17. Tinnevelly ..	64·9	50·4	57·5	54·8	19·1	25·8	27·0
18. Coimbatore ..	53·4	44·3	50·8	63·6	21·9	31·1	29·1
19. Nilgiris.	..	..	..	..	..	21·0	22·0
20. Salem	50·5	47·1	55·0	62·7	25·4	37·9	31·9
21. South Canara ..	33·5	36·4	46·0	49·1	19·5	24·2	20·6
22. Malabar	..	..	..	..	..	..	23·4
Average for the Presidency	42·0	39·9	49·3	55·8	24·0	31·1	29·1
Index numbers representing average prices, taking the average for the years 1849 to 1853 = 100.	133	141	114	100	233	180	192

(d)—*Table showing the prices of cumbu in terms of seers of 80 tolas per rupee.*

Districts.	Average of 5 years from						
	1809 to 1813.	1819 to 1823.	1828 to 1832.	1849 to 1853.	1861 to 1865.	1870 to 1874.	1883-84 to 1887-88.
1. Ganjam	..	..	..	..	31·8	31·0	33·6
2. Vizagapatam ..	50·8	44·8	64·5	73·4	29·7	31·5	30·1
3 Godávari (Rajahmundry) ..	59·1	43·1	61·5	81·7	32·7	37·4	29·2
4. Kistna (Masulipatam) ..	37·0	31·5	49·9	41·5	22·8	25·6	23·2
Guntúr	43·3	31·2	37·0				
5. Nellore	..	..	..	41·1	24·1	27·6	24·2
6. Cuddapah	34·1	28·5	41·5	41·9	17·9	27·5	29·6
7. Anantapur.. ..	38·1	32·2	48·6	41·0	17·4	26·7	27·7
8. Bellary							25·8
9. Kurnool	..	..	..	41·1	17·7	24·0	24·9
10. Madras	37·9	36·2	39·2	46·3	20·7	24·8	23·4
11. Chingleput ..		37·5				24·2	21·5
12. North Arcot ..	32·4	31·8	36·0	50·9	20·8	31·2	27·0
13. South Arcot ..	34·7	39·2	41·9	46·7	24·9	32·7	29·5
14. Tanjore	37·9	43·2	55·5	58·3	26·1	32·1	26·7
15. Trichinopoly ..	38·8	38·4	45·6	49·2	23·1	32·2	27·5
16. Madura	47·6	45·5	48·8	62·2	23·1	29·6	28·6
17. Tinnevelly ..	57·2	43·8	48·8	45·6	17·5	21·4	22·8
18. Coimbatore ..	50·4	41·8	54·1	63·9	22·9	29·0	27·9
19. Nílgiris	..	..	..	..	..	19·3	17·8
20. Salem	43·8	49·0	52·3	59·3	25·3	35·1	27·7
21. South Canara ..	..	..	..	..	..	..	..
22. Malabar	..	..	..	..	..	..	..
Average for the Presidency	42·9	38·6	48·3	53·0	23·4	28·6	26·4
Index numbers representing average prices, taking the average for the years 1849 to 1853 = 100.	123	137	110	100	227	185	200

(e)—*Statement showing the number of padies of paddy sold for a rupee at Palghát for a number of years compiled from the accounts preserved in the family of a rich landlord in Malabar.*

Years.	No. of padies.	Years.	No. of padies.	Years.	No. of padies.
1820	77	1844	59	1868	21
1821	79	1845	57	1869	22
1822	77	1846	59	1870	22
1823	77	1847	58	1871	24
1824	77	1848	59	1872	25
1825	80	1849	63	1873	24
1826	77	1850	61	1874	23
1827	80	1851	60	1875	22
1828	80	1852	57	1876	21
1829	79	1853	55	1877	10
1830	81	1854	32	1878	13
1831	75	1855	25	1879	17
1832	77	1856	31	1880	20
1833	79	1857	30	1881	21
1834	79	1858	29	1882	20
1835	76	1859	22	1883	26
1836	75	1860	22	....	..
1837	75	1861	20	....	..
1838	65	1862	20	....	..
1839	70	1863	21	....	..
1840	71	1864	17	....	..
1841	70	1865	19	....	..
1842	68	1866	15	1890	16
1843	65	1867	21		

(f)—*Statement showing the prices of certain articles of food in* 1853 *as compared with their current prices at Palghát (compiled from the household accounts kept by a large landholder in Malabar).*

Articles.	Quantity.	Price in 1853. RS.	A.	P.	Price in 1891. RS.	A.	P.	Percentage of increase or decrease.
Rice	430 parahs or 2,866⅔ padies.	153	9	2	430	0	0	+ 180
Plantain fruits ..	20,000 No.	28	9	2	50	0	0	+ 79
Green plantains ..	12,005 „	16	1	2	24	0	4	+ 50
Brinjals	5,000 „	5	11	6	12	8	0	+ 90
Cocoanuts	1,261 „	25	4	0	37	12	0	+ 50
Cocoanut-oil	133½ padies.	39	2	4	70	0	0	+ 78
Gingelly-oil	6⅔ „	1	0	0	3	14	3	+ 289
Lamp-oil	33⅓ „	5	9	2	16	4	0	+ 191
Sugar-candy	12½ lb.	1	3	6	0	14	0	— 28
Green-gram	21⅓ padies.	1	2	4	3	4	0	+ 184
White pea	33⅓ „	1	12	7	5	0	0	+ 180
Red-gram	22 „	1	2	4	3	2	4	+ 175
Horse-gram	2 „	0	1	2	0	4	0	+ 243
Salt	100 „	4	5	10	18	12	0	+ 329
Pepper	50 lb.	2	0	0	14	0	0	+ 600
Mustard	17⅓ padies.	1	4	7	3	9	9	+ 180
Turmeric	3⅓ „	0	13	9	1	4	0	+ 45
Dry chillies	40 „	0	13	9	1	12	0	+ 103
Curd	773⅓ „	24	13	9	33	2	4	+ 33
Milk	173⅓ „	5	11	5	32	8	0	+ 468
Ghee	10 „	4	4	7	15	0	0	+ 250
Betel-leaves	3,750 bundles.	24	0	0	37	8	0	+ 56
Areca-nut	225 lb.	31	11	5	63	0	0	+ 50
Tobacco	50 „	2	2	11	10	0	0	+ 358

NOTE.—A padi is a measure of capacity containing 130 tolas of rice.
A parah = 6⅔ Macleod seers containing 128 tolas of rice each.

(g)—*Statement showing the prices of different articles of food, &c., at Súlúr (a large village 7 miles from Coimbatore) compiled from the village accounts preserved by an old Kurnam or Village Accountant in the Coimbatore District.*

Articles.	Years.	Quantity.	Price. RS. A. P.
Rice	1820-21	13 Madras measures	1 0 0
	1832-33	Do.	0 11 7
	1846-47	Do.	1 1 4
	1851-52	Do.	0 11 7
	1853-54	Do.	0 13 0
	1854-55	Do.	1 2 6
	1888-89	Do.	2 2 8
Cholum	1820-21	13 vallams or 26 Madras measures.	1 0 0
	1829-30	Do.	0 5 4
	1834-35	Do.	0 14 3
	1840-41	Do.	0 6 6
	1845-46	Do.	0 6 6
	1846-47	Do.	0 12 3
	1855-56	Do.	0 13 0
	1888-89	Do.	1 10 0
Ragi	1847-48	33 Madras measures	1 0 0
	1856-57 *	Do.	2 1 0
	1888-89	Do.	2 1 0
Horse-gram	1845-46	32 Madras measures	1 0 0
	1847-48	Do.	0 13 6
	1888-89	Do.	2 0 0
Bengal-gram	1843-44	16 Madras measures	1 0 0
	1853-54	Do.	1 5 4
	1862	Do.	2 14 6
	1888-89	Do.	2 0 0
Tobacco	1822-23	One maund	0 8 0
	1832-33	Do.	0 8 0
	1888-89	Do.	2 0 0
Dholl or redgram	1851-52	$18\frac{3}{8}$ Madras measures	1 0 0
	1888-89	Do.	2 10 0
Jaggery	1834-35	One maund	0 14 0
	1839-40	Do.	0 11 0
	1841-42	Do.	0 9 7
	1888-89	Do.	1 0 0
Gingelly-seed	1853-54	16 Madras measures	1 0 0
	1888-89	Do.	2 0 0
Gingelly-oil	1851-52	One small podi	0 2 3
	1888-89	Do.	0 5 4
Castor-oil	1851-52	One small podi	0 2 8
	1888-89	Do.	0 6 8
Cotton	1822-23	One maund	0 11 2
	1834-35	Do.	0 6 5 to 0 8 0
	1840-41	Do.	0 12 0
	1852-53	Do.	0 10 0
	1853-54	Do.	0 8 0
	1862-63	Do.	1 6 5
	1888-89	Do.	1 9 7

* (Famine year).

(h)—*Statement showing the prices of food-grains at certain stations in the Coimbatore district, obtained from certain old cadjan accounts kept by merchants and landholders.*

Grains.	Quantity.	Years.	Price. RS. A. P.
		Karúr.	
Paddy	One kalam (36 Madras measures).	1830-31, a famine year.	0 12 0
		1835-36	0 8 0
		1890	2 10 7
		Dhárápuram.	
Paddy	51 Madras measures ..	Prior to 1840	1 0 0
		1888	3 7 10
Cholum	48 do. ..	Prior to 1840	1 0 0
		1888	1 12 7
Ragi	54 do. ..	Prior to 1840	1 0 0
		1888	2 0 4
		Palladam.	
Cholum	One podi (230 Madras measures).	1837-38	5 0 0
		1838-39	6 2 9
		1839-40	6 8 0
		1888-89	14 6 0
Ragi	One podi	1837-38	5 0 0
		1888-89	14 6 0

(i)—*Statement showing the prices of articles of food, &c., in* 1890 *as compared with those about* 1800 *in the village of Singánallúr (5 miles from Coimbatore) compiled from the accounts preserved by the Kurnam or Accountant of the village.*

Articles.	Quantity.	Price in 1800. RS. A. P.	Price in 1890. RS. A. P.
Paddy	1 salagai or 60 measures of 140 Rs. weight.	1 7 6	5 0 0
Cholum	Do. ..	1 1 7	5 0 0
Cumbu	Do. ..	1 1 7	4 8 0
Ragi	Do. ..	1 1 7	4 8 0
Horse-gram	Do. ..	1 1 7	5 0 0
Ghee	1 podi	0 8 0	1 4 0
Dry chillies	12 measures	0 3 0	0 2 0
Tobacco	1 bundle, 200 Rs. weight.	0 2 0	0 8 0
Cotton	1 maund	0 0 9	0 1 6
Gingelly-oil	1 measure	0 4 0	0 10 8
Lamp-oil	Do.	0 4 0	0 13 4
Brass	1 seer or 24 Rs. weight.	0 8 0	0 5 0
Copper	Do. ..	0 10 0	0 6 0
Lead	Do. ..	0 4 0	0 8 0
Bullocks	Each	20 0 0 to 25 0 0	70 0 0 to 80 0 0
Sheep and goats	Do.	0 12 0 to 1 4 0	5 0 0 to 7 0 0

(j)—*Statement showing the mahanum prices of paddy per Tanjore kalam (24 Madras Measures) for a series of years in the Tanjore District.*

Years.	Price.	Years.	Price.	Years.	Price.
	RS. A. P.		RS. A. P.		RS. A. P.
1823 ..	0 13 6	1844 ..	0 8 4	1865 ..	1 7 9
1824 ..	0 13 8	1845 ..	0 11 2	1866 ..	1 8 4
1825 ..	0 8 7	1846 ..	0 10 5	1867 ..	1 4 0
1826 ..	0 5 11	1847 ..	0 7 4	1868 ..	1 4 6
1827 ..	0 5 9	1848 ..	0 6 2	1869 ..	1 0 4
1828 ..	0 9 8	1849 ..	0 7 1	1870 ..	0 12 9
1829 ..	0 8 0	1850 ..	0 7 3	1871 ..	1 0 6
1830 ..	0 7 4	1851 ..	0 7 4	1872 ..	0 15 1
1831 ..	0 7 3	1852 ..	0 7 7	1873 ..	1 3 5
1832 ..	0 10 0	1853 ..	0 12 10	1874 ..	1 1 0
1833 ..	0 12 0	1854 ..	0 10 6	1875 ..	1 0 7
1834 ..	0 3 7	1855 ..	0 12 10	1876 ..	1 15 11
1835 ..	0 7 4	1856 ..	0 10 4	1877 ..	1 12 5
1836 ..	0 11 9	1857 ..	1 0 3	1878 ..	1 12 10
1837 ..	0 8 6	1858 ..	1 4 8	1879 ..	1 1 5
1838 ..	0 8 10	1859 ..	0 12 4	1880 ..	1 0 7
1839 ..	0 8 5	1860 ..	1 1 0	1881 ..	0 13 8
1840 ..	0 6 3	1861 ..	1 1 10	1882 ..	0 13 3
1841 ..	0 4 4	1862 ..	0 13 10	1883 ..	0 15 3
1842 ..	0 6 1	1863 ..	1 3 4	1884 ..	1 5 0
1843 ..	0 8 0	1864 ..	1 6 1		

The mode of calculating the average current selling price for each mahanum is as follows:—Paddy grown in Tanjore consists of two main species — kar, the early crop, and pasanum, the later crop; the cultivation of kar constitutes about one-fifth of the entire wet cultivation of the Tanjore delta and the practice is therefore to make up the general average by taking one-fifth of the average price of kar and four-fifths of that of pasanum. The averages are struck from actual sales in villages belonging to each mahanum; for kar from 1st November to 31st January and for pasanum from 1st February to 20th May. The village sales are returned by the kurnam every five days, and from them the Tahsildar compiles a return every ten days and transmits it to the Collector's office, where the averages are struck. These returns of sales were prescribed with a view to determine the village prices for the purpose of fixing the demand under the olungu system under which the land revenue demand depended on the price of grain every year. After the abolition of the olungu system the returns were continued for the purpose of calculating the value of melvaram share of the grain due to the Tanjore Ranees in the villages belonging to them. As the Collector is now no longer Receiver of the Rajah's estate, the returns appear to have been since discontinued.

(k)—*Statement showing the prices of articles of food, &c., in 1892, as compared with those in 1797 at Manjeshwar, a village 10 miles from Mangalore, compiled from the 'Black books' kept there.*

Articles.	Quantity.	Price in 1797. RS. A. P.	Price in 1892. RS. A. P.
Paddy	Per moorah of 42 pucka seers.	0 9 0	1 4 0
Rice (Jeera) 1st sort ..	Do. ..	2 0 0	5 0 0
Do. 3rd sort ..	Do. ..	1 8 0	4 0 0
Rice, muscaty, 3rd sort ..	Do. ..	1 4 0	3 8 0
Green gram	Do. ..	1 7 4	3 4 0
A kind of pulse called 'pigeon pea' out of which dholl is prepared	Do. ..	1 13 2	3 4 0
Dholl	Do. ..	2 12 0	4 0 0
Black gram 'Phaseolus Mungo.'	Do. ..	1 7 4	3 4 0
Horse-gram	Do. ..	1 0 0	3 4 0
Salt	Do. ..	0 12 0	3 8 0
Cows' ghee	Per seer of 24 tolas ..	0 3 8	0 7 0
Buffaloes' ghee	Do. ..	0 1 9	0 5 4
Oil, cocoanut	Per maund of 28 lb. ..	1 12 0	4 0 0
Cocoanuts	Per 100	1 0 0	3 8 0
Jaggery (sugar-cane) ..	Per maund of 40 seers of 24 tolas each.	1 4 0	2 0 0
Gingelly seeds	Per seer of 80 Tolas ..	0 1 0	0 2 0
Mustard seeds, country ..	Do. ..	0 1 0	0 2 0
Turmeric	Do. ..	0 1 4	0 4 0
Tamarind	Per maund of 28 lb. ..	0 12 0	1 4 0
Chillies, country ..	Do. ..	2 0 0	4 0 0
Sugar	Do. ..	5 12 0	4 0 0
Chunam	Per moorah of 42 pucka seers.	0 6 0	0 5 0
Pepper	Per maund of 28 lb. ..	2 0 0	6 0 0
Areca-nuts	Per candy	18 0 0 to 22 0 0	60 0 0 to 80 0 0
Beaten rice	Per seer of 80 tolas	0 0 6	0 1 0
Bamboos	Per 100	2 0 0	12 0 0 to 25 0 0
Tin	Per seer of 24 tolas	0 6 0	0 8 0
Copper	Per maund of 28 lb. ..	20 0 0	15 0 0
Coir yarn	Per 40 yards	0 0 1	0 0 3

(D.)—*Trade.*

(a)—*Foreign trade :—Value of exports and imports in million Ṙx.* (*Rx*=10 *Rs.*).

Years.	Exports from						Imports to						Total Exports and Imports.					
	Madras.	Other parts of Indian Empire.				Total, Indian Empire.	Madras.	Other parts of Indian Empire.				Total, Indian Empire.	Madras.	Other parts of Indian Empire.				Total, Indian Empire.
		Bengal.	Burma.	Bombay.	Total.			Bengal.	Burma.	Bombay.	Total.			Bengal.	Burma.	Bombay.	Total.	
Average of five years ending—																		
1838-39 ..	1·1	6·1	..	4·1	10·2	11·3	·7	3·3	..	3·4	6·7	7·4	1·8	9·4	..	7·5	16·9	18·7
1843-44 ..	1·3	8·2	..	4·7	12·9	14·2	·8	5·4	..	4·3	9·7	10·5	2·1	13·6	..	9	22·6	24·7
1848-49 ..	1·7	9·7	..	5·6	15·3	17	1·1	6·3	..	4·8	11·1	12·2	2·7	16	..	10·5	26·5	29·2
1853-54 ..	1·8	10·6	..	7·6	18·2	20	1·3	7·9	..	6·7	14·6	15·9	3·1	18·5	..	14·3	32·8	35·9
1858-59 ..	2·3	13·1	..	10·5	23·6	25·9	2·2	13·2	..	11·4	24·6	26·8	4·5	26·3	..	21·9	48·2	52·7
1863-64 ..	4·3	14·9	* 1·5	23·1	38·9	43·2	3·4	16·1	* ·5	21·1	37·6	41	7·7	31	* 2	44·2	76·5	84·2
1868-69 ..	5·7	19·5	2·2	30·3	52	57·7	4	20·2	1	24·1	45·3	49·3	9·7	39·7	3·2	54·4	97·3	107
1873-74 ..	6·4	24	2·9	24·5	51·4	57·8	4	18·7	1·4	17·2	37·3	41·3	10·4	42·7	4·3	41·7	88·7	99·1
1878-79 ..	6·8	27	4·1	25·2	56·3	63·1	4·1	20·8	2·4	21	44·2	48·3	10·9	47·8	6·5	46·2	100·5	111·4
1883-84 ..	8·1	33·8	6·5	32	72·3	80·4	4·6	24·1	3·6	29·5	57·2	61·8	12·7	57·9	10·1	61·5	129·5	142·2
1888-89 ..	9·3	35·4	6·3	39·2	80·9	90·2	5·7	25·6	4·5	39·4	69·5	75·2	15	61	10·8	78·6	150·4	165·4

* Average for three years.

(b)—*Statement showing the growth or increase of Sea-borne Trade in relation to the Revenue derived from Customs duties therefrom, and of the quantity of salt sold and exported with the rates of sale per maund of* $82\frac{2}{7}$ *lb. in relation to the receipts derived therefrom in the Madras Presidency from* 1800-01 (*In million £ and million lb.*)

Official years.	Customs and land transit duties.	Value of sea-borne trade.			Salt.			Remarks.
		Foreign trade.	Coasting trade.	Total.	Receipts.	Sale rate per Indian Maund of $82\frac{2}{7}$ lb.	Quantity sold and exported.	
1	2	3	4	5	6	7	8	9
	£	£	£	£	£		LB.	
1800-01	·19	No information.			·02		No information.	
1801-02	·31				·02			(*a*) In the original returns, the trade is given in Sicca rupees and transposed into English money at the rate of 2*s.* 3*d.* from 1800-01 to 1810-11.
1802-03	·35	1·9	2·5	(*a*) 4·4	·03			
1803-04	·40	2·6	2·1	4·7	·03			
1804-05	·54	1·6	2·5	4·1	·04			
1805-06	·35	2·0	2·4	4·4	·18	9 annas 4 pies, or 0·7 farthings per lb.	309	
1806-07	·26	1·3	2·3	3·6	·21		399	
1807-08	·25	1·6	3·4	5·0	·26		410	
1808-09	·30	1·5	2·0	3·5	·26		321	
1809-10	·38	1·3	2·0	3·3	·28	14 annas, or 1 farthing per lb.		
Average of 1st Decade ..	·34	1·7	2·4	4·1	·13		360	
1810-11	·42	2·0	1·7	3·7	·34		354	
1811-12	·43	2·2	1·2	(*b*) 3·4	·34		377	(*b*) From 1811-12 to 1818-19, the returns are given in Arcot rupees, $3\frac{1}{2}$ Arcot rupees being held equal to a pagoda, which is equivalent to 8*s.*
1812-13	·46	1·5	1·7	3·2	·37		368	
1813-14	·47	1·3	1·4	2·7	·33		368	
1814-15	·54	1·5	1·2	2·7	·31		290	
1815-16	·51	1·7	1·0	2·7	·31		264	
1816-17	·52	1·5	1·1	2·6	·29		249	
1817-18	·51	1·7	1·1	2·8	·29		293	
1818-19	·51	1·7	1·1	2·8	·35		323	(*c*) From 1819-20 to 1834-35 the returns are rendered in Madras rupees, which varies but slightly from Arcot rupees, one rupee being equivalent to 2*s.* 1*d.*
1819-20	·54	1·3	1·1	(*c*) 2·4	·36		330	
Average of 2nd Decade ..	·49	1·6	1·3	2·9	·33		322	

(b)—*Statement showing the growth or increase of Sea-borne Trade in relation to the Revenue derived from Customs duties, &c.*—cont.

Official years.	Customs and land transit duties.	Value of sea-borne trade.			Salt.			Remarks.
		Foreign trade.	Coasting trade.	Total.	Receipts.	Sale rate per Indian Maund of $82\frac{2}{7}$ lb.	Quantity sold and exported.	
1	2	3	4	5	6	7	8	9
	£	£	£	£	£		LB.	
1820-21	·57	1·3	1·1	2·4	·31	9 annas 4 pies, or ·7 farthings per lb.	385	
1821-22	·63	2·0	1·2	3·2	·37		470	
1822-23	·62	1·8	1·0	2·8	·34		446	
1823-24	·57	1·8	1·3	3·1	·36		458	
1824-25	·54	2·0	2·2	4·2	·33		472	
1825-26	·55	2·3	2·3	4·6	·36		472	
1826-27	·54	1·7	1·8	3·5	·33		428	
1827-28	·57	2·4	1·3	3·7	·35		500	
1828-29	·61	2·0	1·5	3·5	·40	14 annas, or 1 farthing per lb.	382	
1829-30	·59	2·4	1·5	3·9	·47		409	
Average of 3rd Decade ..	·58	2·0	1·5	3·5	·36		442	
1830-31	·58	1·5	1·3	2·8	·44		382	
1831-32	·46	1·9	1·5	3·4	·35		377	
1832-33	·42	1·8	1·5	3·3	·33		394	
1833-34	·38	1·5	2·2	3·7	·37		531	
1834-35	·42	1·7	1·7	3·4	·38		465	
1835-36	·42	1·7	2·1	(d) 3·8	·35		367	(d) From 1835-36 to date the returns are made out in Company's rupees, which have been always taken at 2*s*.
1836-37	·47	2·0	2·3	4·3	·37		368	
1837-38	·40	1·8	1·9	3·7	·38		360	
1838-39	·41	1·9	2·1	4·0	·40		381	
1839-40	·41	2·1	2·3	4·4	·40		384	
Average of 4th Decade ..	·43	1·8	1·9	3·7	·38		401	

(b)—*Statement showing the growth or increase of Sea-borne Trade in relation to the Revenue derived from Customs duties, &c.*—cont.

Official years.	Customs and land transit duties.	Value of sea-borne trade.			Salt.			Remarks.
		Foreign trade.	Coasting trade.	Total.	Receipts.	Sale rate per Indian Maund of 82$\frac{2}{7}$ lb.	Quantity sold and exported.	
1	2	3	4	5	6	7	8	9
	£	£	£	£	£		LB.	
1840-41	·43	2·0	2·6	4·6	·38	14 annas, or 1 farthing per lb.	367	
1841-42	·41	2·2	2·3	4·5	·40		428	
1842-43	·43	2·0	2·2	4·2	·40		435	
1843-44	·42	2·0	2·2	4·2	·43		417	
1844-45	·20	2·9	2·6	(e) 5·5	·45	16 annas, or 1·2 farthings per lb.	387	(e) Land transit duties abolished by Act VI of 1844. New Customs Tariff introduced.
1845-46	·17	2·5	2·2	4·7	·47		402	
1846-47	·15	2·6	2·2	4·8	·46		404	
1847-48	·14	2·6	2·0	4·6	·49		407	
1848-49	·10	3·0	1·6	4·6	·45		409	
1849-50	·10	2·4	2·4	4·8	·46		422	
Average of 5th Decade ..	·25	2·4	2·2	4·6	·44		408	
1850-51	·11	2·8	2·2	5·0	·48		418	
1851-52	·12	3·1	2·3	5·4	·48		438	
1852-53	·12	3·6	2·6	6·2	·51		423	
1853-54	·13	3·6	3·3	6·9	·48		425	
1854-55	·12	3·4	2·5	5·9	·49		476	
1855-56	·13	4·2	2·9	7·1	·51		525	
1856-57	·14	5·0	3·1	8·1	·50		483	
1857-58	·14	5·2	4·4	9·6	·57		492	
1858-59	·15	4·9	3·6	8·5	·60	18 annas, or 1·35 farthings per lb.	538	
1859-60	·26	5·5	3·7	9·2	·65		545	
Average of 6th Decade ..	·14	4·1	3·1	7·2	·53		476	

(b)—*Statement showing the growth or increase of Sea-borne Trade in relation to the Revenue derived from Customs duties, &c.*—cont.

Official years.	Customs and land transit duties.	Value of sea-borne trade. Foreign trade.	Coasting trade.	Total.	Salt. Receipts.	Sale rate per Indian Maund of $82\frac{2}{7}$ lb.	Quantity sold and exported.	Remarks.
1	2	3	4	5	6	7	8	9
	£	£	£	£	£		LB.	
1860-61	·30	6·1	4·4	10·5	·71	18 annas, or 1·35 farthings per lb.	550	
1861-62	·23	6·9	4·7	11·6	·87	24 annas, or 1·8 farthings per lb.	524	
1862-63	·20	8·5	4·7	13·2	·91		530	
1863-64	·23	11·4	7·4	18·8	·90		549	
1864-65	·20	11·2	6·3	17·5	1·04		580	
1865-66	·21	12·7	6·2	18·9	1·01	2[illegible] annas, or 1·9 farthings per lb.	646	
1866-67 (*f*)	·19	6·5	5·2	11·7	1·05		597	(*f*) For eleven months only, the closing date of the financial year having been changed from 30th April to 31st March.
1867-68	·25	8·0	4·8	12·3	1·10		534	
1868-69	·28	10·2	5·4	15·6	1·11		575	
1869-70	·28	10·2	4·8	15·0	1·17	32 annas, or 2·4 farthings per lb.	565	
Average of 7th Decade ..	·24	9·1	5·4	14·5	·99		565	
1870-71	·30	9·4	5·2	14·6	1·27		544	
1871-72	·31	11·1	{ 4·7 4·2	15·8 4·2	} 1·31		561	
1872-73	·39	10·3	{ 5·0 3·4	15·3 3·4	} 1·29		548	

(b)—*Statement showing the growth or increase of Sea-borne Trade in relation to the Revenue derived from Customs duties, &c.*—cont.

Official years.	Customs and land transit duties.	Value of sea-borne trade.			Salt.			Remarks.
		Foreign trade.	Coasting trade.	Total.	Receipts.	Sale rate per Indian Maund of 82⅐ lb.	Quantity sold and exported.	
1	2	3	4	5	6	7	8	9
	£	£	£	£	£		LB.	
1873-74	·34	11·1	5·6 4·3	16·7 4·3	1·30	32 annas, or 2·4 farthings per lb.	535	
1874-75	·32	11·0	5·3 4·0	16·3 4·0	1·33		592	
1875-76	·31	12·3	4·6 3·9	16·9 3·9	1·35		570	
1876-77	·25	11·2	9·5 7·0	20·7 7·0	1·29		525	
1877-78	·20	9·9	12·9 7·2	22·8 7·2	1·14		476	
1878-79	·21	10·1	7·1 3·4	17·2 3·4	1·46	43 annas, or 3·2 farthings per lb.	438	
1879-80	·23	11·4	5·7 3·2	17·1 3·2	1·58		473	
Average of 8th Decade ..	·28	10·8	6·5 4·5	17·3 4·5	1·33		526	
1880-81	·25	11·9	5·4 3·7	17·3 3·7	1·56		466	
1881-82	·20	12·3	5·7 2·8	18·0 2·8	1·47		470	
1882-83	·10	13·5	5·2 3·5	18·7 3·5	1·39	35 annas, 2·6 farthings per lb.	511	
1883-84	·11	14·3	6·2 3·9	20·5 3·9	1·39		552	
1884-85	·10	14·2	6·4 4·2	20·6 4·2	1·38		541	

(b)—*Statement showing the growth or increase of Sea-borne Trade in relation to the Revenue derived from Customs duties, &c.*—cont.

Official years.	Customs and land transit duties.	Value of sea-borne trade. Foreign trade.	Coasting trade.	Total.	Salt. Receipts.	Sale rate per Indian Maund of 82$\frac{2}{7}$ lb.	Quantity sold and exported.	Remarks.
1	2	3	4	5	6	7	8	9
	£	£	£	£	£		LB.	
1885-86	·09	13·4	6·5 5·0	19·9 5·0	1·45	35 annas, or 2·6 farthings per lb. (1885-86 to 1887-88)	561	
1886-87	·13	15·2	6·9 4·1	22·1 4·1	1·42		553	
1887-88	·15	15·8	6·9 4·7	22·7 4·7	1·44		561	
1888-89	·17	16·5	6·9 4·7	23·4 4·7	1·65	43 annas, or 3·2 farthings per lb. (1888-89 to 1889-90)	582	
1889-90	·18	18·2	6·8 4·6	25·0 4·6	1·76		579	
Average of 9th Decade ..	·15	14·5	6·3 4·1	20·8 4·1	1·50		537	

NOTE.—From 1800-01 to 1844-45, the duties derived from land transit are not shown separately from those levied on the import and export trade of the Presidency, whether by sea or passing from British to foreign territory and *vice versâ*. Act IV of 1844 abolished the land transit duties and a new customs tariff was introduced. Since 1844, and up to the present date, the customs tariff has undergone constant revision.

2. The total value of foreign and coasting trade has been extracted from the commercial returns of each year from the earliest date for which such records exist. The information, however, in the original returns was given in different kinds of rupees, but notes are inserted in the column of remarks explaining the rates at which they have been converted into sterling value for different periods. Trade with British ports within the Presidency was not recorded for years prior to 1871-72. Of the two sets of figures entered in the column "coasting trade" against the years subsequent to 1870-71, the upper figures are exclusive of the trade with British ports within the Presidency, the lower figures are those of British ports within the Presidency.

3. The district of North Canara was transferred from the Madras to the Bombay Presidency in 1862.

4. The statement was compiled from the statement printed at pages 160 and 161, Appendix I to the Famine Commission Report, 1881, and from information obtained from the Board of Revenue, Separate Revenue.

(c)—*Statement showing the quantity and value of the principal articles of trade exported from and imported into the Madras Presidency by sea for a series of years (quantity and value are given in millions).*

Note.—The statement was compiled from the statistics given in the Madras Manual of Administration and in the Annual Trade Reports.

Years.		Exports.									
		Cotton wool.		Hides and skins.		Coffee.		Indigo.		Sugar.	
		Quantity.	Value.	Quantity.	Value.	Quantity.	Value.	Quantity.	Value.	Quantity.	Value.
1		2	3	4	5	6	7	8	9	10	11
		LB.	RS.	NO.	RS.	LB.	RS.	LB.	RS.	CWT.	RS.
1855-56	..	21	2·5	3	·7	9	·9	2·9	4·3	·49	3·2
1856-57	..	54	7·2	3	1·4	9	·9	2·8	4·7	·54	3·8
1857-58	..	55	8·8	4	2·2	8	·8	2·	3·9	·45	4·1
1858-59	..	39	6·1	5	1·8	11	1·2	1·9	3·6	·34	2·7
1859-60	..	63	9·6	4	1·6	15	1·9	2·5	4·6	·43	3·1
1860-61	..	79	11·3	4	1·7	19	3·2	1·5	2·8	·4	2·9
1861-62	..	88	17·	3	1·4	21	4·7	2·3	4·9	·32	2·5
1862-63	..	62	23·8	4	1·9	20	5·4	2·4	5·2	·26	2·3
1863-64	..	72	44·7	4	2·1	27	6·6	2·	4·	·41	3·3
1864-65	..	73	40·4	4	1·9	31	7·7	1·5	3·3	·38	3·2
1865-66	..	120	48·4	4	2·	35	7·8	1·6	3·5	·42	2·7
1866-67	..	24	9·4	5	2·4	17	4·2	·6	1·4	·28	1·9
1867-68	..	49	12·4	5	2·9	36	8·1	2·2	4·2	·12	·9
1868-69	..	94	21·4	6	3·2	47	10·8	2·6	6·1	·23	1·4
1869-70	..	68	19·1	6	3·6	37	8·8	3·	7·5	·24	1·7
1870-71	..	42	10·6	7	4·1	35	8·3	3·8	8·5	·2	1·4
1871-72	..	75	17·2	8	4·7	57	13·8	5·2	12·1	·33	2·0
1872-73	..	68	15·9	11	6·7	42	11·3	2·9	6·9	·47	3·0
1873-74	..	62	12·8	10	6·2	41	15·2	4·2	8·8	·22	1·2
1874-75	..	80	16·3	8	5·6	37	13·6	2·8	5·7	·46	2·5
1875-76	..	82	16·5	10	10·8	43	16·6	2·5	4·7	·4	1·9
1876-77	..	54	10·7	11	12·9	36	14·3	3·1	5·6	·49	2·5
1877-78	..	17	3·5	12	15·7	33	13·6	1·9	3·9	·41	2·7
1878-79	..	46	10·	10	11·	38	15·6	2·9	5·9	·23	1·4
1879-80	..	57	13·2	11	11·6	38	15·3	4·9	9·5	·31	1·9
1880-81	..	44	10·2	12	13·7	39	15·2	2·8	6·2	·54	3·3
1881-82	..	45	9·8	14	16·2	36	13·6	5·9	12·6	·91	6·1
1882-83	..	73	16·5	15	19·3	38	13·5	3·8	7·8	1·25	7·6
1883-84	..	73	15·2	..	18·4	38	14·5	5·8	11·7	1·48	8·1
1884-85	..	66	14·3	13	16·9	36	12·5	4·7	9·5	1·10	6·1
1885-86	..	41	9·5	15	19·3	41	13·5	5·1	10·5	1·25	6·2
1886-87	..	67	14·7	16	19·4	41	15·2	4·3	8·7	1·13	6·7
1887-88	..	78	18·	17	21·3	30	15·3	4·9	10·	1·13	5·7
1888-89	..	69	16·7	18	21·8	37	18·6	5·5	10·9	1·03	6·
1889-90	..	98	25·4	18	20·7	26	15·7	6·1	11·9	1·35	8·6

(c)—*Statement showing the quantity and value of the principal articles, &c.*—cont.

Years.	Exports—*cont.*									
	Seeds.		Spices.		Rice.		Paddy.		Cotton piece-goods.	
	Quantity.	Value.	Quantity.	Value.	Quantity.	Value.	Quantity.	Value.	Quantity.	Value.
	12	13	14	15	16	17	18	19	20	21
	CWT.	RS.	LB.	RS.	CWT.	RS.	CWT.	RS.	YDS.	RS.
1855-56 ..	·61	1·7	29	2·4	2·6	5·5	·22	·25	..	2·1
1856-57 ..	·71	2·4	21	1·9	2·4	5·1	·29	·36	..	2·
1857-58 ..	1·23	2·9	25	2·4	2·6	5·8	·29	·38	..	2·1
1858-59 ..	·62	2·5	23	1·9	1·8	4·4	·22	·43	..	2·4
1859-60 ..	·36	1·5	38	2·2	2·1	5·2	·27	·43	..	2·1
1860-61 ..	·52	2·3	27	2·9	2·8	6·2	·21	·36	..	1·9
1861-62 ..	·67	2·8	28	3·3	1·5	4·6	·21	·39	..	2·1
1862-63 ..	·89	3·7	28	2·2	1·3	4·5	·21	·42	..	2·
1863-64 ..	·63	2·7	22	2·4	1·5	5·9	·3	·6	..	1·6
1864-65 ..	·72	2·8	22	2·6	1·4	6·1	·3	·86	..	1·6
1865-66 ..	·59	2·3	24	2·6	1·4	6·6	·28	·7	..	2·
1866-67 ..	·10	·5	5	2·1	1·5	8·4	·24	·65	..	2·4
1867-68 ..	·64	3·4	23	2·6	1·7	7·	·27	·65	..	3·4
1868-69 ..	1·07	5·1	25	2·8	1·8	6·9	·31	·78	..	2·3
1869-70 ..	·86	5·	23	2·5	1·5	5·9	·25	·6	..	2·2
1870-71 ..	..	4·9	24	2·6	2·1	7·4	·28	·55	..	2·2
1871-72 ..	..	5·8	34	3·5	2·4	8·5	·31	·6	..	2·5
1872-73 ..	..	4·	32	2·9	2·1	8·8	·29	·59	7·7	2·6
1873-74 ..	..	5·	25	2·7	3·5	12·4	·35	·71	9·1	2·8
1874-75 ..	..	5·4	28	3·4	3·1	10·9	·27	·65	9·8	2·9
1875-76 ..	1·36	5·9	30	4·1	2·4	8·9	·29	·68	7·5	2·8
1876-77 ..	·90	4·9	27	3·7	1·5	6·2	·23	·54	7·	3·2
1877-78 ..	·56	3·5	18	2·9	·8	4·7	·17	·63	5·5	2·8
1878-79 ..	·39	2·5	25	4·2	1·3	7·4	·21	·75	5·2	2·5
1879-80 ..	1·37	7·7	28	4·3	2·2	9·9	·22	·55	5·3	2·2
1880-81 ..	1·49	7·7	30	4·1	2·8	10·	·47	·88	6·3	2·6
1881-82 ..	1·47	7·1	35	4·6	1·7	5·6	·3	·55	6·9	3·
1882-83 ..	1·40	6·5	32	5·4	1·5	4·5	·16	·29	8·3	3·3
1883-84 ..	2·1	10·3	31	5·9	2·2	6·2	·17	·32	11·2	4·
1884-85 ..	1·86	8·8	37	7·6	1·9	6·4	·29	·64	13·1	4·8
1885-86 ..	1·82	8·6	34	7·4	1·4	5·8	·27	·58	15·4	4·2
1886-87 ..	2·01	9·4	43	8·8	1·9	7·1	·26	·49	13·6	4·6
1887-88 ..	2·27	10·6	36	8·1	1·8	6·6	·28	·54	14·6	4·7
1888-89 ..	1·74	9·7	41	8·6	1·9	7·3	·36	·70	13·3	4·4
1889-90 ..	1·92	11·9	38	7·1	2·1	8·3	·30	·62	13·6	4·5

(o)—*Statement showing the quantity and value of the principal articles, &c.*—cont.

Years.	Exports—*cont.*							
	Oils.		Cocoanuts and kernels.		Coir, yarn and rope.		Tobacco.	
	Quantity.	Value.	Quantity.	Value.	Quantity.	Value.	Quantity.	Value.
	22	23	24	25	26	27	28	29
	GALS.	RS.	NO.	RS.	CWT.	RS.	LB.	RS.
1855-56 ..	2·3	·6	..	·8	·12	·3	2	·2
1856-57 ..	2·5	·7	..	·9	·14	·3	2	·2
1857-58 ..	1·6	·9	..	·7	·15	·3	3	·3
1858-59 ..	2·7	·7	..	·8	·11	·3	3	·3
1859-60 ..	2·4	·6	..	1·1	·17	·3	2	·2
1860-61 ..	2·5	1·6	..	1·9	·18	·6	2	·1
1861-62 ..	1·8	1·6	..	3·	·18	·9	2	·1
1862-63 ..	2·8	2·7	..	3·6	·18	1·1	5	·3
1863-64 ..	3·8	3·7	..	3·5	·21	1·1	3	·3
1864-65 ..	2·8	2·5	..	3·6	·18	·9	4	·6
1865-66 ..	1·6	1·5	..	2·1	·13	1·2	3	·5
1866-67 ..	1·1	1·2	..	2·5	·18	1·	2	·3
1867-68 ..	1·8	2·4	..	3·2	·19	1·3	3	·4
1868-69 ..	2·6	4·1	..	3·4	·25	1·7	3	·4
1869-70 ..	2·8	4·	..	3·2	·25	1·8	3	·6
1870-71 ..	1·9	2·8	..	2·2	·18	1·3	3	·4
1871-72 ..	4·2	5·6	..	3·8	·19	1·4	4	·5
1872-73 ..	4·	5·5	..	3·	·24	1·8	3	·6
1873-74 ..	2·3	3·2	..	2·7	·24	1·9	4	·8
1874-75 ..	2·8	3·3	..	3·2	·26	2·	5	·8
1875-76 ..	3·1	3·4	..	* 1·2	·25	1·9	5	·7
1876-77 ..	3·9	3·9	..	* 1·4	·29	2·6	6	1·
1877-78 ..	2·4	3·1	..	* 1·2	·29	2·4	6	1·1
1878-79 ..	2·7	3·8	..	* 1·5	·3	2·6	5	1·1
1979-80 ..	3·6	4·2	..	* 1·7	·24	1·8	7	1·1
1880-81 ..	3·8	4·1	..	3·6	·23	1·6	7	1·3
1881-82 ..	3·5	3·4	..	2·9	·32	2·4	6	1·3
1882-83 ..	2·9	3·1	..	2·6	·32	2·4	7	1·4
1883-84 ..	4·1	4·5	..	3·5	·32	2·4	7	1·4
1884-85 ..	4·9	4·8	..	3·8	·38	2·9	7	1·5
1885-86 ..	3·9	4·	..	3·2	·35	2·7	7	1·3
1886-87 ..	3·7	3·9	..	2·9	·35	2·7	8	1·4
1887-88 ..	4·2	4·4	..	3·9	·32	2·4	9	1·6
1888-89 ..	4·9	5·	..	4·4	·35	2·6	10	2·1
1889-90 ..	4·9	5·1	..	3·7	·43	3·3	8	1·7

* Particulars of kernels not available for these years.

(c)—*Statement showing the quantity and value of the principal articles, &c.*—cont.

Years.		Imports.									
		Cotton piece-goods.		Cotton twist.		Paddy.		Rice.		Metals.	
		Quantity.	Value.	Quantity.	Value.	Quantity.	Value.	Quantity.	Value.	Quantity.	Value.
		30	31	32	33	34	35	36	37	38	39
		YDS.	RS.	LB.	RS.	CWT.	RS.	CWT.	RS.	CWT.	RS.
1855-56	..	·3	2·8	3·9	2·3	·03	·04	·63	2·05	..	1·08
1856-57	..	·5	2·9	4·2	2·3	·21	·36	·43	1·22	..	1·99
1857-58	..	1·2	3·8	3·5	2·1	·21	·35	·28	·82	..	1·91
1858-59	..	2·7	4·4	6·1	3·5	·37	·73	·18	·65	..	2·43
1859-60	..	9·9	4·9	7·4	4·1	·24	·41	·11	·37	..	2·28
1860-61	..	..	6·1	7·	3·9	·29	·55	·21	·75	..	3·03
1861-62	..	..	5·2	6·2	3·8	·34	·72	·67	2·44	..	3·62
1862-63	..	..	6·4	4·	2·6	·27	·56	·93	3·20	..	2·33
1863-64	..	..	10·1	7·	4·5	·37	·80	1·04	3·85	..	3·37
1864-65	..	..	9·6	6·4	6·2	·29	·61	1·05	4·03	..	3·75
1865-66	..	..	11·2	6·5	7·2	·49	1·27	·54	2·51	..	3·18
1866-67	..	42·1	10·2	7·2	7·9	·46	1·39	·27	1·45	..	3·03
1867-68	..	57·9	12·	9·2	8·3	·56	1·42	·35	1·54	..	4·01
1868-69	..	66·9	13·5	10·1	0·1	·53	1·37	·52	2·13	..	4·33
1869-70	..	71·9	12·6	11·7	9·3	·64	1·58	·94	3·79	..	4·67
1870-71	..	94·6	15·	12·9	10·4	·34	·71	·83	2·98	..	3·98
1871-72	..	93·8	15·3	11·7	9·5	·29	·60	·73	2·52	..	3·22
1872-73	..	86·6	14·1	14·3	10·7	·33	·74	·86	3·11	..	2·71
1873-74	..	96·5	15·7	13·2	10·4	·54	1·27	·56	2·04	..	3·13
1874-75	..	79·	13·5	14·1	10·9	·80	2·02	·37	1·38	..	3·59
1875-76	..	88·6	14·3	16·	12·4	·79	2·02	·41	1·55	·43	4·99
1876-77	..	87·3	14·3	16·5	11·3	1·21	3·71	6·	32·76	·36	4·32
1877-78	..	72·4	11·4	14·2	9·8	2·22	7·82	9·21	55·42	·41	4·49
1878-79	..	68·5	10·5	14·1	9·5	1·87	5·99	2·49	13·71	·25	3·13
1879-80	..	86·9	13·3	16·5	12·	1·1	3·03	·61	2·78	·35	3·55
1880-81	..	106·4	16·7	20·2	14·6	·44	·97	·80	2·75	·51	4·70
1881-82	..	110·8	16·9	17·9	12·	·71	1·22	1·63	5·21	·37	3·83
1882-83	..	128·7	20·2	23·5	15·	·76	1·27	1·68	5·28	·37	4·28
1883-84	..	130·7	20·4	19·7	13·7	·53	·99	2·02	6·29	·55	5·59
1884-85	..	147·9	23·4	22·9	14·8	·89	1·65	·99	3·54	·49	5·53
1885-86	..	123·4	18·4	20·3	12·6	1·37	2·85	1·30	4·93	·62	5·61
1886-87	..	177·8	26·3	21·5	13·9	·53	1·06	1·28	4·75	·46	5·17
1887-88	..	139·3	22·1	21·7	13·8	·56	·99	1·48	5·57	·63	5·42
1888-89	..	173·	26·4	23·3	15·4	·36	·62	·98	3·57	·59	4·72
1889-90	..	169·1	26·8	21·5	14·7	·49	·98	·82	3·34	·5	5·78

(d)—*Statement showing the traffic by rail and by canal of the Madras Presidency with other British Provinces, French Territory, Native States and the Chief Sea-port Towns in* 1889-90 (*in millions of Indian Maunds and in millions of Rupees*).

Articles.	Rail-borne external trade.						Rail-borne internal trade.			Total Rail-borne trade.	Trade by canals.	Value of traffic with the French Territory (in millions of rupees).
	Imports into			Exports from								
	Madras Presidency, excluding the sea-port towns.	Madras sea-ports.	Total.	Madras Presidency, excluding the sea-port towns.	Madras sea-port towns.	Total.	Madras Presidency, excluding the sea-port towns.	Madras sea-ports.	Total.			
	I. MDS.	I. MDS.	I. MDS.	I. MDS.	I. MDS.	I. MDS.	I. MDS.	I. MDS.	I. MDS.	I. MDS.	I. MDS.	RS.
Coal and coke	·04	..	·04	·02	·36	·38	·40	·04	·44	·86	..	·03
Cotton, raw	·07	·06	·13	·04	..	·04	·04	·87	·91	1·08	·62	·15
Cotton, manufactured	·04	·01	·05	·05	·07	·12	·50	·06	·56	·73	·07	1·71
Drugs and chemicals	..	..	..	..	..	..	·05	·06	·11	·11	..	·02
Dyes and tans	·06	·07	·13	·03	·01	·04	·14	·27	·41	·58	·10	·19
Grain and pulse	1·55	·31	1·86	·85	·03	·88	2·96	3·15	6·11	8·85	5·10	2·34
Hides and skins	·06	·26	·32	..	·01	·01	·12	·17	·29	·62	·01	·14
Jute	·03	..	·03	·02	·03	·05	·18	·02	·20	·28	·02	..
Liquors	·03	..	·03	·03	·04	·07	·06	·03	·09	·19	..	·05
Metals	·03	·01	·04	·02	·13	·15	·57	·05	·62	·81	·08	·18
Oils	·01	..	·01	·01	·05	·06	·16	·23	·39	·46	} 2·48 {	2·20
Oil seeds	·27	·13	·40	·08	·02	·10	·36	2·07	2·43	2·93		6·53
Provisions	·07	·19	·26	·26	·02	·28	·62	·85	1·47	2·01	..	·23
Salt	·02	..	·02	·11	·27	·38	2·46	..	2·46	2·86	2·28	·01
Spices	·08	·01	·09	·06	·01	·07	·34	·12	·46	·62	..	·31
Stone and lime	..	·01	·01	·04	·01	·05	·09	2·41	2·50	2·56	..	..
Sugar	·10	·05	·15	·14	..	·14	·60	·76	1·36	1·65	·45	·08
Tobacco	..	..	..	·07	..	·07	·11	·06	·17	·24	·17	·17
Other articles	·14	·07	·21	1·24	·18	1·42	1·10	1·68	2·78	4·41	10·06	7·16
Total ..	2·60	1·18	3·78	3·07	1·24	4·31	10·86	12·90	28·76	31·85	21·44	21·50

(e)—*Statement showing the average prices in Madras of the staple commodities of trade.*

Articles.	1844 to 1848.	1849 to 1853.	1854 to 1858.	1859 to 1863.	1864 to 1868.	1869 to 1873.	1874 to 1876.
Imports.	RS.	RS.	RS.	RS.	RS.	RS.	RS.
Shirtings, per piece ..	6·88	6·15	7·25	7·87	12·16	8·41	6·06
Grey shirtings, per 8¼ lb. ..	..	..	..	..	9·56	6·12	5·36
Mule twist, No. 40, per bundle	2·81	2·64	2·8	3·94	5·74	3·69	3·24
Turkey red, Nos. 40 to 60, per bundle of 12 lb. ..	15·46	13·52	14·5	..	..	..	..
Turkey red, Nos. 40 to 60, per bundle of 10 lb. ..	16·22	..	..	21·87	22·26	17·7	15·94
Orange, Nos. 40 to 60, per bundle	..	4·28	..	6·	6·68	4·9	4·54
Do. Nos. 30 to 60, do.	..	3·72	3·78	3·52	..	..	..
Copper sheathing, 16 to 32 oz., per candy	255·3	258·65	321·8	275·7	249·85	212·	..
Copper sheathing, per candy.	..	..	..	..	..	..	265·42
Iron, assorted, per candy ..	23·69	19·8	30·3	22·14	21·63	23·26	..
Do. spelter, do. ..	63·43	42·8	71·15	57·15	62·4	58·5	..
Exports.							
Hides, buffalo, per 100 ..	55·5	42·25	58·75	60·	93·35	133·75	..
Indigo, ordinary, per maund.	..	32·	39·9	45·05	51·7	50·75	40·
Do. good	..	30·37	45·25	51·5	62·35	63·31	..
Sugar, per candy	49·35	33·	28·53	27·37	36·9	33·97	27·42
Linseed, per candy	13·2	12·87	22·37	19·31	26·	24·3	..
Rice, per garce	209·	159·1	246·	304·	360·6	296·	332·5

REMARKS.—Taken roughly, it will be seen that the nominal prices of the articles of import in 1874-76 are about the same as in 1850. From Mr. O'Conor's report on the trade of India for 1890-91, it appears that the prices of staple imports at Calcutta have fallen since 1873 as shown below, taking the prices in 1873 to be represented by 100.

—	Grey shirtings, 8¼ lb.	Mule Twist.		Copper sheathing.	Iron, flat, bolt, &c.	Total.
		White, No. 40.	Turkey red, No. 40.			
March 1873	100	100	100	100	100	500
June 1874	97	92	106	95	108	498
March 1875	86	92	102	103	93	476
,, 1876	86	90	92	99	79	446
January 1877	78	90	85	92	67	412
,, 1878	73	78	87	86	60	384
,, 1879	76	75	78	80	56	365
,, 1880	81	84	75	83	73	396
,, 1881	82	82	69	81	56	370
,, 1882	78	84	69	89	71	391
,, 1883	82	74	54	80	60	350
,, 1884	75	74	62	77	62	350
,, 1885	76	72	58	64	54	324
,, 1886	84	67	57	57	50	315
,, 1887	81	62	57	65	53	318
,, 1888	79	75	59	90	61	364
,, 1889	81	75	57	98	65	376
,, 1890	76	74	57	69	79	355
,, 1891	74	70	56	71	62	333
August 1891	76	66	57	75	61	335

Information regarding variations in the Madras prices is not available, but there is little doubt that prices in Madras have fallen in about the same proportions as in Calcutta.

(f)—Statement showing the Value of certain articles of Export and Import deduced from the declared values of the articles entered in the Sea-borne Trade Returns of the Madras Presidency.

Years.	Rice and Paddy—Exports.			Cocoanuts and Kernels—Exports.			Cotton Twist—Imports.	
	Value of rice per cwt.	Value of paddy per cwt.	Rate of export duty.	Number of cocoanuts per rupee.	Value of kernels per cwt.	Rate of export duty.	Value—Rupee per lb.	Rate of duty.
	RS.	RS.			RS.			
1855-56 ..	2·04	1·13	....	75	3·92	....	·577	
1856-57 ..	2·12	1·25	....	75	3·94	....	·539	
1857-58 ..	2·17	1·29	....	75	..	....	·612	
1858-59 ..	2·36	1·93	....	75	3·97	....	·576	14th March 1859 to 11th March 1860—5 per cent. *ad valorem.*
1859-60 ..	2·41	1·57	2 annas per maund of $82\frac{2}{7}$ lb.	76	3·96	3 per cent. (*ad valorem*).	·564	
1860-61 ..	2·21	1·69	Do. do. ..	55	6·21	Do. do. ..	·552	12th March 1860 to 22nd April 1862—10 per cent.
1861-62 ..	3·01	1·85	Do. do. ..	39	8·68	Do. do. ..	·616	
1862-63 ..	3·50	1·93	Do. do. ..	40	8·77	Do. do. ..	·642	23rd April 1862 to 9th March 1882—3½ per cent.
1863-64 ..	3·21	1·99	Do. do. ..	40	7·93	Do. do. ..	·649	
1864-65 ..	4·19	2·91	Do. do. ..	39	8·22	Do. do. ..	·962	From 10th March 1882—free.
1865-66 ..	4·56	2·47	3 annas per maund (12th April to 14th July 1865).	36	10·31	Do. do. ..	1·097	
1866-67 ..	5·54	2·69	2 annas per maund (15th July 1865 to 5th March 1867). 3 annas per maund from 6th March 1867.	..	12·96	Do. do. ..	1·096	
1867-68 ..	4·01	2·39	Do. do. ..	..	..	Free from 6th March 1867.	·906	

(f)—*Statement showing the Value of certain articles of Export and Import deduced from the declared values of the articles, &c.*—cont.

Years.	Rice and Paddy—Exports.			Cocoanuts and Kernels—Exports.			Cotton Twist—Imports.	
	Value of rice per cwt.	Value of paddy per cwt.	Rate of export duty.	Number of cocoanuts per rupee.	Value of kernels per cwt.	Rate of export duty.	Value—Rupee per lb.	Rate of duty.
	Rs.	Rs.			Rs.			
1868-69 ..	3·92	2·48	3 annas per maund from 6th March 1867.	39	10·10	....	·907	
1869-70 ..	4·	2·45	Do. do. ..	35	10·59	....	·793	
1870-71 ..	3·62	1·99	Do. do. ..	35	10·76	....	·808	
1871-72 ..	3·16	1·92	Do. do. ..	40	8·72	....	·809	
1872-73 ..	4·07	2·03	Do. do. ..	48	7·28	....	·750	
1873-74 ..	3·57	2·04	Do. do. ..	43	9·13	....	·785	
1874-75 ..	3·57	2·42	Do. do. ..	45	8·62	....	·769	
1875-76 ..	3·63	2·36	Do. do. ..	41	Particulars not available	....	·773	
1876-77 ..	4·02	2·38	Do. do. ..	41		....	·688	
1877-78 ..	5·74	3·68	Do. do. ..	32		....	·691	
1878-79 ..	5·69	3·48	Do. do. ..	29		....	·673	
1879-80 ..	4·55	2·54	Do. do. ..	44		....	·731	
1880-81 ..	3·54	1·86	Do. do. ..	48	8·46	....	·721	
1881-82 ..	3·22	1·84	Do. do. ..	47	8·27	....	·622	
1882-83 ..	2·95	1·80	Do. do. ..	41	10·14	....	·637	
1883-84 ..	2·90	1·86	Do. do. ..	35	10·82	....	·695	
1884-85 ..	3·45	2·17	Do. do. ..	46	8·40	....	645	
1885-86 ..	4·05	2·15	Do. do. ..	40	9·01	....	·622	
1886-87 ..	3·76	1·89	Do. do. ..	42	9·45	....	·643	
1887-88 ..	3·60	1·90	Do. do. ..	40	9·95	....	·637	
1888-89 ..	3·73	1·96	Do. do. ..	43	8·60	....	·666	
1889-90 ..	3·94	2·08	Do. do. ..	43	9·27	....	·683	

(g)—*Statement showing the Net Imports of Gold and Silver into India for a series of years (in Million Rx. Rx. = 10 Rs.).*

Years.	Net imports.		
	Gold.	Silver.	Total.
1834-35	..	..	1·8
1835-36	..	..	2·1
1836-37	..	..	1·8
1837-38	..	..	2·3
1838-39	..	..	2·6
1839-40	..	..	1·5
1840-41	..	..	1·4
1841-42	..	..	1·7
1842-43	..	..	3·2
1843-44	..	..	3·8
1844-45	..	..	3·1
1845-46	..	..	1·9
1846-47	0·8	1·4	2·2
1847-48	1·0	−0·5	0·5
1848-49	1·4	0·3	1·7
1849-50	1·1	1·3	2·4
Total ..	..	..	34·0
1850-51	1·2	2·1	3·3
1851-52	1·2	2·9	4·1
1852-53	1·2	4·6	5·8
1853-54	1·1	2·3	3·4
1854-55	0·7	..	0·7
1855-56	2·5	8·2	10·7
1856-57	2·1	11·1	13·2
1857-58	2·8	12·2	15·0
1858-59	4·4	7·8	12·2
1859-60	4·3	11·1	15·4
1860-61	4·2	5·3	9·5
1861-62	5·2	9·1	14·3
1862-63	6·8	12·6	19·4
1863-64	8·9	12·8	21·7
1864-65	9·8	10·1	19·9

Years.	Net imports.		
	Gold.	Silver.	Total.
1865-66	5·7	18·7	24·4
1866-67	3·8	7·0	10·8
1867-68	4·6	5·6	10·2
1868-69	5·2	8·6	13·8
1869-70	5·6	7·3	12·9
1870-71	2·3	0·9	3·2
1871-72	3·6	6·5	10·1
1872-73	2·5	0·7	3·2
1873-74	1·4	2·5	3·9
1874-75	1·9	4·6	6·5
Total ..	93·0	174·6	267·6
1875-76	1·5	1·6	3·1
1876-77	0·2	7·2	7·4
1877-78	0·5	14·7	15·2
1878-79	− 0·9	4·0	3·1
1879-80	1·8	7·8	9·6
1880-81	3·6	3·9	7·5
1881-82	4·9	5·3	10·2
1882-83	4·9	7·5	12·4
1883-84	5·5	6·4	11·9
1884-85	4·7	7·2	11·9
1885-86	2·8	11·6	14·4
1886-87	2·1	7·2	9·3
1887-88	3·0	9·2	12·2
1888-89	2·8	9·3	12·1
1889-90	4·6	11·0	15·6
Total ..	42·0	113·9	155·9
1890-91	5·6	14·2	19·8
Grand Total from 1850-51 ..	140·6	302·7	443·3

(h)—*Statement showing the number of Factories in the Madras Presidency in* 1889-90.

Nature of Industry.	Number of mills or factories.	Nominal capital (if a joint-stock company).	Number of spindles.	Average daily number of persons employed. Through-out the year.	Average daily number of persons employed. In the working season.	Annual outturn. Quantity.	Annual outturn. Value.	—
		RS.					RS.	
Cotton mills worked by steam ..	8	51,00,500	169,123	5,647	..	181,052 cwt. of cotton worked up	..	
Jute mills	1	..	1,543	711	..	38,266 cwt. of jute	..	
Breweries	2	..	..	..	..	447,404 gallons		
Bone crushing factories	6	..	..	..	..	160 tons	7,237	
Coffee works	23	..	..	1,429	6,166	18,506,465 lb.*	98,34,449	
Cement works	1	..	..	198	233	60,000 cwt.	1,20,000	
Cotton presses and weaving establishments (other than mills).	41	..	..	1,120	1,929	95,725,531 lb., 223,850 yards ..	..	
Flour mills	1	..	..	20	..	....	15,000	
Ice factories	2	..	..	34	20	874 tons	46,359	
Indigo factories	6	..	..	27	580	153 maunds	34,775	
Indigo vats	6,393	..	..	863	88,225	47,762 maunds	50,88,958	
Iron and brass foundries	5	..	..	349	..	12,051 cwts.	1,11,819	
Mineral and ærated water factories..	12	..	..	114	20	80,386 bottles	66,762	
Oil mills	17	..	..	780	..	90,463 cwt.	10,10,482	
Rice mills	1	1,17,500	..	..	60	61,865 cwt.	64,600	
Rope works	4	..	..	61	116	Lb. 176,767, 1,200 to 1,600 bales of coir yarn and fibre, and 1,098 rolls of coir matting.	41,000	
Silk filatures	1	95,000	..	60	..	1,920 lb.	21,120	
Sugar factories	6	..	..	1,318	746	27,922 cwt.	3,71,258	Outturn of only two factories.
Tanneries	7	..	..	505	20	13,336 cwt.	11,55,544	
Timber mills	3	..	..	126	..	....	90,700	
Tobacco firms and factories ..	32	..	..	1,203	454	90,119,992 cigars	7,14,110	

* Also 3,932,244 lb. of cinchona, cardamoms, pepper, ginger, &c., valued at Rs. 6,48,945.

NOTE.—This statement cannot be considered complete or strictly accurate.

(E.)—*Taxation.*

(a)—*Statement showing the growth of Revenue or Taxation in the Madras Presidency from* 1800-01. *In Millions Rx. (Rx. = 10 Rs.).*

Items of Revenue.	1800-01.	1801-02.	1802-03.	1803-04.	1804-05.	1805-06.	1806-07.	1807-08.	1808-09.	1809-10.	Average for 10 years ending 1809-10.	1810-11.	1811-12.	1812-13.	1813-14.
1	2	3	4	5	6	7	8	9	10	11	12	13	14	15	16
State Revenue or Taxation.															
1. Land Revenue .. .. 2. Moturpha or tax on trades, houses, &c., and the income and assessed taxes .. 3. Abkári farms and excise	2·46	3·82	4·01	3·90	3·99	4·15	3·80	4·04	4·05	4·17	3·84	3·99	3·90	3·96	3·99
4. Tobacco monopoly in Malabar & S. Canara	·19	·31	·35	·10	·54	·35	·26	·25	·30	·38	·34	·42	·43	·46	·47
5. Customs and land transit duties ..	·02	·02	·03	·03	·04	·18	·21	·26	·26	·28	·13	·34	·34	·37	·33
6. Salt receipts	..	..	..	..	..	..	..	..	..	·01	..	·03	·03	·03	·03
7. Stamps	..	..	..	..	..	..	..	..	..	..	..	..	..	..	..
8. Provincial rates	..	..	..	..	..	..	..	..	..	..	..	..	..	..	..
9. Forest	..	..	..	..	..	..	..	..	..	..	..	..	..	..	..
10. Registration	..	..	..	..	..	..	..	..	..	..	..	..	..	..	..
Total ..	2·67	4·15	4·39	4·33	4·57	4·68	4·27	4·55	4·61	4·84	4·31	4·78	4·70	4·82	4·82
11. Miscellaneous	·87	·58	·33	·32	·32	·33	·33	·38	·36	·53	·43	·46	·45	·47	·47
Total ..	3·54	4·73	4·72	4·65	4·89	5·01	4·60	4·93	4·97	5·37	4·74	5·24	5·15	5·29	5·29
Other than State Revenue or Taxation.															
12. Village service fund	..	..	..	..	..	..	..	..	..	..	..	..	..	..	..
13. Local funds, general	..	..	..	..	..	..	..	..	..	..	..	..	..	..	..
14. Local funds, special	..	..	..	..	..	..	..	..	..	..	..	..	..	..	..
15. Municipal taxation	..	..	..	..	..	..	..	..	..	..	..	..	..	..	..
Total ..	..	..	..	..	..	..	..	..	..	..	..	..	..	..	..
Grand Total, excluding miscellaneous ..	2·67	4·15	4·39	4·33	4·57	4·68	4·27	4·55	4·61	4·84	4·31	4·78	4·70	4·82	4·83
Grand Total, including miscellaneous ..	3·54	4·73	4·72	4·65	4·89	5·01	4·60	4·93	4·97	5·37	4·74	5·24	5·15	5·29	5·29
Population	..	..	..	..	..	..	..	..	..	..	..	..	..	..	..

(a)—*Statement showing the growth of Revenue or Taxation in the Madras Presidency from* 1800-01. *In Millions Rx.* (*Rx.* = 10 *Rs.*)—cont.

Items of Revenue.	1814-15.	1815-16.	1816-17.	1817-18.	1818-19.	1819-20.	Average for 10 years ending 1819-20.	1820-21.	1821-22.	1822-23.	1823-24.	1824-25.	1825-26.	1826-27.	1827-28.
	17	18	19	20	21	22	23	24	25	26	27	28	29	30	31
State Revenue or Taxation.															
1. Land revenue															
2. Moturpha or tax on trades, houses, &c., and the income and assessed taxes ..	3·89	3·61	3·83	3·85	3·80	3·79	3·86	3·74	3·71	3·77	3·74	3·76	3·98	3·67	3·60
3. Abkári farms and excise															
4. Tobacco monopoly in Malabar & S. Canara															
5. Customs and land transit duties	·54	·51	·52	·51	·51	·54	·49	·57	·63	·62	·57	·54	·55	·54	·57
6. Salt receipts	·31	·31	·29	·29	·35	·36	·33	·31	·37	·34	·36	·33	·36	·33	·35
7. Stamps	·04	·04	·04	·05	·05	·05	·04	·06	·06	·06	·06	·06	·06	·06	·06
8. Provincial rates	..	..	..	..	..	..	..	..	..	..	..	..	..	..	..
9. Forest	..	..	..	..	..	..	..	..	..	..	..	..	..	..	..
10. Registration	..	..	..	..	..	..	..	..	..	..	..	..	..	..	..
Total ..	4·78	4·47	4·68	4·70	4·71	4·74	4·72	4·68	4·77	4·79	4·73	4·69	4·95	4·60	4·58
11. Miscellaneous	·54	·63	·68	·68	·65	·66	·57	·72	·79	·79	·77	·75	·76	1·38	·77
Total ..	5·32	5·10	5·36	5·38	5·36	5·40	5·29	5·40	5·56	5·58	5·50	5·44	5·71	5·98	5·35
Other than State Revenue or Taxation.															
12. Village service fund	..	..	..	..	..	..	..	..	..	..	..	..	..	..	..
13. Local funds, general	..	..	..	..	..	..	..	..	..	..	..	..	..	..	..
14. Local Funds, special	..	..	..	..	..	..	..	..	..	..	..	..	..	..	..
15. Municipal taxation	..	..	..	..	..	..	..	..	..	..	..	..	..	..	..
Total ..	..	..	..	..	..	..	..	..	..	..	..	..	..	..	..
Grand Total, excluding miscellaneous ..	4·78	4·47	4·68	4·70	4·71	4·74	4·72	4·68	4·77	4·79	4·73	4·69	4·95	4·60	4·58
Grand Total, including miscellaneous ..	5·32	5·10	5·36	5·38	5·36	5·40	5·29	5·40	5·56	5·58	5·50	5·44	5·71	5·98	5·35
Population	..	..	..	..	..	..	..	..	..	13,476,923	..	..	..	..	..

(a)—*Statement showing the growth of Revenue or Taxation in the Madras Presidency from 1800-01.* *In Millions Rx.* (*Rx.* = 10 *Rs.*)—cont.

Items of Revenue.	1828-29.	1829-30.	Average for 10 years ending 1829-30.	1830-31.	1831-32.	1832-33.	1833-34.	1834-35.	1835-36.	1836-37.	1837-38.	1838-39.	1839-40.	Average for 10 years ending 1839-40.
	32	33	34	35	36	37	38	39	40	41	42	43	44	45
State Revenue or Taxation.														
1. Land revenue									3·30	2·89	3·15	3·24	3·22	..
2. Moturpha or tax on trades, houses, &c., and the income and assessad taxes .. (items 1–3 combined in cols. 32–39)	3·65	3·52	3·73	3·46	3·25	2·94	3·18	3·25	·10	·10	·10	·11	·10	3·41
3. Abkári farms and excise									·17	·17	·18	·18	·23	..
4. Tobacco monopoly in Malabar & S. Canara	·07	·07	..	·07	·06	·07	·07	·07	·07	·08	·08	·08	·09	..
5. Customs and land transit duties ..	·61	·59	·58	·58	·46	·42	·38	·42	·42	·47	·40	·41	·41	·43
6. Salt receipts	·40	·47	·36	·44	·35	·33	·37	·38	·35	·37	·38	·40	·40	·38
7. Stamps	·06	·05	·06	·05	·04	·04	·04	·04	·04	·05	·05	·05	·05	·04
8. Provincial rates	..	..	..	..	..	..	..	..	..	..	..	..	..	..
9. Forest	..	..	..	..	..	..	..	..	..	..	..	..	..	..
10. Registration	..	..	..	..	..	..	..	..	..	..	..	..	..	..
Total ..	4·79	4·70	4·73	4·60	4·16	3·80	4·04	4·16	4·45	4·13	4·34	4·47	4·50	4·26
11. Miscellaneous	·78	·71	·82	·76	·31	·31	·32	·32	·15	·49	·48	·48	·47	·41
Total ..	5·57	5·41	5·55	5·36	4·47	4·11	4·36	4·48	4·60	4·62	4·82	4·95	4·97	4·67
Other than State Revenue or Taxation.														
12. Village service fund	..	..	..	..	..	..	..	..	..	..	..	..	..	..
13. Local funds, general	..	..	..	..	..	..	..	..	..	..	..	..	..	..
14. Local funds, special	..	..	..	..	..	..	..	..	..	..	..	..	..	..
15. Municipal taxation	..	..	..	..	..	..	..	..	..	..	..	..	..	..
Total ..	..	..	..	..	..	..	..	..	..	..	..	..	..	..
Grand Total, excluding miscellaneous ..	4·79	4·70	4·73	4·60	4·16	3·80	4·04	4·16	4·45	4·13	4·34	4·47	4·50	4·26
Grand Total, including miscellaneous ..	5·57	5·41	5·55	5·36	4·47	4·11	4·36	4·48	4·60	4·62	4·82	4·95	4·97	4·67
Population	..	..	..	..	..	..	..	..	..	13,697,396	..	..	..	..

(a)—*Statement showing the growth of Revenue or Taxation in the Madras Presidency from* 1800-01. *In Millions Rx.* (*Rx.*= 10 *Rs.*)—cont.

Items of Revenue.	1840-41.	1841-42.	1842-43.	1843-44.	1844-45.	1845-46.	1846-47.	1847-48.	1818-49.	1849-50.	Average for 10 years ending 1849-50.	1850-51.	1851-52.	1852-53.
	46	47	48	49	50	51	52	53	54	55	56	57	58	59
State Revenue or Taxation.														
1. Land revenue	3·27	3·30	3·28	3·26	3·38	3·46	3·59	3·65	3·65	3·48	3·43	3·52	3·61	3·69
2. Moturpha or tax on trades, houses, &c., and the income and assessed taxes ..	·10	·10	·11	·11	·11	·12	·11	·11	·11	·11	·11	·11	·12	·12
3. Abkári farms and excise	·19	·19	·21	·23	·23	·23	·22	·23	·25	·25	·22	·24	·24	·24
4. Tobacco monopoly in Malabar & S. Canara	·08	·08	·09	·03	·09	·09	·09	·09	·07	·09	·09	·08	·09	·06
5. Customs and land transit duties ..	·43	·41	·43	·42	·20	·17	·15	·14	·10	·10	·25	·11	·12	·12
6. Salt receipts	·38	·40	·40	·43	·45	·47	·46	·49	·45	·46	·44	·48	·48	·51
7. Stamps	·05	·05	·05	·05	·04	·02	·02	·03	·04	·04	·04	·05	·05	·05
8. Provincial rates	..	..	..	..	..	..	..	..	..	..	..	..	..	..
9. Forest	..	..	..	..	..	..	..	..	..	..	..	..	..	..
10. Registration	..	..	..	..	..	..	..	..	..	..	..	..	..	..
Total ..	4·50	4·53	4·57	4·58	4·50	4·56	4·64	4·74	4·67	4·53	4·58	4·59	4·71	4·79
11. Miscellaneous	·47	·48	·52	·49	·50	·45	·49	·47	·48	·47	·48	·50	·52	·53
Total ..	4·97	5·01	5·09	5·07	5·00	5·01	5·13	5·21	5·15	5·00	5·06	5·09	5·23	5·32
Other than State Revenue or Taxation.														
12. Village service fund	..	..	..	..	..	..	..	..	..	..	..	..	..	..
13. Local funds, general	..	..	..	..	..	..	..	..	..	..	..	..	..	..
14. Local funds, special	..	..	..	..	..	..	..	..	..	..	..	..	..	..
15. Municipal taxation	..	..	..	..	..	..	..	..	..	..	..	..	..	..
Total ..	..	..	..	..	..	..	..	..	..	..	..	..	..	..
Grand Total, excluding miscellaneous ..	4·50	4·53	4·57	4·58	4·50	4·56	4·64	4·74	4·67	4·53	4·58	4·59	4·71	4·79
Grand Total, including miscellaneous ..	4·97	5·01	5·09	5·07	5·00	5·01	5·13	5·21	5·15	5·00	5·06	5·09	5·23	5·32
Population	..	..	..	..	..	..	..	..	..	..	..	..	22,031,697	22,857,855

(a)—*Statement showing the growth of Revenue or Taxation in the Madras Presidency from* 1800-01. *In Millions Rx.* (*Rx.* = 10 *Rs.*)—cont.

Items of Revenue.	1853-54.	1854-55.	1855-56.	1856-57.	1857-58.	1858-59.	1859-60.	Average for 10 years ending 1859-60.	1860-61.	1861-62.	1862-63.	1863-64.	1864-65.	1865-66.
	60	61	62	63	64	65	66	67	68	69	70	71	72	73
State Revenue or Taxation.														
1. Land revenue	3·40	3·49	3·41	3·59	3·68	4·18	4·09	3·66	3·97	4·15	4·24	4·30	4·18	4·30
2. Moturpha or tax on trades, houses, &c., and the income and assessed taxes ..	·11	·11	·10	·10	·11	·11	·11	·11	·20	·29	·23	·17	·15	·07
3. Abkári farms and excise	·25	·24	·23	·23	·27	·29	·29	·26	·31	·33	·38	·40	·40	·41
4. Tobacco monopoly in Malabar & S. Canara	Abolished under Act IV of 1853.													
5. Customs and land transit duties ..	·13	·12	·13	·14	·14	·15	·26	·14	·30	·23	·20	·23	·20	·21
6. Salt receipts	·48	·49	·51	·50	·57	·60	·65	·53	·71	·87	·91	·90	1·04	1·01
7. Stamps	·05	·05	·07	·07	·08	·08	·09	·07	·15	·31	·21	·24	·27	·30
8. Provincial rates	..	..	..	..	..	..	..	..	..	..	..	..	..	..
9. Forest	..	..	..	..	..	..	..	..	..	..	..	..	..	..
10. Registration	..	..	..	..	..	..	..	..	..	..	..	..	..	..
Total ..	4·42	4·50	4·45	4·63	4·85	5·41	5·49	4·77	5·64	6·18	6·17	6·24	6·24	6·30
11. Miscellaneous	·56	·43	·83	·83	·83	·85	1·06	·70	1·03	·83	·76	·79	·77	·66
Total ..	4·98	4·93	5·28	5·46	5·68	6·26	6·55	5·47	6·67	7·01	6·93	7·03	7·01	6·96
Other than State Revenue or Taxation.														
12. Village service fund	·04	·04	·04	·05	·04	·06	·06	·05	·06	·06	·07	·07	·05	·06
13. Local funds, general	..	..	..	..	..	..	..	..	..	..	..	·02	·03	·03
14. Local funds, special	..	..	..	..	..	..	..	..	..	..	..	..	·03	·04
15. Municipal taxation	..	..	..	..	..	·02	·02	·02	·02	·02	·02	·03	·03	·03
Total ..	·04	·04	·04	·05	·04	·08	·08	·05	·08	·08	·09	·12	·14	·16
Grand Total, excluding miscellaneous ..	4·46	4·54	4·49	4·68	4·89	5·49	5·57	4·82	5·72	6·26	6·26	6·36	6·38	6·46
Grand Total, including miscellaneous ..	5·02	4·97	5·32	5·51	5·72	6·34	6·63	5·52	6·75	7·09	7·02	7·15	7·15	7·12
Population	..	..	..	..	24,656,509	..	..	..	..	..	26,539,052	..	..	..

(a)—*Statement showing the growth of Revenue or Taxation in the Madras Presidency from* 1800-01. *In Millions Rx.* (*Rx.* = 10 *Rs.*)—cont.

Items of Revenue.	1866-67.	1867-68.	1868-69.	1869-70.	Average for 10 years ending 1869-70.	1870-71.	1871-72.	1872-73.	1873-74.	1874-75.	1875-76.	1876-77.	1877-78.	1878-79.
	74	75	76	77	78	79	80	81	82	83	84	85	86	87
State Revenue or Taxation.														
1. Land Revenue	3·65	4·24	4·07	4·48	4·16	4·40	4·44	4·69	4·45	4·64	4·55	3·29	3·50	4·97
2. Moturpha or tax on trades, houses, &c., and the income and assessed taxes ..	..	·09	·06	·13	·14	·25	·11	·07	Abolished.					·08
3. Abkári farms and excise	·43	·51	·49	·57	·42	·59	·57	·62	·61	·60	·63	·56	·47	·5[illegible]
4. Tobacco monopoly in Malabar & S. Canara						Abolished under Act IV of 1853.								
5. Customs and land transit duties ..	·19	·25	·28	·28	·24	·30	·31	·39	·34	·32	·31	·25	·20	·21
6. Salt receipts	1·05	1·10	1·11	1·17	·99	1·27	1·31	1·29	1·30	1·33	1·35	1·29	1·14	1·46
7. Stamps	·28	·35	·37	·41	·29	·40	·40	·43	·47	·49	·50	·50	·49	·53
8. Provincial rates	..	..	..	..	..	..	..	..	..	..	..	..	..	·61
9. Forest	..	..	..	..	..	..	·04	·04	·05	·04	·04	·04	·04	·06
10. Registration	..	..	..	..	..	·03	·04	·03	·03	·04	·04	·04	·04	·05
Total ..	5·60	6·54	6·38	7·04	6·24	7·24	7·22	7·56	7·25	7·46	7·42	5·97	5·88	8·56
11. Miscellaneous	·65	·97	1·13	1·04	·86	·97	·87	·64	·94	·91	·94	1·08	1·10	1·35
Total ..	6·25	7·51	7·51	8·08	7·10	8·21	8·09	8·20	8·19	8·37	8·36	7·05	6·98	9·91
Other than State Revenue or Taxation.														
12. Village service fund	·09	·08	·09	·14	·08	·16	·18	·20	·20	·21	·22	·20	·20	·22
13. Local funds, general	·04	·14	·22	·23	·01	·21	·25	·40	·40	·40	·39	·32	·32	·43
14. Local funds, special	·03	·04	·04	·05	·04	·05	·05	·05	·05	·05	·06	·04	·04	·02
15. Municipal taxation	·04	·11	·11	·11	·05	·11	·12	·12	·12	·11	·12	·12	·13	·13
Total ..	·20	·37	·46	·53	·22	·53	·60	·77	·77	·77	·79	·68	·69	·80
Grand Total, excluding miscellaneous ..	5·80	6·91	6·84	7·57	6·46	7·77	7·82	8·33	8·02	8·23	8·21	6·65	6·57	8·71
Grand Total, including miscellaneous ..	6·45	7·88	7·97	8·61	7·32	8·74	8·69	8·97	8·96	9·14	9·15	7·73	7·67	10·06
Population	..	..	..	..	..	31,597,872	..	..	..	..	..	..	..	..

(a)—*Statement showing the growth of Revenue or Taxation in the Madras Presidency from* 1800-01. *In Millions Rx.* (*Rx.* = 10 *Rs.*)—cont.

Items of Revenue.	1879-80.	Average for 10 years ending 1879-80.	1880-81.	1881-82.	1882-83.	1883-84.	1884-85.	1885-86.	1886-87.	1887-88.	1888-89.	1889-90.	Average for 10 years ending 1889-90.
	88	89	90	91	92	93	94	95	96	97	98	99	100
State Revenue or Taxation.													
1. Land Revenue	4·95	4·39	4·67	4·69	4·82	4·85	4·48	4·90	4·85	4·94	4·85	5·03	4·81
2. Moturpha or tax on trades, houses, &c., and the income and assessed taxes ..	·08	·12	·05	·05	·05	·05	·04	·05	·15	·17	·17	·18	·09
3. Abkári farms and excise ..	·62	·59	·63	·65	·65	·66	·77	·88	·92	·97	1·05	1·14	·83
4. Tobacco monopoly in Malabar & S. Canara	Abolished under Act IV of 1853.												
5. Customs and land transit duties ..	·23	·28	·25	·20	·10	·11	·10	·09	—·13	·15	·17	·18	·15
6. Salt receipts	1·58	1·33	1·56	1·47	1·39	1·39	1·38	1·45	1·42	1·44	1·65	1·76	1·50
7. Stamps	·54	·47	·55	·54	·52	·56	·57	·59	·58	·60	·61	·65	·58
8. Provincial rates	·69	·65	·55	·62	·64	·67	·61	·68	·65	·69	·70	·76	·66
9. Forest	·06	·04	·07	·08	·09	·10	·12	·12	·13	·14	·15	·16	·11
10. Registration	·05	·04	·06	·06	·06	·06	·08	·09	·09	·09	·10	·10	·08
Total ..	8·80	7·34	8·39	8·36	8·32	8·45	8·15	8·85	8·92	9·19	9·45	9·96	8·81
11. Miscellaneous	1·31	1·01	1·17	1·17	1·14	1·15	1·11	1·15	1·25	1·34	1·16	1·41	1·20
Total ..	10·11	8·35	9·56	9·53	9·46	9·60	9·26	10·00	10·17	10·53	10·61	11·37	10·01
Other than State Revenue or Taxation.													
12. Village service fund	·26	·21	·26	·31	·31	·33	·31	·33	·32	·34	·34	·37	·32
13. Local funds, general	·47	·36	·42	·44	·46	·48	·45	·50	·49	·50	·51	·55	·48
14. Local funds, special	·02	·04	·02	·02	·02	·02	·02	·03	·03	·03	·03	·03	·02
15. Municipal taxation	·16	·12	·16	·17	·17	·17	·19	·19	·19	·20	·20	·21	·19
Total ..	·91	·73	·86	·94	·96	1·00	·97	1·05	1·03	1·07	1·08	1·16	1·01
Grand Total, excluding miscellaneous ..	8·98	7·93	8·57	8·55	8·51	8·64	8·36	9·07	9·14	9·42	9·68	10·20	9·02
Grand Total, including miscellaneous ..	10·29	8·94	9·74	9·72	9·65	9·79	9·47	10·22	10·39	10·76	10·84	11·61	10·22
Population	..	..	30,827,113	..	..	..	..	..	..	..	..	35,630,440	..

NOTE.—(1) Since 1878-79, the Local funds, General (item 13) and the Village Service fund, (item 12) have been incorporated in the General Financial Accounts and the revenue under these heads have been entered, a portion under Land Revenue, and the remainder under Provincial rates. The receipts for these years have, however, also been separately given for purposes of comparison with the revenue of the previous years. The revenue under these heads having been thus twice entered in the statement for the years subsequent to 1878-79, the sum of the several totals exceeds the figures entered against the grand totals by the amounts entered against "Local funds, General," and "Village Service fund."

(2) Since 1878-79, the figures entered against "Local funds, Special" represent only the collections of the Cattle Pound fund, which has not been incorporated in the Financial Accounts.

(3) Prior to 1870-71, the receipts from forests and registration were included under miscellaneous (item 11).

(4) For details of items 12 to 15—*vide* next statement (*b*).

(5) The figures in this statement have been taken from the statement printed at pages 150 and 151 of the Famine Commission Report, Appendix I, and from the Finance Accounts of the Government of India.

(b)—*Statement showing the growth of the various kinds of Local and Municipal taxation from the year* 1853-54 *in the Madras Presidency.*
In Millions Rx. (*Rx.* = 10 *Rs*).

Items of Revenue.	1853-54.	1854-55.	1855-56.	1856-57.	1857-58.	1858-59.	1859-60.	1860-61.	1861-62.	1862-63.	1863-64.	1864-65.	1865-66.
1	2	3	4	5	6	7	8	9	10	11	12	13	14
Village Service Funds.													
Prescriptive allowances	·04	·04	·04	·05	·04	·06	·06	·06	·06	·07	·07	·05	·06
Service cess in lieu of direct fees	..	..	..	..	..	..	..	..	..	..	..	..	..
Total ..	·04	·04	·04	·05	·04	·06	·06	·06	·06	·07	·07	·05	·06
Local Funds, General.													
Rate on rent value of land	..	..	..	..	..	..	..	..	..	..	·01	·02	·02
House-tax in villages for educational purposes.	..	..	..	..	..	..	..	..	..	..	..	..	..
Tolls and ferries	..	..	..	..	..	..	..	..	..	..	·01	·01	·01
Total ..	..	..	..	..	..	..	..	..	..	..	·02	·03	·03
Local Funds, Special.													
Pound fund	..	..	..	..	..	..	..	..	..	..	..	·01	·02
Fishery rents	..	..	..	..	..	..	..	..	..	..	..	·01	·01
Jungle conservancy	..	..	..	..	..	..	..	..	..	..	..	·01	·01
Total ..	..	..	..	..	..	..	..	..	..	..	..	·03	·04
Municipal.													
Taxation in the city of Madras	..	..	..	..	..	·02	·02	·02	·02	·02	·03	·03	·03
Taxation of Provincial Municipalities ..	..	..	..	..	..	..	..	..	..	..	..	..	..
Total ..	..	..	..	..	..	·02	·02	·02	·02	·02	·03	·03	·03
Grand Total ..	·04	·04	·04	·05	·04	·08	·08	·08	·08	·09	·12	·14	·16

(b)—*Statement showing the growth of the various kinds of Local and Municipal taxation from the year* 1853-54, *&c.*—cont.

Items of Revenue.	1866-67.	1867-68.	1868-69.	1869-70.	1870-71.	1871-72.	1872-73.	1873-74.	1874-75.	1875-76.	1876-77.	1877-78.
	15	16	17	18	19	20	21	22	23	24	25	26
Village Service Funds.												
Prescriptive allowances	·09	·08	·09	·14	·16	·14	* ·14	* ·14	* ·16	* ·14	* ·12	Not available.
Service cess in lieu of direct fees	..	..	..	..	..	·04	* ·04	* ·04	* ·05	* ·05	* ·05	..
Total ..	·09	·08	·09	·14	·16	·18	* ·20	* ·20	* ·21	* ·22	* ·20	·20
Local Funds, General.												
Rate on rent value of land	·03	·12	·20	·21	·19	·23	·37	·37	·37	·36	·30	·29
House-tax in villages for educational purposes	..		..	..	..	..	·01	·01	·01	..	..	..
Tolls and ferries	·01	·02	·02	·02	·02	·02	·02	·02	·02	·03	·02	·03
Total ..	·04	·14	·22	·23	·21	·25	·40	·40	·40	·39	·32	·32
Local Funds, Special.												
Pound fund	·01	·02	·02	·02	·02	·02	·02	·02	·02	·02	·02	·02
Fishery rents	·01	·01	·01	·01	·01	·01	·01	·01	·01	·01	Trnsfd. to "Irrigation."	
Jungle conservancy	·01	·01	·01	·02	·02	·02	·02	·02	·02	·03	·02	·02
Total ..	·03	·04	·04	·05	·05	·05	·05	·05	·05	·06	·04	·04
Municipal.												
Taxation in the city of Madras	·04	·04	·04	·04	·04	·04	·04	·04	·04	·04	·05	·06
Taxation of Provincial Municipalities ..	..	·07	·07	·07	·07	·08	·08	·08	·07	·08	·07	·07
Total ..	·04	·11	·11	·11	·11	·12	·12	·12	·11	·12	·12	·13
Grand Total ..	·20	·27	·46	·53	·53	·60	·77	·77	·77	·79	·68	·69

* These figures do not make up the totals for the reason that certain items (such as percentage on water rates) have been credited to the Village Service fund, which had not been shown separately in the accounts under either head.

(b)—*Statement showing the growth of the various kinds of Local and Muncipal taxation from the year* 1853-54, *&c.*—cont.

Items of Revenue.	1878-79.	1879-80.	Average of 10 years ending 1879-80.	1880-81.	1881-82.	1882-83.	1883-84.	1884-85.	1885-86.	1886-87.	1887-88.	1888-89.	1889-90.	Average for 10 years ending 1889-90.
	27	28	29	30	31	32	33	34	35	36	37	38	39	40
Village Service Funds.														
Prescriptive allowances	·15	·16	..	·16	·18	·17	·18	·17	·18	·18	·19	·18	·18	·18
Service cess in lieu of direct fees	·07	·10		·10	·13	·14	·15	·14	·15	·14	·15	·16	·19	·14
Total ..	·22	·26	·21	·26	·31	·31	·33	·31	·33	·32	·34	·34	·37	·32
Local Funds, General.														
Rate on rent value of land	·40	·44	..	·38	·40	·42	·43	·40	·45	·43	·43	·43	·45	·42
House-tax in villages for educational purposes	..	..	..	..	..	..	..	..	..	..	·01	·01	·02	·01
Tolls and ferries	·03	·03	..	·04	·04	·04	·05	·05	·05	·06	06	·07	·08	·05
Total ..	·43	·47	·36	·42	·44	·46	·48	·45	·50	·49	·50	·51	·55	·48
Local Funds, Special.														
Pound fund	·02	·02	·02	·02	·02	02	·02	·02	·03	·03	·03	·03	·03	·02
Fishery rents	Trnsfd. to "Irrgn."		·01	Transferred to "Irrigation."									..	..
Jungle conservancy	Trnsfd. to "Forests."		·01	Transferred to "Forests."									..	..
Total ..	·02	·02	·04	·02	·02	·02	·02	·02	·03	·03	·03	·03	·03	·02
Municipal.														
Taxation in the city of Madras	·05	·07	..	·07	·07	·07	·07	·09	·09	·09	·09	·09	·09	·08
Taxation of Provincial Municipalities ..	08	·09	..	·09	·10	·10	·10	·10	·10	·10	·11	·11	·12	·11
Total ..	·13	·16	·12	·16	·17	·17	·17	·19	·19	·19	·20	·20	·21	·19
Grand Total ..	·80	·91	·73	·86	·94	·96	1·00	·97	1·05	1·03	1·07	1·08	1·16	1·01

NOTE.—The return has been compiled from the statement printed at 'page 152 of Appendix I, of the Famine Commission Report and from the departmental administration reports.

(c)—*Statement showing the growth of the Land Revenue and extension of occupied area of land fully assessed in the Madras Presidency.*

(*In Million £ and Million Acres*—1 £ = *Rs.* 10).

—	1852-53.	1853-54.	1854-55.	1855-56.	1856-57.	1857-58.	1858-59.	1859-60.
1. Land revenue realized according to financial statements presented to Parliament. £	3·69	3·40	3·49	3·41	3·59	3·68	4·18	4·09
2. Current land revenue demand as given in the revenue returns, including South Canara and Malabar. (a) Revenue of zemindari or permanently-settled estates. £	0·50	0·50	0·50	0·50	0·50	0·50	0·50	0·51
(b) Revenue not permanently settled, including "Miscellaneous," "Water-rates," &c. £	3·20	2·92	3·07	3·22	3·35	3·26	3·61	3·53
Total £ ..	3·70	3·42	3·57	3·72	3·85	3·76	4·11	4·04
3. Total cultivators' holdings of fully-assessed lands in ryotwari tracts showing the area in acres and assessment thereon, according to the annual revenue returns, excluding the districts of North and South Canara in each year, and including the district of Malabar after 1865-66. (a) Dry or unirrigated lands. Area acres ..	9·80	9·33	9·41	9·70	10·35	Details not available.	11·01	11·48
Assessment £ ..	1·23	1·17	1·23	1·32	1·41		1·41	1·42
Rate of assessment per acre in shillings and pence.	2—6·1	2—6·1	2—7·3	2—8·6	2—8·6		2—6·6	2—5·6
(b) Wet or irrigated lands under consolidated assessment. Area acres ..	2·56	2·58	2·36	2·43	2·57		2·70	2·78
Assessment £ ..	1·59	1·65	1·49	1·60	1·63		1·78	1·52
Rate of assessment per acre in shillings and pence.	12—5·2	12—10·4	12—7·6	13—2·5	12—7·9		13—2	10—11·4
(c) Garden lands. Area acres ..	0·41	0·31	0·39	0·39	0·39		0·35	0·38
Assessment £ ..	0·20	0·17	0·19	0·20	0·20		0·17	0·17
Rate of assessment per acre in shillings and pence.	10—1	10—10·5	10—1·2	9—11	9—10·9		9—6·5	8—11·5
(d) Extra assessment or additional revenue. (1) Water-rate and charge for lands converted from dry to wet. £	..	..	..	0·06	0·07	0·07	0·07	0·06
(2) Charge for second crop on wet lands. £	..	.	..	0·04	0·06	0·04	0·08	0·08
Total holdings in ryotwari tracts. Area acres ..	12·77	12·22	12·16	12·52	13·31	13·66	14·06	14·64
Assessment £ ..	3·32	3·00	2·91	3·22	3·37	3·40	3·51	3·25
Rate of assessment per acre in shillings and pence.	4—8·7	4—10·9	4—9·5	5—1·9	5—0·6	4—11·8	4—11·7	4—5·4

(c)—*Statement showing the growth of the Land Revenue and extension of occupied area of land fully assessed, &c.*—cont.

—			1860-61.	1861-62.	1862-63.	1863-64.	1864-65.	1865-66.	1866-67.	1867-68.
1. Land revenue realized according to financial statements presented to Parliament.		£	3·97	4·15	4·24	4·30	4·18	4·30	3·65	4·24
2. Current land revenue demand as given in the revenue returns, including South Canara and Malabar.	(a) Revenue of zemindari or permanently-settled estates.	£	0·51	0·51	0·51	0·51	0·51	0·51	0·51	0·51
	(b) Revenue not permanently settled, including "Miscellaneous," "Water-rates," &c.	£	3·50	3·72	3·78	3·83	3·74	3·80	3·90	3·69
		Total £ ..	4·01	4·23	4·29	4·34	4·25	4·31	4·41	4·20
3. Total cultivators' holdings of fully-assessed lands in ryotwari tracts showing the area in acres and assessment thereon, according to the annual revenue returns, excluding the districts of North and South Canara in each year, and including the district of Malabar after 1865-66.	(a) Dry or unirrigated lands.	Area acres ..	11·80	12·44	12·96	13·64	14·05	14·66	14·04	15·44
		Assessment £ ..	1·42	1·45	1·47	1·48	1·53	1·63	1·63	1·68
		Rate of assessment per acre in shillings and pence.	2—4·7	2—4·3	2—3·2	2—2	2—2·1	2—2·7	2—2	2—2
	(b) Wet or irrigated lands under consolidated assessment.	Area acres ..	2·86	2·95	3·08	3·06	3·08	3·58	3·57	3·57
		Assessment £ ..	1·52	1·59	1·60	1·56	1·56	1·75	1·73	1·73
		Rate of assessment per acre in shillings and pence.	10—8·1	10—8·7	10—4·3	10—2·5	10—1·5	9—9·3	9—8·2	9—8·2
	(c) Garden lands.	Area acres ..	0·39	0·39	0·40	0·36	0·20	The classification into "Gardens" has been discontinued since 1865.		
		Assessment £ .	0·16	0·16	0·16	0·14	0·09			
		Rate of assessment per acre in shillings and pence.	8—4·4	8—4	8—2·8	7—9·9	9—2			
	(d) Extra assessment or additional revenue.	(1) Water-rate and charge for lands converted from dry to wet. £	0·07	0.06	0·09	0·10	0·10	0·13	0·13	0·13
		(2) Charge for second crop on wet lands £.	0·05	0·06	0·07	0·07	0·05	0·05	0·05	0·05
	Total holdings in ryotwari tracts.	Area acres ..	15·05	15·78	16·44	17·06	17·33	18·24	18·51	19·01
		Assessment £ ..	3·22	3·32	3·39	3·35	3·33	3·37	3·54	3·59
		Rate of assessment per acre in shillings and pence.	4—3·3	4—2·5	4—1·4	3—11·1	3—10·2	3—10·7	3—9·8	3—9·3

(c)—*Statement showing the growth of the Land Revenue and extension of occupied area of land fully assessed, &c.*—cont.

—	1868-69.	1869-70.	1870-71.	1871-72.	1872-73.	1873-74.	1874-75.	1875-76.
1. Land revenue realized according to financial statements presented to Parliament. £	4·07	4·48	4·40	4·44	4·69	4·45	4·64	4·55
2. Current land revenue demand as given in the revenue returns, including South Canara and Malabar. (a) Revenue of zemindari or permanently-settled estates. £	0·51	0·51	0·51	0·51	0·51	0·51	0·51	0·51
(b) Revenue not permanently settled, including "Miscellaneous," "Water-rates," &c. £	3·80	4·00	4·09	3·94	4·04	3·91	4·14	3·90
Total £ ..	4·31	4·51	4·60	4·45	4·55	4·42	4·65	4·41
3. Total cultivators' holdings of fully-assessed lands in ryotwari tracts showing the area in acres and assessment thereon, according to the annual revenue returns, excluding the districts of North and South Canara in each year, and including the district of Malabar after 1865-66. (a) Dry or unirrigated lands. Area acres ..	15·64	16·00	16·34	16·08	16·10	15·95	16·23	16·28
Assessment £ ..	1·69	1·73	1·75	1·71	1·69	1·68	1·71	1·72
Rate of assessment per acre in shillings and pence.	2—1·7	2—1·7	2—1·5	2—1·5	2—1	2—1·2	2—1·2	2—1·2
(b) Wet or irrigated lands under consolidated assessment. Area acres ..	3·57	3·61	3·65	3·60	3·64	3·68	3·73	3·74
Assessment £ ..	1·72	1·72	1·73	1·69	1·70	1·69	1·70	1·70
Rate of assessment per acre in shillings and pence.	9—7·7	9—6·5	9—6·2	9—4·7	9—4·1	9—1·7	9—1·2	9—1·2
(c) Garden lands. Area acres .. Assessment £ .. Rate of assessment per acre in shillings and pence.	The classification into "Gardens" has been discontinued since 1865.							
(d) Extra assessment or additional revenue. (1) Water-rate and charge for lands converted from dry to wet. £	0·14	0·15	0·17	0·18	0·20	0·22	0·25	0·24
(2) Charge for second crop on wet lands £.	0·05	0·06	0·06	0·06	0·07	0·07	0·09	0·06
Total holdings in ryotwari tracts. Area acres ..	19·21	19·61	19·99	18·68	19·74	19·63	19·96	20·02
Assessment £ ..	3·60	3·66	3·71	3·64	3·66	3·66	3·75	3·72
Rate of assessment per acre in shillings and pence.	3—9	3—8·7	3—8·5	3—8·4	3—8·5	3—8·7	3—9·2	3—8·6

(c)—*Statement showing the growth of the Land Revenue and extension of occupied area of land fully assessed, &c.*—**cont.**

—			1876-77.	1877-78.	1878-79.	1879-80.	1880-81.	1881-82.	1882-83.
1. Land revenue realized according to financial statements presented to Parliament. £			3·29	3·50	4·97	4·95	4·67	4·69	4·82
2. Current land revenue demand as given in the revenue returns, including South Canara and Malabar.	(a) Revenue of zemindari or permanently-settled estates. £		0·51	0·51	0·51	0·51	0·51	0·51	0·51
	(b) Revenue not permanently settled, including "Miscellaneous," "Water-rates," &c. £		3·14	3·96	4·10	4·03	4·02	3·95	4·01
	Total £ ..		3·65	4·47	4·61	4·54	4·53	4·46	4·52
3. Total cultivators' holdings of fully-assessed lands in ryotwari tracts showing the area in acres and assessment thereon, according to the annual revenue returns, excluding the districts of North and South Canara in each year, and including the district of Malabar after 1865-66.	(a) Dry or unirrigated lands.	Area acres ..	16·22	16·17	16·04	15·30	15·13	14·98	15·29
		Assessment £ ..	1·73	1·71	1·71	1·65	1·64	1·64	1·67
		Rate of assessment per acre in shillings and pence.	2—1·5	2—1·2	2—1·2	2—1·7	2—2	2—2·2	2—2
	(b) Wet or irrigated lands under consolidated assessment.	Area acres ..	3·74	3·83	3·86	3·87	3·80	3·79	3·80
		Assessment £ ..	1·69	1·72	1·73	1·73	1·72	1·71	1·72
		Rate of assessment per acre in shillings and pence.	9—·05	8—11·5	8—11·3	8—11·3	9—0·5	9—0·5	9—0·5
	(c) Garden lands.	Area acres ..	The classification into "Gardens" has been discontinued since 1865.						
		Assessment £ ..							
		Rate of assessment per acre in shillings and pence.							
	(d) Extra assessment or additional revenue.	(1) Water-rate and charge for lands converted from dry to wet. £	0·21	0·24	0·27	0·27	0·26	0·24	0·25
		(2) Charge for second crop on wet lands £	0·05	0·09	0·08	0·08	0·08	0·07	0·08
	Total holdings in ryotwari tracts.	Area acres ..	19·96	20·00	19·90	19·17	18·93	18·77	19·09
		Assessment £ ..	3·68	3·76	3·78	3·73	3·70	3·66	3·72
		Rate of assessment per acre in shillings and pence.	3—8·2	3—9·1	3—9·6	3—10·7	3—10·8	3—10·8	3—10·7

(c)—*Statement showing the growth of the Land Revenue and extension of occupied area of land fully assessed, &c.*—**cont.**

—			1883-84.	1884-85.	1885-86.	1886-87.	1887-88.	1888-89.	1889-90.
1. Land revenue realized according to financial statements presented to Parliament. £			4·85	4·48	4·90	4·85	4·94	4·85	5·03
2. Current land revenue demand as given in the revenue returns, including South Canara and Malabar.	(a) Revenue of zemindari or permanently-settled estates. £		0·51	0·51	0·51	0·51	0·51	0·51	0·51
	(b) Revenue not permanently settled, including "Miscellaneous," "Water-rates," &c. £		4·12	3·87	4·13	4·23	4·28	4·30	4·34
	Total £ ..		4·63	4·38	4·64	4·74	4·79	4·81	4·85
3. Total cultivators' holdings of fully-assessed lands in ryotwari tracts showing the area in acres and assessment thereon, according to the annual revenue returns, excluding the districts of North and South Canara in each year, and including the district of Malabar after 1865-66.	(a) Dry or unirrigated lands.	Area acres ..	15·56	15·59	15·99	16·39	16·52	16·66	16·93
		Assessment £ ..	1·68	1·68	1·70	1·72	1·72	1·73	1·74
		Rate of assessment per acre in shillings and pence.	2—2	2—1·7	2—1·5	2—1·2	2—1	2—0·7	2—0·7
	(b) Wet or irrigated lands under consolidated assessment.	Area acres ..	3·83	3·85	3·89	3·93	3·98	4·06	4·11
		Assessment £ ..	1·73	1·74	1·75	1·77	2·00	2·03	2·06
		Rate of assessment per acre in shillings and pence.	9—0·5	9—0·5	9—0·	8—3·7	10—0·5	10—0·	10—0·
	(c) Garden lands.	Area acres ..	The classification into "Gardens" has been discontinued since 1865.						
		Assessment £ ..							
		Rate of assessment per acres in shillings and pence							
	(d) Extra assessment or additional revenue.	(1) Water-rate and charge for lands converted from dry to wet. £	0·26	0·26	0·27	0·29	0·09	0·08	0·08
		(2) Charge for second crop on wet lands. £	0·08	0·07	0·08	0·09	0·08	0·08	0·08
	Total holdings in ryotwari tracts.	Area acres ..	19·33	19·44	19·88	20·32	20·50	20·72	21·04
		Assessment £ ..	3·75	3·75	3·80	3·87	3·89	3·92	3·96
		Rate of assessment per acre in shillings and pence.	3—10·1	3—10·2	3—9·7	3—9·5	3—9·5	3—9·5	3—9·2

For Remarks see next page.

NOTE.—This statement cannot be carried before 1852-53, as detailed information does not exist in a complete form prior to that year.

2. Item No. 1 represents the *actual realizations* of land revenue for each year, which are the same as the *current demand* (item No. 2) for that year, *minus* any sums left uncollected within the year, *plus* collections of arrears of former years. This explains the discrepancies between items 1 and 2.

3. Item No. 2 (*a*) represents the fixed land revenue demand on the zemindari or permanently-settled estates, assessed at a lump sum on each estate. The total area of these estates is about 27½ millions of acres, but the areas occupied and cultivated by tenants within them not being known, they have been excluded from item No. 3.

4. When lands in zemindaris and whole inam villages receive water from Government works of irrigation, they pay water-rate in addition to their fixed assessment. This water-rate now amounts to £50,000 a year, and is included in item 2 (*b*).

5. Item No. 2 (*b*) comprises all heads of land revenue demand other than the fixed assessment of the zemindari estates. The principal item is the revenue of lands held at full assessments direct from Government or ryotwari lands (item No. 3 (*a*), (*b*), (*c*)), the other items are water-rates (items 3 *d* (1 and 2)) and those referred to in Note 4 *supra*, quit-rents on lands and villages partially exempt from assessment (in area about 8 million acres) amounting to £ 280,000 and numerous minor items known as land revenue "*Miscellaneous*" about £300,000.

6. Item No. 3 does not include the figures for North and South Canara for each year and for Malabar up to 1865-66 as the areas have not been shown in the revenue returns.

7. Ryotwari lands were, up to 1864-65, classified under the Madras revenue system into lands assessed as "dry," "wet," and "garden" and the class "garden" was abolished in that year. Lands which are irrigated by works which are private property (as for instance, wells constructed by the landholder) are assessed at dry or unirrigated rates and have been entered under item 3 (*a*) since 1865-66 and lands irrigated from Government works of irrigation are assessed at wet rates and are shown under item 3 (*b*). In order to exhibit the direct return from certain large irrigation works constructed by Government, such as the Godávari and Kistna anicut systems, the charge for water supplied from them was, till 1887-88, shown in the revenue returns as water-rate separately from the land assessment and the water-rate amounted to about £200,000 annually. In 1865 lands watered by private wells were relieved of any impost beyond the "dry" rate and all lands were classed as either "dry" or "wet." This accounts for the disappearance of "garden" lands since 1865-66.

8. The areas entered under item No. 3 represent the extent of holdings, not of cultivation, of *fully-assessed* lands. In ordinary years about 88 per cent. of the area held in ryotwar settlement is under the plough and 12 per cent. fallow or pasture.

9. The amount and the rate of assessment per acre of the different classes of lands entered under items 3 (*a*), (*b*) and (*c*) show the regular ordinary assessment of fully-assessed lands. But under certain circumstances an extra charge on account of the use of water may be made either on dry lands, water-rate (item 3 (*d*. 1), or on wet lands, an extra charge when a second crop is grown (item 3 (*d*. 2), because the ordinary "consolidated" assessment (so called as including both soil and water-rate) is calculated on one crop only. As already expained in note 7 the large decrease under water-rate 3 (*d*. 1), is due to the water-rate charged on wet lands in the Godávari and Kistna districts having been since 1887-88 consolidated into wet assessment.

10. 1853-54. Very disastrous year.
1854-55. Assessments previously reduced in nine districts to the extent of £113,749.
1859-60. Olungu method of adjusting the commutation prices of grain in Tanjore and Tinnevelly abandoned for regular settlement.
1862-63. North Canara transferred to Bombay; revenue demand, £110,000; cultivated area not known.
1864-65. Rates of assessment reduced in Trichinopoly, and land watered from wells relieved of special water-rate.
1865-66. Area and assessment for Malabar first shown in the accounts in this year. Dry 381,815 acres, assessment £59,442 and wet 381,151 acres, assessment £ 116,086; distinction of garden and other minor classification of lands disappear in the accounts from this date.
1871-72. Unfavorable year.
1876-77 to 1877-78. Famine years; large remissions or suspensions of revenue demands were made in consequence.

11. The statement has been compiled from the Revenue Settlement Reports and the Finance and Revenue Accounts of the Government of India.

(d)—*Statement showing the value of land in certain districts of the Madras Presidency.*

(1)—*Statement showing the average value of land per acre in the Tanjore District.*

Years.	Wet lands.	Remarks.
	RS.	
1823-24	12	The values for the years up to 1862-63 have been deduced from the values entered in the deeds of sale and mortgage of lands paying revenue to Government, which passed through the Collector's office under the system of mirasi registry, which formerly prevailed in the district.
1824-25	12	
1825-26	15	
1826-27	9	
1827-28	9	
1828-29	25	
1829-30	13	
1830-31	15	
1831-32	16	
1832-33	13	
1833-34	19	
1834-35	18	
1835-36	18	
1836-37	19	
1837-38 ...	23	
1838-39	20	The selling prices for the years subsequent to 1862-63 have been deduced from the values given in the deeds of sale registered in the Registration offices.
1839-40	23	
1840-41	27	
1841-42	27	
1842-43	26	
1843-44	24	
1844-45	26	
1862-63	39	
1868-69	151	
1869-70	160	
1870-71	148	
1871-72	138	
1872-73	132	
1873-74	146	
1874-75	126	
1875-76	153	
1876-77	180	
1877-78	172	

(2)—*Table showing the selling prices of land in certain villages in the Tanjore District per acre.*

Taluk.	Village.	1838-39.	1840.	1885–88.	Remarks.
		RS.	RS.	RS.	
Shiyáli ...	Alakudi	21	25	235	The selling prices for the years 1838-39 and 1840 are the values deduced from the prices for which lands were sold for arrears of revenue. Those for 1885–88 are the averages deduced from the sale deeds registered in Registration offices.
Do. ...	Valluvakkudi .	8	20	170	
Do. ...	Kilangunar ...	31	38	300	
Do. ...	Keelayur	42	62	272	
Do. ...	Cadavasal	20	21	132	
Kumbakónam	Yaragraharam ...	47	48	483	
Do. ..	Kadichambadi ...	38	40	409	
Do. ...	Valangiman .	12	30	241	
Do. ...	Tillayambur .	11	72	392	
Tanjore ...	Perambuliyur	108	108	672	
Do. ...	Vaithinathampalli	42	129	547	

(3)—*Table showing the prices paid in the Tinnevelly District for the same lands at different sales ascertained from Registration records.*

Shermádevi, Ambásamudram Taluk.—Survey No. 1343, nunjah acres 0·74, sold in 1865 for Rs. 330, fetched Rs. 1,102-8-0 in 1890.

Shembagavamapadi, Nánguneri Taluk.—Survey No. 120 (*a*) and (*c*), extent acres 0·64, sold in 1866 for Rs. 116, was resold in 1885 for Rs. 200.

Vadakkuvimananallur, Ambásamudram Taluk.—Survey No. 634, nunjah acres 0·30, sold in 1868 for Rs. 182, fetched Rs. 275 in 1889.

Anuppankulam, Sátúr Taluk.—Punjah field survey No. 9 (*b*), acres 3·3, sold in 1872 for Rs. 98, fetched Rs. 290 in 1889.

Gopalasamudram, Ambásamudram Taluk.—Nunjah field No. 286, 8 cents., sold in 1874 for Rs. 50, fetched Rs. 262-8-0 in 1882.

Shembayavampari, Nánguneri Taluk.—Survey No. 51 (*b*) and 112 (*c*), nunjah acres 1·21, sold in 1875 for Rs. 297, fetched Rs. 825 in 1889.

Anaikulam, Srivilliputur Taluk.—Punjah No. 156 (*b*), acres 1·95, sold in 1870 for Rs. 50, fetched Rs. 100 in 1879.

(4)—*Table showing the prices paid in the Coimbatore District for the same lands on the several occasions when they changed hands, ascertained from Registration records.*

1. *Anuparpallayam.*—11·18 acres of punjah lands (survey Nos. 26, 37 and 38), were sold in 1860 for Rs. 225; a portion of the lands, *i.e.*, survey No. 37, measuring 5·47 acres, was sold in 1882 for Rs. 500.

2. *Kumarapalayam.*—Survey Nos. 57, 58 and 59 (extent 6·1 acres) of nunjah lands, were sold in 1848 for Rs. 1,200. They were resold in 1877 and 1880 for Rs. 1,900.

3. *Kurichi.*—Survey Nos. 370, 452 and 454 (extent acres 8·42 of nunjah lands), sold in 1858 for Rs. 750, were resold in 1887 for Rs. 1,850.

4. *Devarayapuram.*—Survey Nos. 55 and 56, acres 8·62 of punjah lands, sold in 1847 for Rs. 200, were resold in 1876 for Rs. 300.

5. *Ramanathapuram.*—Survey Nos. 138, 143 and 153, extent 6·97 acres of nunjah lands, were sold in 1855 for Rs. 350. A portion of the lands (No. 143) measuring 2·87 acres, was resold in 1876 for Rs. 1,300.

6. *Vellalur.*—Survey Nos. 225 and 226, extent 9·10 acres of punjah lands, sold in 1849 for Rs. 30-8-0, were resold in 1885 for Rs. 200.

7. *Sanganur.*—Punjah land, Nos. 248, 249 and 250, sold in 1863 for Rs. 50, fetched Rs. 200 in 1884.

8. *Kumaralingam.*—Paimash Nos. 30 and 39, extent 2·2 cawnies, were sold in 1847 for Rs. 225. No. 39 alone was resold in 1876 for Rs. 550 and in 1890 for Rs. 900.

9. *Avalappampatti.*—Paimash No. 37, extent 3·14 vallams of punjah land, sold in 1852 for Rs. 716, fetched in 1881 Rs. 1,000.

10. *Kallapuram.*—Paimash Nos. 233 and 234, extent cawnies 2-14-2, sold in 1872 for Rs. 500, fetched in 1890 Rs. 1,500.

11. *Kallapuram.*—Paimash No. 248, sold in 1873 for Rs. 100, fetched in 1890 Rs. 600.

12. *Mevadi.*—Paimash Nos. 186, 116 and 38, sold in 1876 for Rs. 600, fetched Rs. 800 in 1890.

13. *Nunjahthothakurichi.*—Field No. 203, wet acres 0·75, was sold in 1876 and 1880 for Rs. 200 and in 1890 for Rs. 250.

14. *Nunjahthothakurichi.*—Field No. 31, wet acres 1·5, was sold in 1876 for Rs. 375 and Rs. 400 and in 1879 for Rs. 550 and Rs. 450.

(5)—*Statement showing the prices of lands per acre in the Coimbatore District, deduced from the statistics relating to applications for transfer of revenue registry (extracted from the Coimbatore District Manual).*

Years.	Erode taluk.			Coimbatore taluk.		Pollâchi taluk.		Udamalpet taluk.	
	Wet.	Dry.	Garden.	Wet.	Dry.	Wet.	Dry.	Wet.	Dry.
	RS.	RS.	RS.	RS.	RS.	RS.	RS.	RS.	RS.
1850-51	23	9	69	...	...	...	...	...	...
1855-56	32	3	31	...	...	...	...	...	...
1860-61	111	7	39	...	...	...	...	...	...
1865-66	222	14	80	...	...	...	...	...	...
1870-71	296	15	130	...	...	86	20	271	23
1873-74	...	...	..	119	18	55	32	189	24
1875-76	364	16	90	200	13	66	18	276	32
1878-79	...	...	...	109	11	92	30	633	24
1880-81	285	14	77	155	17	163	33	185	28
1882-83	369	15	99	136	7	208	33	241	30

(6 —*Statement showing the average prices of lands per acre in the several taluks of the Coimbatore District, deduced from the sale-deeds registered in the Registration offices from* 1878-79 *to* 1882-83.

Taluks and divisions.	Wet.	Dry.	Garden.
	RS.	RS.	RS.
Aravakurchi	405	15	59
Avanáshi	117	13	31
Bhaváni	73	15	45
Dhárápnram	500	11	34
Erode	366	25	88
Karúr	277	14	83
Kollegál	113	37	...
Kángyám	100	16	78
Mettupálaiyam	123	8	55
Palladam	162	23	52
Perundurai	50	21	...
Pollâchi	145	25	62
Satyamangalam	249	19	55
Udamalpet	294	22	57
Average for the district ...	266	20½	45

(7)—*Statement showing the prices of land per acre in the Kurnool District, deduced from the values entered in the sale-deeds registered in the Registration offices during the years 1882–86.*

Taluks and divisions.	Wet lands.			All lands.		
	RS.	A.	P.	RS.	A.	P.
Kurnool	47	3	2	10	11	7
Rámallakót	55	4	0	11	4	8
Pattikonda	......			6	13	11
Pyápali	42	14	4	12	2	0
Koilkuntla	54	2	6	18	11	4
Owk	60	2	8	23	14	9
Sirvel	43	9	8	14	2	5
Nandyál	85	1	9	22	8	11
Atmakúr	18	15	9	11	10	2
Nandikótkur	70	14	11	12	13	3
Kalwa	220	0	2	18	0	8
Márkápur	47	12	6	15	15	3
Cumbum	63	4	0	23	7	9
Giddalur	49	12	11	21	6	0
	......			16	1	3

(8)—*Statement showing the sale value of lands per acre in the Anantapur District, deduced from sale-deeds registered in the years 1878-79 to 1885-86.*

—	Wet.	Garden.	Dry.
	RS.	RS.	RS.
Whole district exclusive of Tadpatri ...	45	27	6
Tadpatri taluk	82	61	16
Whole district	47	33	10

(e)—*Table showing the ratio of Government assessment to gross produce of lands.*

(1)—*Statement showing the average outturn of lands per acre (Class IV) on which the assessment was based by the Settlement Department in the Chingleput District.*

Sorts.	Wet 3rd group, Madras measures.	Dry 1st group, Madras measures.	Remarks.
1st, Best	840	444	Varagu and ragi.
2nd, Good	720	380	
3rd, Ordinary	600	316	
4th, Inferior	530	286	
5th, Worst	460	246	

(2)—*Statement showing the value of outturn per acre, of each sort of land under class IV, for wet and dry, in the Chingleput District, at the commutation rates adopted by the Revenue Settlement Department.*

—	Value of outturn.	One-sixth deduction for wet and one-fourth for dry lands.	Cultivation expenses.	Remainder.	Rate.
			Wet.		
	RS. A. P.	RS. A. P.	RS. A. P.	RS. A. P.	RS. A. P.
1st	27 9 0	4 9 6	11 0 0	11 15 6	6 0 0
2nd	23 10 0	3 15 0	9 12 0	9 15 0	5 0 0
3rd	19 11 0	3 4 0	8 8 0	7 14 6	4 0 0
4th	17 6 3	2 14 4	7 8 0	6 15 11	3 8 0
5th	15 1 6	2 8 3	6 8 0	6 1 3	3 0 0
			Dry.		
1st	15 8 6	3 14 1	5 8 0	6 2 5	3 0 0
2nd	13 3 6	3 4 10	5 0 0	4 14 8	2 8 0
3rd	10 14 7	2 11 8	4 10 0	3 8 11	1 12 0
4th	9 13 3	2 7 4	4 6 0	2 15 11	1 8 0
5th	8 6 1	2 1 6	4 2 0	2 2 7	1 0 0

NOTE.—The commutation rate for paddy was Rs. 105, for varagu Rs. 89, for ragi Rs. 142. The commutation price is taken at 12½ per cent. loss than market prices.

(3)—*Statement showing the average yield, the cultivation expenses and the rent per acre in the United Kingdom and in the Madras Presidency.*

—	United Kingdom.		Madras Presidency.	
	Wheat.	Barley.	Dry.	Wet.
	£ s. d.	£ s. d.	RS. A. P.	RS. A. P.
Value of produce	8 17 0	7 11 9	8 0 11	25 7 1
Cultivation expenses	5 2 2	4 1 8	3 3 10	9 8 9
Rent	1 14 9	1 11 1	1 3 2	5 1 9
Rates and taxes	0 2 4	0 2 3	......	......
Total ...	1 17 1	1 13 4	1 3 2	5 1 9
Ratio of rent to produce ...	19·63	20·48	14·87	20·08
Farmer's profit	1 17 9	1 16 9	3 9 11	10 12 7

NOTE.—The figures for the United Kingdom were worked out from the statistics published in the Report of the Royal Commission on Agriculture, and those for the Madras Presidency from the Settlement calculations, the produce being valued at the commutation rates assumed by the Settlement Department.

(4)—*Statement showing the extent of Ryotwar or fully assessed lands leased out for money rent in the Coimbatore District in* 1889, *the Government assessment thereon and the rent stipulated to be paid to the proprietors (prepared from the Registration statistics).*

Names of Sub-district.	Dry lands.						Garden lands (*i.e.*) dry lands with wells on them.						Wet lands.					
	Number of leases.	Extent of land leased.	Amount of Government assessment.	Amount of rent.	Assessment per acre.	Rent per acre.	Number of leases.	Extent of land leased.	Amount of Government assessment.	Amount of rent.	Assessment per acre.	Rent per acre.	Number of leases.	Extent of land leased.	Amount of Government assessment.	Amount of rent.	Assessment per acre.	Rent per acre.
		ACRES.	RS.	RS.	RS.	RS.		ACRES.	RS.	RS.	RS.	RS.		ACRES.	RS.	RS.	RS.	RS.
Kumarapalaiyam ...	4	53	57	109	1·1	2·1	3	13	18	81	1·4	6·2	1	1	6	5	6	5
Ganapathi	13	112	156	660	1·4	5·9	11	50	80	666	1·6	13·3	...	...	...	...	...	...
Gudalur	12	65	86	452	1·3	7·0	18	130	192	1,318	1·5	10·1	...	...	...	...	...	...
Mettupalaiyam ...	1	5	5	10	1·0	2·0	4	37	26	175	·7	4·7	4	15	103	800	6·8	53·3
Pollachi	36	419	410	1,380	1·0	3·3	14	322	303	1,073	1·0	3·3	5	21	116	662	5·5	31·5
Anaimalai	5	36	35	144	1·0	4·0	...	..	..	...	...	...	2	31	110	390	3·6	12·6
Udumalpet	17	193	215	805	1·1	4·1	39	656	772	4,005	1·1	6·1	3	17	85	740	5·0	43·5
Dharapuram	17	302	257	541	·8	1·8	23	381	392	1,862	1·0	4·7	1	6	47	142	7·8	23·6
Aravakurichi	4	43	38	75	·9	1·7	5	83	57	248	·7	3·0	...	...	...	...	...	...
Karur	4	15	11	80	·7	5·3	4	37	28	189	·7	5·1	81	124	986	4,892	8·0	40·0
Kodumudi	9	82	75	217	·9	2·7	6	83	75	354	·9	4·2	2	3	18	165	6·0	55·0
Erode	7	39	39	116	1·0	3·0	3	27	63	365	2·3	13·5	2	2	33	122	16·5	61·0
Perundurai	8	51	58	75	1·1	1·5	13	133	187	693	1·4	5·2	...	...	...	...	...	...
Bhavani	5	51	55	160	1·0	3·1	9	72	89	653	1·2	9·1	...	...	...	...	...	...
Gopichettipalayam ...	1	8	12	40	1·5	5·0	2	6	8	72	1·3	12·0	1	4	43	195	10·7	48·7
Satiamangalam ...	2	14	15	135	1·0	9·6	3	31	31	290	1·0	9·3	...	...	...	...	...	...
Avanashi	4	33	35	185	1·0	5·6	14	153	187	717	1·2	4·6	...	...	...	...	...	..
Sulur	26	270	296	1,196	1·1	4·4	29	370	479	3,120	1·3	8·4	6	21	174	976	8·3	46·5
Palladam	41	519	517	2,006	1·0	3·9	62	614	627	3,610	1·0	6·0	..	...	...	..	...	...
Kangayam	32	424	294	837	·7	2·0	29	354	305	915	·8	2·6	...	...	...	...	...	..
Kollegal	1	4	4	4	1·0	1·0	...	...	...	...	...	...	...	...	...	...	...	...
Coimbatore Registrar's Office	21	346	248	869	·7	2·5	10	123	140	749	1·1	6·1	21	130	611	2,630	4·7	20·2
Total ...	270	3,084	2,918	10,096	0·94	3·2	301	3,675	4,059	21,155	1·1	5·7	129	375	2,332	11,719	6·2	31·2

NOTE.—In all these cases, the lessor pays the Government assessment on the lands leased, out of the rent which is stipulated to be paid entirely in money.

(5)—*Tables showing the cost of Cultivation, &c., for an acre of certain grains in the Sátúr Taluk of the Tinnevelly District, published by the Madras Agricultural Department.*

(a) *Gingelly.*

	RS.	A.	P.
3 ploughings requiring 4 pairs of cattle ...	2	0	0
Sowing	0	12	0
Seed	0	4	0
1 ploughing through the crop, 1 pair ...	0	8	0
Reaping, 6 men	1	0	0
Threshing for 3 days, 6 men	1	0	0
	5	8	0
Assessment	1	0	0
Total ...	6	8	0
Value of outturn (1½ kotahs or 144 measures at 7 measures a rupee)	20	8	0
Balance ...	14	0	0

(b) *Cumbu following cumbu for a Sanghili or 3·64 acres.*

	RS.	A.	P.
3 ploughings, 14 pairs of cattle	7	0	0
Sowing, 4 pairs	3	0	0
Seed (cumbu, mochai, tattampayaru, kallup-payaru, green-gram, castor)	2	0	0
Bullock hoeing, 3 pairs	1	8	0
Reaping, 16 men	2	8	0
Watching	1	0	0
Total ...	17	0	0
Value of produce—			
6 kotahs of cumbu	48	0	0
1 kotah of pulses, &c.	7	0	0
4 cart-loads of straw	12	0	0
Total ...	67	0	0
Balance on 1 Sanghili ...	50	0	0
Or on one acre ...	14	0	0

(c) *One Sanghili (3·64 acres) of cumbu after cotton.*

	RS.	A.	P.
Sowing, 4 pairs	3	0	0
Seed	0	8	0
Bullock-hoeing, 3 pairs	1	8	0
Reaping, 16 men	2	8	0
Watching	1	0	0
Total ...	8	8	0

	RS.	A.	P.
Outturn—			
4 kotahs of cumbu	32	0	0
3 cart-loads of straw	9	0	0
Total ...	41	0	0
Balance on one Sanghili ..	32	8	0
On one acre ...	9	4	0

(d) *One acre of cholum grown as a fodder crop.*

	RS.	A.	P.
Seed, 30 measures	2	0	0
Sowings	0	12	0
Reaping, 12 men	2	0	0
Total ...	4	12	0
Outturn—			
3 cart-loads at Rs. 4-8-0 each	13	8	0
Balance ...	8	12	0

(e) *One acre of cholum grown as a grain crop.*

	RS.	A.	P.
3 ploughings, 4 pairs	2	0	0
Sowing	0	12	0
Seed	0	6	0
Ploughing the crop	0	8	0
Reaping, 6 men	1	0	0
Total ...	4	10	0
Outturn—			
Cholum, 2½ kotahs	15	0	0
3 cart-loads of straw	9	0	0
Total ...	24	0	0
Balance ...	19	6	0

(f) *One Sanghili* (3·64 *acres*) *of varagu grown as a mixed crop.*

	RS.	A.	P.
3 ploughings	7	0	0
Sowing, 4 pairs	3	0	0
Seed—			
Varagu, 24 measures	1	8	0
Red-gram, 2½ measures	0	6	0
Castor, 2½ measures	0	6	0
Bullock-hoeing, 3 pairs	1	8	0
Weeding, 24 women	2	0	0
Reaping, 32 men	5	6	0
Threshing	2	8	0
Total ...	23	10	0

	RS.	A.	P.
Outturn—			
20 kotahs of varagu	90	0	0
12 merkals of castor	5	0	0
12 merkals of red-gram	4	0	0
3 cart-loads of straw	9	0	0
40 bundles of castor plants	2	0	0
40 bundles of red-gram	2	0	0
Total ...	112	0	0
Balance for one Sanghili ...	88	6	0
Balance for one acre ...	25	0	0

(g) *One acre of Bengal-gram.*

2 ploughings, 3 pairs of cattle	1	8	0
Sowing, 2 pairs	1	8	0
Sower (1)	0	3	0
Seed, 7 measures	0	12	0
Harvesting, 6 men	1	0	0
Threshing	0	4	0
Total ...	5	3	0
Outturn—			
36 measures	15	0	0
Balance ...	9	13	0

(h) *One acre of horse-gram.*

Seed, 6 measures	0	8	0
Sowing, 1 pair	0	12	0
Harvesting, 6 men	1	0	0
Threshing, 2 men	0	6	0
Total ...	2	10	0
Outturn—			
1 kotah of horse-gram	6	0	0
6 merkals of castor	2	0	0
Stemps and pods	1	0	0
Total ...	9	0	0
Balance ..	6	6	0

(i) *One acre of Cotton.*

	RS.	A.	P.
3 ploughing requiring 5 pairs	2	8	0
Seed	0	4	0
Manure ($\frac{1}{6}$ of the value of 20 cart-loads) ...	1	8	0
Sowing	0	12	0
3 weedings	1	8	0
Watching the crop	0	8	0
Clearing the plants	0	12	0
	7	12	0
Assessment	1	8	0
Total ...	9	4	0
Outturn of uncleaned cotton $1\frac{1}{2}$ podis (of 328 lb. each) at Rs. 22 a podi	33	0	0
3 cart-loads of plants	1	8	0
Total ...	34	8	0
Balance or profit ...	25	4	0

NOTE (1). The Government assessment of an acre of land as regards (b), (c), (d), (e), (f), (g) and (h) may be taken at one rupee.

(2). The season in the year to which the outturn given in the above tables relates is reported to have been particularly good.

(f)—*Remarks on the alleged increase in the price of Salt due to the Salt Excise System.*

The evil features of the monopoly system of salt manufacture are the following.

2. Under the monopoly system the Government undertakes a work for which private agency is better fitted. The Government cannot by means of its officers manufacture salt as cheaply as private individuals, under the stimulus of self-interest, can. I do not put this on the *laissez faire* or any other abstract principle, but on the experienced results of the monopoly system when it was in force. There are certainly cases in which Government can advantageously undertake the supply of services to the community, for instance, the Postal service, the Telegraph, and perhaps in this country even Railways. These are all cases in which the work to be done is spread over such large tracts of country, and is of such invariable routine character as to make its regulation by general rules issued by a Government department possible and desirable. In these cases, the work done by the officers of the department in different parts of the country is such that the failure or laxity on the part of one of them is liable to immediate detection and exposure by throwing out of gear almost instantaneously the work of those similarly employed in other parts. No one will maintain that salt manufacture is a business of this kind. As in agriculture, so in the manufac-

ture of salt, profit to the manufacturer depends on the minute attention given to details at every stage of the process of production and on the small and individually almost inappreciable saving in cost effected in a hundred ways.

3. It may perhaps be argued that even under the monopoly system the Government employs the ryots to manufacture the salt and recognizes to some extent a right of occupancy in these ryots, who may be supposed to have an interest in making as much salt and as cheaply as possible. This, however, is not the case, and it is exactly in this respect that the monopoly system grievously fails. The quantity to be manufactured by each ryot is fixed at the commencement of the manufacturing season by a Government officer, and any outturn in excess of the quantity required by Government must be destroyed. The ryot has thus no certainty as to the quantity of salt he will be allowed to manufacture in coming years, or even as to whether he will be permitted to manufacture at all; for manufacture must be closed if the stocks in the factory in question and adjoining factories are sufficient. He cannot, therefore, look beyond the immediate present in any of his arrangements for carrying on manufacture and is practically reduced to the position of a labourer paid at a fixed rate on the quantity of salt which the Government chooses to take. The variableness of the seasons renders salt manufacture a somewhat precarious industry; and the monopoly system makes it still more precarious.

4. The salt, whether good or bad, must be taken by Government when it is not below a certain standard in quality; and in years in which the outturn, owing to unfavourable season, is deficient, any salt that is delivered must be accepted. As the Government pays at the same rate for good and bad salt, the incentive to the production of good salt is weakened. It is to the interest of the Government officer having large stocks of bad salt to force it on the public by withholding the sales of good salt until the former are got rid of. This very frequently happened when the monopoly system was in force throughout the Presidency. It is no doubt true that the portion of the population which cares for good salt is at present a small one, but small as it is, it is increasing. Under the monopoly system there is no chance of the taste of the higher classes of the community for good salt at increased prices finding satisfaction, and the result must be that so long as the system is in force, the demand for good salt will be smothered, unless the Government undertakes to supply salt of different qualities at different costs to suit the tastes of the different classes of consumers. This, it is hardly necessary to say, will be a chimerical undertaking and lead to peculation and waste. That any part of the community should be debarred from getting salt of good quality when it is willing to pay for it, is a considerable grievance, and the grievance is all the greater when it is remembered that good salt is really cheap salt too. For instance, A manufactures salt containing 96 per cent. sodium chloride and 4 per cent. impurities, while B turns out salt with 99 per cent. chloride of sodium and 1 per cent. impurities. Under the excise system if each man be allowed to sell the salt at such price as he can get for it, A may realize for his salt 3 annas and B 4½ annas over and above the duty of Rs. 2-8-0 paid to

Government. As, however, B's salt contains a little over 3 per cent. more of sodium chloride than A's, the purchaser of A's salt saves in duty more than he loses in cost price, and, on the whole, gets a better article for a lower price. Under the monopoly system both kinds of salt would be sold at exactly the same price, 3 annas per maund ex-duty, and the person wishing to obtain by legal means the better kind of salt might chance to obtain it as a matter of favour, but could not get it for money.

5. The rates of kudivaram, that is, the prices paid by Government for salt delivered to it under the monopoly system, are fixed and to a great extent independent of the changes in the rates of wages for labour prevailing in the particular localities. This would not be a great grievance if the ryots were allowed to regulate production each year according to their own calculations as to probable demand, so that they might recoup the losses of one year from the gains of another. It is true that the rates of kudivaram have sometimes been raised, but this is done only after it is demonstrated to the satisfaction of the higher authorities that the ryots could not possibly manufacture and deliver salt at the rates in force. This is not an easy process. Moreover, there is considerable difference between the costs of salt of pans situated near the platforms and of those at a great distance, the cost of carriage in the latter case being higher than in the former. The Government officers cannot take into account all these differences and increase or decrease the kudivaram in the way in which private manufacturers can. I find from the last annual report of the Salt Department that Messrs. Arbuthnot and Company and other firms who have entered into contracts with manufacturers in the Chingleput factories for short periods have agreed to pay in addition to the fixed kudivaram additional sums varying apparently with reference to the increased cost of manufacture in, or of transport of salt from, particular pans.

6. The selling of salt at a fixed price whether it is good or bad, light or heavy, gives room for the play of individual preferences or partialities and consequent demoralization of the subordinate officers in the factories. An example will make my meaning clear.. It is a well known fact that traders prefer to buy light salt as they can make a greater profit out of it than out of heavy salt; the reason is that people purchase salt by the measure and light salt measures more than heavy salt, the difference being sometimes * as much as 20 per cent. The sale of salt by measurement instead of weighment is sometimes erroneously ascribed to the machinations of traders who seek to earn a profit by deceiving ignorant purchasers and giving them short weight. Traders do, no doubt, sometimes take undue advantage of the ignorance of purchasers, but in this instance it seems to me probable that even if they reformed their ways and attempted to sell by weighment, the purchasers who have long been accustomed to purchase by measurement would imagine that fraud was intended and would not take the salt. However desirable it may be that salt should be retailed by

* NOTE.—It appears from the administration report of the Salt Department for 1890-91, that eight factories in the Bombay Presidency have made special arrangements for the production of light salt in order to meet the demand for it in this Presidency.

weight and not by measure, any attempt to bring about this result by coercive measures, rendering penal the sale of salt by measure in the thousands of petty bazaars throughout the Presidency, will be attended with great risk of oppression to the poorer classes of the population whose interests are intended to be safe-guarded ; and the Government cannot undertake legislation of this kind with a light heart. This question is intimately connected with the scheme for the introduction of greater uniformity in the measures and weights in use in this Presidency, which, I believe, is now under the consideration of Government. If it is decided to take action in this direction, the measure will, I presume, be adopted tentatively in the larger towns at first and gradually extended to rural tracts, the duty of enforcing the regulations prescribed being entrusted to popular bodies, such as Municipal Councils and Local Fund Union Panchayats. However this may be, there is the fact that light salt finds greater favour with the trade than heavy salt, and this fact gives the former a higher value. Under the monopoly system, it was in the power of the subordinate officers of the department to sell the light salt to their friends and benefit them, while heavy salt fell to the lot of others. No doubt the heaps were sold in the order of the numbers assigned to them, but information as to which heaps contained light salt was not easily procurable by all intending purchasers, and it would be nothing strange if particular persons succeeded in getting the light salt to the exclusion of others. It comes then to this, viz., that, whereas under the monopoly system the additional, it may be adventitious, value borne by light salt was appropriated either by accident or by design by certain favored persons among purchasers, under the excise system it is enjoyed by the person who is justly entitled to it, viz., the producer.

7. While the monopoly system on the one hand throws upon Government the serious responsibility of adjusting supplies to demand with reference to the evershifting conditions of trade, it deprives Government of the only means of judging whether and when, such an adjustment is necessary, as it substitutes an artificial for a natural price which, under ordinary circumstances, serves as an unerring index pointing to the necessity of increasing or contracting supplies. This is an evil of great magnitude, and now that owing to the extension of communications and the cheapening of the cost of carriage, almost all parts of the country have been brought into trade relations with one another and rendered sensitive to trade influences, it seems to me to be perfectly idle for a Government department to undertake the duty of regulating salt production. To put the same thing in another way. The salt trade cannot be isolated from trade in other commodities, because salt is generally brought inland as a return load by traders who take grain or other articles to the coast, and a change in the demand for those articles reacts on the demand for salt. In private trade under natural conditions the adjustment of supplies to demand is automatic, that is to say, traders and manufacturers who may know nothing about the causes in the changes in the conditions of supply and demand all over the country of any commodity, set about making arrangements for increasing or diminishing supplies by simply taking as their guide the rise or fall

in prices. The Government officers would need to be almost omniscient to perform this function efficiently without the aid afforded by the natural course of prices.

8. The Government by selling salt produced at different places at a uniform price, without reference to the cost of production or the conditions of demand and supply, bolsters up inferior factories and handicaps the better sources, the result being on the whole increase in the cost of salt and loss to the community.

9. The monopoly system has not the effect of steadying prices, as is commonly believed. On the contrary, though under it salt is sold at a uniform price when it leaves the factory, outside the factory the prices are subjected to fluctuations all the more violent, because the factory price is kept down at an artificial level. The result is that the trader benefits at the expense of the producer, except in cases in which both occupations are combined in the same person. The truth of the above observations will be seen from the following example. Take 3 factories A, B and C, at a distance of 20 miles from each other north to south. When there are sufficient stocks in these factories and the facilities of communications are equal, each factory will supply all places within a distance of 10 miles north and south, besides tracts which are at less distance from it than from other factories. If stocks are deficient in A and the demand great, and Government continue selling salt at 3 annas a maund, there is sure to be a run on the factory. When the salt is all sold out, traders from A and the regions supplied by it will have to go to B, and though they may get the salt at 3 annas a maund, the cost of carriage will have increased. Meanwhile the factory at A having been denuded of salt, the retail prices at that station will have enormously risen. Under the excise system what would happen is this. When the stocks in A are insufficient to meet the demand, the price of salt in A will rise to such an extent as to make it profitable for traders in some of the tracts served by A to go to B for the salt. This will again affect the price in B and then in C and so on all along the line. The result is that no factory will be absolutely denuded of salt, producing panic and violent perturbations in retail prices, but stocks will be conserved as long as practicable, a diversion of trade being effected in various directions.

10. The above remarks, I repeat, are not based merely on theoretic considerations, but on actual experience. The report of the Salt Commission and the annual reports of the administration of the Salt Department are full of instances of factories having been denuded of salt in the manner pointed out.

11. In view of the grave evils inherent in the monopoly system, we should be justified in giving preference to the excise system, even if it were attended with some increase of price to the consumer; but has there really been an increase of price and over what? The cost price under the monopoly system has been assumed to be 3 annas for the last 30 years, and this rate has acquired in popular estimation a sort of prescriptive right to be regarded as the normal cost notwithstanding changes in the rates of wages, in the value of money, and in the conditions of trade. Even when the Salt Commission

made their calculations, the cost of salt in Madras was found to be more than 3 annas a maund, and salt was sold by Government at the Madras depôt really at a loss. Assuming, however, for the sake of argument, that 3 annas correctly represented the cost price of salt at the time when the monopoly system was displaced by the excise, it will be seen that no fair comparison can be made between that rate and the present excise prices without taking the following considerations into account and making due allowances for them :—

1*st.*—Since 1881 the sales of salt in consequence of demand from tracts outside the Presidency, chiefly Orissa, and increase of population which amounts to 15·6 per cent., have increased from 56 to 69½ lakhs of maunds or by 24 per cent., while the number of factories at work was greatly reduced shortly before 1881. The increased produce would to some extent have had to be raised at more than proportionate cost, even if the monopoly system had been continued throughout the Presidency. That this must be the case is clear from statements contained in the administration reports of the Salt Department which go to show that the officers of the department find very great difficulty in procuring labour for working the extensions of factories recently sanctioned.

2*nd.*—The prices of excise salt include three items of charges which the monopoly rate of 3 annas excludes, though these charges fall eventually on the consumers under either system. The items are—

(*a*) The additional price paid to the producer at the factory instead of to the trader on account of the inadequacy of stocks to meet the demand as pointed out in paragraph 9 *supra.*

(*b*) The additional price paid for light salt (paragraph 6 *supra*).

(*c*) The additional price paid for good salt (paragraph 4 *supra*).

For example, the price of excise salt at Surlá in the Ganjam district was 4 annas 3 pies a maund in 1890-91. The high price was due to the restriction, owing to insufficient stocks, of inland sales at Ganjam (which by the way is a *monopoly* factory) and the consequent diversion of trade to Surlá. Salt at Ganjam is sold by Government at a fixed price of 4 annas (*not* 3 annas), and sales are allowed only on certain days and in restricted quantities to prevent depletion of stocks. The consequence is that traders have to go to Surlá and get their salt at an enhanced price incurring probably enhanced cost of carriage at the same time. All this enhanced cost is recouped by the traders by enhancing the price of salt to the consumers whether the salt has been obtained from Ganjam or Surlá. Nevertheless the factory price of a maund is only 4 annas at Ganjam, while that at Surlá is 4 annas 3 pies, and this shows that the factory price of excise salt may be higher than the monopoly rate though really the price paid by the consumer may be less under the former than under the latter system. Examples of cases of salt commanding higher or lower prices according as they are light or heavy abound in the Madras depôt, where the price of salt varies from 4 to 7 annas a maund. The reason for the preference for light salt has already been explained. In the Madras retail market also salt is sold at different prices with reference to the quality of the article.

12. What after all is the increase of cost of excise salt at present? The cost is 4 annas a maund for the whole Presidency as compared with the hypothetical 3 annas under the monopoly system. In the Masulipatam division it is only 2 annas 8 pies. It seems to me that, making sufficient allowance for the considerations above pointed out, prices are really cheaper now than under the monopoly system. A comparison of retail prices in 1889 with the prices before 1880 shows that retail prices are in most places lower now than under the monopoly system. Moreover, a difference of one anna per maund of 80 lb. makes no difference in retail prices, as these are quoted at so much per Madras measure of say 4 lb., and the increase of one anna per maund would be equivalent to only an increase of price of a Madras measure by less than one-half of a pie. This fact should be borne in mind in judging of the real effect of a sudden temporary pressure of demand on inadequate stocks and consequent rise of prices, which pressure of demand, be it noted, must happen quite as frequently as, if not more frequently, under the monopoly than under the excise system.

13. It is now unnecessary to advert to the circumstances which led to the enhancement of the price of salt in 1885 and 1886, soon after the introduction of the excise system. The causes of the rise in price were fully investigated by Government in 1888, aud though the views of the Salt Department have been at variance with those of Government on this subject, I am not aware that a single argument has been brought forward tending in any way to shake the conclusions arrived at by Government after full enquiry. As regards the measures adopted by Government to remedy the evils that had arisen, there can be but one opinion, viz., that the measures have been eminently successful. The retail price of salt to the consumer has not increased beyond what it was under the monopoly system. On the contrary, if an exact calculation were possible, it would probably be found that prices have gone below what they would be at the present time under the monopoly system. A fairer distribution of profits between the manufacturers and the traders has been brought about and the profits of middlemen have to some extent been cut down. The old argument that capitalists restrict production has been shown to be entirely unfounded, the "*dittam*" or regulation of the quantity manufactured being now found to have been fixed with a view to secure the *maximum* production and not with a view to restrict it. Many licensees work their salt pans independently of capitalists and store and sell salt on their own account. There is full competition among the capitalists themselves. This, I believe, is the case even in Madras where the average price is 5 annas 2 pies a maund. Salt at this station always costs more than the monopoly price of 3 annas, and the additional 2 annas and 2 pies includes this excess as well as the extra value of light as well as of good salt as already explained. I do not think therefore that any material reduction in the price of salt at Madras can be looked for.

14. The monopoly system is sometimes defended on the ground that as the Government levies on salt a duty amounting to nearly 20 times the cost price, it is bound to see that the cost to the consumer is not unduly enhanced. The assumption underlying this statement is

that under the monopoly system it is possible for Government to have control over the price of salt. This assumption, as I have above shown, is unfounded. It seems to me that if the salt tax is an evil, it is an aggravation of that evil to levy it under the monopoly system. The Government has, however, with a view to prevent an undue enhancement of price by combinations of traders, accumulated reserve stocks, and these stocks have completely fulfilled their purpose. The necessity for this arrangement arose from the sudden substitution of the excise for the monopoly system which was in existence for over three-quarters of a century, and I believe that in the course of a few years more, their maintenance will be found to be unnecessary. The object is not to drive capitalists out of the salt trade; what is desired is that there should be sufficient competition among them. There is not likely to be any danger of extensive combinations among the capitalists, such as that which arose at Madras in 1885 and 1886 under very special circumstances. Temporary local combinations may of course occasionally occur, but their effect will be evanescent. The danger now seems to be rather in the direction of Salt Department imposing unnecessary restrictions on the prices charged by salt manufacturers or of bringing the reserve stocks to sale with a view to reduce prices below what they would be under natural conditions when there is full competition, instead of keeping the reserve for use as a heroic remedy on extraordinary occasions, such as, for instance, would justify Government in importing grain to tracts suffering from distress. Government reserve stocks under the excise system, though objectionable on principle and justifiable only as a temporary expedient to repair mistakes committed in the past, have not practically operated to the prejudice of the excise manufacturers, because the Government has not hitherto interfered with the course of salt trade and has allowed traders a large range of prices to base their calculations upon. The loss incurred by Government by maintaining the stocks is also very trifling when compared with the revenue derived by Government from the salt duty. If, however, Government were to enter into direct competition with excise manufacturers, it would simply lead to the extinction of the excise and to the rehabilitation of the monopoly system, which is a consummation greatly to be regretted in the interests of the public for the reasons I have already explained.

15. There are three conditions essential for the proper working of the excise system, viz., *first*, the restrictions imposed on manufacturers should not be greater than are absolutely necessary for the protection of the revenue; *secondly*, there should be no obstacles interposed to the opening of new pans, and additional storage room should be provided on a liberal scale under adequate guarantees in all factories; *thirdly*, small traders should receive the same countenance and assistance as large traders from both salt and Railway officials when they want to purchase salt and send them by the railway. I do not know what the policy of the Salt Department in respect of these matters latterly has been, but I have no doubt that, if they are looked at from the point of view of the convenience of the producers as well as of the Salt Department and adequately provided for, the excise system will in the course of a few years be able to stand on its own

legs, and to dispense with the artificial support of Government reserve stocks. The completion of the East Coast and other railways now in progress will also materially help to bring about this result. The excise system has now justified itself and what is wanted for its complete success is a continuity of policy. If this is ensured, there is no reason why Madras should not secure a large share in the Bengal salt trade, driving out Liverpool salt from thence. The question of substitution of excise for Government monopoly was first mooted by the Cheshire Salt Chamber of Commerce, in the hope that a market might thereby be opened in Madras for their salt, and the prejudice against the excise system is to some extent due to this circumstance. The probability, however, is that Madras salt will eventually drive out English salt from Bengal. Salt is sent from England to Bengal as ballast, but if a trade springs up between Madras and Bengal in Bengal coal, it would be profitable to send Madras salt as a return load. The Government would do well to do all that lies in its power to develop an export trade in Madras salt, and this can be done only under the excise system. If the English salt syndicate persists in artificially raising the price of English salt shipped to Bengal, it would be materially assisting the Madras manufacturers to compete in the Bengal market. Germany, Aden and Arabia have been sending salt to Bengal during the last 3 or 4 years; and Madras, which is so much nearer to Bengal than these countries and has so many facilities for the manufacture of good salt, ought, under proper arrangements, to be able to secure to itself the bulk of the Bengal salt trade.

Statement No. I.

Quantity of salt manufactured and sold and the balance remaining in stock in the East Coast factories in each year from 1881-82 *to* 1890-91.

In lakhs of maunds. 1 maund = 82⅚ lb.

Years.	Manufacture.	Sale.	Stocks at the end of each year.
1881-82	60·42	56·00	75·89
1882-83	66·54	62·55	76·44
1883-84	59·83	65·35	63·28
1884-85	74·87	64·89	67·08
1885-86	57·20	67·34	51·27
1886-87	48·40	65·91	28·04
1887-88	88·67	68·24	47·03
1888-89	89·94	70·69	63·25
1889-90	92·42	71·58	80·21
1890-91	87·23	69·50	94·20

STATEMENT No. II.

Average factory price of salt per maund.

—	1885-86.		1886-87.		1887-88.		1888-89.		1889-90.		1890-91.	
	AS.	P.	AS.	P.	AS.	P.	AS.	P.	AS.	P.	AS.	P.
Chatrapur	3	2	3	5·7	6	0·6	5	10·9	4	1	4	3·6
Chicacole	3	6·6	4	5·6	9	2·6	5	9·8	4	3	3	11·5
Masulipatam	3	6·6	4	9·5	4	11·09	3	11·2	3	3	2	8
Nellore	3	0	3	9·9	3	3·6	3	6·7	3	7	3	5·3
Chingleput	5	4·8	6	8·2	6	3·2	5	4·1	5	2	5	0·5
Negapatam	3	10·9	7	1·0	6	2·2	4	11·6	4	3	4	5
Tinnevelly	5	0·9	6	1·0	6	1·7	4	4·3	4	3	3	7
Average ..	..		5	7·3	6	1·1	4	9·8	4	4	4	0·2

NOTE.—The excise system was introduced in a small number of factories in 1882–1884. In 1885-86 the system was brought into force in nearly all the Madras factories. The season in 1885-86 and 1886-87 was unfavorable for salt manufacture, and the outturn in those years was very small as compared with the ordinary outturn. The result was depletion of stocks and consequent enhancement in the price of salt.

STATEMENT No. III.

Retail price of salt in seers of 8 tolas per rupee.

—	1879.	1880.	1889.	1890.
Ganjam	11·85	11·81	12·33	11·40
Vizagapatam	10·24	10·58	11·69	11·70
Godávari	12·54	11·98	12·00	12·01
Kistna	12·91	12·80	13·19	13·11
Nellore	12·70	12·60	12·34	12·80
Cuddapah	13·89	13·92	12·34	12·20
Anantapur	12·95	12·81	11·14	11·60
Bellary			11·87	11·90
Kurnool	12·06	12·53	11·36	11·50
Madras	13·88	13·75	12·31	13·00
North Arcot	12·12	12·33	11·31	11·40
South Arcot	14·09	14·28	11·58	11·60
Tanjore	12·27	12·52	12·62	12·80
Trichinopoly	12·20	12·13	12·46	12·42
Madura	13·80	13·64	13·47	13·48
Tinnevelly	13·95	14·74	14·68	14·80
Coimbatore	11·78	12·12	11·98	12·50
Salem	11·82	11·94	13·43	13·28
South Canara	11·55	11·51	13·17	13·50
Malabar	10·55	9·79	11·69	11·70
Average ..	12·48	12·52	12·35	12·44

NOTE.—From January 1878 to 10th March 1882, the duty on salt was Rs. 2-8-0 a maund; and on the latter date it was reduced to Rs. 2 a maund. The duty was again raised to Rs. 2-8-0 in January 1888 and continues at this rate at present.

(g)—*Remarks on the Abkári Administration of the Madras Presidency.*

The principles formulated by the Secretary of State for India in regard to abkári administration and accepted by the House of Commons during the recent debate on this question are stated in the letter of the Government of India of 16th May last to be as follows:—

(1) Any extension of the habit of drinking among Indian populations is to be discouraged.

(2) The tax on spirits should be as high as may be possible without giving rise to illicit methods of making and selling liquor.

(3) Subject to the above considerations, a maximum revenue should be raised from a minimum consumption of intoxicating liquors.

2. The discouragement of drinking is thus the primary object aimed at in abkári arrangements. A *total prohibition* of the consumption of liquors among classes of people addicted to the use of them would, however, cause great hardship and be incapable of enforcement even if desirable. The drinking classes in such a case would almost to a certainty supply themselves with liquor by illicit distillation and smuggling, and get demoralized by law-breaking as well as drinking. The object in view is therefore sought to be attained by subjecting liquors to a high duty, so high as to act as a check on consumption, and yet not so high as to cause an outbreak of illicit distillation or smuggling, which cannot be coped with except by employing preventive establishments at enormous cost. The limit of taxation which satisfies the above conditions is not the same in all places but varies in different places, and even in the same place at different times, according to idiosyncrasies of race, taste and lawless habits, climatic differences, efficiency of prevention, facilities for illicit distillation and other circumstances; and the problem of excise administration consists in finding this limit for the different parts of the country and adjusting the duty with reference to it.

3. Revenue is not to be the main object in abkári arrangements, that is to say, it is not to be developed by lowering the duty and extending consumption of intoxicating liquors, but by enhancing the duty and restricting consumption. Subject to this condition, it is a desirable object to develop the revenue (1) by pushing up taxation to the limit already referred to, (2) by taking care that as little of the realizable revenue as possible is diverted from the coffers of the State and absorbed by middlemen or others to whom privilege of sale, &c., of liquors may be granted. The taxation of liquors has this great advantage over other forms of taxation of commodities in general consumption, viz., that while the latter are objectionable in that and in so far as they restrict consumption, the former is beneficial for that very reason.

4. The following facts will show that the principles and considerations above adverted to have been steadily kept in view in all abkári arrangements in this Presidency during the last 15 or 20 years, and that this Government may justly claim to have attained, in spite of difficulties met with at the outset, a very considerable measure of success in the application of those principles.

5. The Presidency contains an area of about 140,000 square miles with a population of nearly 31 millions. Of this area about 20,000 square miles, containing a population of nearly a million, comprise what are called the Agency tracts in the Ganjam, Vizagapatam and Godávari districts. These tracts are hilly and jungly and inhabited by uncivilized, wild races; and it is not open to Government to adopt scientific methods of administration in these places. Throughout the Agency tracts, toddy (fermented palm juice) is now left untaxed. During the Rumpa rebellion in 1880, the oppressions of the toddy renters was alleged as one of the reasons for the *emeute*. In Ganjam, Khonds are allowed to distil spirits for domestic consumption and not for sale. It was at one time thought that Uriya distillers in the Khond country were spreading drunkenness among the Khonds and steadily and surely winning their lands; and they (Uriyas) were prohibited from distilling or selling liquor there. Recent reports from the Collector, however, show that the Khonds do not distil liquor themselves, but employ clandestinely Uriya distillers to manufacture for them and that the prohibition above referred to has given rise to considerable illicit traffic in liquor. The question of allowing Uriyas to distil under proper safeguards and strict control is now under the consideration of the Abkári department. In Vizagapatam the Abkári privileges in some of the tracts are leased out to contractors, and in others kept under amani management, that is to say, the supply and sale of liquor is made under the supervision of Government officers. In the Rumpa country in the Godávari district little or no spirit is consumed. In some of the other Agency villages in this district the privilege of sale of spirit is leased out to contractors; in others again to the villagers themselves for lump sums. It will not be possible to control the traffic in liquor in the Agency tracts on the principles laid down by the Secretary of State, and these tracts must be put aside so far as the present inquiry is concerned. There is, however, no reason to think that drunkenness is on the increase in these regions.

6. Confining our attention to the portions of the Presidency (comprising an area of nearly 120,000 square miles with a population of about 30 millions) in which it is practicable to regulate the taxation of liquor on the principles laid down by the Secretary of State, the following very brief account will show the steps taken during the last 20 years for introducing sound methods of abkári administration. The liquors principally drunk in this Presidency are, 1st, country spirits, 2ndly, imported liquors and liquors manufactured in the country and excised at the customs rate of duty and otherwise dealt with for purposes of taxation in the same manner as imported liquors, and, 3rdly, toddy or fermented palm juice.

7. *Country spirits* consumed are distilled either from jaggery (crude sugar) or toddy (palm juice). Toddy spirit is in use in the Godávari, Malabar and South Canara districts and in the coast taluks of the Kistna district and the two taluks of the Kurnool district east of the Nallamalai hills, viz., Cumbum and Márkápur. In some of the plain taluks of the Vizagapatam district spirit distilled from mowha flowers (*Bassia latifolia*) and also spirit distilled from rice are consumed. In the remaining portions, jaggery spirit is drunk.

8. Twenty years ago, the systems of abkári administration in force were very primitive and the privilege of manufacturing and selling spirits in large areas, usually districts, was leased out to contractors for lump sums, and the spirit was manufactured in stills scattered all over the country according to the rude methods and appliances in use among native distillers. The liquor was sold in sanctioned shops, but practically there was no limit to the number of shops that might be opened. In accordance with the provisions of the Abkári Act, a minimum price was no doubt fixed below which liquor could not be sold, but as the minimum price was fixed without any reference to the alcoholic strength of the liquor sold, it was of no use whatever. In short, there was no attempt made to regulate taxation or to ascertain and control consumption, and contractors were practically allowed to do what they liked in the way of extending consumption.

9. The obvious remedy for this state of things was the substitution for the renting system of an arrangement under which out-stills could be suppressed and manufacture concentrated in large distilleries easily guarded, the revenue being realized by a duty of excise adjusted with reference to alcoholic strength on every gallon of spirit issued therefrom. Before, however, this system of central distilleries, known locally as the "excise system," could be introduced into any particular district, it was necessary to make sure of two conditions, viz., 1st, that when out-stills were suppressed distillers able and willing to construct the necessary buildings and manufacture spirit cheaply on a large scale by using scientific methods and appliances would be forthcoming, and, 2ndly, that the expenses of distribution of liquor from a central distillery to the outlying parts of districts in which facilities for illicit distillation were great did not so enhance the cost of liquor to the consumers as to drive them to supply themselves with it illicitly.

10. Accordingly, "the excise system" was first experimentally tried in selected districts between the years 1869—74. The results showed that no difficulty was likely to be experienced in finding distillers, provided that the areas over which they were given the privilege of selling liquor were sufficiently extensive to enable them to do a large business. In 1875-76, the "excise system" was introduced into further portions of the Presidency with certain modifications, the chief of which was that the distiller or contractor who was given the monopoly privilege of manufacture and sale within a district was required to guarantee a minimum revenue from the duty leviable on the spirit issued for consumption, the object in view being to prevent his making all his profit in the easily manageable portions of his farms, leaving the distant outlying portions to the illicit distiller and the smuggler. The contractor was charged with the duty of maintaining sufficient establishments to prevent illicit practices and smuggling. He was bound to sell the spirit at certain maximum and minimum prices prescribed by Government. The minimum limit was intended to prevent the contractor lowering the price to such an extent as to unduly extend consumption, and the maximum limit to prevent his running up the price so high in particular localities as to cause hardship to the drinking classes and drive them to illicit practices in obtaining supplies of liquor. The minimum prices were

fixed in such a manner as to leave a reasonable profit to the contractor after paying the duty and defraying the cost of liquor, of distillation, of establishments, of remuneration to vendors, &c., according to an assumed standard, and the maximum prices were fixed somewhat higher so as to leave a margin for the contractor to enable him to adapt prices to the actual circumstances of the different parts of his farm.

11. The concentration of distillation and the introduction of the guaranteed revenue system, as the system above described was called, was easy in all districts in which jaggery spirit was consumed, and it was extended in 1875 and 1878 to all the districts of the Presidency excepting those mentioned in paragraph 7 as districts in which toddy spirit is chiefly drunk. In the inland taluks of the Vizagapatam district in which mowha spirit is drunk, the excise system was introduced in 1875, but was withdrawn in 1878 as it did not work well there.

12. The guaranteed revenue system (which is still retained in Bombay) was in force until 1884-85, when the abkári arrangements were again completely remodelled with reference to the recommendations of the Abkári Committee, which was appointed by Government in 1884. It was found that this system had done its work in the way of introducing and familiarizing native distillers with improved methods and appliances in the manufacture of spirit, but was operating prejudicially to sound abkári administration in other respects. Its failure was mainly attributable to three causes, viz., *first*, the large size of the farms generally comprising entire districts, which shut out all but the largest capitalists from the competition for the contracts, and enabled a few rich European firms to combine to keep down the bids for the guaranteed revenue, and to make unduly large profits from the more easily managed portions of the farms, neglecting altogether the outlying parts; *secondly*, the realization of the revenue wholly in the shape of a uniform fixed duty throughout the farms without regard to the often widely varying conditions of the tracts comprised within them, and the artificial regulations imposed by Government as regards retail prices of liquor, which, as already observed, were based on hypothetical data as regards cost of liquor and other items liable to considerable fluctuations in different tracts of country and from year to year; and, *thirdly*, the entrusting to the contractors the duty of maintaining sufficient establishments for the prevention of illicit distillation, while at the same time no police powers were or could be conceded to these establishments which were not under official control and discipline. The large monopolists had very generally neglected to maintain the establishments they were bound to employ or to provide adequate facilities for the supply of liquor to the more difficult and less accessible portions of their farms; they had closed large numbers of shops previously existing, and in the remaining shops they had cut down the allowance of the retailers to such an extent as to drive them to seek their remuneration in illicit practices, such as giving short measure, dilution, &c.; and by charging the maximum prices in the populous portions of the farms and spending as little as possible on their management, they had reaped enormous profits, a very considerable portion of which should, under proper arrangements, have come to Government in the shape

of taxation. The result was a considerable decline in the revenue, while at the same time there was reason to suppose that the real consumption had increased and not decreased.

13. The object of the reforms initiated in 1884 was to provide a remedy for these evils. To ensure sufficient personal attention being paid by the renters to all parts of the farms and to admit of the smaller capitalists with local knowledge competing for them, the size of the farms had to be reduced; but as it would, at the same time, have been distinctly a retrograde step to allow small renters to establish stills of their own for the supply of tracts served by central distilleries, the expedient was adopted of separating the privileges of manufacture and sale, which had hitherto been leased out conjointly. As regards the former, the policy has been to leave the manufacture and supply of spirits to licensed vendors "free" wherever possible, that is to say, to make it cease to be a monopoly and to permit any one, who chooses to embark in the business of distillation, to obtain a license to work a distillery and to sell the liquor manufactured to licensed vendors at prices mutually agreed upon between them from time to time and not fixed by Government. The existence of sufficient competition between distillers being essential to the success of this scheme, it was experimentally tried at first in a limited number of localities, and being found to answer was extended to all the districts brought under the excise system with the exception of a few special tracts where, owing to the absence of railway communications or other causes, the privilege of manufacture is still, for the present, granted as a monopoly. The principal advantages of the "free supply" system, as it is called, are that it affords encouragement to distillers to lay out capital in the adoption of the most recent improvements in the methods of manufacture, without the fear, so long as they comply with excise regulations, of having the right of distillation taken out of their hands after any definite period, as would be the case when the privilege is granted as a monopoly; that by reducing the cost of liquor, it increases the margin left for the Government taxation out of the price realizable from the consumers, and that it enables licensed vendors to exercise some choice as to the distillers from whom they can purchase their liquor, and thus to adapt the liquor supplied by them to some extent to the tastes of the consumers. The duty of maintaining preventive establishments has been undertaken by Government. The realizable taxation varies, as already pointed out, in different parts of the country, depending as it does on the habits of the people, the price which they can pay and the facility with which illicit liquor can be made with impunity; and in order to obtain the highest duty that it is possible to get in different localities, the taxation was divided into two portions; the first being the still-head duty payable when the liquor leaves the distilleries and fixed at rates sufficiently low to enable the renters of the vend farms to suppress the sale of illicit liquor where necessary, and the second being the lump sums paid for the privilege of sale by the vend-farmers and determined by public competition. By these arrangements the total taxation leviable in different places is intended to adapt itself to their varying circumstances by a natural process; and when, by the combined action of the preventive establishments maintained by Government and of the renters working in their own interest to displace illicit by licit consumption, unhampered by artificial

restrictions as regards maximum and minimum prices, illicit dealings in liquor have been suppressed, it is expected that the way will be clear for equalizing the still-head duty throughout the country and levelling it up to the import rate; in other words, increasing the fixed and decreasing the variable portion of the total taxation. The intention is eventually to dispense altogether with middlemen, with monopoly privileges for the sale of liquor also and to make the taxation consist of the still-head duty and shop rents. This plan has been adopted in towns, but as it is not possible to abolish middlemen all at once in rural tracts, the size of the vend farms has been gradually reduced in view to middlemen being finally got rid of.

14. Since 1884 very considerable progress has been made in bringing the improved excise system into force throughout the Presidency; it was of course introduced at once into the districts in which the "guaranteed revenue" system was in force; it was also extended to the Kurnool district with the exception of the Cumbum and Márkápur taluks in 1885-86; to the upland taluks of the Kistna district in 1886; to the five Municipal towns of the Malabar district in 1886-87; to the inland taluks of the Vizagapatam district and into the Mangalore taluk of the South Canara district and into the taluks of Chirakal, Kottayam, Calicut and Pálghat of the Malabar district in 1888-89. It is under contemplation to introduce it into Cumbum and Márkápur taluks of the Kurnool district and Gudiváda, Vissanapet and Núzvíd taluks of the Kistna district from next April. Within the next two or three years it will probably be in force in all parts of the Presidency excepting, of course, the Agency tracts. The difficulty has hitherto been to devise arrangements under which the excise system can be worked in districts in which toddy spirit is consumed. In these districts distillation is practised by almost every toddy-drawer and its suppression requires large preventive establishments. Toddy required for distillation is, moreover, expensive to carry long distances and gets spoilt if kept long. The plan introduced into the taluks of the Malabar district at the suggestion of Mr. Galton may, however, be considered to have solved the problem. The plan is to establish distilleries in central localities, where palm-trees are abundant, and to permit the distiller to work subsidiary stills in the vicinity, from which weak spirits could be passed by the distillery officer to the central distillery for redistillation. Centralization of distillation of toddy spirit necessitates the employment of strong preventive establishments and it is found convenient to work it in connection with the tree-tax system (to be noticed in connection with toddy arrangements) which likewise requires strong establishments to work it.

	Area in sq. miles.	Population.
Tracts under the excise system ...	106,000	25,425,000
Tracts in which the excise system has been ordered to be introduced from 1st April next	4,000	473,000
Total ...	110,000	25,898,000

15. The number of distilleries in the tracts under the excise system is 20, of which 17 are worked under the "free supply" and 3 under the "monopoly supply" system. In all these distilleries spirit is manufactured by the method of continuous "close distillation." It was at one time feared that Messrs. Parry and Company, who work a

large distillery at Nellikuppam in the South Arcot district in connection with their sugar factory there and manufacture spirit cheaply from molasses, would be able under the "free supply" system to establish a practical monopoly and then enhance the price of liquor unduly and thus diminish the margin left out of the retail price for the Government duty. Experience has, however, since shown that there is keen competition among distillers for the custom of licensed vendors in "free supply" areas and that the danger apprehended is not likely to arise.

16. There can be no doubt that since 1883-84 both the duty realized and the price of liquor in excise districts have increased. The average duty for the districts in which the excise system was in force in 1883-84 was Rs. 3-2-6 per gallon of proof strength. In 1887-88 the duty realized in the same districts was Rs. 4-8-3 per gallon, of which Rs. 2-13-10 represented the duty levied at the still-head and Rs. 1-10-5 the incidence per gallon of the rents paid by vend farmers and shopkeepers for the privilege of sale. The highest excise duty leviable under law is Rs. 5 per proof gallon. For the current year the still-head duty has been enhanced considerably in several districts and therefore a much larger portion of the taxation will be realized in the shape of still-head duty than in 1887-88.

17. To determine the effect of the excise system on consumption of liquor, the circumstances of the several districts must be separately examined. The following are the facts connected with each district :—

Ganjam, exclusive of Agency tracts.—The consumption in 1875-76 was 38,849 proof gallons, in 1883-84 it had increased to 41,836 gallons. Since then it has been rapidly diminishing; in 1886-87 it was 24,579 gallons; 1887-88, 24,170 gallons; and in 1888-89, 24,044 gallons. The duty per proof gallon which was Rs. 1-15-0 had increased to Rs. 3-11-9 in 1887-88 and to Rs. 3-6-4 in 1888-89.

Vizagapatam, exclusive of Agency tracts.—The consumption in the coast taluks of the district was 16,905 gallons in 1875-76, 11,227 gallons in 1883-84, 26,479 gallons in 1886-87 and 29,133 gallons in 1887-88. The increase in these taluks in the later years is entirely due to the stoppage of smuggling from the inland taluks where liquor was sold cheaply by the contractors under the renting system. Under the old law the transport of spirit in quantities not exceeding one quart was permissible and considerable quantities were thus transported from the rented to the excise taluks with a view to evade the higher duty leviable in the latter. The Abkári Act of 1886 has enabled Government to put a stop to this practice by prohibiting the transport of liquor in however small quantities from the rented to the excise tract. The excise system having been introduced into the interior taluks also from 1888-89, the consumption for the whole district has declined from 68,472 gallons in 1887-88 to 36,323 in 1888-89. The duty realized in 1887-88 and 1888-89 was Rs. 3-4-10 and Rs. 5-7-1, respectively, per proof gallon against Rs. 2-10-0 in 1875-76.

Godávari.—No reliable statistics of consumption are available for this district which has not yet been brought under the excise system. In this as in other tracts in which the out-still system is retained the consumption is very large, being 80 proof gallons per 1,000 of the population, a rate nearly double of that in excise tracts. There is nothing to show that consumption has increased since 1875-76. When the arrangements for concentrating distillation of toddy spirit are introduced in this district, there will be an enormous decrease in consumption. Mr. Bliss has been directed to visit the Northern districts and submit proposals for placing the Abkári administration there on an improved footing, which, it is hoped, will be done at an early date.

Kistna.—The excise system was introduced into the upland taluks of this district only in 1886-87 and reliable statistics of consumption for previous years are not available. The consumption in 1887-88 was very high, 141 gallons per 1,000 of the population, but it must have been much higher under the out-still system. A reduction in the consumption should be brought about by a *gradual* enhancement of the still-head duty in this district. Since 1888-89 the duty has been raised from Rs. 1-1-2 to Rs. 1-14-0 per gallon London proof. As the upland taluks of this district are surrounded by tracts in which the renting system is still maintained, it is necessary, in order to prevent smuggling, that the duty should not be fixed very high at the outset, but when the coast taluks are also brought under the excise system, as it is hoped that they will shortly be, the duty can be considerably enhanced.

Nellore.—In 1875-76 the consumption was 27,403 proof gallons; it has been gradually increasing since 1883-84; in that year it was 38,859 gallons, in 1886-87, 39,813 gallons, and in 1887-88, 42,106 gallons. In 1888-89, however, it went down to 39,240 gallons. The increase, as compared with the earlier years is due to the suppression of illicit distillation and smuggling, which is known to have been prevalent chiefly in the zemindari portions, and this is shown by the fact that the consumption per head of the population * in this district is much lower than in the adjacent districts. The duty, which was Rs. 2-3-9 per proof gallon in 1875-76, amounted to Rs. 4-9-1 in 1887-88 and to Rs. 4-6-6 in 1888-89.

	Gallon per head of the population.
* North Arcot	·50
Cuddapah	·42
Kurnool	·58
Nellore	·32

Cuddapah.—The excise system was introduced into this district in 1878. The consumption under renting system in 1875-76 was reported at 66,848 gallons. In 1878-79, the year after the famine during which this district had suffered very severely and lost more then one-fifth of its population, the consumption was 41,172 proof gallons. Since then the consumption has been 50,205 gallons in 1883-84, 43,614 in 1886-87, 46,703 in 1887-88 and 47,541 in 1888-89. The duty has risen from Rs. 3-1-2 per gallon in 1878-79 to Rs. 5-1-2 in 1887-88 and Rs. 4-14-9 in 1888-89.

Bellary Cantonment.—In 1875-76, the consumption was 33,460 gallons. In 1883-84 it had increased to 46,164 gallons; in 1886-87 it fell to 37,531 gallons; it rose in 1887-88 to 42,685 owing to favorable season and fell again to 38,487 gallons in 1888-89. The duty per gallon has risen from Rs. 3-13-6 in 1875-76 to Rs. 5-8-11 in 1887-88 and Rs. 5-0-1 in 1888-89. The consumption in this town fluctuates with the strength of the garrison.

Bellary district, exclusive of the Cantonment, and Anantapur district.—The excise system was introduced into these districts in 1878-79. If the consumption reported under the renting system in 1875-76 can be relied on, it must have been very high—119,375 proof gallons. In 1883-84, or 5 years after the famine in which these districts severely suffered, the consumption was 53,615 gallons; in 1886-87, 48,637 gallons; in 1887-88, 63,179 gallons; and in 1888-89, 50,990 gallons. The duty realized in 1888-89 amounted to Rs. 4-11-8 per gallon in the Bellary district including the cantonment and to Rs. 4-4-5 in the Anantapur district.

Kurnool District.—In the taluks west of Nallamalai hills the excise system was introduced in 1885-86. The consumption has been as follows:—1885-86, 35,438 gallons; 1886-87, 41,282 gallons; 1887-88, 38,798; and 1888-89, 28,022. The high consumption in 1886-87 appears to have been due to the large numbers of laborers employed on railway works which have since been completed. The duty realized in 1888-89 was Rs. 4-14-9 per gallon.

Madras Town.—The consumption of Puttai and Colombo arrack within the Municipal limits in 1875-76 was 114,402 gallons. In 1877-78, when the famine was at its height, the consumption rose to 127,101 gallons owing to the activity of the grain trade. In 1883-84 it was 126,628 gallons. In 1887-88 the consumption rose to 136,673 gallons owing to the strike among toddy-drawers during a portion of the year and consequent increase in the sales of arrack. In 1888-89 consumption fell to 129,802 gallons.

Chingleput District.— The consumption in the Chingleput district was in 1888-89, 57,483 against 57,795 gallons in 1875-76.

North Arcot.—The consumption in this district has been as follows:—90,765 gallons in 1875-76; 76,647 in 1883-84; 91,157 gallons in 1887-88; and 91,323 gallons in 1888-89. The duty realized has risen from Rs. 3-3-3 per gallon, London proof, in 1875-76, to Rs. 5 per gallon in 1888-89.

South Arcot.—The consumption in this district has been 50,437 gallons in 1875-76; 55,514 gallons in 1883-84; 74,981 gallons in 1886-87; 80,670 gallons in 1887-88; and 95,740 gallons in 1888-89. The rapid increase in the later years is entirely due to the employment of preventive establishments and other arrangements made with a view to put a stop to the smuggling of liquor which for several years past was going on from the French territory of Pondicherry into the adjoining taluks of the South Arcot district. In fact the French Government was deriving a large revenue from consumption of liquor in British territory. The French and British villages are so interlaced with one another that a large population in the British taluks were drinking French liquor which was sold at much lower prices than the British liquor. Partly owing to a rise in the price of French spirit and partly owing to fall in the price of spirit sold in shops within British territory, the latter spirit is now enabled to compete with the former, and much of the revenue which the French Government was illegitimately making from consumption in British territory now finds its way, as it ought to, into the British treasury. The price* of British liquor consumed is, however, higher than the French liquor consumed before, and there is no reason to think that actual consumption has really increased. The rate of consumption in the South Arcot district (53 gallons per 1,000 of the population) is about the same as that in the adjoining district of North Arcot (50 gallons per 1,000 of the population), the conditions of which are similar to those of the former. The French Government are getting alarmed at the diminution of the revenue they have been deriving for several years and are thinking of imposing a high duty on country spirits as well as on imported brandies. If they do this, they will be benefiting their revenue and placing a check on the enormous consumption of liquors within their territory—a consumption which is little less than a scandal and has no parallel in any portion of the British territory. Until they see the wisdom of this policy the British frontier taluks must suffer as regards abkári administration by the proximity of the French territory. Negotiation with the French Government for an assimilation of the systems of abkári administration in their territory with that in force in British territory was tried before but it led to no result, as the French Government returned evasive answers, being apparently loath to give up the revenue they were deriving from British consumption. Now that it has been shown to them that they can no longer rely on this revenue, it is to be hoped that they will see that, by working the abkári administration on sound principles, they can improve the revenue, and, at the same time, promote the interests of sobriety and morality.

	Price per gallon of 30° under-proof. RS. A. P.
* In French shops	2 6 6
In shops on the British side of the frontier ...	2 4 0

Tanjore.—The consumption in this district has been as follows:—1875-76, 36,564 gallons; 1883-84, 33,875 gallons; 1887-88, 37,045 gallons; and 1888-89, 39,100 gallons. Much arrack is not drunk in this district, the favorite drink of the lower classes being toddy. The rate of consumption of arrack per head of the population is about one-third of that of the adjoining district of South Arcot. The duty realized in 1888-89 was Rs. 3-11-0 per gallon against Rs. 2-13-9 in 1875-76.

Trichinopoly.—The consumption has been—1875-76, 39,092 gallons; 1883-84, 36,314 gallons; 1887-88, 32,157 gallons; 1888-89, 35,282 gallons. The duty realized has risen from Rs. 2-12-11 in 1875-76 to Rs. 4-3-8 in 1888-89.

Madura.—In 1875-76, when the abkári revenue of this district was managed under the renting system, the consumption of arrack was reported to have been 75,003 gallons. In 1883-84 the consumption under the excise system was 46,742 gallons; in 1887-88, 42,477 gallons; and in 1888-89, 48,225 gallons. The rate of consumption per head of the population is less than that in the northern districts and there is considerable smuggling and illicit distillation in the zemindari portions. The increase in consumption in 1888-89 appears to be due to large numbers of laborers employed on the works connected with the Periyár project. The duty realized in 1888-89 was Rs. 4-5-1 per gallon.

Tinnevelly.—In this district also, the arrack revenue was managed under the renting system in 1875-76, when the consumption of arrack was reported by the renters to have been 73,794 gallons. In 1883-84 the consumption was 36,462 gallons; in 1887-88, 21,718 gallons; and in 1888-89, 26,506 gallons. The rate of consumption of arrack in this district is the lowest in the Presidency. The duty realized in 1888-89 was Rs. 3-15-4 per gallon.

Coimbatore.—The consumption in this district has been as follows:—1875-76, 59,944 gallons; 1883-84, 47,594 gallons; 1887-88, 38,183 gallons; and 1888-89, 46,148 gallons. The duty realized has risen from Rs. 2-9-10 per gallon in 1875-76 to Rs. 4-15-5 in 1888-89.

Nilgiris.—In this district the consumption of arrack has been as follows:—1875-76, 23,255 gallons; 1883-84, 37,217 gallons; 1887-88, 36,212 gallons; 1888-89, 31,918 gallons. The consumption in 1883-84 was considerably in excess of that in 1875-76, but the * principal towns in the district have been growing of late years. It is also understood that, as the cultivation of poppy, which was carried on to some extent by the Badagas, was suppressed when the Opium Act was introduced in 1880, they have taken to drinking liquors. Since 1883-84, however, there has been a decline in the consumption of country spirits. The duty realized has risen from Rs. 3-6-11 per gallon in 1875-76 to Rs. 6-0-8 in 1888-89.

	Population in 1871.	Population in 1881.
* Ootacamund ...	9,988	12,335
Coonoor ...	2,498	4,778

Salem.—The consumption in this district has been—1875-76, 76,187 gallons; 1883-84, 53,000 gallons; 1887-88, 54,171 gallons; 1888-89, 52,236 gallons. The duty has risen from Rs. 3-9-3 per gallon in 1875-76 to Rs. 4-10-1 in 1888-89.

Malabar and South Canara.—In Malabar, except in the Wynaad, the excise system was only recently introduced into some of the taluks. In South Canara the excise system has been introduced only into one taluk. The introduction of the excise system by raising the price of liquor has undoubtedly tended to check consumption, but reliable statistics are not available for previous years.

18. From the foregoing it will be seen (i) that the "excise" system has been introduced since 1875-76 into the greater portion of the Presidency as rapidly as circumstances permitted; (ii) that the effect of the introduction has been to increase the taxation and with it the price of country spirits and to diminish the consumption much below what it was under the old renting system; (iii) that in most of the "excise" districts the consumption in 1888-89 was very much less than in 1875-76 with the exception of South Arcot and the Nílgiris; (iv) that in South Arcot the increase is due to the measures taken for enabling liquor in British shops to compete with and displace the cheap liquor sold in French shops and which was chiefly consumed in the taluks on the frontier of the Pondicherry territory, and that it does not indicate any increase in drunkenness; (v) that the increase in the Nílgiri district is more than accounted for by the increase in the population; and (vi) that in the Madras town, where it might be expected that consumption would have increased considerably owing to increase of population and other causes, the consumption in 1888-89,

as compared with that in 1875-76, shows only a slight increase. As regards the increase in consumption in 1888-89 observable in a few districts, as compared with that in 1883-84, it should be remembered (i) that since then most portions of the Presidency have had a succession of very good seasons and the Presidency has rapidly recovered from the effects of the famine of 1876–78; and (ii) that, since 1886, the amendment of the Abkári law giving power to prohibit transport of liquor from Native States, &c., even in quantities not exceeding a quart and the preventive establishments employed by Government have rendered it possible to displace illicit by licit consumption.

19. The above remarks refer to "country spirits," by which term is to be understood spirits manufactured in this country and on which the duty levied is below the rate prescribed by the customs tariff for imported liquors and which under present law is Rs. 5 per gallon of London proof strength and in proportion to strength for spirits of other strengths. Spirit manufactured in this country and taxed at the tariff rate is treated in all respects as imported spirit and permitted to be sold in the same shops as the latter. The object is eventually to assimilate the duty on the so-called "country spirit" to that on foreign spirits, that is to say, to abolish the distinction between "country spirit" and "foreign spirit," which is based simply on the rate of duty levied and not on the methods of manufacture. The so-called "country spirit" is in most distilleries manufactured by European process and is really rum and it is taxed at lower rates than the tariff rate, because it is believed that, if the duty were levied at the latter rate, considerable inducement would be offered to illicit distillation and smuggling. In the case of the Madras town and the Nílgiri district, it is possible now to raise the duty on country spirit to the tariff rate and abolish the distinction between "country" and "foreign" liquors and this question is now under consideration.

20. *Foreign liquors.*—Liquors classed as "foreign" consist of (i) imported spirits, wines and malt liquors; (ii) spirit manufactured within the Presidency and excised at the customs tariff rate of Rs. 5 per gallon of proof strength; and (iii) beer brewed in the country and excised at the tariff rate of one anna per gallon. Formerly licenses for sale of "foreign liquors" used to be granted on payment of fixed fees, but licenses for the sale of liquors, except in hotels and refreshment rooms, are put up to auction and the liquors subjected to a heavier duty than before. There are two breweries on the Nílgiris and the consumption of the beer brewed is stated to be extending among the lower classes of natives at Ootacamund and other places on the hills, where toddy is not available and the price of country spirit is high.

21. *Toddy.*—The regulation of the taxation of toddy (fermented palm juice) presents great difficulties. The levy of an excise duty is impossible and the only means available for regulating the tax on this intoxicant with some reference to consumption is to impose a tax on each palm tree tapped, the rate of tax being based on an estimate of the average production of the several descriptions of toddy-producing trees. The tree-tax to some extent performs the function of an excise duty and enables Government to form some judgment as to increase or decrease in consumption from the number of trees tapped

and to enhance the tax wherever it is found that consumption is increasing. The idea was borrowed from Bombay, but in working it care has been taken here to avoid the mistake which was committed in that Presidency of attempting to levy the duty not only on raw toddy but also on toddy spirit by means of the tree-tax. This necessitated the imposition of the tree-tax at rates so high (Rs. 18 annually per cocoanut tree) that they had the effect of suppressing the consumption of raw toddy altogether and compelling classes of the population accustomed to this beverage to drink spirit. The correct principle for working the tree-tax was stated by Mr. Galton when Abkári Commissioner in the following terms: "The true principle appears to be that the taxation in the form of a tree-tax should not exceed what the people can afford to pay upon the beverage, and where, as in some parts of Malabar, toddy constitutes an article of diet and is in fact the ordinary morning meal of some of the laboring classes, taxation must be moderate, or such classes would be deprived of their food. Shop rents serve to enhance the tax on toddy used as an intoxicant and when toddy is used for distillation taxation must be supplemented by other means; if possible by a still-head duty." The tree-tax in the portions of the Presidency in which it has been introduced has been worked strictly on the lines above indicated. The tax imposed, excepting in the town of Madras, amounts to Rs. 3 per cocoanut tree. The tree-tax at this rate is hardly equivalent to a duty of one anna per gallon of fermented toddy which contains sometimes as much as 8 per cent. of alcohol. When palm juice is drawn in vessels coated with lime, fermentation is prevented and the toddy thus drawn is used either for food or for the manufacture of crude sugar. This description of toddy is not taxed. In the Madras town the tree-tax is at the rate of Rs. 6 per cocoanut tree. This rate is not an unduly heavy one for the town of Madras, where considerable quantities of toddy are drunk for purposes of intoxication, and it is desirable to check consumption by raising the price of toddy. The tax was originally at the rate of Rs. 3 per tree and subsequently enhanced to Rs. 4-8-0; this enhancement did not cause any rise in the price of the beverage, but only reduced the profits of the toddy drawers. It has, therefore, been still further enhanced to Rs. 6 per annum during the current year in the town of Madras. It is believed that the increase in the duty levied on country spirit and consequent enhancement of its price have tended to increase the consumption of toddy and that this tendency requires to be checked to some extent. The tree-tax system, which is the only satisfactory system for taxing toddy on sound principles, is being gradually introduced. It has now worked well in the portions of the Presidency in which it is in force and its extension throughout the whole of the Presidency is only a question of time. It requires considerable establishments for marking the trees on which the tax is to be levied, and as the organization of the establishments entails considerable labour on the Abkári department the work has to be done gradually. In the tracts in which the tree-tax system is in force the toddy-shops are sold by auction every year, excepting in the Madras town and the Malabar district, where fixed fees are levied. In South Canara a regular tree-tax system has not been introduced, but the toddy-drawers are granted licenses to tap any number of trees they like on payment of fixed fees; the licenses are not transferable and tapping under them of trees by persons other than those whose names are specified in the license is not permitted. This plan is obviously inferior to the tree-tax system, as there is no limit to the number of trees tapped under each license and no reliable estimate can be formed of the quantity of toddy drawn or of the incidence of taxation. The only advantages of this system are that it renders the employment of expensive establishments for marking the trees tapped unnecessary and prepares the way for the introduction of the tree-tax. The fees levied on each license have gradually been enhanced, but they still fall far short of what would be payable if the tree-tax, such as exists in Malabar, were introduced. In other portions of the Presidency the old renting system as regards toddy is still retained, but the size of the toddy farms in like manner with arrack farms has been reduced everywhere in order to ensure the renters effectually coping with illicit tapping and unlicensed sale of toddy. In towns middlemen have been dispensed with and toddy shops are sold by auction.

22. In some of the towns, however, the consumption of spirit appears to have increased considerably since 1882-83. A great part of the increase is no doubt accounted for by the increase of urban population in recent years, but the price of liquor in some towns during portions of the year appears to have been lower than in the rural tracts. In the town of Vellore, for instance, prices of spirit of 30° under proof appear to have ranged from Rs. 2-8-0 to Rs. 6 during 1888-89. This would appear to indicate that the shopkeepers are endeavouring to force sales during festivals, &c., by lowering prices unduly. When the abkári arrangements for the next year come to be settled, it will be a question for consideration whether the still-head duty on spirit issued for consumption in these towns should not be considerably enhanced with a view to compel the shop-keepers to sell their liquor during all portions of the year at rates which are not unduly low.

Towns.	Consumption in 1882-83.	Consumption in 1888-89.	Rate per head of the population, 1888-89.
	GALS.	GALS.	
Nellore... ...	9,044	12,174	·442
Adóni	3,659	7,236	·332
Conjeeveram ...	4,784	8,931	·239
Vellore... ...	7,970	13,746	·367
Kumbakónam...	4,195	7,770	·155
Madura ...	7,466	12,191	·165
Dindigul ...	2,698	5,660	·399

23. The number of shops for the sale of liquors licensed in 1887-88 compares with the number in 1875-76 as follows:—Country spirits 22,549 against 20,062; toddy 20,140 against 19,671; foreign liquors 931 against 965. The number of licenses to sell arrack in the Malabar district was 4,422 in 1887-88 against 1,119 in 1875-76, and licenses to sell toddy were 4,152 against 1,262. If the figures for Malabar are excluded, it will be seen that the number of arrack shops in the remaining districts show a decrease of 425 and toddy shops show a decrease of 2,812. The peculiar circumstances of Malabar render the maintenance of a large number of shops necessary. The people are not congregated in villages, but have their homesteads in the midst of their farms and palm groves. Palm trees are most abundant, and the distillation of toddy spirit, which is both easy and

inexpensive, is universally practised. Illicit distillation carried on in a country, where the houses are detached and situated each in its own garden, removed from observation, must of course be difficult of detection in the absence of very strong preventive establishments. Prior to 1884-85 under the renting system unlicensed sales were very common, the renters contenting themselves with levying a fee from the vendors and leaving them to do what they liked. With a view to suppress this illicit traffic it was necessary that places should be freely licensed and steps taken to enforce the requirements of the law as regards sales in licensed places only. This accounts for the large increase in the number of shops in this district in recent years up to 1887-88. Of late, however, the tree-tax and excise systems have been introduced into portions of the district and large preventive establishments organized to detect and prevent illicit practices. This has made it possible to reduce the number of shops very much, the reduction in 1888-89 amounting to no less than 2,000. The Collector expects that there will be a further decrease of 1,000 shops during the current year. The regulation of the number of shops has perhaps been the most vulnerable part of the abkári arrangements in this Presidency. Under the renting system and also the guaranteed excise system, which was one of big monopolies, it was necessary that the contractors, who were charged with the duty of preventing illicit distillation and smuggling, should be allowed considerable discretion as regards the number of shops to be maintained. During the last few years the Government has, however, employed preventive establishments of its own, and the facts as regards illicit consumption in the different parts are being pretty well ascertained. It is therefore now possible to regulate the number of shops with reference to the requirements of different localities and the Commissioner of Salt and Abkári Revenue has been devoting considerable attention to the subject. He has recently directed that the number of shops, in towns especially, where illicit practices are easy of detection, should be considerably reduced. The Government has insisted on large reductions in the number of shops in the rural tracts also, and before long the number of shops will in all probability be reduced to one-half of what it is now. As in this Presidency, however, toddy and arrack are sold in different shops, the total number of shops maintained must be larger than in provinces where the two kinds of liquor are allowed to be sold in the same shop.

24. The net abkári revenue of this Presidency since 1878-79 has been as follows :—

	Lakhs of rupees.
1878-79	56·72
1879-80	57·31
1880-81	54·49
1881-82	58·29
1882-83	57·84
1883-84	57·82
1884-85	68·42
1885-86	77·21
1886-87	81·79
1887-88	88·19
1888-89	95·13

Since 1883-84 it will be seen that the revenue has increased by 37·31 lakhs or 64 per cent.

25. The facts stated above will, I believe, place it beyond doubt that the abkári administration of this Presidency has for several years past been conducted on sound principles. The revenue has doubtless increased considerably, but it has been obtained by pushing up taxation and reducing consumption and not by pushing up consumption. The ascertainment of the limit, to which the taxation in the several parts of the Presidency can be carried, is a tentative process and it would be rash to assert that in no instance was a mistake committed. On the whole, however, there is no reason to think that consumption is now higher than it was 15 years ago, and there is distinct evidence to show that in most parts of the Presidency it is very much less. The assertion, which one sometimes hears to the contrary, is not the result of a proper investigation of the conditions of the past or study of comparative statistics, but of a newly awakened consciousness to the evils of drinking in the abstract. It has been truly remarked: "Those who have lately become conscious of certain facts are apt to suppose that they have lately risen. After a changed state of mind has made us observant of occurrences we were before indifferent to, there often results the belief that such occurrences are more common than they were." I believe that most of the difficulties connected with abkári administration have now been surmounted and that very little remains to be done beyond persevering in the policy hitherto pursued. The excise system and the tree-tax system must of course be introduced into the remaining portions of the Presidency as quickly as circumstances will permit, and when this has been done, and the shops licensed have been reduced to the smallest number possible, consistently with the requirements of the population to be served, and the duty is enhanced from time to time in places where the consumption shows a tendency to increase, the Government will have done in the way of reducing consumption all that it is possible for it to do. The consumption of liquor by the laboring classes fluctuates with the state of the agricultural season from year to year and in prosperous times shows a tendency to increase. This tendency can be checked only by the diffusion of elementary education among the lower classes. This being so, it is a question for consideration whether a fixed percentage of the increase of revenue (nearly 38 lakhs within the last 5 years) contributed chiefly by the working classes should not be set apart for advancing elementary education. The Government of India now take 75 per cent. of the revenue derived from excise.

26. There are three classes of persons who condemn the abkári arrangements in this Presidency. The first comprises philanthropists who, being impressed with the evils which the spread of drunkenness has wrought in England, feel anxious lest a similar state of things should be brought about by Government arrangements in India, more especially as religious prejudices among large classes of the population, which formerly told in favour of sobriety, are gradually wearing away. Their fears, so far as this Presidency is concerned, are not well-founded, and if they knew the facts they would doubtless be ready to admit that Government is working in the same direction as

themselves. The second class of persons are the distillers and big monopolists who have had their enormous profits reduced by the new arrangements. Their dislike to the new order of things is, of course, very natural. The third class are the toddy-drawers and professional distillers who find their hereditary occupation going out of their hands and who have to seek new means of livelihood. They undoubtedly suffer hardship, but it is temporary, and their interests are opposed to those of the general public.

Postscript.

The above note was written in November 1889 or two years ago. I will briefly state below what improvements have since been effected in the abkári administration :—

(1) Excluding the agency tracts, the "excise system" (*vide* para. 14) is in force in about 110,000 square miles out of the 120,000 square miles comprised within the Presidency.

(2) The tree-tax system (*vide* para. 21) has been further extended and it is in force in 28,000 square miles of country.

(3) The average rate of duty per gallon of country spirits, proof strength, which was Rs. 2-13-7 in 1875-76 was Rs. 3-15-9 in 1888-89, Rs. 4-2-1 in 1889-90 and Rs. 4-6-1 in 1890-91.

(4) The consumption of country spirits has fallen considerably during recent years and as compared with 1875-76 the consumption in 1890-91 was only 5 per cent. more notwithstanding an increase of more than 10 per cent. in the population.

Millions of proof gallons.

1875-76	1·27
1888-89	1·38
1889-90	1·43
1890-91	1·33

(5) The number of shops both in the towns and in the rural tracts has been enormously reduced.

		1875-76.	1888-89.	1889-90.	1890-91.
Country spirit shops.	40 towns ...	...	...	899	524
	Rest of the Presidency.	...	...	14,026	12,230
	Total ...	20,062	17,532	14,925	12,754
Toddy shops		19,761	26,180	21,684	19,415
	Grand Total ...	39,823	43,712	36,609	32,169

(6) The taxation per head of the population of duty on country spirits and on toddy has increased as shown below :—

Per head of population.

——	1875-76	1888-89.	1889-90.	1890-91.
	RS. A. P.	RS. A. P.	RS. A. P.	RS. A. P.
Country spirits	0 1 10	0 2 2	0 2 6	0 2 7
Toddy	0 1 1	0 1 10	0 2 0	0 2 4

(7) The revenue derived from country spirits and toddy has increased.

——	In lakhs of rupees.			
	Country spirits.	Toddy.	Country spirits and toddy combined.	Total.
1888-89	46	40	8	94
1889-90	54	44	5	103
1890-91	57	51	1	109

(8) The consumption of imported liquors, excluding liquors manufactured in the country on the European method, in 1890-91 compares with that in 1875-76 as shown below :—

——	In thousands of gallons.	
	1875-76.	1890-91.
Imported spirits	208	203
Wines	102	61
Malt liquor	196	540
Country brewed beer	80	379
Total ...	586	1,183

The above table shows that the consumption of spirits and wines has decreased, while that of malt liquors has considerably increased. Regarding the causes of the increase Mr. O'Conor in his trade review for 1889-90, says : " Various causes in combination may be assigned for this remarkable augmentation. The character of the beer has changed and many are able to drink the lighter qualities now imported who were unable to drink the heavier beers of former years. There has been a great increase in the classes of European population accustomed to drink beer habitually,—artizans, workers in mills and factories, men employed on railways and in land and coasting steamers and so forth. There has also been created a taste for beer among the Madras coolies who work for high wages in Burmah and return annually to Madras with their earnings. The strength of the British army has been largely augmented and the prices of beer have materially fallen. But it is hardly likely that these causes alone can have brought about such a sudden development in consumption, and the most effectual cause may perhaps be sought in competition. The English brewers keenly felt the competition of the German and Austrian brewers, and actively sought to retain a market which seemed to be undermined from without by continental and from within by Indian beer." The total population of the Presidency has increased by 14 per cent. since 1871 and the European and Eurasian population by 11·4 per cent.

(9) On the whole, there has been great decrease in consumption by the introduction of the "excise system," and the assertion that drunkenness is spreading is entirely without foundation so far as this Presidency is concerned.

(h) 1—*Statement showing the Number of Offences reported in* 1850 *and* 1890 *in the Madras Presidency.*

—	1850.	1890.
1. Offences against person—		
(*a*) Affecting life	352	799
(*b*) Hurt	437	14,079
(*c*) Rape	75	82
(*d*) Assault	167,063	32,725
(*e*) Other offences	...	2,629
Total ...	167,927	50,314
2. Offences against property—		
(*a*) Robbery and dacoity	1,314	899
(*b*) Theft	14,715	19,424
(*c*) Other offences	6,541	23,948
Total ...	22,570	44,271
3. Other offences	7,263	19,447
4. Offences against special and local laws	...	121,181
Grand Total ...	197,760	235,213

(h) 2—*Statement showing the Number of Cases instituted before Criminal Courts in the Madras Presidency.*

—	1850.	1890.
Number of cases filed before the Village Police	12,678	11,529
Number of cases filed before the District Police (answering to the present 2nd and 3rd Class Magistrates) ..	171,584	169,490
Number of cases filed before the Magistracy (the present 1st-class Magistrates)	10,151	41,730
Number of cases committed to the Sessions Courts .	914	1,040
Number of cases committed to the High Court	115	51
Total ..	195,445	223,840

NOTE.—Out of 41,730 cases filed before 1st-class Magistrates in 1890, 35,606 were before the Presidency Magistrates.

(h) 3—*Statement showing the Number of Civil Suits instituted in the Presidency of Madras in* 1850 *and* 1889.

—	1850.	1889.
1. Village Punchayats	14	...
2. Village Munsiffs	11,107	53,733
3. District Punchayats	8	...
4. District Munsiffs	52,708	151,498
5. Revenue Courts	...	6,656
6. Cantonment Court of Small Causes		354
7. Agency Courts	...	912
8. Sudder Ameens	12,691	...
9. Subordinate Judges	4,816	14,017
10. District Judges	48	641
11. Presidency Court of Small Causes	...	26,824
12. High Court	...	371
Total ...	*81,392	255,006
Number of suits for lands, houses and other fixed property	6,347	44,242
Number of suits for arrears of rent or revenue	1,239	6,656
Number of suits for money, allowances and personalities.	70,841	204,108
Total ...	78,427	255,006
Total value of suits, Rs.	54,82,053	3,74,59,396
Average value, Rs.	70	146

* Includes suits "referred," for which particulars are not available.

(i)—*Statement showing the incidence of taxation in the Madras Presidency.*

Heads of revenue.	Gross revenue in lakhs of rupees.			Incidence per head of the population.		
	1852-53.	1872-73.	1889-90.	1852-53.	1872-73.	1889-90.
				RS. A. P.	RS. A. P.	RS. A. P.
Land revenue, including receipts from Forests and Tobacco monopoly	375·1	475·3	519	1 8 0	1 8 3	1 7 3
Provincial rates, including Municipal taxation	...	75·1	107·9	...	0 3 10	0 4 10
Salt	50·4	128·5	175·7	0 3 3	0 6 6	0 7 11
Excise (including Abkári and Opium) ...	24·2	61·7	114	0 1 6	0 3 4	0 5 4
Customs	12·1	39·4	18·1	0 0 9	0 2 1	0 0 9
Assessed taxes (Moturpha)...	11·8	7·3	18·3	0 0 9	0 0 4	0 0 9
Stamps	4·8	42·6	65	0 0 3	0 2 2	0 3 0
Registration	...	3·3	10·3	...	0 0 2	0 0 5
Total ...	478·4	833·2	1,028·3	1 14 6	2 10 8	2 14 3

NOTE (1).—The incidence for 1852-53 has been arrived at by assuming the then population of the Presidency to have been 25,000,000.

(j)—*Statement showing the Expenditure of the Madras Presidency in* 1889-90 *as compared with that in* 1849-50. 000 *omitted.*

Items.	1849-50.	Items.	1889-90.
	RS.		RS.
1. Land Revenue, Sayer, Abkári and Tobacco—		1. Land Revenue and Abkári—	
(a) Salaries and allowances to the Members of the Board of Revenue, officers of account, &c. ...	237	(a) Salaries and allowances to the Members of the Board of Revenue and Civil Officers of Account and Audit ...	404
(b) Charges of collecting the revenues, &c. ...	4,110	(b) Charges of collecting the revenue, &c.	4,217
(c) Purchase and charges of tobacco	265	(c) Revenue Survey and Settlement	930
(d) Tanjore sinking funds and interest on Tanjore bonds	493	(d) Land Records and Agriculture	56
		(e) Inam Commission ...	14
(e) Allowances and assignments payable out of the revenues in accordance with treaties or other engagements ...	5,112	(f) Allowances to District and Village Officers ...	3,660
		(g) Assignments and compensations	1,240
		(h) Territorial and political pensions	918
Total ...	10,217	Total ...	11,439
2. Customs	215	2. Customs	212

NOTE.—The figures for 1849-50 have been taken from Appendix 1 to the report from the Select Committee on Indian territories in 1852. The figures for 1889-90 are taken from the Financial and Revenue Accounts for that year.

(j)—*Statement showing the Expenditure of the Madras Presidency in* 1889-90 *as compared with that in* 1849-50. 000 *omitted*—cont.

Items.	1849-50.
	RS.
3. Salt—	
(*a*) Purchase of salt ...	234
(*b*) Purchase of salt manufacturer's share ...	333
(*c*) Establishment and contingencies	233
(*d*) Compensation	13
Total ...	813
4. Assessed taxes	...
5. Forest	...
6. Stamps	50
7. Registration	...
8. Mints	100
9. Interest on loans and deposits including the Tanjore Redemption Fund ...	533
10. Post Office	434
11. General administration ...	887
12. Residents and Political-Agents	141
13. Ecclesiastical establishments	292
14. Education	113
15. Courts of Law	2,361
16. Police	977
17. Jails	...
18. Medical (hospitals, &c.) ...	124
19. Scientific and minor departments	30
20. Pensions, donations to charitable institutions, &c. ...	1,175
21. Marine charges	123
22. Miscellaneous	270
23. Military charges including buildings	25,247
24. Public Works—	
(*a*) Repairs to tanks, &c.	970
(*b*) Buildings, roads, &c.	719
Total ...	1,689
Grand Total ...	45,741

Items.	1889-90.
	RS.
3. Salt	
(*a*) Salt purchase and freight	168
(*b*) Purchase of salt manufacturer's share ...	115
(*c*) Establishment, contingencies, &c.	1,324
Total ...	1,607
4. Assessed taxes	31
5. Forest	1,162
6. Stamps	248
7. Registration	661
8. Mints	...
9. Interest	80
10. Post Office	1,395
11. General administration, including charges on account of Local Funds and Municipal establishments.	1,356
12. Political Agents	83
13. Ecclesiastical establishments	347
14. Education, including Local Funds and Municipal expenditure	2,290
15. Courts of Law	4,128
16. Police (public safety) ...	3,987
17. Jails	800
18. Medical	3,337
19. Scientific and minor departments	350
20. Pensions, donations to charitable institutions, &c.	1,350
21. Marine charges	83
22. Miscellaneous	2,480
23. Military charges including buildings	34,750
24. Public Works—	
(*a*) Railways, working expenses and capital expenditure ...	5,021
(*b*) Buildings and roads ...	5,813
(*c*) Irrigation including capital outlay ...	4,574
(*d*) Establishments, &c. ...	2,689
Total ...	18,097
Grand Total ...	90,273

NOTE.—The figures for 1849-50 have been taken from Appendix 1 to the report from the Select Committee on Indian territories in 1852. The figures for 1889-90 are taken from the Finance and Revenue Accounts for that year.

(F.)—*Statistics relating to the improvement or the reverse in the standard of living of the different classes of the population.*

(a)—*Comparative table showing the number of persons (males) engaged in the several occupations in* 1871 *and* 1881 *in the Madras Presidency (extracted from the Report on the Census of* 1881).

	Male population, 1871.	Male population exclusive of Pudukota, 1881.
1. Persons engaged in the general and local government of the country	126,104	193,450
2. Do. in defence of the country	34,319	22,882
3. Do. in learned professions, literature, art and science, with their immediate subordinates	154,848	185,070
4. Do. in entertaining or performing personal offices to man	36,277	104,639
5. Persons who buy, sell, keep or lend houses or goods of various kinds including bankers, money-lenders and money changers	425,116	176,544
6. Persons engaged in the conveyance of men, animals, goods and messages	63,376	163,342
7. Persons possessing or working the land or engaged in producing grain, fruit, grasses, animals or other products	5,211,178	6,453,839
8. Persons engaged about animals	38,042	106,380
9. Do. in art and mechanical productions.	89,585	150.337
10. Do. in working and dealing in the textile fabrics and dress	755,676	720,404
11. Do. in food and drinks	223,520	391,048
12. Do. in animal substances	5,253	63,281
13. Do. in vegetables	58,906	153,617
14. Do. in minerals	288,001	116.934
15. Laborers and others (branch of labor undefined) ...	2,295,917	510,585

NOTE.—The classification of occupations in the Census of 1881 was different from that adopted in 1871. In framing the above table, attempt has been made to re-classify the population of 1871 on the principles adopted in 1881. The rusults cannot, however, be fully relied on.

2. The very considerable increase in the number of persons engaged in "Personal service," item 4, will be noted. In regard to this, the Census report says: "Increased contact with western ways, the incidents of railway travelling, competition in business, have all led to the greater development of personal services as a group of industries. The words 'hotel' and 'club' have grown into the native language and the things they mean have come into existence within the last few years. For the well-to-do traveller, the choultry of tradition has, with its gratuitous shelter (and sometimes gratuitous entertainment), given place in every town to the private hotel, where the traveller is entertained for payment; while the Brahmin traveller, who formerly crept up the coast ten miles a day and cooked his rice at the chattram, now readily embarks in a steamer and shares with his paid fellow-clerk (*sic*) the services of a travelling cook of his own caste." The number of persons engaged in "Personal service" is, however, still only 1 in 139

in the Madras Presidency, while it is 1 in 14 in England, and this to some extent affords an indication of the number of wealthy persons needing personal services in the two countries.

3. The great decrease observable in the mercantile men and general dealers, item 5, is attributed to erroneous classification. The figures for 1881 include—mercantile men 78,268, and other general dealers 107,902. The first head comprises 46,041 merchants, 21,544 money-lenders and money-changers and 3,707 brokers. The number of merchants is absurdly overstated, as there are only 16,000 merchants in England, the most commercial country in the world.

4. The increase in the number of persons engaged in connection with land, item 7, is merely nominal, as the figures of 1881 evidently include agricultural laborers shown under the head "Laborers and others (branch of labor undefined)" in the Census of 1871.

5. The decrease in the number of "Persons working and dealing in textile fabrics and dress," item 10, is the result of the declining condition of the weaving industry owing to the competition of the Manchester cotton goods and also, latterly, to some extent of the machine-made goods from Bombay. The imports of cotton twist, which amounted to 4 millions of pounds in 1855-56, increased to 13 millions in 1870-71 and they are now (1887-88) 21½ millions. The imports of piece-goods increased from 825,406 pieces and 311,815 yards in 1855-56 to 94,600,201 yards and 11,469½ dozens in 1870-71 and to 139,360,368 yards and 1,150,450 pieces in 1887-88. While the weaving trade is a poor industry, it affords employment to a large number of persons, probably half a million males as the women and children of weavers' families all work in the looms. That this is not a profitable industry may be inferred from the fact that among the weaving castes only 3 in every 1,000 of the males are returned as subsisting by "property." In 1871, the Board of Revenue instituted inquiries into the state of the weaving industry in this Presidency and the results are given in their Proceedings, dated 28th June 1871, No. 2605. The conclusion then arrived at was that the weaving industry was in a fairly healthy condition. The number of looms at work (279,220) showed an increase of nearly 42 per cent. as compared with the number of looms at work between 1856-57 and 1860-61 and on which the moturpha tax was levied, but the returns for the earlier period were imperfect and not to be relied on. The Board estimated the real increase at between 20 and 25 per cent. and attributed this result mainly to the abolition of the vexatious and inquisitorial moturpha tax. The total quantity of twist worked up into cloth was taken at 31½ million pounds, of which 11½ millions, or 36½ per cent., was imported and the rest country-made.

Another inquiry was instituted in 1889 by the Board of Revenue on a reference from the Government of India calling for "fairly accurate statistics of the area and probable outturn of cotton" in the Madras Presidency, and the results are embodied in the Proceedings of the Board of Revenue, No. 39, dated 12th February 1890, Revenue Settlement, Land Records and Agriculture. The average area under the cotton crop was ascertained to be 1¾ million acres, and the probable annual outturn was fixed at 87¾ million pounds, or at 50 pounds of clean cotton per acre with reference to the quantity of cotton clothing required per head of the population and having regard also to the exports and imports of cotton and cotton cloth manufactured. The quantity of cotton used locally was estimated at 28¾ million pounds, 13⅓ millions being used by the spinning and weaving mills at work in the Presidency and the remainder being used by the poorer classes for spinning into the thread used for making coarser cloths used by the rural population. The number of hand looms at work in the Presidency was estimated at 300,000, and the quantity of twist worked up into cloth at 34½ millions of pounds, of which 19 millions, or 55 per cent., were imported, 1 million mill-spun and the remaining 14½ millions hand spun in the country.

6. In the number of persons engaged in the other occupations specified in the statement, it will be seen that there has been a very large increase; that in items 6, 12 and 14 may be particularly noticed. The increased facilities of communication between different parts of the country have led to a great increase in the number of carts and other conveyances, and railways, here as elsewhere, have not in any way reduced their number, but on the other hand have since increased it. Under item 12, the fish-curing industry is gaining in importance since 1881 on account of new facilities granted for the use of duty-free salt in fish-curing operations. The large increase in the imports of metals (valued at 11 lakhs of rupees in 1855-56, 40 lakhs in 1870-71, and 54 lakhs in 1887-88) and the great reduction in the cost of the articles has led to an extension of the demand for them and the prosperity of the metal industry. Among the persons included under item 14, 76,469 were gold and silver smiths, or 1 male goldsmith for every 408 of the total population, while in England there is only 1 goldsmith for every 1,200 inhabitants.

(b)—*Statement showing the varieties of Tenure held direct from Government during the official year* 1889-90 *in the Madras Presidency.*

Nature of tenure.		Number of estates.	Number of villages.	Number of holders or shareholders.	Gross area in acres.	Average area of each estate.	Average assessment of each estate.
		NO.	NO.	NO.	ACRES.	ACRES.	RS.
1. Great Zemindaries paying more than Rs. 50,000 revenue to Government.	Held by individuals under law of primogeniture.	14	9,183	14	6,783,549	484,539	1,96,906
	Held by individuals and families under ordinary law.	1	269	1	116,102	116,102	59,928
2. Large Zemindaries paying from Rs. 50,000 to Rs. 5,000 revenue to Government.	Under law of primogeniture.	50	9,837	51	8,280,030	165,601	14,363
	Under ordinary law.	78	1,475	124	1,088,943	13,961	20,511
3. Zemindaries paying from Rs. 5,000 to Rs. 100 revenue ...		612	3,162	929	2,506,258	4,095	1,482
4. Small Zemindaries other than those of cultivating communities paying less than Rs. 100.		94	429	116	275,047	2,926	54
5. Peasant proprietors paying separately *		2,848,710	26,728	4,615,740	21,133,179	7	14
6. Holders of wholly or partially revenue free tenures.	In perpetuity ...	433,298	28,247	778,197	8,135,537	19	11
	For life or lives ...	5,361	1,121	8,949	102,237	19	8
7. Landholders who have redeemed the revenue		550	181	651	4,767	9	¼
8. Purchasers of waste lands		464	138	495	27,436	59	82
Total ...		3,289,232	80,770	5,405,267	48,453,085	15	16

* For details see statement.

Classes of puttahs.	Number of single puttahs.	Joint puttahs.		Total number of puttahs.	Total assessment.	Average assessment for each puttah.
		Number.	Number of ryots holding them.			
					RS.	RS. A. P.
Ryots paying under Rs. 10 to Government	1.419.869	150.825	1.308.939	1.870,694	71,86.747	3 13 6
Do. between Rs. 10 & 30	443,678	227,712	810,068	671.390	1,12,90,515	16 11 5
Do. do. Rs. 30 & 50	109.322	53,898	288,033	163,220	60,98,921	37 5 10
Do. do. Rs. 50 & 100	68,397	32.630	143.152	101,027	67,49,731	66 12 11
Do. do. Rs. 100 & 250	26.998	11.889	49,278	38.887	55,73,105	143 5 1
Do. do. Rs. 250 & 500	4.701	2.011	9,403	6,712	21,74,052	323 14 6
Do. do. Rs. 500 & 1,000	1,292	440	2,877	1.732	11,18,110	645 8 11
Do. do. Rs. 1,000 and upwards	318	107	956	425	6,55.304	1,541 14 3
Total ...	2.074,575	779,512	2.612.706	2,854,087	4,08,46,485	14 4 11

(c)—*Statement showing the number of transfers of Revenue estates during the year* 1889-90.

Nature of Estate.	Number of transfers			Total area in acres transferred		
	By order of Court.	By sale for arrears of revenue.	By private contract or gift.	By order of Court.	By sale for arrears of revenue.	By private contract or gift.
Zemindaris or permanently-settled estates	4	2	32	36,571	2,675	54,908
Ryotwar holdings	971	5,140	107,424	7,409	13,070	356,374
Inam tenures	208	194	5,200	1,334	1,416	43,765
Total ...	1,183	5,336	112,656	45,314	17,161	455,047

(d)—*Statement showing the classification of the incomes on whicl the*

Classified items.	Incomes from Rs. 500 to Rs. 2,000 per annum. Districts. Number of assessees.	Districts. Amount of assessment.	Presidency Town. Number of assessees.	Presidency Town. Amount of assessment.	Total. Number of assessees.	Total. Amount of assessment.	Incom ,s of Rs. District. Number of assessees.	District. Amount of assessment.
PART I.								
		RS.		RS.		RS.		RS.
(*a*) Salaries, &c., paid by Government.	3,971	57,645	1,208	15,665	5,179	73,310	1,295	1,31,778
(*b*) Do. by local authorities.	1,141	10,655	177	2,996	1,318	13,651	61	4,315
(*c*) Do. by Companies, &c.	2,645	33,793	1,010	16,393	3,655	50,186	533	39,573
Total, Part I ...	7,757	1,02,093	2,395	35,054	10,152	1,37,147	1,889	1,75,666
PART II.								
(*a*) Banking Companies ...	41	781	41	1,104	82	1,885	21	2,609
(*b*) All other Companies ...	4	102	6	181	10	283	18	14,259
Total, Part II ...	45	883	47	1,285	92	2,168	39	16,868
PART III.								
(*a*) Interest on securities of the Government of India.	...	99	...	861	...	960	...	11,962
(*b*) Do. on all other securities.	...	...	...	...	...	...	...	265
Total, Part III ...	...	99	...	861	...	960	...	12,227
PART IV.								
(*a*) *Professions*—								
(1) Fine Arts	33	591	3	50	36	641	...	...
(2) Barristers, pleaders, and other legal practitioners.	1,020	18,686	14	401	1,034	19,087	220	24,607
(3) Medicine	18	307	7	179	25	486	1	191
(4) Other professions ..	237	3,537	23	544	260	4,081	27	4,188
Total (*a*) ...	1,308	23,121	47	1,174	1,355	24,295	248	28,986
(*b*) *Commerce*—								
(1) Agents, brokers, bankers, and contractors.	974	18,172	58	1,939	1,032	20,111	229	30,765
(2) General merchants ...	3,152	46,213	...	62	3,152	46,275	235	35,819
(3) Piece-goods merchants.	1,659	26,076	68	1,320	1,727	27,396	91	8,250
(4) Grain merchants ...	3,280	48,623	7	132	3,287	48,755	137	14,263
(5) Indigo merchants ..	439	6,096	3	90	442	6,186	15	1,147
(6) Salt merchants ...	125	1,909	...	...	125	1,909	19	4,753
(7) Money lending and changing.	13,329	2,01,487	56	1,555	13,385	2,03,042	1,210	1,46,761
(8) Other merchants ...	719	10,081	...	225	719	10,306	65	9,451
Total (*b*) ...	23,677	3,58,657	192	5,323	23,869	3,63,980	2,001	2,51,209
(*c*) *Transport, &c.*—								
(1) Cart and carriage builders and owners and livery stable-keepers.	107	1,374	23	520	130	1,894	4	950
(2) Ship or boat owners ...	139	2,046	6	192	145	2,238	42	6,290
(3) Hotel and inn-keepers and others.	59	905	4	126	63	1,031	10	917
Total (*c*) ...	305	4,325	33	838	338	5,163	56	8,157

Inc. me-tax was collected in the Madras Presidency during the year 1890-91.

2,000 a. d upwards per annum.				Total.					
Presidency Town.		Total.		Districts.		Presidency Town.		Total.	
Number of assessees.	Amount of assessment.	Number of assessees.	Amount of assessment.	Number of assessees.	Amount of assessment.	Number of assessees.	Amount of assessment.	Number of assessees.	Amount of assessment.
	RS.		RS.		RS.		RS.		RS.
682	78,975	1,977	2,10,753	5,266	1,89,423	1,890	94,640	7,156	2,84,063
22	2,849	83	7,164	1,202	14,970	199	5,867	1,401	20,837
323	33,340	856	72,913	3,178	73,366	1,333	49,733	4,511	1,23,099
1,027	1,15,164	2,916	2,90,830	9,646	2,77,759	3,422	1,50,240	13,068	4,27,999
21	24,643	42	27,252	62	3,390	62	25,747	124	29,137
9	6,933	27	21,192	22	14,361	15	7,114	37	21,475
30	31,576	69	48,444	84	17,751	77	32,861	161	50,612
...	54,134	...	66,096	...	12,061	...	54,995	...	67,056
...	3,116	...	3,381	...	265	...	3,116	...	3,381
...	57,250	...	69,477	...	12,326	...	58,111	...	70,437
...	65	...	65	33	591	3	115	36	706
47	15,435	267	40,042	1,240	43,293	61	15,836	1,301	59,129
7	1,488	8	1,679	19	498	14	1,667	33	2,165
5	1,410	32	5,598	264	7,725	28	1,954	292	9,679
59	18,398	307	47,384	1,556	52,107	106	19,572	1,662	71,679
51	24,647	280	55,412	1,203	48,937	109	26,586	1,312	75,523
14	22,762	249	58,581	3,387	82,032	14	22,824	3,401	1,04,856
29	11,950	120	20,200	1,750	34,326	97	13,270	1,847	47,596
...	197	137	14,460	3,417	62,886	7	329	3,424	63,215
4	866	19	2,013	454	7,243	7	956	461	8,199
2	251	21	5,004	144	6,662	2	251	146	6,913
26	8,893	1,236	1,55,654	14,539	3,48,248	82	10,448	14,621	3,58,696
...	57	65	9,508	784	19,532	...	282	784	19,814
126	69,623	2,127	3,20,832	25,678	6,09,866	318	74,946	25,996	6,84,812
2	1,288	6	2,238	111	2,324	25	1,808	136	4,132
1	234	43	6,524	181	8,336	7	426	188	8,762
3	771	13	1,688	69	1,822	7	897	76	2,719
6	2,293	62	10,450	361	12,482	39	3,131	400	15,613

Statement showing the classification of the incomes on which the Income ,ax

Classified items.	Incomes from Rs. 500 to Rs. 2,000 per annum.						Incom s of Rs.	
	Districts.		Presidency Town.		Total.		Districts.	
	Number of assessees.	Amount of assessment.	Number of assessees.	Amount of assessment.	Number of assessees.	Amount of assessment.	Number of assessees.	Amount of assessment.
(*d*) *Trade*—		RS.		RS.		RS		RS.
(1) Dealers in agricultural produce.	1,816	24,943	78	1,710	1,894	26,653	41	10,605
(2) Dealers in animals, animal and vegetable substances, not food, food and salt.	1,328	18,010	34	1,061	1,362	19,071	32	3,323
(3) Dealers in precious stones, &c.	273	4,101	7	287	280	4,388	11	1,108
(4) Dealers in spirits and opium.	314	4,780	7	2,421	321	7,201	19	1,693
(5) Dealers in dress, &c. ...	954	13,905	3	1,192	957	15,097	45	3,759
(6) Dealers in other articles.	3,931	54,765	232	6,479	4,163	61,244	133	15,128
Total (*d*) ...	8,616	1,20,504	361	13,150	8,977	1,33,654	281	35,616
(*e*) *Manufacture*—								
(1) Manufacture of cotton, silk and woollen goods.	1,199	15,986	...	...	1,199	15,986	38	4,039
(2) Builders and artizans ...	50	588	5	251	55	839	..	...
(3) Manufacture of salt ...	168	3,007	...	...	168	3,007	32	3,351
(4) Manufacture of spirits, &c.	1	15	...	...	1	15	1	417
(5) Manufacture of metals, &c.	328	4,716	9	193	337	4,909	29	3,304
Total (*e*) ...	1,746	24,312	14	444	1,760	24,756	100	11,111
(*f*) *Property*—								
(1) House proprietors ...	361	6,579	195	4,854	556		63	7,150
(2) Newspaper proprietors.	3	75	...	42	3	11,433	...	...
(3) Printing press proprietors.	21	361	9	177	30	117	...	...
						538	17	3,396
(4) Taxable Estate holders.	7	126	...	...	7	126		
Total (*f*)	392	7,141	204	5,073	596	12,214	80	10,546
Total, Part IV ..	36,044	5,38,060	851	26,002	36,895	5,64,062	2,766	3,45,625
Grand Total, Parts I, II, III, & IV.	43,846	6,41,135	3,293	63,202	47,139	7,04,337	4,694	5,50,386

* Inclusive of Rs. 22 relating to the tax on salaries paid by local

REMARKS.—

Number of persons assessed to income-tax in 1890-91	56,809
Total taxable income	Rs. 6,51,21,760
Average income assessed per head	Rs. 1,148
Average assessment per head	Rs. 28-10-6
Number of ryots paying assessment of Rs. 250 and upwards	8,869
Total assessment	Rs. 39,47,466

w... collected in the Madras Presidency during the year 1890-91—cont.

2,000 and upwards per annum.				Total.					
Presidency Town.		Total.		Districts.		Presidency Town.		Total.	
Number of assessees.	Amount of assessment.	Number of assessees.	Amount of assessment.	Number of assessees.	Amount of assessment.	Number of assessees.	Amount of assessment.	Number of assessees.	Amount of assessment.
	RS.		RS.		RS.		RS.		RS.
2	208	43	10,813	1,857	35,548	80	1,918	1,937	37,466
16	4,121	48	7,444	1,360	21,333	50	5,182	1,410	26,515
2	4,659	13	5,767	234	5,209	9	4,946	293	10,155
3	4,628	22	6,321	333	6,473	10	7,049	343	13,522
1	890	46	4,649	999	17,664	4	2,082	1,003	19,746
35	6,194	168	21,322	4,064	69,893	267	12,673	4,331	82,566
59	20,700	340	56,316	8,897	1,56,120	420	33,850	9,317	1,89,970
...	...	38	4,039	1,237	20,025	...	...	1,237	20,025
1	117	1	117	50	588	6	368	56	956
...	...	32	3,351	200	6,358	...	...	200	6,358
1	1,792	2	2,209	2	432	1	1,792	3	2,224
...	130	29	3,434	357	8,020	9	323	366	8,343
2	2,039	102	13,150	1,846	35,423	16	2,483	1,862	37,906
54	8,729	117	15,879	424	13,729	249	13,583	673	27,312
4	1,468	4	1,468	3	75	4	1,510	7	1,585
2	221	2	221	21	361	11	398	32	759
...	...	17	3,396	24	3,522	...	...	24	3,522
60	10,418	140	20,964	472	17,687	264	15,491	736	33,178
312	1,23,471	3,078	4,69,096	38,810	8,83,685	1,163	1,49,473	39,973	10,33,158
1,369	3,27,461	6,063	8,77,047	48,540	11,91,521	4,662	*3,90,685	53,202	*15,82,206

authorities for which classwar particulars are not available.

Average assessment per ryot ...	Rs. 445
Number of ryots paying assessments of Rs. 500 and upwards ...	2,157
Total assessment ...	Rs. 17,73,414
Average assessment per ryot ...	Rs. 822
Number of income-tax payers per 100,000 of the population ...	165
Number of ryots paying Rs. 250 and upwards per 100,000 ...	26
Number of ryots paying 500 and upwards per 100,000 ...	6

(e)—*Statement showing the amount of Government stock (public debt) held by Europeans and Natives, respectively, in* 1834, 1850 *and* 1888, *througho*[illegible] *India.*

—	Europeans.	Natives.	Total.
	Rx.	Rx.	Rx.
1834	20,439,870	7,225,360	27,665,230
1850	21,981,447	12,271,140	34,252,587
1888	70,895,590	24,065,239	94,960,829

NOTE.—(*a*) The amounts entered for 1888 do not include the special loans from the Gwalior Durbar, &c.

(*b*) The amount of stock actually presented for payment of interest was Rx. 54,582,992, Rx. 36,657,560 by Europeans, and Rx. 17,925,432 by Natives. The amount of enfaced notes held in London was Rx. 21,682,105. The balance of principal not presented for interest, viz., Rx. 18,695,732, was ratably distributed among Europeans and Natives in the proportion of the amounts presented by each for payment of interest.

(f)—*Statement showing the transactions of the Presidency, District and Post Office Savings Banks in India.*

Years.	Number of Deposits.			Amount of Deposits including interest in thousands of rupees.		
	Europeans.	Natives.	Total.	Europeans.	Natives.	Total.
				RS.	RS.	RS.
1857-58 ...	...	...	...	...	...	3,898
1862-63 ...	...	...	...	...	...	4,167
1867-68 ...	12,565	16,310	28,875	3,165	3,607	6,772
1872-73 ...	13,631	28,236	41,867	4,915	8,558	13,473
1877-78 ..	17,208	48,378	65,586	5,113	12,172	17,285
1882-83 ...	20,232	68,614	88,846	7,815	23,321	31,136
1889-90 ...	53,416	343,790	397,206	11,562	57,393	68,955

NOTE.—District Savings and Post Office Savings Banks were established in 1871-72 and 1886-87 respectively.

(g)—*Statement showing the Number and Value of Money Orders issued.*

Year.	Number of Orders.		Value of Orders in thousands of rupees.	
	India.	Madras.	India.	Madras.
			RS.	RS.
1867-68	120,107	9,794	6,816	528
1872-73	269,435	30,086	12,921	1,131
1877-78	259,680	36,192	9,847	1,333
1882-83	2,594,364	554,939	66,231	8,315
1889-90	6,750,000	847,852	1,46,500	17,212

(h)—*Comparative statement of the rates of value of labour per diem in the several districts of the Madras Presidency for certain yea compiled from schedules of rates in force in the Public Works Department.*

Description of labour.	Per	Ganjam.	Vizagapatam.	Godávari.	Kistna.	Nellore.	Cuddapah.	Bellary.	Kurnool.
1	2	3	4	5	6	7	8	9	10
Skilled labour.		RS. A. P.	RS. A. P.	RS. A. P.	RS. A. P.	RS. A. P.	RS. A. P.	RS. A. P.	RS. A. P.
Bricklayers .. .. 1859-60 .. 1874 ..	Each ,,	0 4 11½ 0 5 4 0 6 0	0 4 1 0 6 0 0 5 6	0 4 5¼ 0 7 0 0 6 0	0 4 11⅓ 0 8 0 0 7 0	0 5 9½ 0 7 6 0 7 0	0 5 5⅗ 0 10 0 0 8 0	0 6 3 3/16 0 10 0 0 12 0	0 6 1 1/13 0 10 0 0 8 0
Recent years since 1883 ..	,,	0 7 0 0 8 0	0 5 6 0 6 0	0 7 0 0 8 0	0 6 0 0 7 0 0 8 0	0 10 0 0 7 0 0 6 0	0 8 0 0 12 0 0 10 0	0 10 0 0 12 0	0 10 0 0 12 0
Carpenters .. .. 1859-60 .. 1874 ..	,, ,,	0 4 7¼ 0 6 0 0 7 0	0 3 11⅗ 0 5 6 0 5 0	0 4 8⅕ 0 7 0 0 6 0	0 5 1 4/7 0 8 0 0 6 0	0 5 2¼ 0 10 0 0 7 0	0 5 7½ 0 10 0 0 8 0	0 6 1 5/16 0 8 0 0 12 0	0 6 4 2/13 0 8 0 0 7 0
Recent years since 1883 ..	,,	0 7 0 0 8 0	0 5 0 0 5 6 0 5 0	0 6 0 0 8 0	0 8 0 0 12 0	0 12 0 0 8 0 0 6 0	0 10 0 0 12 0	0 10 0 0 12 0	0 10 0 0 12 0
Smiths .. .. 1859-60 .. 1874 ..	,, ,,	0 4 2½ 0 6 6 0 5 4	0 4 3 0 7 0 0 5 6	0 5 0 13/30 0 7 0 0 6 0	0 5 1 4/7 0 6 0 0 8 0	0 5 0⅔ 0 10 0 0 7 0	0 5 4 10/11 0 10 0 0 8 0	0 6 4½ 0 8 0 0 12 0	0 6 5 7/13 0 12 0 0 10 0
Recent years since 1883 ..	,,	0 6 0 0 8 0	0 7 0 0 6 0	0 7 0	0 7 0 0 8 0	0 12 0 0 10 0 0 6 0	0 10 0 0 12 0	0 10 0 0 12 0	0 14 0 1 0 0

(h)—*Comparative statement of the rates of value of labour per diem in the several districts of the Madras Presidency, &c.*—cont.

Description of labour.	Per	Chingleput.	North Arcot.	South Arcot.	Tanjore.	Trichinopoly.	Madura.	Tinnevelly.	Coimbatore.
	11	12	13	14	15	16	17	18	19
		RS. A. P.	RS. A. P.	RS. A. P.	RS. A. P.	RS. A. P.	RS. A. P.	RS. A. P.	RS. A. P.
Skilled labour.									
Bricklayers .. 1859-60 ..	Each	0 6 6$\frac{9}{10}$	0 6 6$\frac{21}{26}$	0 6 2$\frac{7}{19}$	0 6 4$\frac{2}{3}$	0 5 11$\frac{1}{3}$	0 5 6$\frac{6}{7}$	0 5 0$\frac{6}{13}$	0 6 8$\frac{11}{28}$
1874 ..	,,	0 6 6 0 7 0	0 9 0 0 7 6	0 8 0 0 7 0	0 9 0 0 6 0	0 5 0 0 6 0 0 8 0 0 12 0	0 12 0	..	0 10 0 0 9 0
Recent years since 1883 ..	,,	0 6 0 0 8 0	0 6 0 0 10 0 0 8 0 0 12 0	0 8 0 0 10 0 0 12 0	0 6 0 0 8 0	0 8 0 0 10 0 0 7 0 0 6 0	0 7 0 0 10 0	0 8 0 0 12 0	0 9 0 0 10 0
Carpenters .. 1859-60 ..	,,	0 7 3$\frac{9}{10}$	0 7 2$\frac{5}{26}$	0 5 11$\frac{10}{13}$	0 6 7$\frac{3}{4}$	0 5 11$\frac{1}{3}$	0 4 11$\frac{4}{7}$	0 4 1$\frac{6}{13}$	0 6 11$\frac{13}{28}$
1874 ..	,,	0 7 0 0 8 0	0 10 0 0 8 0	0 10 0 0 9 0	0 9 0 0 5 0	0 6 0 0 8 0 0 12 0	0 12 0	0 8 0 0 10 0 0 12 0	0 12 0 0 10 0
Recent years since 1883 ..	,,	0 8 0 0 10 0	0 7 0 0 10 0 0 8 0 0 12 0	0 10 0 0 12 0 0 8 0	0 8 0 0 10 0	0 10 0 0 12 0 0 8 0 0 6 0	0 8 0 0 10 0	0 6 0 0 12 0	0 9 0 0 12 0
Smiths .. 1859-60 ..	,,	0 7 1$\frac{7}{20}$	0 7 1$\frac{5}{13}$	0 6 0$\frac{12}{19}$	0 6 7$\frac{1}{3}$	0 6 3$\frac{1}{3}$	0 4 10$\frac{6}{7}$	0 3 9$\frac{6}{31}$	0 5 10$\frac{1}{28}$
1874 ..	,,	0 9 0 0 8 0	0 11 0 0 8 0	0 8 0 0 9 0	0 6 0 0 8 0	0 12 0 0 8 0 0 6 0	0 12 0	0 12 0 0 8 0	0 10 0 0 8 0
Recent years since 1883 ..	,,	0 8 0 0 12 0	0 8 0 0 12 0	0 11 0 0 12 0 0 8 0	0 8 0 0 10 0	0 10 0 0 12 0 0 8 0 0 6 0	0 9 0 0 10 0	0 7 0 0 12 0	0 9 0 0 12 0

(h)—*Comparative statement of the rates of value of labour per diem in the several districts of the Madras Presidency, &c.*—cont.

Description of labour.	Per	Salem.	North Canara.	South Canara.	Malabar.	Civil Architect (Madras).	Garrison Engineer.	Wellington (Nilgiris).	Bangalore.
	20	21	22	23	24	25	26	27	28
Skilled labour.		RS. A. P.	RS. A. P.	RS. A. P.	RS. A. P.	RS. A. P.	RS. A. P.	RS. A. P.	RS. A. P.
Bricklayer .. .. 1859-60 ..	Each	0 6 11 5/14	0 6 9 3/14	0 7 0 2/3	0 6 5 13/16	0 7 1 1/2	0 7 6	0 9 6	0 5 10 1/2
1874 ..	,,	0 8 0 0 9 0	..	0 14 0 0 12 3	0 12 0 0 8 0	0 7 0 0 8 0	..	0 10 6 0 12 0	0 8 0 0 7 0
Recent years since 1883 ..	,,	0 10 0 0 12 0	..	0 12 0 0 14 0	0 10 0 0 12 0 0 13 0	0 6 6 0 7 0	..	1 0 0 0 15 0 0 14 0 0 8 0	0 8 0 0 9 0 0 7 0
Carpenters .. .. 1859-60 ..	,,	0 6 8 22/25	0 7 2 4/7	0 7 0	0 6 3 5/8	0 7 3	0 9 0	0 10 6	0 5 10 1/2
1874 ..	,,	0 8 0 0 9 0	..	0 14 9 0 12 3	0 10 0 0 12 0	0 7 6 0 8 6	..	0 10 6 0 12 0 0 14 0	0 8 0 0 7 0
Recent years since 1883 ..	,,	0 10 0 0 12 0	..	0 12 0 0 14 0	0 8 0 0 12 0 0 10 0	0 8 0 0 12 0	..	1 0 0 0 14 0 0 10 0	0 8 0 0 12 0
Smiths .. .. 1859-60 ..	,,	0 6 4 13/14	0 6 7 3/7	0 6 6 2/3	0 5 5 1/8	0 6 9	..	0 11 0 1/2	0 5 10 1/2
1874 ..	,,	0 9 0 0 10 0	..	0 12 0 0 10 0	0 10 0 0 12 0	0 7 6 0 8 0	..	0 10 6 0 12 0 0 14 0 1 0 0	0 10 0 0 9 0
Recent years since 1883 ..	,,	0 10 0 0 12 0	..	0 14 0 0 12 0	0 8 0 0 10 0	0 8 0 0 12 0	..	1 4 0 1 0 0	0 10 0 0 12 0

(h)—*Comparative statement of the rates of value of labour per diem in the several districts of the Madras Presidency, &c.*—cont.

Description of labour.	Per	Ganjam.	Vizagapatam.	Godavari.	Kistna.	Nellore.	Cuddapah.	Bellary.	Kurnool.
1	2	3	4	5	6	7	8	9	10
		RS. A. P.	RS. A. P.	RS. A. P.	RS. A. P.	RS. A. P.	RS. A. P.	RS. A. P.	RS. A. P.
Unskilled labour.									
Adult coolies .. 1859-60 ..	Each	0 1 4½	0 1 2$\frac{9}{14}$	0 2 0$\frac{3}{16}$	0 2 0	0 1 10$\frac{12}{19}$	0 2 0	0 1 11¾	0 2 0$\frac{4}{13}$
1869 ..	,,	..	..	..	0 3 1	0 2 6	..	..	..
1874 ..	,,	0 2 0	0 2 0	0 3 0	0 3 6	0 2 6 0 2 0	0 2 6	0 4 0	0 2 8
1878 ..	,,	0 1 4 0 1 8	0 2 0 0 2 6 0 3 0	0 2 6 0 5 0	0 2 6 0 3 0	0 2 6 0 3 0	0 2 0 0 2 9 0 3 0	0 2 0 to 0 4 0	0 2 3 0 3 0
Recent years since 1883 ..	,,	0 2 0	0 2 0	0 3 0	0 3 0 0 3 6	0 2 0 to 0 4 0	0 4 0	0 3 0	0 3 0
Boys .. .. .. 1859-60 ..	,,	0 0 9	0 0 8$\frac{4}{7}$	0 1 3	0 1 4$\frac{5}{21}$	0 1 0½	0 1 2$\frac{1}{12}$	0 1 2$\frac{5}{16}$	0 1 0$\frac{3}{13}$
1874 ..	,,	0 1 0	..	..	..	..	..	0 1 6	..
1878 ..	,,	0 0 8 0 0 9	0 0 8 0 0 10	0 1 0 0 1 3	0 1 0 0 2 6	0 1 0 0 1 3	0 1 0 0 1 6	0 1 0 0 1 6	0 1 3 0 1 4
Recent years since 1883 ..	,,	0 1 0	0 1 0	0 1 6	0 1 6 0 1 9	0 1 3 to 0 1 6	0 1 6	0 1 6	0 1 6
Women .. .. 1859-60 ..	,,	0 0 11⅓	0 0 10$\frac{3}{7}$	0 1 6	0 1 4$\frac{16}{21}$	0 1 3$\frac{1}{19}$	0 1 3¼	0 1 2$\frac{11}{16}$	0 1 3$\frac{11}{13}$
1874 ..	,,	0 1 3	0 3 0	..	..	..	..	0 2 0	..
1878 ..	,,	0 0 10 0 1 3	0 0 10 0 1 4	0 1 6 0 2 0	0 1 6 0 2 6	0 1 4 0 2 0	0 1 3 0 2 0	0 1 4 0 2 0	0 1 8 0 1 9
Recent years since 1883 ..	,,	0 [illegible] 6	0 1 0	0 1 6	0 2 0 0 2 3 0 3 0	0 1 3 to 0 2 0	0 2 0	0 2 0	0 2 0

(h)—*Comparative statement of the rates of value of labour per diem in the several districts of the Madras Presidency, &c.*—cont.

Description of labour.	Per	Chingleput.	North Arcot.	South Arcot.	Tanjore.	Trichinopoly.	Madura.	Tinnevelly.	Coimbatore.
	11	12	13	14	15	16	17	18	19
Unskilled labour.		RS. A. P.	RS. A. P.	RS. A. P.	RS. A. P.	RS. A. P.	RS. A. P.	RS. A. P.	RS. A. P.
Adult coolies .. .. 1859-60 ..	Each	0 2 4$\frac{1}{3}$	0 2 4$\frac{8}{13}$	0 2 0	0 2 6	0 1 10	0 2 0	0 1 11$\frac{1}{13}$	0 2 1$\frac{13}{15}$
1869 ..	,,	..	..	..	..	..	..	..	0 4 1$\frac{1}{2}$
1874 ..	,,	0 3 0	0 2 6	0 4 0	0 3 6 0 4 0	0 2 0 0 2 6 0 3 0	0 4 0	0 2 0 0 4 0	0 4 0
1878 ..	,,	0 2 2 0 2 6	0 2 2 0 2 4 0 2 6	0 2 6 to 0 4 6	0 2 0 to 0 4 6	0 3 6 0 4 0	0 2 6 0 5 4	0 3 0 0 3 4	0 4 0 0 8 0
Recent years since 1883 ..	,,	0 3 0	0 3 0 0 2 6	0 3 0 0 2 6	0 4 0 0 3 6	0 2 6 0 3 6	0 3 0	0 4 0	0 4 0
Boys .. .. .. 1859-60 ..	,,	0 1 2$\frac{2}{3}$	0 1 0$\frac{3}{13}$	0 1 6	0 1 4$\frac{4}{9}$	0 1 0$\frac{2}{3}$	0 1 0	0 1 0$\frac{10}{13}$	0 1 1$\frac{3}{7}$
1874 ..	,,	0 1 3 0 1 6	..	..	0 2 0	0 1 6	0 2 0	0 1 0 0 2 0	0 1 6
1878 ..	,,	0 1 0	0 1 1 0 1 2 0 1 3	..	0 0 9 to 0 2 0	..	0 1 0 to 0 2 8	0 1 0 0 1 6	0 0 10 to 0 2 0
Recent years since 1883 ..	,,	0 1 6 0 1 3	0 1 3 0 1 6	0 1 6	0 2 0	0 1 0 0 1 6	0 1 3	0 2 0	0 1 6
Women .. .. 1859-60 ..	,,	0 1 4$\frac{4}{5}$	0 1 3$\frac{1}{2}$	0 1 3	0 1 0 0 1 5$\frac{2}{3}$	0 1 1	0 1 0	0 1 0$\frac{8}{13}$	0 1 1$\frac{2}{3}$
1874 ..	,,	0 1 6 0 2 0	0 1 6	..	0 2 6 0 3 0	0 2 0	0 2 0	0 2 0 0 3 0	0 2 0
1878 ..	,,	0 1 8 0 2 0	0 1 8 0 2 0	..	0 1 6 0 2 6	0 2 0	0 1 3 to 0 2 8	0 1 6 0 2 3	0 1 6 0 2 6
Recent years since 1883 ..	,,	0 2 0	0 2 0 0 1 9	0 2 0 0 1 6	0 2 0	0 1 6	0 1 6	0 2 6	0 2 0

(h)—*Comparative statement of the rates of value of labour per diem in the several districts of the Madras Presidency, &c.*—cont.

Description of labour.	Per	Salem.	North Canara.	South Canara.	Malabar.	Civil Architect (Madras).	Garrison Engineer.	Wellington (Nilgiris).	Bangalore.
	20	21	22	23	24	25	26	27	28
		RS. A. P.	RS. A. P.	RS. A. P.	RS. A. P.	RS. A. P.	RS. A. P.	RS. A. P.	RS. A. P.
Unskilled labour.									
Adult coolies — 1859-60	Each	0 2 $0\frac{2}{3}$	0 2 $8\frac{2}{7}$	0 2 $4\frac{2}{3}$	0 2 $8\frac{1}{16}$	0 3 6	0 3 $7\frac{1}{4}$	0 3 6	0 2 0
1869	"	..	..	0 3 4	0 4 6	..	..	..	..
1874	"	0 2 6	..	0 3 3	0 5 0	0 3 6	..	0 6 0	0 3 0
1878	"	0 2 0 0 3 6	..	0 2 9 to 0 4 0	0 4 0 to 0 8 0	0 2 6 to 0 4 0	..	0 5 0	0 3 0
Recent years since 1883	"	0 3 0	..	0 4 0	0 4 0 0 3 0	0 3 0	..	0 4 0 0 5 0	0 4 0
Boys — 1859-60	"	0 1 $0\frac{2}{7}$	0 1 $7\frac{2}{3}$	0 1 6	0 1 $5\frac{3}{16}$	0 2 0	0 2 $2\frac{1}{2}$	0 2 3	[illegible] 1 2
1874	"	0 1 0	..	..	..	0 1 9	..	0 4 6	..
1878	"	0 1 0 0 1 6	..	0 2 0 0 3 0	0 1 6 to 0 4 0	0 1 9 0 2 6	..	0 2 0 0 3 0	..
Recent years since 1883	"	0 1 3	..	0 2 4 0 2 6	0 1 6 0 2 0	0 2 0	..	0 2 6 0 3 0	0 2 0
Women — 1859-60	"	0 1 $0\frac{4}{7}$	0 1 $7\frac{3}{7}$	0 1 $4\frac{2}{3}$	0 1 $5\frac{3}{4}$	0 2 6	0 2 $7\frac{1}{4}$	0 2 6	0 1 2
1874	"	0 [illegible] 4	..	..	..	0 2 0	..	0 3 0	..
1874	"	[illegible] 1 [illegible] 0 2 0	..	0 2 0 0 3 0	0 1 6 0 3 0	0 1 6 0 2 0	..	0 3 0 0 4 0	0 1 8
Recent years since 1883	"	0 1 [illegible]	..	0 2 6 0 2 8	0 2 0 0 2 6	0 2 6	..	0 3 0 0 3 6	[illegible] 2 0

(i)—*Statement showing the pressure of population on the land in the several districts of the Madras Presidency.*

Districts.	Number of persons to a square mile according to the Census of 1891.	Average size of a ryotwar holding.	Average assessment of a ryotwar holding.	Proportion of dry and wet acreage to total ryotwar holdings.		Proportion of unoccupied waste to total ryotwar holdings.	Average rate of assessment per acre of occupied land.		Average rate of assessment per acre of unoccupied land.		Ratio of working population to total population.	Ratio of agricultural to working population.	Ratio of females to total agricultural and working population.
				Dry.	Wet.		Dry.	Wet.	Dry.	Wet.			
		ACRES.	RS.				RS. A. P.	RS. A. P.	RS. A. P.	RS. A. P.			
Ganjam	226	7·8	11·8	54	46	17	1 4 5	2 14 6	1 0 3	2 5 7	54	60	40
Vizagapatam ..	164	12·6	29·0	68	32	7	0 15 11	5 5 3	1 10 10	4 14 10	70	65	42
Godávari ..	235	10·2	19·6	39	61	15	1 13 8	2 12 10	0 6 7	1 12 3	49	59	26
Kistna	220	11·8	17·4	85	15	17	1 7 5	3 12 3	0 15 4	4 14 3	50	62	29
Nellore	166	9·2	18·5	76	24	29	1 3 8	4 7 10	0 9 9	4 4 9	53	63	33
Cuddapah ..	145	7·4	9·5	90	10	30	0 12 3	7 1 3	0 6 4	4 14 7	61	71	40
Anantapur ..	134	14·6	11·2	93	7	45	0 10 2	5 0 3	0 11 6	4 2 1	60	74	40
Bellary	151	15·1	13·1	97	3	39	0 10 2	5 0 3	0 7 0	3 9 5	59	69	40
Kurnool	109	11·6	12·6	97	3	30	0 15 4	6 7 1	0 8 10	4 15 8	54	59	33
Madras	15,515	..	..	..	..	..	..	..	..	..	34	7	21
Chingleput ..	400	7·0	18·0	38	62	19	1 8 7	3 13 0	0 14 5	2 11 2	50	61	25
North Arcot ..	286	3·6	9·5	66	34	29	1 6 4	5 12 5	1 0 9	4 14 4	52	69	33
South Arcot ..	414	3·8	9·4	77	23	41	1 11 5	5 5 10	1 9 1	4 5 3	49	78	31
Tanjore	600	6·6	25·1	25	75	8	1 4 0	4 15 2	1 0 1	2 8 4	48	64	32
Trichinopoly ..	379	6·2	8·3	84	16	20	0 15 6	4 6 9	1 0 10	3 4 6	53	73	36
Madura	271	5·5	9·6	83	17	23	1 5 1	4 4 2	0 15 8	3 6 0	59	71	45
Tinnevelly ..	356	7·1	12·9	83	17	6	0 13 3	10 4 10	0 8 8	5 3 9	52	63	37
Coimbatore ..	254	10·2	12·0	96	4	16	0 14 7	7 7 1	0 9 7	4 11 10	58	64	44
Nilgiris	104	26·6	19·0	97	3	40	0 8 7	2 4 0	0 10 9	2 14 10	61	63	37
Salem	260	6·6	9·6	92	8	31	1 2 8	5 14 6	0 13 9	3 13 11	60	67	46
South Canara ..	270	..	..	..	..	18	..	..	..	..	55	74	43
Malabar	475	4·1	9·4	49	51	41	..	..	..	..	47	53	39
Average ..	251	7·2	12·9	79	21	26·36	1 1 3	4 11 8	0 11 2	4 2 2	61	70	42

REMARKS.—(1) The number of persons to a square mile entered for Ganjam, Vizagapatam and Godávari is inclusive of the Agency Tracts in these districts; excluding the Agency Tracts, the number is 326, 452 and 407 respectively.

(2) The figures in the last 3 columns refer to the population of 1881, similar information as per Census of 1891 not being available yet.

(3) A comparison of the average rates of assessment of occupied and unoccupied cultivable lands will show whether the land available is of very inferior quality or not.

(4) The extent to which women are employed in field labour may, to some extent, be taken as a measure of the standard of living in the district.

(j)—*Statement showing the total acreage, classification of areas, irrigated crops, current fallows, and the number of live-stock, carts, ploughs and boats in the Madras Presidency during the year* 1889-90.

(1) *Total acreage.*

		Millions of acres.
(*a*) Area according to Survey Department	...	91·03
(*b*) Deduct.	(1) Feudatory and Tributary States.	0·97
	(2) Area for which there are no returns	30·29
(*c*) Net area by Survey Department	... ...	59·77

(2) *Classification of net area.*

(*a*) Forests	... ...	11·13
(*b*) Not available for cultivation	... ...	11·85
(*c*) Available for cultivation	... ...	8·02
(*d*) Current fallows	... ...	4·97
(*e*) Cropped during the year	... ...	23·80
(*f*) Area irrigated during the year.	(1) Government canals ...	2·70
	(2) Private channels	0·03
	(3) Tanks	2·31
	(4) Wells	1·17
	(5) Other sources	0·18
	Total area irrigated ...	6·39
(*g*) Crops irrigated.	(1) Wheat	0·005
	(2) Other cereals and pulses ...	5·61
	(3) Miscellaneous food crops ...	0·57
	(4) Non-food crops	0·21

(3) *Acreage under crops.*

(*a*) Cereals and pulses.	(1) Rice	6·46
	(2) Wheat	0·02
	(3) Other food grains including pulses	14·10
(*b*) Oil-seeds	... ...	1·91
(*c*) Sugarcane	... ...	0·06
(*d*) Fibres ...	(1) Cotton mixed and unmixed.	1·64
	(2) Other sorts	0·05
(*e*) Indigo	... ...	0·45
(*f*) Coffee	... ...	0·05
(*g*) Tea	... ...	0·005
(*h*) Tobacco	... ...	0·10
(*i*) Cinchona	... ...	0·01
(*j*) Miscellaneous crops.	Food	0·36
	Non-food	0·905
(*k*) Total area of crops cultivated	... ...	26·12
(*l*) Area cropped more than once	... ...	2·32
(*m*) Actual area cropped (k-l)	... ...	23·80

(4) *Number of live-stock, &c.*

	Number in millions.
(*a*) Cows and bullocks	11·02
(*b*) Buffaloes	3·46
(*c*) Horses and ponies	0·05
(*d*) Mules and donkeys	0·12
(*e*) Sheep and goats	12·06
(*f*) Carts	0·44
(*g*) Ploughs	2·50
(*h*) Boats	0·02

(k)—*Extracts from Dr. Macleane's Manual of Administration on the economic condition of the labouring classes.*

Arcot, North.—The population is mainly rural. The ordinary agriculturist is strongly attached to his native village and rarely leaves it except to attend some religious festival. The railway has worked very considerable changes, and by raising the value of agricultural produce has materially improved the condition of the cultivating classes along the line. In the towns stone houses are not uncommon, but all the villagers and the vast majority of the urban population live in mud buildings. The household furniture of the ordinary cultivator, herdsman and small trader consists merely of a bed of wooden planks (visoopalagay), a bench and one or two boxes. The land under cultivation is reported at 578,731 acres (dry 377,715 and wet 201,016) or only 13 per cent. of the district area. Most of the individual holdings are very small, paying less than Rs. 25 per annum. A cultivator paying more than that may be called a moderately large holder, while those paying more than Rs. 100 per annum are few in number and wealthy. The profits derivable from a holding of 5 acres average from Rs. 8 to Rs. 10 per mensem. From ragi the people make porridge (sankaty) which constitutes the ordinary food of the masses. Rice, though sometimes mixed as a luxury with the cheaper grains, is eaten as a regular meal only by the wealthy. Male labourers earn from Annas 2 to Annas 2-8 per diem and females about half as much. The wages of a working goldsmith or blacksmith are 6 annas a day; of carpenter or bricklayer 6 annas to 8 annas. The rate of interest for money lent on personal security varies from 12 to 36 per cent. per annum. On the security of personal goods it averages 12 per cent. and with a lien on crops 18 per cent. From 6 to 8 per cent. is considered a fair return for money invested on land.

Arcot, South.—With a holding of 5 acres, the peasant is not so well off as a retail shopkeeper, making a net income of Rs. 8 a month. The mass of cultivators, however, hold less, and although the expenses of an ordinary cultivator with a wife and 3 children may be calculated at only Rs. 3-0-0 to Rs. 4-8-0 per mensem, they are as a rule in debt. Twenty acres would be considered a large holding; less than 2 acres reduces the cultivator to a hand-to-mouth subsistence. Under the regulations in force, cultivable waste is being annually taken up for casuarina and cashewnut. Agricultural and day-labouring males earn Annas 2-8 to Annas 3-4 per day and females about half as much. Smiths, bricklayers, carpenters obtain 6 annas a day on the average.

Since 1850 wages have risen 50 per cent., in some cases 75 per cent. A comparison of prices of food-grains in the years 1850-51, 1860-61 and 1870-71, all average years, shows a general rise in the second decade with a fall in the third decade. The district contains a large number of field labourers called padials of the Pariah caste, who receive payments in kind and are, as a rule, farm hands engaged by the season, but sometimes permanently attached to the estate. The mass of cultivators are tenants with rights of occupancy terminable at their own option. On private estates the cultivators, where not padials, are tenants-at-will, paying rent to the intermediate landlord, sometimes in cash but often in kind and liable to ejectment at the end of the season. The rates of interest vary from 12 to 24 per cent. on the security of personal goods; from 6 to 9 per cent. on large transactions and from 12 to 18 per cent. on personal security with a lien on a crop. 5 to 6 per cent. would be considered fair return for money invested on land.

Bellary and Anantapur.—Prices have for many years been steadily rising, and, where money payments obtain, agricultural labourers and ordinary artisans now receive double and even treble the wages given before 1850. The field labourers, however, are as a rule paid in kind and the rise of prices has not affected them. In other cases the cultivator class has benefited, the cotton-growers notably, many of whom during the American war made considerable fortunes. Rice during 1840–50 averaged 24 lb. for Annas 8, between 1850–60 rose to 20 lb., and since 1860 has averaged 10 lb. for Annas 8; cholum during the same period rose from 58 to 38 and 23 lb. for Annas 8; and ragi from 62 to 46 and 25.

Canara, South.—The ruling retail prices of food-grains, &c., in 1883-84 per garce of 9,600 lb., were for best rice Rs. 400; paddy Rs. 148; gram Rs. 237. The wages of day labourers have increased since 1850, an ordinary male labourer being now paid Annas 3 and a female Annas 2 a day instead of Annas 2 and Annas 1½, respectively, in 1850. Smiths and bricklayers who in that year obtained Annas 4 now get Annas 8 and carpenters now get Annas 8 who then got Annas 6. The Holeyas, answering to the Pariahs of Madras and the Ruhans of Bombay, are a class who live by hire as unskilled labourers. They are paid in paddy or rice, and their wages are subject to deductions on account of debts contracted to meet the expenses of marriage. In gathering the harvest and storing it up they are not paid so much per day but receive $\frac{1}{11}$ of the crop; so also for preparing rice from paddy, they receive 6 lb. of rice for preparing 84 lb. At the time of transplanting and reaping, females are largely employed and are generally paid 4 lb. of rice per day. Before the British rule the Holeyas were the slaves of the Wurgdars and even to this day they remain in a state of modified serfdom; but the coffee estates are drawing large numbers from their original homes and labour market is being largely ruled by the ordinary laws of supply and demand.

Godávari.—In 30 years the population has doubled, and, thanks to the splendid system of navigable irrigation works, the agriculture and commerce of the district are in a most prosperous condition. Great improvement has taken place of late years in the quality of the food-grains raised in the district owing to the extension of irrigation by canals. A farm, 100 acres in extent, would be considered a large holding for an agriculturist, one of 30 acres a middlesized one, and one of 5 acres a very small one. Government tenants have a permanent right of occupancy so long as they pay the Government assessment. In zemindari estates, on the other hand, the cultivators are mostly yearly tenants. A number of landless labourers are employed in cultivation, paid sometimes in money and sometimes at a fixed rate in grain, but never by a regular share of the crop. Wages have more than doubled since 1850. A carpenter, smith or bricklayer now earns Annas 8-1 in towns and Annas 7-5 in villages and an agricultural labourer 3 annas. Women employed in weeding and transplanting are paid at from one-half to two-thirds of the rates for men, while the children receive a lower rate. Paddy or unhusked rice, which in 1850 was returned at Rs. 24 per garce (9,860 lb.), is now (1884) worth Rs. 68 per garce.

Kistna.—The people of the district are generally poor, but an exception must be made in the case of the ryots of the delta, who are, as a rule, very well off. Throughout the delta the houses are, as a rule, built with brick-walls and tiled or terraced roofs; in other parts they are of mud walls with terraced roofs. Rice is the food of all classes in the delta, but only the well-to-do people use it in other parts of the district. The total monthly expenditure of a prosperous shopkeeper's family, consisting of 5 persons, would be about Rs. 14 and that of an ordinary peasant about Rs. 8. The district contains numerous wells. The daily wages of coolies and agricultural labourers in 1850 were from Anna 1 to Annas 2; in 1876 from Annas 1-3 to Annas 4 and Annas 1-4 to Annas 3, respectively. Bricklayers and carpenters from Annas 4 to Annas 6 and Annas 5 to Annas 8 a day, respectively, while 16 years ago they earned Annas 2-6 to Annas 4 and Annas 2 to Annas 4, respectively. In 1883-84 skilled labourers—average, Annas 7, others, Annas 4.

Malabar.—The peasantry of Malabar are no exception to the general rule, dividing this class into those who borrow and into those who lend. The borrowers among the actual cultivators are much more numerous than the lenders, and borrowing, owing to certain characteristics in the prevailing tenure, is rapidly on the increase. The wages of artisans and labourers have been steadily increasing. Coolies, who in 1800 earned 1 anna and in 1850, 2 annas, earned in 1876-77, 5 annas a day, and skilled workmen, whose wages in 1850 varied from 5 to 6 annas earned in 1876-77 from 8 to 10 annas. Agricultural labourers are always paid in kind at the daily rate of 5 lb. of rice for a man and 4 lb. for a woman.

Tanjore.—Wages of agricultural labour are almost invariably paid in grain. The ordinary rates are three-fourths of a merkal or 3·87 lb. of paddy (giving about $2\frac{1}{2}$ lb. of clean rice) per diem for a trained labourer, male or female, and one-half merkal for inferior adult labourers; boys and girls receive half the rates. In towns, wages are paid in money, the ordinary daily rate for an adult male being Annas $4\text{-}4\frac{3}{16}$ in 1841-42 to Rs. 1-13-0 * in 1876-77, for children 1 anna each. Skilled labourers, such as bricklayers, stone-masons, carpenters and smiths are paid according to the nature of the work from 5 to 8 annas a day. The money

* Sic.

wages in all these cases are generally twice as high as it was twenty-five years ago and in some cases the increase is still greater. Prices of all articles of food have risen in about the same ratio. The village sales of paddy, the staple produce of the district, on which the original commutation rate for the assessment of irrigated land was calculated, show that the average price of the Tanjore kalam equal to 12 merkals or 62 lb. has varied from Annas 7 in 1850-51 to Rs. 1-7-0 in 1875-76. Landless labourers constitute about one-half the adult male population of the district and of these nearly two-thirds are engaged in agriculture. They are chiefly Pullers and Pariahs who are permanently attached to the farms. The remainder are low-caste Sudras, who have immigrated from time to time from the Marava country lying between the Cauvery delta and Cape Comorin.

Coimbatore.—Agricultural day-labourers or coolies earn 3 annas per diem, women 2 annas and children 1 anna. Blacksmiths, bricklayers, carpenters receive from Annas 6 to Annas 14 per diem. Since 1850 the rate of wages for skilled labour has risen from 25 to 80 per cent. and prices of food have doubled. Rice which in 1850 was selling at Rs. 1-8-0 per maund (80 lb.) now sells at Rs. 3; cholum formerly Annas 10-8 per maund now costs Rs. 1-6-0; wheat once Rs. 1-8-0 per maund now sells at Rs. 3-4-0; salt has risen from Rs. 2-1-8 per maund to Rs. 2-15-3; and country liquor (arrack) now sells from Rs. 3-4-0 to Rs. 4-4-0 per gallon.

Kurnool.—The ryots, as a rule, cultivate their own lands. Owners of very large holdings sublet some of their lands and employ labourers on others. The wages of day labourers and artisans are usually paid in kind. When paid in cash, coolies receive from Annas 2-6 to Annas 3 a day; blacksmiths, bricklayers, carpenters Annas 4 to Annas 12. The average price of best rice in 1883-84 was Rs. 3-3-8 and of cholum Rs. 1-4-1 per maund of 80 lb.

Nellore —The average prices of produce per maund (80 lb.) were rice Rs. 3, inferior food-grains Re. 1, indigo Rs. 149, cotton Rs. 15. The daily rates of wages are, skilled labour 12 annas at Ongole and Kanigiri, 6 annas in most places, and 4 annas in some; for unskilled, Annas 6 at Atmakúr, Annas 2-6 in most places and Annas 1-6 in some.

Salem.—On a holding of 2 acres *wet* and 3 acres of *dry* land the net profit would not probably exceed Rs. 60 per annum or Rs. 5 a month. The mass of the peasantry are in debt. The habit of indebtedness is so ingrained in their nature that if they all started fair tomorrow, 50 per cent. would be in debt again in a year. One man is held to be sufficient for the ordinary daily labour on a farm of 3 acres of wet or 6 acres of dry land, if assisted in the heavy work of planting, weeding, reaping and threshing. His wages would be 480 measures of grain per annum = Rs. 12-8-0 *plus* an annual money payment of Rs. 3, the wages in the northern being lower than in the southern taluks. Twenty-seven measures of seed are required for an acre of wet and 6 measures for an acre of dry land. The highest Government wet rate in the district is Rs. 14 per acre and the lowest is Rs. 11-9-0, exclusive of local cesses; the highest for *dry* lands being Rs. 5 and the lowest Annas 4. The customary rates of wages for unskilled labour are, for men Annas 2; for women Annas 1-6; for children, male or female, Pies 10. The Wodder or Navvy caste get twice as much, but they do generally task work, by which they gain more than by daily wages. The wages of a working goldsmith vary with the value of the materials, but may be taken on an average to be Annas 8 per diem. A blacksmith gets Annas 8; a carpenter from Annas 8 to Annas 10; bricklayers from Annas 6 to Annas 10. During the 10 years ending 1874, the prices at Salem town per garce or 9,360 lb. in February and March, when the ryots sell, averaged Rs. 103 for rice and Rs. 115 for cholum or great millet.

Tinnevelly.—In 1883-84 the average rates of wages were for unskilled labour in towns Annas 2-10 and in villages Annas 2-4 a day. The price of rice in the same year was Rs. 3-12-11 per maund (80 lb.) and of cumbu, the staple food of the district, Rs. 1-9-2.

Trichinopoly.—Agricultural labourers are generally paid in grain. From 1881-82 to 1883-84 their money wages averaged Rs. 5-5-0 a month. The wages of common masons, carpenters and smiths averaged Rs. 15-2-1 a month. The average price of second-sort rice during the 5 years ending 1883-84 was 15·23 imperial seers for 1 rupee; in 1879-80, 12·05; in 1880-81, 14·34; in 1881-82, 16·31; in 1882-83, 16·10; in 1883-84, 17·36 seers for 1 rupee. Similarly the price of cumbu (the staple food) in the 5 years ending 1873 varied from 15 to 43; in 1879 from 15 to 23; in 1880 from 23 to 30; in 1881 from 24 to 34; in 1882 from 28 to 39; in 1883 from 30 to 43 seers for 1 rupee. An imperial seer equals 2·2046 lb.

Vizagaptam.—Prices of grain have risen very considerably during the last few years. The rate of wages has also risen, but not in the same proportion.

(1)—*Opinions of certain gentlemen on the present economic condition of the people as compared with their past condition.*

(1) *Note by C. Nagojee Row, Esq., B. A., Inspector of Schools, Northern Circle.*

People who talk of the poverty of India do so in a very vague way. The country is poorer than it was 30 years ago; it is poorer than England, France or Germany; it is not so rich as it might be under more favorable conditions—these are three distinct propositions having no necessary connection with each other; but newspaper writers and others who write about the poverty of our country mean now one of these things and now another, and do not, I fear, carefully distinguish between the different propositions.

One may admit the two latter statements without admitting the first, but even with regard to the statement that India is poorer than most European countries, I wish to state that drawing inferences as regards the happiness of people from the production or value of production per head of population alone is not quite safe. The necessities of the people of different countries, the climatic conditions under which they live, the sort of house accommodation, and the kind and quantity of food, which they require for comfortable living, should also be taken into account along with production in judging of the relative well-being of different communities, and, if these things and the distribution of wealth among the various classes are considered, I doubt very much whether the bulk of the Indian population is so very badly off when compared with the bulk of the English people. Dr. Dhanakoti Raju, who has just returned from Europe, is of opinion that the condition of the lower classes in India is really much better than that of the corresponding classes in England.

I readily admit the proposition that India might be richer than it is. If the cost of administration were less, home manufactures encouraged, our interests not sacrificed, as they sometimes are, to English interests, and the people more energetic, more intelligent and more enterprising, the country would no doubt be very much wealthier than it is at present.

With reference to the opinion commonly expressed that this country has been growing poorer, I can only give my general impressions and what appear to me to be reasonable deductions from well-known facts. I shall at first refer to the condition of the land-owning classes. It is admitted that Government had formerly the greatest difficulty in collecting revenue and in inducing people to keep lands under cultivation. The reason was that prices were so low that the ryots found great difficulty in realizing, by the sale of the surplus produce of their lands, money sufficient to meet the Government or Zemindar's demand. The land had consequently little or no value. Now, no such difficulty is experienced; every inch of good land is under cultivation and the price of produce and land, I am informed, has quadrupled during the last 30 years. The opening out of the country by means of roads, railways and canals and the establishment of steamer communication have brought the markets of the world within the reach of the Indian ryot, and he has no difficulty in disposing of the produce of the land which remain over and above his requirements. Assuming that the ryots of the present day are not more extravagant than their fathers, and admitting that every year they grow more than they require for their consumption, it follows that they should be richer now than they were 40 years ago. Security of property is one of the inducements to lay by money. When an individual or a community gets richer, there is generally perceptible a rise in the standard of living, and this is noticeable everywhere among the agricultural classes, but notably so in the Godávari and Kistna districts, which are exceptionally favored. An intelligent friend, who remembers the state of things 40 years ago, states that, while ryots then lived in poor mud huts, had nothing better than earthen pots, no jewels and no furniture, they now live in tiled houses, wear better and more clothing, have a number of silver and gold ornaments, and even some furniture. This, he says, is a certain proof of some wealth. The staple food of the people is now rice, whereas it was formerly ragi or cholum. Another sign of prosperity is that the better class of ryots, instead of selling produce immediately after harvest to pay Government and other demands, generally store it up, and sell it when prices go up. They have credit, too, now and find no difficulty in raising loans when they wish to do so. With the landowners agricultural laborers have prospered. They get plenty of work in the cultivating season; and in the dry weather, repairs to, and clearance of, the numerous irrigation and navigation channels in these districts give them occupation. The prosperity of the agricultural community implies also the prosperity of the trading community.

Against the prosperity of the agricultural and trading classes, however, is to be set the pressure which the landless and old manufacturing classes are feeling. The condition of the weavers is everywhere lamentable. Their occupatiom is gone; and they have not had time enough to reconcile themselves to their new lot and to adapt themselves to changed circumstances. The extinction of native manufactures means, I suppose, the loss of so much wealth to the community and suffering to the manufacturing classes; but the net result of British administration up to now has been an increase, and not a decrease of national wealth. This is the impression of most people whom I have consulted. I have no figures at hand to establish this.

It is true the cost of administration has considerably increased of late, the public debt has swelled, and the fall in the value of the rupee is telling heavily on our finances; making allowances for these and the increase in taxation they imply, the country, owing to the security it enjoys and the facilities afforded for transport of produce and goods, is very much better off now than it was in 1850.

The increase in the area of land under tillage, the starting and successful working of spinning and weaving mills, and the discovery of coal in several parts of the country, are all factors in the question.

(2) *Note by S. Seshaiyar, Esq., B.A., Professor, Government College, Kumbakónam.*

I examined some bundles of old accounts in the possession of some of the merchants of this town. The information to be gathered from them is not as satisfactory as one could wish it were. Still there does not appear to be any doubt about certain broad facts.

1*st.*—Brass and copper vessels are much cheaper now than they were between 30 and 40 years ago. The average price of brass wrought into vessels, such as தாம்பாளம் and கங்காளம், &c., was 8 annas a seer, or, in other words, 7 seers for a pagoda, whereas now it is 11 or 12 seers, and, 4 years ago before the Paris Syndicate raised by compact the price of coppor, it sold at 14 seers the pagoda. Copper was likewise dearer in the same ratio. Roughly it may be said that the price of brass and copper vessels has cheapened by between 30 and 40 per cent. This is due, of course, to the enormous importation of metallic sheets from Europe. Formerly they had to make brass here. It is a mixture of copper and tin. And there is the notion that brass pots and other vessels of those days were purer in quality and more durable. Everywhere, even in villages, and among the lower classes of the population, the journeymen laborers included, brass pots, plates and bronze cups have taken and are taking the place of the earthen vessels. Even for cooking purposes they use the metallic vessels.

2*nd.*—As regards clothing, there is no doubt that Manchester goods are steadily driving out of the market the home-woven cloths, and this is because of the great cheapness of the former. It is difficult to compare the prices of these days with those that obtained thirty years ago. Still, roughly, it may be estimated that cloths of nearly the same quality are cheaper by 40 per cent. Then a ten, six, as it is called a தோவத்தி and அங்கவஸ்திரம், of *rough kind* could not be had for less than Rs. 1-12-0; 8 yards of jaconet will now do for it, and you can get it at annas 2 and pies 3 a yard, *i.e.*, Rs. 1-2-0 the whole. Country-spun cloths are dearer than Manchester manufactures or those of Bombay mills; but even for them the yarn is all English. In towns, at all events, 80 per cent. of the male population buy Manchester cloths. The higher classes of females in this part of the country wear country manufactures of the silk and colored kind. Comparison of prices here seems almost hopeless; fashion has changed so enormously during these 30 or 40 years. Looking into a large bundle of sales of cloths, I find that female cloths, 99 per cent. of them, varied in price between Rs. 3 and 7. These cloths have been substituted by others whose average price may be put down at least at Rs. 10. These, of course, are much prettier in appearance, and contain far more of silk. I am not prepared to say that cloths of the same quality would be cheaper now than in those days. What of cheapness in the material used may be made up by the increased rates of wages, but one thing is certain that the better classes wear clothing now nearly three times as costly as those worn by their grandmothers. This fact may in itself be worth noting. The lower classes, including the working classes—by *lower* I don't mean lower by caste, but chiefly by wealth—are much more decently clothed than they ever were. For Rs. 1-12-0 or Rs. 2 they get a female cloth, of cotton entirely—the work of Bombay mills or English; they get a cloth of the same pattern as the கொரநாடு cloth. Within my own knowledge in this town, *i.e.*, during the last 20 years, the dress of the lower classes has vastly improved; and this improvement is more than half of it due to cheapness of clothing.

And just a few words on the economic question you are busy with. I have no idea of the results you have arrived at, or even of the exact lines on which you have been working. Still I shall venture to say a few words, although I know that the question has to be looked at from various points of view.

I have a pretty vivid recollection of how things were in South Arcot and in this district 35 years ago when a boy. I had opportunities of travelling through South Arcot and Tanjore. I have travelled, too, over the same parts of the country recently. In the villages, substantial brick-built houses have now taken the place of thatched houses of old; brass and copper vessels, as also of bronze and tin, are used where earthen and wooden vessels were used; clothing is decidedly better, far more elegant and costly; and five times at least more of gold and silver jewellery than in former days. I am not prepared to say that everywhere in the country it is so. But it is so in most places I have visited. Whether people are more wealthy or not, there is far more display of wealth now than there was in days when I was a boy of ten. And almost every intelligent elderly man I have conversed with has told me the same as his observation. Another significant fact is the rise in the price of land in this district as elsewhere. Forty years ago a relation of mine who owned lands near Karikal, sold 15 velies or 100 acres of land for Rs. 2,000, and the same would sell now at Rs. 20,000, *i.e.*, ten-fold. Confining ourselves to the last 50 years only, I am not inclined to believe in the cry of increasing poverty of the country. Beyond a shadow of doubt, people are now better fed, better clothed and better housed. Whether the country might not be far richer, were it not for this or that, is another question which it is needless to enter into. But at the same time I may mention there are certain vices which are rapidly developing and which need arresting—1st, falsehood, 2nd drunkenness, 3rd, want of thrift. These vices are not confined to towns, but are on the increase in villages also. On the bearing of these on the future economy of the country it is useless for me to dwell.

(3) *Changes in Godávari District since the construction of Anicut.—Noted by S. Nathamunni Mudaliar, Esq., Pensioned Tahsildar, Godávari District.*

The construction of the anicut across the Godávari is a great boon to this part of the country. This mighty work was commenced in 1846 and completed in about 1850. Previous to its construction, the district depended on rain and rain-fed tanks and the fitful supply of water from the river. Paddy was not so plentiful as now. The cultivation of paddy varied with the diversity of the seasons. In years of drought, famine was the inevitable lot of the people and both men and cattle suffered. Since its construction, the district is intersected with canals, useful not only for purposes of agriculture, but also for navigation. There are two main canals in the Western delta—the Ellore and Narsápur canals. In the Central delta, there is one—the Amalapore canal. In the Eastern, there are five—the Samalcottah, Cocanada, Coringa, Mandapeta and Bank canals. There is also a Bank canal in each of the other deltas. All these are navigable, and from these proceed a number of irrigation channels and paddy transplantation has immensely increased. Sugar plantation, which was rare in this district, is now to be seen almost everywhere. The extent of cultivation is acres 794,829 as given in the jamabandi report for fasli 1297 (1887-88).

2. For the transport of produce thus plentifully raised, there is considerable facility afforded by the introduction of canals, and this has resulted in the increase of price of every article. In 1854, when the Western canals were only in progress, and I first went to Narsápur, the price of paddy on that side was only Rs. 6 or 8 for a putty of 200 kunchams (533 Madras measures or 66 merkals). Now it is Rs. 20 and it sometimes rises to Rs. 24. In the famine of 1876 and 1877, the price rose to Rs. 50, there having arisen a great demand for it from different parts of the country. The introduction of coasting steamers in addition to navigable canals afforded easy passage for transhipment of goods. The wealthier classes were much benefited and the condition of ryots was so much improved by the general high prices that instead of being in the hands of sowcars, they were sowcars themselves. Even now, the majority of them are not in their hands. They have enough to pay for Government dues. The rich ryots lend money largely on inam lands, taking them on long leases. The inamdars in general, being poor Brahmins, are not capable of cultivating the lands themselves, while the ryots have means enough for carrying on extensive cultivation. They have enough of cattle, ploughs and laborers. The famine of 1876 and 1877 brought in a considerable number of poor people from the neighbouring districts of Vizagapatam and Ganjam, who found employment here in various ways.

They engaged themselves as field laborers, coolies, palanquin bearers and domestic servants. This rendered labor cheap. Most of them have remained here permanently, and some are so far improved in their condition as to become farmers themselves.

3. Besides the staple article of paddy, there are other crops, such as gingelly and ragi, which take canal water when timely rains fail. Chillies, turmeric, onions and garlic also take canal water and are charged as wet crop. Tobacco is another article which is largely raised in these parts. The finest tobacco is from the Lankas (islands) in the river. This is exported to Moulmein and other places. The Lankas are sold by auction for 3 or 5 years for considerable sums. They are so sold periodically because of the baneful or beneficial effects of inundation almost every year. Some are swept away, while others are enlarged and enriched by accretions and rich deposit of alluvial soil.

4. The vast increase in agriculture by irrigation has very materially improved the condition of ryots. They have learnt to build substantial and fashionable houses and upstair buildings unlike their former thatched and slovenly ones. There has been considerable improvement in the manufacture of jaggery. Iron mills for extracting juice from sugar-cane are in general use now in the place of wooden ones, which are not so effective in getting out all the juice. There has not been any improvement in the implements of tilling. The ploughs of old are still in use, which do not furrow the land deep. Some years back, the Swedish plough was brought into this district and several experiments were made, but this was found too heavy for the ordinary bullocks here and the attempt to introduce it failed. Even the richer ryots found no use with it, for the land here requires no great tilling; it is flooded with canal water for some time before tilling and the land easily turned up and transplanted. A second crop is also raised, but it is of inferior quality. It is only of 3 months' growth from February to April and is chiefly used by the laboring classes. The land has become very valuable. An acre of land sells from Rs. 100 to Rs. 300, and the inams from Rs. 200 to Rs. 500.

5. Prior to anicut, the joint-rent system was in use. Each village was rented out jointly to the ryots of the village, and the leading men and men of substance were held responsible for the payment of Government dues. On account of paucity of produce owing to failure of rain, the Amarakam, as the leasing out was called, was a matter of very great difficulty. Nobody used to come forward to take up the village or a portion of it, and the Tahsildars used to force it on some men of substance. It was really a painful sight. Now, the land has acquired so much value by irrigation that almost every inch of land is taken up and the Government dues easily paid. There is great competition among ryots to secure a right to the land. They come forward with darkhasts even at the end of the fasli, offering to pay the assessment for the whole year, though they could derive no benefit in that year. The renting system has entirely disappeared except in the hill tracts, and the ryotwari has taken its place. By this system, each ryot deals directly with the Government and reaps all the benefit of his labor. He commands more respect now, enjoys more comforts, wears better clothes and lives in a more comfortable way.

6. In the hill tracts, the joint-rent system is in use, but the villages are given away for a fixed sum and not rented out for a term of years as was the case before the disturbance of 1879. The condition of the people in these parts is also much improved. The rioting of 1879 compelled the Government to clear the jungles and lay roads. The communication to the hill tracts being more easy now, the hillmen have come more in contact with the people in the plains and learnt the real value of things which they used to dispose of at a very cheap rate in their own places or in the periodical markets on the outskirts near the plains. Tamarind, myrobolams, soapnuts, hill-oranges, timber, honey and wax are the chief products of those parts. The price of these articles has risen considerably, and the hillmen are in a much better condition than before. Paddy is also in use in these parts, the clearance of jungles and communication by roads having rendered cart traffic easy. The food in general use here is chiefly paste from tamarind seeds, mango seeds and toddy from jiluga trees, which yield toddy abundantly. Jonna is also in use in some parts. Transplantation of paddy is carried on under tanks in some places, the people having learnt it from those in the plains. Survey and settlement are also begun to be made. This will gradually find its way into the more interior and the people will become more settled. Their education is also attended to now. Local Fund schools are established in certain localities and there is also a Superintendent of Hill schools.

7. The Local Fund Act has greatly added to the convenience of the people everywhere. Roads have multiplied; the indigenous schools considerably improved and their number increased; sanitation attended to; tanks and wells dug even in remote places. The number of village schools has so considerably increased that there are now four Deputy Inspectors (Sub-Assistants) and one Assistant Inspector for the whole district in the place of one Deputy Inspector some 7 or 8 years ago. There is besides an Inspecting Schoolmaster for each taluk. The Sub-Assistant Inspectors are stationed, one at Narsápur, another at Ellore, a third at Rajahmundry and a fourth at Cocanada. The district is considerably in advance in this respect also.

8. The improvement in all directions which has been the source of happiness to the people has also been the source of great litigation. Much of people's money goes to swell the revenue of civil courts and to fill the pleaders' purse. People are more reckless in their proceedings and squander away their money, caring only to win their cause, good or bad. The country is in every way in a prosperous condition and it is quite unlike what it was prior to the construction of the anicut. Sir Arthur Cotton, to whose genius this gigantic work owes its existence, seems to have estimated the land revenue of the district at 22 lakhs and expected to realize 50 or 60 lakhs when the whole project was complete, as will be seen from the Manual of the district. Now, from the jamabandi report for fasli 1297, the land revenue appears to be 38 lakhs and odd. Other cesses, peishcush from zemindari estates, quit-rent on inam and inam villages, come up to 14 lakhs and odd. Salt, abkári, opium, ferry fund and income-tax amount to upwards of 6 lakhs. The grand total of the revenue of the district from all sources reaches nearly that amount which the great benefactor, Sir Arthur Cotton, roughly estimated some 40 years ago. The present

project of Lord Connemara of connecting this part of the country with Madras by means of railroads will still more develope the resources of the country and secure that felicity to the ill-favored aborigines of Ganjam and Vizagapatam districts which their southern fellow-beings invariably enjoy.

9. The only class that seems to have suffered is the weaver class. Cloths of different descriptions are being imported from foreign countries, and as they are cheaper being machine made, the demand for country cloths is much lessened. Only coarser cloths are now woven here. The finer sorts of Uppada are also not in so much use. Calcutta cloths find a more ready sale.

(4) *Note by K. Subbarayudu, Esq., Deputy Collector, Bellary District.*

I have finished the jamabandi of the division by the end of June last and my examination of section I of the famine analysis village registers has also been nearly completed. The result of the enquiries made by me is that, as compared with their state 30 or 40 years back, both the agricultural and trading classes seem to have made an advance, and not retrogression, on the whole. Many an old ryot has informed me that 40 or 50 years back there was much more jungle and waste about this part of the country than is the case now, and they attribute the gradual spread of cultivation to gradual increase in population. Of course, this part of the country cannot be said to be a densely-populated one even now, but there seems no doubt whatever that the population has been steadily increasing year after year; and but for the sudden and terrible check it received during the famine of 1876—78, when a good proportion of the then existing population died, there is no doubt that the present population of this part of the country would have been much more than what it now is.

Many of the old people I have talked to on the subject have expressed an opinion that, although the extent under occupation is growing with the population, the lands have not been yielding as much now as they used to do some 40 or 50 years back; and, when questioned as to what could be the reason for the reduction in the yielding power of land, they explain that when they were young they observed that the agricultural classes were constantly changing their holdings at intervals of 2 or 3 years, giving up old lands and taking up new ones, as there were then immense extents of jungle and waste available all round, whereas they cannot and would not do it now; so that there is more permanency about holdings now than 40 or 50 years ago. The above explanation given by the ryots for reduction in the yielding power of land seems quite reasonable, as the same piece of land if cultivated year after year without intermission cannot naturally be expected to yield as much as if left waste for an interval or as a piece of virgin soil.

People say that another main feature of change now apparent is that, whereas about 40 or 50 years ago there used to be only a few important ryots and sowcars scattered here and there in villages and taluks, each having at times a number of families depending upon him as so many parasites, the present aspect is that wealth and importance are more generally distributed over the part of the country, thus showing that all classes are now enjoying more independence than before, and that the sweets of liberty have been tasted even by the lowest orders. Even in other respects, the people on the whole seem to be enjoying more material comforts than in days past. The introduction of the machine-made goods into the market, although it has more or less interfered with some of the native industries such as weaving, &c., has no doubt done the masses and the public at large a world of good by placing cheap and ready-made goods almost at their doors. The fact, moreover, that, unlike in former days, people now dare to enjoy any wealth they possess more freely and openly, also bears testimony to the fact that there is now more peace prevailing about the country than in the old days when, some people say, people would not dare to wear even the jewels they possessed or build big and comfortable houses to live in, for fear of robbers and dacoits. It seems also quite a fact that the bulk of the peoples' wealth—both cash and jewels—used to be under ground in former days and not in current use as now, and the fact that we are still coming across instances of hidden treasure and valuables here and there all over the province goes to show that in times past people thought their safes could only be under ground and never above it.

The opening of the railways and telegraph lines and postal communications have also been a source of great relief and alleviation to the people in several ways.

As regards the condition of an *average* ryot in this part of the country, my own experience and impression is that, provided the country is not visited with anything like a severe drought or famine necessitating the grant of dry remissions, he gets on tolerably well without any kind of distress, living easily from hand to mouth. And had it not been for the heavy expenses they have to incur now and then in connection with marriage ceremonies occurring in their families, there is no doubt the condition of the average ryots in this part of the country would have been much better. Many an old ryot has told me that occasional marriages occurring in a ryot's family from time to time have been draining away from his pocket more than anything else, and that, however miserly and economical an average ryot may be at other times, he will be obliged to spend some hundreds of rupees, never less than two, as I am given to understand, for a daughter's or a son's marriage. They say the figure generally ranges from Rs. 200 to Rs. 500 in the case of an ordinary ryot. It appears that these costly marriages generally necessitate borrowing, and the ryot, though with much reluctance, is obliged to go and open an account with the ever-safe sowcar on account of these marriages. Debts incurred by ryots from sowcars are oftener conditioned to be liquidated *in kind* by annual instalments, and the rates of prices fixed on the produce supplied by him being at times even lower and cheaper than what are colloquially termed కాపుధరలు or the harvest season rates, the ryot necessarily loses a good deal in this direction also in the long run. As he is dunned by the sowcar for the payment of the instalment due at the harvest season, the ryot cannot think of laying by any excess quantities of grain, &c., produced on his lands until he finds high prices ruling in the market, so that the fruit of the ryot's labor is in several instances really enjoyed more by the sitting sowcar than by the plodding ryot. It is thus that ryots generally find themselves entangled in the sowcar's hands; and once a ryot is so entangled, it seems really a very difficult matter for him to get out again. The account once opened generally continues to run on, and occasional unfavorable seasons and slight droughts, which seem to be more common in the Ceded Districts than elsewhere, tend to contribute to the permanency of the connection formed by the ryot with the sowcar so that the sowcar seems to have become a necessary evil with the average ryot.

As I have already stated before, the ryot class people have no doubt made an advance on the whole and not retrogression, and enjoy more material comforts now than before, but there seems to be a change in only one point which they do not seem to relish at all. I mean the severity of the forest law, which they seem to complain has curtailed many a concession they were enjoying before in that direction. In fact, they had no restraint whatever in that direction in times past either under grazing or under fuel or timber. The ryot class people, however, do not seem to understand the ultimate good that the forest law is intended or expected to do to the country.

Now, as regards the trading classes, there does not, to my mind, seem the least doubt that, as compared with times past, they have grown both in quantity and quality. The method of business that a sowcar or merchant adopts in these rural parts seems to me to be such that, once starting in business, he hardly experiences a failure. They generally undertake to deal in different things, and what little they rarely lose in one is generally more than counterbalanced by their gain in others. They are, moreover, a proverbially economical and simple class of people in these parts, and are generally unknown to luxuries of any kind. Traders, unlike the agricultural classes, are, furthermore, people who gain throughout all seasons. They have not that distinction between a good and a bad season which a ryot has, and, in fact, a bad season or a regular famine does a trader more good than a favorable one. The enclosed memorandum, containing statistics as far as available, as regards income to the Adóni Municipality from professional tax and tolls as also the number of cotton bales pressed in the three cotton presses here, would also show that, excepting bad seasons, trade here has been on the increase on the whole.

As regards recovery of this part of the country from the effects of the famine of 1876—78, my humble opinion is that it has very nearly recovered. Compared with the extent of Government assessed land under occupation before the last famine of 1876–78, similar extent now under occupation in this division consisting of the Adóni and Alúr taluks is about 28,500 acres less. But of this difference as much as nearly 19,000 acres is already under "Sivaijama" or unauthorized cultivation, and there seems no doubt whatever that that, as well as even the still outstanding difference, will come under *permanent* holding before long. In this connection it is also to be remembered that some extents of assessed land under occupation previous to the famine of 1876—78 have since been included in the forest reserves formed, and that some of the lands so included are such as would have already been under occupation had they not been so included in reserves.

Statement showing income to the Ádóni Municipality from professional tax and tolls.

Years.	Income from tax on arts.	Income from tolls.
	RS.	RS.
1880-81	2,861	3,112
1881-82	3,146	2,650
1882-83	3,354	3,991
1883-84	3,872	3,700
1884-85	3,577	4,350
1885-86	3,710	3,200
1886-87	4,729	3,950
1887-88	4,200	4,249
1888-89	* 3,748	5,870
1889-90	4,856	5,615

Statement showing number of bales pressed at the Cotton Presses in Ádóni.

Year.	Number pressed at the two presses of Messrs. Dymes and Co. and Sabapathy Mudaliar and Co.	Number pressed at all the three presses including the press of Messrs. Framjee and Co.	Remarks.
1881	10,263	3rd Company's not available.	
1882	17,506	Do.	
1883	15,838	Do.	
1884	14,663	20,964	
1885	4,268	5,946	Particularly bad season.
1886	17,202	20,667	
1887	18,982	22,090	
1888	15,485	18,899	
1889	26,832	38,095	
1890	13,309	17,735	Up to 30th July 1890.

N.B.—The price of a pressed bale of cotton ranges between Rs. 80 and Rs. 90.

(5) *Note by A. Sabapathy Mudaliar, Esq., Bellary.*

The condition of the agricultural population two or three years before the famine was the best that was ever known owing to the high prices of cotton which ruled during the American war. But after the famine, with a few exceptions, they (people) were reduced almost to

* Reduction due to some amount having been left uncollected at the close of the year which, however, is included in the figure for 1889-90.

beggary. During the past 4 or 5 years they have been gradually recovering their lost position.

Dry land was then sold at Rs. 50 to 100 per acre; now the price of wet land is Rs. 30 to 40 for lands irrigated by the Hagari, and Rs 100 to 150 for lands irrigated by the Tungabhadra.

This year (1890) the cotton and cholum crops having been exceptionally favorable and the cotton crops having ripened simultaneously in almost every place, the laboring classes have benefited thereby to an enormous extent. The wages which were paid were three times as high as those ordinarily paid. This was the only year in which it was known that the laborers were not found to be enough in number to cope with the work. The extension of cultivation and the railways running through the district have enhanced wages cent. per cent. as compared with ordinary times before the current year. Wages are low as compared with what they were before the *famine.*

The condition of the agricultural classes as a whole has not generally improved in the same way as that of laboring classes owing to deficient rainfall in the Bellary district, which is due to the denudation of forests; with the exception of the agricultural classes, the commercial and artisan classes are better off than they were before. The agricultural classes have to pay higher wages to coolies.

The increase in the number of cotton presses and mills in the surrounding districts has been the cause of giving technical knowledge to lots of males and females, who are able to earn exceptionally high wages, *i.e.*, 10 to 15 rupees per man per month and 6 to 10 rupees per woman, who do work on the piece-work system. The position of the artisan class is also very much improved, such as masons, stone-dressers, carpenters and blacksmiths, who are required in large numbers to meet the demand from the factories and the railways. In their case also the wages have gone up quite 50 per cent., if not more. The ordinary wages for masons, carpenters and blacksmiths used to be 8 annas, but it is now over 12 annas according to capacity and qualifications.

The prosperity of the people in general is shown by the large demand there is for both imported and locally-manufactured goods. The starting of the mills in India has been the cause of cheapening the prices of piece-goods and yarn by at least 30 per cent. as compared with what it was about 10 years ago.

Imported cloth goods now chiefly consist of the finer varieties, not the coarser kind generally used by the people.

The weaving industry is going down. -The higher classes use the finer varieties of imported cloth, and the lower classes prefer locally-manufactured mill cloth.

In the Bellary Spinning and Weaving Mill, there are 100 looms, but only 50 are being now worked. In course of time the whole number will be utilized. The whole number will produce on an average 1,000 lb. of manufactured cloth every day. The production of yarn will be about 4,000 lb. daily, of which 1,000 lb. will be made into cloth if all the looms are worked.

Prices.

—	Before the recent rise in exchange.	Ten years ago.	Twenty years ago.
	RS. A. P.	RS. A. P.	RS. A. P.
Cloth for males, better sorts ..	4 1 0	3 12 0	3 8 0
Cloth for males, coarse	0 9 0	0 7 0	0 6 0
Dungary cloth	1 13 0	1 4 0	1 2 0
Cloth for females, coarse, colored.	2 2 0	1 12 0	1 10 0
Brass and copper vessels per seer of 21 tolas.	4 to $4\frac{1}{4}$ annas.	$5\frac{1}{2}$ annas.	7 annas.
Iron, per 20 maunds or 500 lb.	17 to $17\frac{1}{2}$ rupees up to the year before last. For 11 months last year, 23 to 30 rupees.	..	About 20 years ago, 35 rupees.
Glassware	From $\frac{1}{2}$ to $\frac{1}{3}$ of what it was before.	..	..

(6) *Note by R. Subbramania Aiyar, Esq., B.A., District Registrar, Tinnevelly.*

Changes in the value of land.—There is no ready and easy means of tracing out the various sales to which particular lands have been subjected in the course of the past 25 years. The only course open was to see by going through a good number of instruments of sale in the registers whether they contained any references to previous sales affecting the same properties Even this was not attended with complete success. The lands mentioned in the previous and subsequent sales are not wholly identical. Prior to 1874, the lands were not described by their Survey numbers, and there is no means of knowing as to what Adangal numbers correspond to the present Survey numbers. Besides, the price of the same land is not distinctly ascertainable in all the years, as such lands are found intermingled with others in subsequent transactions, or only a portion detached and alienated. In ascertaining the price of one acre of average nunjah and punjah, recourse was had to the method of ascertaining the price of any piece of land in one year, and finding out the value of the same land in subsequent years, or of lands in proximity to it, bearing the next previous or succeeding number. The fluctuation in prices is noticed to be not based on any principle, and the only explanation which can be rendered for this is that the price varies according to the grain produced by it, *i.e.*, in famine years and those of ordinary scarcity the value of grain being rather high, the productive lands go for a very high price, and others fetch only an inconsiderable amount. Further, it appears that there is a general tendency for the increase in the number of landholders, which means diminution in the extent held by individuals, and consequently each man is able to devote better attention to lands under his care, which, therefore, in their improved condition, rise in value. As civilization advances, the artisans, such as carpenters, bricklayers, smiths, &c., find enough of work for them, and an increasing demand for them has tended to increase the rate of their wages nearly three-fold during the last 25 years. Persons who were allowed 3 annas a day before now earn 8 to 10 annas. Most of these people who can earn money by hard labor are in a position to save enough to purchase lands and live comfortably.

On account of increase in population, there is undoubtedly an increase both in the number of agriculturists and in the extent of land cultivated, as most of the waste lands are now rendered cultivable for ordinary nunjah crops. And the bigger vakils and other well-to-do people, instead of hoarding up their money or lending it out on interest, prefer investing it in lands which they consider safe. Moreover, the chief agricultural classes of Southern India have been impoverished by their constantly running into debts on account of their lavish expenditure on the occasions of marriages and deaths, when their agricultural resources are stinted, and when they are too lazy or too uncondescending to take to other industrial professions. The result is the higher classes, who were sole landholders before, have now to give up their land little by little, whereas the poor laboring classes have acquired land by dint of their economical savings. As agricultural profession is found to be more safe and secure by the lower classes, they lay out their earnings on landed property. It is this tendency that partly causes the rise in the value of land in spite of deficiency of its yield.

The gradual increase in population, a population depending entirely upon agriculture for their livelihood, contributes as much to this rapid increase in the value of lands as the artificial improvements brought to bear from time to time upon the productiveness of the lands themselves. More than 30 years ago changes in the ownership of holdings will compare by an extreme minimum if viewed in connection with the rapidly-increasing divisions of property at the present day, and the nature of the tenures under which they are held. The causes seem to be more or less due to the increased resources of the country, to the enterprise of the enlightened section of the community, and to the hard competition of the times. There has been more accumulation of capital, and more of the nature of sinking funds than what the history of a past age will teach us. In certain directions, the increased value of land is due to the improved productive nature of the soil, and to the facilities afforded by irrigational works. The idea of acquisition helps the idea for permanent property, and owing to competition in the same market, the values are generally very high. The value of the land in general has thus increased, and the increase is due to the desire for permanent property in some shape at any cost. In short, accumulation of wealth, increased investment, competition, and over-population contribute to the rise in the value of land.

In what directions the agricultural class has progressed.—The agricultural class embraces three sets of people—

(1) Landholders who do nothing more than let their lands and collect the rents.

(2) Those who have some lands of their own which they cultivate themselves, and who also take up lands from others on lease, if circumstances would permit it.

(3) Those who have no lands of their own, but only cultivate the lands of others on different terms of leases.

Those coming under the second and third class have improved their status by yearly fresh acquisition of land, and by converting waste lands into cultivable ones. With the exception of a small percentage who are engaged in trade, the major portion of those falling under the first class are by degrees growing poorer and poorer by selling or mortgaging their property. And it is the cry of this section of the population that is likely to be the cause of the general impression that the condition of the agricultural classes is going down.

The general feeling of the agricultural classes is one of satisfaction with their lot ; this satisfaction can be said to be unalloyed if the rigour of the forest laws were mitigated, and nature were less fickle in the matter of water-supply—rain. The general want of rain in season has driven these classes to the necessity of sinking wells. Lands that were 30 years ago wastes overgrown with shrubs, &c., are now under cultivation. The extension of railway and other communications has not failed to bring in their train to the cultivator advantages which were wanting 30 years ago. He now carries the products to the market, where he secures the highest price possible. He is no more under the painful necessity of parting with the fruits of his labor for a nominal price. The mode of cultivation, the mechanism employed in the act of raising water and of turning up the soil, &c., have, however, remained practically the same as they were 30 years ago. The conservative instinct of the Indian cultivator abhors all innovation in these directions, and he rightly or wrongly prefers *his* mode and mechanism to all others.

The people are happy in the safety they enjoy under the good Government of the country. A good Government has brought safety along with it, and hence property has been rendered more secure, and there is nothing of that dread of life or of the prospect of losing property, which places the ryot in eternal anxiety, in the absence of an organized form of Government.

In what directions the agricultural class has deteriorated.—The causes of deterioration are—

(1) Heavy marriage expenses.

(2) Factious spirit and consequent expensive litigation.

(3) The neglect of the ryots to give any sort of rest to the cultivable lands.

(4) The lands are not as of old well manured, the consequence being a low yield with increased population.

Notwithstanding the safe and peaceful situation of the country, there has been some diminution among the agricultural classes. To be a ryot is considered among the so-called enlightened section something akin to being a serf in an enslaved country. Various other professions have been called in aid, and agriculture has been partially abandoned among the gentry who have taken to the renting system. Many of the population have gone to other places in pursuit of varieties of trade or professions. Reservation of callings to one particular set is gradually dying out. And with the spread of education, less regard is paid to aristocratical authority, and the village panchayat system has almost ceased to be an institution of the country.

Given the same laws, the same situation, and the same form of Government as that of a highly advanced country, what will be the situation of the ryot now if he does not go in for the foreign importations of the market for the desire of keeping up appearances, for the interchange of callings, or for the affectation of the many foibles which now attend on him ? One other great feature which adds to his misery is the laxity of the abkári rules, the spread of stills and shops, and the encouragement given to wholesale and retail systems, which place the juice at the door of the ryot at cheap rates. Again there are the forest and salt laws, the one depriving him of the use of the forest, and the other stinting the supply of the necessary of life to himself and to his cattle. In this aspect of the question, the condition of the ryot may fairly be said to have deteriorated.

Other industries.—As regards other industries, some show improvement, some are stationary, and others show decline. The mason, the carpenter, the blacksmith, and the brass-smith are now prosperous more than before. The potter has remained in the same position as 30 or 25 years ago. It is in the case of the weaver that one finds almost complete collapse. The weaver stands helpless before the gigantic array of machines and machine-made cloths of the mighty Manchester, and realizes in the application to India of the principles of free-trade the plain fact that his ruin is not far off, and cries for protection.

Native industrial arts have generally declined. They were in times gone by held in deservedly high esteem and every encouragement was given to the proprietors by the former rulers of the country. With the beginning of English rule, and the importation of machinery, from the cooking stove to the locomotive engine, native industrial arts received a death-blow, and there are now glasses for lotas, and the shining chintz for the thick elegant cotton fabric of the native dealer. Government seems to have felt the necessity of reviving them wherever possible. In this district, trade in senna leaves, jaggery, and cotton seems to be the most flourishing at present, as the labor bestowed on them is attended with more profit.

General Remarks.—That the agricultural classes are on the whole improving there is no doubt. There are larger areas now under cultivation. Greater number of people find a living in agriculture. Larger varieties of things are grown. Large landed properties found accumulated in a few hands are now split up and spread over a larger number of hands. The condition of the actual cultivators is much better than what it was some twenty years ago; some big mirasidars may perhaps be seen ruined here and there; but it is no proof of the agricultural classes as a whole going down.

Before the beginning of the present generation, the agricultural population of the country was divisible into only two sections—the landlords and the tillers of the soil. The relation between these two classes was anything but satisfactory. The landlord had the "lion's share" of the produce of the soil; and he allowed only a pittance just to keep the body and the soul together of the toiling cultivator. The landlord maintained the cattle, supplied the expenses of cultivation, seed, manure, &c., while all the manual labor was done by the cultivator, and he was paid at the harvest season about a twelfth of the produce (குறுணி ஆறுபடி for a kottah), as it is called in this portion of the country. This, together with a pittance of other சுவதந்திரம், would not give a family of three or four souls more than 8 kottahs a year of paddy at the highest, which quantity is barely sufficient to maintain the family. For this payment, the landlord exacted other work too from him. He must do all the menial services for the landlord's well-being utterly unconnected with cultivation. The landlord would usurp anything found with his tenant which would be of any use to him. In fact, the landlord would get everything for his living without paying anything for the same—labor and materials for his well-being.

Thus the condition of the cultivator was far worse than what it is at present, while that of the landlord was undoubtedly far better. In addition to this comparatively larger share in the income, the landlord's domestic economy was much greater. Luxuries were unknown. Expenses of litigation far less. Differences of civil rights settled in the village panchayat without much cost. The less complicated laws of the Revenue Department placed redress at a much less cost to the landlord. Thus the landlord was a great saving party, while the cultivator was only a toiling machine, without any saving of his own.

The work of the present generation is the complete change of this state of the relation between the landlord and the cultivator, and the creation, or more appropriately the increase and strengthening, of a middle class of people who are landlords and cultivators in one. The original landlord has grown now lazier by his frequent visits to towns and the importations to his very door of the luxuries of the town, &c.; his life has become more expensive. His uncalled for luxuries, unnecessary litigation, the complicated and expensive laws, all these expenses combined with the reduced income noted below have brought down the condition of the landlord on the one hand, and on the other hand, the daily increasing independence of the cultivator, his boldness to refuse to give the landlord anything more than his actual due, using his time and labor to more profitable things, his savings, &c., have enabled him to buy cattle of his own to meet the expenses of cultivation from his own pocket without depending on the mercy of his usurious landlord, who, saved of these services, is paid a much less share of the produce.

The said cultivators have gone on further. They began to advance sundry sums to their landlords, and have bought, in most cases, small bits of land of their own, which they cultivate themselves, and obtain all the produce without a sharer. Many working people of other professions and castes have invested their savings in purchasing lands, and they have taken to cultivation in addition to their original profession.

The second class of people, besides cultivating their own lands, take a lease of the lands of the first class of ryots, and cultivate them and obtain a share of the cattle they maintain, and of the cultivator if they can. In many cases, these men sub-rent such lands to the third class of people, and obtain a profit on both sides by this bargain. The second class of people, being men of some substance, have greater credit with the first class of people on the one hand, and being fellow workers on the field, are found to be less oppressive and more convenient for the third class to deal with; and hence they are used as middlemen by the first and the third classes. It is this second and third classes of people that reap the full benefits of the advantages of the British rule, and it is those falling under the first class, if they do not pursue other ways of getting money, and if they waste their time, energy and money in useless luxury, &c., that are going down.

All the advance made during this generation is in no way proportionate to the intentions of the Government and their trouble and expenses in establishing colleges and training institutions at the Presidency towns to introduce into the country the scientific modes of cultivation of the Western nations. The country has adopted only such portions of the advantages which the force of the surrounding circumstances in their natural course have driven the people to adopt, and nothing more. It is still left to the future politico-economic statesmen to find suitable ways to introduce into the country the more profitable modes of scientific cultivation, and to the sympathising scientist to devise means suitable to the low state of the poor country to induce and lead its children step by step to reap the advantages of a scientific agriculture.

That trade, manufacture, and handicrafts have increased a great deal during the present generation no one would dare to oppose. The introduction of the railways, the improved roads, and easy communications, the establishment of the village post offices, the increased demand and supply, have tended to increase every class of trade from the petty retail sales in the streets and villages to wholesale commerce. The variety of things bought and sold in these days, and their quality, and quantity compared with those found in the markets some twenty years ago, show a great deal of advance. A larger number of people are employed now in these trades. Persons of every caste take up the trades suitable to their means and ability. The first class of agricultural population noted above are seen here and there using their time and money to their advantage in trading. Those of the second and third classes, too, carry on petty inland trades during the time they are free from their work on their lands. Persons of other ancestral professions have cast off their prejudices, and freely take up trading if they find it more convenient and paying than those of their forefathers.

Manufacture and handicraft.—Here again the quality and the quantity of the work turned out, and the variety of such work done in these days, are far higher than what they were during the last generation. The caste which, in the majority of cases among the natives, distinguishes the professions is now fast fading away. It is needless here to enumerate the several branches of industry that are improved, and that are newly started and starting up. Suffice it to say that our artisans and manufacturers successfully imitate the works of the western nations, and produce the necessary articles nearly equal in quality and durability to those of their teachers and sell them much cheaper. The hands that used to be idle or to be content with the making of rude articles and low prices now find ample work and good samples, and a ready sale to pay their labors.

In conclusion, it may safely be stated that the state of the country is much better than what it was some twenty or twenty-five years ago in every respect—agriculture, manufacture, and commerce. The tillers of the soil, the artisans, the manufacturers, and the traders—petty and wholesale—are, as shown above, getting strengthened day after day in their natural course. Whatever may be said of the proportion of increase under these heads to the attempts, inducements, and training afforded by Government, and whatever may be thought about the causes of the shortcomings in this proportion, the fact lies bare to every observer that the lower and middle classes, *i.e.*, the working classes, are now much better off than what they were during the last generation, though not as much as they ought or would be expected to be under the particular attention paid by our Western rulers to improve their condition by the establishment of several colleges and training institutions all over the country. The fault is not of the poor classes, but it is due to the indifference of their richer brethren, who, instead of teaching and leading them, look to their own selfish ends, or spend their energies and wealth in questionable directions.

(7) CONDITION OF THE WEAVING INDUSTRY IN MADURA.

Note by V. Rajagopala Chariar, Esq., B.A., B.L., District Registrar, Madura.

Number of silk weavers' houses.—The town of Madura is divided into ten Municipal wards. Of these ten wards the silk weavers occupy the 1st, 2nd, 3rd, 4th and 9th wards, and the number of silk weavers' houses may be roughly estimated at 5,000 or so. Houses are multiplying in these wards and the fresh additions are generally thatched huts occupied by the laboring classes. It would appear that weavers from other parts of the district, finding no occupation in their respective places, have migrated to the town of Madura and settled themselves down here. The records of the Municipal office show that about 281 new houses have been erected in these wards.

2. *Number of silk weavers in the town.*—The silk weavers as a class are a very prolific people. They are said to multiply more rapidly than the other classes. Fixing, therefore, the inmates of each house to be from 4 to 5, the silk weavers' population of the town of Madura may be roughly estimated to be between 20,000 to 25,000 including females and children. Of these, about 10,000, including females, may be said to belong to the actual cooly class who earn their living by daily wages. Next to these come the petty traders who number from 400 to 500 families. Some of these sell threads, having purchased them in retail from the bigger merchants; some again sell lace in retail; some advance small sums of money to the holders of looms and order a small supply of cloths and sell them to the richer merchants. Some are brokers who collect cloths manufactured in the town and sell them either to the merchants in the town or to those abroad and very few are capitalists who have any very large trading concerns. The last class may almost be counted on one's fingers and it is said they are likely to be only between 10 and 20 on the whole. It is the brokers who form a comparatively large number. Some of the silk weavers have become agriculturists, finding that the profession of weaving does not pay. Their holdings are small and they only eke out their maintenance from the results of the agricultural labor. Some are said to keep carts and

bulls and to be employed in collecting sand from the river for building purposes.

3. *Their average income.*—Of the class of merchants, those who get profit of about Rs. 100 and more per month are only 5 or 6; about 20 or 30 get from Rs. 50 to Rs. 100 and those who get from Rs. 5 to Rs. 20 are about 400 or 500. The profession of brokers is not very remunerative. A broker makes a profit of one anna on every rupee, but to earn a profit of 30 or 40 rupees in a month he has to employ two agents—one to go about the town and watch the progress of the cloths entrusted to the laborers and another to keep accounts. Very often he has to borrow money and pay the weavers in advance.

The average income of a cooly family is Rs. 5 a month and it never goes higher than Rs. 10 a month. Females also work; some are employed in preparing the threads for weaving, some in the dyeing of cloths and others in the marking of spots or what is called sundadis. Boys of 12 years and more also earn wages and generally get from one rupee upwards.

4. *The quantity of cloths manufactured in the town, their different kinds and the average values thereof.*—The number of looms in the town is about 3,500. About four cloths can be woven from a loom in a month. This gives a total of 14,000 cloths per month for the whole town.

The different kinds of cloth manufactured are the following:—

Palukka selais—Of the value of Rs. 2 to Rs. 3½.

Urumals—Of the value of Re. 1 to Rs. 6 per taw or tari, consisting of 8 each.

Plain male cloths with silk borders—Of the value of Re. 1 to Rs. 4.

White laced head kerchiefs dyed—Of the value of Rs. 7 to Rs. 12, the charge for dyeing being Rs. 2 or Rs. 3 in excess.

Chittadais—Of the value of Rs. 3 to Rs. 8.

Female cloths of sorts.—The ordinary ranging from Rs. 6 to Rs. 20 and special cloths from Rs. 40 to Rs. 80.

Upper cloths—Of the value of Rs. 10 to Rs. 15.

Rs. 500 is the highest value of a cloth which has ever been made in Madura. Merchants of their own accord do not order for cloths of value of more than Rs. 80 to Rs. 100. The cloths made ordinarily range from Rs. 6 to Rs. 10 only in value.

The introduction of cotton twist from England, of lace from France, as well as of even the dyeing stuff from Bombay has considerably affected the value of the cloths made in the town and necessarily the wages to the coolies and the profits to merchants. Of the 14,000 cloths above mentioned as being made in a month in the town, for 7,000 to 10,000 cloths the inferior brass lace is used and the value of these do not go over Rs. 6 at the utmost. Their average price may be fixed at Rs. 2½ per cloth and this gives the sum total of Rs. 17,500 to 25,000. The average value of an ordinary cloth with good lace may be fixed at Rs. 7 and supposing that good lace is used for the remaining 4,000 cloths, their approximate value amounts to Rs. 28,000. Thus the total value of cloths made in the town in a month may be fixed at Rs. 50,000 to Rs. 60,000.

To get an impression of how much of this sum of Rs. 60,000 actually benefits the townsmen and how much goes to other countries and places, what the component parts of a Madura cloth are must be examined. Let me take for illustration an ordinary white cloth which is sold in the town for Rs. 10. The different items which go to make this sum of Rs. 10 may be described as follows :—

	RS.	A.	P.
Value of the thread	1	0	0
Cost of preparing the same for weaving .	0	2	0
Profit earned by the merchant who sells the thread	0	1	0
Cost of fastening the thread to the loom ...	0	1	0
Wages for weaving thread into a cloth ...	1	4	0
Value of the lace	6	0	0
	8	8	0
Merchants' profits including brokerage	1	8	0
Total ...	10	0	0

When this cloth is dyed the excess charge is as follows :—

	RS.	A.	P.
For the first and rough coloring	0	12	0
For the making of spots	0	12	0
For dyeing them over again	0	12	0
Miscellaneous	0	4	0
Total ...	2	8	0

Thus the great portion of the value of a cloth goes for the lace which is manufactured in France. Then by the cotton twists used, it is the English merchants who are benefited. The dye is also prepared abroad and the greater portion of Rs. 1-12-0 spent for dyeing goes also to other hands. The portion of Rs. 12-8-0 which actually circulates among the townsmen may be taken at the highest to be from Rs. 4 to Rs. 5 or one-third of the value of the cloth. This calculated with reference to the Rs. 60,000 worth of cloth yields a total amount of Rs. 24,000 to Rs. 30,000 and this amount may roughly be fixed to be the sum earned from the industry by cooly upwards to the richest merchant. Deducting again Rs. 5,000 or so as being the profits earned by merchants, there remains Rs. 25,000 to be distributed amongst 5,000 families, giving an average of Rs. 5 per family, the amount mentioned above, as being the average income of a family. Generally speaking the industry is becoming day by day less profitable to the actual working classes. The causes thereof are not far to seek. Prior to the importation of cotton twist, some fifty years ago, it would appear there were in the town of Madura 2,000 to 3,000 families employed in spinning out threads. This vocation has entirely ceased now. Again, prior to the importation of lace there were 500 Mussulman families engaged in making lace, and in their place there are, it would appear, only 10 families employed in making country lace. The preparation of coloring materials was at least done locally till a year or two ago, but this too has been superseded by the Bombay article. As a necessary result of the cessation of all these vocations, the labor is now directed entirely in one direction towards weaving, and it is in consequence very cheap. What used to be paid for at Rs. 2 in former years is now remunerated by 1 rupee only.

Even as regards the merchant class, the general complaint is that the trade does not pay. It may be that a larger number of cloths are now made than before, but what merchants make as profit by reason of the cheapness of the commodity and keenness of competition seems to be considerably less than what it was in former years. A cloth which was sold for Rs. 60 is now sold for only Rs. 30.

As a curious illustration of how the importation of the English-made goods has affected the local weaving industry, it may be mentioned that the weavers themselves of the town of Madura do hardly use the cloths woven by them. Mulls and piece-goods have taken the place of the home-made articles and if the richer class should seek for some country cloths, it is the Conjeeveram cloths that are made use of. The females likewise use the *Thombu*, and if they seek for some better country-made cloths, they purchase the Koranadu cloths. Thus it happens that one or two per cent. of the town-made articles are sold in the town itself and the rest are sent abroad.

The habits and manners of the silk weavers as a class.—Silk weavers as a class lead a simple life. Their food is simple and consists of cholum, cumbu and other dry grains. Rice is used by comparatively few persons only. Their clothing is simple. The females wear a cloth of Rs. 2 worth only, except on festive occasions, when they wear the Koranadu cloths. House accommodation is necessary for their profession, and each endeavours, therefore, first, to secure a house for himself. They are not also without the desire for ornaments. Even the poorest household are mentioned to have some gold jewels. A silk weaver's property consists generally of his house and ornaments. Marriage is costly with them. About Rs. 63 must be paid to the bride even by the poorest man. To meet this item of expenditure, almost every cooly before he enters on his profession begins to subscribe to some CHIT transaction or other and to save out of his hard earned wages 1 rupee or so to be paid monthly for a series of years extending from five to seven. Before he earns his prize in his turn, necessity, however, often compels him to borrow, mortgaging his chit amount and the house owned by him. It is such documents that are registered in large numbers in the town offices of Madura. There is another peculiarity about these silk weavers. They seldom borrow from other than their castemen. In case of loans of large sums, probably they may resort to the Nattukkottai chetti, but all ordinary loans are contracted from one of their own community.

In addition to the town of Madura, the weaving industry is carried on in the following places in the district—Dindigul, Paramakudi, Palni, Tirumangalam and Aruppukóta. In Dindigul only laced cloths are made to the value of Rs. 10 or so. In other places rough country cloths only are made. In all the stations, the industry is said to be declining so much so that weavers from these places come up to Madura for employment and overcrowd the market.

(8) The Condition of the Laboring Classes.

Note by H. Subbaraya Aiyar, Esq., Deputy Collector, Coimbatore District.

I have had ample opportunities of observing and judging of the condition of the labouring classes during the last three decades, and can confidently say that it has materially improved in every way. Agricultural labourers consist of two classes (1) the permanent farm servants, and (2) those employed temporarily on daily wages when agricultural operations are carried on extensively.

The farm labourer is paid monthly and in kind, and is also given, to cultivate on his own account, small plots of land belonging to his master. He also receives small presents and loans on occasions of festivals and marriages, besides a certain percentage of the produce harvested. He is also permitted to work elsewhere during certain months in the year when there is no work in the fields or on the threshing ground, and thereby earn what little he can additionally. The temporary labourer is paid either, in kind or in money or both. There was a time, within my own memory, when the labouring classes chiefly depended for work on agricultural operations in the year, and when these were over, they found it very difficult to maintain themselves. Now the demand for work, in the fields owing to increased cultivation, in the Imperial and Local Fund departments, in the Railway department, in the coffee, tea and cinchona estates, in the cotton presses, weaving and spinning mills and in other various departments of trade and agriculture, has become so great within the last thirty or forty years, that the labouring classes do not find it difficult to obtain employment freely on increased wages during the prosperous years. The labourers, especially in the maritime districts, have also begun to emigrate freely in large numbers to foreign countries, where they find work on higher wages, and thereby secure competence.

The rise in the price of food grains and other necessaries of life, the steady increasing demand for work, the development of trade, the large scope now offered for emigration, the high mode of living suitable to the period of advancement and civilization, and the fashion of the day to naturalize whatever is foreign--all these have undoubtedly enhanced the rate of wages, not only for the skilled, but also for the unskilled labourer, to a considerable extent. In localities where low caste labourers, owing to caste prejudices, are unable to compete with caste labourers, the latter, as a rule, demand exorbitant rates of wages and are getting themselves enriched more than the former. I have generally found a harmonious, and on the whole, sympathetic relations existing between the landholders and the labouring classes both in the districts in which I have served and in those which I have seen.

As far as I have seen and known of the condition of the labouring classes, I may safely say it is not what it was thirty or forty years ago, but has materially improved in several respects, and is improving, and will, I believe, improve steadily. Those who once formed the landless class, the petty traders, the artizans and the weavers who have chosen to work in the fields and elsewhere, have now acquired landed property to some extent; the exact extent I am unable to say, as I have no records with me to ascertain it. But reference to the records of the registry offices, as well as to the records of the villages, will, I am sure, furnish ample evidence regarding the same.

If at all there is any class of people who are getting deteriorated, it is the peasant proprietary class, who do not work in the fields themselves owing to religious scruples and caste prejudices, but depend for work on the labouring classes; and next to these come those who depend upon the munificence of the well-to-do classes and earn their livelihood by rendering religious and other services. I am really at a loss to find any remedial measures to improve their condition; and, unless they resort to labour, they must die out.

(m)—*Tables showing the Income, Expenditure, Scale of Diet, &c., in different Countries.*

(1) *Statement showing the amount of Imports and Exports of all Nations measured by value (extracted from "Mulhall's History of Prices").*

—	Millions Sterling.					Per inhabitant in 1884.
	1850.	1860.	1870.	1880.	1884.	
	£	£	£	£	£	£
Great Britain	193	376	547	698	686	19·0
France	75	167	227	339	315	8·4
Germany	105	160	212	315	331	7·0
Russia	32	46	100	121	114	1·3
Austria	29	51	83	128	137	3·5
Italy	26	46	74	96	99	3·4
Spain and Portugal ...	20	30	41	64	74	3·5
Holland	44	56	71	121	144	34·2
Belgium	35	48	64	116	116	20·3
Scandinavia	17	30	42	55	66	7·4
Europe	576	1,010	1,461	2,053	2,082	7·0
United States	64	137	172	309	276	4·9
South America	38	62	85	101	104	3·9
India	18	69	104	138	157	·8

For India 10 Rs. = £ 1.

(2) *Table showing the Income, the Amount of Taxes paid and the proportion of Taxes to Income in some of the European Countries ("Mulhall's History of Prices").*

—	Income, Millions Sterling.			Percentage of Agricultural to Total Income.	Taxes, Millions Sterling.	Ratio of Taxes to Income.
	Agricultural.	Non-agricultural.	Total.			
	£	£	£		£	
United Kingdom	263	984	1,247	21	88	7·1
France	435	530	965	44	142	14·7
Russia	482	366	848	57	92	10·8
Italy	174	171	345	52	62	18·0
Spain	133	85	218	60	35	16·0
Europe	2,476	3,102	5,578	44	632	11·3
India	360	180	540	67	48	8·9

(3) *Table showing the Wages of the Working Classes and the National Income in France (extracted from the article on "the wages of the working classes and the national income in France," published in the "Journal of the Royal Statistical Society for March* 1891").

Average wages per diem.	Men. s.	d.	Women. s.	d.
Country districts	2	1	1	4
Provincial towns	2	10	1	5
Paris	4	6	2	2

Millions.		Production. Million £.
17·7	Agricultural population	400
19·3	Non-agricultural population	435
37·0		835

Distribution of Incomes.

Millions.	Working classes.	Million £.
3·4	Agricultural labourers	80
3·8	Industrial and commercial workmen	144
1·1	Employés and other persons receiving wages ...	40
2·0	Domestics	56
10·3	Total wages and salaries	320
3·7	Small landowners, artizans, transport agents, soldiers, sailors, minor functionaries, schoolmasters, &c., whose resources do not exceed the maximum wages of the *ouvrier* ...	160
	Capitalists properly so called.	
1·7	Landowners	420 (bracketed)
1·0	Manufacturers, merchants, &c.	
1·0	Rentiers and members of the liberal professions	
17·7	Total	900

The capitalist classes get £112 per family after payment of the services of domestics and of taxation.

(4) *Table showing the Distribution of Incomes of Great Britain and Ireland.* (*Mr. Giffen.*)

—	Persons.	Incomes.		
	Millions.	Agricultural. Million £.	Non-agricultural. Million £.	Total. Million £.
I.—*Great Britain.*				
Income-tax incomes	1·4	90	486	576
Upper and middle classes below income-tax ...	1·5	23	84	107
Manual labourers	11·6	70	445	515
Total ...	14·5	183	1,015	1,198
II.—*Ireland.*				
Income-tax incomes ...	0·1	10	16	26
Upper and middle classes below income-tax	0·3	7	4	11
Manual labourers	1·6	20	15	35
Total ...	2·0	37	35	72
Grand Total ...	16·5	220	1,050	1,270

(5) *Statement showing the Cost of living per inhabitant (extracted from "Mulhall's Dictionary of Statistics").*

Daily Expenditure.

—	Pence per inhabitant.					
	Food.	Clothing.	Rent.	Taxes.	Sundries.	Total.
United Kingdom	9·0	2·6	2·2	2·4	4·6	20·8
France	7·0	2·2	1·8	2·7	1·7	15·4
Germany	6·5	1·8	1·2	1·9	1·4	12·8
Russia	4·1	1·0	0·4	0·8	0·3	6·6
Austria	5·8	1·6	0·8	1·2	0·7	10·1
Italy	4·2	1·0	0·6	1·4	0·4	7·6
Spain	4·6	1·2	0·7	1·5	0·4	8·4
Belgium and Holland ...	6·7	2·1	1·1	1·7	2·2	13·8
Scandinavia	6·0	1·6	0·9	1·2	1·4	11·1
Europe	6·0	1·6	1·1	1·6	0·9	11·2
United States	7·0	3·1	1·8	2·0	1·7	15·6

(6) *Table showing the Cost of living of the English Labourer and Mechanic per annum ("Mulhall's Dictionary of Statistics").*

Items.	Labourer.			Mechanic.		
	1792.	1823.	1883.	1792.	1823.	1883.
	£	£	£	£	£	£
Bread, meat, &c.	16	17	20	18	20	22
Groceries	2	3	5	4	6	8
Rent	2	3	4	3	4	6
Clothing, &c.	7	8	8	17	22	24
Total ...	27	31	37	42	52	60

(7) *Statement showing the relation between wages and food (extracted from "Mulhall's Dictionary of Statistics").*

—	Shillings per week.		
	Wages.	Food.	Ratio of food expenses to wages earned.
			PER CENT.
Great Britain	31	14	45
France	21	12	57
Germany	16	10	62
Belgium	20	12	60
Italy	15	9	60
Spain	16	10	62
United States	48	16	33
Australia	40	11	27

(8) *Statement showing the scale of diet prescribed in Jails in the Madras Presidency (Jail Code).*

(*a*)—The daily diet scale for European and East Indian long-term prisoners is as follows:—

Articles.		Labouring prisoners.	Females and non-labouring male prisoners.
Bread	Oz.	18	16
Meat, uncooked	,,	$4\frac{1}{2}$	3
Potatoes	,,	8	6
Vegetables	,,	6	6
Flour	,,	5	...
Suet	,,	$\frac{3}{4}$	...
Salt	,,	1	$\frac{3}{4}$
Rolong or syce meal	,,	2	...
Dholl meal	,,	1	1
Coffee	Pint	1	1
Tea	,,	1	1
Sugar	Oz.	$2\frac{1}{2}$	$1\frac{1}{2}$
Onions	,,	1	1
Pepper	,,	$\frac{1}{10}$	$\frac{1}{10}$
Mint and parsley	...	$\frac{1}{8}$	$\frac{1}{8}$
Rice	Oz.	5	5

On Mondays, Wednesdays and Sundays, vegetables and dholl meal are not given and rice is reduced to 4 oz. in the case of labouring prisoners and increased to 6 oz. in the case of non-labouring prisoners. On these days meat is increased to 7 oz. in the case of the first and to 4 oz. in the case of the second. On Saturdays instead of potatoes three additional ounces of rice are given, and $\frac{1}{2}$ oz. of curry-powder is substituted for mint, parsley and pepper. The allowance of firewood is 2 lb. per diem.

(*b*)—The daily diet scale for Native Convicts is as follows :—

Labouring prisoners.

	oz.	
Grain—		
Ragi, Cholum, Cumbu } sifted flour or without husk	24	
Dholl	2	
Butter-milk, tyre	10	Three days a week, not mutton days.
Ghee or oil	$\frac{1}{2}$	
Tamarind	$\frac{1}{2}$	
Salt	$\frac{3}{4}$	
Curry-powder	$\frac{1}{2}$	
Vegetables	4	
Onions	$\frac{1}{2}$	
Garlic	30	grains on mutton days.
Mutton or fish	5 oz.	without bone or $2\frac{1}{2}$ oz. of salt fish three days in the week.
Firewood	$1\frac{1}{4}$ lb.	

Remarks.—Females and non-labouring male prisoners get 20 oz. of grain instead of 24 oz. and 4 oz. of mutton instead of 5 oz. Any of the three grains may be used. 25 oz. of cumbu is to be considered as equivalent to 24 oz. of ragi or cholum. Labouring prisoners are to have two substantial meals, before going to work, and on returning from it, with a third light meal at midday. No rice less than six months' old is to be issued to prisoners. Dholl must be carefully husked. The allowance of fresh vegetables may be increased on the recommendation of the medical officer to any reasonable extent that can be supplied by the Jail garden. The weight of vegetables must be calculated after the stalks, skins and refuse have been separated, and only good succulent vegetables are to be used. The allowance of salt may, in times of epidemic cholera, be increased by order of the medical officer. The allowance of meat must be estimated without bone. Good ordinary grass-fed mutton or goats' flesh should be supplied. When dried or salt-fish is used, $2\frac{1}{2}$ oz. will be considered=5 oz. of fresh fish. Brahmins and other non meat-eating *castes* may be allowed 1 oz. of ghee or oil or 2 oz. of dholl with 10 oz. of butter-milk on meat days in lieu of mutton. In districts where cocoanuts are plentiful, 2 oz. of copra may be given in lieu of $\frac{1}{2}$ oz. of oil or ghee. Mango pickles may be substituted for tamarind when procurable. All kinds of grain used must be good, of thin kind and nutritious, not too new nor too old, and the quantity should be a fair average of the produce of the local markets. All unripe, mildewed or weevil eaten grain must be rejected and the grain should be free from all external impurities.

(9) *The particulars noted below have reference to the scale of diet in use among the ryot-population in a village near Coimbatore.*

The cost of food of Brahmin and other high *castes* per male adult in villages may be taken to be Rs. 3-12-0 per mensem or 2 annas per diem. Among labourers of the lower castes, the ordinary cost is about Rs. 1-12-6, or 1 anna per head per diem. The particulars are shown below :—

Higher castes.	RS.	A.	P.
Rice	2	0	0
Salt	0	1	6
Dholl	0	1	6
Chillies	0	0	6
Tamarind	0	1	0
Black gram (powdered)	0	2	0
Butter-milk	0	2	6
Ghee	0	5	0
Kerosine-oil for light...	0	2	6
Gingelly-oil	0	2	0
Firewood	0	8	0
Vegetables	0	1	0
Total ...	3	11	6

Lower castes.	RS.	A.	P.
Cholum	1	0	0
Horse gram	0	1	0
Salt	0	1	6
Chillies	0	0	6
Onions	0	0	6
Sundries	0	1	0
Kerosine-oil	0	1	6
Gingelly-oil	0	2	0
Tamarind	0	0	6
Betel leaves, areca nut and tobacco ...	0	4	0
Total ...	1	12	6

Vegetables, firewood, &c., are seldom purchased.

(10) *Scale of weekly diet to Soldiers and Convicts (Mulhall).*

—	Ration.	Nitrogenous.	Carbon.
	LB.	LB.	LB.
British soldiers in England	25·7	2·46	4·84
British soldiers in India	20·0	2·33	4·52
English convicts } in England	22·2	1·38	4·99
Farm labourers } in England	22·1	1·82	5·11

The 25·7 lb., the allowance of British soldier in England, is made up as follows :—

	LB.
Bread	7·0
Cooked meat	3·5
Vegetables	7·0
Sugar	0·7
Sundries	7·5
Total ...	25·7

(11) *Frankland's table of food required to lift a male adult (weighing 10 stones) 10,000 feet.*

	Quantity.	Cost.		Quantity.	Cost.
	LB.	D.		LB.	D.
Milk	8·02	15	Bread	2·35	5
Apples	7·82	12	Rice	1·34	5
Fish	6·37	25	Flour	1·31	4
Potatoes ..	5·07	4	Arrowroot	1·29	15
Beef	3·58	36	Oatmeal	1·28	3
Ham	3·00	38	Cheese	1·15	12

(12) (*Lyons' food tables*).—*The following is the quantity of cereals and pulses required by an adult weighing* 110 *lb.* (*the average weight of labourers in this country*) *for his nourishment. To cereals* ½ *oz. of fat or oil or ghee and not less than* ½ *oz. of salt should be added.*

——	Hard labour diet.	Light labour diet.	Subsistence scale.
	oz.	oz.	oz.
(1) Rice	16·61	14·77	14·91
Pulses	7·11	5·97	3·78
	23·72	20·74	18·69
(2) Cholum	17·85	15·86	16·03
Pulses	5·87	4·88	2·66
	23·72	20·74	18·69
(3) Cumbu	19·56	17·46	15·55
Pulses	4·16	3·28	3·14
	23·72	20·74	18·69
(4) Ragi	18·54	16·45	14·63
Pulses	5·18	4·29	4·06
	23·72	20·74	18·69
(5) Wheat	23·72	20·74	18·69
(6) Wheat	12·30	10·40	10·93
Rice	8·30	7·39	7·46
Pulses	3·12	2·95	0·30
	23·72	20·74	18·69

The above tables are based on the nourishment required by a labourer in England whose average weight is 150 lb. It is assumed that the work done and the nourishment required vary directly as the weight and no allowance is apparently made for the smaller quantity of food required in hot climates.

In calculating the cost of food, the value of rice may be taken to be 30 lb., of the dry grains 50 lb., of wheat 15 lb., and of dholl 25 lb., per rupee.

SECTION VI.—CERTAIN ALLEGED EVILS IN THE PRESENT ECONOMIC POSITION AND REMEDIAL MEASURES CONSIDERED.

(A).—LAND SETTLEMENTS.

(1) *Remarks on the method adopted by the Settlement Department for calculating the outturn of lands and its money value for fixing the Government assessment on the lands.*

In his "Memorandum on the Revision of Land Settlements in the N.-W. Provinces" by Mr. (now Sir) Auckland Colvin, written in 1872 when he was Secretary to the Board of Revenue in those Provinces, he has forcibly pointed out the impracticability of valuing lands for the purpose of assessing the land tax by endeavouring to ascertain the net produce of different qualities of soil. He remarks:—

"It is impossible to form an accurate conception of the process of assessment in these Provinces until one very general, but very important, error is explained. Because, in theory, the Government which we succeeded asserted a right to a share in the gross produce of the land, it is very frequently assumed that a settlement should still rest on a calculation of the gross produce, the cost of cultivation and the net yield of every field. The land is represented to be a kind of *tabula rasa* on which the settlement officer may frame any estimates he likes of capabilities and outturn. Hence, we hear of the necessity of settlement officers being experts in agricultural matters; of the rise in revenue bearing no ratio to the alleged rise in prices; of the ruinous waste of revenue involved in our settlements, and so on. It must be stated here once for all, that with the gross produce of the land, as the basis of assessment, the settlement officer in the North-West, except in tracts where rents are paid in kind, has little or nothing to do."

The plan of finding out the net produce of each field was tried in the N.-W. Provinces and was given up as impracticable. The following extracts from the report of the Saharanpore Settlement officer quoted in Sir Auckland Colvin's memorandum very clearly illustrate the difficulty in ascertaining the gross and net produce of soils.

Saharanpore Settlement officer.—"I have not made any use of the facts brought out by the actual cutting and weighing of the crop in 1864-65, because, as will be seen by the average rates, the jumma which would thus be gained would be the enormous sum of Rs. 16,96,824, the present jumma being Rs. 8,29,155 and my proposed jumma (the utmost assessable in my opinion) Rs. 8,88,699. This fact appears to me sufficient to show the fallaciousness of such data; and I proceed to show the reasons for their being so fallacious and do so at some length, as my action in the matter has been questioned:—

"(*a*) Too small an area could be appraised by a European officer. When so small a plot as one-tenth of an acre is taken as the measure of the whole, an enormous number of fields must be appraised in order that, by the rule of averages, the little errors in excess in one part may be checked by the reverse kind of errors in another part. But it takes about three hours to cut and weigh the crop of a field on the spot. On an average this operation can only go on simultaneously in two fields at a time. For the 'Khureef' there are less than two and for the 'Rubbee' less than one month available for the purpose, that is, some seventy-six working days ; *i.e.*, no more than 152 different fields can be appraised by the European Officer, even if he gives up two-thirds of the time available for inspecting his villages ; and you must recollect what pressure was put on me to finish this work speedily. Bearing in mind that it is necessary to find out the average produce of some dozen and-a-half different kinds of crop on eight different classes of soil irrigated and unirrigated, it is easy to see what a small basis of calculation can be obtained for each soil ; add to this, the fact that the appraisement had to be made in 41 groups of villages by two officers within the limit of one year, and that till the inspection was over it could not be ascertained how these groups would be divided, and the impossibility of procuring broad enough data for the calculation is apparent. . . . .

"(*b*) The native officials to whom part of the task was entrusted, with the wish of avoiding the imputation of lowering the apparent assets of a village, fell into the opposite extreme, and in spite of orders to choose in each village, at least one good, one average and one inferior field, rejected all the really bad fields.

"(*d*) The native officials taking the soils as given in the settlement papers, in many cases put down as *meesum* that which had not been manured for many years.

"(*e*) No allowance can be made for the numerous *tukm sokht* fields where seed is annually sown on the mere chances of a favorable fall of rain.

"(*f*) No allowances can with any certainty be made for the little unproductive places at the corners and edges of fields ; nor do I see how to make accurate allowances for the charges of weighing and carriage which fall on the Zemindars and the latter of which varies with the distance from the bazaar. Nor can it be ascertained what amount the Zemindar is forced by his necessities to sell at the low harvest price and what portion he can reserve till the price rises.

"(*g*) The appraisement of the inferior crops—bajra, mote, oorud, lobia, mundwa, &c., in the Khureef ; gram, mussoor, &c., in the Rubbee —is particularly difficult. The produce has to be exposed for days to the wind and sun before the grain can be separated. Who is to watch during this time ? It was the Zemindar's (peasant proprietor's) interest of course, to lower the apparent outturn, and I could feel no confidence in the result of an operation which I had not witnessed throughout with my own eyes ; yet this was in most cases incompatible with the task of inspecting fresh villages every morning. The consequence was the appraisement was far too much limited to the better classes of crops,—cotton and mukkee for the Khureef, wheat and barley for the Rubbee. This was the case in Mr. Daniell's pergunahs as well ; but of course to make such an operation a true measure of the actual outturn, the several crops must be cut in the same proportion in which they are grown.

"(*h*) I found that there was a decided difference in the weight of a crop according as it was cut at the commencement or end of the harvest. The grain was drier and lighter at the end than at the beginning; consequently the outturn of crops cut at the commencement of the season was unduly overstated. What allowance to make on this account I know not; yet a difference of a couple of seers in the produce of one-tenth of an acre comes to a serious amount on the whole. . . . ."

In the Madras settlements the grain experiments were really very few, considering the number of soils and of crops the outturn of which had to be ascertained. To take the two districts in which the number of experiments was the largest, viz., Nellore and Coimbatore. In Nellore, the experiments were made during seven years. The number was for jonna 2,771, for aruga 425 and for paddy 2,230. This amounts to hardly one experiment for each sort of soil (and there are 66 of them) in a year for each taluk which is oftentimes bigger than an English county. In Coimbatore, 1,542 experiments were made as regards the outturn of the three dry grains—cumbu, cholum and ragi—in five taluks in two years. The number hardly amounts to one for each grain for each sort of soil.

The cultivation expenses are even more difficult to ascertain. The cost of cultivation varies with agricultural skill and efficiency of labour in different localities and with the characteristics of different castes of laborers in the same locality. In some of the Madras settlements the cultivation expenses were not ascertained for each variety of soil; it was ascertained with more or less accuracy for one sort of soil and increased or decreased in proportion to the assumed outturn in the case of other soils. This was particularly the case in Kurnool and the same method has been proposed to be adopted in the case of Tanjore. In his "Analysis" of the agricultural statistics of the Kurnool district, Mr. Benson points out the fallaciousness of this method. He remarks that "the system of calculating the working expenses of the ryot by which these decrease in proportion to the assessed value of the land is radically wrong," and that "in fact, within certain limits the expenses for the production of the standard crop of jonna vary rather inversely to the quality of the land dealt with."

The quotations of prices of food grains for the old years on the average of which the commutation rates are based cannot also be relied upon as accurate. These prices are given in terms of garce (a measure of capacity containing 3,200 Madras measures), and the Board of Revenue found in 1885 that the local officers had committed many mistakes in converting the quotations in terms of local measures into quotations in terms of garce. The following are instances. In Ganjam the local measures were converted to garce at the rate of 1,600 tooms to a garce. The toom, however, is not a measure of uniform capacity throughout the district, its contents in rice varying from 240 to 280 tolas at the several stations. The conversion is correct only as regards those stations in which the toom of 240 tolas rice is in use. In Cuddapah a garce was assumed to be equivalent to 3,200 local measures of 132 tolas each or one-tenth more than its real contents. In Kurnool the three varieties of local measures of 86, 114 and 132 tolas, were converted into garce at the same rate, viz., 3,200 measures. In South Arcot 3,200 local measures of 140$\frac{2}{3}$ tolas rice were assumed to be equivalent to a garce which is thus taken to be one-seventh larger than it is. In Tanjore no uniform principle was adopted, the conversion being effected at the rate of 116 kalams or 2,784 local measures in some taluks and in others at the rate of 133$\frac{1}{3}$ kalams or 3,200 local measures. The contents in rice of the measures in use in this district being either 133 or 144 tolas, the garce was assumed to contain 10 and 20 per cent. more than it really does. The Board had the prices in terms of garce for years subsequent to 1873 re-calculated with reference to the retail prices recorded since that year, but as regards the prices of the previous years on which the commutation rates adopted for the settlements already concluded are based, it was found impossible to apply any corrections to them.

These considerations are sufficient to show the almost insuperable difficulties met with in effecting land valuations and the imperfect character of the data which have to be made use of for the purpose.

(2) ***Statement showing the increase or decrease in the occupied area and in the assessment caused by the introduction of the Survey and Settlement.***

District.	Area. As per Revenue Accounts.	Area. As per Survey.	Area. Difference.	Area. Percentage.	Assessment. As per Revenue Accounts.	Assessment. As per Settlement.	Assessment. Difference.	Assessment. Percentage.	Remarks.
	ACS.	ACS.	ACS.		RS.	RS.	RS.		
Ganjam	280,572	336,167	+ 55,595	20	6,55,732	7,20,449	+ 64,717	10	
Vizagapatam	93,652	105,751	+ 12,099	13	2,16,613	2,49,743	+ 33,130	15	
Godávari { Western Delta	142,558	183,390	+ 45,832	32	5,75,143	8,50,564	+ 2,75,421	48	(a)
Godávari { Eastern and Central Deltas and Uplands	Not available.	390,709			11,35,259	12,43,578	+ 1,08,319	10	(a)
Total ...		579,099			17,10,402	20,94,142	+ 3,83,740	22	
Kistna { Masulipatam	391,844	399,402	+ 7,558	2	5,76,474	8,75,051	+ 2,98,577	52	(a)
Kistna { Guntúr	1,291,547	1,394,363	+ 103,316	8	24,21,589	25,91,289	+ 1,69,700	7	
Total ...	1,683,391	1,794,265	+ 110,874	7	29,98,063	34,66,340	+ 4,68,277	16	
Nellore	910,352	910,078	− 274	...	17,10,412	18,98,568	+ 1,88,156	11	
Cuddapah	1,161,613	1,258,540	+ 96,927	8	15,19,259	16,27,135	+ 1,07,876	7	
Kurnool	1,121,553	1,226,413	+ 104,860	9	12,87,123	13,27,500	+ 40,377	3	
Chingleput	488,646	544,093	+ 55,447	11	13,57,612	14,10,576	+ 52,964	4	
North Arcot	627,027	706,056	+ 79,029	13	17,47,530	17,81,257	+ 33,727	2	
Salem	1,048,239	1,208,588	+ 160,349	15	17,29,016	17,97,381	+ 68,365	4	
Coimbatore	2,192,940	2,336,046	+ 143,106	7	24,51,880	26,56,792	+ 2,04,912	8	
Trichinopoly	647,245	764,496	+ 117,251	18	15,82,074	11,94,018	− 3,88,056	− 25	
Tinnevelly	1,299,296	1,396,644	+ 97,348	7	25,25,366	24,73,398	− 51,968	− 2	
Madura	874,082	941,825	+ 67,743	8	15,75,468	15,82,577	+ 7,109	0·5	
Nílgiris	64,150	112,589	+ 48,439	75	33,632	68,559	+ 34,927	103	(b)
Total ...	12,635,316	{ 13,829,941 390,709	+ 1,194,625	9	2,31,00,182	243,48,435	+ 12,48,253	5	

(a) The increase of revenue by settlement includes water-rate on lands brought under cultivation by means of water taken from anicut works in the Godávari and Kistna Deltas recently constructed. The water-rate was at first tentatively fixed at Rs. 3 per acre and was raised to Rs. 4 per acre at the time when the new settlement was introduced. The increase is also due to some extent to lands under the influence of the Godávari and Kistna anicuts having been assessed at a higher rate, in view of the prospective advantages of irrigation from the anicut works.

(b) The increase of revenue by settlement is due to the imposition of a pepper corn rent on a large area of waste land included under private holdings, which, under the previously existing revenue system, was charged for only when cultivated.

(3) *Extract from Mr. Giffen's article on "Taxes on Land," printed in his "Essays on Finance," 1st Series.*

"Clearly, if the phenomena of the last thirty years are about to be repeated—and there is a reasonable chance that they will be, for there is no sign of check to the growth of population or the increase of machinery and inventions—it is much to be wished that a better system should, if possible, be at work than has hitherto existed, for securing to the nation a portion of the augmenting value of its soil. The problem, however, is excessively difficult, and I doubt very much whether Mr. Mill's own suggestion, which must be first considered, will be found, as a general measure, to answer the purpose. It is in effect a proposal to go straight to the end in view—that the State should inquire at prescribed intervals what is the augmenting rental of land, and make a charge upon the owners of some definite portion of that augmentation. If there is no increase of rental due to general causes, there will be no increase of tax, and owners who object will have the opportunity of surrendering their estate on what Mr. Mill's enemies must admit will be full compensation. One objection to this proposal is that it is almost wholly novel in European countries, at least where the art of taxation has been most carefully studied, and is least of all fitted for a country in the circumstances of England. Mr. Mill has apparently in view the ideal of the *Foncier* taxes on the continent, in which the process is for the State at a certain date to impose a lump charge on the whole land of the country in proportion to its estimated value, and then apportion this charge among the various localities and parts of soil in the country, by a carefully arranged *Cadastre*. But there is nothing more tedious in fact than the completion of a *Cadastre*, or unequal when it is completed. Even in France, which has set the example in these *Foncier* taxes, the new *Cadastre*, which was commenced forty years ago, was only completed the other day, and while it was being put into operation the value of the whole land subject to it was changing. It is hardly possible to imagine that even if in England we could give that attention to the nice adjustment of competing qualities of land or property, which could alone make the basis of French direct taxes endurable, we should be content to await the slow development of a pretentiously perfect, but really imperfect, *Cadastre* for a period of 40 years. It is a still more fatal objection that such taxes do not appear to draw. It is officially estimated in France that the annual value of real property has increased since 1821 from £64,000,000 to £160,000,000, which is quite comparable with the increase in England. But while the rates have risen in England from about £10,000,000 to £17,000,000, the special land tax of France has only risen from £11,720,000 to £12,280,000, including the additional hundredths imposed for local purposes, as well as the 'principal' of the tax. The special tax of England is thus more elastic and effective than the special tax of France, which is proposed as a model. Besides, if these objections could be got over, if it could be shown that an improved *Cadastre* is easily possible, and is capable of frequent renewal, there would remain the objection that such a tax, so imposed, might interfere with the enjoyment of private property in an inexpedient manner. It would be very difficult to re-assure individuals against the operations of the tax assessors.

Every few years they would foresee a demand of an indefinite amount, depending on many points of taste and opinion, and they would only have the alternative of paying or surrendering their property to the State. Careful as Mr. Mill is to suggest safe-guards, the essential nature of the transaction would be such as to destroy confidence in the continuity of private right in some particular plot of land. The apprehensions might in the main be unfounded, but their existence would be a public calamity, unless the theory is admitted that the abolition of private property would be beneficial, which in some localities it might be.

"Turning from this suggestion, I think there is much to be said in favor of our present special taxes on land, imperfect as we have shown them to be. They have permitted the growth of an immense mass of value in the hands of individuals only, and at a very recent date there was a sudden reduction of the burden, by which a small class received a considerable gain. But with all their imperfections, they have the merit of elasticity. They are set apart for the discharge of certain branches of expenditure ; and, without fluctuating so widely as to disturb property rights, they may be increased materially, and so reserve for the State some portion, however insignificant it may be, of the augmenting value of property. This is no small merit, especially when compared with the model of the continental land taxes, which have no such capacity of expansion. It is an additional convenience, that, as the branches of expenditure which are thrown specially on this property are local, local administration and local taxation can be associated. In this view, the rates are, in fact, a happy English invention, by which different and unconnected advantages are obtained in a rough practical fashion, and as it is a familiar system we have another obvious reason for trying to make the most of it. Could not something more be made of it ? It will be of some use perhaps if the discussion of the principles on which the burden is imposed makes it clear that no injustice is now committed—that the support of a certain burden of expenditure is a condition of the enjoyment of the property which the State may properly impose. Every one knows the condition beforehand, and as it is quite a calculable one, notwithstanding the loud talk of the increase of rates and the addition of new rates, there is no inexpediency in it as a too heavy restriction on the enjoyment of private property in land. But the discussion, I think, may do more, and justify the imposition of new charges which are convenient for local administration. As the tendency of the functions of local Government is to increase, and the additional expense has not yet proved commensurate with the increase of the value of property, we have a security in the recognition of this principle, both for the reservation to the State of a part of that value—though, I fear, a most inadequate part—and for the safety of private property against any great disturbance. If I might venture to make a suggestion, there is one new charge which escapes notice, and which might very properly be treated as a branch of local expenditure; the army for home defence ought to be locally maintained. For many reasons it is important that a good deal of local management and self-government should be associated with the organization of our militia and volunteers and the charges might very properly fall on the rates. This would not only relieve the Imperial army estimates of a heterogeneous charge, but by really associating localities with the work, would contribute much to the strength and vitality of our home system of defence. There is another way in which something more could be made of the present system. Under the hap-hazard methods and want of principle which have hitherto prevailed, the local rates have gradually been relieved of a large portion of the burden which properly falls upon them. On one pretext or another the Imperial exchequer has been drawn on for 'grants' amounting annually in England to a million and a quarter, by which the growth of the local burden has been retarded —or in other words, the individual landowner has been permitted to retain a larger share than otherwise he would retain of the augmenting value of land. Good reasons, I think, have been furnished for putting a stop to this system, if rates continue to be the form of our special tax. The proper course would now be to institute a mode of discontinuing the grants by degrees, according to a defined scale, and so reimpose on property a burden which it has escaped." *

(4) ***Statistics showing the amount of taxes on land in various countries and its ratio to total agricultural production (extracted from "Mulhall's Statistical Dictionary").***

Countries.	Taxes.	Agricultural production.	Tax percentage.
	Millions £.	Millions £.	
England	16·2	157	10·3
Scotland	1·9	40	4·8
Ireland	2·7	54	5·0
United Kingdom	20·8	251	8·3
France	21·8	460	4·8
Germany	12·7	424	3·0
Austria Proper	8·6	175	4·9
Italy	14·2	204	7·0
Belgium	1·53	55	2·8
Holland	1·08	39	2·8
Egypt	4·89	35	14·0
India	23·4	400	5·8
	109·0	2,043	5·4

In the United Kingdom the taxes on agriculture are distributed as follows :—

Taxes.	England.	Scotland.	Ireland.	Total.
	Millions £.	Millions £.	Millions £.	Millions £.
Tithes	4·05	...	...	4·05
Rates	8·30	1·40	2·10	11·80
Income-tax	1·20	·20	·25	1·65
Land-tax	1·05	·05	..	1·10
Duties and stamps	1·60	·25	·35	2·20
	16·20	1·90	2·70	20·80

* **Note.**—It should be remembered that Mr. Giffen's remarks in the concluding portion of the above extract were made in 1871, before the present agricultural depression and the great fall in the rent-value of lands had set in, in England.

In France the taxes levied in 1874 were distributed as follows :—

	Millions £.
National	4·8
Departmental	4·8
Indirect	8·6
Roads, &c.	3·6
	21·8

The rental of land in France was estimated in 1874 at 158 millions £.

(B).—Tenure of Ryots in Zemindaries.

(1) *Extracts from the remarks of the Madras Board of Revenue on the relative rights of Zemindars and Tenants.*

In Proceedings, dated 2nd December 1864, No. 7843, the Board reviewed the history of the relative rights of Zemindars and ryots and arrived at the following conclusions, viz. :—

"That in the earliest times of which we have record, the right of the State to a share in the produce of the land was *limited*, and that this limit was such as to leave a sufficient margin for the growth of a valuable property in the land appertaining to the occupant, whose right to retain possession on payment of the limited share was inviolable and hereditary;

"That a fixed limit was equally maintained by the Muhammedan conquerors;

"That the origin of the Zemindar's office was comparatively a modern one, and that whatever its origin, the Zemindars derived their rights from the State, which could not confer more than it had possessed and exercised;

"That the State asserted, and often in later times exercised, the power of resuming the exercise of its rights from the Zemindars without thereby altering the terms and conditions of the ryot's tenure;

"That any increase in the rate of the Zemindar's demand on the ryots was only justified by the Zemindar on the plea that the State had raised its demands on him, although this ground was by no means a sufficient foundation for any increase in the *rate;* inasmuch as the State share collected by the Zemindar could be legally increased by *extension* of cultivation, and its value enhanced by improvements in the cultivation, and when the superior kind of crops were grown, and as the State demand on the Zemindar was not fixed, though his percentage of the State share of the produce might have been so;

"That the notorious prevalence of excessive receipts by the Zemindars from the ryots induced the Nazims of the Empire to raise the State demands on the Zemindars, which measure again excited the Zemindars still further to exact from the ryots, till the latter were ground down to penury, or exasperated to resistance. Hence the Zemindars were themselves impoverished, so long as, and where the officers of the Empire were able to maintain their authority over them; or they fattened on extortion where the influence and authority of the Empire or its lieutenants had grown weak. In neither case was the State benefited;

"That the object steadily kept in view by the framers of the Permanent Settlement was to remedy these crying evils by re-adjusting matters; in order to which they proposed to relinquish to the Zemindars an ample allowance for their personal benefit, out of the average State demand in past years on the Zemindari, and to fix the Zemindar's payment unalterably for ever, leaving to him all the benefits derivable from extension of cultivation and improvements in the culture of the lands, but to restrict his demands on the ryot to the rate or share established for Government by prescription, which rate was to be registered in the village by officers appointed for the purpose; while the actual demand on the individual ryot was to be recorded in a puttah or written engagement in accordance with this established rate or share, which puttahs when granted not 'without limit of time' but 'for one year,' should be renewable at its close, or be in force till renewed;

"That a limited time (six months) was allowed to each Zemindar *after* the Permanent Settlement of the State demand on his Zemindari, for the necessary arrangements with the ryots, after which time he became liable to fine if he failed to grant puttahs to ryots on demand;

"That when disputes arose regarding the *rates* to be specified in those puttahs, whether of assessment in specific quantities of grain or sums of money for a specified extent of land, or of shares in the produce, they were to be determined with reference to the rates in force in the particular case in the year *preceding* the Permanent Settlement of the State demand, or where that was not ascertainable, then according to the rates in force in the case of neighbouring land of similar quality;

"That no ryot can be ejected from his holding, so long as he pays, or is willing to pay, this established rate;

"That the Collector has summary powers to give decisions in such cases in a *quasi* judicial capacity, and may refer them for the decision of Punchayet when the parties agree;

"That appeals lie by regular suit to the Courts from the Collector's decisions, but that the Punchayet's decision is final where unimpeachable on the ground of corruption."

(2) *Note on Judicial decisions affecting the rights of Zemindari Ryots.*

It is noteworthy that the decisions of the Madras High Court which really jeopardized the status of Zemindari ryots were not passed with reference to Zemindari ryots, but with reference to Government ryots. The decisions in Chockalinga Pillai *versus* Vythilinga Pandara Sannadi and Mrs. Jessie Foulkes *versus* Rajarathna Mudely (VI Madras High Court Reports, pages 164, &c., and 175, &c.) are supposed to have rendered the tenure of Zemindari ryots precarious. In the first case, the tenant on whose behalf occupancy right was claimed was a porakudi and the landlord was a Government ryot entitled to *kudivaram* and not *melvaram*. In the second case, the so-called puttadar was the lessee of the melvaram rights of a mittadar.

In neither case, therefore, was there a presumption in favor of permanent occupancy right according to the common law of the country. This has been laid down in subsequent decisions of the Madras High Court. In the case reported in Indian Law Reports, V Madras, page 345, the High Court observe: "It has never been the law in any part of India, of which we have experience, that a mere farmer of revenue or proprietary right acquires a right of occupancy." Both in this case and in the case reported in Indian Law Reports, VII Madras, page 374, the High Court further hold that *primâ facie* porakudis are tenants from year to year, and that a claim on the part of porakudis to hold land permanently should be proved to have originated either in grant or prescription. The case in which the permanent occupancy right of ryots was called in question was Fakir Mahammed *versus* Tirumala Chariar (Indian Law Reports, I Madras, page 205) decided by a Full Bench composed of Sir Walter Morgan, Chief Justice and Messrs. Holloway and Innes, Judges, Mr. Innes dissenting. The decision was that an ordinary puttadar under Government is merely a tenant from year to year, and that the rules of the Board of Revenue asserting the contrary did not constitute rights enforceable at law. Mr. Innes pointed out the true state of the case, viz., that the ryot does not derive his title from the puttah, but from *occupation* of the land and registry of his name in the registers of landed property kept under Regulation 26 of 1802; that puttah is not a lease but merely a memorandum showing the revenue payable for each year on the holding with reference to changes in the extent of land newly taken up or relinquished, and remissions of revenue granted on account of loss of crop, &c.; and that by the common law of the country, a ryot holding land under this tenure is entitled to hold it as long as he pays the regulated assessment, or is evicted *in due course of law* for default. In a subsequent case reported in Indian Law Reports, IV Madras, page 174, decided by Messrs. Muthusami Aiyar and Tarrant, it was ruled that it was incumbent on the Mittadar to show that the *kudivaram* right as well as the *melvaram* right vested in him, so as to entitle him to eject the ryots in the mittah on notice, as tenants from year to year, and that there was nothing to show that the Mittadar was the proprietor in the sense that the *kudivaram* right belonged to him. Again in Subraya Mudeli *versus* Sub-Collector of Chingleput (Indian Law Reports, IV Madras, page 303), Sir Charles Turner observed that a puttah issued by Government will, unless it is otherwise stipulated, be construed to endure so long as the ryot pays the revenue he has engaged to pay. Mr. Innes laid down that the right of Government is only a right to a charge on the land, and a right to forfeit, *by due course of law*, the title of the person who does not pay the charge. In the Secretary of State *versus* Nunja (Indian Law Reports, V Madras, page 163) decided by Sir Charles Turner and Mr. Muthusami Aiyar, they stated "we see strong reason to doubt whether the view of the majority of the Court in that case (Fakir Mahammed *versus* Timmala Chariar) was right and when an occasion arises, we should propose that the ruling be reconsidered by the Full Bench." It is difficult to say whether the principle involved in the dictum of Sir Charles Turner that a puttah issued by Government, unless otherwise stipulated, will be construed to endure so long as the ryot pays the revenue he has engaged to pay will be applied to Zemindari ryots. In Venkatagopal *versus* Rangappa (Indian Law Reports, VII Madras, page 365) decided by a Full Bench, the Madras High Court review the legislation in regard to landlords and tenants, but do not afford any indication of what their decision would be on the above point. The High Court in their judgment state that the permanent settlement regulations of 1802 had placed the rights of Zemindari ryots on an assured basis, and Regulations IV and V of 1822 jeopardized these rights. The statement seems to reverse the facts. The intention of the Regulations of 1822 undoubtedly was to prevent any doubt being cast upon the rights of the ryots by the provision in the permanent settlement regulations which declared Zemindars to be "proprietors of the soil." Further in this case, the High Court presumed an "implied contract" for the payment of a money-rent for the simple reason that the ryot had paid a money-rent at a certain rate for 14 years, though he objected to the payment of the money-rent as being excessive, and stated that he was prepared to divide the crop with the mittadar at the usual rates of varam. This he was entitled to do under clause 3 of section 11 of Act VIII of 1865. If the money-rent represented the money value of the mittadar's share of the crop at certain assumed rates, the clause gives the option to the ryot of rendering the rent at the rates demanded or of falling back upon a division of the crop when the parties could not agree to its future money valuation. The fact that for 14 years it suited the ryot to pay the money rates demanded, owing to the prices of produce then prevailing, would not show that he impliedly contracted to pay at the same rates when prices had fallen and were expected to fall further. In Polu *versus* Ragavammal (Indian Law Reports, XIV Madras, page 52) the High Court followed the ruling in Venkatagopal *versus* Rangappa, but in this instance it was the landlord and not the tenant that claimed payment of rent in kind.

(3) *Extract from the Report of Mr. Forbes on the condition of the Zemindari Ryots in the Ganjam district.*

Mr. Forbes writing in 1866 as Collector of Ganjam says, "I will now add a few words on the comparative merits of the ryotwari and Zemindari tenures as regards the condition of the tenants. In Ganjam, the assessment on ryotwari lands held under Government is light, and a series of years of very remunerative prices had enabled the ryots to accumulate substance; they had begun, prior to the famine, to achieve an independence before unknown to the class and to hold their own with the sowcar, in bargains for produce; had it not been for this circumstance, we should have had to choose between agricultural depopulation and the alternative of maintaining the whole class, as we have already maintained more than 20,000 souls.

"The Government ryot in Ganjam pays a light rent, and his interests are cared for by the preservation of the existing sources of irrigation.

"The 13 Oorya Zemindars of Ganjam are, with few exceptions, the most grasping landholders and the least enlightened proprietors in the world; they take 50 per cent. of the crops and lay out little or nothing in improving or even in maintaining irrigation works. They rack-rent their villages to middle-men, and the under-tenants are consequently deprived of all chance of accumulating capital, and are little better than serfs of the soil; the bulk of the ryots in Zemindari estates would hail a change to Government management with joy. I limit these remarks to the Zemindari system as it is worked here. There may be liberal native landlords in other districts, whose policy produces different results; but in the Ganjam Zemindaries, the profits of the soil are divided between the ryot, the Zemindar, the renter and the Government. In the Government taluks, the ryot and the Government divide the produce, the ryot taking by far the larger share. There can be no question which class lives under the more favorable conditions, and in fact, when the famine fell upon Zemindari estates, the misery and mortality were far greater than in Government taluks."

(4) *Extract from the Report of Mr. Cotton on the condition of the Ryots in the Kalahasti Zemindari, in the North Arcot district, quoted by Mr. W. Digby in his Memorandum on private relief in the Madras Famine* 1877, *p.* 129, *Appendix I, to the Report of the Famine Commission.*

"The Maderpauk division is the southern portion of Kalahasti Zemindari of the North Arcot district. The division contains 178 villages, not including hamlets; the population of which in 1871 amounted to 73,085; half to two-thirds of these are ryots, or people who earn their livelihood by agricultural pursuits. The greater number of the ryots, of whom the population chiefly consists, are always exceedingly poor, much more so, than in villages belonging to Governmont, for the following reasons:—The ryot who ploughs and cultivates the land has no real right of occupancy, and hence has no interest in improving his land by sinking wells and manuring it. The effects of this system can be seen at once by comparing the Inam villages of the Zemindari, with those directly under the Zemindar's control. In the fields of the former there are wells, the land is manured, and the owner consequently gets good crops and is generally well to do, living in a good substantial house. In the fields of the latter, there are no wells; and the fields having no fixed occupants are not manured, and give but a poor return to the labour expended on their cultivation; the villages (*sic in origine*) attached to the lands bear invariably a poverty-stricken look.

"The Zemindar, Venkatappa Naidu, C.S.I., collects his revenue, not in money, as is done in Government villages, but in kind. The Zemindar is supposed to receive one-half of the outturn of the crop and the cultivator is supposed to receive the other; but he rarely gets more than a quarter, the other quarter generally going to the subordinate Zemindari officials. What remains to the cultivator, after paying everything, is hardly sufficient to keep him and his family in food till the next harvest; so that, it is a case of living from hand to mouth. If the crops fail for one year for want of water or other causes, most of the cultivators are left absolutely destitute; and not only the cultivators and their families, but also the coolies, who, though not actually cultivating themselves, earn their livelihood by working for those that do. The cultivator, when his crops fail, has to use the seed, that he had put by for sowing, as food; when this is exhausted, he sells his bullocks, &c., and having spent the money received from these, he is without any resources. He is unable to raise money on his fields from the sowcar, as he has no rights of occupancy; therefore his last hope is to get an advance from the Zemindar; failing this, he leaves his village and seeks work as a cooly elsewhere. This is what happened last year. In November we had excellent rains, but owing to the exhaustion of the cultivators, the fields remained unploughed. The Zemindar gave no advances, or to such a small extent that they were useless. Many ryots had already left their villages, and others were preparing to do so; roofless houses were seen in all directions and some small villages were entirely deserted."

(5) *Extract from the Administration Report of the Pudukota State for* 1881-82 *by the Dewan-Regent Mr. A. Sashiah Shastriar, C.S.I., describing the evils of the system of collecting the Government assessment on land in kind by a division of the crops raised.*

"I have already remarked that the prevailing revenue system was the 'amani.' A very large portion of the lands under cultivation and believed to be of the best kind were held under this system. *The property in these lands was vested in the sirkar.* The ryots were in most cases tenants-at-will and theoretically could be turned out without their consent. The transfer or sale of such lands was void at law. The crop raised by the ryot (at his own expense generally, and at times assisted with seed-grain from sirkar) was shared half and half* between him and the sirkar. He moved his share to his own house and carried the sirkar share to the granaries provided for the purpose, and if there were none, kept it in his own house either in trust, or under the lock and key of the responsible sirkar village officers. These were the main features of the system, and to one who knows no more, they must appear on their face to be very just indeed. What could be more fair? The ryot and the sirkar, by sharing the crop equally, share equally the vicissitudes of season and market.

2. "During a life-long career of service, I have had opportunities of watching closely the evils of the sharing system in all its varied forms in many districts of the Madras Presidency, as well as in Travancore, and my experiences have been of an interestingly sad kind. To tell the whole tale would occupy more space than would be justifiable in this place. I shall, therefore, content myself with stating briefly what is the case in this State.

3. "The system is saturated with evils and frauds of a grave nature.

(*a*) "The ryots having no heritable or transferable property never cared to cultivate the amani lands in due season. If you saw a bit of cultivation at the tail-end of the season, the chances are it is 'amani.' Ryots prefer infinitely to cultivate other lands held on different tenures, such as inam, jeevithem and money assessed lands. To prevent this, a penal agreement is forced from them to the effect that they would not fail to cultivate the 'amani' lands first.

---

* This is the prevailing proportion, but it varied in special cases, sometimes two-fifth and sometimes half and so on.

(b) "As soon as the ears of the grain make their appearance, an army of watchers called kanganies (literally eye-watchers) is let loose. As they get no pay for the duty and are for the most part the old militia of the country, on whom this kind of work is imposed since fighting time had departed, and get a grain fee on the crop they watch, their watch is at best often lax.

(c) "When the crop arrives towards maturity, it is the turn of sirkar village officers and the village headmen (called mirasidars here) to go round the fields and note down estimates of the crop. That there is considerable wooing and feeing at this stage goes for the saying. As in other matters, so in this, the race is to the rich and woe to the poor.

(d) "As soon as the village officers have done and reported the first estimate, down come special estimators from the taluk cutcherries to check the first estimate. Their demands have equally to be satisfied. Then comes the business of obtaining permission to cut and stack the crops. Here again another stage, where much feeing and grudge-paying take place. If permission is delayed just two days, an adverse shower of rain irreparably damages the crop on the field, or over-exposure to the sun renders the grain unmarketable.

(e) "Then comes the threshing and division of the grain on the threshing-floor. What takes place then may be imagined. If the outturn is less than the estimate, the ryot is made responsible for the *difference* without any further ado. If it is more, woe be to the *estimators*. The result in the latter case is often that the difference is made away with and shared half and half between the ryot and the officers concerned. During all this time the unpaid army of the watchers continues on duty.

(f) "Now the sirkar grain is removed to the granaries. Is all danger over now? By no means. A fresh series of frauds commences. The granaries have neither impregnable walls, nor are their locks Chubb's patents. The half-famished vettiyan, the hereditary watchman of the village, mounts guard, and he and the village headmen are personally held responsible for any deficiency which may occur on the re-measurement of the grain *out* of the granary. It often happens the poor vettiyan, stung by hunger, is driven to certain deeds much against his conscience. Scaling over the mud walls or forcing open the too easily yielding village locks, he helps himself from time to time to what his urgent wants may dictate. It is not often he is able to replace, even if he was so minded, what he has appropriated before the day of reckoning comes. This comes sometimes soon and sometimes late, depending on the time when the paddy is required for sirkar purpose, or for sale to purchasers. When it does come, there is crimination and recrimination without end, the vettiyan charging the mirasidars, and the mirasidars the vettiyan. The sirkar officials, to vindicate its robbed rights, come down heavily on both, and often both are ruined. If the misappropriation is made in very small quantities, the way of replacement is very ingenious; a quantity of chaff or a quantity of loose earth or a quantity of big-grained sand is put in to make up the measure.

(g) "Time passes and the months denoting favorable markets come round. There now remains the business of disposing of the sirkar grain from the granaries. Simple as it may appear, enormous difficulty is experienced, and we have to face another series of frauds now on the part of the taluk or superior officers. Tenders are invited, but only a few come and bid low. Tenders are again invited but to no better purpose. At last come upon the scene a set of unscrupulous fraudulent tradesmen or relatives or friends of those in authority, or mere speculators professing to give security, which is really worthless. These men bid higher prices and take up the grain in lots they require. They remove the grain, but make no payment down, but enter into promises to pay value in eight instalments and profess to give due security for the fulfilment of the promise. It not unfrequently happens that the purchaser decamps and his surety is found to have followed suit or found to be hollow. The money due on the sales to the relatives and friends of the officers outstands the longest. If, to avoid these troubles, the grain is taken direct to the nearest market to be there sold outright for cash, few could be induced to pay the market price, the sirkar grain being notoriously bad crop and unscrupulously adulterated.

"Such is a brief *résumé* of the beauties of the 'amani' system. Complaints against the system on the part of the poorer ryots were rife. The State was ringing with the news of the plunder practised every day. Honest-minded higher officers found themselves helpless to apply a remedy. The evils in all their realities came home to me. To knock the system on the head was the only remedy possible, and to this I had to apply myself as soon as I had ascertained the wishes of the people and had the leisure to begin. A beginning was made to substitute money assessments. It met with success and would have been carried through but for the unfortunate character of the season which deterred the ryots from entering into immediate arrangements. The plan adopted will be described in the next report."

(6) *Suggestions as to amendments to be made in the law of landlord and tenant in the Madras Presidency.*

The following are the matters for which provision should be made in a law regulating the relations between Zemindars and ryots. The two main interests in the land are the melvaram and the kudivaram; and the two classes of land are "ryoti" or aiyan or peasant land, and pannai or kamar or private or domain land. In the former, the Zemindar has the melvaram right alone, and in the latter, he has both the melvaram and the kudivaram right. The distinction is well known throughout the Presidency, and is recognized by the common law of the country. Advantage should be taken of the distinction, and the relative rights of landlords and tenants should be defined on this basis. There would then be 4 classes of persons to be dealt with, viz., 1st, melvaramdar or the superior holder next after Government; 2nd, tenure holders or persons who have interests carved out of the melvaram; 3rd, the ryot proper or the possessor of the kudivaram right; and 4th, sub-ryots or persons holding under ryots interests carved out of the kudivaram. The second and fourth classes do not require any specific protection, and their rights may be left to be defined by contracts and the operation of the general law of prescription, there being no presumption in their case according to the common law in regard to acquisition of permanent occupancy rights, except by grant or prescription. What the proposed law has to do is to define the relations of ryots proper to the melvaramdar immediately above them. The provisions to be made in their case are these :—

I. *As regards fixity of tenure.* (i) All lands to be presumed to be ryoti unless the contrary is shown; (ii) continuous possession as tenant of land, for 12 years, originally private, to convert it to ryoti land; (iii) all occupants of ryoti land to be considered to have permanent occupancy right in it; (iv) no occupant of ryoti land to be evicted except by a decree of court; (v) waste lands to be granted by the melvaramdar to the resident ryots in the first instance and failing them to strangers, on ryoti tenure on terms applicable to lands of similar description and quality in the village; (vi) ryots and melvaramdars to be entitled to apply to the Collector for a measurement of the holdings and determination of the classification of lands as ryoti or private; (vii) the melvaramdar to be entitled to apply to the court for permission to enclose waste land and add it to private land for the purpose of forming plantations, or growing jungles, and the application to be granted after giving notice to the ryots and hearing their objections in the manner provided in the Forest Conservancy Act, and making sufficient allowance for *bonâ fide* increase of cultivation and pasturage requirements of the ryots; (viii) Government to have power to order the survey of any estate whenever this may be deemed necessary in the interests of public peace, to determine once for all what lands are *ryoti* and what *private ;* the cost to be charged to the melvaramdar and the ryots in defined proportions determined by the Collector with reference to the relative values of the interests of the melvaramdar and the ryots in the lands, and payable in instalments not exceeding 10 per cent. of the rent payable to the Zemindar; (ix) in private lands, the melvaramdar's rights to be governed by the ordinary laws of property and contract.

II. *As regards enhancement of rents and right to make improvements.* (i) Occupants of ryoti land not to be compelled to pay more than the customary rate of rent whether in money, grain or share of the crop, and not more than a "fair and equitable" rent in any case, *i.e.*, a rent which leaves to the ryot enough to reimburse him for the cost of labour and cultivation together with a fair farming profit; (ii) the rent paid during the last 3 years to be considered "fair and equitable" unless the contrary be shown; (iii) the occupant of ryoti land to be at liberty to adopt any mode of cultivation he thinks fit, provided he pays a rent determined with reference to the *standard* crop of the village; (iv) he is to have the prior right to make permanent improvement to the land, and failing him, the melvaramdar is to have the right; (v) where the value of a ryoti holding becomes enhanced by the ryot's improvement he is to have the whole benefit of it; (vi) where the value becomes enhanced by the melvaramdar's improvement, the melvaramdar is to have the whole benefit, due allowance being made for any increase of cost of cultivation and for fair profit on such cost; (vii) where the increased value of the holding is due to water supplied by Government and the charge for water is directly paid by the ryot, the latter is to have the whole benefit; and if the Zemindar undertakes to pay for the water, the additional charge leviable from the ryot to be fixed under general rules as regards the collection of water rate fixed by Government; (viii) where there is an increase in the productive powers of land by natural causes, increased agricultural skill and knowledge, discovery of cheap chemical manures, &c., the benefit is to be enjoyed by the ryot; (ix) when there is an increase in the money value of the holding due to enhanced prices of standard produce, the melvaramdar is to be entitled to claim additional rent not exceeding two-thirds of the proportionate increase in the rent, the remaining third being intended to defray the increased cost of cultivation, &c., due to increased price of produce; (x) enhancement by voluntary agreement not to exceed 2 annas in the rupee or 12½ per cent., whether in money or grain, the agreement to be in writing and registered; (xi) rent once enhanced by voluntary agreement or decree of court not to be liable to be enhanced again for 15 years; (xii) the court to be authorized to decree that increased rent to which the melvaramdar is entitled shall be imposed by gradual increments to prevent hardship to the ryot; (xiii) the ryot to be allowed abatement of rent for deficiency in the area of holding and also for loss of produce by natural causes in cases in which he is entitled to remission according to usage; (xiv) melvaramdar or the ryot to be entitled to apply to the court for the conversion of grain rents into money-rents; (xv) Government to frame rules and make arrangements for fixing the standard produce with reference to which rent is to be regulated and for periodical publication of lists of prices of produce, and (xvi) the above provisions not to apply to "private lands" of the melvaramdar.

III. *As regards the right to transfer or sub-let holdings.* (i) Right of transfer to be freely allowed to occupant of ryoti land, but the Zemindar to have a prior lien on the land transferred for unpaid balance of rent next after Government revenue, the balance, however, exceeding 3 years' rent not being enforceable against the land. Tenants of private land not to have any transferable right; (ii) sub-letting not to be allowed for more than 9 years at a time; (iii) melvaramdars to maintain a register of ryots paying rent to them and to register transfers of holdings by decree of Court or private contract, the transferor to continue liable for rent till the transfer is registered.

IV. *As regards the remedies to be provided for the recovery of rents.* (i) Landlord to be authorized to proceed under the special law for the recovery of rent only in cases in which he has tendered a puttah to the tenant such as the latter is bound to accept; (ii) the landlord's right to distrain to be limited to ungathered products or gathered products stored on the farm or the threshing-floor; (iii) an occupancy ryot not to be ejected for non-payment of rent but his interest in the land to be sold, the sale being free of encumbrances on the kudivaram right, not created with the landlord's consent; (iv) a tenant of private land to be liable to ejectment; (v) Government to be empowered to invest any officer of Government with the powers of a court under the special law.

V. *As regards the duties of landlords.* (i) Landlord not to levy any unauthorized cesses or dues in money or labor beyond what may be specified in the puttah; (ii) landlord to keep irrigation works in order and liability to be enforced on complaints from ryots by carrying out the necessary repairs and levying the cost from him; (iii) village establishments within the landlord's estate to be maintained in a state of efficiency.

(7) *Extract from Sir Henry Maine's speech on the Panjab Tenancy Bill before the Legislative Council of India in October* 1868.

As regards the hardship of requiring strict proof in a court of justice of the existence of customary rights and privileges under conditions which preclude settled authority and regular government, and the necessity for inferring the existence of such rights and customs from the facts ascertained as regards whole tracts of country, and not in individual cases, the following extracts from Sir Henry Maine's speech on the Panjab Tenancy Bill before the Legislative Council of India in October 1868 may be usefully consulted.

"Property in land which had little or no value before annexation (of the Panjab) has now a very great and distinct value, and the real struggle obviously is whether, in the case of occupancy tenants, the new profits shall be divided between them and the landlords, or shall wholly go to the landlords. The position, therefore, of the two parties to this contention in the Settlement Courts was this: on the one side, you had very ignorant men, asked very difficult questions as to indistinct ideas of old date. On the other, you had witnesses, a shade better educated, more thoroughly aware of the matter in hand, but under the strongest temptation to adapt their testimony to their interests. . . . .

"I observe, for example, that in a great number of cases the persons under examination, whether landlords, tenants or witnesses, were asked whether a particular person had a right to do a particular thing, and the point was frequently put for decision to the committees who acted as referees. I do not mean to say that the word 'right' was invariably used, but the questions constantly implied the notion of a right, or some shade of it. Now, every body who has paid even a superficial attention to the subject is aware that there is no more ambiguous term than 'right,' and no idea less definite. I do not suppose that in the Oriental *patois* in which the questions were asked, the word is less equivocal than in the cultivated European languages, and yet in Europe it is only the strictest and severest jurists who speak of rights with accuracy. *Primâ facie*, when you ask whether a class had rights of a particular kind, you mean *legal* rights; but *legal* rights imply a regular administration of fixed laws, and there was confessedly no such administration under Sikh rule. Yet I find Settlement Officers enquiring about rights of eviction or enhancement, without explaining (and apparently without being conscious of the need of explaining) whether the rights in question were of the nature of *legal* rights, or whether *moral* rights were meant, or whether what was intended was merely the physical power of the stronger to do what he pleased with the weaker. And these difficult and ambiguous questions—questions which in reality sometimes involved highly refined abstractions—questions which I do not hesitate to say that, even if I had been cognizant of the facts, I could not myself have answered without fuller elucidation of their meaning—were put to ignorant and uneducated men, to men, therefore, who, like all ignorant men, are capable only of thinking in the concrete and in connection with actual facts, and were put, moreover, with reference to a state of facts which ceased to exist twenty years ago. Perhaps, Sir, it may be said that the rights about which enquiry was made were customary rights—rights arising under a custom. But here, so far from having my ideas cleared, I find myself in greater difficulties than ever. For it appears to me, that in the papers relating to the recent Panjab Settlement, the word 'custom' is used in a sense certainly unknown to jurisprudence, and I believe also, to popular usage. A custom is constantly spoken of, as if it were independent of that which is generally, if not universally, considered to be the foundation of a custom. According to the understanding of lawyers, and I should have said according to the understanding of all men, barbarous or civilized, the foundation of a custom is habitual practice, a series of facts, a succession of instances, from whose constant recurrence a rule is inferred. But the writers of these papers perpetually talk of customs of eviction, or of enhancement, or of rack-rent, and in the same breath admit the non-existence of any practice of the kind alleged. Some broadly state that there never was an instance of the customary right being exercised; nearly all allow that its exercise was as rare as possible, nor do they attempt to show that the rare instances of its exercise were not simple acts of violence. . . . . . I do not pretend to have an exhaustive acquaintance with the voluminous literature of Indian revenue settlements; but I know something of it, and I think I can see that the old investigators of Native customs proceeded on a mode of enquiry which is perfectly intelligible. They enquired for the most part into practices and into facts, not into vague opinions. They inferred a rule from the facts they believed themselves to have discovered, and then they stereotyped it. No doubt they may have made mistakes. They may have generalised too rapidly, may have neglected local exceptions, and may have made a usage universal which was only general or even occasional."

N.B.—The occasion for the above speech was the following: Soon after the Panjab was annexed, there was a revenue settlement of the Province and in the course of it, large numbers of tenants were, after enquiry, declared to possess permanent occupancy rights. Twenty years later, there was a revision of settlement, in which it was alleged that a mistake was committed in declaring the tenants to have occupancy rights, and that further enquiry showed that they were merely tenants-at-will, and it was proposed that those who had been recognized as permanent tenants should be transferred to the latter class. Sir Henry Maine protested against the injustice of the proposal and pointed out that the results of the earlier enquiry were likely to be more correct than those of the later.

(8) *Extract from Sir Frederick Pollock's "English Land Laws."*

As regards the successive steps by which "common land," held as separate property not by individuals but by communities, became saleable and marketable property, Sir Frederick Pollock remarks in his "English Land Laws" as follows :

"In old times it could not be disposed of by the holder, but a custom gradually arose of alienating it by will, and perhaps by purchase, within the limits of the family. Freedom of alienation became greater as the bonds of the village community or township and of the family were loosened. The order of the steps would be of this kind :—First, no alienation but only inheritance; then, alienation within the family, but with the consent of the possible heirs as well as the community; lastly, the consent of the community would become a mere form. Where a lord of the manor had acquired the powers of the community, he probably acquired among them the veto on alienation which in historic times he certainly possessed. In this later shape also, the restriction became a formality, but not an empty one. The lord's consent to alienation could not be refused if the accustomed dues and fines were paid."

The steps in the transition of common to individual property have been the same in India, except that freedom of bequest is an idea quite foreign to Hindu law and has come into existence within a very recent period.

As regards the English "copy-holder," Sir F. Pollock states that he is a tenant of a manor, who is said to hold his tenement "at the will of the lord according to the custom of the manor." This means that the tenant's rights are nominally dependent upon the will of the lord; but the lord is bound to exercise his will according to the custom, so that the tenant is really as safe as if he were an absolute owner. The tenant's title is evidenced by the records of the lord's court. The tenant cannot cut timber or open mines, and he has to pay a heriot on succession,—give the best beast or the best chattel.

As regards the origin of the copy-hold tenure Sir F. Pollock observes "Blackstone's account is 'copy-holders are in truth no other than villeins, who by a long series of encroachments on the lord have at last established a customary right to those estates which were held absolutely at the lord's will.' It would be nearer the truth to say that by a long series of encroachments and fictions the lords and lawyers acting in the interest of the lords got people to believe that the lord's will was the origin of those ancient customary rights which before were absolute."

The following is the account given of the manner in which the English law of landlord and tenant was developed :—

"The truth is, and it may as well be stated at this point, that the law of landlord and tenant has never, at least under any usual conditions, been a law of free contract. It is a law of contract partly express, partly supplied by judicial interpretation, and partly controlled by legislation, and sometimes by local custom. So far as the terms and conditions are express, they are in the vast majority of cases framed by the landlords or their advisers. The tendency of judicial interpretation has also been, until lately, to incline the scale of presumption in favor of the landlord on doubtful points; and the same may be said of the ruling tendency of legislation down to the middle of the present century. The allowance of local customs, which might have done much to redress the balance if taken up betimes, depends on the tendency of the judges. When special customs were looked on as a kind of natural enemies of the common law, and strict proof of them was required, they got little help in court. Probably many tenants in past times failed to establish customary rights, or have been discouraged by the failure of others from asserting them, in cases where the decision would now be the other way."

As regards the rights of the lord of the manor to the waste, Sir F. Pollock says, "the waste of the manor is, in modern legal theory, so much of the lord's land as his predecessors have not found it worth while to take into cultivation on their own account or to let out to tenants." The tenants enjoyed various privileges over these lands, and these liberties have ripened into rights. This theory reverses the facts, but not without some qualifications. "A great many of the manors, now or formerly existing, represent ancient communities in which, little by little, the authority of the community was engrossed by the most considerable man in it, until he became the lord and the other landholders became his dependents. But a manor might also be formed without going through the earlier stages at all. Free dependents and emancipated serfs might gather round a lord until they formed a community comparable in size to the old free township. Under such conditions we should expect usages to spring up imitated from those of the old communities, and modelled as far as possible on them; but these usages would, in such a case, really owe their force to the permission and consent of the lord, as they were feigned to do by the theory of the lawyers in the case where the lord was only an overgrown member of the township. Thus we have a possible class of cases in which the theory to some extent answers to the real facts."

(9) *Note on the discussions in the Madras Presidency as regards the preferential rights of Mirasidars and resident ryots to cultivate waste lands in their villages as against strangers and the final settlement of the question.*

Mirasi claims were cropping up continually in the first half of the century and produced quite a literature of their own which will be found collected in Mr. Huddleston's compilation, entitled "Papers on Mirasi Right." These claims were troublesome to deal with for several reasons. In the first place, the traditional feelings of the early English administrators, derived from the state of landed property in their own country, was opposed to the recognition of such claims, incompatible as they seemed with the right of Government to claim a large share of the produce of land, which was denominated *rent* and which entitled it, according to English notions, to be regarded as the absolute proprietor of land. There was much also in the state of the country to favor such an impression. These Mirasi claims were of a pronounced type only in a few districts and in others, they were vague and undefined, and in some to all appearance, hardly a trace of them had been left. In some of the southern districts, notably in Chingleput and Tanjore, the Mirasi right was in full operation; in several other districts it was in various stages of decay, although a traditional feeling in regard to it still existed; in others again, especially in the Northern Circars, even this traditional feeling had become effaced. Wherever by previous mis-government and heavy assessments, land had lost all saleable value and the greater portion of arable land was out of cultivation, and the efforts of the officers of Government were directed towards saddling the ryots with more land than they could cultivate, as was the case under the Dittam system in the dry districts, Mirasi rights would rather be a burden than a privilege; and the longer this state of things continued the less would be the chance of the ryots asserting their rights. In the few favorably circumstanced districts in which land had some saleable value, these rights would be clung to with great tenacity. This was exactly what happened. The result was two schools of writers on Indian land tenures, one asserting that land was the property of Government and the ryots merely cultivating tenants, and the other, that the ryots were proprietors of the land they cultivated. The Government of the day was called upon to decide between these two conflicting theories and a discussion was kept up for nearly 40 years. There was one incident of the Mirasi tenure which almost all engaged in the discussion were unwilling to admit (viz., the absolute right of the Mirasidars to waste lands), as being inconsistent with the right of Government to levy its share of the crop as revenue. The Mirasidars claimed the right to keep the waste lands uncultivated themselves and to prevent Government from finding other ryots to cultivate them. Such a right, in the interests of revenue and of the general public, the Government could not acknowledge. The Government was willing, however, to acknowledge the right of the Mirasidars to hold the lands they cultivated so long as they paid the assessment; nay more, it was willing to concede the same right even to new cultivators and it reduced the heavy assessments wherever it was necessary to create a substantial interest for the ryot in the soil. As regards waste lands whenever there was any demand for them it was willing to acknowledge the rights of the Mirasidars so far as to give them the refusal, before granting them to strangers, but in this respect it would treat the old Mirasidars and the new puttadars in the same way. Government recognized mirasi rights only to this extent, but if the Mirasidars had any further rights they were to establish them before the judicial tribunals. In the language of the Board of that day, by this decision the question of Mirasi rights was "set at rest." The following quotations from "Papers on Mirasi Right" establish this position:—

In their Despatch, dated 28th July 1841, the Court of Directors stated that "without entering upon a discussion of the respective rights of Government and the Mirasidars over the waste lands (a point still under the consideration of the superior tribunal to which the case has been appealed), it will be enough for us to state our opinion that it is desirable that in all cases where Payacarries propose to cultivate the waste lands of a Mirasi village, their proposal should be in the first instance communicated to the Mirasidars, to whom, in the event of their being willing to cultivate, or to give security for the revenue assessable on the land, the preference should be given. We consider that the Government has a clear right to the revenue to be derived from the conversion of waste lands into arable, but we, at the same time, think it preferable that this object should be obtained, whenever practicable, without the intrusion of strangers into the village community."

In their Proceedings, 11th November 1841, the Board remarked as follows :—" Under this view of the case, it is not considered *expedient* to raise abstract questions of the extent of the Mirasidars' rights in regard to the village waste. No opinion on these points would be binding upon any court of law in which the questions might be mooted by parties dissatisfied with the *dictum* of the Revenue authorities, and it seems quite unnecessary to raise the question with a view to its solution by the highest legal authorities, unless it could be shown that under the existing practice the interests of Government are compromised or injured.

" Mr. Kindersley's first question is whether in default of means or desire of Mirasidars to exercise their right of cultivating the waste, their consent is necessary before the Government can grant the land for cultivation to a stranger. To this the Board can only reply, that it is the custom generally to give the option of occupation to the Mirasidars and to the *kadeem ryot* where no Mirasi exists, in preference to a stranger. It matters not what the law may be on this point; much of the revenue practice is founded on custom, and the practice is both, the Board believe, favorable to Government and in accordance with the feelings and sentiments of the people.

" The second question is to the effect whether the offer of strangers can be accepted by Government if more favorable than that of the Mirasidars ? To this the Board answer, *most unquestionably it cannot.* The admission of such a practice would virtually set aside the prescribed remission of assessment on the redemption of waste existing in every Province.

" The Board cannot conceive a case in which the interests of Government can suffer materially by the continuance of the system that now prevails. If the Mirasidars can, by themselves or through others, undertake the cultivation of all the reclaimable lands of their village and pay the established dues of Government, no loss is sustained by the State. If they cannot do this or if they neglect to do it, then the rule is to give the land as well as the Toondoovarum thereon to any stranger who chooses to undertake it. Thus the right of Government which is *simply the right to claim the authorized assessment* is abundantly protected.

" The only possible profit or advantage that Government could derive in assuming the right to dispose of waste land for cultivation without reference to the Mirasidars or ancient cultivators would consist in the sums they might derive, over and above the legitimate annual land-tax, by selling to the best advantage the right of occupancy, as the ryots now do in some instances. The assertion of such a right, *even if it was upheld by judicial decision*, would lead, it is believed, to much *discontent* and *dissatisfaction*, and be powerless in the main as a means of raising revenue."

In the Despatch of the Court of Directors, dated 3rd July 1844, they remarked " from the perusal of the decree of the Provincial Court, it appears to us that that tribunal has declared the law to be in accordance with what, in para. 55 of our Despatch, dated 28th July 1841, we desired might be generally adopted in practice in similar cases, viz., that when proposals were made by Porakudi ryots for waste lands in

Mirasi villages, they should, in the first instance, be communicated to the Mirasidars, to whom in the event of their being willing to cultivate or to give security for the revenue assessable on the lands, the preference should be given.

"In the case which has now been brought under discussion, this course was not adopted by the Collector, and it would appear that the question still remains undecided, whether Government possesses the right, in the event of the Mirasidars refusing to cultivate or to give security for the revenue, to alienate waste lands in Mirasi villages to Porakudi cultivators either for a term or in perpetuity. We trust, however, that *on all occasions care will be taken that the just rights of the Mirasidars shall be respected.*"

In G.O., dated 1st March 1849, Government said, "The Right Honorable the Governor in Council has only to observe, in reference to the foregoing Proceedings of the Board of Revenue, that the principle which the Honorable the Court have laid down for the guidance of this Government, in the disposal of waste lands, is, that the ryots of the village in which the waste land is situated should invariably have the option of holding it for cultivation on certain terms. If they refuse, the Collector is justified in giving such land to strangers."

The Court of Directors in their Despatch, dated 17th December 1856, remarked as follows :—

"In para. 27 you have referred to the rights of Mirasidars over the waste lands of their villages, and you observe that 'under moderate assessment' land 'will become valuable, the rightful holders will occupy it themselves, sub-letting it or part of it, and will no longer quietly submit to its being given away to those who have no rightful interest in it.'

"The question involved in this para. is one of very considerable importance and it would appear that you now propose to deal with it in a manner at variance with the practice which has hitherto prevailed. We desire that in the disposal of waste land you will be guided by the principles laid down in para. 55 of our Despatch of the 28th July 1841, 3rd July 1844, &c.

"We see no reason to change the opinions respecting the rights of Mirasidars which we entertained when these paras. were written. Whenever, as in Tanjore, any remains of Mirasi right have survived to the present time and have actual existence, we do not desire that it should be interfered with, but where, as in the greater portion of your Presidency, it has fallen into desuetude, and has only been known in name ever since we have obtained possession of the country, we think that it would be unwise and inexpedient to make any attempt for its revival.

"When applications for waste land are made by strangers, they should be communicated to the resident ryots of the village, whether claiming to be Mirasidars *or not*, and the option should be given to them of engaging for it, finding security for the payment of the assessment. Should they or any of them think fit to do so, they would of course be at liberty either to cultivate the land themselves or sub-let it; but the payment should be strictly enforced, in order, on the one hand, to prevent transactions in the nature of land jobbing, and on the other, to deter the villagers from engaging for land merely for the purpose of excluding others who might be desirous of holding it direct from Government, but who objected to take it as their sub-tenants. In cases where the resident ryots should refuse to engage for the waste lands of their village, Government may exercise the right of granting them to the persons applying, who would then hold the same position and possess the same rights in all respects as the other ryots of the village."

In G.O., 5th June 1857, Government remarked "we apprehend that the views on this subject recorded by Sir Thomas Munro would be generally acceded to, viz., that Mirasidars had no rights over lands reclaimed by others without their agency, and that their rights in regard to immemorial waste were good against strange ryots but not against the Government; and it was the established rule, prescribed by your Honorable Court, that waste land in a village was not to be given to a stranger until it was first offered to and refused by the *resident ryots* or Mirasidars."

The Board in their Proceedings, dated 15th July 1857, observed as follows:—"The Board trust that as regards the provinces, *the question is now so far set at rest* by the decision of the Court of Directors, as to guide the Revenue officers and that when the old residents of a village, whether they call themselves Mirasidars *or not*, decline to cultivate (or else pay for) waste land, the usual puttahs may be given to durkhastdars without forcing them to become sub-tenants of the old residents, and that the influence which the so-called Mirasidars have hitherto exercised in keeping much land out of the occupation of others though not occupying themselves, may be put an end to."

The above extracts make it clear that the Court of Directors told the ryots somewhat as follows:—

"You claim a lot of things under the description of Mirasi rights. We cannot find out what they exactly are and how far you are justly entitled to them. There is one thing we gladly recognise; it is your right to hold the land you cultivate. There is another thing also we will concede; it is that whenever we receive an offer to cultivate waste land in your village, we will give you the option of taking it up yourselves, should you be willing to do so. We mean to concede this right not only to you who call themselves Mirasidars, but to ryots of all descriptions, for we do not know what your mirasi means, and we are not going to be bothered with any further discussions on that subject. We wish to see all puttadars, whether belonging to the class of ancient Mirasidars or recently created, placed on an equal footing so far as it is in our power to do so; and certainly the preferential right which we wish to give them is not only in accordance with long standing custom but also public policy. You must clearly understand that we will not indulge your dog-in-the-manger spirit of neither cultivating the waste lands yourselves nor allowing strangers to cultivate them, thus preventing extension of cultivation and increase of our revenue. If you think you can establish such a right you may do so before the Court of Justice."

This is no doubt a rough and ready solution of a much vexed question, but it has been acted upon and acquiesced in for the last 30 years and has now become a part of the common law of the country, even if it was not so before. The rule was passed in the spirit of compromise allowing to Mirasidars such rights as they possessed if they were found not to be inconsistent with good policy, and the same policy required that all puttadars should be treated alike to put an end to interminable disputes as to whether a puttadar was an ancient occupant or a Payacari. The well-known work of Sir Henry Maine on Village Communities has established the fact that throughout the whole of India, and probably throughout the whole of the ancient world, property in land was vested in village communities whose rights extended not only to cultivated lands, but also to the waste lands of the village, and customs and forms of property derived from this tenure survive to this day in the greater part of India. Regarding waste lands Sir H. Maine writes as follows:—"The waste or common land of the village community has still to be considered. One point of difference between the view taken of it in the East and that which at all times seems to have been taken in Europe deserves to be specially noted. The members of the Teutonic community appear to have valued the village waste chiefly as pasture for their cattle, and possibly may have found it so profitable for this purpose as to have deliberately refrained from increasing that cultivated portion of it which had been turned into the arable mark. These rights of pasture vested in the commoners are those, I need scarcely tell you, which have descended but little modified to our own day in our own country; and it is only the modern improvements in the methods of agriculture which have disturbed the balance between pasture and tillage, and have thus tended to multiply Inclosure acts. But the vast bulk of the natives of India are a grain and not a flesh eating people. Cattle are mostly regarded by them as auxiliary to tillage. The view, therefore, generally taken (as I am told) of the common-land by the community is that it is that part of village domain which is temporarily uncultivated, but which will some time or other be cultivated and merge in the arable mark. Doubtless it is valued for pasture, but it is more especially valued as potentially capable of tillage. The effect is to produce in the community a much stronger sense of property in common-land than at all reflects the vaguer feeling of right which, in England at all events, characterises the commoners. In the later days of the East India Company, when all its acts and omissions were very bitterly criticised, and amid the general re-opening of Indian questions after the military insurrection of 1857, much stress was laid on the great amount of waste land which official returns showed to exist in India, and it was more than hinted that better government would bring these wastes under cultivation, possibly under cotton cultivation, and even plant them with English colonists. The answer of experienced Indian functionaries was that there was *no* waste land at all in India. If you except certain territories which stand to India Proper much as the tracts of land at the base of the Rocky Mountains stand to the United States—as for example, the Indo-Chinese province of Assam—the reply is substantially correct. The so-called waste lands are part of the domain of the various communities which the villagers, theoretically, are only waiting opportunity to bring under cultivation. Yet this controversy elicited an admission which is of some historical interest. It did appear that, though the Native Indian Government had for the most part left the village communities entirely to themselves on condition of their paying the revenue assessed upon them, they nevertheless sometimes claimed (though in a vague and occasional way) some exceptional authority over the wastes; and acting on this precedent, the British Government, at the various settlements of land revenue, has not seldom interfered to reduce excessive wastes and to re-apportion uncultivated land among the various communities of a district."

This extract makes it clear that the waste lands are not unreservedly at the disposal of Government. They in the first instance belong to the ryots in common, but the State occasionally interferes for the protection of its rights. In the present case, it has done so by ruling that the land will be given away to a stranger if the resident villages are not willing to cultivate it.

The passages quoted from Sir H. Maine's work are almost identical with G.O., dated 27th May 1856, No. 667, in which it is stated :—"The waste land in this country in the villages of the plains at least is certainly not the property of Government or the State in the absolute sense in which the unoccupied land in the United States and some of the British Colonies is so. The village communities claim an interest in it and that interest has been universally admitted though not accurately defined. To put up the waste to sale, entirely ignoring that prior right of the village communities, would be to introduce a totally new practice; and *it would certainly be regarded by the common feeling of the country as an invasion of existing rights.*"

In former times, if the Government thought that waste lands remained uncultivated through the fault or negligence of those entitled to cultivate them, the offending parties would have been coerced to do their duty. Menu says "If land be injured by the fault of the farmer himself, as if he fails to sow it in due time, he shall be fined ten times the king's share of the crop, that might otherwise have been raised; but only five times as much if it was the fault of his servants without his knowledge." Under the present *régime* of personal freedom, the coercive power which can no longer be applied is transmuted into a power to declare the right to cultivate the lands forfeited, when an offer is made by a stranger to cultivate such lands, and the Mirasidars after due notice are unwilling to cultivate them and pay the revenue assessed thereon.

(10) *Extract from the speech of the Honourable Mr. Ilbert in the Legislative Council of India on the Bengal Tenancy Bill in* 1885.

"The Bengal ryot is not the same thing as the English farmer; he is something widely different from him. But he presents many curious and instructive points of resemblance to the English customary tenant of some six or seven centuries ago. The rights and powers claimed by the Zemindar are not unlike those once claimed by the feudal lord of the manor; the privileges, duties, liabilities of the ryot resemble in some important particulars those which once belonged to the English customary tenant and which were gradually developed into the status either of the free-holder or copy-holder. In the phrase which is still technically applied to the English copy-holder, viz., that he holds 'at the will of the lord according to the custom of the manor,' we discern echoes of the controversies which once raged round the customary tenant of the English manor and which still rage round the position of the Bengal ryot—controversies in which the assertion of high proprietary rights on the part of the landlord is set against the assertion of strong customary privileges on the part of the tenant. If we were to pursue the investigation further we should find equally suggestive analogies. The bewildering multitude of tenures with local variations of nomenclature and incidents finds its parallel in the multitude of subordinate interests in land which are recorded in the Domesday Survey, the English record of rights in the 11th century. Again it is well known that there is no point in English legal history which is more obscure than the question of extent to which and the circumstances under which alienation of land was legally recognised and actually took place before the 13th century. But in the midst of this obscurity, one fact is clearly established, viz., that such alienation as took place assumed the form not of sale but of subinfeudation or sub-letting, and the extent to which this sub-letting was carried was distasteful to the superior lords. We know that at the instance of the great lords a famous statute was passed to stop sub-letting; we know that while the intention of the statute was to stop sub-letting, its effect was to legalize free sale, that it enabled the fee simple tenant to alienate his interest without consulting his lord and that it has since become the foundation of modern English law of the sale of land. If there had been a Hansard in the days when the statute "Quia Emptores" became law, he might perhaps have supplied us with additional arguments for and against the comparative merits and demerits of sub-letting and free sale.

"However, I do not intend to weary the Council with any elaborate historical disquisition. My object in touching on these analogies between the past and the present is not to demonstrate—what has been demonstrated to satiety—that the application of the modern English landlord and tenant law to the relation of Zemindar and Ryot would be both an anachronism and a political blunder; but also to illustrate some of the exceptional difficulties which surround any attempt either to declare or to amend the law bearing on those relations. For to say that the Bengal ryot is still living in an age which to us Englishmen has become an age of the past is to present only one side of the picture; there is another side to it. Side by side with the landlord who exercises, and is content to exercise, his old customary rights so far as they are compatible with the modern system of Government, we have the auction purchaser who has bought his rights as a commercial speculation, and thinks only how he can turn them to the best advantage. Side by side with the hereditary tenant, cultivating and living on his land, we have the enterprizing planter who has got his lease and wishes to work it so as to extract from the land the greatest possible profit in the smallest possible time. The modern theory of competitive rents is jostling the old practice of customary rates; the new fashion of terminable leases is threatening to displace ancient occupancy rights. The 13th century is being brought face to face with the 19th and is striving with more or less success to understand and accommodate itself to its ways. The cultivator for subsistence is giving way before or developing into cultivator for profit; those who have walked in the dim twilight of custom are emerging into the hard and fierce glare of law as administerd by the Courts. The ideas, habits and customs of widely different ages and widely different civilizations are being thrown into a common crucible and are assuming new and strange forms. We cannot arrest this process of change; we cannot predict with certainty the rate at which it will progress or the direction which it will take if left to itself. All that we can do is to endeavour by such means as are at our disposal to guide it in the right direction, to ease off the abruptness of the transition from the old to the new, from an age of feudalism to an age of industrialism; to bridge over the gulf between status and contract, to prevent custom from being too violently ousted by competition; to see that rules based on commercial transactions between hard and keen men of business are not applied to the ignorant and unlettered peasant, when he is unable to understand them or to use them.

"Can we afford to stand aside and let things drift, trusting that they may somehow come out right in the end? Such may be a policy which would commend itself to some of the influential classes in the country, to men of the strong hand and the long purse; but such is not the policy which the British Government has ever ventured or ever can venture to adopt; such is not our conception of the duty which we owe to the millions whom Providence has confided to our care. We are responsible for the introduction into this country of forces, which threaten to revolutionize its social and economical system; we cannot fold our hands and let them work in accordance with nature's blind laws. We must, to the best of our ability, endeavour to regulate and control their operations, and in so doing it is inevitable that we should occasionally interfere in a manner and to an extent which, to those whose institutions have not for long ages undergone the strain imposed by foreign conquest or foreign immigration, may not unnaturally appear difficult to justify or explain.

"That in so doing we should be charged with ignoring or violating the laws of political economy is a matter of course. We do not violate or ignore those laws; on the contrary, the whole of our action as a State in legislation of this kind is based on a recognition and appreciation of the laws which regulate the production and distribution of wealth, just as the whole of our action as a State in dealing with famine is based on the recognition and appreciation of the laws, so far as they are discoverable, which regulate the occurrence of famines. We do not ignore these laws; but we proceed on the view that their operation is capable of being modified and controlled by human action.

"Assuming, then, that interference is justifiable and necessary, what kind of interference is possible and expedient; what kind of legislation is suitable to the circumstances with which we have to deal? Must we not admit, are we not always being compelled to admit, that it is a legislation of opportunism? For a transitional period final legislation is neither appropriate nor possible. What we have to do is to establish a *modus vivendi*, a working arrangement not merely between conflicting interests but between the customs, habits, ideas and ways of different ages and different forms of civilization. Our legislation must contain much that is in the nature of expedients, adjustments, compromises; it will inevitably contain provisions which will be to political economists a stumbling block, and to lawyers—I will say even to law-lords—foolishness—but which for all that may be based on good, sound common sense."

(C).—Agricultural Indebtedness, its causes and remedies.

(1) *Statement showing the classification of mortgages of immovable property registered in the year* 1891 *in the Madras Presidency according to the periods for which they run.*

Term of mortgage.	Simple mortgages.						Mortgages with possession.						Total number of mortgages.					
	Less than Rs. 100		Rs. 100 and upwards.		Total.		Less than Rs. 100.		Rs. 100 and upwards.		Total.		Less than Rs. 100.		Rs. 100 and upwards.		Total.	
	No.	Percentage.	No.	Percentage.	No.	Percentage.	No.	Percentage.	No.	Percentage.	No.	Percentage.	No.	Percentage.	No.	Percentage.	No.	Percentage.
No term	18,646	18·1	17,473	14·9	36,119	16·4	5,549	9·8	4,245	9·3	9,794	9·6	24,195	15·2	21,718	13·3	45,913	14·1
One year or less ...	45,905	44·6	42,864	36·5	88,769	40·3	4,757	8·6	4,057	8·9	8,814	8·7	50,662	31·9	46,921	28·8	97,583	30·3
Between 1 and 2 years.	15,954	15·5	19,063	16·3	35,017	15·9	4,286	7·6	3,216	7·0	7,502	7·4	20,240	12·7	22,279	13·7	42,519	13·2
„ 2 and 3 do.	10,955	10·6	15,163	12·9	26,118	12·0	10,916	19·8	8,172	17·9	19,088	18·7	21,871	13·8	23,335	14·3	45,206	14·1
„ 3 and 4 do.	3,734	3·6	7,340	6·3	11,074	5·0	4,061	7·2	3,841	8·4	7,902	7·8	7,795	4·9	11,181	6·9	18,976	5·9
„ 4 and 5 do.	2,545	2·5	5,464	4·7	8,009	3·6	5,290	9·4	5,273	11·5	10,563	10·3	7,835	4·9	10,737	6·6	18,572	5·8
„ 5 and 6 do.	894	0·9	2,238	1·9	3,132	1·4	2,452	4·3	2,396	5·2	4,848	4·8	3,346	2·1	4,634	2·8	7,980	2·5
„ 6 and 7 do.	388	0·4	1,140	1·0	1,528	0·7	2,049	3·6	1,872	4·1	3,921	3·9	2,437	1·5	3,012	1·8	5,449	1·7
„ 7 and 8 do.	303	0·3	970	0·8	1,273	0·6	756	1·3	723	1·6	1,479	1·4	1,059	0·7	1,693	1·0	2,752	0·8
„ 8 and 9 do.	217	0·2	575	0·5	792	0·3	805	1·4	877	1·9	1,682	1·7	1,022	0·6	1,452	0·9	2,474	0·8
„ 9 and 10 do.	274	0·3	884	0·7	1,158	0·5	1,517	2·7	1,387	3·0	2,904	2·8	1,791	1·1	2,271	1·4	4,062	1·2
„ 10 and 11 do.	135	0·1	354	0·3	489	0·2	695	1·2	674	1·5	1,369	1·4	830	0·5	1,028	0·6	1,858	0·6
„ 11 and 12 do.	438	0·4	566	0·5	1,004	0·5	7,499	13·3	3,907	8·6	11,406	11·2	7,937	5·0	4,473	2·8	12,410	3·9
Twelve years and above	2,586	2·5	3,165	2·7	5,751	2·6	5,489	9·8	5,089	11·1	10,578	10·3	8,075	5·1	8,254	5·1	16,329	5·1
Total ...	102,974	100	117,259	100	220,233	100	56,121	100	45,729	100	101,850	100	159,095	100	162,988	100	322,083	100

(2) *Statement showing the classification of lenders, the purposes of loans, and the rates of interest charged on loans compiled from deeds of mortgage of immovable property without possession and from simple bonds registered in* 1889, 1890 *and* 1891 *in the districts of Kistna, Nellore, Cuddapah, Kurnool, Bellary, and Anantapur, North Arcot, South Arcot, Coimbatore and Tinnevelly.*

Items.	Number of mortgages of Rs. 100 and upwards.				Number of mortgages of less than Rs. 100.			Simple bonds.	Percentage.			
	Rs. 100—500.	Rs. 501—1,000.	Over Rs. 1,000.	Total.	Rs. 1—50.	Rs. 51—99.	Total.		Mortgage Rs. 100 and above.	Mortgages below Rs. 100.	Simple bonds.	All transactions.
Profession of lenders—												
Agriculturists	19,177	1,538	441	21,156	13,508	6,846	20,354	8,140	61	65	64	63
Non-agriculturists	10,453	1,014	334	11,801	6,076	3,686	9,762	4,106	34	31	32	32
Ryots combining other professions with agriculture.	1,641	203	58	1,902	891	530	1,421	474	5	4	4	5
Total ...	31,271	2,755	833	34,859	20,475	11,062	31,537	12,720	100	100	100	100
Purposes of loans—												
Renewal of subsisting mortgages.	4,094	515	175	4,784	1,603	1,861	3,464	867	} 61·0	51·7	44·7	55·0
Discharge of other debts	8,676	987	347	10,010	3,574	2,841	6,415	2,666	}			
Payment of Court decrees ...	244	33	10	287	110	87	197	84	1·2	1·0	1·1	1·2
Court expenses	101	7	8	116	39	55	94	88	·5	·5	1·1	·7
Purposes of trade	287	41	17	345	134	40	174	317	1·4	·9	4·1	1·6
Purchasing lands and houses ...	1,986	176	39	2,201	794	521	1,315	357	9·1	6·9	4·5	7·5
Purchasing cattle and cultivation expenses.	526	22	6	554	838	327	1,165	556	2·3	6·1	7·0	4·4
Sinking wells and improving lands.	239	15	3	257	143	62	205	107	1·1	1·1	1·3	1·1
Payment of Government assessment.	216	12	4	232	184	94	278	188	·9	1·5	2·4	1·3

(2) *Statement showing the classification of lenders, the purposes of loans, and the rates of interest charged on loans compiled from deeds of mortgage of immovable property without possession and from simple bonds registered in* 1889, 1890 *and* 1891 *in the districts of Kistna, &c.*—continued.

Items.	Number of mortgages of Rs. 100 and upwards.				Number of mortgages of less than Rs. 100.			Simple bonds.	Percentage.			
	Rs. 100—500.	Rs. 501—1,000.	Over Rs. 1,000.	Total.	Rs. 1—50.	Rs. 51—99.	Total.		Mortgage Rs. 100 and above.	Mortgages below Rs. 100.	Simple bonds.	All transactions.
Purposes of loans—*cont.*												
Marriages	1,528	62	10	1,600	911	514	1,425	477	6·5	7·5	6·1	7·0
Funerals	48	2	1	51	63	23	86	18	·2	·4	·3	·3
Other household purposes ...	1,890	144	39	2,073	1,644	696	2,340	781	8·5	12·2	9·9	10·1
Other purposes ...	1,618	115	27	1,760	1,329	627	1,956	1,381	7·3	10·2	17·5	9·8
Total ...	21,453	2,131	686	24,270	11,366	7,748	19,114	7,887	100	100	100	100
Purpose not stated	9,818	624	147	10,589	9,109	3,314	12,423	4,833	...	...	...	...
Grand Total ...	31,271	2,755	833	34,859	20,475	11,062	31,537	12,720	...	...	...	...
Rates of interest on loans—												
Below 6 per cent. per annum ...	115	23	20	158	41	36	77	149	·5	·3	1·4	·6
From 6 to below 9 per cent. per annum.	1,401	404	182	1,987	322	265	587	555	6·5	2·1	5·5	4·6
From 9 to below 12 per cent. per annum.	4,[illegible]73	907	303	5,683	1,093	1,227	2,320	911	18·5	8·5	9·0	13·1
12 per cent. per annum	13,798	888	207	14,893	6,865	4,404	11,269	4,994	48·3	41·2	49·3	45·2
Over 12 and below 18 per cent. per annum.	4,369	144	24	4,537	2,926	1,724	4,650	1,362	14·8	17·0	13·5	15·5
18 per cent.	1,957	60	7	2,024	2,711	852	3,563	1,176	6·5	13·0	11·6	10·0
Over 18 and up to and including 24 per cent. per annum.	1,230	27	7	1,264	2,505	1,007	3,512	788	4·1	12·9	7·8	8·2

(2) *Statement showing the classification of lenders, the purposes of loans, and the rates of interest charged on loans compiled from deeds of mortgage of immovable property without possession and from simple bonds registered in* 1889, 1890 *and* 1891 *in the districts of Kistna, &c.*—continued.

Items.	Number of mortgages of Rs. 100 and upwards.				Number of mortgages of less than Rs. 100.			Simple bonds.	Percentage.			
	Rs. 100—500.	Rs. 501—1,000.	Over Rs. 1,000.	Total.	Rs. 1—50.	Rs. 51—99.	Total.		Mortgage Rs. 100 and above.	Mortgages below Rs. 100.	Simple bonds.	All transactions.
Rates of Interest on loans—*cont.*												
Over 24 per cent. per annum ...	266	6	2	274	1,097	291	1,388	184	·8	5·0	1·9	2·8
Total ...	27,609	2,459	752	30,820	17,560	9,806	27,366	10,119	100	100	100	100
Grain interest	2,367	90	13	2,470	2,342	758	3,100	816	...	...	...	...
No interest	1,295	206	68	1,569	573	498	1,071	1,785	...	...	...	...
Grand Total ...	31,271	2,755	883	34,859	20,475	11,062	31,537	12,720	...	...	...	...

NOTE 1.—The above statement was compiled from the statistics furnished from each of the offices of the districts named for 100 mortgages of Rs. 100 and upwards, 100 mortgages of value less than Rs. 100, and of 100 bonds irrespective of the total number registered. Applying the proportion of agriculturist to the non-agriculturist lenders arrived at from these figures to the total number of mortgages and bonds registered in the several districts, and assuming, as we may, that the lenders in cases of mortgages with possession are agriculturists, it is found that in 80 per cent. of the registered transactions the lenders are agriculturists. The percentages for the districts examined are found to be Tinnevelly 87, Coimbatore 82, South Arcot 73, Nellore 71, Kistna 70, Cuddapah and North Arcot 66, Bellary and Anantapur 53.

NOTE 2.—Cases in which it is not clear whether the purpose of the loan was to discharge other debts or whether the documents were renewals of subsisting mortgages have been included under the former head. From the statistics relating to the offices where the information is precisely given, it appears that the number of mortgages of the former class is nearly double that of the latter.

NOTE 3.—From a number of documents examined in the Malabar District, it is found that the general rate of interest on loans is 12 per cent.

NOTE 4.—In South Canara the rates of interest have been on an examination of registered documents, found to be as follows:—

—	Loans below Rs. 100.	Loans between Rs. 100 and Rs. 500.	Loans between Rs. 500 and Rs. 1,000.	Loans above Rs. 1,000.
Before 1835	12 p. c. per annum.	12 p. c.	9 to 12 p. c.	6 to 7 p. c.
Between 1835 and 1865	8 to 12 p. c.	10 to 12 p. c.	7 to 10 p. c.	6 to 8 p. c.
Between 1865 and 1892	10 to 12 p. c.	8 p. c.	$6\frac{1}{2}$ p. c.	6 p. c.

From the 'black books' preserved at Manjeshwar, a town 10 miles from Mangalore, it appears that the rate of interest was over 12 per cent. and near 18 per cent. per annum about the beginning of the century.

(3) *Statement showing the aggregate and average values of different classes of documents registered in the year* 1891–92 *in the Madras Presidency.*

Districts.	Population in thousands.	Sales of immoveable property.									
		Less than Rs. 100 in value.			Rs. 100 and above in value.			Total.			
		Number of documents.	Aggregate value in lakhs of Rs.	Average value per document, Rs.	Number of documents.	Aggregate value in lakhs of Rs.	Average value per document, Rs.	Number of documents.	Aggregate value in lakhs of Rs.	Average value per document, Rs.	Aggregate value per thousand of population, Rs.
1. Madras	452	291	·16	57	1,844	24·74	1,341	2,135	24·90	1,167	5,504
2. Ganjam	1,589	2,792	1·30	46	2,252	7·66	340	5,044	8·96	178	564
3. Vizagapatam	1,943	1,052	·47	45	1,873	10·80	576	2,925	11·27	385	580
4. Godávari	1,952	6,700	3·04	45	6,312	20·53	325	13,012	23·57	181	1,208
5. Kistna	1,855	4,887	2·46	50	5,073	14·41	284	9,960	16·87	169	776
6. Nellore	1,464	3,130	1·30	41	2,119	5·85	276	5,249	7·15	136	489
7. Cuddapah	1,272	7,125	2·98	42	3,292	6·94	210	10,417	9·92	95	780
8. Bellary and Anantapur	1,608	4,107	1·72	42	2,981	7·53	252	7,088	9·25	130	575
9. Kurnool	818	3,021	1·24	41	1,551	3·21	207	4,572	4·45	97	545
10. Chingleput	1,137	5,872	2·45	42	3,630	12·26	338	9,502	14·71	155	1,292
11. North Arcot	2,180	12,468	5·25	42	6,998	19·42	277	19,466	24·67	126	1,131
12. South Arcot	2,163	16,135	6·61	41	6,791	17·77	262	22,926	24·38	106	1,127
13. Tanjore	2,228	11,315	5·08	45	12,255	55·37	452	23,570	60·45	256	2,713
14. Trichinopoly	1,373	7,493	3·09	42	5,191	17·48	336	12,684	20·57	162	1,535
15. Madura	2,608	10,829	4·59	42	9,522	31·97	335	20,351	36·56	180	1,226
16. Tinnevelly	1,916	13,497	5·72	42	13,026	44·80	344	26,523	50·52	190	2,637
17. Coimbatore	2,005	7,896	3·04	38	8,116	29·99	369	16,012	33·03	206	1,647
18. Salem	1,963	7,332	2·91	39	5,135	13·47	262	12,467	16·38	131	835
19. Nilgiris	100	374	·14	38	211	3·15	1,494	585	3·29	564	3,302
20. South Canara	1,056	484	·21	43	1,379	11·18	811	1,863	11·39	611	1,078
21. Tellicherry	2,653	427	·19	44	1,049	5·36	511	1,476	5·55	376	722
22. Calicut		1,553	·65	42	1,973	10·56	535	3,526	11·21	318	
Total ...	34,335	128,780	54·60	42	102,573	374·45	365	231,353	429·05	185	1,220

(3) *Statement showing the aggregate and average values of different classes of documents registered in the year* 1891–92 *in the Madras Presidency*—continued.

Districts.	Mortgages of immovable property.										All documents relating to movable and immovable property.			
	Less than Rs. 100.			Rs. 100 and above.			Total.							
	Number of documents.	Aggregate value in lakhs of Rs.	Average value per document, Rs.	Number of documents.	Aggregate value in lakhs of Rs.	Average value per document, Rs.	Number of documents.	Aggregate value in lakhs of Rs.	Average value per document, Rs.	Aggregate value per thousand of population, Rs.	Number of documents.	Aggregate value in lakhs of Rs.	Average value per document, Rs.	Aggregate value per thousand of population, Rs.
1. Madras	139	·08	57	2,302	25·92	1,126	2,441	26·00	1,065	5,745	7,608	88·72	1,166	19,605
2. Ganjam	2,384	1·25	52	2,704	10·72	389	5,088	11·97	235	753	13,276	28·44	214	1,789
3. Vizagapatam	986	·53	54	3,286	13·81	420	4,272	14·34	336	738	11,007	40·55	368	2,087
4. Godávari	5,955	3·04	51	8,670	30·90	356	14,625	33·94	232	1,739	42,188	90·80	215	4,652
5. Kistna	2,888	1·75	60	5,308	19·84	374	8,196	21·59	263	1,163	24,154	48·59	201	2,618
6. Nellore	2,464	1·35	54	3,316	10·50	316	5,780	11·85	205	809	15,038	26·14	173	1,785
7. Cuddapah	1,143	·59	52	1,182	3·07	260	2,325	3·66	158	288	14,870	18·57	125	1,459
8. Bellary and Anantapur	2,161	1·14	53	4,435	13·74	310	6,596	14·83	225	926	16,149	29·57	183	1,838
9. Kurnool	1,786	·93	52	1,768	4·25	241	3,554	5·18	146	634	9,388	13·41	143	1,639
10. Chingleput	6,812	3·16	46	5,197	15·45	297	12,069	18·61	155	1,636	24,380	40·26	165	3,541
11. North Arcot	13,177	6·38	48	9,856	25·07	254	23,033	31·45	136	1,442	47,503	74·58	157	3,420
12. South Arcot	18,203	8·30	46	10,220	24·61	240	28,423	32·91	116	1,521	56,929	68·14	120	3,150
13. Tanjore	13,352	6·52	49	18,601	62·79	337	31,935	69·31	217	3,110	72,969	180·82	248	8,115
14. Trichinopoly	7,723	3·67	47	8,461	25·44	300	16,184	29·11	180	2,121	34,971	64·85	185	4,724
15. Madura	25,704	12·07	47	22,476	38·20	303	48,180	80·27	166	3,077	76,630	155·50	203	5,961
16. Tinnevelly	22,174	10·88	49	25,390	70·67	279	47,564	81·55	171	4,256	84,944	167·57	197	8,745
17. Coimbatore	12,155	5·39	44	14,085	37·24	264	26,240	42·63	162	2,126	51,336	100·18	195	4,996
18. Salem	8,887	4·12	46	7,956	17·64	222	16,843	21·76	129	1,127	34,582	51·85	150	2,642
19. Nilgiris	110	·06	50	242	3·15	1,304	352	3·21	912	3,217	1,245	9·78	786	9,805
20. South Canara	947	·48	51	4,396	30·38	691	5,343	30·86	577	2,922	19,712	73·62	373	6,971
21. Tellicherry	11,580	3·74	32	8,567	22·54	263	20,147	26·28	130	3,099	56,643	58·50	103	7,379
22. Calicut	23,720	6·91	29	14,998	49·01	325	38,718	55·92	144		87,586	137·23	157	
Total ...	184,450	82·34	44	183,416	584·94	313	367,866	667·28	181	1,933	803,105	1,567·66	195	4,565

NOTE.—(1) The figures for Ganjam, Vizagapatam and Godávari are exclusive of those for the Agency tracts comprised in those districts.

(2) In Malabar leases are, in some cases, classified as mortgages owing to the difficulty of clearly distinguishing the two classes of documents. The average value per document is low in this district, as a large number of counterparts, whose value is discarded from the statistical returns, are registered with their originals, and the average value is calculated with reference to the total number of documents including counterparts.

(3) In the Zemindari districts in the north sales and mortgages refer mostly to inam lands and house properties, as the right of transfer by Zemindari ryots of their holdings is not recognised by Zemindars.

(4) The small number of sales in Malabar and South Canara is due to the difficulty of alienation of family property under the Marumakkatayam and Alyasantana systems. In these districts the transfers take the form of leases and mortgages.

(4) *The following account of the methods of business adopted by firms of Nattukottai Chetties established in Karúr (Coimbatore District) in lending money to ryots has been furnished by the Sub-Registrar of Karúr.*

There are twelve firms of Nattukottai Chetties established at Karúr for lending money. Of these firms, four are wealthy and have dealings to the extent of a lakh of rupees each. The investments of others vary from about Rs. 10,000 to Rs. 50,000. The richest of them has banks in Rangoon, Madura and Madras, and it is from one of his agents that the information given below was obtained.

When a ryot applies to the Chetties for a loan, which is not done in writing, his name is noted down, and careful inquiries are made as to whether the property owned by him will be sufficient security for the loan. Villagers known to be respectable, and having transactions with them, supply the Chetties with the necessary information on the point. Village officers are consulted in cases of doubt, and all deeds relating to the property upon which his claims rest are demanded and examined. The Chetties are more ready to advance money on the security of lands in the actual possession and enjoyment of the ryot by right of purchase or mortgage, than on the security of inherited property, as there are chances of claims being disputed in the latter case. Encumbrance certificates from registration offices are very rarely, if ever, required. (There has not been a single application for general search in this year on this account.) The Chetties and their agents have made themselves thoroughly acquainted with the condition of the ryots living in the vicinity of Karúr. The help of the village officer is sought only where reliable information cannot be had from other available sources. As a rule, a ryot who has already had transactions with the bankers introduces the applicant, and, if necessary, becomes his surety. The applicant has not to wait for more than a week unless the amount is large, say Rs. 1,000. Promissory notes and simple bonds are accepted only when the applicant is a well known and respectable man. Mortgage deeds with personal security are the rule.

The Chetties do not keep any treasury in their banks, and there is never more than a thousand rupees in reserve in the richest firm. They are supplied with money according to requirements by their brethren in Madras, with whom they keep accounts current. When a loan is applied for, clients already owing are pressed hard and the advance is made from recoveries; when this is not possible, or when there is a likelihood of a longer delay than a week, money is obtained from Madras.

There are forty Nattukottai Chetties in Madras who supply their brethren in the mofussil with sums of money whenever required, bearing rates of interest which vary every month. These sums the mofussil Chetties are at liberty to return without any restrictions as to time of repayment. But, as a rule, all debts recovered are remitted at once to Madras, unless there is demand for fresh loans. The Madras Chetties belong to one and the same sect and place as those in the mofussil, and are therefore acquainted with the character and solvency of the latter to enable them to judge as to how much can be safely advanced. The rates of interest charged by the Madras firms on their mofussil bankers vary according to demand every month. About the first of every

Tamil month the forty Chetties meet in their temple and resolve as to what rate should be adopted for the month. This is generally done by a reference to the rates that prevailed in the same month in the previous year. The actual rates charged during the last three years are given below:—

	Rate of interest charged.					
	1890.		1891.		1892.	
	A.	P.	A.	P.	A.	P.
Chittirai (April and May)	15	3	13	0	13	3
Vaiyasi (May and June)	14	0	12	0	12	6
Ani (June and July)	11	9	10	6	11	3
Adi (July and August)	10	6	9	6	9	6
Avani (August and September) ...	8	0	7	6		
Purattasi (September and October) ...	8	0	7	6		
Arpisi (October and November) ...	8	0	7	6		
Kartigai (November and December)	8	6	8	0		
Margali (December and January) ...	10	6	10	0		
Tai (January and February)	13	0	12	6		
Masi (February and March)	14	0	15	0		
Panguni (March and April)	14	0	14	3		

The balances outstanding to the credit of the Madras firms bear interest month by month according to the rates then prevailing and not according to any fixed rate. The average interest for a year under these calculations will be about 8 per cent. Every seven months the interest is added to the balance and compound interest according to rates as above stated is calculated. The mofussil Chetties take care, therefore, to keep no account unpaid for more than seven months. This is the main reason for the terms of repayment in their stipulations with ryots being always short. One of the Chetties here gets money from Rangoon occasionally, but the rate of interest being higher there it is not preferred to Madras. Remittances are made by currency notes, and hundis where possible.

The establishment of each banker consists only of an agent or kanakapillai (accountant) who does much of his business. Most of the Chetties remain in Karúr for about eight months in a year and transact their business in person. During their absence the kanakapillais are empowered to make loans and recover debts subject to conditions differing according to the character and experience of the men. The richest bankers have agents of their own class and do not stay in Karúr long, the agents doing all their business. No securities are taken from them. . . . . . who is the richest pays his agents Rs. 500 a year each besides undergoing their boarding expenses. Kanakapillais get from Rs. 10 to Rs. 20 a month and keep their accounts in cadjan leaves. Their services are availed of in writing documents, and they have also to go about the villages collecting interest due. Debtors do not pay interest every month, though in the documents they agree to do so; generally once in every three months or so it is collected. The profit and loss are determined once every three years with some; with others the periods vary.

There is no particular season in which debts are recovered. During the harvest seasons the ryots are pressed for payment, but they prefer to keep what is harvested and sell the produce during the dearest season to obtain a larger price. The payments are made throughout the year according to individual convenience.

The loans granted under the special well rules at a small rate of interest were mostly in the months of March, April and May last, when a Deputy Collector was specially deputed to this taluk for the purpose. That these loans have affected the transactions of Nattukottai Chetties will be clear from the number of documents executed and registered in their favor in those months. The number of documents executed in favor of five of the important Chetties in the three months in 1891 and 1892 have been compared, and it is found that while the total number registered in 1891 was 88, the number has fallen to 30 in 1892. The rates of interest have not, however, shown any decline. The sums lent amounted in a large number of cases to from Rs. 100 to Rs. 500, and in very rare instances to Rs. 1,000. The average rate of interest for the former class is Rs. 1-4-0 or 15 per cent. per annum. Deducting the interest which the Chetties have to pay to their bankers in Madras, there is a net gain of about 7 per cent. This does not, however, express the full extent of their profit as some of them have invested funds with the Madras bankers and share their profits also. Moreover it is not always with remittances from Madras that they carry on their business. Sums of Rs. 1,000 or Rs. 2,000 are got from their private funds at Devakóta in the Madura district, the central seat of Nattukottai Chetties. A deed for Rs. 1,800 in May 1892 bears rate of interest at 12 annas per mensem, the rate chargeable in Madras being about 14 annas in the month; this at first sight seems inexplicable. But as the interest is here levied throughout the whole term at a fixed rate, and as the high rates in Madras are payable only for two or three months, the same sum bearing about 9 annas rate in July and August, the profit at the close of the term will be large.

(5) *The account given by Mr. Warden, Collector of Malabar in* 1801, *of usurious money-lenders in Pálghat.*

"The cultivating ryot is obliged at the end of the year to borrow money to purchase seed for the ensuing year's cultivation. To obtain this money, there being no one else to lend him, he is driven to the necessity of applying for it to a Putter (Pálghat Brahmin), the greedy nature of whose disposition is beyond anything I ever knew or heard of. That your Board may be able to form some idea of it, I shall here beg leave to state the hardships to which a ryot borrowing money from one of these Putters is frequently subjected.

"Let it be supposed that a ryot borrows from him 50 fanams at the latter end of the year to purchase seed for sowing. The price of batty (paddy) at this time is generally about 1½ parahs the fanam, at which rate he will get 75 parahs. He then passes a note to the Putter (who will not otherwise lend him a kaas) promising to return his 50 fanams within four months at 3 per cent. interest per mensem, in batty on his reaping the first crop at the price at which it may be then current. This current price is never less than 3 parahs, and sometimes 3½ and 4 parahs the fanam—let it be reckoned at 3. At the expiration of the four months the loan of 50 fanams with interest will amount to 58 fanams, the value of which in grain at 3 parahs the fanam will be 174 parahs. The ryot at this period has to pay the Sircar revenue, and is at the same time dunned by his Brahmin creditor whom the proportion of the produce will not allow to satisfy in full. The Brahmin, however, is content with receiving two-thirds of his grain, which will be 116 parahs, and for the remaining one-third or 58 parahs he will exact a new bond from the ryot (who will pass it to avoid a civil prosecution with which his creditor threatens him) promising to pay the value of the grain in a specified month at the latter end of the season (with the same usurious interest as above said) in *money* at the rate at which grain may be *then* selling. The price, as I have above mentioned, is about 1½ parahs the fanam. Thus allowing six months' interest, the sum to be paid in lieu of 58 parahs will amount to 47 fanams, so that in the course of about ten or twelve months, for the loan of 50 fanams or 75 parahs of paddy, although the ryot has paid 116 parahs, he does not return his debt in a greater sum than 3 fanams or 4½ parahs of paddy. Cases of this nature have come before me, when the poor ryot has been driven to the extremity of distress, and at last prosecuted with all the severity imaginable by his avaricious and unrelenting creditor."

The following particulars have been furnished by the Sub-Registrar of Pálghat as to the nature of usurious money-lending transactions carried on by Moplahs at present :—

"Usurious transactions of the nature described by Mr. Warden continue to be carried on in Pálghat and some other parts of the Malabar district.

"The people taking such loans are agriculturists of very small or almost of no credit who eke out a struggling existence by cultivating other peoples' lands for a season. Mr. Warden's account describes a transaction from the beginning and traces it through two stages. The documents now obtainable in regard to such transactions evidence only a certain stage in the progress of the loan operation and the deficiencies in them have to be supplied by oral statements. Translations of two subsisting bonds are appended ; of which one marked A evidences a transaction entered into for the first time between the parties and the other marked B relates to a loan in the second stage of its progress and forms the note passed by the debtor to the creditor for the balance found due after a settlement of the account in regard to a loan of 80 parahs of paddy made in Edavam (May-June) 1066. The loan in its original stage is stated to have carried interest at 4 parahs for 10 parahs a year. In neither of the documents is seen any provision made for interest after default of payment. In all such cases, however, it is a recognized rule to get a stipulation made for the return of the paddy in money when the price of paddy is at a maximum. (In Pálghat the price of paddy has in these two years ruled at a parah the fanam in the harvest season ; and at the latter end it varied from 5¾ to 6¼ edangalies the fanam)."

A.—Document executed by A to B. I have this day borrowed from you in cash Rs. 10 ; and I promise to pay for this amount 35 parahs of paddy within the 30th Tulam 1068 (November 1892), at a parah the fanam ; and shall thereupon take back this document, dated the 9th Mithunam, 1067 (July 1892).

B.—Simple mortgage executed by A to B.—In settlement of previous accounts you find myself indebted to you in 57 parahs 6 edangalies of paddy. This 57 parahs 6 edangalies of paddy I shall return to you before the 30th of Vrischikam, 1068 (December 1892), with interest at 5 parahs for every 10 parahs of paddy (*i.e.*, 50 per cent.) and shall take back this document, dated the 7th Mithunam, 1067 (14th July 1892).

"At Ottapálam, a station on the Railway, the business is said to be very briskly carried on by the Moplahs and the following case is adduced in illustration of the terms of the business :—

"A ryot, in order to furnish himself with a stock of paddy for paying the wages of his laborers, borrows of a Moplah in Mithunam (June-July) 50 parahs of paddy which for the borrower is then priced at Rs. 25, on the condition that when the first crop is harvested in Kanni (September-October) he will repay the principal and the interest at 2 per cent. per mensem in paddy at 4 edangalies in excess of the market rate. Under the terms of this agreement, in Kanni, when paddy sells at 12 edangalies the fanam, the borrower has to pay for the 27 rupees which then becomes due, $\frac{27 \times 3\frac{1}{2} \times 16}{10}$ or 151 parahs 2 edangalies of paddy. The borrower whose gross produce at the time is not more than 250 parahs is not able to pay and the lender is not really anxious to receive the whole amount of the debt. But the creditor being the person to be on the spot first, and his demand being more inperious than that of the landlord, the ryot gives him 100 parahs at once and agrees to pay the remainder in *money* calculated on the price that may be found to be current in the succeeding Dhanu when the price of paddy rises to 8 edangalies the fanam. In Dhanu, thus, the ryot finds himself indebted to the Moplah in $\frac{51\frac{1}{5} \times 10}{8}$ or 64 fanams, which is $18\frac{2}{7}$ rupees. At that part of the year he has neither money nor paddy with which to discharge the debt; and he then makes a third promise that for the 64 fanams he will give paddy on the harvesting of the Makaram crop when the price of paddy falls to a parah the fanam. In Makaram the ryot's indebtedness amounts to 64 fanams which he is unable to clear simultaneously with his paying his rent in full. Being anxious to retain his land for the next year's cultivation, he now desires to keep himself in the good graces of his Jenmi and so hands over to him the greater portion of his produce. The land which the ryot is assumed to cultivate is capable of sowing 25 parahs and the gross produce that the land brings in to him is estimated at 250 + 200 or 450 parahs. He has to pay as rent 200 parahs for the year. With this produce he is unable to meet in full the demands of either the Jenmi or the Moplah, and to both of them he finds himself indebted. Supposing the ryot to conciliate the Moplah by paying him 32 parahs at once and agreeing to pay money for the balance at 8 annas the parah in Mesham, the result to the ryot is that after paying the Moplah 132 parahs for the original loan of 50 parahs, he finds his original debt reduced at the end of the year by only 9 rupees. The Jenmi may occasionally remit the balance, but the Moplah never does.

"The above account is given by one well acquainted with the place and the people and vouched to be correct and represents transactions of but a milder type."

(6) *Extract from Buchanan's "Journey through Mysore, Canara and Malabar*, 1801."

The following is the account given by Dr. Buchanan as to the terms on which advances were usually made by merchants on the sea coast to ryots in the interior on account of commercial produce to be delivered after harvest :—

"Farmers of prudence and substance, such as the Moplahs mostly are, receive no advances for pepper; but when their pepper is fit for market, sell it to the best advantange and deliver it at the seaport at from Rs. 120 to Rs. 125 a candy of 640 lb. The case is, however, different with most of the Hindus, who, in Malabar, are as remarkable for a thoughtless profusion as in other parts they are penurious. Between 12th of June and of 13th September, the Mussulman traders come from the coast and enter into written engagements with those who are willing to receive advances. The cultivators agree to deliver a certain quantity of peper for which the trader pays down immediately from 13 to 15 fanams a tulam or from Rs. 65 to Rs. 75 a candy. Should the cultivator, at the crop season, be unable to deliver the quantity for which he contracted, he must pay for the deficiency at the market price, which is generally Rs. 120 to Rs. 125 a candy. As he is seldom or never able to pay this in cash, he gives a note of hand, engaging to deliver pepper for the amount of the price of the deficiency, at the rate of 1 tulam for 13 to 15 fanams; but no interest is charged. Indeed the profits of the trader are immense; as for an advance of 15 fanams for six months, he gets a profit of 10; and it is evident that the risk is very small. Should a merchant not consent to receive the pepper on account of its being bad, the cultivator may sell it to any person that he pleases and give the proceeds to the merchant. Should these not amount to the market price, he gives a note of hand for the balance, which is considered as part of the advance for next year. It is evident that the interest of the merchant is to keep up a high nominal price, even should he, in selling the pepper to foreigners, be obliged to allow a large discount; for all the balances due by the farmer are paid in, what is called, the market price. The present market price is Rs. 125 a candy or £2-1-5 a cwt. It is sometimes as low as Rs. 100, and at others rises to double that sum.

"The cultivators, when questioned concerning the reason that can induce them to take up money on terms so disadvantageous, attribute it entirely to the land tax; for every evil in Malabar is ascribed to that as its source. . . . . . At length, I found that the real cause of the Hindus disposing of their pepper at this low rate is a festival called 'Onam,' which is celebrated in the month of Singham. At this, the Hindus expend in drinking and finery everything which they can raise."

As regards the arrangements now usually entered into by merchants with cultivators in regard to the delivery of commercial produce, such as pepper, cocoanuts and coffee, the Registrar of the Tellicherry district, in which these crops are extensively grown, reports as follows :—

"About fifty years ago it was the practice for Moplahs on the sea coast to go to the interior and advance money to tenants at Rs. 60 or

Rs. 70 a candy, when pepper was selling at Rs. 120 in the town. It is also true that they were made to pay for the deficient quantity at the market rate or to give a note of hand engaging to deliver pepper at the next harvest for the amount settled at Rs. 60 or Rs. 70 a candy. This mode of advance has become changed for various reasons. Formerly, there were no cartable roads in the district and the facility of communication between the coast, where the merchants generally lived, and the interior, was wanting. Further, Moplah traders were not many and money was also scarce. Now the state of things is quite the reverse. As the advance of time has brought on so many changes, it must have reacted on the old practice which was ruinous to tenants. They have now grown more intelligent and civilized. They now freely go to towns and learn the market price daily. The present method of advance, as described below, must have been brought on by natural course to suit the convenience of the purchaser and seller. It is a well known fact that tenants in Malabar have no proprietary right in the soil and cannot therefore give sufficient guarantee for the money advanced. In cases of non-fulfilment of engagements, merchants must have found considerable difficulty in recovering the amount. On the other hand, tenants must also have seen their own ruin in such bargains.

"I made careful enquiries among merchants who deal extensively in pepper and coffee. They borrow large sums from the banks and hand them to various middlemen (Moplahs generally) who live in the interior and have moderate means. The rate of interest charged by the bank is generally 12 per cent. per annum or even less. These middlemen are charged at 24 per cent. by merchants and agree to give, for principal and interest, pepper at market rates. They go to different pepper gardens in their neighbourhood, estimate the crops on pepper vines and purchase them for ready money from tenants who are in need of it. Pepper is generally plucked from vines from 15th January to 15th February. One would be able to judge the quantity and quality of the crop from September forward. The middlemen commence to purchase the crop from August and September. The more it grows to maturity the higher its price rises for two reasons. The merchant has not much to lose in the shape of interest on the sum paid beforehand. Secondly, he will be in a better position to see the state of the crop. He is always shrewd enough not to lose and makes a net profit of 20 per cent. on his borrowed capital in four or five months. He, first of all, estimates the crop by edangalies (nearly equal to Madras measures). For every 100 edangalies of undried pepper, he agrees to pay Rs. 9 or Rs. 10. Seven hundred edangalies of undried pepper, if dried, will be a little more or less than a candy, according to the quality of the crop. He has to bear all charges for plucking and other incidental expenses required for drying and taking it to the market. The rate of purchasing raw pepper on the vines will vary according to the nature of the market in seaport towns and the demand of wholesale merchants. While petty merchants make a clear profit of not less than 20 per cent. on their outlay in five months, big merchants in the town have a profit of 1 per cent. per mensem on their borrowed capital from the bank. The middlemen, about the end of February, deliver pepper to wholesale merchants for the amount borrowed and for its interest at

24 per cent. at market rates. If they fail to do so, the contract is enforced with a small additional amount calculated at a certain rate per candy for the disappointment caused. Even the loss of 20 per cent. on a sum expected in a few months is ruinous to a tenant. Why he foregoes this amount will be explained further on.

"*Coffee.*—It should not be supposed that Europeans alone have coffee gardens in Wynaad. Jenmies and small farmers rear coffee plants on their parambas and waste lands according to their means and circumstances. The soil is virgin and fertile and the climate congenial to their growth. The petty jenmies and tenants are in need of money like those who farm pepper gardens at the foot of the hills. The middlemen first estimate coffee crops and purchase them for a price which would give them not less than 20 per cent. profit on their outlay. The expenses of plucking, &c., are borne by them. The wholesale merchants in the town purchase coffee for the market price, from petty traders who have received advance, in adjustment of principal and interest which is generally not less than 24 per cent. The processes of purchasing and selling coffee are similar to those detailed above for pepper. The above method is not applicable to European planters who generally borrow large sums from the bank directly for expenses of cultivation and for the payment of coolies in their gardens.

"*Cocoanut.*—The process is the same. But it is purchased by the thousand. If 1,000 cocoanuts are expected to be sold at Rs. 25 in January, the pre-payment for the same quantity is Rs. 15 to Rs. 17 in September. In this case the petty traders' profit will be about 30 per cent. on the outlay. Their risk is greater and they are almost entirely at the mercy of the tenants who generally have nothing and oftentimes not even the trees to pledge. Hence under this head advances to tenants are not made for large sums. In cases of failure to fulfil the engagement, legal steps are taken to enforce the contract according to the penal rates stipulated therein.

"I do not mean to say that the old practice of advancing money on pepper, coffee and cocoanuts has died out entirely. It has almost gone out and there may be rare occurrences in the interior parts. By the new method the connection between petty traders and tenants ceases and is renewed annually. While the latter are not much harassed the former do not lose their profit largely. It is found convenient to both parties."

As to the question why small farmers and tenants receive advances on crops on disadvantageous terms instead of harvesting the produce and selling it on their own account when the price is high, the Registrar remarks that the reason for this is not to be found in the heaviness of the land tax or extravagant expenditure during the "Onam" feast as suggested by Dr. Buchanan, but in the great poverty of the lower classes of the cultivators due to the system of landholding under the Marumakattayam law. It is not to the interest of the karnavan or the head of a Malabar family who is uncontrolled in regard to the disposal of the income of the property to invest money either on improvements to property or in helping tenants with advances. The tenants are, as a rule, rack-rented and have to pay heavy renewal fees whenever kanom mortgages are renewed. The Nairs, as a class, do not engage in trade which is almost entirely in the hands of the Moplahs.

(7) *Extract from a report on the indebtedness of the agricultural classes furnished by the Acting Registrar, South Arcot District.*

1. Ryots (or those that are engaged in agriculture) are divisible into three classes; farm servants, farmers and proprietors. The first class have no credit except with their employers to a very limited extent. They till the soil for the landlords either for monthly grain wages, for kalam (that which is left in the threshing ground, after it is imperfectly swept), partly for kalam and partly for grain wages, or for kalam and a small share (of grain harvested). They can get advances from their employers to the extent of the wages they are likely to earn in the course of the year, or an advance for marriage of about Rs. 20. This latter sum is not repaid, nor is interest charged upon it, when the servant leaves his masters' service. It is difficult to dismiss him without forfeiting the advance unless the servant transfers his services to another master in the same village, when, by mutual understanding among the villagers, he is required and enabled to refund the sum advanced.

The credit of the farmers is nearly co-extensive with their annual profits and that of the proprietors with nearly 70 per cent. of the value of their property. The so-called farmers are persons of very little means, possessing only a pair of cattle, a plough and a hut. Their extraordinary expenses are generally defrayed from their savings. The large borrowing class are all proprietors of land and their credit has considerably improved during the last twenty years owing to the rise of prices. In the sub-district of Panruti, and, I believe, also in the whole district, the last class only are numerous. . . . . . .

2. In the neighbourhood of Panruti, cumboo, paddy and ground-nut are raised, the first two for home consumption, and the last almost wholly for export. The money-lenders chiefly live at Panruti. They make advances from time, to time, but, specially before the Kartiga festival of Tiruvannámalai, for buying cattle. The advances are in small sums by account-current, but when they reach a respectable figure, a stamped bond or mortgage-deed is obtained. The conditions are that the advances should be repaid within a year or two; that the price should be the lowest prevailing at the commencement of the harvest season; and a highly penal rate of interest from 2 to 6¼ per cent. per mensum be paid for default. No interest is charged for repayments in time. It is said that the penal interest is not always exacted, except when the claim has to be enforced in a Court. This is the practice of the petty, though numerous, class of money-lenders. Comparatively large but temporary loans are also granted upon jewels, indigo, paddy, &c. The rate of interest in these cases is between 6 and 12 per cent. Loans on personal credit are allowed only to traders and to customers of goods. No interest is charged on such loans so long as they remain account debts. Larger proprietors make loans of grain to petty farmers about July or so, repayable at the harvest time with profit or interest at one-fourth of the principal. Allusion to this custom is found in the reports of the Sub-Registrars of Chidambaram and Tindivanam, and I also find it prevalent in the Chingleput district. Money loans are also granted upon, what is called, paddy interest, *i.e.*, at so many kalams

per Rs. 100, irrespective of the price of paddy at the time it is paid. Compound interest is very unusual in any case.

3. *Result of the system.*—Much misapprehension prevails as to the character of money-lenders or as to the result of borrowing. Human nature is the same at all times and at all places, and where there is a difference it is wholly due to the influence to which it is subject. A capitalist will willingly pay a premium to purchase a 4 per cent. Government security; but is very reluctant to lend money at 12 per cent. to a near relation. He is not capricious and it will not be difficult to know his motive. The much-abused Marwadies risk their money on personal credit, and interest cannot be the same where the risks are not. Professional money-lenders have no longing for lands, because their avocation is not agricultural. When they buy, they do so against their will for want of other buyers, and sell them when they can. The position of the agricultural borrowers has greatly improved and that of the professional money-lenders has deteriorated during the last quarter of a century. The value of money having fallen or that of the agricultural produce risen, the money lent is returned when it is not worth as much as when it was given. The value so far is transferred from the one class to the other . . . . * This will show that the money-lender has been a blessing instead of a curse, and he has been improving, unconciously though it be, the position of the agriculturists in his own district. I have experience of two or three districts, and I am able to state that the improvement is marked and perceptible to all unprejudiced observers. Nearly half of the huts that existed twenty-five years ago have disappeared, and tiled houses have taken their places. Houses which were tiled then have changed their dimensions and appearance now. So in clothing and other comforts. Agriculturists have in their turn become money-lenders and have learnt to dispense with the aid of the professional money-lenders to a very great extent. The improvement in material prosperity can be easily gauged by the fall in the interest, which was then 12 per cent. at least (then called charitable or தர்மவட்டி), is now nearly 6 per cent. Time has come when ryots are able to take advantage of any help that may be rendered to them to organize a system of mutual credit on the lines that will hereafter be explained. Farm servants are a diminishing class. Their ambition is to become farmers. By getting a small loan for purchasing one bullock or two, by industry and economy, they become in time proprietors of a plough and a pair of cattle and are able to maintain themselves independently. As farmers, they are able to repay their loans which, as servants, they were not. By dint of exertion and thrift, they are even able to purchase a small piece of land and attain the status of proprietors. Rich landlords, on the other hand, have been losing ground. The sons by partition get only a fraction of their patrimony, while their family and expenditure are, in many cases, equal to, or greater than, those of their parents. They involve themselves in debt and have ultimately to part with their lands. They become poor and by hard necessity understand their position and try to lift themselves with those who were originally poor. The lands are passing from

* This seems to be too high an estimate.

them to vakils and Government officials. Of the four systems of credit here alluded to, the result of lending money, at so much per cent., is very advantageous to the borrower. Grain interest is demandable by small capitalists who have to purchase paddy for their consumption. It is generally favorable to the lender and is not had recourse to, except in an emergency. *Vasi* or *Nanji* (the latter means one-fourth share), apparently very disadvantageous to the borrower, is not really so. The grain is advanced in June or July and is repaid in February or March. The duration of the loan is about nine months and the interest, if the value and condition of paddy be the same, is nearly 3 per cent. We have, however, to allow for the difference in the price which itself is sometimes nearly 25 per cent. in favour of the borrower. We have also to allow for the dryage of the paddy at the time of repayment. This comes to nearly 15 to 20 per cent.* The ryots prefer this kind of payment to money payment. The only advantage to the lender is that there is no excuse for putting off the payment when the harvest is realized.

"Repayment in kind, at the time of harvest without interest, is apparently advantageous to the ryot and sometimes is really so. He gets as much for his grain as he would otherwise have if he sold the crops when they are gathered. His gain consists in the interest on the money borrowed for the period between the date of the loan and that of the harvest. In consideration of this, he has to abstain from selling his grain to others and from selling it at a time when it would fetch the best price. Taking into account his necessitous condition, the sacrifice is nominal. The lenders can buy paddy at the time of the harvest and pocket the difference if they can. That they are not able to do so indicates the real position. The lenders have to pay simply to purchase a custom and this is no doubt proof that the ryots are able to dictate their own terms and money is easy."†

(S) *Tenant right in Java : extracted from an article from one of the English Newspapers quoted in the "Indian Economist,"* 1870.

"We can very well understand the excitement created in Holland by the passing of the Agrarian Bill for the Dutch Indian possessions; and there can be little doubt its conservative opponents are right in proclaiming it the precursor of a social revolution. It seems to decide the question, which has been so long and hotly debated in the Parliament at the Hague and signs the death-warrant of the Dutch Colonial System. Independently of the radical changes introduced in that system by the bill, the very fact of foreign witnesses being invited behind the scenes—of the working of Dutch Colonial policy being laid bare to public opinion—seems to make the inevitable revolution in it merely a question of time. That that revolution must have come sooner or later was certain. Its advocates had all the arguments

* This seems to be too high an estimate.

† This is somewhat too broadly stated. It is necessity that makes ryots part with their grain soon after harvest and the lenders make a profit out of this. The ryots in general, however, are now better able to hold out for a price than they were before.

on their side except utilitarian ones. The telling and hitherto conclusive reply of their opponents has been that their present system pays and pays enormously. Not only is there no difficulty whatever in establishing an equilibrium in Javanese budgets, but Javanese labour and taxation contribute immediately to the home treasury. Now the new measure not merely introduces the wedge—that was done some time ago, when free labour was admitted on the new railway works,—but drives it home into the very roots of the system; one or two blows more must follow in local sequence and it will be rent into fragments. The two leading features of the Dutch system are the ownership by the State of all the lands in the island, and forced labour. With regard to the former, the Dutch, on their occupation, found the native princes enjoying all over the soil of their dominions what resembled much more nearly actual ownership than a bare feudal superiority. Stepping into their places and rights, they pensioned these local magnates, and governed or oppressed from behind their names. The Dutch Resident drew the lion's share of the gains: the native prince had a handsome commission and the whole unpopularity for his share. If he were slack in turning the screw, he abdicated under pressure in favour of some member of his family, with an hereditary claim equally unimpeachable with his own. All the island is administered on this footing, with the exception of a couple of quasi-independant states, ruled by puppets under the eyes of a Dutch garrison. The whole population is not only bound down to the soil, but limited rigorously as to the productions to be raised upon it. Over certain districts the cultivator cannot exercise his discretion, but must satisfy Government inspectors on their periodical visits that he grows a certain number of trees of a certain kind. His produce is brought into Government markets, and bought at Government prices, and the margin between the sums it fetches in Java and at Amsterdam is always great and often fabulous. Then, in one form or another, Javanese labour is absolutely at the service of the State, and the marvellous prosperity of the island—regarding the matter from a Dutch, not a Javanese, point of view—dates from the impulse given to this principle by General Vanden Bocsh. Be it observed, it is a system highly practical and profitable, but essentially vicious; and, with this radical defect in it, that if you once subject it to criticism you invite its condemnation in all its parts. Modification can only lead on to annihilation. We presume the party who has carried the measure in the House will have the power and the will to see that it is carried out in the colonies, although we may well imagine the local officials will offer it all the opposition they dare. It is not pleasant seeing nearly absolute power tempered down to constitutional authority, the rich salaries and allowances passing into the crucible of reform. A paradise as the island is, in some ways, it wants strong counter-inducements to the climate to make life in Java an enviable thing; and if the Dutch residents have had to work and think, and turn night to day, hitherto at least they have lived in the license and luxury of Oriental despots, and enjoyed the slavish reverence of their subjects. Now if the revenues dwindle to or below the point at which they stood before Vanden Bocsh set to work on them with his rough and ready finance system, officials will find themselves the victims of their economical home Government; and, moreover, the proposed changes will probably suggest a very material reduction in their numbers.

"Article 62 provides that land leases may be granted for periods not exceeding 75 years. It invites, in fact, to the immigration and colonization which for so long have been studiously discouraged. It assures extreme fixity of tenure, and offers every facility for converting occupation into permanent property. It admits and confirms the strange principle of native ownership, and permits, under certain restrictions, that land shall vest in foreigners, or be rented by them. Holland, in short, throws open to all the world the rich garden she has hitherto made a close monopoly of, and renounces the right of the crown —a right at once shadowy and substantial—to all the lands cultivated by the natives. There can be no doubt the conservatives are right in saying it will annihilate the present system of cultivation, and it will be hopeless to think of maintaining the Government monopoly of markets. No European colonist would dream of farming, subject to the condition that some three-fourths of his fair profits should become legally the property of the State—that he should have to sell for half a dollar in Java what the telegraph informed him was selling for four in Holland. And although the natives have hitherto been treated and have regarded themselves as an inferior caste, it would be impossible to attempt to make distinctions on a point on which they are sure to be so sensitive as the pocket. The Government system must go, and with it the Government profits. How far land leases and taxation may replace them is another question, and one that, when we contrast results from the British and the Dutch Indies, cannot be answered very hopefully for the Dutch treasury. We are told the Dutch conservatives are uneasy as to the advent of English adventurers and its consequences. We have no doubt the restrictions referred to have been naturally arranged so as to impose some check on that. It would be contrary to human nature, and to Dutch nature especially, to suppose that all of a sudden they should push free-trade and self-abnegation to sentimental lengths. But, in any case, of all the climates in the East, the climate of Java is among the most trying to Europeans; and that consideration alone, we should fancy, would operate against any such influx as the Dutch affect to apprehend. That the bill will endanger their hold on their colonies we do not believe. On the contrary a weak State always does wisely to shelter itself behind 'the principles of eternal justice;' and daring filibusterers, or even acquisitive Governments, have lost an excellent chance of having public opinion in their favour in a crusade against the task-master of the Malay race. And for Malays, when the islands have ceased to be closed colonies, the Dutch may venture to turn their tardy attention to raising their Eastern subjects in the social scale. Hitherto they have not merely been neglected, but degraded as a matter of policy; for an enlightenment among the population was absolutely incompatible with the system of serfdom and *corvée* on which they were governed. It is impossible to deny that Holland may have legislated away her splendid colonies' income; but we have every reason to believe she has strengthened her hold on her colonies. Better perpetuate a connection that must always be profitable than continue a scandal of civilization, and gains as insecure and uncertain as great speculative profits generally are. [The truth seems to be that the system of semi-slavery has broken down and that a change is absolutely necessary. Why should the Dutch fear an influx of English planters? They would soon make the mountains of Java what the mountains of Ceylon are, to the detriment not of the Dutch but English Colony]."

(9) *Description of a Swiss Land Credit Bank.*

An extract from a paper read to the Statistical and Social Inquiry Society of Ireland, by Mr. M. O'Brien, printed as Appendix A to the Third Report of the Royal Commission to inquire into the depression of Trade and Industry (1886).

The demand for legislation to facilitate the lending of public money on small plots of land in Ireland makes a description of the constitution and operation of a Continental Land Credit Bank of some interest.

Mr. H. D. MacLeod, in his lectures on credit and banking, says—

"Many banks in Central Europe have been founded for the purpose of making advances to cultivate land, and a very large portion of the advance in agriculture during the last 130 years has been due to them."

The provisions of the French Civil Code, the principles of which have been adopted in many other countries, make land a suitable security for bankers' loans, which it is not under English law.

In the report of the Royal Commission of 1857 on registration of titles, the following sentence (p. 46) occurs, and is applicable to land as banking security:—

"It has been well said that the greatest condemnation of the existing system of lending money on land is the reluctance which bankers, the natural traders in loans, have to lend on mortgage or judgment. The security which they refuse, careless trustees, ignorant people who have savings, and widows and others who have some small provision, are advised to accept, and in this way the whole risk of bad security is thrown on the classes least able to bear it."

The Land Credit Bank of the State of Vaud (*Caisse hypothecaire cantonate, Vaudoise*) was established for the purpose of granting advances on the security of real property to the agricultural classes. As the entire canton is owned and occupied in very small parcels, the advantages of the bank extended to the whole community. The control and management of the bank is in the hands of the following three bodies:—

(1) A council of 20, of whom 10 members are named by the executive government and 10 are elected by the bank shareholders with a President, who must be a member of the Government; the council meets at least once in six months.

(2) A committee of supervision, consisting of the President of council, and 4 members named by the council, meeting at least twice a month.

(3) A directorate, consisting of a chief director, 2 managers, and 2 assistants; they meet at the chief office at least three times a week, and must not be related to each other. The Secretary of the bank is selected by the Government from among the permanent officials of the State.

The following figures are taken from the report of the bank for the year ending 31st December 1883, and are given in round numbers :—

The resources of the bank consisted of—

	£
(1) Paid up capital in £20 shares (the State must be the proprietor at least of 1,000 shares)	380,000
(2) The funds obtained by the issue of debentures in amounts of £20, £40 and £200	790,000
(3) The funds of the State Savings Bank, on which 4 per cent. interest is guaranteed	835,000
(4) Sundry convertible securities, cash, &c.	80,000

According to the constitution of bank, loans can only be made on real or *quasi*-real property, and by preference on agricultural and pastoral properties. The following classes of loans are made :—

(1) On real estate, for terms varying from 9 to 53 years, repayable by a sinking fund, varying according to the term, from 10 per cent. to ½ per cent., the interest being calculated at 4½ per cent.

(2) On real estate for not less than five years; but without sinking fund repayment; at the expiration of this time repayment cannot be required unless a year's notice has been given.

(3) On assignment of mortgage debts and deposit of the bankers own debentures.

During 1883, 4½ per cent. interest was charged on loans with a commission of from ½ to ¼ per cent.; £12 is the smallest amount lent.

Four per cent. is paid, the debentures issued and outstanding debentures issued at 4½ and 4¼ per cent. are being paid off.

At the ending of 1883, the bank had 17,533 debentures of the aggregate value of £790,000 in circulation, and had 9,087 loans outstanding of the aggregate value of £1,899,400.

During 1883 its chief operations were the issue of 1,026 new loans amounting to £219,500; and the cancelling of loans repaid amounting to £162,183, the issue of 1,264 new debentures at 4 per cent., and the paying off of 588 4½ and 4¼ per cent. debentures of the value of £39,700. It had property of the value of £60,000 in liquidation, and during the year had disposed of £18,880 worth of these estates. The realization of such property is, the directors report, the most difficult part of their work, requiring great care and watchfulness of the market, lest by too many sales in any locality they should increase the depression which had now for some years prevailed in the market for land.

The bank pays 4 per cent. for the Savings Bank funds; a trifle over 4 per cent. on the whole on its debentures and 4 per cent. on its paid up shares; after providing for these fixed charges, three-fifth of the net profit is divided among the shareholders, and the remaining two-fifth between the bank's officers and the reserve funds.

For 1883 the bank had a net profit of £7,304, which was disposed of in the following manner :—

	£
One per cent. to the holders in addition to the fixed interest of 4 per cent.	3,800
To the reserve fund	1,638
To a special reserve for depreciation of property in liquidation	1,200
Bonus to the bank officers	620
Carried forward	46
Total ..	7,304

Management expenses amounted to £2,500, taxes and sundries to £1,100.

In round numbers the bank handles about £2,000,000, and on this sum earns about 10*s.* per £100. The shareholders are content with the modest return of 5 per cent. The business can scarcely be called very remunerative, but is kept up for the public convenience by the countenance of the State, its credit, and partial guarantee, and by special laws to facilitate operations. The receivers of taxes throughout the canton act as agents for the bank and the Savings Bank.

Even the modest return of 5 per cent. could not be earned were it not for the facility and certainty with which loans can be charged upon land. Imagine the Solicitor of an English county making 1,000 investigations of title each year and the cost of such investigations and of the mortgage-deeds in case the loans were made.

The term "mortgage" is not properly applicable to loans secured upon land under the system prevailing in countries subject to the principles of French Civil Code, for the legal estate in the land is not conveyed to the lender as under the English system; but as the word "mortgage" and *hypothèque* are almost exclusively used in connection with loans upon real property, it is convenient to treat them as equivalent, although the legal ideas underlying the two words are different. The description given by Mr. Jenkins, Assistant Agricultural Commissioner, of the system of transfer and mortgage in France, Belgium, the Netherlands and Denmark is equally applicable to most of Switzerland.

"The transfer of landed property is done by means of a system of book-keeping, coupled with an official map on which every plot of land is marked and numbered; a registration office exists in each district; and an intending purchaser can ascertain in a short time the official acreage of any particular field; the name of the registered owner, the amount and nature of any mortgage or other charges upon it. No transaction connected with the land is authentic (in other words legally executed) unless it is duly registered at the district office. The proceeding is perfectly simple and effective."

In Vaud the following books are kept for each commune in connection with the official maps :—

(1) A register of parcels (*registre Foncier*).

(2) A register of owners and their properties (*registre cadastrale or cadastre*).

(3) A register of loans of land (*controle des hypothèques*).

(4) A register of rights, easements, temporary interests (*controle des charges immobilières*).

If an owner wishes to borrow, say, 100 francs or £40, and charge his property with that amount, he furnishes with his application to the bank his title, consisting of an extract from the *Cadastre*, and certificate endorsed thereon by the Registrar of Loans and Charges. The expense of obtaining this would not usually exceed 2*s*. The loan having been agreed to, an *acte* would be drawn by a Notary for 5 francs to the effect that the borrower admits his liability, and charges his land with the amount in favour of the lender. This is represented to the Registrar, and the charge recorded against for a fee of from 1*s*. to 2*s*. The charge can be fully or partially erased when paid off in full or in part or can be assigned to a person for similar trifling fees.

Special laws, in addition to Vaudois Civil Code, have been recently passed in order to facilitate the obtaining of loans on land, and in these laws the interests of borrowers have been preferred to those of lenders.

The preamble of a law (*Loi concernante l'obligation hypothecaire à terme*) passed in 1874 recites that the wants of the country require that greater facilities should be given for obtaining loans upon land, and this law legalized a new and special form of *hypothèque* for a term of years not less than five. At the expiration of this term, or at any subsequent period, the lender cannot require repayment, except after a year's notice; the borrower may pay off the loan or any part, being not less than one-third of the original loan, on giving three months' notice. Instead of making repayment when legally demanded, the debtor may require the creditor to assign his right of action to any other person who may be willing to take it up. These loans may be paid off by a sinking fund not exceeding 10 per cent. annually on the loan.

The 16th section of this law promised the establishment of a Land Credit Fund, and, in fulfilment of this promise, a special decree reorganized a previously existing loan fund and constituted the present Land Credit Bank.

The bank is restricted to make loans on real estate, preference is to be given to, and the greater part of the bank's resources lent on, rural and agricultural properties. Loans must not be made for more than two-thirds of the capital value of vineyard land, where the growing vines constitute a considerable portion of the value, and are capable of removal or deterioration; in other cases three-fourths value may be lent. In case of unpunctual payment, interest at the rate of 6 per cent. is charged on the overdue annuity.

The general council of the bank, on which the executive government has a preponderating influence, is charged with the duty of laying down each year the general lines on which business is to be carried on, fixing the rates of interest and providing that the greater part of the loans shall be made on rural properties and repayable on the sinking fund system.

The land debenture (*obligation foncière*) is one of the chief instruments used by these land credit banks, and the Vaudois Bank derives nearly half of its resources from the issue of these debentures in exchange for deposits. They are issued in amounts of £20, £40, and £200, with interest coupons attached, payable to particular persons and transferable by endorsement or payable to bearer and transferable by delivery; they are repayable at par after three years on three months' notice being given to the holder.

They are recommended as safe and suitable investment for persons of small means, municipalities and friendly societies. The law permits trust moneys to be invested in them, without application to any legal tribunal. The security for these debentures is the whole amount of property mortgaged to the bank and the paid-up share capital of the bank on which the State guarantees 4 per cent. interest. The numerous mortgage debts of various amounts due to the bank, and each secured on a certain special property are, as it were, converted into stock and issued in amounts found to suit the convenience of the public.

The whole amount of the bank's transactions may seem small; but it is to be remembered that its operations are confined to a district and population which are not as large as some counties in Ireland. The county of Antrim, exclusive of the borough of Belfast, is about the same size and has about the same population as *Canton de Vaud*.

The success of this bank earning for its shareholders the modest dividend of 5 per cent. is due to the countenance and guarantee of the State not so much as to the system of land transfer and registration of charges, without which its operations could not be carried on at all.

The effect of the State aid extends its operations and keeps the rate of interest charged somewhat lower than it otherwise would be. The State aid would be of little avail if the general law was not adapted to the needs of the country, making transfer and registration charges so easy, that price of the land is quoted by the yards and sales are made with quite as much facility and with same certainty as to costs as sales of shares and stock in this country.

Transfer of land by deed in comparison with transfer on the record of title system seems as antiquated and cumbrous as the use of metal in bulk in place of coin. In the one case the metal must be assayed and weighed at every transfer; in the other its quality and weight are known at sight.

Under a perfected system of recording titles it is seldom that the title cannot be kept written up. Its state and ownership can be ascertained at a glance, and a legal certificate can be obtained in a few minutes. The delays and uncertainty of the other system are only too familiar to persons in this country who have had dealings with lands.

Another Swiss Land Credit Bank, the "*Banque Foncière de Jura*," without any State aid or guarantee, also pays 5 per cent. on its paid-up capital. Its head-quarters are at Delémont, the most prosperous part of the Canton of Berne. This Bank, however, charges from $4\frac{3}{4}$ to 5 per cent. for most of its loans and pays from $4\frac{1}{4}$ to $4\frac{1}{2}$ on all its debentures. Money is obtained on its debentures so easily that it has abandoned a contemplated increase of its paid-up capital. In their report for 1883, the directors say that the interest and annuities due have been satisfactorily paid and that notwithstanding the great depreciation in the value of land, not only in the Jura, but throughout the whole of Switzerland and adjoining countries, they have been enabled to sell properties on their hands without loss and sometimes at a profit.

Mr. H. D. MacLeod, in his *Lectures on Credit and Banking*, claims for the system of cash credits, as practised in Scotland, similar advantages to those of the Continental Land Credit Banks. There is, however, a very great difference, which is due to the superior system of transfer and mortgage under the Continental codes of law. The "Cash credit" is given on personal security and for a short term. In the case of the Continental *hypothèque* the land is the security; the loans can be made for long terms and at a lower rate of interest.

Although 5 per cent. may appear to be a very small return for a banking business as compared with the earnings of English and Irish banks, it is in reality a very good return for an investment on the security of real estate, and must be considered in this light when contrasted with earnings of a speculative business, such as an ordinary bank.

Mr. Thorold Rogers says it has been estimated that conveyance of real estate in the United Kingdom is mulcted in law charges, exclusive of taxes, to the extent of £12,000,000 annually :—

"Such charges are not only a present loss, but the system under which they are permitted brings about and perpetuates an insecurity from which properly registered titles would be free."

Whether the estimate of £12,000,000 be correct or not, there can be no doubt that the legal charges on the conveyancing and charging of lands are enormous, not in proportion to the work done, for the evil consists in there being so much work, such cumbrous method of performing what might be done, and what is done in other countries, so much more simply, certainly, expeditiously and cheaply.

The reported failures of the many attempts at reform in Ireland by means of "purchase clauses" may not be considered universally due to the want of a simple system of transfer and charging. Transfer of land ownership from one class to another may be effected on a large scale by a liberal system of State loans; but it is essential to the success of the system sought to be established that the laws relating to transfer and loans on lands should be radically changed. Under those at present in force, loans of small amounts on land are unsafe; they are made on a bad security, no matter how much the value of the land may exceed the amount of the loan, for the security can neither be sold or charged, nor can loans be recovered without delay, and great and uncertain expense.

(D).—Decay of Domestic Industries, Absence of Diversity of Occupations, &c.

(1) *Extracts from a Reply published in the* Madras Mail *of the 7th and 9th February* 1893, *to certain criticisms contained in an article published in the* Calcutta Review *for January* 1893, *headed "Agricultural History in Madras, and What it teaches us."*

* * * *

I. *Why was a period of* 40 *years taken for gauging the progress made?*—The reviewer sees some deep design on the part of Lord Connemara in having proposed that a memorandum should be prepared furnishing materials for forming a judgment as to the results of the last 40 years of British administration on the economic condition of the Presidency. The reviewer agrees with me, however, in thinking that "there can be no two opinions as to the very great advance made by the country" during this period, but supposes that no one in his senses ever asserted the contrary. To this it is perhaps sufficient to reply that there are persons—intelligent and well-meaning persons too—who, mainly because they have not had facilities for studying the question in all its details, have asserted the contrary for the last 20 years and more; and an inquiry as to whether there is any, and, if so, what truth in their statements is by no means superfluous. The reviewer's idea is that, having regard to the effects of improved and cheaper internal and external communications which should have stimulated enormously its greatest industry, viz., agriculture, a much shorter period should have been taken for review, and that no more suitable period could be found than the last 20 years. It is, of course, easy to object to any period that might be taken, either on the ground that it is too long or too short; but the reasons for taking a period of 40 years are sufficiently obvious. For one thing, a period of 20 years is far too short to gauge the effects of economic forces in operation, of new laws, institutions, methods of Government and administrative measures in any country, and it is emphatically so in a country in which a great famine occurs once in 100 years, and scarcities of greater or less intensity every 12 years or so, and in which the institutions and the habits of the people change slowly. The reviewer admits that the disastrous famine that occurred 7 years after the commencement of the period which he contends should have been taken for review was the severest known during the present century, that it threw back the Presidency "to an enormous extent," and that such a visitation is not ascribable to the defects of British administration. Barely 13 years have passed since this catastrophe occurred, and it would clearly be absurd to select this period specially for gauging the effects of British rule on the condition of the population. The middle of the century, on the other hand, is a suitable starting point in every way for the purposes of a comparison such as that proposed to be instituted. During the first quarter of the century the efforts of the British Government were directed towards introducing order and tranquillity in the territories newly acquired and in carrying out land settlements. The second quarter witnessed the acute agricultural depression,—due, in the main, to the substitution of a *regimé* of cash payments for one of barter and the insufficiency of the currency to meet requirements under the altered condition of things,—the effects of which I have endeavoured to describe in the Memorandum. The East India Company was at its wit's end to find the wherewithal to carry on the administration of the country and the wars which were undertaken under the pressure of necessity or otherwise for the consolidation of the Empire; the initiation of improvements on an extensive scale during this period was, therefore, out of the question. It was about 1850, then, that almost every species of reform and improvement had its commencement—the construction of railways, roads, anicuts and canals, the establishment of schools and Universities, the constitution of Legislative Councils and the enactment of Codes of Laws, the reorganisation of the Police and the Magistracy, the revision of revenue establishments, the abolition of restrictions on trade, the settlement of lands held on favorable terms but uncertain or doubtful titles, the alleviation of burdens on land, and a host of other reforms;

and within 8 years after the commencement of this period the direct Government of the Indian Empire was transferred from the East India Company to the Crown. The gold discoveries in California and Australia, of course, made the carrying out of these reforms possible, by stimulating foreign trade, causing an influx of the precious metals, and replenishing an insufficient currency. From 1850 to 1870 under the stimulus of the exceptionally high prices of commodities which ruled, the causes of which I have explained in my Memorandum, there was enormous expansion of cultivation and trade, and the period was one of unexampled, if inflated, prosperity. After 1870 prices suddenly fell and gave a check to cultivation, and the famine that followed was one of appalling severity and strained the resources of the country to the utmost. From a national point of view, the first period comprised the "fat" years and the second the "lean" ones, and in a country where the "fat" and "lean" years come in almost regular succession, the proper method to adopt in estimating the normal advance made is not to take either period by itself, but to take the combined period as a whole. This is what I have done.

II. *Reviewer's analysis of the statistics of the acreage of holdings.*—The reviewer's procedure in taking a period of 20 years for gauging the general advance made by the country under British administration is about as reasonable as the conduct of a man who, to estimate the advance in general health made under a course of hygienic treatment by a patient subject to periodical attacks of fever which occasionally assumes a malignant form, compares the state of his health when it was at its best with the state at which it is a short time after he has suffered from one of the most malignant of such attacks. For the more limited purpose of finding out how far the country has, under the impetus given by good administration, been enabled to recover from the disastrous effects of the late famine, a comparison for a shorter period would doubtless be legitimate, but in that case the period taken should not be the last 20 but the last 10 years. If such a comparison be made, it will be found that the country is rapidly recovering from the effects of the late famine. In 1875 the ryotwar holdings amounted to 20 million acres, of which 16·3 millions consisted of unirrigated and 3·7 millions of irrigated land. The famine which commenced in 1876 lasted till 1878, while its immediate after-effects continued down to 1882. By 1882, the accounts were cleared of holdings which had been entered in the names of ryots who had deserted or died, and the total area was reduced to 18·8 millions of acres, of which 15 millions of acres consisted of lands classed as unirrigated and 3·8 millions of lands classed as irrigated. In 1890, the acreage of holdings had increased to 21 millions—16·9 millions of unirrigated land and 4·1 millions of irrigated land. The advance made in 8 years was 11·7 per cent.—12·6 per cent. in unirrigated and 8 per cent. in irrigated land. These figures have doubtless to be discounted on account of excess of area found in holdings over and above the area entered in the revenue accounts according to the old measurements in districts resurveyed subsequent to 1882; but this excess area is very small. The only districts in which the new survey areas were introduced between 1882 and 1890 were portions of Cuddapah, South Arcot, Madura and Ganjám, the Wynaad and the whole of the North Arcot district except one taluk, and Vizagapatam.

I have not with me ready to hand exact statistics showing the excess area discovered by remeasurement in the tracts, but there can be no doubt that it cannot exceed 300,000 acres, or about one-seventh of the increase in the area of holdings. Against this has to be set off the extent of lands cultivated but not included under holdings for various reasons; the excess of such cultivation in 1890 over 1882 in the 7 districts greatly affected by the famine was 240,000 acres, or 300,000 acres for the whole Presidency. The increase of population during the 8 years at the rate of 1·5 per cent. per annum was 12 per cent., and taking the yield of irrigated lands to be between four and five times that of unirrigated lands on an average, the increase in production as measured by the area of holdings has proceeded, so far, as fast as the increase in population. In the Kistna and the Gódávari deltas there was an increase of nearly 250,000 acres, or 30 per cent., in the area irrigated both in Government taluks and zemindari tracts, during the last 8 years, and this means an enormous addition to the food production of the country.

The same result is arrived at by an examination of the statistics returned of acreage actually cultivated. In 1882 the area of unirrigated cultivation was 12·3 million acres, of irrigated cultivation 3·5 million acres—total 15·8 million acres. For 1890, the figures were 14 million acres unirrigated, 3·9 millions irrigated—total 17·9 million acres. The increase in 8 years was 13·8 per cent. in unirrigated, and 11 per cent. in irrigated cultivation, subject to the allowance already referred to on account of the excess area found on remeasurement. There is, however, a large extent of cultivation not brought to account in the register of holdings, and the acreage of this cultivation has increased in later years. There is, besides, extension of second crop cultivation and of cultivation with the aid of well irrigation to be taken into account. It must further be remembered that during the period in question the taking up of poor lands thrown out of occupation during the late famine has been discouraged in two ways, viz., first by the imposition of substantial assessments on the lowest class of lands instead of the nominal pepper-corn assessments that used to be levied under the old settlements; and, secondly, the large extent of lands taken up by the Forest Department for fuel and fodder reserves. About 200,000 acres were taken up in the Bellary and Anantapur districts alone. Large extents of lands have similarly been reserved in other districts.

Apart from the cardinal objection already stated to comparing the statistics of holdings in 1890 with those of 1870, the reviewer has overlooked many important considerations and committed several errors in carrying out his analysis. Taking the Presidency as a whole, with the exception of South Canara, the nominal area of ryotwar holdings, as shown in the accounts, increased from 19·6 millions of acres in 1870 to 21 millions of acres in 1890, *i.e.,* 7 per cent. (not 12 per cent. as stated by the reviewer). The values of irrigated and unirrigated lands differ so enormously that we should be drawing very erroneous conclusions from these figures if we do not consider the increase in the irrigated and unirrigated areas separately. For instance, in 1890, the 16·9 millions of acres of unirrigated lands comprised within holdings were assessed to the revenue at only 174·6 lakhs of rupees, while 4·1 millions of acres of irrigated land were assessed at 205·7 lakhs of rupees, or in other words, acre for acre, irrigated, land is worth nearly

5 times as much as unirrigated land, supposing that the assessment bears a uniform ratio to the rental, which, of course, can be taken to be true only as a very rough approximation. The increase in the unirrigated area was from 16 millions to 16·9 millions, or 5·6 per cent. and in the irrigated area from 3·6 millions to 4·1 millions of acres, or by 14 per cent. The increase thus shown has to be discounted on account of excess area found in holdings only in districts which have been surveyed between 1870 and 1890, and districts which have not yet been surveyed, or which were surveyed prior to 1870, remain untouched by this consideration. These latter districts are the Gódávari, the Masulipatam portion of the Kistna district comprising the Kistna delta, Tanjore, Trichinopoly, Malabar, Bellary and Anantapur, the larger portion of the South Arcot and the Kurnool districts, *i.e.*, they include nearly all the districts in which the tracts commanded by the great irrigation systems are situated, or in which areas classed as wet largely predominate. The survey increase in the remaining districts may, on a rough calculation, be estimated at 160,000 acres in irrigated and 800,000 acres in unirrigated land. The real increase in the unirrigated land is thus reduced to 100,000 acres or ·6 per cent., and in the irrigated land to 340,000 acres, or 10 per cent. If the two classes of land be reduced to a common denomination by taking 5 acres of unirrigated land as equal to an acre of irrigated land, the increase in holdings in the 20 years amounts to 5 per cent., while the increase in population during the same period has been 14 per cent.

* * * *

The course of prices.—A most important consideration, which the reviewer entirely overlooks in his examination of the pressure of population on the land, is the course of prices. In the 10 years ending 1870, the prices ruled highest, this result being due to the fact that the quantity of precious metals received into the country as the value of merchandise exported and as the proceeds of loans raised in England for carrying out railways and irrigation works, was largely in excess of the requirements of this country for purposes of currency. The average price of second sort paddy during this period was Rs. 172 per garce. After 1870, the price suddenly fell, and the average for 6 years prior to the famine of 1877 was reduced to Rs. 141. During the famine, of course, prices rose enormously and the average price for the whole decade reached the level of that of the previous decade. The prices for the decade ending 1890 have, however, averaged only Rs. 142. The prices during the last 2 years have been higher, but this is due to the drought which has prevailed over large portions of the Presidency and the consequent failure of crops. What is stated above as regards the price of paddy is more or less true of other food-grains, for the prices of these food-grains move in sympathy with those of paddy, subject to the qualification that as their consumption is confined to special tracts, the rise or fall in their prices in years of scarcity or plenty, as the case may be, is in a greater ratio than the rise or fall in the price of paddy. Now increased pressure of population can only mean the inability of the supplies of food to overtake the demand and the rise of the price of food as a consequence. The prices of food-grains have not risen in normal years above the level of the years immediately preceding the famine. So recently as 1887, the price of paddy, second sort, went down as low as Rs. 128 per garce, the lowest point it had reached during the previous 30 years. If the purchasing power of silver had risen, this result would be consistent with increased pressure of population; but the purchasing value of silver has really fallen by more than one-third, or nearly 35 per cent., as compared with gold, and absolutely by at least 20 per cent. This being so, supposing other things were equal, the prices of food-grains should have risen in the same ratio. When, however, we find that there has been in recent normal years no rise in the prices of food-grains at all, the conclusion is irresistible that the increased pressure of the population on the means of subsistence is so far a mere figment of the imagination.

Actual cultivation and holdings.—Further instances of the reviewer's unfair and inconclusive reasoning are found in his remarks on the proportion borne by the area of actual cultivation to the acreage of ryotwar holdings, the increase of the land-tax, and the sub-divisions of holdings. Prior to the famine of 1877--78, the ratio of the area of cultivation to holdings was 88·2 per cent. on an average, and in 1890 the ratio was 85·2 per cent. The fall in the ratio is taken by the reviewer as indicative "of a decided retrogression in the ability of the ryots to carry on the cultivation of their holdings." To ordinary minds, a fall in the ratio in normal years would be proof of the fact of the pressure on land having been lightened and not increased, for, were the latter the case, the land-owners who were unable to cultivate portions of their holdings would relinquish such portions, and increasing difficulty would be felt in realising the Government dues, leading to forced sales for the recovery of arrears of revenue. This is not only not the case, but the very opposite of it is true. The area of land sold for arrears of land-tax has been constantly diminishing during recent years, while the revenue itself is collected with the greatest punctuality. The area sold in 1890 was 23,615 acres out of a total area of holdings of 21 million acres; more than half of this area consisted of valueless land on the margin of cultivation taken up or relinquished by the ryots according to the exigencies of the season, and was purchased by Government for nominal prices averaging less than 2 annas per acre. The true reason, however, for the fall in the percentage is the fact that prior to 1874 the statistics of acreage of cultivation included portions of demarcated fields left waste which are now excluded. In 1871 the extent of portion of fields left waste amounted to 325,000 and in 1872 to 500,000 acres or 1½ and 2½ per cent., respectively, of the total area of holdings. In the calculations given in my Memorandum, I accordingly made an allowance of 2 per cent. on this account. The reviewer, who has not thought it necessary to take the trouble of investigating the question fully, has summarily rejected my estimate as "without justification."

* * * *

IV. *Pressure of population.*—What then are the actual present position and immediate future prospects as regards pressure of population? I have dwelt at some length in my Memorandum on the various considerations bearing on the question, but as the reviewer has ignored most of them, confining his attention almost exclusively to the single consideration of the extension of the area of cultivation, it is desirable even at the risk of repetition to consider the question as a whole. The first point requiring consideration is the normal rate of increase of population in this country. In the decade ending 1890 the population increased by 15 per cent. or 1·44 per cent. per annum, but the increase during this period was obviously abnormal. The mortality caused by the famine of 1876–78 fell heaviest on the very old and the very young, and birth-rates for the time received a check. The result was that in the surviving population the proportion of aged and juvenile persons was abnormally low, and that of persons of what may be called reproductive ages correspondingly high. Now the increase of population is due to the excess of the births over the deaths. The births during the decade were abnormally high because of the abnormally high proportion of persons of reproductive ages left in the population, and the deaths were abnormally low because the proportion of aged and juvenile persons among whom the death-rate is the highest was abnormally low. The combined effect of both the causes was to enhance the rate of increase of population for a short period far beyond what it would be under normal conditions. The disproportion, however, soon rights itself, and the rate of increase of population resumes its normal level. It is clear, then, that the $1\frac{1}{2}$ per cent. rate is one which is maintained for a brief period shortly after the population has been reduced very considerably by frightful mortality such as that of the famine of 1876–78. This high rate may also be maintained when there is extraordinary accession of prosperity resulting from exceptional circumstances such as the "boom" in the decade ending 1870. In either case, however, the effects must be merely temporary; and I mention this to show that it would not be right to treat the $1\frac{1}{2}$ per cent. rate as if it were normal, and to expect that population would go on increasing at this rate. In the Census Report of British India for 1881, the normal rate of increase was estimated at ·6 per cent. for districts liable to frequent failures of crops and ·8 per cent. for the remainder of the Presidency. Between 1870 and 1890 the population increased by 14 per cent., or ·66 per cent. per annum, and as such a frightful famine of 1877 is not likely to occur except once in a century, 1 per cent. per annum may be safely taken to be the normal rate of increase for this country.

The second question for consideration is: Is the production of the country per head of the population lower now than it was in 1870? If it is, it would *not* necessarily show that the country, notwithstanding the *temporary* check received by it, is not economically progressing in the right direction, and this for two reasons, viz., first, 1870 marks the end of a period of abnormal prosperity, when, owing to the American war and consequent demand for Indian cotton, the Indian produce had trebled in value, and large areas devoted to the production of food-crops were cultivated with cotton crops, and inferior soils were taken up for the cultivation of the former under the stimulus of high prices, and the season in 1870 itself is described in the Government records to have been "conspicuously favorable for agricultural operations;" and, secondly, in about the middle of the period the country was afflicted with a terrible famine which caused a mortality of nearly four millions, and a loss of revenue of 1·2 crores of rupees and entailed on the State an expenditure of $6\frac{3}{4}$ crores of rupees in dispensation of relief to the suffering population. Let us, however, see what the actual facts are. The population increased during the 20 years by about $4\frac{1}{2}$ millions, or 14 per cent. The increase in the area of holdings, allowing for the superior productiveness of irrigated as compared with unirrigated land, and taking into account the survey excess, may be estimated, as we have already seen, at 5 per cent. Is the inference to be drawn (as the reviewer has done) that the income per head of the population is about 10 per cent. less than what it was in 1870, and that the established standard of living has to that extent deteriorated? A little consideration will show that such an inference is opposed to fact. As I have already stated, prices fell from the inflated level they had attained in the sixties so that for the five years preceding the famine of 1876–78 they were 30 per cent. less than the average of the previous decade. Prices now, excluding the last 2 years in which a drought prevailed over considerable portions of the Presidency, are not much above that level. In the year preceding the famine of 1876–78, or, in other words, before 1874, the rate of exchange was at par. Of late years the rate of exchange, that is the value of silver expressed in terms of gold, has fallen by as much as 35 per cent. This divergence in the values of gold and silver is known to be, in the main, due to the fall in the general purchasing power of silver; and taking the latter to be even as low as 20 per cent., the prices in this country, other things being equal, should have risen at least in a corresponding ratio. Prices have not risen appreciably and certainly not in anything like a ratio of 20 per cent. Increased pressure of population means increased demand for food and the rise in prices in consequence; and a consideration of prices, therefore, shows that the pressure has not increased, but, on the contrary, has been lightened. Another gauge of the pressure of the population is the change in the standard of living of the higher and middle classes of the population and also the change in the real wages of the labouring classes as estimated by the quantity of food-grains which the wages, when paid in money, would purchase. No one who has had the least experience of the country will deny that the standard of living has considerably risen during the last 20 years. I have collected together in my Memorandum a large body of evidence on this subject, and my subsequent inquiries only go to show that I understated the real position in this respect. As regards wages of labouring classes, since I wrote my Memorandum, I have obtained information from all parts of the country. Nearly 8,000 contracts for labour registered in the various Registration offices of the Presidency have been examined, and the result goes to show that in no instances have the old customary rates suffered reduction; that in tracts where custom is persistent, the perquisites and extras now given are considerably higher than they were; that in some places grain wages for harvest work have almost doubled, and daily wages have increased, though not to the same extent; that notwithstanding the depressed state of the weaving industry, there is no redundancy of labour as compared with past years; that the complaint among landholders is that it is difficult to get labourers either to work with zeal, or full time for the old rates of grain wages, which is proof of the fact that there is a struggle going on for the re-adjustment and enhancement of the old customary rates of wages; that during the off season when agricultural work is suspended, labourers find other employment to a greater extent than was the case in the past, and that the condition of labourers, except in remote and secluded parts, is one of decided improvement. I have heard it sometimes asserted that while the higher classes and the lowest classes have improved, the middle classes have deteriorated.' Such an assertion carries with it its own refutation. There is no sharp division between the several classes in this country, and the gradations rise or fall by imperceptible degrees, and when there is improvement in the higher and lower strata it stands to reason that it extends all along the line. The classes which work neither with the head nor with the hands have, of course, suffered under the present *régime*. Persons belonging to the middle classes who have not been able to rise to the requirements of the times and keep up with their fellows have also had to sink relatively to a lower position, much to their chagrin and discontent. Barring individual exceptions, that the middle classes as a whole have risen along with the higher and lower classes, there cannot be the slightest doubt.

The question arises, if the condition of the country as a whole has not deteriorated since 1870, but, on the contrary, has improved, and if the area of cultivation has not increased in proportion to the increase in population, how is the additional wealth obtained? The sources of this additional wealth are (1) improved cultivation in tracts of country where the conditions admit of it; (2) extension of cultivation of valuable commercial products; (3) the substitution owing to extension of communications of cultivation of soils in tracts hitherto inaccessible for cultivation of poor soils in tracts which have had all along the advantage of good communications; (4) additional value obtained for commercial produce by reduction in the cost of transport by sea and land; and (5) the saving in the cost at which imported merchandise is obtained both on account of the reduction in the cost of production in the country whence the articles are obtained, and the cost of transport. That these causes have diminished the pressure of population will be seen from the fact that it is in the prosperous districts—Tanjore, Trichinopoly, Malabar, Madura, Tinnevelly and Coimbatore—that the increase in the area of holdings has fallen much short of the increase in population. In Tanjore, though cultivation is not as careful as it ought to be, it is certainly much more careful than it was in times past; manure is made use of to a greater extent than formerly. In the Shiyali taluk, I understand, owing probably to the example set by the late Mr. Krishnasamy Mudelliar, more efficient cattle power is employed for ploughing and the cattle are better fed and less liable to epizootics. In the dry districts the improvement in agriculture has taken the form of extension of well cultivation, which is undoubtedly advancing by rapid strides when the expense and the risk involved in finding suitable sites for wells are taken into account. Manures are also applied to a considerable extent to market garden produce in the vicinity of towns. Mr. Benson, in his analysis of the agricultural statistics of the Kurnool district, notes: "For the irrigated lands near Nandyal, the whole country is swept to find manure. Indigo vat refuse is brought from as far as 20 or 30 miles for use there, and prices varying from Annas 8 to Rs. 5 a cart-load are paid for it. The ryot no doubt appreciates such manures as are known to him, but the number he uses is limited, and above all others, he does not appear to understand the conservation of them. This is perhaps not surprising when it is remembered how modern is any knowledge of the subject." The bats' dung in the Bella Surghum caves is, it appears, collected and carried away by men from Cuddapah. The extension of the cultivation of indigo and of sugar-cane has already been referred to. Groundnut cultivation has brought a considerable accession of wealth to the South Arcot and Chingleput districts and parts of North Arcot, Tanjore and Trichinopoly. The returns of this cultivation are very great and the ryots, especially in the Shiyali taluk of the Tanjore district, are using considerable quantities of manure to prevent possible deterioration of the soil by over cropping. As regards the effect of the extension of communications in the way of bringing fertile soil in remote situations under cultivation, it is a familiar truth not needing demonstration. This fact to some extent acts as a counterpoise to the necessity for poorer lands being taken up for cultivation as population increases. As the Government revenue assessed on lands depends upon the rent value, which again is affected conjointly both by the productive power of the lands and the facilities for taking the produce to market, the fact of fertile lands in remote tracts having been taken up for cultivation could not be discovered merely by a comparison of the revenue rates of the old years with those of recent years. As regards the increased value realised by ryots for commercial produce and the low cost at which imported articles are obtained, the following facts may be noted. Within the last 20 years the value of the foreign sea-borne trade of the Presidency has increased from 10·2 to 18·2 crores of rupees, the increase in the imports being from 4·1 to 6·6 crores and in the exports from 6·1 to 11·6 crores. The development of railways in this country has greatly reduced the cost of transport of goods by land, and the opening of the Suez Canal, the extension of telegraph lines, the improvements and economies effected in the construction and working of steamers have immensely diminished the cost of carriage by sea and the incidental charges. An idea may be formed as to how great the saving is from the fact that the cost of carriage of Cawnpore wheat taken to Calcutta and shipped there to London was reduced between 1879 and 1886 by 9 shillings a quarter, a reduction of 22 per cent. on the value of the wheat in London, viz., 42 shilling a quarter in 1881. The value of the staple imported articles—cotton goods and metals—has greatly fallen, the value at Calcutta being now one-third less than in 1873, although during this period the value of silver has fallen enormously. For more detailed particulars the paragraphs of the Memorandum bearing on the subject should be referred to.

The next question we have to consider is whether there is any *immediate* danger of the increase of population outstripping the increase of production and causing a deterioration in the standard of living. The population, as already observed, may, under normal conditions, be assumed to increase at the rate of one per cent. per annum in this country. The late Sir James Caird was of opinion that "it is possible to obtain such a gradual increase of production as would meet the present rate of increase of population for a considerable time. One bushel per acre gained gradually in 10 years, in addition to a moderate reclamation of cultivable land, would meet the demand of the present growth of population; considering the generally fertile nature of the soil and that, in most parts of India, two crops can be got in the year, this would seem to be a possible result. By these two methods wisely combined, the increase of population may be safely provided for several generations." The experience of the past 20 years to my mind shows incontestably that, extraordinary and unforeseen calamities of such magnitude as the famine of 1877 apart, there is no reason to doubt that by the combined efforts of the Government and the people, the modest estimate put forward by Sir James Caird would be realised, if not exceeded. The Government has already done so much, both directly by the construction of irrigation works and indirectly by the extension of communications, that the tendency of increased pressure of population has been counteracted without imposing on the people the necessity to resort to the cultivation of poorer lands to any considerable extent—a fact which, the reviewer, most erroneously, in my opinion, takes to be evidence of the deterioration of the economic condition of the population. The railway and irrigation projects still under execution—the Tank Restoration Scheme, the Periyar and the Rushikuliya irrigation projects, and the East Coast Railway will immensely develop what are now backward districts and add to the food production not merely of particular tracts but of the country as a whole. The reviewer has very curious ideas about the effect of irrigation works on tracts of country other than those in which they are actually situated, as he remarks tautologically regarding the Kistna and the Góćávari anicuts that they affect "strictly localised areas," ignoring the fact that the Gódávari and Burma rice are being sold at Negapatam in the centre of the Cauvery delta, while considerable quantities of Tanjore rice are exported to Madura and Tinnevelly districts. We have also seen that the real value of food-grains, *i.e.*, the price taking into account the change in the purchasing power of money in terms of which it is expressed, has so far fallen and not risen. On the part of the ryots the improvements effected by them have consisted chiefly in the extension of cultivation by wells and, to some extent, in the cultivation of commercial crops and the adoption of improved methods of cultivation as regards crops for which there is a fairly constant demand in foreign markets, for instance Tinnevelly cotton. As regards cultivation by wells, I have made inquiries in all directions, and there is not the least doubt that it is extending rapidly in Coimbatore, Salem, Madura, Tinnevelly, Chingleput and Trichinopoly districts. Mr. Nicholson, I believe, found that, in some villages in the Tinnevelly district, wells had enormously increased during the last decade. The increase in the Coimbatore district is well known. In one of the zemindaries in the Madura district for which I have information, the number of wells has doubled during the same period. 20,000 wells have been dug within the last 2 years alone with the aid of loans obtained from Government to the extent of upwards of 30 lakhs of rupees, and a very recent inspection of these wells by the Settlement Commissioner showed that they are in good condition and calculated to be of great benefit to the tracts where they have been excavated. The increase of produce due to application of irrigation to land whether the water is obtained from channels, tanks, or wells, must have increased the average rate of outturn per acre and it is absurd on the part of the reviewer to contend that this is not quite as legitimate an increase in the average outturn as the additional produce obtained by the adoption of improved methods of tillage, and of rotation of crops, and by the application of expensive manures. Though there has been some improvement in the latter respects also, it is on too small a scale to be striking.

The reasons why the improvement has taken the form of extension of irrigation either by means of water provided by Government or obtained by the ryots at their expense from wells are not far to seek. Cultivation in this country is dependent on supply of water, while in England the main problem connected with agriculture is drainage. The extreme variations in the quantity of rainfall and the times when it comes down make every other consideration of far less importance than the supply of water in the quantities and at the times required for cultivation. The first great requisite of successful agriculture except in black cotton soils, which are extremely retentive of moisture and yield abundant returns in spite of scanty rainfall, is therefore storage of water or the tapping of subsoil springs. The application of irrigation to crops increases also the produce so enormously in proportion to the cost of the water that no other mode of raising additional produce from land can compete with it. In the case of lands for which means of irrigation are not available, the produce fluctuates greatly from year to year according to the quantity and seasonableness of the rainfall. This great uncertainty operates as a bar to the introduction of improved methods of cultivation, rotation of crops, &c., except in the case of commercial crops for which there is a fairly constant demand in foreign countries, because in the case of a rotation of crops for instance, the year in which a light restorative crop is grown might be one in which the season is very favorable and the year in which the main crop is grown might be one of drought. Again, deep ploughing, which is of great assistance to the crop in times of drought, is not required in times of comparatively good rainfall. Similar considerations apply to irrigation by means of wells. I have found from inquiry in the Coimbatore district that garden cultivation by means of wells cannot be carried on successfully unless the cultivator has some acres of *dry* land attached as an adjunct to his "garden" lands. The reason for this is the following. The labour of lifting water is great and the cultivator has to employ all through the year hired labour and bullocks for the purpose. If the rainfall be abundant in any particular year the cultivation can be carried on to a great extent without lifting water, and in such cases both human labour and cattle power will have to be kept idle, *i.e.*, wasted, unless it is employed in dry cultivation thereby enhancing the cost of cultivation by wells. In dry seasons, on the other hand, when the cultivation has to be carried on mainly with the aid of water baled from wells, the whole labour and cattle power is concentrated on the "garden" lands, and the dry fields are left uncultivated. The profits of cultivation in both the years are nearly the same as the value of produce in the dry season would be higher than in the favorable season, notwithstanding that the area under cultivation in the former year was considerably less than in the latter year. In the same way the proportion of crops, pulses for instance, to cereals, is to some extent determined by the extent to which pulses enter into the diet of the population. These considerations are specially applicable to produce grown for home consumption. As foreign demand is developed owing to extension of communications there will be greater room for regulating the kinds of crops grown so as to obtain the largest outturns from the land. I have alluded to these considerations merely to show why there is so much difficulty in putting into practice the principles of agricultural science under a given set of conditions, and that it is not reasonable to expect any marked improvement in agricultural methods unless there is a change in these conditions. At the same time, foreign demand for agricultural produce is changing the conditions so as to enable the cultivators to cultivate the soil in the manner calculated to make it yield the largest return; and in this way while, on the one hand, foreign trade carries off the ingredients of the soil, it also, by placing more wealth in the hands of cultivators, and by making improved methods of cultivation, by which the waste is repaired, possible, works its own cure.

It is at this stage—a stage to which the country is tending—that Government has to adopt all possible measures to ensure that the ryots do not fall below the requirements of the situation. The chief requisites in the ryots can only be very briefly indicated here. These are (1) enterprise or readiness to seize hold of advantages within their reach; (2) knowledge of agricultural principles and practices; and (3) capital. The first want can be supplied only by education—both high and elementary, high for the richer classes who must be the pioneers in agricultural improvement, and elementary to the poorer classes who must imitate and successfully carry out the improvements demonstrated to be practicable by the former. The second want must be supplied by the establishment of Agricultural Schools and Model Farms at various centres in the country. It would not do to look for any immediate results from the establishment of these schools and farms, any more than from measures for imparting elementary education, but the knowledge acquired in these institutions when it becomes diffused would bear fruit in time so soon as the conditions of any particular tract allow of its practical application with profitable results. The third want must be supplied by the establishment of Agricultural Banks. The poorer ryots are unable now to obtain small sums of money required for various purposes connected with their calling except at rates varying from 12 to 18 per cent. even when they are able to offer unexceptionable security for the loans, and this means that they are debarred from making improvements other than those which yield large returns for a small outlay; and this circumstance must, of course, greatly limit the scope for improvement. Moreover, one of the effects of the present *régime* is to diffuse wealth among the mass of the population and not to concentrate it in a few hands in a form easily available for industrial purposes. Unless measures are adopted by Government, by the provision of banking facilities of a character which commands the confidence of the people, to collect these savings in one mass and make them available to persons in need of money for various industrial enterprises at reasonable rates of interest, the material progress of the country will be greatly retarded. None of these measures, it is almost needless to say, will by itself suffice; they should all go hand in hand and when the external conditions favorable to agricultural improvement come into being, those who are expected to move in that direction will be enabled to seize hold of the opportunities presented. It must further be remembered that agricultural improvement after it has set in cannot go on indefinitely and that real progress must come from continual improvement in the standard of living, which implies the gradual re-adjustment of social usages and institutions that conduce to the increase of population beyond the limits imposed by such standard. It may be that there is no prospect of such a transformation taking place in the near future, but as, at the same time, there is no immediate danger of the increase of production not keeping pace with the increase of population, there is, so far as I can see, no reason to despair that the transformation will take place in due time. Meanwhile, the Government will, by educational agencies—both for the richer and the poorer classes—have to make unremitting efforts to quicken the intelligence and promote habits of enterprise and forethought among the people.

V. *The remedial measures proposed by the reviewer.*—The reviewer, however, does not consider that the remedies for the evils of the present economic position lie either in the institution of Agricultural Banks, or in spreading a knowledge of agricultural principles broadcast through the land. He believes in the necessity for *intensive* farming, and to render progress in this direction possible in the near future, he considers it necessary, in the first instance, to attack certain problems of rural economy. The particular remedies he recommends are the following: First, to check the inordinate increase in the number of pauper ryots and to endeavour to turn the tide the other way, so that the *pauper* ryot may become a *solvent* labourer; secondly, to encourage and enforce the consolidation and enclosure of all holdings, so that cultivation may become economical, and the individual may reap the fruits of his labour; thirdly, to teach the ryot to be self-dependent for the support of his cattle and thus gradually to lead up to the improvement of the tilling power by the rejection of the worthless; fourthly, to encourage the capitalist, instead of the speculative pauper, to embark in agricultural pursuits; and fifthly, to check the export of the raw as contrasted with the manufactured or half-worked produce of the land. I have given the suggestions in the reviewer's own words, as it is very difficult to attach any definite meaning to them. What precise measures Government should take to secure the first of the objects aimed at the reviewer does not explain, but the suggestions sometimes put forward in this connection are that an upset price of say not less than ten times the Government revenue payable should be put upon the land taken up for cultivation, to prevent its being worked in a racking manner and thrown up when exhausted, and that sub-division of holdings below a certain minimum limit should be prevented by legislation. The futility of the proposed restrictions will be apparent on the slightest consideration. Waste lands are now sold in the Bombay Presidency, but no remarkable results have been achieved and no capitalists full of the spirit of agricultural enterprise have come forward to bid for them. In the dry districts, there are lands of little or no value and nobody would pay for them ten times the Government assessment; and capitalists can have no difficulty in getting any quantity of land if they want it. The occupation of the poorer lands has, to some extent, been discouraged by the imposition of substantial assessments on the lowest classes of lands, and large extents of lands in a great many districts have been taken up for fodder and fuel reserves under the Forest Act. The objection to raising the assessments of the lowest classes of lands is the great distress and impoverishment it would cause to existing holders of lands. For instance, if a cultivator owns 80 acres of lands assessed at 4 annas per acre, and if the assessment be raised to Re. 1 per acre he will be simply ruined; he will be turned, in fact, from perhaps a poor ryot into not a solvent labourer, but into a landless labourer without any means or opportunities for procuring subsistence.

The suggestion to fix a minimum limit to sub-division by legislation is equally impracticable. There is no means of enforcing such a striction, and wherever it has been imposed it is found that the law is a dead letter. The Government might, no doubt, refuse to recognise the sub-division for the purpose of recovery of its revenue, but this does not prevent the holding being practically sub-divided for purposes of cultivation, while remaining undivided for purposes of revenue collection. Even if it were thought proper for Government to insist on the holding being the exclusive property of some one of the sharers, and the Government granted it away arbitrarily to him, it would be of doubtful advantage to the favored individual who would be burdened with the liability to pay the other sharers the value of their shares; and the tendency of the legislation would be to compel the sharers to continue as members of a joint family even when they found it advantageous to divide. There would be difficulty also in fixing the minimum limit with reference to the requirements of the several classes of lands, *e.g.*, lands in the vicinity of towns, employed in raising market garden produce, which are highly productive and held in small plots.

Mr. Henry W. Wolff in an article on peasant properties contributed to the *Contemporary Review* for May 1891, makes the following remarks on the failure of legislative attempts to regulate the minimum limit of farms in Germany: "Under the modern Saxon law—similar laws exist in other countries—a 'peasant property' is not divisible beyond a certain minimum area. It is a foolish regulation as the result has shown. For the small plots and the 'rolling'—*i.e.*, detachable—portions fetch throughout the highest prices. Protection, after its wont, has injured the interest which it desired to benefit. Following in the footsteps of the Hanoverian Government, most German Governments have introduced what they call a *Hoeferolle*, a register, *i.e.*, in which peasant owners may inscribe their properties in order to ensure, in cases of intestacy, undivided descent to one heir. That law has in most countries remained a dead letter. One agricultural Minister related to me with glee that he had done better than his short-sighted colleagues. *They* had left the presumption on the side of division. *He* had put it on the side of intact descent. But his shrewdness does not appear to have materially altered the result. The fact is that the proprietors know their own interests far better than do paternal Governments. They find it more to their advantage to curtail their holdings, and to sell at a good price in plots than to retain large showy estates at a loss. Foiled in respect of the *Hoeferolle* the advocates of larger properties now openly propose such preposterous measures as these—enforced devise of undivided properties at much less than their real value, a provision securing mortgagors against notice of repayment except by a sinking fund (spread over many years), and partial exemption from rates and taxes! Could there be a more complete confession of failure? These wise people have been fighting very hard against common sense and Providence. Both alike point out very clearly the way in which a plethora of population can and should relieve itself. They know better. But once more the sea has held its own against meddling Canute." In Germany, as in France, the farms appear to be of very small size. 12½ acres are taken to yield, for a family consisting of 5 persons, corn necessary for subsistence and for seed. 77 per cent. of the holdings are under that average and of this again 58 per cent. are under 5 acres. In Wurtemburg the average size of separate properties is stated to be about three-quarters of an acre. Mr. Wolff quotes the following testimony of a German official in regard to the beneficial effects of small holdings on the industry and thrift of the labouring classes: "The unmistakable advance in productive farming observable in the plain of the Rhine—the district principally affected by the (sub-dividing) *Landrecht*—stands in the closest possible relation to the growing sub-division. The advantage afforded by the fact that every day-labourer in the country may acquire a small plot of land, may, by industry and thrift, add to his modest holding, and eventually raise himself to the position of an independent *Bauer*, cannot be rated too highly; for the prospect of making himself economically independent is one of the most powerful incentives to the exercise of economical virtues. The smallness of the proprietary plots in the plain of the Rhine is accordingly no evil, but rather a direct advantage. Each one of these small cultivators makes it his endeavour to raise from his soil, by the cultivation of 'trade-plants,' of vegetables and the like, the most remunerative crops, and to employ the surplus of his working power as profitably as he can at some trade, at paid day-work or otherwise."

As regards the second of the remedies suggested by the reviewer, the idea that Government can "enforce" the breaking up of the village system and the substitution of homestead farms without a change in rural conditions is entirely chimerical. The proposal evidently owes its origin to a misapplication of the teachings of English Agricultural History to the conditions of rural life in India. There is a good deal of misapprehension as to the nature of the ryots' cultivation which is oftentimes likened to the open field or champion system as it prevailed some centuries ago in England. The last remnants of this cultivation were swept away by the partition of Samudayam lands in the Chingleput district, and no ryot is now hampered in the cultivation of his holding to the best advantage, though the villagers, owing to their poverty, need each other's assistance in connection with the various incidents of rural life. The enclosure and consolidation of holdings were brought about in England by social and economic causes and the Legislature, in so far as it interfered at all in the matter, did so with a view to arrest a too rapid transformation. The leading facts as regards the conditions under which development of English agriculture took place may be very briefly noted. During the middle ages, England had a monopoly of the wool trade, so much so that the revenue required for carrying on the continental wars was derived almost wholly from an impost on wool, the rate levied in emergencies being as high as 100 per cent. *ad valorem*. The trade was a most profitable one and common lands were extensively enclosed and holdings consolidated and turned into sheep-walks, with the result that where hundreds of ploughmen were employed their places were taken by a few shepherds. In the beginning of the sixteenth century thousands of agricultural labourers were thrown out of employment and reduced to a condition of the greatest misery. The Legislature strove to stem the tide by insisting on landlords maintaining a certain proportion of the area of their estates under tillage and the necessary farm buildings, but without effect. Mr.

Prothero, in his book on the Progress of English Farming, mentions that a "Petition in the reign of Henry VIII, states that 50,000 ploughs had been put down. Each on the average maintained 13½ persons. Thus 675,000 persons were thrown out of work when the whole population of the country did not exceed 5 millions." The difficulties of the situation were immensely aggravated by the enormous rise in the price of provisions due to the discovery of the American silver and gold mines and the influx of the precious metals into England; the price of wheat, which in the latter half of the sixteenth century and the first half of the seventeenth averaged 9*s.* 2*d.* per quarter was, 47*s.* 5*d.* a quarter or more than 5 times as much in the latter half of the seventeenth century. Rents rose very high and landlords accumulated great wealth at the expense of the working classes and the wages were kept down by stringent labour laws. Laws were enacted also to put down vagrancy, to compel the able-bodied vagrants to work and to provide relief to the impotent poor. Under these regulations, "all people who used subtle, crafty, and unlawful games and plays, or who feigned a knowledge of physiognomy and palmistry, all those who had no apparent means of support and who were fit for work, all fencers, bear-traders, jugglers, pedlars, tinkers, petty chapmen, and strolling players, all unlicensed scholars or shopmen who were caught begging were considered to be rogues and sturdy beggars." To this period is to be referred the beginning of the system of poor relief which has developed to such enormous proportions in England. In the seventeenth century some schemes for the reclamation of swamps were undertaken and the way was prepared for the introduction of improved methods of agriculture, but the agricultural practices themselves did not undergo any material alteration. The disturbed relations caused by the depreciation of the precious metals and the consequent increase of prices had settled down; capital had accumulated; the efficiency of human labour had increased; the horse was substituded for the ox in ploughing; and the extension of pasture farms and cattle farming had provided increased manure for arable lands. In the beginning of the eighteenth century, there was a rapid advance in agriculture. Several improvements were adopted which, aided by good seasons, increased greatly agricultural production. The wages and the standard of living of the labouring classes rose, and wheat became a necessary article of diet in the place of inferior grains. During the latter half of the eighteenth century the population increased enormously and the progress of manufactures caused a diversion of labour from agriculture to manufactures. Wars and bad seasons had increased prices of food-grains and the enclosure of commons and consolidation of holdings proceeded with redoubled speed. At the end of the eighteenth century prices rose so high as 115*s.* a quarter, with the result that land-owners increased their standard of living, which they were unable to keep up when the prices reached a normal level. The small owners suffered severely and they found it profitable to sell their holdings to large owners and to seek employment for their capital in manufactures, which were assuming large proportions. This diversion of a large part of the population to manufacturing industries rendered it necessary to grow a larger quantity of food with a diminished quantity of human labour and thus materially aided the introduction of machinery. The rapid changes which were taking place, and principally the substitution of machinery in manufactures together with a faulty administration of the poor law, had induced a great amount of pauperism; but the enormous growth of manufactures during the first three-quarters of the century soon gave employment to the surplus population. The use of animal food became general, and the tendency was to convert arable into pasture land and the price of wheat was maintained at a high level. High farming and intensive cultivation were assisted by the high price and the large proportion of lands under pasture. During the last 15 years, however, the price of both wheat and meat has fallen owing to foreign competition, the former from about 48*s.* to about 32*s.*, and the complaint is now general that high farming does not pay in England.

These being the facts connected with the progress of English agriculture—and I have given a very imperfect sketch alluding only to such facts as bear on the question on hand—is there any analogy between the conditions under which large farms became profitable in England and the conditions which exist in this country? In England, it has been calculated that while only 53 men can be supported per 100 acres on a dairy farm, 250 can be maintained on the same acreage of wheat and 683 on a like acreage of potatoes; and yet out of 50 million acres of arable and pasture land in 1880, 25 millions of acres were under permanent pasture, and 11 millions under corn crops in the United Kingdom. In India, it was pointed out by Dr. Buchanan as early as the beginning of the century, that "the religion of the natives is a powerful obstacle in the way of agriculture. The higher ranks of society being excluded from animal food, no attention will, of course, be paid to fattening cattle; without that, what would our agriculture in England be worth? We could have no green crops to restore our lands to fertility, and a scanty manure to invigorate our crops of grain." As to the introduction of machinery, the low value of human labour stands in the way. It has been found that at the present value of labour, no water-pump can compete with the *Picottah* in lifting water from wells. Again, Sir James Caird has pointed out that a square mile of land in England cultivated gives employment to 50 persons in the proportion of 25 men, young and old, and 25 women and boys, and that if four times that number or 200 were allowed for each square mile of cultivated land in India, it would take up only one-third of the people. What is to become, then, of the surplus human labour, if economical methods are extensively employed. Manufactures are not growing on an extensive scale to afford employment to the surplus population, and how are the "pauper" ryots to be transformed into "solvent" labourers? Is the Government to undertake the duty of finding work for the ryots deprived of land or of feeding them at the public cost in normal seasons as it does during famines, or is the surplus labour to be swept away as so much "human rubbish?" The possibility of high farming paying depends on economic conditions, and so long as the conditions are absent, no direct interference of Government for bringing about large farms and consolidation of holdings can be other than mischievous. Large farms are suitable to a country like England, which has to raise food for a population, the bulk of which is engaged in manufacturing industries; and agricultural improvements in this country should obviously follow on lines adopted in European countries where peasant properties prevail, by giving security of tenure, by the diffusion of education among the peasantry, by the establishment of credit Banks, by Agricultural Exhibitions and demonstrations, by the introduction of cottage industries to give employment to the peasant population during the spare time at their disposal, and such other measures as were pointed out by Mr. Nicholson in the admirable preliminary note written by him as Secretary to the Madras Agricultural Committee. European capitalists, with their plethora of capital looking out for opportunities for investment, would not have been slow to embark in the business, if they saw that they had the least chance of competing with native cultivators by adopting *intensive* methods of cultivations ; and I myself personally know some intelligent native landlords, with command of capital, who would be glad to invest a considerable amount in high farming, if they could have a reasonable assurance that the capital laid out would fetch 6 per cent. interest. And we have, in the failure of the Saidapet model farm to achieve profitable results, an impressive warning against extravagant expectations being entertained from intensive farming under present conditions. The model farm was started in 1871 and after 5 years' trial was found to have been worked at a loss of Rs. 6,000 (*vide* Mr. Nicholson's "Preliminary Note," paragraph 42). There is undoubtedly considerable scope for improvement by the introduction of deep-ploughing, better conservation of cattle manure, somewhat better treatment of cattle, and utilisation of inexpensive waste products as manures not now known or suspected to have manurial properties; but such improvements can only come in very gradually. The Government has already, by the reservation of large areas as fuel and fodder reserves, put a check on the taking up of the poorer lands for cultivation and made intensive cultivation to meet the requirements of the growing population to some extent necessary, and it is difficult to see what further steps can be taken in this direction without causing great hardship at present to the great body of the ryots. It should also be remembered that the proposal to encourage the consolidation and enclosure of farms with a view to the introduction of *intensive* farming would go against the proposed legislation to confer security of tenure on zemindari ryots, which is recognised on all hands to be a pressing necessity in the present situation.

The reviewer's third suggestion is not intelligible. If it is intended that grazing farms should be maintained for the support of cattle required for agricultural purposes, it would hardly pay the ryot to do this, seeing that cattle are not fattened in this country for meat, and that it would be profitable to obtain the cattle required for ploughing and draught from professional breeders. If the ryots require a better description of cattle than they now use, and are willing to pay the proper price, doubtless such cattle would be bred in larger numbers than at present. It has been calculated that 5 acres of land have to be kept under grass to feed a single head of cattle properly, and if this estimate is at all correct, it is obvious that it would be ruinous to breed cattle of this description, as 5 acres now produce corn sufficient to feed three human beings. The fourth suggestion is without any special significance, and it is connected with the first and second suggestions already considered. It is not clear what measures the reviewer intends should be taken for carrying out the fifth suggestion, viz., to check the export of raw, as contrasted with the manufactured or half-worked produce of the land. If it is intended that this result should be obtained by the levy of heavy export duties, it would simply destroy the foreign trade of the country as imports must be paid for by the exports. In fact, it is time wasted, considering seriously such crude proposals which violate the most elementary economic considerations.

Concluding Remarks.—I have found no small difficulty in ascertaining what precisely are the reviewer's conclusions as regards the progress made by the country as his reasoning is full of inconsistencies. He admits that there has been "very great advance" during the last 40 years and that the first half of this period was one of "marked and unchecked progress." As regards the second half, he asserts, however, that there is no evidence to show that the production of food is *much* ahead of the demand, although it has increased during the period. He admits, at the same time, that about the middle of the period occurred "the severest famine known in Southern India during the present century" and that this visitation threw back the Presidency "to an enormous extent." Notwithstanding the rapidity with which the Presidency has recovered from the effects of the famine, he calls the period one of agricultural "stagnation," if not of retrogression. The reason assigned for characterising the period as one of stagnation is the fact that the area of ryotwar holdings has not increased in the same ratio as the population. The reviewer in the same breath asserts that the liberty accorded to pauper ryots to take up lands of the poorer qualities which alone now remain unoccupied, or in other words, *extensive* cultivation, is at the root of the evils of the present economic position, and that the occupation of such lands should be checked. He considers that the effects of improved and cheaper internal and external communication during the last 20 years should have stimulated enormously its greatest industry—agriculture—where the products are so bulky and difficult to move. It does not occur to him that the cheapened cost of production and transport due to these causes might have obviated the necessity for falling upon the poorer soils for production, as indeed will be seen to have been the case, when the facts connected with grain wages of the labouring classes, the prices of food-grains, and the standard of living, are taken into account, and that it is a satisfactory feature that the internal and external trade of the country should have increased in the manner it has notwithstanding what he calls the "throwback" of the famine. As the best means of stimulating agricultural production, he recommends that "the export of the raw, as contrasted with the half-manufactured produce of the land" should be checked. Again, for the purpose of diminishing pauperism, he advocates the enforcement of the enclosure and consolidation of holdings, forgetful of the fact that the advantage of large farms consists in the economising of labour, that this economising of labour on any large scale cannot be carried out without much suffering unless there are alternative occupations; that in a country where the labourer himself is the cheapest of machines and manufactures are non-existent, any sudden or great displacement of labour must induce a frightful amount of pauperism and reduce the condition of the lower classes, bad as it is, to a still lower level; that large farms which will deprive the vast majority of the population of all interest in the soil, must necessitate the maintenance of a very costly system of poor relief with all its demoralising features, and that a system of large holdings can be introduced only *pari passu* with the development of industrial occupations, and that for a country where opportunities for employment not connected with agriculture are so few, a system of peasant properties is the best suited. Those who, in common with the reviewer, believe that Government can, by adopting a few measures of a drastic character, pull by main force the teeming millions of the population out of their accustomed grooves determined for them by the economic conditions under which they have to work, and set them going in this or that direction which is considered desirable, will doubtless feel disappointed at the slow rate at which the country has progressed. Those, on the other hand, who take note of the difficulties to be surmounted in raising the economic condition of the population which was as bad as bad could be but 40 years ago; the liability of most parts of the country to the extremes of plenty and dearth alternately—a state of things conducive to careless habits of life and inimical to the formation of habits of steady industry; the tendency of every increase in production to be absorbed in mere increase of numbers unless there is a rise in the standard of comfort; the necessity for the readjustment of time-honoured, religious and social usages for effecting any permanent change in the standard of comfort, and the impossibility of effecting such a change by coercive methods which do not touch the intelligence of the people, will, when they compare the state of things at present with what it was in the past, be gratified to see that the improvement has been so substantial; and will further see more "consolatory signs of decided and vigorous progress" in the future than the reviewer has been able to detect. While recognising that every step in improvement adds to the duties and responsibilities of Government and requires wiser statesmanship than even in the past for guiding the country through the period of transition, and for meeting new evils by methods and measures calculated to influence the growing public intelligence, they will see no reason in the experience of the past to despair that either the Government or the people will rise to the requirements of the future.

*   *   *   *

(2). *Note on the progress of Education in the Madras Presidency between* 1870–71 *and* 1890–91 *by S. Seshaiyar, Esq., B.A., Professor of Kumbakónam College.*

During the past twenty years the Madras Presidency has made indeed a vast progress in education. The most noteworthy features of that progress are (1) the enormous expansion of higher or collegiate education, (2) the rapid diffusion of elementary or primary education among the bulk of the population, and (3) the strong stimulus given to female education.

Prior to 1850, there were few or no English schools in the mofussil. The only institution in the Presidency in which a liberal English education was given was the Presidency College in Madras. It was in 1853 that Government started its first schools for instruction in English at Zillah or Provincial stations. Kumbakónam, Rajahmundry, Calicut and Cuddalore were among the earliest centres chosen for the experiment. The University of Madras was constituted in 1857 and held its first examination for the degree of Bachelor of Arts in 1858. From 1858 to 1871 inclusive, the number of young men who passed the examination for the degree of Arts was 199. In the two decades that followed including 1891, it rose up to the astonishing figure of 2,552. The Bachelor of Arts degree represents the ordinary collegiate course taught in an Indian College, and may, for all practical purposes, be regarded as marking the highest general culture received by the youth of the country. The studies that one pursues after passing the B.A. Examination are either special and technical, such as those pertaining to Law, Medicine, Engineering, &c., or the advanced branches of Mathematics, Philosophy, and the like; to qualify oneself for the higher degree in arts. It is but a small fraction of those who receive the B.A. degree that go up for examination in Honours. The number of those who qualify themselves for the special studies mentioned above must necessarily be limited by the demand of the learned professions for specialists. At present the most crowded of them is Law. Teaching likewise absorbs in its service a large number of the *alumni* of the University. The technical colleges now in existence are all maintained by the State; and they are the Law College, the College of Civil Engineering, the Medical College, the Agricultural College, and the Teachers' College. Looking into the statistics for 1890–91 we find that there were 35 Arts Colleges in the Presidency—First and Second Grades together—with an attendance of 3,200 scholars. These figures indicate a great advance as compared with those of 1870–71 when the number of colleges was 12 with an attendance of only 385 scholars. Again 548 candidates appeared for the B.A. Examination in 1891 as against 65 in 1871; the number of candidates for the F.A. Examination was 531 and 2,052 for the earlier and the later years respectively. These figures are sufficient to show the rate of expansion of collegiate education during the interval under notice. One very satisfactory feature of this development is that learning is no longer the monopoly of any one section of the Indian community. The desire for English education is spreading among all classes. Of the 3,200 students in attendance at the Arts Colleges in 1890–91, 38 were Europeans and Eurasians, 244 Native Christians, 46 Muhammadans, 2,208 Brahmins, 658 non-Brahmin Hindus, and 6 other classes. Nor has the alleged difficulty of finding suitable openings in life for educated men had as yet any appreciable effect on the growing demand for English education. Looking to the efficiency of public service alone, there would yet seem to be open a large field for educated talent. There are indications too that the education given in our colleges is fostering in its recipients a spirit of self-help and manly enterprise. The number of young men who have in recent years taken to commercial pursuits, or have crossed the sea for service in Burma, afford evidence of the new spirit. Nor would there seem to be any foundation in fact for the opinion that the Indian Colleges are rearing up a body of disaffected young men. Those who have had the best opportunities of watching the progress of education in the country and its results are almost unanimous in holding that its influence for good has been marked, considering the short period during which it has been at work.

Equally satisfactory has been the development of what is called secondary education, which comprises a course of studies, extending over six years, in English and in one of the vernacular languages of the country, as also in the elementary portions of History, Geography, Mathematics, Physics and Chemistry. The Matriculation Examination of the Madras University constitutes the final test of the work of what may be designated Anglo-Vernacular schools. The number of candidates who went up for this examination in 1891 was 7,002 as against 1,358 in 1871. The number of pupils under instruction in 1890–91 in all the Anglo-Vernacular schools of the Presidency was nearly 30,000.

One of the recommendations of the Educational Commission was that Government should gradually retire from the field of higher education. So far as the Madras Presidency is concerned, that recommendation has already been carried out in the main. Of the 35 arts colleges existing in 1890–91, 30 were private and aided institutions, and of the 556 secondary schools for boys, only 26 were maintained by Government. Whether the highest or collegiate education could safely be left wholly to private agency might be a question. There are various reasons why it should not be, even if private agencies were financially equal to the task. But experience shows that private effort with some aid from Government is quite equal to the call of secondary education. In this connection, we are bound to mention the incalculable service rendered to the cause of Indian education by European Missionary Bodies. They should justly be regarded as the pioneers of modern Indian civilization. But how long this foreign help might be relied upon is problematical. In the meanwhile, it is satisfactory to note that native communities, Hindu and Muhammadan, are learning the lesson of self-help in education as in other things and may, when the time should come for it, be able to occupy the field that may be vacated by Christian Missions. Another satisfactory feature in connection with educational progress is the steady rise in the fee receipts in colleges and schools. High and middle schools, in most parts of the Presidency, are nearly self-supporting and need only a small percentage of grants from provincial or local funds. Even in colleges the fees cover an appreciable proportion of the total expenditure. In the Government College at Kumbakónam, which is one of the cheapest colleges in the Presidency, the income from fees met in 1890–91 a third of the total cost of the institution. In recent years a considerable share of educational work has devolved on Municipalities and Local Fund Boards. By this means it has become possible to keep up middle and high schools at stations away from capitals of districts where private agencies have not sprung up.

The most striking feature in the history of education between 1870–71 and 1890–91 is the great diffusion of elementary knowledge among the masses of the population. A numerous agency is at work, whose special mission is to carry the rudiments of vernacular education to the simplest villager. Village schools have been organised in nearly all parts of the country and are periodically visited and examined by the inspecting staff of the Educational department. In the Educational Report for 1890–91, Dr. Duncan remarks: "Of the lower primary schools, 2,558 with 140,422 scholars were situated in municipal towns. Omitting them, 19,470 schools with 503,472 scholars were located in non-municipal towns and villages, which, according to the census of 1881, numbered 52,592. Most of the small towns and large villages contain more than one school each. But in many villages the population is too small to maintain a separate school. In view of these facts, only one village in three can be said to be provided with a school." Going back to 1870-71, we find that primary education was then in its infancy: only 1,606 schools had been registered in the official returns for the whole Presidency, and these, with an attendance of 42,299 pupils, earned a grant of Rs. 60,332 from Government. It is clear then that since 1870-71 primary education has been rapidly extending under the combined exertions of Government, Municipalities, and Local Fund Boards. By far the largest share of the financial cost of primary education is now borne by Municipalities and Local Boards. According to the returns for 1890-91 it was no less than five-sixths of the total charge. The most pressing question in connection with primary education is, of course, the question of finance. While there seems to be almost an indefinite scope for the extension, and the improvement in quality, of village schools, the agencies, who now mainly contribute towards their upkeep, are beginning to feel the pressure of cost and complain that they have already gone far enough, in justice to other and more pressing demands upon their resources.

Perhaps the most hopeful sign of the intellectual and moral progress of the country is the encouragement given in recent years to female education. In 1870-71, there were no girl-schools to speak of, except the few that had been started by Christian Missionaries in Madras and a few other stations. In 1890-91, according to the report of the Director of Public Instruction, there were no less than 87,715 girl-pupils under instruction. The number that has gone through the higher courses of school and collegiate study is, as may be expected, very limited; but there are hopeful indications that increasing numbers will soon go up to the higher stages of education. Only two women have as yet taken the degree of Bachelor of Arts in the local University. Sixty-three female candidates went up for the Matriculation Examination in 1890-91, of whom 37 were successful, while 278 candidates appeared for the Higher Examination for Women, of whom 160 passed and obtained certificates. It is a significant fact that even the most conservative classes of the Indian community are coming under the influence of this new education—which, as it spreads wider and wider, would doubtless prepare the way for those much-needed social reforms, for which our reformers are fighting so hard, but now without the support of those who constitute the real strength of Hindu homes.

During the period under review, steps were also taken for encouraging education among Europeans and Eurasians, Muhammadans and other classes who, by reason of their poverty or other cause, were slow to avail themselves of the ordinary facilities for education afforded by the State. On the 31st March 1891 there were 94 schools for Europeans and Eurasians with an attendance of 3,855 boys and 3,152 girls, and 936 schools for Muhammadans with 39,089 pupils under instruction. Municipalities and Local Fund Boards now pay special attention to the education of the backward sections of the community, such as weavers and other handicraftsmen. Night schools have also been started for the sons of these classes, so that those who cannot spare time in the day may be instructed for an hour or so after sun-set. According to the return for 1890-91, there were no less than 609 night schools with an attendance of 11,706 pupils. Schools for Pariahs specially are few as yet: but under the order of Government recently issued, they will soon come into existence.

One of the most important questions for the consideration of Government is technical and scientific education bearing on arts and industries. How the existing arts and industries of the country may be improved or what new ones may be introduced are questions that demand the early attention of Government. At present there exist but a few schools for the benefit of those who seek instruction in arts and industries. The foremost of such institutions is the School of Arts in Madras, in which the attendance in 1890–91 was over 400 pupils, who received instruction in some of the ornamental arts and higher industries. Schools have also been opened in some of the larger trading towns in the mofussil, such as Rajahmundry, Kumbakónam, Negapàtam, Guntúr, Madura and Nazareth, in which drawing, carpentry, and a few other industries are taught. Industrial sections have also been attached to Government Normal Schools in the mofussil. All these appear, however, to be crude and imperfect attempts, pending a satisfactory solution of the question as a whole—beset, as that is, with great difficulties, finance being not the least of them.

In the sketch above given nothing more has been attempted than the barest outline of the progress of education during a period of twenty years, beginning with 1870–71 and ending with 1890–91, the last official year for which statistics were available. Enough, it is believed, has been said to show that education has spread far and wide in the country, and that nearly all classes of the community have come under its influence. There cannot be any doubt that this spread of education will have an important effect on the future economic and moral condition of the people.

(E).—Costliness of Justice.

Statement showing the costs incurred in suits when the amount claimed is Rs. 50 *and below, between Rs.* 50 *and* 100, *between Rs.* 100 *to* 500, *and between Rs.* 500 *and* 1,000.

Nature of Expense.	Amount claimed.				Amount irrecoverable when the claim is				Remarks.
	Rs. 50 and below.	Between Rs. 50 and 100.	Between Rs. 100 and 500.	Between Rs. 500 and 1,000.	Rs. 50 and below.	Between Rs. 50 and 100.	Between Rs. 100 and 500.	Between Rs. 500 and 1,000.	
	RS. A. P.	RS. A. P.	RS. A. P.	RS. A. P.	RS. A. P.	RS. A. P.	RS. A. P.	RS. A. P.	
1. Court-fee	3 12 0	7 8 0	37 8 0	75 0 0	...	...	...	...	The figures represent the average of original and small cause suits (contested).
2. Vakil's fee	3 0 0	6 0 0	25 0 0	50 0 0	0 8 0	1 0 0	...	...	
3. Stamp for vakalat ...	0 8 0	0 8 0	0 8 0	0 8 0	...	...	...	...	
4. Process fee (number of witnesses, 3 to 5 on an average).	1 8 0	1 8 0	2 8 0	3 8 0	...	...	...	...	
5. Batta for witnesses ...	1 8 0	1 8 0	3 0 0	4 0 0	...	...	...	...	
6. Expenses by the party for feeding the witnesses.	1 8 0	1 8 0	5 0 0	5 0 0	1 8 0	1 8 0	5 0 0	5 0 0	
7. Notice fee to defendants.	1 0 0	1 0 0	1 0 0	1 8 0	...	...	...	...	
8. On account of two adjournments on an average.	3 0 0	3 0 0	21 0 0	25 0 0	3 0 0	3 0 0	10 0 0	10 0 0	
9. Writing fee for Vakil's Gumastah.	1 0 0	1 0 0	2 0 0	2 0 0	1 0 0	1 0 0	2 0 0	2 0 0	
10. Copies of depositions or documents from other offices.	0 8 0	0 8 0	1 8 0	1 8 0	0 8 0	0 8 0	1 8 0	1 8 0	
11. Stamps for the above...	0 8 0	0 8 0	1 8 0	2 0 0	...	...	...	...	
12. Party's travelling expenses.	2 0 0	2 0 0	4 0 0	5 0 0	2 0 0	2 0 0	4 0 0	5 0 0	

13. Copy of judgment and decree in stamps.	0 8 0	0 8 0	1 8 0	1 8 0	0 8 0	0 8 0	1 8 0	1 8 0	
14. Stamps for the above...	0 8 0	1 8 0	1 8 0	1 8 0	...	...	...	...	
15. Stamps for applications, &c., in the course of the trial of the suit.	0 2 0	1 0 0	2 0 0	2 0 0	...	...	...	...	
16. For issuing commission, &c. (1 out of 100 cases)	...	...	..	...	...	...	...	...	Such instances being rare, the expenses are not shown.
17. Charges for warrants, &c.	1 0 0	1 0 0	2 0 0	2 0 0	...	...	...	...	
18. For default of party ...	...	...	...	...	...	...	...	...	No cost is entered against this item, as the chances of the party paying the costs of the other side and obtaining costs from the other side are even.
19. For execution applications, 3 or 4 times for attachment.	2 0 0	2 0 0	2 0 0	4 0 0	...	...	...	...	
20. For attachment ...	2 0 0	2 0 0	2 0 0	2 0 0	...	...	...	...	
21. Vakil's fee	1 0 0	1 0 0	6 4 0	12 8 0	1 0 0	1 0 0	...	...	
22. Proclamation for sale.	1 0 0	1 0 0	1 0 0	1 0 0	...	...	...	...	
23. Warrant of arrest ...	2 0 0	2 0 0	2 0 0	2 0 0	...	...	...	...	
24. Application for money, &c.	0 8 0	0 8 0	0 8 0	0 8 0	0 8 0	0 8 0	0 8 0	0 8 0	
25. Batta for debtor in Civil Jail.	2 0 0	2 0 0	5 0 0	5 0 0	...	...	...	...	
26. Receipt stamps ... 27. Sundry expenses ...	1 8 0	1 8 0	3 0 0	5 0 0	1 0 0	1 0 0	2 8 0	4 8 0	
28. For loss of time (not calculated).	...	...	...	...	...	...	...	...	
Total ...	33 14 0	42 8 0	133 4 0	214 0 0	11 8 0	12 0 0	27 0 0	30 0 0	

Note.—Even in case of success the party will not get the amounts shown in the last 4 columns.

This statement has been prepared by a Judicial officer having experience in the districts of Tanjore, Trichinopoly and Tinnevelly, with reference to contested suits (ordinary and small causes). In districts where the territorial limits of District Munsifs are larger, the amounts incurred for the travelling and other expenses of parties and witnesses will be more and the amount irrecoverable necessarily greater. The figures are necessarily conjectural, but care has been taken to make the estimate as moderate as possible.

(F).—Local Fund and Municipal Administration, &c.

Extracts from the remarks of Sir Alfred Lyall in regard to the political inexpediency of Government relinquishing its right to control the management of religious institutions in this country (Sir Alfred Lyall's "Asiatic Studies").

Sir Alfred Lyall has pointed out that from a political point of view it was a mistake for the Indian Government to have relinquished its right to control religious endowments. The following are extracts from his remarks:

"In India they have no conception of the animosity against Establishment which has been fostered in England by Acts passed to enforce unity of religious profession and uniformity of clerical teaching, by the old attempts to drive wandering sects like sheep into one fold under one official shepherd. As there has never been one nation or one religion in India, so a national church establishment, excluding all others, has never been imagined. That the Sovereign should provide decently for his own persuasion is regarded as natural and decorous; that he should distribute revenue allotments (or continue them) to every well-defined religious community is thought liberal; that he should administer to all religious properties and interests is right and proper; that he should ignore them all and provide not even for his own faith would be a policy comprehensible only by those who had studied English polemics, and one without precedent in Asia. . . . ."

"It has been said latterly, and with some reason, that the English Government acted prematurely, and upon incomplete knowledge of all the considerations involved, when it resolved to sever the ancient chain which bound the religious institutions of each province round the feet of the Government which annexed them, and when we thus, in liberating ourselves from being plagued with old-world fancies, threw away the repute and leadership which accrued to the Sovereign of India from being universally recognized as the authority whose *congé d'élire* was required, or whose arbitration was accepted, in all nominations and successions to important religious office or estate. In the Madras Presidency the superintendence of 'no less than seven thousand six hundred Hindu establishments had hitherto been vested in the officers of Government; and this was more than a nominal superintendence; the people regarded the district officer as the friendly guardian of their religion.' Speaking of the aversion of the people to the abandonment by Government of the management of a famous pagoda (Tirupati) in North Arcot, the district magistrate wrote: 'No persuasion or reasoning could effect a change in the resolution they had taken; the management of this pagoda, they said, had been in the hands of the ruling power for ages back; the innovation proposed was contrary to established custom, and if persisted in, religious worship in their temple would cease. . . .'

"At first we were over-careful to conciliate native prejudices by showing official respect and deference to rites and ceremonies of a nature largely repugnant to European habits of thought in such matters; and we were far too anxious to prove that we had no notion of giving umbrage to powerful creeds by favoring Christianity, which had no political importance. This overshot the mark, and naturally displeased European opinion; so we gave way to a strong re-action, and at one time we borrowed from the religious politics of Great Britain to an extent which laid us open to complaints that the English Government in its endeavour to assume an impartial and irresponsible attitude towards all religions, had not sufficiently regarded the material interests of the native creeds and rituals, or their prescriptive claims upon the ruler, whoever he may be, of their country. . . .

"In England an assurance of neutrality would probably mean that the Government had determined to have nothing whatever to do with the affairs, temporal or spiritual, of any sect or creed; in India, the declaration is generally taken to convey a welcome guarantee that the Queen will not favor one religion more than another; but it is not so welcome if it is found to mean the complete renunciation by their governors of all direct authority or headship over the management of the temporal interests of their religions. Such a course of action is foreign to all historic experience of the relations between secular and ecclesiastical authorities throughout Asia. It may be the only course now open to the English in India; nevertheless another might be learned from observing the organization of all great Asiatic Governments, and from the example of every ruler over divers tribes and nationalities —namely, that in certain conditions of society the immediate authority and close supervision of a monarch over the powerful religious interests with which he has to reckon at every step, is a matter of political expediency, not an affair of doctrine or opinion, but a recognized duty of the State. To relinquish this position is to let go at least one real political advantage which accrues to us from our attitude of perfect neutrality, that of enabling us to superintend and guarantee the religious administration of all sects with entire impartiality, and with the confidence of our subjects. There is no reason whatever to regret the abolition of the old *régime* under which public officers were literally agents and managers for religious institutions; that system was rightly condemned. But to cut away all the historic ties between Church and State, to free Asiatic religions from every kind of direct subordination to the executive power, would be to push the principle further in India, where it is not understood and has no advocates, than has as yet been attempted even in any country of Europe, where it is supported by a large and increasing party."

GOVERNMENT OF MADRAS.

REVENUE DEPARTMENT.

READ—the following letter from Diwan Bahadur S. SRINIVASA RAGHAVAIYENGAR Avergal, to the Secretary to Government, Revenue Department :—

Adverting to your demi-official communication of the 5th March 1892, I have the honour to submit a complete copy of my "Memorandum on the Progress of the Madras Presidency during the last Forty Years."

2. The collection and reduction of the necessary statistics and the preparation of the second part of the memorandum took up more time than I had anticipated, and I was able to complete the work only last May notwithstanding that I took privilege leave for three months in the beginning of this year for the purpose.

3. I should be wanting in my duty if I did not bring to your notice the valuable assistance rendered to me by M.R.Ry. C. Sarvothama Row, B.A., travelling clerk of my office, and M.R.Ry. R. Saminathaiyar, B.A., head clerk in the Revenue Secretariat. The heavy work of compilation and reduction of statistics under my directions and the correction of the proofs devolved on Sarvothama Row, and but for the assistance cheerfully afforded by him at all times I should have found it impossible to do this special work along with my official duties. R. Saminathaiyar made abstracts of official and other papers required for the earlier portions of the memorandum, and I have utilised his high mathematical attainments and sound knowledge of economic principles in getting some of the intricate calculations checked.

ORDER—dated 20th October 1893, No. 915, Revenue.

Miccellaneous.

With the foregoing letter Diwan Bahadur S. Srinivasa Raghavaiyengar, C.I.E., submits to Government, in a complete form, his "Memorandum on the Progress of the Madras Presidency during the last Forty Years of British administration." Although bearing this modest title, the work is indeed a compendious history of the period to which it relates, compiled with great industry and care mainly from official records, but embodying also the results of independent inquiries. The task which the author at the request of His Excellency the then Governor Lord Connemara undertook to perform, and which, in the opinion of His Excellency the Governor in Council, he has very successfully accomplished, was "to examine whether the economic condition of the Madras Presidency, and especially of the agricultural classes, has improved or deteriorated during the last forty years, and whether, if there has been improvement, it is proceeding on right lines."

2. After describing briefly the state of the country and the condition of the people in former centuries, and, from the information available, drawing the conclusion that the government of former rulers was generally oppressive, the author proceeds to consider the state of the Presidency at the end of the eighteenth century, when most of the provinces of Southern India were acquired by the British. The position at this time is described thus: "In the earlier centuries, although the country had suffered from frequent wars, it had, with some intervals of anarchy, the advantage of a more or less settled government. In the eighteenth century, however, the completest anarchy prevailed, and the position of the people was miserable in the extreme. In the Zemindar and Poligar countries the only limit to the exactions to which the ryots were subject was their ability to pay; the customary share of the produce belonging to Government was nominally half, but additional taxes were levied on various pretexts, reducing the share enjoyed by the ryots to one-fifth or one-sixth." Such was the state of the country when the government thereof was assumed by the English; the condition of the agricultural classes, who formed the bulk of the population, is said to have been abject and demoralized to the last degree.

3. The next section is devoted to a description of these classes under British administration during the first half of the present century. Efforts were made on all sides to improve the position of the ryot, but frequently without success. The substitution of payment of Government dues in money for the former system of payment in kind, led to much inconvenience and hardship owing to the insufficiency of the currency to meet the increased "duty" thrown upon it by the change, and prices steadily fell. The period of 20 years from 1834 to 1854 was one of great agricultural

depression on account of the low prices of grain, and, during the 30 years which preceded this period, progress was retarded by five successive famines. During the early years of the century metalled roads were unknown, and wheel-traffic, except for short distances, did not exist. Trade was hampered by want of communications and the means of transport and was confined to the narrowest local limits. The general improvement of communications throughout the country may be said to date from the report of the Public Works Commission issued in 1852.

Section IV.

4. The author then proceeds to review the principal facts bearing upon the condition of the agricultural classes from the middle of the century to the present time. About the year 1854 the period of agricultural depression came to an end and a time of great prosperity began. The demand abroad for Indian commodities largely increased—the result of several causes, such as the discovery of gold in Australia and California, the Crimean war, and, above all, the Civil war in America which increased enormously the demand for Indian cotton. Exports, which in 1840–41 amounted to only 13½ millions sterling, rose in 1864–65 to 68 millions. Silver flowed into the country and large loans—especially for the construction of railways and other public works—were raised in England, of which it is calculated that about one-half was expended on wages in India. The result was that the currency was replenished and the prices of Indian produce rose to three times what they had been in the years immediately preceding 1850. During this period, moreover, many administrative reforms were introduced. The police was organised upon a new footing; the Settlement Department was constituted for the purpose of alleviating the heavy burthens on land and of removing inequalities in assessments; the revenue and magisterial establishments were revised and village accounts were simplified; and, above all, an enormous impetus was given to the construction of public works, notably works of irrigation. With increased demand, the wages of labour rose in proportion to prices.

5. The period of high prices continued till about 1870, when a re-action took place. At this time several new and unfamiliar forms of taxation were resorted to, chiefly of a "local" character, and, while still suffering from the effects of falling prices, the country was visited by the terrible famine of 1876–78. The cost of this calamity, including revenue remitted, amounted to 8 millions sterling and the loss in population was nearly 4 millions.

6. Having reviewed the condition of the agricultural classes before and after the establishment of British power, the author proceeds,* by the help of statistics, to examine what progress has been made during the last 40 years, and he divides the subject into the following heads :—

* Section V.

(*a*) population ;
(*b*) area of cultivation ;
(*c*) prices of produce ;
(*d*) improvement in the processes of production and in communications ;
(*e*) foreign and domestic trade ;
(*f*) taxation ; and
(*g*) the standard of living of the different classes of the population.

The figures of the census of 1891 show that during the last decade the population of the Presidency increased by $4\frac{3}{4}$ millions or by 15·6 per cent.; and assuming—as seems reasonable—that no such famine as that of 1876–78 will recur within a century, the author calculates the normal increase of population under present conditions to be not much less than 1 per cent. per annum. That the bulk of the population is not devoid of the means of subsistence is the necessary inference from this high rate of increase. Upon the question whether the advance in area cultivated has been equal to the increase in population, the author finds, upon the data available, that since 1852 the increase in area cultivated has been 25, 41, and 138 per cent. of dry, wet, and well lands respectively, and that the increased production has been very considerable. In regard to prices, the conclusions arrived at are that from 1828 to 1853 prices rapidly declined until they were 25 per cent. below those which ruled in the early years of the century; that between 1853 and 1865 they rose till they were twice as high as at the beginning of the century; that from this level they declined by about 20 per cent. after 1870; and that the average prices of the five years previous to 1890 show a slight increase over those of the lustrum ending with 1874. The author gives some interesting statistics showing the vast improvements which have been made in communications and the effect produced thereby upon trade and prices, especially in the levelling of prices in times of local scarcity. By the development of communications the abolition of transit duties and of customs duties, trade, both internal and external, has advanced by enormous strides. In illustration of this statement the port of Tuticorin is cited. The value of the trade of this port has risen from 23 lakhs in 1830 to 232 lakhs in 1889–90. In regard to taxation the incidence (including land revenue) per head of the population has risen from Rs. 1–14–6 in 1852–53 to Rs. 2–10–8 in 1872–73 and Rs. 2–14–3 in 1889–90, *i.e.*, by 51 per cent. since 1852; but of the increased revenue raised a large proportion has been laid out on works of public utility, such as communications, education, irrigation, and medical relief. In considering the standard of living, the author has roughly divided the population into four classes, viz., the agricultural classes, non-agricultural labourers, professional and mercantile classes, and artizans and small traders. He calculates that one-fifth of the ryotwari land revenue is contributed by agriculturalists who are primarily labourers, but who supplement wages by cultivating small holdings; about one-third is contributed by peasant proprietors, who, for the most part, till their own land; one-third by farmers who employ hired labour; and the remainder by the class who can afford to let their lands and generally do so. With a holding of 8 acres of ordinary dry land it is calculated that a ryot should be able to support his family, not indeed in luxury, but according to the standard of living which obtains among the ryot population. The average money value of the food of an adult labourer is estimated at Rs. 20 per annum and the remuneration of a permanont farm servant at twice the cost of his feeding and clothing expenses. So far as the non-agricultural class of labourers is concerned, it admits of no question that their condition has greatly improved. With the development of trade the members of the mercantile and professional classes have largely increased and these are in a prosperous condition. The wages of artizans, in spite of the decline of some native handicrafts, have greatly risen, and the demand for luxuries, which are provided by the skill of the brass-smiths, goldsmiths, carpenters and masons, is increasing directly with the wealth of the country. In considering the standard of living, the author quotes the opinions of a number of gentlemen who have had exceptional opportunities of observation and concludes that there is ample evidence that the standard has risen. Tiled and terraced houses are rapidly taking the place of thatched roofs; metal utensils are largely superseding earthen vessels even among the lower classes; better and more clothes are worn, and considerable sums are now spent upon the education of their children by persons of small means; and although it is true that every one feels that his means are inadequate to satisfy his wants, it is not that his wealth has not increased, but that his wants have increased more rapidly still. That the standard of living generally has risen very considerably during the last 40 years, must indeed be patent to every impartial observer, and the Government fully concurs with the conclusions at which the author has arrived. In discussing the pressure of population upon the soil, the author points out that it is precisely in those districts, such as Tanjore, where the population is most dense, that all classes, not excepting the lowest, are the most prosperous, and he calculates that the area at present under cultivation is ample for the maintenance of the population and that the area still left for extended cultivation is very considerable. He quotes Sir James Caird that "it is possible to obtain such a gradual increase of production in India as would meet the present rate of increase of population for a considerable time." Here, however, the author wisely remarks that the increase of production has its limits, and for a permanent improvement in the standard of living and the general condition of the masses a change in the habits of the people in regard to early marriages is a necessary requisite. The next question discussed is one which, for some time past, has engaged public attention, viz., "whether the greater portion of the population suffer from a daily insufficiency of food." Upon this question, after inquiring in this connection how much is sufficient, the author, who finds that as to certain broad facts there can be no doubt, states his conclusions as follows:—(1) the great majority of the population is very poor when judged by a European standard; (2) compared with the condition of the people fifty years ago there has certainly been improvement in the material condition of the population, the advance consisting mainly of a rise in the standard of living of the upper strata of society and a reduction in the percentage which the lowest grades bear to the total population; (3) the very lowest classes still live a hand-to-mouth existence, but, not being congregated in towns, they have a better physique than one would expect to find in them, considering their resourcelessness and the frequency of crop failures, on which occasions they have to pick up a scanty subsistence as best they can; and (4) the economic condition of the country, as a whole, though improving, is at best a low one and is such as to tax the energies and statesmanship of Government to the utmost in devising suitable remedies for its amelioration. From these conclusions the Government is by no means disposed to dissent; they recall, however, the recorded observations of Sir Thomas Munro, made nearly a century ago, whereby he cautions the governing authorities of that day against expecting to effect in a generation a revolution in the habits of the people of India which in European countries it took centuries to accomplish. This part of the volume concludes with a valuable comparison between the economic condition of India and that of European countries and closes with the hope that, having regard to the wonderful improvement which has taken place in England during the last three centuries, a similar advance in prosperity may be attainable here.

7. In the next place the author proceeds to consider* certain alleged evils in the present economic position and to suggest certain remedial measures. Prominent among the suggestions here made are those which relate to the principles recently enunciated for the revision of land assessments in future years. The author points out that while it would be impossible to have rules regarding revisions of assessment conceived in a more liberal spirit than those at present in force, yet these rules are not generally known and that it is very necessary that they should be widely published. Before doing so, however, he considers it essential that the initial standard schedule of prices, with reference to which future revisions of assessment are to be regulated, should be fixed. He shows that the commutation prices adopted for the existing settlements have been calculated in different ways and should not therefore be taken as the standards for the future revision of assessments with reference to prices. He suggests that the average prices of a definite period prior to each settlement should be taken as the initial standard, and that the prices thus arrived at should be compared with those of a like period preceding any future revision. His Excellency the Governor in Council regards this suggestion, as well as that which would ensure the publication in the official Gazettes of the rules regarding the revision of assessments, as sound and practical, and proposes to take action in the direction indicated without loss of time. The Government considers, however, that there is no need for legislation in this matter.

* Section VI.

8. The proposals to improve the position of zemindari tenants on the one hand, by the amendment of the law of land-lord and tenant, and on the other to arrest the rapid dismemberment of zemindari estates have been anticipated by Government. A draft Tenancy Bill and a draft Encumbered Estates Bill have been recently drawn up and will be introduced into the Legislative Council at a very early date.

9. The remarks regarding the advantages of banking facilities are of a practical character. The question of establishing what are known as Agricultural Banks has been

under the consideration of Government for some time past, a special officer, Mr. Nicholson, having been deputed to make inquiries concerning the constitution and working of such banks on the continent of Europe and to report to Government upon the subject generally. Similarly as regards Agricultural education, which has engaged the earnest attention of the Madras Government for the last 30 years, His Excellency the Governor in Council hopes soon to be in a position to determine what further steps should be taken for its extension, the action of the Government having been held in abeyance for some time past pending the disposal by the Government of India of Dr. Voelcker's report. The Educational Department will be requested to consider the observations and suggestions on the subject of "technical education." * It may, however, be remarked that Government is at the present time in communication with the Director of the Geological Survey of India with a view to the deputation of a special officer to inquire into the mineral resources of the Presidency, and it is probable that work will be begun at an early date in the district of Salem. Doubtless the fish-curing industry is susceptible of development, but the author is hardly correct in supposing that it is at present altogether in the hands of the poorest classes. Having examined under the head of "costliness of justice" the system under which justice, civil and criminal, is administered, the writer concludes with a chapter upon "Local and Municipal administration and Legislation affecting local usages." Although the idea of combination for public purposes of persons belonging to different castes and creeds is a new one in this country, it must be admitted that considerable success has attended the efforts made to introduce an efficient system of self-government in local affairs by the constitution of District and Taluk Boards and Municipal Councils. With a view to the further development of the usefulness of these bodies the author makes several suggestions which are worthy of consideration. The proposal that to secure for the office of Chairman in Municipalities persons trained in public business the Government should lend the services of Deputy Collectors, Tahsildars, &c., to the Councils for employment in that office, seems to His Excellency the Governor in Council to be a step of a somewhat retrograde character, and, although in exceptional cases, the suggestion might, perhaps, be adopted, the Government is not disposed to accept it as a general rule. On the other hand the Government fully concurs with the author in considering that further advance in

* Sections 104 and 105.

the direction of local self-government is to be looked for only by entrusting to local bodies more and more of the work of real administration, and the suggestions as to the manner in which these bodies might be utilized in advising the Government in regard to legislation upon social matters, appear to His Excellency the Governor in Council to be of much practical value. In the last paragraph of this chapter the question of legislation for the control of native religious endowments is mooted. Upon this it is only necessary to observe that the manner in which these institutions are now administered has long been acknowledged to be unsatisfactory and that the Government has at present under its consideration a draft Bill to provide for the more efficient control of such endowments.

10. The author concludes his valuable "Memorandum" with some "general remarks in regard to the considerations to be borne in mind in estimating the value of the results achieved." He points to the condition of the country at the beginning of the century "devastated by wars, famines and bands of plunderers," and rightly observes that to understand the full significance of the change which has come over the country, one has to contrast what he sees at present, unsatisfactory as it may appear from some points of view, with the state of things described above, and, having indicated some of the evils which are inseparable from progress, records his opinion that "what remains to be done is gradually to widen the foundations of Local Government and make it strike deeper roots into society, so as to enable it to adjust its institutions to its needs as they arise, without weakening in any way the power of the Central Government to maintain a due balance between rival interests and creeds and for interfering effectually when there is danger of such balance being disturbed," and, referring to the change which has taken place in the feeling of the educated classes, who are now apt to complain that progress does not proceed fast enough, states his conviction that "the progress which has been made under the new *régime* during the short time it has been in force—fifty years is a brief interval in the life of a people—is little short of marvellous." With this conclusion His Excellency the Governor in Council fully concurs.

11. Having thus noticed the salient features of this valuable work and expressed his general concurrence with the conclusions arrived at by the author, His Excellency the Governor in Council desires to record his high appreciation

of the very efficient manner in which Mr. Srinivasa Raghavaiyengar has accomplished a difficult and arduous task. That he has been able, without interruption of his duties as Inspector-General of Registration, to compile this volume and to collect the statistics comprised in the appendices is an indication not only of indefatigable industry but also of the keen interest with which he has pursued his investigations. Above all the thanks of Government are due to him for the valuable suggestions for improving the future administration of the Presidency with which the author concludes his interesting "Memorandum." The Government also notes with approval the valuable assistance afforded to the author by M.R.Ry. R. Swaminathaiyar and M.R.Ry. C. Sarvothama Row.

(True Extract.)

(Signed) E. GIBSON,
Ag. Secretary to Government.